CORRIGENDUM

Publication: "Europe in figures – Eurostat yearbook 2010"
ISBN 978-92-79-14884-2
ISSN 1681-4789
Cat. No. KS-CD-10-220-EN-C

Corrections and updates are highlighted in yellow.

1) Page 301, the penultimate paragraph:

> Information on **median earnings** are based on gross annual earnings, and represent the median earnings of full-time employees in enterprises with 10 or more employees. **Low wage earners** are full-time employees that earn less than two thirds of the median gross annual earnings.

2) Page 304,

   a) The titles of the two figures:

   > **Figure 5.11:** Median earnings, 2006 ([1])
   > (median gross annual earnings of full-time employees, EUR)

   > **Figure 5.12:** Low wage earners – full-time employees earning less than two thirds of the median gross annual earnings, 2006 ([1])
   > (% of employees)

   b) The structure of earnings survey data, on which both figures are based, has become available through the data code earn_ses_adeci; the source for both figures can be updated to:

   > *Source:* Eurostat (earn_ses_adeci)

   c) Figure 5.12: the value for Iceland has been updated to 13.4 %.

3) Page 308, table 5.11, the indicator "Low wage trap – single person without children" erroneously had the data for the indicator "Unemployment trap", which was duplicated (provided to the left of the low wage trap in the table). The corrected and updated table (data extracted on 24.11.2010) is provided overleaf.

   As a consequence of the updated data the penultimate paragraph on page 303 should be changed to:

   > Tax wedge data for 2002 and 2007 show little overall change in the EU-27, however the tax wedge has fallen in 18 of the Member States and remained unchanged in Spain. The tax wedge only increased between these two years in eight of the Member States, most notably by 2.0 percentage points in the United Kingdom, although the tax wedge there remained below the EU-27 average.

Table 5.11: Tax rate indicators on low wage earners
(%)

	Tax wedge on labour cost		Unemployment trap		Low wage trap - single person without children		Low wage trap - one earner couple with two children	
	2002	2007	2002	2007	2002	2007	2002	2007
EU-27	42.2	42.0	75	77	46	48	56	58
Belgium	50.5	50.0	87	85	57	59	48	48
Bulgaria	36.2	32.3	76	76	21	19	54	19
Czech Republic	41.5	40.6	67	67	38	37	72	44
Denmark	39.9	39.3	91	90	83	81	105	102
Germany	48.1	47.8	75	74	53	57	66	84
Estonia	40.2	38.7	50	63	28	24	74	11
Ireland	16.7	15.0	71	74	42	49	74	85
Greece	35.7	36.8	56	59	20	22	16	16
Spain	35.7	35.7	80	82	26	26	16	14
France	47.4	45.4	80	78	37	44	59	61
Italy	43.0	42.6	61	73	32	36	-11	-10
Cyprus	17.3	11.9	55	61	7	6	74	115
Latvia	42.2	41.2	87	87	32	32	100	73
Lithuania	43.1	41.2	59	80	36	30	94	58
Luxembourg	29.0	29.9	86	87	51	53	108	108
Hungary	48.2	46.0	68	81	39	37	60	55
Malta	17.7	17.9	59	61	17	20	11	30
Netherlands	39.1	40.7	70	81	64	68	77	81
Austria	43.1	44.1	67	68	36	38	83	65
Poland	41.4	41.8	82	78	65	63	79	68
Portugal	32.3	33.0	81	82	21	23	66	61
Romania	44.6	41.8	61	71	30	30	29	24
Slovenia	43.2	40.9	84	81	43	51	96	67
Slovakia	40.8	35.6	71	44	32	24	124	30
Finland	40.9	38.2	82	75	65	57	100	100
Sweden	46.8	43.3	87	82	58	47	94	81
United Kingdom	28.7	30.7	68	68	58	57	61	85
Turkey	41.5	41.8	:	:	:	:	:	:
Iceland	22.6	23.4	71	82	37	39	79	57
Norway	35.2	34.2	75	76	39	35	91	93
Switzerland	27.3	27.0	:	:	:	:	:	:
Japan	23.2	:	58	58	20	21	140	136
United States	28.0	27.5	71	70	28	28	59	50

Source: Eurostat (tsiem050, earn_nt_unemtrp and earn_nt_lowwtrp)

Statistical books

Europe in figures

Eurostat yearbook 2010

EUROPEAN COMMISSION

Europe Direct is a service to help you find answers
to your questions about the European Union.

Freephone number (*):

00 800 6 7 8 9 10 11

(*) Certain mobile telephone operators do not allow access to 00 800 numbers or these
calls may be billed.

More information on the European Union is available on the Internet (http://europa.eu).

Cataloguing data can be found at the end of this publication.

Luxembourg: Publications Office of the European Union, 2010

ISBN 978-92-79-14884-2
ISSN 1681-4789
Doi: 10.2785/40830
Cat. No. KS-CD-10-220-EN-C

Theme: General and regional statistics
Collection: Statistical books

Printed in Belgium

PRINTED ON ELEMENTAL CHLORINE-FREE BLEACHED PAPER (ECF)

Foreword

Official statistics play a fundamental role in today's society. Public administrations, policymakers, economic operators, markets, researchers and citizens rely on high quality statistics to describe developments in the economic, social, environmental and cultural spheres as accurately as possible.

Impartial, objective, timely and easily accessible statistical information is essential in order to enable well informed decisions based on an accurate and relevant picture of society. Statistical information underpins the transparency and openness of policy decisions; official statistics are therefore a public good and a basis for the smooth functioning of democracy.

Eurostat, the statistical office of the European Union, ensures the development, production and dissemination of harmonised statistics at a European level. Eurostat gets most of its data from the national statistical authorities in the Member States. It then processes, analyses and disseminates that data, following common statistical concepts, methods and standards. Eurostat also supports and encourages the development of similar statistical systems within countries neighbouring the European Union, driving thereby a process of statistical harmonisation.

At a European level, statistics are increasingly important for the definition, implementation, monitoring and evaluation of policies. Europe needs a plethora of statistical data which meet the highest possible standards in terms of quality. For example, reliable statistics are needed to assess macro-economic developments such as inflation, employment and government finances. European statistics thus constitute an essential information tool for monitoring strategic objectives, in particular through the use of principal European economic indicators (PEEIs), sustainable development indicators, structural indicators, and employment and social policy indicators.

The first chapter in this edition of the Eurostat yearbook concentrates on national accounts statistics, which – due to the financial and economic crisis of 2008/2009 – have frequently been in the media spotlight. This spotlight chapter provides a broad overview of the national accounts system and uses that can be made of these economic statistics, focusing on quarterly data to analyse the economic downturn.

I hope this publication will encourage you to use Eurostat's data for your information needs and daily work. Please consult our website at http://ec.europa.eu/eurostat which offers you free access to nearly all Eurostat data and publications.

Walter Radermacher
Director-General, Eurostat

ABSTRACT

Europe in figures – Eurostat yearbook 2010 – presents a comprehensive selection of statistical data on Europe. The yearbook may be viewed as an introduction to European statistics and provides guidance to the vast range of data freely available from the Eurostat website at: http://ec.europa.eu/eurostat.

Most data cover the period 1998-2008 for the European Union and some indicators are provided for other countries, such as candidate countries to the European Union, members of EFTA, Japan or the United States (subject to availability). With just over 450 statistical tables, graphs and maps, the yearbook treats the following areas: the economy, population, health, education, the labour market, living conditions and welfare, industry and services, agriculture, forestry and fisheries, trade, transport, the environment, energy, science and technology, and Europe's regions. This edition's spotlight chapter covers national accounts statistics – with a particular focus on the economic downturn observed during 2008/2009.

Editor-in-chief

Jukka Piirto
Eurostat, Unit D4 - Dissemination

Editors

Diana Ivan, Annika Johansson Augier, Veronika Lang
Eurostat, Unit D4 - Dissemination

Contact details

Eurostat,
Statistical office of the European Union,
Bâtiment Joseph Bech,
5, rue Alphonse Weicker
2721 Luxembourg
E-mail: estat-user-support@ec.europa.eu

Production

This publication was produced by Informa sàrl

For more information please consult

Internet: http://ec.europa.eu/eurostat

Data extracted

September 2009

Acknowledgements

The editor-in-chief and the editorial team of the Eurostat yearbook would like to thank all those who were involved in its preparation. The yearbook could only be published thanks to the support of the following colleagues:

Eurostat, the statistical office of the European Union

Directorate C: National and European accounts

C1 National accounts methodology; statistics for own resources: Gallo Gueye, Christian Ravets

C2 National accounts – production: Roberto Barcellan, Christine Gerstberger, Jukka Jalava, Andreas Krüger, Peter Ritzmann, Jenny Runesson

C3 Public finance: Luca Ascoli, Rasa Sodeikaite

C4 Balance of payments: Franca Faes-Cannito, Mushtaq Hussain, Olaf Nowak, Luca Pappalardo, Konstantia Petridou

C5 Government and sector accounts; financial indicators: Denis Leythienne, Alessandro Lupi, Peter Parlasca, Gilles Thouvenin, John Verrinder

C6 Remuneration and pensions; purchasing power parities: Lars Svennebye

Directorate D: External cooperation, communication and key indicators

D5 Key indicators for European policies: Vincent Tronet, Andrea Scheller

Directorate E: Sectoral and regional statistics

E1 Farms, agro-environment and rural development: Ludivine Baudouin, Catherine Coyette, Carla Martins, Pierre Nadin, Johan Selenius

E2 Agriculture and fisheries: Fausto Cardoso, Garry Mahon, Ole Olsen, Iulia Paula Pop, Franco Zampogna

E3 Environmental statistics and accounts: Jürgen Förster, Julie Hass, Christian Heidorn, Marilise Wolf-Crowther

E4 Regional statistics and geographical information: Teodóra Brandmüller, Berthold Feldmann, Oliver Heiden, Pedro Jorge Martins Ferreira, Åsa Önnerfors, Baudouin Quennery, Gunter Schäfer, Daniela Scirankova

E5 Energy: Antigone Gikas, Christian Kroeppl

E6 Transport: Jonas Noreland, Hans Strelow

Directorate F: Social and information society statistics

F1 Population: Piotr Juchno, Monica Marcu, Katya Vasileva

F2 Labour market: Luis Biedma, Simone Casali, Beate Czech, Arturo de la Fuente Nuño, Sabine Gagel, Daniele Giovannola, Remko Hijman, Ingo Kuhnert

F3 Living conditions and social protection: Maria Liviana Mattonetti, Anna Rybkowska

F4 Education, science and culture: Marta Beck-Domzalska, Bernard Felix, Dominique Groenez, Angeles Hermosa-Lopez, Lene Mejer, Tomas Meri, Sergiu Pârvan, Reni Petkova, Fernando Reis, Veijo Ritola, Paolo Turchetti, Håkan Wilen

F5 Health and food safety; crime: Lucian Agafiței, Elodie Cayotte, Anne Clemenceau, Bart De Norre, Elisabeth Rohner-Thielen, Geoffrey Thomas

F6 Information society; tourism: Christophe Demunter, Anna Lööf, Martti Lumio, Petronela Reinecke, Heidi Seybert, Maria Smihily, Hendrikus Storm, Albrecht Wirthmann

Directorate G: Business statistics

G2 Structural business statistics: Aleksandra Stawińska, Brian Williams

G3 Short-term statistics: Digna Amil, Liliana Apostol, Anastassios Giannoplidis, Carmen Lipp-Lingua, Liselott Öhman, Jane Schofield, Sarmite Visocka

G5 International trade – production: Gilberto Gambini

G6 Price statistics: Tatiana Mrlianova, Christine Wirtz

European Free Trade Association (EFTA)

Directorate-General for Translation of the European Commission

Publications Office of the European Union

Contents

Contents

Introduction

The Eurostat yearbook

Europe in figures – Eurostat yearbook 2010 provides users of official statistics with an overview of the wealth of information that is available on Eurostat's website and within its online databases. It belongs to a set of general compendium publications and, of these, it provides the most extensive set of analyses and detailed data. Europe in figures has been conceived as a publication that provides a balanced set of indicators, with a broad cross-section of information.

Structure of the publication

Europe in figures is divided into an introduction, a spotlight chapter, 13 main chapters and a set of annexes. The main chapters contain data and/or background information relating to the full range of Eurostat data, while the spotlight chapter in this edition focuses on national accounts statistics. Each subchapter starts with an introduction containing background information and policy relevance, followed by some details regarding definitions and data availability and then a commentary on the main findings. The core of each subchapter is a set of tables and graphs that have been selected to show the wide variety of data available for that particular topic; often these include information on how important benchmark indicators have developed during recent years within the European Union (EU), the euro area and the Member States. Users will find a great deal more information when consulting the Eurostat website, which contains subject-specific publications and online databases. The

publication closes with a set of annexes that contain details of classifications, a list of statistical symbols, abbreviations and acronyms, and a subject index.

Files on the Eurostat website

The Eurostat website has a dedicated section for the yearbook, which contains the PDF version of the publication as well as all tables and graphs in MS Excel format. The PDF version of the publication allows direct access through a set of hyper-links to all of the data tables and databases that were used in the production of this publication, see: http://epp.eurostat.ec.europa.eu/portal/page/portal/publications/eurostat_yearbook.

Data extraction, coverage and presentation

The statistical data presented in the yearbook were extracted at the start of September 2009 and represent data availability at that time. There are a few specific tables/graphs where the data had to be extracted at a later date – where this was the case, the extraction date is mentioned under the table or graph in question. The accompanying text was drafted during October and November 2009.

Due to its complex nature, data collection, data processing and the subsequent release of information either online or in publications often means that a significant amount of time may elapse between the collection of data and its publication/release; this can vary from a few weeks

in the case of short-term monthly indicators to several years for complex, ad-hoc surveys. There is a release calendar, which provides details of the schedule for releasing euro-indicators (a collection of the most important monthly and quarterly indicators), available at: http://epp.eurostat.ec.europa.eu/portal/page/portal/release_calendars/news_releases. For other data sets, the meta-data provided on the Eurostat website gives information relating to the frequency of surveys and the time that may elapse before data is published/released.

The Eurostat website is constantly being updated, therefore it is likely that fresher data will have become available since the data was extracted for the production of this publication. It is possible to access the latest version of each data set through hyper-links that are provided as part of the source under each table and graph.

This publication usually presents information for the EU-27 (the 27 Member States of the EU), the euro area (based on 16 members), as well as the individual Member States. The order of the Member States used in the yearbook generally follows their order of protocol; in other words, the alphabetical order of the countries' names in their respective original languages; in some graphs the data are ranked according to the values of a particular indicator.

The EU-27 and euro area aggregates are only provided when information for all of the countries is available, or if an estimate has been made for missing information. Any partial totals that are created are systematically footnoted. Time-series for these geographical aggregates are based on a consistent set of countries for the whole of the time period (unless otherwise indicated). In other words, although the EU only had 25 Member States since early 2004 and has only had 27 Member States since the start of 2007, the time-series for EU-27 refer to a sum or an average for all 27 countries for the whole of the period presented, as if all 27 Member States had been part of the EU in earlier periods. In a similar vein, the data for the euro area are consistently presented for all 16 members, despite the later accessions of Greece, Slovenia, Cyprus and Malta, and Slovakia to the euro area. As such, unless otherwise stated, the data for the euro area covers the 16 Member States that share the euro as a common currency as of November 2009 (Belgium, Germany, Greece, Spain, France, Ireland, Italy, Cyprus, Luxembourg, Malta, the Netherlands, Austria, Portugal, Slovenia, Slovakia and Finland).

When available, information is also presented for the candidate countries of Croatia, the former Yugoslav Republic of Macedonia and Turkey, as well as for EFTA countries, Japan and the United States. In the event that data for these non-member countries does not exist, then these have been excluded from tables and graphs in order to save space; however, the full set of 27 Member States is maintained in tables, with footnotes being added in graphs for those Member States for which information is missing.

In the event that a reference year is not available for a particular country, then efforts have been made to fill tables and graphs with previous reference years (these exceptions are footnoted); generally, an effort has been made to go back two reference periods.

Eurostat online databases contain a large amount of meta-data that provides information on the status of particular values or data series. In order to improve readability, the majority of this has been omitted when constructing the tables and graphs.

The following symbols are used, where necessary:

Italic	value is a forecast, provisional or an estimate and is therefore likely to change
:	not available, confidential or unreliable value
–	not applicable or zero by default
0	less than half the final digit shown and greater than real zero

Breaks in series are indicated in the footnotes provided under each table and graph.

Eurostat – the statistical office of the European Union

Eurostat is the statistical office of the European Union, situated in Luxembourg. Its task is to provide the EU with statistics at a European level that enable comparisons between countries and regions. Eurostat's mission is '*to provide the European Union with a high-quality statistical information service*'.

As one of the Directorates-General of the European Commission, Eurostat is headed by a Director-General. Under him are seven Directors responsible for different areas of activity (Directorates as of November 2009):

- Cooperation in the European Statistical System; resources;
- Quality, methodology and information systems;
- National and European accounts;
- External cooperation, communication and key indicators;
- Sectoral and regional statistics;
- Social and information society statistics;
- Business statistics.

In 2009, Eurostat had around 900 posts; of these some 73 % were civil servants, 8 % were seconded national experts, and 19 % had other types of contracts. Eurostat's executed budget was around EUR 66 million in 2008 (excluding costs of statutory staff and administrative expenses) of which EUR 48 million was used for the implementation of the statistical programme, while EUR 18.5 million was sub-delegated to Eurostat by other Directorates-General.

Since the creation of a European statistical body in 1952, there has always been a realisation that the planning and implementation of European policies must be based on reliable and comparable statistics. As a result, the European Statistical System (ESS) was built-up gradually to provide comparable statistics at EU level. For this

purpose, Eurostat does not work alone, as the ESS comprises Eurostat and the national statistical institutes (NSIs) and other national authorities responsible in each Member State for European statistics.

Regulation (EC) No 223/2009 (¹) of the European Parliament and of the Council of 11 March 2009 on European statistics establishes a new legal framework for the development, production and dissemination of European statistics. The Regulation states that European statistics shall be developed in conformity with the statistical principles set out in Article 285(2) of the Treaty and further elaborated in the European statistics Code of Practice, namely, that: *'the production of Community statistics shall conform to impartiality, reliability, objectivity, scientific independence, cost-effectiveness and statistical confidentiality; it shall not entail excessive burdens on economic operators'*.

Article 7 of the same Regulation establishes the European Statistical System Committee (ESSC), which is at the heart of the ESS, stating the Committee *'shall provide professional guidance to the ESS for developing, producing and disseminating European statistics'*. The ESSC is chaired by the European Commission (Eurostat) and composed of representatives from the national statistical institutes of the Member States. The national statistical institutes of EEA-EFTA countries participate as observers, as may representatives of other European/international bodies, for example the ECB or the OECD.

To meet the challenges associated with the adoption of the Regulation, Eurostat aims:

- to provide other European institutions and the governments of the Member States with the information needed to implement, monitor and evaluate Community policies;
- to disseminate statistics to the European public and enterprises and to all economic and social agents involved in decision-making;
- to implement a set of standards, methods and organisational structures which allow comparable, reliable and relevant statistics to be produced throughout the Community, in line with the principles of the European statistics Code of Practice;
- to improve the functioning of the European Statistical System, to support the Member States, and to assist in the development of statistical systems on international level.

Eurostat and its partners in the ESS aim to provide high-quality, impartial, reliable and comparable statistical data. Indeed, access to reliable and high-quality statistics and Eurostat's obligation for trustworthiness is enshrined in law. European statistics should be provided to all types of users on the basis of equal opportunities, such that public administrations, researchers, trade unions, students, businesses and political parties, among others, can access data freely and easily. Access to the most recent statistics, as well as an expanding archive of information, is guaranteed through free access to Eurostat databases on its website.

The data collected, harmonised and reported upon by Eurostat have been agreed through a well-defined political process at European level, in which the Member States are deeply involved. Most surveys and data collection exercises are based on European regulations or directives that are legally binding. In order to do this, comparisons of data between

(¹) For more information: http://eur-lex.europa.eu/LexUriServ/LexUriServ.do?uri=OJ:L:2009:087:0164:0173:en:PDF.

countries require comparable statistics that, in turn, demand the use of a common *statistical language*. This language has to embrace concepts, methods and definitions, as well as technical standards and infrastructure, in order to achieve harmonisation. This is Eurostat's *raison d'être* – and sums up what the ESS is all about.

In order to provide an independent overview of the European Statistical System as regards the implementation of the European statistics Code of Practice, the European Statistical Governance Advisory Board (ESGAB) was set up; it is composed of seven independent members and started its work in March 2009. Its main task is to prepare an annual report for the European Parliament and the Council on the implementation of the Code of Practice by Eurostat and by the European Statistical System as a whole.

The European Statistical Advisory Committee (ESAC) is composed of 24 members representing users, respondents and other stakeholders of European statistics (including the scientific community, social partners and civil society), as well as institutional users (like, for example, the European Parliament and the Council). This committee is entrusted with ensuring that user requirements as well as the response burden on information providers and producers are taken into account when developing Community statistical programmes.

A practical guide to accessing European statistics

The simplest way of accessing Eurostat's broad range of statistical information is through the Eurostat website (http://ec.europa.eu). Eurostat provides users with free access to its databases and all of its publications in PDF format via the Internet. The website is updated twice per day and gives access to the latest and most comprehensive statistical information available on the EU, its Member States, its candidate countries and EFTA countries.

For full access to all of the services available through Eurostat's website, it is recommended that users should take a few minutes to register from the homepage. Registration is free of charge and allows access to:

- tailor-made e-mail alerts providing information on new publications or statistics as soon as they are online;

- enhanced functionalities of the databases (save queries and make bulk downloads).

The information on Eurostat's website under the heading of 'Statistics' is structured according to a set of 'themes', which may be accessed from the 'Statistics' tab that is consistently present near the top of each webpage; it provides links to:

- EU policy indicators (see the end of this introduction for more details);
- general and regional statistics;
- economy and finance;
- population and social conditions;
- industry, trade and services;
- agriculture and fisheries;
- external trade;
- transport;
- environment and energy;
- science and technology.

For each of these themes, the user is presented with a range of different sub-topics (for example, within the population and social conditions theme there are sub-topics for population, health, education and training, the labour market, living conditions and social protection, crime and criminal justice, and culture). These sub-topics are presented as hyper-links that take the user to a dedicated section on the subject, with information generally presented for data (main tables, and databases), publications, legislation, methodology and other background information.

Access to data

Data navigation tree

The majority of Eurostat's statistics may be accessed from the data navigation tree, at: http://epp.eurostat.ec.europa.eu/portal/page/portal/statistics/search_database; alternatively, there is an icon at the right-hand end of the top menu bar 🍃 on each webpage that can be used to switch to the data navigation tree.

The data navigation tree is based on the statistical themes presented above and is collapsible. It has two main branches:

- **Tables** offers a selection of the most important Eurostat data in a user-friendly way. All data are presented in simple two- or three-dimensional tables, generally with European aggregates and data for the Member States on the y-axis and time on the x-axis. Tables can be viewed using an interface called TGM – tables, graphs and maps (icon 🗺) – where data can be visualised as graphs or maps in

addition to a standard, tabular presentation. Data can be downloaded (icon 🖥) from TGM in various formats (XLS, HTML, XML and TSV).
- **Database** contains the full range of public data available on the Eurostat website. These data are presented in multi-dimensional tables with selection features that allow tailor-made presentations and extractions. The interface for databases is called the Data Explorer (icon 🗃) and this provides an intuitive way to select and organise information. Data can be downloaded (icon 🖥) from the Data Explorer in various formats (XLS, TXT, HTML, PC AXIS, SPSS and TSV).

In addition, the data navigation tree has three special branches, where specific items from the two main branches – Tables and Database – have been collected: Tables on EU policy, New Items and Recently Updated Items.

Eurostat data codes – easy online access to the freshest data

Eurostat data codes, such as tps00001 and nama_gdp_c ([2]), allow the reader to easily access the most recent data on the Eurostat website. In this yearbook these codes are given as part of the source below tables and figures.

In the PDF version of this yearbook the reader is led directly to the freshest data when clicking on the hyper-links that form the data code(s). Readers of the paper version can access the freshest data directly by using typing a standardised hyper-link into a web browser, http://ec.europa.eu/eurostat/product?code=<data_code>&mode=view, where <data_code> is to be replaced by the

---

([2]) There are two types of data codes:
  - Tables (accessed using the TGM interface) have 8-character codes, which consist of 3 or 5 letters – the first of which is 't' – followed by 5 or 3 digits, e.g. tps00001 and tsdph220.
  - Databases (accessed using the Data Explorer interface) have codes that use an underscore '_' within the syntax of the code, e.g. nama_gdp_c and proj_08c2150p.

data code in question. The data is presented either in the TGM or the Data Explorer interface.

The data codes can also be fed into the 'Search' function of Eurostat's website, which is found in the upper right corner of the Eurostat homepage, at http://ec.europa.eu/eurostat.

The results from such a search present related dataset(s) and possibly publication(s) and metadata. By clicking on these hyperlinks users are taken to product page(s) (³), which provide some background information about each dataset/publication or set of metadata. For example, it is possible to move directly to the data from the data product page by clicking the TGM or Data Explorer icons presented under the 'View table' sub-heading.

Note that the data on the Eurostat's website is frequently updated.

Note also that the description above presents the situation as of April 2010.

Policy indicators

Aside from the main tables and databases, there exists a group of policy indicators that may be accessed from the 'Statistics' tab, covering:

- euro-indicators/principal European economic indicators (PEEIs);
- structural indicators;
- sustainable development indicators;
- employment and social policy indicators.

More details on each of these are provided at the end of this introduction.

Statistics Explained

Statistics Explained is part of the Eurostat website. It is a wiki-based system that presents statistical topics in an easy to understand way. Together, the articles make up an encyclopaedia of European statistics, which is completed by a statistical glossary that clarifies the terms used. In addition, there are numerous links provided to the latest data, further information, and metadata, making Statistics Explained a portal for regular and occasional users alike.

Statistics Explained can be accessed via a link on the right-hand side of Eurostat's homepage, or directly at: http://epp.eurostat.ec.europa.eu/statistics_explained.

In April 2010, Statistics Explained contained around 200 different articles and over 800 glossary items; its content and user-friendliness will be expanded regularly. Users may find articles using a set of navigational features in the left-hand menu; on the top-right menu bar of Statistics Explained it is possible to find options that make it possible, among others, to print, forward, cite, blog or share content easily.

(³) The product page can also be accessed by using a hyper-link, for example, http://ec.europa.eu/eurostat/product?code=<data_code>, where <data_code> is to be replaced by the data code in question.

Other utilities

Finally, users may access two additional utilities for viewing data from the Eurostat homepage. The **business cycle clock** (BCC) is an interactive tool that shows how economic indicators evolve in close proximity to one another. Moving as a 'cloud' of indicators, some have a clear lead in development – for example, economic sentiment – whereas others lag behind – for example, unemployment. These and other dynamic patterns can be visually observed, and can help the user to understand today's and yesterday's economics. The BCC tool can be consulted via the following link: http://epp.eurostat.ec.europa.eu/cache/BCC2.

The **country profiles interface** offers the possibility to visualise major statistical indicators, of different countries and/or EU aggregates, in a user-friendly map-based presentation. The interface can be accessed via the following link: http://epp.eurostat.ec.europa.eu/cache/BCC2.

Publications

Eurostat produces a variety of publications, all of which are available on the Eurostat website in PDF format, free of charge. As with the 'Statistics' tab that is available at all times for accessing data, there is a 'Publications' tab that is always accessible near the top of each webpage for accessing material in PDF format; the publications are organised under Eurostat's nine statistical themes.

There are a variety of different types of publication, ranging from news and data releases to more in-depth analyses in the form of statistical books. Among the most interesting collections are:

News releases – rapid updates providing information about the release of key data;

Statistics in focus and Data in focus – relatively short publications which present up-to-date summaries of the main results of statistical surveys, studies and analyses;

Pocketbooks – handy, pocket-sized publications presenting main indicators for a particular theme;

Statistical books – a collection of comprehensive studies; usually quite lengthy, providing analyses, tables and graphs for one or more statistical themes;

Methodologies and working papers – for specialists who want to consult methodologies, nomenclatures, or specific studies relating to a particular data set.

Alternatively, some Eurostat publications are also printed or made available on CD-ROM or DVD; these can be ordered from the website of the EU bookshop (http://bookshop.europa.eu) or through sales agents in the Member States. The bookshop is managed by the Publications Office (http://publications.europa.eu).

Reference metadata

The ESMS (Euro SDMX Metadata Structure) is a format based on the Statistical Data and Metadata eXchange (SDMX) Content Oriented Guidelines, which were adopted in January 2009 by seven international organisations at a worldwide level. The ESMS uses a subset of 21 cross domain concepts (plus sub-concepts) and is the new standard for reference metadata in the ESS. It puts emphasis on quality-related information (containing concepts such as accuracy, comparability, coherence and timeliness).

Reference metadata may be accessed either from the heading 'Metadata' which appears in the left-hand menu after selecting the 'Statistics' tab, or directly from the data navigation tree, where the following icon ⊞ is used to signify its availability.

User support

Eurostat and the other members of the ESS have set up a system of user support centres – European Statistical Data Support (ESDS). These exist in 22 of the Member States, Croatia, Norway, Switzerland and Turkey. In order to offer the best possible and personalised support, requests should, whenever possible, be addressed to the relevant national support centre. The mission of each centre is to provide free of charge additional help and guidance to users who are having difficulty in finding the statistical data they require. The list and addresses of all support centres can be reached via the Help-TAB on Eurostat's homepage.

Specific requests can be addressed to this network, via the Eurostat website at:

https://ec.europa.eu/eurostat/xtnetassist/login.htm (requires a user log-in).

Eurostat's service for journalists

Statistics make news and they are essential to many stories, features and in-depth analyses. Printed media, as well as radio and TV, use Eurostat data intensively. Eurostat's press office puts out user-friendly news releases on a key selection of data covering the EU, the euro area, the Member States and their partners. All Eurostat news releases are available free of charge on the Eurostat website at 11 a.m. (C.E.T.) on the day they are released. Just under 200 press releases were published in 2009, of which approximately three quarters were based on monthly or quarterly euro-indicators; other releases covered major international events and important Eurostat publications.

Eurostat's media support centre helps professional journalists find data on all kinds of topics. Journalists can contact media support for further information on news releases and other data (tel. (352) 4301-33408; e-mail: Eurostat-mediasupport@ec.europa.eu).

Linking statistics to European policies

Effective economic and political decision-making depends on the regular supply of reliable information. Statistics are one of the principle sources of such information, providing quantitative support to the elaboration and implementation of policies. Statistics are also a powerful tool for communicating with the general public.

The information needs of politicians require constant interaction between policymakers and statisticians: the former formulate their needs for data, and the latter attempt to adapt the statistical production system so as to fulfil those needs. In this fashion, new policies lead to improvements in statistical production, both in terms of enhancing the quality of existing indicators and of creating new ones.

Whereas politicians require aggregated indicators which provide a synthetic and clear picture of the different phenomena they are interested in, statisticians tend to deal with less aggregated basic data. Statisticians therefore have to transform, synthesise and model basic data in order to increase data readability and extract signals (i.e. indicators).

Over recent years, a number of policies have substantially influenced Eurostat's priorities and activities:

- economic and monetary union (EMU) and the creation of the euro area (1999);
- the Lisbon Strategy (2000, revised in 2005), including the open method of coordination on social inclusion and social protection;
- the EU Sustainable Development Strategy, EU SDS (2001, renewed in 2006);

Economic and monetary union and the setting-up of the European Central Bank (ECB) required a broad range of infra-annual short-term statistics to measure economic and monetary developments within the euro area and to assist in the implementation of a common monetary policy. Effective monetary policy depends on timely, reliable and comprehensive economic statistics giving an overview of the economic situation. Such data are also needed for the assessment of the business cycle.

Europeans place a high value on their quality of life, including aspects such as a clean environment, social protection, prosperity and equity. In recent years the European Council has focused on a

number of key areas intended to shape the future development of the EU. While the goal of the Lisbon Strategy is for the EU to '*become the most competitive and dynamic knowledge-based economy in the world, capable of sustainable economic growth with more and better jobs and greater social cohesion*', the Sustainable Development Strategy is concerned with the continuous improvement of quality of life, both for current and future generations, through seeking a balance between economic development, social cohesion and protection of the environment.

Eurostat has responded to politicians needs in these areas by developing four sets of 'EU policy indicators' that may be accessed from the 'Statistics' tab that appears near the top of every webpage on the Eurostat website. There are a set of dedicated sections on Eurostat's website that are devoted to these indicators and they are accessible from Eurostat homepage, by selecting 'Statistics' on the top menu bar. These four sets of data may be summarised as:

- **euro-indicators**, of which the principal European economic indicators (PEEIs) are the core, for monetary policy purposes; this is a collection of monthly and quarterly data, useful to evaluate the economic situation within the euro area and the EU. Euro-indicators are available on the Eurostat website at: http://ec.europa.eu/eurostat/euroindicators.
- **structural indicators**, for the (revised) Lisbon Strategy are used to underpin the European Commission's analyses in an annual progress report to the European Council; these assess

the longer-term progress being made within the EU in the domains of employment, innovation and research, economic reform, social cohesion, and the environment, as well as the general economic background. The Lisbon Strategy is being revised and transformed into the EU 2020 Strategy for the period after 2010 which entails a substantial revision of the structural indicators. Structural indicators are available on the Eurostat website at: http://ec.europa.eu/eurostat/ structuralindicators.

- **sustainable development indicators**, for the EU Sustainable Development Strategy extend across a wide range of issues affecting the quality of life, in particular looking at ways to reconcile economic development, social cohesion and the protection of the environment. Sustainable development indicators are available on the Eurostat website at: http://ec.europa.eu/eurostat/ sustainabledevelopment.

- **employment and social policy indicators**, for monitoring and reporting in relation to employment and social policy. These indicators are designed to address a range of different issues, such as employment guidelines, the open method of coordination on social inclusion and policy protection, the education and training programme, and i2010 (the European information society for growth and employment). Employment and social policy indicators are available on the Eurostat website at: http://epp.eurostat.ec.europa.eu/portal/ page/portal/employment_and_social_ policy_indicators/introduction.

Euro-indicators/PEEIs

Since October 2001 the euro-indicators/ PEEIs web pages have been a reference point for all users of official statistics dealing with short-term data. They were initially conceived as an independent website, available in parallel to the Eurostat website; however, since October 2004, they have been integrated with the remaining content on Eurostat's website. It is possible to access euro-indicators/PEEIs data from the 'Statistics' tab visible in the menu near the top of the screen on each webpage, or directly via the euro-indicators/PEEIs dedicated section pages at http://ec.europa.eu/eurostat/euroindicators. It is also possible to e-mail the euro-indicators/PEEIs team at: ESTAT-EUROINDI-CATORS@ec.europa.eu.

Euro-indicators/PEEIs aim to supply business-cycle analysts, policymakers, media, researchers, students, and other interested users with a comprehensive, well structured and high quality set of information which is useful for their daily activities. The core of euro-indicators/ PEEIs comprises a set of statistical indicators giving an accurate and as timely as possible overview of the economic evolution of the euro area, the EU, and the individual Member States. The euro-indicators/PEEIs dedicated section contains the following additional products and services intended to assist in the understanding and analysis of data:

- selected principal European economic indicators (PEEIs);
- background;
- news releases;
- data;
- publications;
- information relating to seminars/conferences.

Data

The data presented in euro-indicators/PEEIs are built around a set of the most relevant statistics, called principal European economic indicators (PEEIs), a complete list of which can be found in the European Commission's Communication (2002) 661 (⁴). They are structured in three main parts:

- selected principal European economic indicators (containing a set of 22 most relevant and timely short-term economic indicators for the euro area and the EU) directly accessible on the euro-indicators/PEEIs homepage;
- short-term indicators (included as the first branch of the 'Main tables' on the data navigation tree);
- European and national short-term statistics database (included as the first branch of the 'Database' section on the data navigation tree – under the heading of 'General and regional statistics' – as European and national short term indicators (euroind).

	Release date		Unit	Reference period					
	latest	next							

European Union * **Euro Area **** Print

	Release date latest	next	Unit	2007q03	2007q04	2008q01	2008q02	2008q03	2008q04
GDP in volume	07/04/2009	15/05/2009	% (Q/Q-1)	0.7	0.6	0.5	-0.1	-0.3	-1.5
			% (Q/Q-4)	2.8	2.5	2.0	2.3	1.1	-1.6
Private final consumption in volume	07/04/2009	03/06/2009	% (Q/Q-1)	0.7	0.4	0.2	-0.2	0.0	-0.4
			% (Q/Q-4)	2.4	2.2	2.0	1.4	0.8	-0.5
Investments in volume	07/04/2009	03/06/2009	% (Q/Q-1)	1.2	1.3	0.3	-1.0	-1.1	-3.3
			% (Q/Q-4)	4.6	4.3	2.8	2.7	-0.1	-5.1

				2008m10	2008m11	2008m12	2009m01	2009m02	2009m03
External trade balance	17/04/2009	18/05/2009	mio euro	-18721.0	-19781.0	-13865.9	-21763.5	-13053.9	(:)

				2007q03	2007q04	2008q01	2008q02	2008q03	2008q04
Current account- Total	22/04/2009		mio euro	-33161	-21568	-46160	-73196	-67416	-57288

				2008m10	2008m11	2008m12	2009m01	2009m02	2009m03
Inflation (HICP all items)	16/04/2009		% (M/M-1)	0.0	-0.4	-0.2	-0.6	0.5	0.3
			% (M/M-12)	3.7	2.8	2.2	1.8	1.8	1.3

Both the main tables for short-term indicators and the Euroind database are divided into the following eight domains:

- balance of payments;
- business and consumer surveys;
- consumer prices;
- external trade;
- industry, commerce and services;
- labour market;
- monetary and financial indicators;
- national accounts.

(⁴) For more information: http://eur-lex.europa.eu/LexUriServ/LexUriServ.do?uri=COM:2002:0661:FIN:EN:PDF.

Publications and working papers

The main publication in this domain is called 'Eurostatistics'. It is a monthly release that presents a synthetic picture of the economic situation together with detailed statistical analysis of the latest economic events for the euro area, the EU, and the Member States. The latest issue of 'Eurostatistics' is accessible from the homepage of the euro-indicators/PEEIs dedicated section. Previous issues are also accessible – click on the 'publications' link in the left-hand menu from within the euro-indicators/PEEIs dedicated section. Under the same heading of 'publications', users may also access a collection of 'selected readings' and 'working papers', containing both methodological and empirical studies on statistical improvements and analyses of European data.

Quality reports

Since 2001, the Euroind database has been subject to monthly quality monitoring. The results of this assessment are presented in a detailed online publication called 'State of affairs', also accessible from the 'publications' link in the left-hand menu of the euro-indicators/PEEIs dedicated section. A synthesis of this monthly assessment is presented in another publication, entitled the 'Monitoring report', accessible from the same location.

Structural indicators

At the Lisbon European Council in the spring of 2000, the EU set itself the following strategic goal for the next decade: '*to become the most competitive and dynamic knowledge-based economy in the world, capable of sustainable economic growth with more and better jobs and greater social cohesion*'.

The European Council recognised the need to regularly discuss and assess progress made in achieving this goal on the basis of a commonly agreed set of structural indicators and to this end, invited the European Commission to draw up an annual spring report on progress being made. This report was based on the evolution of structural indicators in the following areas:

- general economic background;
- innovation and research;
- economic reform;
- employment;
- social cohesion;
- environment (since 2002).

For the first time, in 2004, the European Commission presented a shortlist of 14 structural indicators which were included in the statistical annex to its spring report to the European Council. This shortlist was agreed with the European Council; its concise layout makes it easier to present policy messages and the Member States' positions with regard to the key Lisbon targets. The same shortlist indicators were presented in the annexes of subsequent annual progress reports to the European Council.

The Lisbon Strategy entered a new phase as of the spring of 2005, with the spotlight on delivering results, focusing on growth and jobs. By submitting national reform programmes, Member States have accepted a new responsibility, setting out detailed commitments for action. At the same time, Community programmes specify what has to be done at an EU level. National reform programmes provide

the basis for the reform agenda, prioritising growth and employment.

The EU is revising the Lisbon Strategy for the period after 2010: The new 'EU 2020 Strategy' will focus on overcoming the recession and moving towards a low-carbon, knowledge-based society. This transformation involves a substantial revision of the set of structural indicators including the short list.

Shortlist of structural indicators

General economic background

- GDP per capita in PPS
- Labour productivity per person employed

Innovation and research

- Youth educational attainment level by gender
- Gross domestic expenditure on R & D (GERD)

Economic reform

- Comparative price levels
- Business investment

Employment

- Employment rate by gender
- Employment rate of older workers by gender

Social cohesion

- At-risk-of-poverty rate after social transfers by gender
- Long-term unemployment rate by gender

- Dispersion of regional employment rates by gender

Environment

- Greenhouse gas emissions
- Energy intensity of the economy
- Volume of freight transport relative to GDP

More information regarding structural indicators may be found on Eurostat's website at: http://ec.europa.eu/eurostat/structuralindicators. Alternatively, for further information, contact Eurostat's structural indicators coordination team, at: estat-structuralindicators@ec.europa.eu.

Sustainable development indicators

The EU Sustainable Development Strategy (EU SDS), adopted by the European Council in Gothenburg in June 2001, and renewed in June 2006, aims to continuously improve quality of life, both for current and for future generations, through reconciling economic development, social cohesion and protection of the environment. A set of sustainable development indicators (SDI) has been developed to monitor progress in the implementation of the strategy. The indicators are organised under ten themes (and sub-themes) that reflect different political priorities (cf. first column of Table 2).

In order to facilitate communication, the set of indicators has been built as a three-level pyramid.

Table 1: Framework for sustainable development indicators

Indicator level	Hierarchical framework	Indicator types
Level 1	Lead objectives	11 headline indicators are at the top of the pyramid. They are intended to monitor the 'overall objectives' of the strategy. They are well-known indicators with a high communication value. They are robust and available for most EU Member States for a period of at least five years.
Level 2	SDS priority objectives	The second level of the pyramid consists of ca. 30 indicators related to the operational objectives of the strategy. They are the lead indicators in their respective subthemes. They are robust and available for most EU Member States for a period of at least three years.
Level 3	Actions/explanatory variables	The third level consists of ca. 80 indicators related to actions outlined in the strategy or to other issues which are useful to analyse progress towards the SDS objectives. Breakdowns of level-1 or -2 indicators are usually also found at level 3.
Contextual indicators	Background	Contextual indicators are part of the SDI set, but they either do not monitor directly any of the strategy's objectives or they are not policy responsive. Generally they are difficult to interpret in a normative way. However, they provide valuable background information on issues having direct relevance for sustainable development policies and are useful for the analysis.

This distinction between the three levels of indicators reflects the structure of the renewed strategy (overall lead objectives, operational priority objectives, and actions/explanatory variables) and also responds to different kinds of user needs. The three levels of the pyramid are complemented with contextual indicators, which do not monitor directly the strategy's objectives, but provide valuable background information for analysis. The SDI data set also describes indicators which are not yet fully developed but which will, in the future, be necessary to get a more complete picture of progress, differentiating between indicators that are expected to become available within some years, with sufficient quality ('indicators under development'), and those to be developed in the longer term ('indicators to be developed').

The table below presents the current situation of progress being made for the headline indicators.

Table 2: Headline sustainable development indicators and progress being made within the EU

SDI theme	Headline indicator	EU-27 evaluation of change (since 2000)
Socioeconomic development	Growth of GDP per capita	☀️
Climate change and energy	Greenhouse gas emissions ([1])	☁️
	Consumption of renewables	☁️
Sustainable transport	Energy consumption of transport relative to GDP	🌤️
Sustainable consumption and production	Resource productivity	☀️
Natural resources	Abundance of common birds ([2])	🌤️
	Conservation of fish stocks ([3])	⛈️
Public health	Healthy life years ([4])	🌤️
Social inclusion	Risk of poverty ([4])	🌤️
Demographic changes	Employment rate of older workers	🌤️
Global partnership	Official development assistance ([5])	⛈️
Good governance	[No headline indicator]	⋮

 Clearly favourable change/on target path

 No or moderately favourable change/ close to target path

 No or moderately favourable change/close to target path

 No or moderately favourable change/ close to target path

([1]) EU-15.
([2]) Based on 19 Member States.
([3]) In north east Atlantic.
([4]) EU-25, from 2005.
([5]) From 2005.

Source: Eurostat

More information regarding sustainable development indicators may be found on the Eurostat website: http://ec.europa.eu/eurostat/sustainabledevelopment, or by contacting: estat-sdi@ec.europa.eu. There is also a comprehensive publication on the subject, 'Sustainable development in the European Union: 2009 monitoring report of the EU Sustainable Development Strategy', available at: http://ec.europa.eu/eurostat/product?code=KS-78-09-865&mode=view.

Employment and social policy indicators

This section presents various indicators covering different areas of employment and social policy. The indicators are used to monitor and report upon progress being made in relation to several EU policies, relating to:

- employment;
- social inclusion and social protection;
- education and training;
- information society.

European Employment Strategy

The European Employment Strategy (EES) is the employment section of the Lisbon Strategy. Since its launch in 1997 indicators have been used for the assessment of Member States' progress on implementing the employment guidelines that have been developed under the EES, and that are proposed by the European Commission and approved by the European Council.

Most of the indicators for monitoring and analysis of the employment guidelines are provided by Eurostat. However, for the time-being the coherent presentation of these indicators is under development. For more information on

the list of indicators as well as the EES, please refer to the website of the Directorate-General for Employment, Social Affairs and Equal Opportunities, at: http://ec.europa.eu/social/main.jsp?catId=101&langId=en.

Open method of coordination on social inclusion and social protection

The Lisbon Strategy also gave rise to the open method of coordination (OMC) that provides a framework for political coordination (without legal constraints) in relation to social inclusion and social protection issues. This is a flexible and decentralised method, which involves:

- agreeing on common objectives which set out high-level, shared goals to underpin the entire process;
- agreeing to a set of common indicators which show how progress towards these goals can be measured;
- preparing national strategic reports, in which Member States set out how they will plan policies over an agreed period to meet the common objectives;
- evaluating these strategies jointly through the European Commission and the Member States.

The indicators can be accessed directly from the Eurostat website, through the left-hand menu of the dedicated section covering employment and social policy indicators, that may be found by clicking on the 'Statistics' tab near the top of the screen on each webpage. The indicators are currently divided into four strands, covering:

- overarching indicators;
- indicators of the social inclusion strand;

- indicators of the pension strand;
- indicators of the health and long term care strand.

Common indicators allow a comparison of best practices to be made and also measure progress being made towards the common objectives. For more information about the open method of coordination on social inclusion and social protection, please refer to the website of the Directorate-General for Employment, Social Affairs and Equal Opportunities, at: http://ec.europa.eu/social/main.jsp?catId= 753&langId=en.

Education and training

To ensure their contribution to the Lisbon Strategy, the ministers of education from the various Member States adopted in 2001 a report on the future objectives of education and training systems agreeing for the first time on shared objectives to be achieved by 2010. A year later, a ten-year work programme was endorsed (Education and training 2010). As with the indicators above relating to social inclusion and social protection, these indicators are also implemented through the open method of coordination, using similar procedures to set objectives, exchange good practices, and finally to measure progress that is being made. On 25 May 2007 the Council adopted conclusions on a coherent framework of 16 core indicators for monitoring progress towards the Lisbon objectives in education and training.

This programme has three overall objectives:

- improving the quality and effectiveness of education and training systems;
- facilitating access to education and training systems;

- opening up EU education and training systems to the wider world.

Indicators and methodology are available on the Eurostat website as part of the dedicated section covering employment and social policy indicators. For the period up to 2010, the education and training programme covers the following core indicators:

- four-year-olds in education;
- early school-leavers by gender;
- literacy in reading, mathematics and science;
- upper-secondary completion rate of young people;
- numbers of higher education graduates;
- life-long learning by gender – percentage of the adult population aged 25 to 64 participating in education and training;
- ICT skills:
  - Individuals' level of computer skills;
  - Individuals' level of Internet skills;
- public expenditure in education as a percentage of GDP.

It is likely that the programme will be extended to cover the period through to 2020, following the conclusions of a Council meeting on 12 May 2009 ([5]). Indeed, five new benchmark goals have already been defined for 2020, by which time:

- an average of at least 15 % of adults should participate in lifelong learning;
- the share of low-achieving 15-years olds in reading, mathematics and science should be less than 15 %;
- the share of 30-34 year olds with tertiary educational attainment should be at least 40 %;

([5]) For more information: http://eur-lex.europa.eu/LexUriServ/LexUriServ.do?uri=OJ:C:2009:119:0002:0010:EN:PDF.

- the share of early leavers from education and training should be less than 10 %;
- at least 95 % of children between four years of age and the age for starting compulsory primary education should participate in early childhood education.

For more information on the programme through to 2010, please refer to the website of the Directorate-General for Education and Culture, at: http://ec.europa.eu/education/lifelong-learning-policy/doc28_en.htm.

European Information Society for growth and employment

The final heading within this section covers the information society. The eEurope action plan was launched under the Lisbon Strategy and included a set of benchmarking indicators on Internet and broadband take-up, as well as the use of online services. Within the context of the renewed Lisbon agenda, a strategic framework for a European information society for growth and employment (i2010) was launched. The benchmarking framework for measuring progress in relation to the programme was set up and approved in April 2006; it contains a set of core indicators and provides for flexible modules on specific issues to be defined each year.

Annual Community surveys on ICT usage in households and by individuals are a major source of information for monitoring many of the aims of the i2010 Strategy. The data presented on Eurostat's website as part of the dedicated section covering i2010 indicators is divided into four main themes:

- developments of broadband;
- advanced services;
- inclusion;
- public services.

For more information on the i2010 programme in general and more specifically upon the benchmarking exercise, please refer to the website of the Directorate-General for Information Society, at: http://ec.europa.eu/information_society/eeurope/i2010/index_en.htm.

On 9 November 2009 a new benchmarking initiative was endorsed, providing the conceptual framework for the collection of statistics on the information society as well as a list of core indicators. For more information, please refer to: http://ec.europa.eu/information_society/eeurope/i2010/docs/benchmarking/benchmarking_digital_europe_2011-2015.pdf.

In the spotlight – national accounts: key macro-economic indicators for monitoring the economic and financial crisis

Each year Eurostat's yearbook presents a topic that is of particular importance for European policy making. In 2010, the spotlight is on national accounts as a key instrument for monitoring and analysing the current state of the economic situation in the European Union (EU) and deriving appropriate national and European policy responses to the worst global financial and economic crisis since the 1930's.

Indeed, the bursting of the bubble in United States' mortgage markets that developed into a global financial market confidence crisis after the bankruptcy of Lehman Brothers in the autumn of 2008 had severe repercussions on the economic performance of many economies, including the EU-27 Member States. Central banks, financial supervisors and governments around the world had to take bold actions to stabilise the financial system and support their economies.

In Europe, the European Central Bank (ECB) acted in concert with other central banks to provide the financial system with additional liquidity; additional impetus was given to the economic recovery as interest rates remained at historically low levels. The European Commission launched the European Economic Recovery Plan (EERP) in December 2008 to restore confidence and bolster demand through coordinated actions. The total value of this package amounted to around EUR 200 000 million, equivalent to 1.5 % of the EU-27's GDP. The European Investment Bank (EIB) also responded to the economic crisis by increasing its annual level of financing by around EUR 15 000 million over two years. In May 2009, the European Commission built on recommendations of a high-level expert group (chaired by Jacques de Larosière) to present a Communication setting out the basic architecture for a new European financial supervisory framework, with the target of having this operational in 2010. In parallel, many European governments took their own actions to stabilise their financial systems and supported their own economies with measures targeted at labour and product markets, such as short-time work or incentives to replace old cars (in particular, those that damaged the environment). However, increased fiscal stimuli and falling government revenues from income and consumption taxes increased public deficits above the ceiling of 3 % in most Member Stares, triggering the excessive deficit procedure (EDP) in accordance with the provisions of the stability and growth pact (SGP), and raising new policy challenges.

As information derived from national accounts and other macro-economic indicators have a crucial role for policymaking, this spotlight chapter starts with a presentation of the main elements of the European system of national and regional accounts (ESA), providing an explanation of the various types of accounts and balance sheets that make up this framework, for example the sector accounts and government finance statistics.

The next section presents some of the policy areas that rely on the availability of high quality national accounts data. These include notably the use of national and quarterly accounts for business cycle analysis, for example, to develop and monitor macro-economic policies, to support monetary policy decisions, and to analyse the development of public finances, particularly in the context of the stability and growth pact. ESA data also provide a basis for structural policies, for example in the context of the Lisbon Strategy and the EU 2020 Strategy. Another example presented is the use of regional accounts as the basis for the allocation of expenditure for the structural funds or the assessment of the results of regional and cohesion policy.

The third section uses national accounts data and related data to present an analysis of recent economic developments. A selection of macro-economic data, many of which are taken from quarterly national and sector accounts, presents a profile of the economic and financial crisis. The analysis notably shows the impact on output, investment, consumption, income, saving and wealth, as well as economic sentiment, inflation and unemployment. One advantage in comparison with the analysis traditionally presented in the subsequent chapters of this yearbook is that the majority of the data used in this spotlight chapter is presented for a quarterly frequency – and in some cases monthly frequency – instead of annual data, thereby allowing a more timely and nuanced analysis of the business cycle. The section closes with a presentation relating to the statistical implications of the financial and economic crisis.

The final section reviews the main challenges that lie ahead for national accounts and some of the responses that are already being developed and implemented. It notably presents efforts made to improve national accounts standards through the update of the system of national accounts (SNA) at a global level, as well as at the European level, by the revision of the ESA. The chapter concludes with a section that looks beyond the use of GDP as a single number to 'summarise what is happening in the economy', and presents a number of initiatives to complement traditional national accounts indicators in order to be able to combine economic, social and environmental measures. In September 2009, two initiatives in this domain were unveiled, both of which underline the need to extend the traditional use that is made of national accounts statistics: the European Commission's Communication on 'GDP and beyond' and the so-called 'Stiglitz Report' on the measurement of economic performance and social progress.

1. National accounts – an overview

National accounts are a system of accounts and balance sheets that provide a broad and integrated framework to describe an economy, whether a region, a country, or a group of countries. For internationally comparable national accounts this system needs to be based on common concepts, definitions, classifications and accounting rules, in order to arrive at a consistent, reliable and comparable quantitative description of an economy. National accounts provide systematic and detailed economic data useful for economic analysis to support the development and monitoring of policy-making. This section provides a brief description of various types of accounts.

1.1 General features of national accounts

National accounts record economic activities in a systematic manner, distinguishing actors belonging to institutional sectors such as households, corporations and government. The system describes the various transactions or other changes in assets (flows) during a period of time as well as the level (normally at the end of a period of time) of stocks. A particular focus on the monitoring of fiscal policies in the EU is reflected through the development of government finance statistics (Point 1.7). The recent financial and economic crisis has also underlined the importance of financial accounts (Point 1.8), which present financial transactions, other changes in financial assets or liabilities, and financial balance sheets. Furthermore, national accounts serve as the foundation of a broader statistical system. This is the case for social and economic statistics in general (Section 4), and for satellite accounts in particular (Point 1.10).

The European system of national and regional accounts

The European system of national and regional accounts ([6]) known by the abbreviation ESA is fully consistent with the worldwide guidelines on national accounting, namely the system of national accounts (SNA): the SNA is published jointly by the United Nations, the Commission of the European Communities, the International Monetary Fund, the Organisation for Economic Cooperation and Development and the World Bank.

The ESA is not restricted to annual national accounting, but applies also to quarterly accounts and regional accounts, and these three types of accounts are presented under Points 1.2, 1.3 and 1.9 below. The ESA consists of two main sets of tables, namely the input-output framework/accounts by industry and the sector accounts, which

([6]) For more information: http://circa.europa.eu/irc/dsis/nfaccount/info/data/ESA95/en/esa95en.htm.

are presented under Points 1.5 and 1.6. The ESA also encompasses concepts of population and employment (Point 1.4) that are relevant for both the sector accounts and the input-output framework.

The compilation of the accounts

National accounts are compiled separately by each Member State, more specifically by the national statistical office or another institution appointed by the government, for example, the national central bank. The accounts are the result of a process of integration of data from many sources, for example, statistical surveys of businesses and households and administrative data. European national accounts are compiled by Eurostat by combining Member States' national accounts. For this purpose countries are required to provide Eurostat with a pre-specified data set according to a fixed transmission timetable.

1.2 Annual accounts

Annual data constitute the core of the national accounts system, both regarding their level of detail and their use for the estimation of quarterly data (see Point 1.3). Data within the national accounts domain encompasses information on the gross domestic product (GDP) and its components, final consumption aggregates, income, savings and employment. Breakdowns exist for certain variables by economic activity (as defined by the activity classification, NACE), investment products, final consumption purpose and institutional sectors. Further explanations on definitions and data availability as well as some main findings in relation to annual national accounts are presented within Subchapter 1.1 of this yearbook, as part of the chapter on the economy.

Box 1: gross domestic product (GDP)

The most frequently used measure for the overall size of an economy is gross domestic product (GDP). GDP at market prices is the total monetary value of the production activity of all producer units within a certain area (for example, a national territory), no matter whether the units are owned by nationals or foreigners.

GDP, and in particular GDP per capita, is one of the main indicators used for general economic analysis, as well as spatial and/or temporal comparisons.

GDP can be defined and calculated in three ways:

- **the output approach:** as the sum of gross value added of the various institutional sectors or the various industries, plus taxes and less subsidies on products;
- **the expenditure approach:** as the sum of final uses of goods and services by resident institutional units (final consumption and gross capital formation), plus exports and minus imports of goods and services;
- **the income approach:** as the sum of the compensation of employees, net taxes on production and imports, gross operating surplus and mixed income.

Figure 1 provides an example of one of the most common analysis of data from national accounts. The analysis of GDP across countries is facilitated by studying GDP per capita, so removing the influence of the absolute size of the population. GDP per capita is often considered as a broad economic indicator of living standards, despite the fact that this is not the main purpose of such an indicator. An index of GDP per capita in relation to the EU average (set to equal 100) can be derived: if the index of a country is higher/lower than 100, this country's level of GDP per head is above/below the EU-27 average. Such comparisons of the economic activity of countries should ideally be made using a series that reflects the purchasing power of each currency, rather than using market exchange rates, and as a result this indicator is generally expressed in purchasing power standards (PPS).

Figure 1: GDP per capita in purchasing power standards (PPS), 2008 (¹) (EU-27=100)

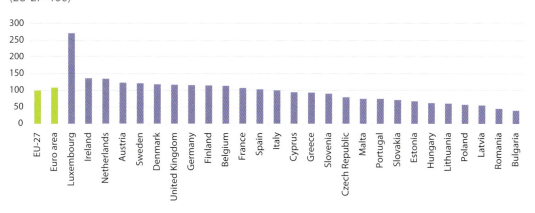

(¹) Greece, provisional; Austria and Romania, forecasts; Slovakia, estimate.

Source: Eurostat (tsieb010)

1.3 Quarterly accounts

The motivation for quarterly accounts stems from some of the shortcomings of annual data that make them unsuitable for the purpose of supporting short-term economic analysis, for example:

- ongoing economic policy decisions, which require prompt information on economic developments are inadequately supported, especially for the current year;
- business cycle fluctuations are not adequately captured because the average period of the cycle does not generally coincide with calendar years;
- there is a long delay after the end of the reference period before the figures are published.

Quarterly accounts have the advantage of being able to provide a coherent set of indicators on both non-financial and financial economic activity that are available with a short time lag. They have thus been developed to form an integral part of the system of accounts. A chapter on quarterly national accounts was introduced in the 1995 version of the ESA and Eurostat published a separate manual, a 'Handbook on quarterly accounts' in 1999. This aims to ensure that quarterly accounts adopt the same principles, definitions and structure as the annual accounts, subject to certain modifications, due to the period of time covered.

However, quarterly data follow a simplified scheme because the purpose of quarterly accounts is to track movements in key macro-economic aggregates, not to provide the same structural detail of the economy as the annual accounts, and to aid rapid compilation, recognising that there are less data available quarterly. Some further particularities of the quarterly accounts include the treatment of seasonality, and ensuring consistency between quarterly and annual accounts.

The statistical methods used for compiling quarterly accounts may also differ quite considerably from those used for the annual accounts. They can be classified in two major categories: those based on the availability at quarterly intervals, with appropriate simplifications, of similar sources to those used to compile the annual accounts; and indirect procedures based on time disaggregation of the annual accounts data in accordance with mathematical or statistical methods relying on appropriate quarterly indicators. In some systems, the annual accounts are a by-product of the quarterly system and there is no separate annual calculation.

The increasing role that the quarterly accounts have assumed in recent years demonstrates their importance for short-term economic analysis and justifies the increasing efforts devoted to compiling them. As all Member States compile quarterly accounts, EU-27 and euro area aggregates are, in principle, obtained through the aggregation of the data from the Member States. Eurostat regularly estimates the quarterly EU accounts from annual EU accounts using quarterly information that is available from the Member States. The main reason for this approach is the strong demand for timely quarterly accounts, as business cycle analysis requires quarterly results for the EU-27 and in particular the euro area much earlier than the arrival of data for the last of Member States. Eurostat publishes GDP flash estimates about 45 days after the end of each quarter and more detailed breakdowns with the first and second regular estimates after 65 days and 105 days. Quarterly estimations of employment figures are released after 75 days and 105 days and quarterly sector accounts after 120 days. A broad selection of figures based on quarterly national accounts data are presented under Point 3.1.

1.4 Employment

Employment and population have traditionally been considered auxiliary variables in national accounts, intended to calculate ratios per inhabitant or per employed person. The importance of employment within the system has increased, and is now considered as a key short-term economic indicator. Employment in national accounts is the result of the integration of data from many sources, and should be estimated simultaneously to and consistently with other national accounts variables, like output and the compensation of employees.

However, it should be kept in mind that employment figures in national accounts may differ from those produced by labour market statistics, such as the labour force survey (LFS), which also provides data on employment and unemployment, broken down by gender or other characteristics of the individual. The ESA distinguishes resident persons in employment (the national scope) from employment in resident production units (the domestic scope): the difference is significant for geographical areas with large cross-border flows of persons employed. Notably the LFS focuses on resident households, and so is closer to the national scope definition in the ESA, but there are also other differences between the ESA and LFS employment data.

Figure 2 presents the evolution of employment in the EU-27 and the euro area –consistent with the national accounts concepts. Using seasonally adjusted data, the figure illustrates that the number of persons employed progressively accelerated over the past decade until the economic and financial crisis provoked a setback in European labour markets from mid-2008.

Figure 2: Employment index, domestic concept, seasonally adjusted (2000=100)

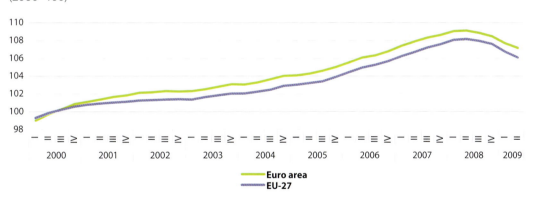

Source: Eurostat (namq_aux_pem)

1.5 Supply, use and input-output tables

The supply and use framework is the part of the national accounts system which focuses on the production and use of goods and services in an economy. It reflects the activities of industries in which intermediate products and primary inputs (such as labour and capital) are required. Supply and use tables show where and how goods and services are produced and to which intermediate or final use they flow.

The input-output framework consists of three types of tables: supply and use tables, symmetric input-output tables and tables linking the supply and use tables to the sector accounts; these are an integral part of the ESA. Compilation issues and harmonised solutions are presented in the Eurostat manual of supply, use and input-output tables.

These tables describe the production process (such as the cost structure and the generation of income) by industry or activity and the use of goods and services (output, imports, exports, final consumption, intermediate consumption and capital formation by product group). Within the national accounts system the supply, use and input-output tables offer the most detailed portrait of an economy's production and use activities and also provide a consistent framework for balancing national accounts.

These tables show among others:

• the structure of the costs of production and the value added, which is generated in the production process;
• the inter-dependencies of industries;
• the flows of goods and services produced and used within the national economy;
• international trade in goods and services with the rest of the world.

Supply tables record how products are made available in an economy: this may be output from a range of domestic industries or imports.

Table 1: Simplified supply table

Products	Industries: 1, 2, …, n	Imports	Total
1	Matrix of the	Imports of	Total supply
2	output of each product	each product	(output + import)
	by each industry		of each product
⋮			
n			
Total	Total output	Total	Total
	by each industry	imports	supply

In a similar manner the use of the same list of products can be analysed differentiating the use for intermediate consumption of domestic industries or final uses such as final consumption, fixed capital formation or exports. Use tables also show the components of value added (such as compensation for employees or consumption of fixed capital) by industry. The framework must fulfil two identities. The output of each industry is equal to the sum of intermediate consumption plus value added. For each product, total supply (output plus imports) equals the sum of intermediate consumption, final consumption, gross capital formation and exports.

Table 2: Simplified use table

| | Industries: 1, 2, ..., n | Final uses | | | | Total |
		Final consump-tion	Gross fixed capital formation	Change in inventories	Exports	
Products 1 2 ⋮ n	Matrix of the intermediate consumption of each product by each industry	Final consump-tion of each product	Gross fixed capital formation of each product	Change in inventories of each product	Exports of each product	Total use (intermediate consumption + final uses) of each product
Value added **— compensation of employees** **— consumption of fixed capital** **— net operating surplus**	Matrix of the value added components by each industry					Total value added of each product
Total	Total output by each industry: intermediate consumption + value added	Total final uses by category				Total use

A symmetric input-output table is a product-by-product (or industry-by-industry) matrix: it rearranges both supply and use in a single table with a single, identical product (or industry) classification applied for both rows and columns.

1.6 Sector accounts

Sector accounts provide, by institutional sector, a systematic description of the different stages of the economic process, from production through to the use of income and financial and non-financial accumulation. The sector accounts also include balance sheets to describe the stocks of assets, liabilities and net worth. The European Central Bank (ECB) and Eurostat publish quarterly EU and euro area accounts by institutional sector, and recently key indicators for Member States have also been published.

Macro-economic developments, such as economic growth and inflation, are driven by the actions of the individual economic subjects in an economy. The institutional sectors combine institutional units with broadly similar characteristics and behaviour: households and non-profit institutions serving households (NPISHs), non-financial corporations, financial corporations, and government. Grouping economic subjects with similar behaviour into institutional sectors helps to understand the functioning of the economy.

Transactions with non-residents and the financial claims of residents on non-residents, or vice versa, are recorded in a separate account referred to as the rest of the world.

Figure 3: Shares of institutional sectors in key aggregates, EU-27, 1999-2008 average (%)

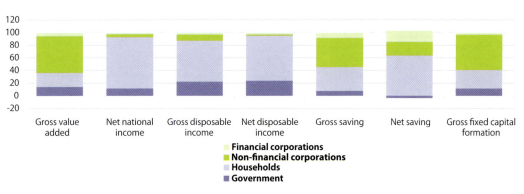

Source: Eurostat (nasa_simplif) and European Central Bank (ECB)

Figure 3 presents the shares of institutional sectors in key national accounts aggregates. The households sector comprises all households and household firms, such as sole proprietorships and most partnerships that do not have an independent legal status. Therefore, the households sector, in addition to consumption, also generates output and entrepreneurial income. For presentational reasons, non-profit institutions serving households (NPISHs), such as charities and trade unions, are grouped in the European accounts with households; their economic weight is relatively limited. The non-financial corporations sector comprises all private and

public corporate enterprises that produce goods or provide non-financial services to the market. Accordingly, the government sector excludes non-market public enterprises and comprises central, state (regional) and local government and social security funds. The financial corporations sector comprises all private and public entities engaged in financial intermediation, such as monetary financial institutions (predominantly banks), investment funds, insurance corporations and pension funds. A selection of data based on quarterly sector accounts is presented under Point 3.1.

1.7 Government finance statistics

Government finance statistics (GFS) present the economic activities of government in a harmonised and comparable way. GFS may differ noticeably from nationally-specific budget or public accounting presentations as far as the scope of units and the recording of transactions are concerned. The GFS present revenue, expenditure and deficit, as well as transactions in assets, liabilities, other economic flows, and balance sheets. They are fully consistent with the general government sector within the national accounts, but have a different (integrated) presentation for users.

The GFS attract particular attention as they form the basis for fiscal monitoring in Europe, notably statistics related to the excessive deficit procedure (EDP).

The EDP is defined by Article 104 of the Treaty on European Union (the so-called Maastricht Treaty), which foresaw the creation of the euro. The Treaty obliges Member States to comply with budgetary discipline by adhering to two criteria: a deficit to GDP ratio and a debt to GDP ratio not exceeding reference values of 3 % and 60 % respectively, as defined in the Protocol on the EDP annexed to the Treaty; these reference values are based on GFS concepts. The government deficit is the net lending/net borrowing of government as defined in the ESA, adjusted for the treatment of interest relating to swaps and forward rate agreements. Government debt is defined as the total consolidated gross debt at nominal value in the following categories of government liabilities: currency and deposits, securities other than shares excluding financial derivatives, and loans.

Figure 4: Government deficit and debt as a percentage of GDP, four-quarter moving average, EU-27 (%)

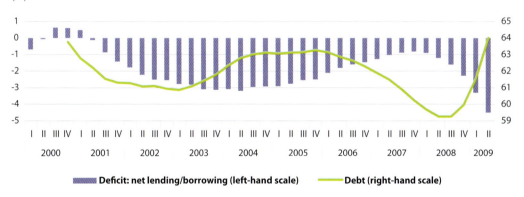

Source: Eurostat (gov_q_ggnfa and gov_q_ggdebt)

The ESA95 manual on government debt and deficit (MGDD) provides interpretation and guidance to establish agreed methodological practices for the measurement of government deficit and debt. The European Commission is responsible for providing the data used for the EDP, and within the European Commission this task is undertaken by Eurostat on the basis of GFS statistics provided by the Member States.

Figure 5: Government deficit, net borrowing (-)/lending (+) as a percentage of GDP (¹)
(%)

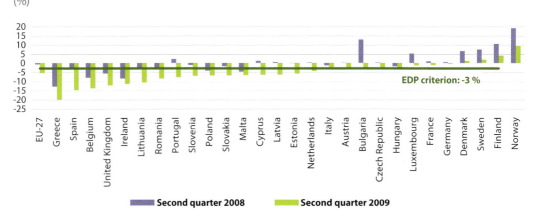

(¹) Germany and France, fourth quarter of 2007 and fourth quarter of 2008; Belgium, first quarter of 2008 and first quarter of 2009.

Source: Eurostat (gov_q_ggnfa)

Figure 6: Government debt as a percentage of GDP
(%)

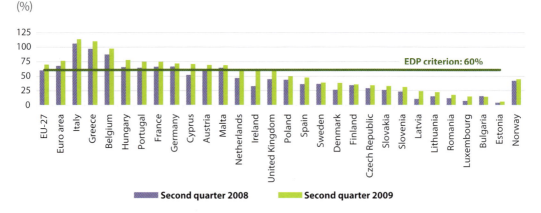

Source: Eurostat (gov_q_ggdebt)

1.8 Financial accounts

Within the ESA, financial accounts show financial transactions, holding gains and losses, other changes in financial assets or liabilities, and the financial balance sheets. The compilation of these accounts is the subject of a manual on sources and methods for the compilation of ESA95 financial accounts. Most transactions involving the transfer of ownership of goods or assets or the provision of services have some counterpart entry in the financial account. The counterpart may take the form of a change in currency or transferable deposits, an account receivable or payable (for example, a trade credit) or some other type of financial asset or liability. Moreover, there are many transactions that are recorded entirely within the financial account, where one financial asset is exchanged for another or a liability is repaid with an asset. Such transactions change the distribution of the portfolio of financial assets and liabilities and may change their total amounts but do not affect net lending/net borrowing.

Accounts on financial transactions show how the surplus or deficit on the capital account is financed by transactions in financial assets and liabilities. Thus, the value of the balance of the financial account (net acquisition of financial assets less net incurrence of liabilities) is equal, in theory, to net lending/net borrowing, the balancing item of the capital account. The financial account indicates how net borrowing sectors obtain resources by incurring liabilities or reducing assets, and how net lending sectors allocate their surpluses by acquiring assets or reducing liabilities. The account also shows the contributions to these transactions of the various types of financial assets, and the role of financial intermediaries.

In addition, accounts on nominal holding gains/losses show the gains/losses on a given quantity of an asset/liability as the change in value for the owner of that asset/liability as a result of change in prices or exchange rates. Any changes in financial assets and liabilities that are not due to financial transactions, holding gains and losses or reclassifications are recorded as other changes in volume, for example, write-offs of bad debt.

Financial balance sheets are statements of the value of assets and liabilities at a particular point in time: the balancing item is net worth or, in the case of the whole economy, national wealth – the aggregate of non-financial assets and net claims on the rest of the world.

Financial accounts form an important tool for analysing financial flows taking place between well-defined institutional sectors within the economy, and between those institutional sectors and the rest of the world, and for assessing financial interrelationships within the economy and vis-à-vis the rest of the world at a particular point in time. Because of their link with the capital and use of income accounts, financial accounts serve as an important instrument to monitor the transmission process of monetary policy. The completeness of financial accounts makes possible the analysis of monetary aggregates as well as the analysis of longer-term financial investments and sources of finance. Consequently, the financial accounts provide a way of examining the financial effects of economic policy and assistance for decisions regarding future

policy. They can be used to investigate factors influencing the holdings of and transactions in, different types of financial instruments, for example, changes in interest rates.

For financial institutions the financial account shows the large amounts of funds which are channelled through them as financial intermediaries. The scale of this makes it important to be aware of changes in their sources of funds and in their use of those funds. The transactions of financial institutions reflect the liquidity, current and capital expenditure of other sectors, and the financing of the government sector net cash requirement.

The financial balance sheets show the financial worth of each sector of the economy at a particular point in time. The changes from previous balance sheets illustrate both the change in the valuation of different instruments (for example, as stock markets move or currency exchange rates change) and the changing portfolios resulting from the financial transactions of the sectors. This allows the measurement of so-called 'wealth effects' through the change in the market prices of assets.

1.9 Regional economic accounts

Regional accounts are a regional specification of the corresponding accounts of the total economy. A full set of accounts at the regional level implies treating each region as a separate economic entity. In this context, transactions with other regions become external transactions. Conceptual difficulties partly explain why regional accounts are limited to recording production activities by industry and to accounts for some institutional sectors like households.

Nevertheless, regional accounts do provide information in particular on regional GDP, regional gross value added and some other indicators by industry. As already noted for national accounts it is common to present GDP as an average per inhabitant and for regional statistics the distinction between place of work and place of residence is therefore particularly significant. Regional GDP measures the economic output achieved within regional boundaries, regardless of whether this was attributable to resident or non-resident employed persons. The analysis of GDP per inhabitant is therefore only straightforward if all employed persons involved in generating GDP are also residents of the region in question. In areas with a high proportion of inbound commuters, regional GDP per inhabitant can be extremely high and conversely it can be relatively low in the surrounding regions. Regional GDP can be used to identify regional disparities within and between countries, as well as convergence between regions. A map of regional GDP per inhabitant is presented in Chapter 13.

1.10 Satellite accounts

For some uses, the concepts in the ESA are insufficient and may need to be supplemented. One of the ways this can be done in a coherent manner is through the development of satellite accounts. Satellite accounts can show more detail where necessary, or they may enlarge the scope of the accounting system by adding non-monetary information, or they may change some basic concepts – for example, by enlarging the concept of capital formation. Generally, satellite accounts follow the basic concepts and classifications of the national accounting system, only deviating when the specific purpose of the satellite account requires a modification.

Satellite accounts may include stocks and flows which are not readily observable in monetary terms (or without a clear monetary counterpart) as these are not well served by the core national accounts system. Examples are measuring time usage for production within households, or information on the number of pupils or time spent in education, or the health of trees as an indicator of pollution. Satellite accounts offer a possibility to link such statistics in non-monetary units to national accounts by using the classifications employed in the standard framework for these non-monetary statistics. This linkage can then facilitate the analysis of interactions between the standard national accounts information and the information in satellite accounts.

One example of a satellite account where considerable development has been made within the United Nations and the EU is environmental accounts, which are a tool to analyse the links between the environment and the economy. These can be used, for example, to analyse to what extent our current production and consumption patterns are degrading natural resources, or to measure the environmental effects of economic policy measures. Some information and data relating to environmental accounts is presented in Subchapter 11.5.

Another example of satellite accounts is the tourism satellite account for which a new joint methodological framework was released in 2008 by the United Nations, Eurostat, the OECD and the World Tourism Organisation (WTO).

The extent of the use of satellite accounts is growing, and these accounts will likely have a more prominent place in the revised ESA, for example, for social protection statistics – see Point 4.3.

2. Main users of national accounts statistics

European institutions, governments, central banks as well as other economic and social bodies in the public and private sectors need a set of comparable and reliable statistics on which to base their decisions. National accounts can be used for various types of analysis and evaluation. For instance, an analysis of the structure of the economy can be used to show the level or share of value added and employment in each industry, or the final consumption expenditure dedicated to different product groups. Analysis may focus on specific parts or aspects of an economy – for example, banking and finance, or the role of government. National accounts may also be analysed over time to show changes in an economy, for example, the development of GDP, or a comparison of the structure of two economies. The use of internationally accepted concepts and definitions also permits an analysis of different economies, such as the interdependencies between the economies of the EU, or a comparison between the EU and non-member countries. This section portrays some of the main uses and users of national accounts data.

2.1 Business cycle and macro-economic policy analysis

One of the main uses of national accounts data relates to the need to support European economic policy decisions and the achievement of EMU objectives with high-quality short-term statistics that allow the monitoring of macro-economic developments and the derivation of macro-economic policy advice. For instance, one of the most basic and long-standing uses of national accounts is to quantify the rate of growth of an economy, in simple terms the growth of GDP. However, national accounts are used much more widely than this. Core national accounts figures are notably used to develop and monitor macro-economic policies, while detailed national accounts data can also be used to develop sectoral or industrial policies, particularly through analysis of input-output tables. In some economies national accounts have been used to develop and monitor economic plans. Among the European institutions, national accounts are used in a wide range of areas, including to support monetary policy decision-making, economic research and policy analysis, macro-economic forecasting, and fiscal surveillance.

The ECB and European Monetary Union

Since the beginning of the EMU in 1999, the European Central Bank (ECB) has been one of the main users of national accounts. The primary objective of the ECB and its single monetary policy is the maintenance of price stability in the euro area, and in this respect the key indicator is inflation, measured through the harmonised index of consumer prices

(HICP). The ECB's strategy for assessing the risks to price stability is based on two analytical perspectives, referred to as the 'two pillars': economic analysis and monetary analysis. A large number of monetary and financial indicators are thus evaluated in relation to other relevant data that allow the combination of monetary, financial and economic analysis, for example, key national accounts aggregates and sector accounts. In this way monetary and financial indicators can be analysed within the context of the rest of the economy. As detailed under Point 1.6, the ECB and Eurostat have joined forces to produce European sector accounts on an annual and quarterly basis, which link financial and non-financial statistics and include consistent financial balance sheets. They provide a large range of indicators on the development of the economic situation in various institutional sectors, for example regarding income, expenditure, investment and outstanding debt for households, or the level of investment and debt of non-financial corporations.

Economic policy analysis

The European Commission is another main user of national accounts across a wide range of areas. Its services regularly use these data for designing and assessing their policies. The Directorate-General for Economic and Financial Affairs (DG ECFIN) develops research tools and analyses data to guide and support policy-making in the European Commission in general. One area of key research is the functioning of economic and monetary union, however, the analyses conducted covers a broad range of issues from financial stability or an assessment of economic convergence in the context of enlargement, to how structural reforms contribute to macro-economic performance or the economic implications of ageing populations. The research tools that underpin DG ECFIN's work on economic policy coordination and surveillance include macro-economic and econometric models, business and consumer surveys, economic databases and macro-economic forecasts.

Macro-economic forecasting

DG ECFIN also produces the European Commission's macro-economic forecasts twice a year, in the spring and autumn. These forecasts cover all EU Member States in order to derive forecasts for the euro area and the EU-27, but they also include outlooks for candidate countries, as well as some non-member countries. Each forecast has at least a two-year time horizon (with an additional year added each autumn) covering the current year and the next. In between the spring and autumn forecasts, interim forecasts are produced in which an update of real GDP growth and inflation is estimated for the seven largest Member States and for the current year only. While the biannual forecasts are built on detailed country by country analysis, interim forecasts are largely prepared using indicator-based models.

Fiscal policy and the stability and growth pact

The analysis of public finances through national accounts is another well established use of these statistics. Within the EU a specific application was developed in relation to the convergence criteria for EMU, two of which refer directly to public finances. These criteria have been defined in terms of national accounts figures, namely, government deficit and government debt relative to GDP.

As noted under Point 1.7 above, the Treaty on European Union (Maastricht Treaty) established limits for government deficits and debt. Under the provisions of the stability and growth pact (SGP) the Member States have to submit annual stability (convergence) programmes, showing how they intend to achieve or safeguard sound fiscal positions in the medium-term, taking into account the impending budgetary impact of population aging and other factors. The European Commission assesses these programmes and the Council gives its opinion on them. The SGP also governs the excessive deficit procedure (EDP): the EDP is triggered when the deficit breaches the 3 % GDP threshold of the Treaty. If it is decided that the deficit is excessive in the meaning of the Treaty, the Council issues recommendations to the Member States concerned to correct their excessive deficits and gives a timeframe for doing so. Non-compliance with the recommendations triggers further steps in the procedures, including the possibility of sanctions for euro area Member States.

However, it should be noted that these two criteria relating to public finances do not synthesise all the information about public finances, and a much broader range of indicators (than these two headline figures) is considered useful for monitoring purposes – for example, the composition of revenue raising activities and the purposes for which government expenditure is made.

2.2 Regional, structural and sectoral policies

As well as business cycle and macro-economic policy analysis, there are other policy-related uses of ESA data, notably concerning regional, structural and sectoral issues.

Regional policy

The allocation of expenditure for the structural funds is partly based on regional accounts. Furthermore, regional statistics are used for ex-post assessment of the results of regional and cohesion policy.

The EU's regional policy aims to strengthen economic, social and territorial cohesion by reducing differences in the level of development among regions and Member States. For the period 2007-2013 a budget of EUR 347 410 million is foreseen ([7]), equivalent to more than one third of the whole EU budget. The main concerns of the policy for 2007 to 2013 are:

* convergence – 81.5 % of the funds available;
* (regional) competitiveness and employment – 16 % of the funds available;
* territorial cooperation – 2.5 % of the funds available.

Convergence regions are NUTS ([8]) level 2 regions whose GDP per inhabitant (measured in purchasing power standards and on the basis of a three year average) is less than 75 % of the EU-25 average; in other words, the poorest regions and Member States. These 84 regions (based on regions according to the 2003 version of the NUTS classification) have a total population of 154 million inhabitants.

All other NUTS level 2 regions, of which there are 168, are eligible under the regional competitiveness and employment objective, which aims to strengthen competitiveness, attractiveness and employment. Special financing will be provided to 13 'phasing-in' regions as they formerly had the equivalent status to convergence regions.

Several instruments are used to implement regional policy, notably the European Regional Development Fund (ERDF) and the Cohesion Fund. The ERDF operates in all Member States but is concentrated on the poorest regions and co-finances investments and training. The Cohesion Fund mainly co-finances transport networks and environment projects. Member States whose gross national income per inhabitant is less than 90 % of the EU average are eligible: for the period 2007-2013 the Cohesion Fund concerns the Member States that joined the EU in 2004 and 2007, as well as Greece and Portugal; Spain is eligible to a phase-out fund.

Analysis of structural reforms

Encouraging more growth and more jobs is a strategic priority for both the EU and the Member States, and is part of the revised Lisbon and EU 2020 strategies. In support of these strategic priorities, common policies are implemented across all sectors of the EU economy while the Member States implement their own national structural reforms. The effects of these policies and reforms may spread across the EU as a result of the economic links between Member States. To ensure that this is as beneficial as possible, and to prepare for the challenges that lie ahead,

([7]) For more information: http://ec.europa.eu/regional_policy/policy/fonds/index_en.htm.

([8]) NUTS: common classification of territorial units for statistics.

the European Commission rigorously analyses all these policies.

Agricultural policy

The European Commission conducts economic analysis contributing to the evolution of the Common Agricultural Policy (CAP) by analysing the efficiency of its various support mechanisms and developing a long-term perspective. This includes research, analysis and impact assessments on topics related to agriculture and the rural economy in the EU and non-member countries, in part using the economic accounts for agriculture (satellite accounts).

2.3 Target setting, benchmarking and contributions

Target setting

Policies within the EU are increasingly setting medium or long-term targets, whether binding or not. For some of these, the level of GDP is used as a benchmark denominator, for example, setting a target for expenditure on research and development at a level of 3 % of GDP.

Another example concerns official development assistance (ODA), which consists of grants or loans that are undertaken by the official sector with promotion of economic development and welfare in the recipient countries as the main objective.

The EU agreed to increase its ODA as a step towards the 0.7 % target set by the United Nations. In 2005 the EU made additional commitments to collectively reach official development assistance of 0.56 % of GNI by 2010, underpinned by an individual target of 0.17 % for the 12 newest Member States and 0.51 % for the others, with those Member States that have already reached their targets keeping higher aid levels.

Budgetary contributions

National accounts are also used to determine EU resources. The basic rules on the system of the EU's resources are laid down in a Council Decision (currently 2000/597/EC, Euratom). The overall amount of own resources needed to finance the budget is determined by total expenditure less other revenue. The total amount of own resources cannot exceed 1.24 % of the gross national income of the EU.

Own resources can be divided into the following categories:

- Traditional own resources consist of customs duties, agricultural duties and sugar levies. These own resources are levied on economic operators and collected by Member States on behalf of the EU. However, Member States keep 25 % as a compensation for their collection costs.

Table 3: National contribution by Member State and traditional own resources collected on behalf of the EU, 2007
(EUR million)

	VAT-based resource	GNI-based resource (¹)	UK correction	Traditional own resources	Total	Total (% of GNI)
EU-27 (²)	19 441	73 915	59	16 573	109 988	0.9
Belgium	469	1 986	233	1 685	4 372	1.3
Bulgaria	46	163	21	61	291	1.0
Czech Republic	200	704	84	179	1 167	1.0
Denmark	333	1 394	163	330	2 219	1.0
Germany	3 635	14 654	294	3 127	21 710	0.9
Estonia	27	96	11	43	177	1.2
Ireland	276	972	120	218	1 586	1.0
Greece	698	1 947	146	230	3 020	1.4
Spain	1 723	6 073	752	1 290	9 838	1.0
France	3 114	11 216	1 327	1 333	16 989	0.9
Italy	2 030	9 144	1 163	1 687	14 024	0.9
Cyprus	25	88	11	46	170	1.1
Latvia	35	118	15	31	199	1.0
Lithuania	47	158	20	45	271	1.0
Luxembourg	53	202	21	19	296	1.0
Hungary	138	547	75	111	870	0.9
Malta	9	33	4	12	57	1.1
Netherlands	936	3 401	92	1 874	6 303	1.1
Austria	409	1 565	43	201	2 218	0.8
Poland	509	1 746	216	338	2 809	1.0
Portugal	269	940	114	137	1 460	0.9
Romania	162	682	86	159	1 089	0.9
Slovenia	56	198	23	83	359	1.1
Slovakia	85	303	42	91	519	1.0
Finland	261	1 088	132	149	1 629	0.9
Sweden	487	1 949	41	438	2 915	0.9
United Kingdom	3 410	12 551	-5 189	2 657	13 429	0.7

(¹) For simplicity of the presentation, the GNI-based own resource includes the adjustment for certain justice and home affairs (JHA) policies where Member States choose not to participate.
(²) Total UK correction payments are not equal to zero on account of exchange rate differences.

Source: EU budget report 2007, European Commission

- The own resource based on value added tax is levied on Member States' VAT bases, which are harmonised for this purpose in accordance with Community rules. The same percentage is levied on the harmonised base of each Member State. However, the VAT base to take into account is capped at 50 % of each Member State's GNI. This rule is intended to avoid that the less prosperous Member States pay out of proportion to their capacity, since consumption and hence VAT tend to account for a higher percentage of a country's national income at relatively lower levels of prosperity. The contributions by the Member States for the VAT resource are largely affected by national accounts figures, as these are used to calculate the average VAT rate.

- The resource based on gross national income is used to balance budget revenue and expenditure, in other words, to finance the part of the budget not covered by any other sources of revenue. The same percentage rate is levied on each Member States' GNI, which is established in accordance with Community rules.

National accounts also assist in the calculation of the correction applied for the United Kingdom's contribution. The financing of the reimbursement by the other Member States is calculated on the basis of each country's share in the EU's total gross national income, with upper thresholds applied for some Member States.

Other international organisations

As well as being used to determine budgetary contributions within the EU, national accounts data are also used to determine contributions to other international organisations, such as the United Nations. Contributions to the United Nations' budget are based on gross national income along with a variety of adjustments and limits ([9]).

2.4 Analysts and forecasters

National accounts are also widely used by analysts and researchers to examine the economic situation and developments. Financial institutions' interest in national accounts may range from a broad analysis of the economy to specific information concerning savings, investment or debt among households, non-financial corporations or other institutional sectors. Social partners, such as representatives of businesses (for example, trade associations) or representatives of workers (for example, trade unions), also have an interest in national accounts for the purpose of analysing developments that affect industrial relations. Among other uses, researchers and analysts use national accounts for business cycle analysis and analysing long-term economic cycles and relating these to economic, political or technological developments.

([9]) Resolution adopted by the General Assembly 61/237.

3. The impact of the economic and financial crisis

Following the description of the various types of national accounts as well as their main uses and users, this section aims to demonstrate how national accounts data and related indicators can be used to monitor and analyse the recent evolution of the business cycle –for example, focussing on the economic and financial crisis.

This section starts with a presentation of the main GDP aggregate, before an analysis of external trade, output, income, consumption and investment, as well as developments for savings and wealth (from the sector accounts). The remaining analysis looks at a range of other economic indicators, such as economic sentiment, inflation and unemployment, in relation to the development of GDP. The indicators presented focus on economic developments over a period of close to ten years and, more specifically, on the impact of the financial and economic crisis (as shown by the most recent data available at the time of writing). This section concludes with a point in relation to statistical implications of the financial and economic crisis.

3.1 The impact of the recession – as measured by national accounts aggregates

As noted in the previous section, national accounts provide a tool for business cycle analysis. The indicators that are presented in this section show the considerable impact of the economic and financial crisis. Focussing mainly on aggregated data for the EU-27 economy, but

presenting also some snapshots in relation to the most recent situation observed in the Member States, the data presented in this section drawn from national accounts illustrate how the economic and financial crisis has impacted upon various sectors of the economy. Whereas this section focuses on quarterly data, which is more suited to an analysis of the business cycle, further analysis based on annual data from national accounts may be found in Chapter 1: more specifically, Subchapter 1.1 presents an analysis of GDP and its main components, while Subchapter 1.2 presents Government finance statistics.

GDP growth

Taking a medium-term perspective, Figure 7 shows quarter on quarter changes in GDP since 2000 for the EU-27. While positive growth rates were recorded each and every quarter until the middle of 2008, the negative growth rates in the final quarter of 2008 and the first quarter of 2009 were greater in magnitude than any of the growth rates recorded in earlier years, underlying the severity of the recession. In fact these were the first negative rates of change since the series began in 1995 and it is widely acknowledged that this is the worst global recession since the 1930's. The most recent rates of change available show that the strength of the recession weakened during 2009 and estimates for the third quarter of 2009 show a return to growth in the EU-27 as a whole.

However, the economic downturn was not homogeneous across the EU. Looking at the changes in GDP volumes compared with one year earlier, Figure 8 shows the great diversity in the intensity of the economic downturn between Member States: while the Baltic Member States all experienced particularly strong negative rates of change, Poland still continued to record economic growth.

Figure 7: GDP, change on previous quarter, EU-27
(%)

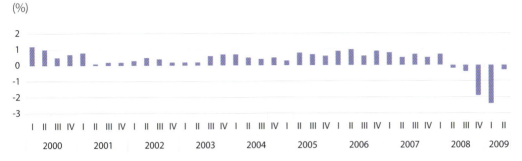

Source: Eurostat (namq_gdp_k)

Figure 8: GDP, change on same quarter of previous year, second quarter 2009 (¹)
(%)

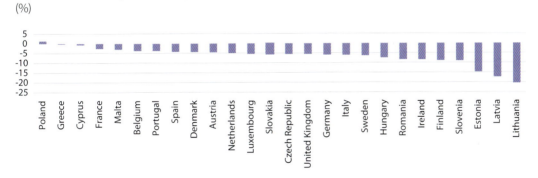

(¹) Bulgaria, not available; Denmark, Estonia, Ireland and Luxembourg, first quarter 2009.

Source: Eurostat (namq_gdp_k)

External trade

The global dimension of the economic crisis is clearly demonstrated by the evolution of external trade. Figure 9 illustrates that external trade in goods and services grew faster than GDP in the EU-27 from 2002 to the beginning of 2008. From this date, reductions in levels of external trade were more pronounced than the contraction in GDP. Furthermore, the level of GDP appeared to be stabilising in the middle of 2009, whereas external trade flows were still falling, albeit at a slower rate than in the second half of 2008.

Figures 10 and 11 show that the relative importance of imports and exports varies significantly across countries, and that the drop in imports was generally slightly more significant than the drop experienced for exports during the second quarter of 2009.

Figure 9: Indices of GDP and external trade, EU-27 (2000=100)

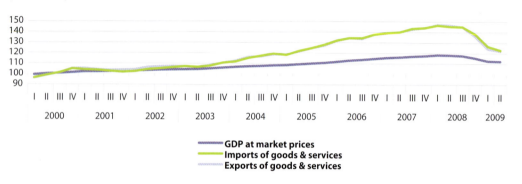

Source: Eurostat (namq_gdp_k)

Figure 10: Exports, change on same period of previous year, second quarter 2009 (%)

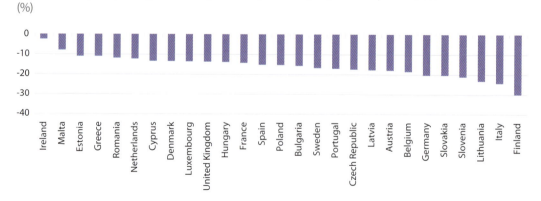

Source: Eurostat (namq_gdp_k)

Figure 11: Imports, change on same period of previous year, second quarter 2009 (%)

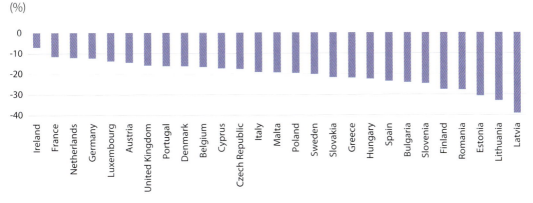

Source: Eurostat (namq_gdp_k)

Production, consumption and investment

The contraction in international trade may be cited as one of the main reasons for falling demand within the global economy. Industrial output in the EU-27 dropped sharply from the beginning of 2008. Figure 12 shows that the decline in industrial output was also much sharper than that recorded for GDP (industrial output fell by around 18 % overall from the first quarter of 2008 to the second

quarter of 2009). The decline in retail sales was more modest, but in both cases, there were again significant variations across Member States (see Figures 13 and 14).

An analysis of expenditure (see Figure 15) confirms that the decline in final consumption expenditure (mainly of households and government) was relatively modest in comparison, but investment (shown as gross fixed capital formation) declined at a particularly rapid pace across the EU during the recession.

Figure 12: Indices of GDP and industrial and retail trade output, EU-27 (2000=100)

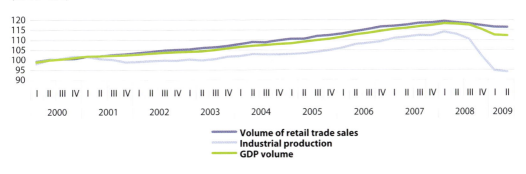

Source: Eurostat (sts_inpr_q, sts_trtu_q and namq_gdp_k)

Figure 13: Industrial production, change on same period of previous year, second quarter 2009 (¹) (%)

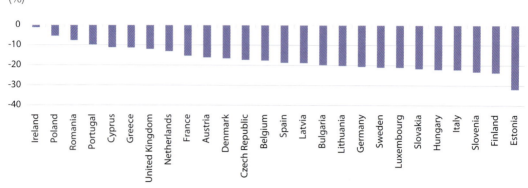

(¹) Belgium and Bulgaria, estimates; the Czech Republic, Greece, Cyprus, the Netherlands and Slovenia, provisional.

Source: Eurostat (sts_inprgr_q)

Figure 14: Retail trade volume of sales, change on same period of previous year, second quarter 2009 (¹) (%)

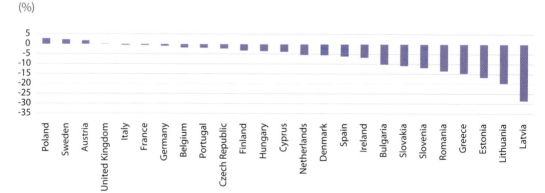

(¹) Luxembourg and Malta, not available; Spain, Italy, Cyprus and the Netherlands, estimates; Belgium, the Czech Republic, Germany and Austria, provisional.

Source: Eurostat (sts_trtugr_q)

Figure 15: Indices of GDP, consumption and investment, EU-27
(2000=100)

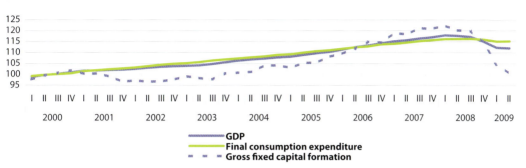

Source: Eurostat (namq_gdp_k)

3.2 The impact of the recession – as measured by European sector accounts

More detailed insights on trends affecting different types of economic agents during the recession can be gained from the sector accounts. Figures 16 to 18 indicate the contribution of the institutional sectors to changes in value added, capital formation, and lending/borrowing. Non-financial corporations generally deliver the largest contribution to value added (and GDP) growth, but their contribution is quite volatile. The contribution of households normally fluctuates less, partly because of the stabilising influence of the imputed rent on owner-occupied dwellings. Nevertheless, during recession in 2008/2009 the contribution of households to value added growth fell, and in fact turned negative from the final quarter of 2008.

Gross capital formation includes principally investment in fixed assets (buildings, machinery) but also changes in inventories. The overall growth of gross capital formation is mainly driven by developments in the non-financial corporations sector and, to a lesser extent, by households (dwellings). Gross capital formation is relatively volatile in all sectors, and during the recession in 2008/2009 households and non-financial corporations recorded negative rates of change for this indicator.

The difference between savings plus net capital transfers, on the one hand, and gross capital formation, on the other hand, is net lending if positive or net borrowing if negative. During the period shown in Figure 18 the EU-27 has been a net borrower from the rest of the world, and the extent of this borrowing increased from the beginning of 2005. Over the period shown, households were net lenders as were financial corporations in most quarters (note that the figure in fact shows cumulated values for four quarters), while non-financial corporations were net borrowers, as were governments most quarters. The increase in net borrowing during the recession in 2008/2009 results in large part from particularly strong growth in government net borrowing. The remainder of this section reviews developments in the corporate, household or government sectors, focussing mainly on wealth effects.

Figure 16: Growth of gross value added (GVA) by sector, EU-27 (¹)
(%)

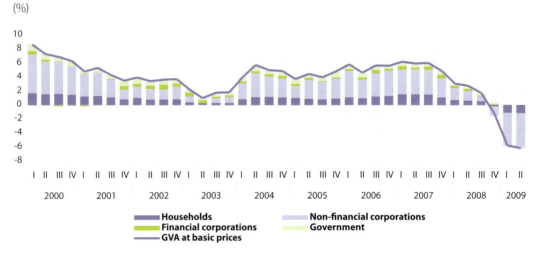

(¹) Annual percentage change.

Source: Eurostat (nasq_sector)

Figure 17: Growth of gross capital formation by sector, EU-27 (¹)
(%)

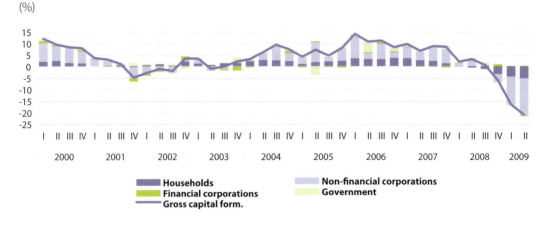

(¹) Annual percentage change.

Source: Eurostat (nasq_sector)

Figure 18: Net lending (+)/net borrowing (-) by sector, EU-27 (¹)
(%)

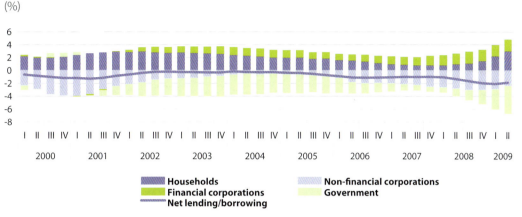

(¹) Percentage of GDP, based on four-quarter-cumulated sums.

Source: Eurostat (nasq_sector) and European Central Bank (ECB)

Corporations

The net financial wealth of corporations is the ultimate property of the owners/shareholders of corporations, mainly households. As such it is useful to analyse this before accounting for shares and other equity on the liabilities side. Figures 19 and 20 show the rate of change of net financial wealth adjusted in this way for financial and non-financial corporations, along with the changes in the main components. As for household financial wealth (see below), in recent periods other changes in prices and volumes have moved from positive to negative rates of change.

Figure 21 analyses the net financial wealth of non-financial corporations both on the assets and liabilities side, and confirms that the main movement in net financial wealth was changes in the value of shares and other equity.

Whereas for households the investment rate is expressed relative to disposable income, for non-financial corporations it is expressed relative to value added. Figure 22 indicates how the investment rate in the EU-27 increased between 2004 and the middle of 2008 as the growth of gross fixed capital formation outstripped that of value added. This situation was subsequently reversed with relatively large negative rates of change recorded for gross fixed capital formation from the final quarter of 2008.

Figure 19: Financial corporations, annual rates of change in financial assets, liabilities and wealth, euro area (¹)
(%)

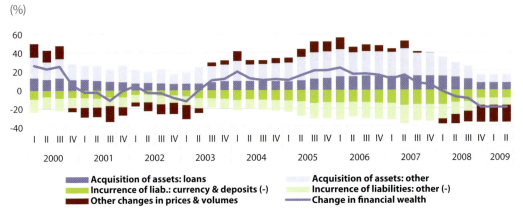

■■■ Acquisition of assets: loans
▨▨▨ Incurrence of liab.: currency & deposits (-)
■■■ Other changes in prices & volumes
▨▨▨ Acquisition of assets: other
▨▨▨ Incurrence of liabilities: other (-)
—— Change in financial wealth

(¹) Excludes shares and other equity liabilities; acquisitions, liabilities and change in wealth are all presented net.

Source: European Central Bank (ECB)

Figure 20: Non-financial corporations, annual rates of change in financial assets, liabilities and wealth, euro area (¹)
(%)

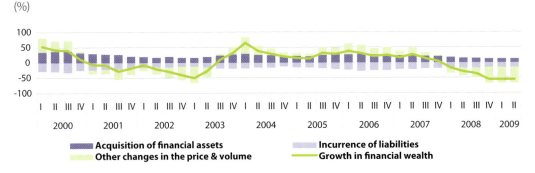

▨▨▨ Acquisition of financial assets
▨▨▨ Other changes in the price & volume
▨▨▨ Incurrence of liabilities
—— Growth in financial wealth

(¹) Except shares and other equity liabilities; acquisitions, liabilities and change in wealth are all presented net.

Source: European Central Bank (ECB)

Figure 21: Non-financial corporations, stock of financial assets, liabilities and wealth, euro area (¹)
(%)

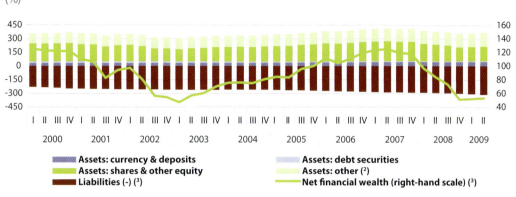

(¹) Percentage of net value added, based on four-quarter-cumulated sums.
(²) Insurance technical reserves, financial derivatives, loans granted and other accounts receivable.
(³) Except shares and other equity liabilities.

Source: European Central Bank (ECB)

Figure 22: Non-financial corporations, investment rate and annual rate of change in gross fixed capital formation and value added, EU-27
(%)

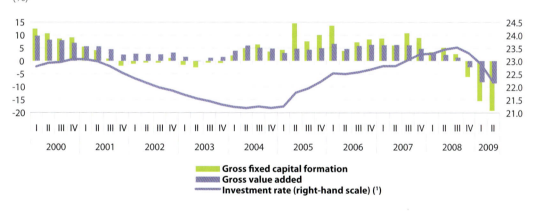

(¹) Percentage of gross value added, based on four-quarter-cumulated sums.

Source: Eurostat (nasq_sector)

Households

The main contribution to households' income growth is provided by the compensation of employees, while operating surplus and mixed income (which accrues to self-employed households and home owners) generally has the next highest contribution. Both of these sources recorded negative rates of change during the recession, most notably in the first two quarters of 2009. Net property income (interest received minus interest paid, dividends, etc) and net social benefits are normally the most volatile components; the latter is also affected by the position in the business cycle and its growth was particularly large in the first two quarters of 2009.

If households' gross disposable income increases faster than their consumption the household saving rate increases, and this has been observed in the EU-27 since the middle of 2008 – see Figure 24 – with consumption expenditure actually falling in the final quarter of 2008 and the first half of 2009. The saving rate is a key indicator for the household sector: short-term increases in the household saving rate are often linked with pessimistic expectations about the economic future, while longer term variations are generally driven by changes in the labour market or interest rates movements. Household savings (and also borrowing) may be used to finance investment in fixed assets (see

Figure 25). When households' gross disposable income grows slower than their investment in fixed assets (principally dwellings) the investment rate increases: this occurred between 2003 and 2007 in the EU-27, with the reverse situation in 2008 and the first half of 2009. Figure 26 summarises the development of the rate of change of households' savings and investment within the EU-27, with the level of saving increasing significantly accompanied by a fall in investment in the most recent quarters.

The households sector has the greatest wealth of all sectors, composed of residential property as well as other non-financial and financial assets. Focusing on financial wealth, changes in the net financial wealth of households are influenced to some extent by their net acquisitions of financial assets and their net incurrence of liabilities, for example, loans for property purchases. Furthermore, changes in the price of households' financial assets (notably changes in share prices) play an important part in the overall change in net financial wealth: in the euro area this net financial wealth fell throughout 2008 and the first half of 2009 (see Figure 27), driven by falls in the value of their assets. Figure 28 shows the composition of households' net financial wealth, and how in particular falling values of shares and other equity reduced household wealth in 2008 and 2009.

Figure 23: Households, growth of gross disposable income by component, EU-27 (¹)
(%)

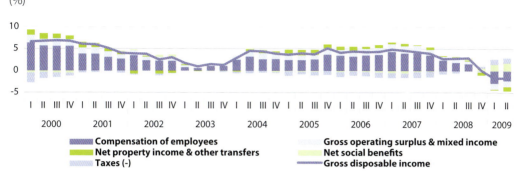

- ▨ **Compensation of employees**
- ▨ **Net property income & other transfers**
- ▨ **Taxes (-)**
- ▨ **Gross operating surplus & mixed income**
- ▨ **Net social benefits**
- **Gross disposable income**

(¹) Annual percentage change.

Source: Eurostat (nasq_sector)

Figure 24: Households, saving rate and the annual rate of change of income and consumption, EU-27
(%)

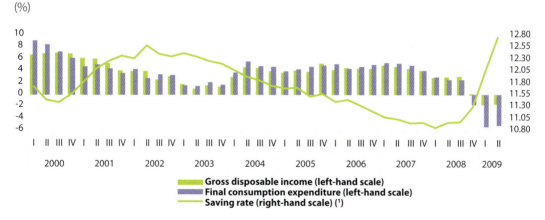

- ▨ **Gross disposable income (left-hand scale)**
- ▨ **Final consumption expenditure (left-hand scale)**
- **Saving rate (right-hand scale) (¹)**

(¹) Percentage of gross disposable income including net adjustment for the change in net equity of households in pension funds reserves, based on four-quarter-cumulated sums.

Source: Eurostat (nasq_sector)

Figure 25: Households, investment rate and the annual rate of change of income and capital formation, EU-27
(%)

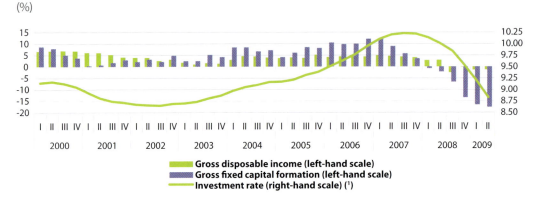

Gross disposable income (left-hand scale)
Gross fixed capital formation (left-hand scale)
Investment rate (right-hand scale) (¹)

(¹) Percentage of gross disposable income including net adjustment for the change in net equity of households in pension funds reserves, based on four-quarter-cumulated sums.

Source: Eurostat (nasq_sector)

Figure 26: Households, saving and investment, change on same period of previous year, EU-27
(%)

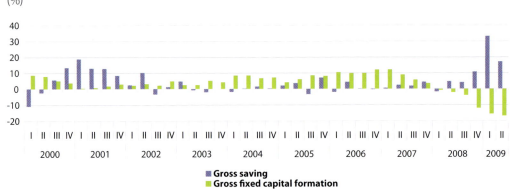

Gross saving
Gross fixed capital formation

Source: Eurostat (nasq_sector)

Figure 27: Households, change in financial assets, liabilities and net financial wealth, euro area (%)

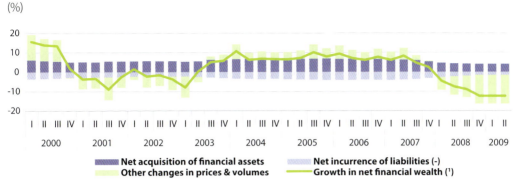

(¹) Annual rate of change.

Source: European Central Bank (ECB)

Figure 28: Households, financial assets, liabilities and net financial wealth, euro area (¹) (%)

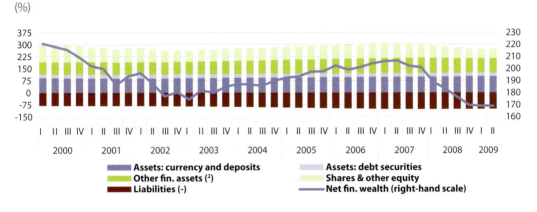

(¹) Percentage of gross disposable income, including net adjustment for the change in net equity of households in pension funds reserves, based on four-quarter-cumulated sums.
(²) Insurance technical reserves, financial derivatives, loans granted and other accounts receivable.

Source: European Central Bank (ECB)

Governments

Government borrowing and debt within the EU-27 increased strongly during 2008 and the beginning of 2009 as governments responded to the economic and financial crisis – see Figure 29. Figure 30 presents the development of net lending/borrowing (right axis) as well as an analysis of the main categories of receipts and payments of the government sector (left axis). The receipt side records taxes less subsidies on production and current taxes on income and wealth. The payment side records notably compensation paid to government employees and social contributions less benefits that account for the surplus/deficit of the social security system (including public pension schemes). During 2008 and 2009 net borrowing by governments in the EU-27 increased, largely because

net revenue from production taxes less subsidies fell and net payments for social security increased along with other payments. Figure 31 shows the separate figures for contributions receivable and benefits payable from social security systems: as a share of GDP both of these increased during 2008 and 2009, with benefits payable growing faster. Figure 32 provides a similar analysis for taxes on production and imports and subsidies: despite falling GDP, taxes on production and imports as a share of GDP fell from 2007, while subsidies were relatively stable.

The net financial wealth of governments in the euro area is shown in Figure 33, along with an analysis of assets and liabilities. The increase in the negative net wealth seen in the last quarter of 2008 was mainly due to a large increase in debt.

Figure 29: Government debt and deficit as a percentage of GDP, EU-27
(%)

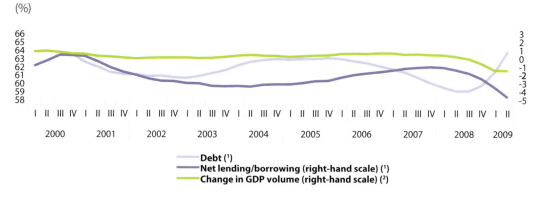

(¹) Percentage of GDP, based on four quarters average.
(²) Change on previous quarter (seasonally adjusted).

Source: Eurostat (gov_q_ggnfa, gov_q_ggdebt and namq_gdp_k)

Figure 30: Government, income and expenditure components, EU-27 (¹)
(%)

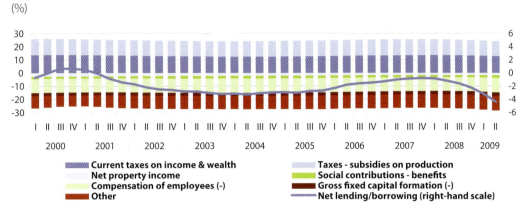

(¹) Percentage of GDP, based on four quarters cumulated sums.

Source: Eurostat (nasq_sector) and European Central Bank (ECB)

Figure 31: Government, social contributions and benefits, EU-27 (¹)
(%)

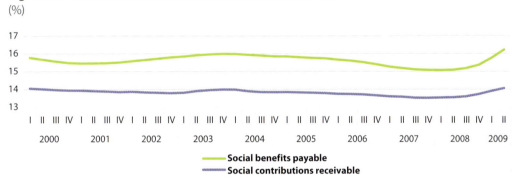

(¹) Percentage of GDP, based on four quarters cumulated sums.

Source: Eurostat (gov_q_ggnfa)

Figure 32: Government, taxes and subsidies, EU-27 ([¹])
(%)

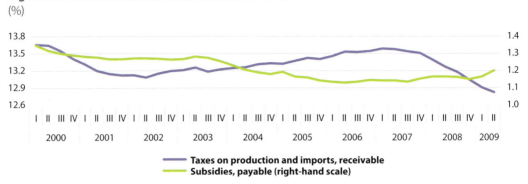

(¹) Percentage of GDP, based on four quarters cumulated averages.

Source: Eurostat (gov_q_ggnfa)

Figure 33: Government, stock of financial assets, liabilities and net financial wealth, euro area ([¹])
(%)

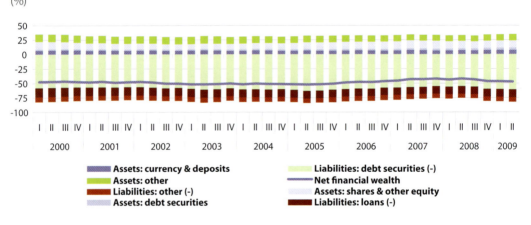

(¹) Percentage of GDP, based on four quarters cumulated sums.

Source: European Central Bank (ECB)

3.3 The impact of the recession – as measured by other macro-economic indicators

National accounts indicators are often used to complete the overall picture described by other short-term indicators and, being usually at the end of the statistical process, national accounts statistics can often give greater detail, as well as a coherent and integrated structure to the signals provided by other macro-economic indicators (such as economic and business sentiment indicators, inflation, employment/unemployment). Information relating to annual statistics is provided for many of these indicators later in this publication: for example, Subchapters 1.3, 1.4 and 1.5 present interest rates, consumer prices and balance of payment statistics; Subchapters 5.1

and 5.2 present statistics on employment and unemployment.

Economic sentiment

The economic sentiment indicator (ESI) is an important indicator to anticipate changes in the economic business cycle. The European Commission's Directorate-General for Economic and Financial Affairs (DG ECFIN) conducts regular harmonised surveys for different sectors of the economy in the Member States. The ESI is compiled as a weighted average of five confidence indicators concerning industry, construction, retail trade, services, and consumers. Figure 34 shows how the ESI started its most recent fall in 2007, earlier than GDP, while growing confidence returned in the second quarter of 2009.

Figure 34: GDP and the economic sentiment indicator, EU-27
(%)

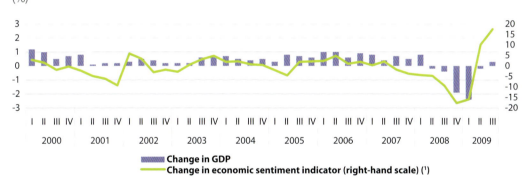

(¹) The monthly economic sentiment indicator has been averaged to a quarterly index.

Source: European Commission, Directorate-General for Economic and Financial Affairs

Inflation

Inflation is another timely indicator on the state of the economic business cycle, as changes in the balance between demand and supply for consumer goods and services are typically reflected in the evolution of prices. Within the EU, inflation is measured by the harmonised index of consumer prices (HICP), which is calculated according to a harmonised approach and a single set of definitions that result in a comparable measure of inflation across the euro area, the EU, the EEA, as well as other non-member countries (including candidate countries). These statistics provide the official measure of consumer price inflation in the euro area for the purposes of monetary policy and assessing inflation convergence (as required under the Maastricht criteria).

In this respect, it is interesting that Figure 35 shows a relatively long period of stable price inflation and unchanged ECB refinancing rates between 2003 and the beginning of 2006. Subsequently, interest rates in the euro area broadly doubled in

relation to monetary tightening, while the harmonised index of consumer prices rose significantly in 2007 and 2008 in part due to increased oil prices and also food prices. As the financial and economic crisis resulted in a sharp economic contraction, the ECB proceeded with significant cuts in the refinancing rate and HICP inflation fell from broadly 4 % to nearly zero within a year. By the summer of 2009 the HICP stabilised at a relatively low rate of change and the ECB's refinancing rate was also kept stable at 1 %.

Comparing the respective rates of HICP inflation between September 2008 and 2009, Figure 36 and Table 4 show that inflation varied significantly across the EU Member States, but that all countries experienced a significant drop in their inflation rates. The decline was most noteworthy for the Baltic countries and Bulgaria where inflation had reached double-digits in September 2008. One year later, several EU Member States, notably Ireland, Portugal and Estonia recorded negative inflation rates, while the annual rate of change was almost unchanged in Poland.

Figure 35: Inflation, interest rates and quarterly GDP
(%)

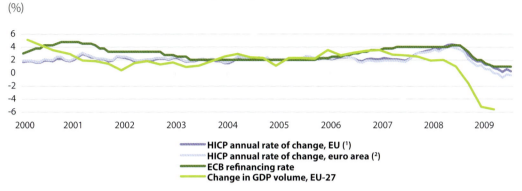

━━━━ HICP annual rate of change, EU (¹)
━━━━ HICP annual rate of change, euro area (²)
━━━━ ECB refinancing rate
━━━━ Change in GDP volume, EU-27

(¹) The data refer to the official EU aggregate, its country coverage changes in line with the addition of new EU Member States and integrates them using a chain index formula.
(²) The data refer to the official euro area aggregate, its country coverage changes in line with the addition of new EA Member States and integrates them using a chain index formula.

Source: Eurostat (prc_hicp_manr, irt_cb_m and namq_gdp_k)

Figure 36: HICP, annual rate of change
(%)

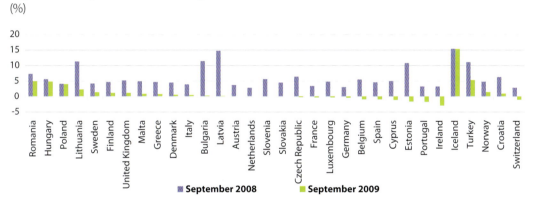

■ **September 2008**   ■ **September 2009**

Source: Eurostat (prc_hicp_manr)

Table 4: HICP, annual rate of change
(%)

	2008			2009								
	Oct	Nov	Dec	Jan	Feb	Mar	Apr	May	Jun	Jul	Aug	Sep
EU (¹)	3.7	2.8	2.2	1.8	1.8	1.3	1.3	0.8	0.6	0.2	0.6	0.3
Euro area (²)	3.2	2.1	1.6	1.1	1.2	0.6	0.6	0.0	-0.1	-0.7	-0.2	-0.3
Belgium	4.8	3.2	2.7	2.1	1.9	0.6	0.7	-0.2	-1.0	-1.7	-0.7	-1.0
Bulgaria	11.2	8.8	7.2	6.0	5.4	4.0	3.8	3.0	2.6	1.0	1.3	0.2
Czech Republic	5.7	4.1	3.3	1.4	1.3	1.7	1.3	0.9	0.8	-0.1	0.0	-0.3
Denmark	3.8	2.8	2.4	1.7	1.7	1.6	1.1	1.1	0.9	0.7	0.7	0.5
Germany	2.5	1.4	1.1	0.9	1.0	0.4	0.8	0.0	0.0	-0.7	-0.1	-0.5
Estonia	10.1	8.5	7.5	4.7	3.9	2.5	0.9	0.3	-0.5	-0.4	-0.7	-1.7
Ireland	2.7	2.1	1.3	1.1	0.1	-0.7	-0.7	-1.7	-2.2	-2.6	-2.4	-3.0
Greece	4.0	3.0	2.2	2.0	1.8	1.5	1.1	0.7	0.7	0.7	1.0	0.7
Spain	3.6	2.4	1.5	0.8	0.7	-0.1	-0.2	-0.9	-1.0	-1.4	-0.8	-1.0
France	3.0	1.9	1.2	0.8	1.0	0.4	0.1	-0.3	-0.6	-0.8	-0.2	-0.4
Italy	3.6	2.7	2.4	1.4	1.5	1.1	1.2	0.8	0.6	-0.1	0.1	0.4
Cyprus	4.8	3.1	1.8	0.9	0.6	0.9	0.6	0.5	0.1	-0.8	-0.9	-1.2
Latvia	13.7	11.6	10.4	9.7	9.4	7.9	5.9	4.4	3.1	2.1	1.5	0.1
Lithuania	10.7	9.2	8.5	9.5	8.5	7.4	5.9	4.9	3.9	2.6	2.2	2.3
Luxembourg	3.9	2.0	0.7	0.0	0.7	-0.3	-0.3	-0.9	-1.0	-1.5	-0.2	-0.4
Hungary	5.1	4.1	3.4	2.4	2.9	2.8	3.2	3.8	3.7	4.9	5.0	4.8
Malta	5.7	4.9	5.0	3.1	3.5	3.9	4.0	3.4	2.8	0.8	1.0	0.8
Netherlands	2.5	1.9	1.7	1.7	1.9	1.8	1.8	1.5	1.4	-0.1	-0.1	0.0
Austria	3.0	2.3	1.5	1.2	1.4	0.6	0.5	0.1	-0.3	-0.4	0.2	0.0
Poland	4.0	3.6	3.3	3.2	3.6	4.0	4.3	4.2	4.2	4.5	4.3	4.0
Portugal	2.5	1.4	0.8	0.1	0.1	-0.6	-0.6	-1.2	-1.6	-1.4	-1.2	-1.8
Romania	7.4	6.8	6.4	6.8	6.9	6.7	6.5	5.9	5.9	5.0	4.9	4.9
Slovenia	4.8	2.9	1.8	1.4	2.1	1.6	1.1	0.5	0.2	-0.6	0.1	0.0
Slovakia	4.2	3.9	3.5	2.7	2.4	1.8	1.4	1.1	0.7	0.6	0.5	0.0
Finland	4.4	3.5	3.4	2.5	2.7	2.0	2.1	1.5	1.6	1.2	1.3	1.1
Sweden	3.4	2.4	2.1	2.0	2.2	1.9	1.8	1.7	1.6	1.8	1.9	1.4
United Kingdom	4.5	4.1	3.1	3.0	3.2	2.9	2.3	2.2	1.8	1.8	1.6	1.1
Croatia	5.7	4.5	2.8	3.2	3.8	3.4	3.5	2.5	1.9	1.2	1.5	0.9
Turkey	12.0	10.8	10.1	9.5	7.7	7.9	6.1	5.2	5.7	5.4	5.3	5.3
Iceland	17.9	19.8	21.0	21.9	21.6	19.9	16.3	15.7	16.7	16.5	16.0	15.3
Norway	5.1	3.3	2.6	2.6	2.8	2.6	2.9	2.9	3.5	2.2	1.8	1.4
Switzerland	2.6	1.2	0.3	-0.1	-0.1	-0.7	-0.6	-1.1	-1.2	-1.4	-1.0	-1.1

(¹) The data refer to the official EU aggregate, its country coverage changes in line with the addition of new EU Member States and integrates them using a chain index formula.
(²) The data refer to the official euro area aggregate, its country coverage changes in line with the addition of new EA Member States and integrates them using a chain index formula.

Source: Eurostat (prc_hicp_manr)

Employment and unemployment

Employment figures typically lag many of the other indicators that are used for business cycle analysis, as an economic expansion or downturn usually takes some time to pass through into the labour market. Figure 37 illustrates that employment in the EU-27 only started to decline in the second half of 2008, whereas the EU-27 unemployment rate reached a low point at the beginning of 2008 (the same period when quarterly GDP in volume terms peaked). The number of unemployed persons rose strongly during 2008 and 2009: at the time of writing the latest data (January 2010) shows that the unemployment rate continues to increase, alongside slowly growing quarterly GDP.

Figures 38 and 39, as well as Table 5 give a detailed picture of how the situation varies across Member States. They clearly show that the labour market has been most severely affected in the Baltic countries, Spain and Ireland, while the increase in unemployment between the second quarter of 2008 and 2009 was relatively modest in a number of Member States, most notably Germany (where increased use was made of short-time work in order to reduce the number of redundancies).

Figure 37: Indices of GDP, employment and unemployment, EU-27 (2000=100)

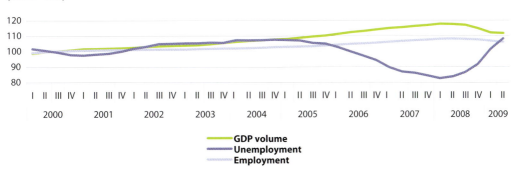

Source: Eurostat (namq_gdp_k, lfsi_grt_q and une_nb_q)

Figure 38: Employment, change on same period of previous year, second quarter 2009 (¹)
(%)

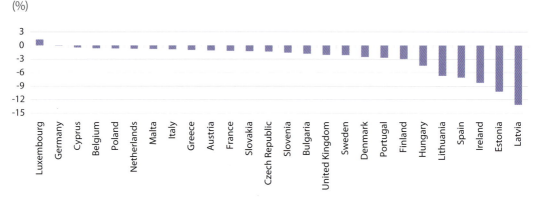

(¹) Romania, not available.

Source: Eurostat (lfsi_grt_q)

Figure 39: Unemployment rate
(% of the labour force)

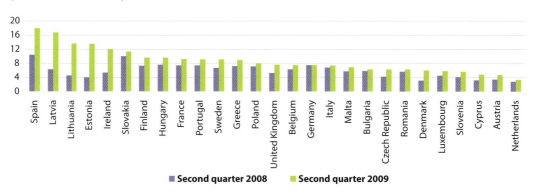

■ **Second quarter 2008** ■ **Second quarter 2009**

Source: Eurostat (une_rt_q)

Table 5: Unemployment rate, seasonally adjusted
(% of the labour force)

	2006	2007				2008				2009		
	IV	I	II	III	IV	I	II	III	IV	I	II	III
EU-27	7.8	7.4	7.2	7.1	6.9	6.7	6.8	7.0	7.5	8.2	8.8	9.1
Euro area	8.0	7.7	7.5	7.4	7.3	7.2	7.4	7.6	8.0	8.8	9.3	9.6
Belgium	8.0	7.8	7.9	7.0	7.1	6.9	6.7	7.4	7.0	7.7	7.7	7.9
Bulgaria	8.4	7.6	7.0	6.8	6.2	6.1	5.9	5.3	5.2	6.0	6.3	7.2
Czech Republic	6.6	5.9	5.4	5.1	4.9	4.5	4.3	4.3	4.5	5.5	6.3	6.9
Denmark	3.7	4.1	3.7	3.9	3.4	3.2	3.1	3.3	3.8	4.7	5.9	6.1
Germany	9.2	8.8	8.5	8.3	8.0	7.6	7.3	7.2	7.1	7.3	7.6	7.6
Estonia	5.5	5.1	5.2	4.3	4.0	4.0	4.1	6.5	7.7	11.0	13.3	:
Ireland	4.3	4.4	4.6	4.6	4.7	4.7	5.3	6.4	7.7	10.3	12.1	12.6
Greece	8.7	8.6	8.4	8.2	8.0	7.8	7.5	7.5	7.9	8.8	9.2	:
Spain	8.3	8.1	8.0	8.4	8.6	9.2	10.5	11.9	14.0	16.5	17.9	18.9
France	9.0	8.8	8.5	8.2	7.9	7.6	7.7	7.9	8.3	8.9	9.4	9.8
Italy	6.5	6.0	5.9	6.2	6.4	6.6	6.8	6.8	6.9	7.4	7.4	:
Cyprus	4.2	4.2	4.0	3.8	3.8	3.7	3.5	3.5	3.7	4.4	5.2	5.6
Latvia	6.2	6.5	5.9	6.2	5.5	6.1	6.2	7.5	10.2	13.2	16.4	18.7
Lithuania	4.9	4.7	4.3	4.1	4.1	4.5	4.8	6.3	8.1	11.0	13.8	:
Luxembourg	4.6	4.4	4.1	4.1	4.2	4.4	4.8	5.1	5.3	5.8	6.3	6.5
Hungary	7.6	7.2	7.1	7.3	7.9	7.6	7.7	7.8	8.1	9.2	9.7	9.6
Malta	6.8	6.7	6.4	6.4	6.2	5.9	5.9	5.9	6.1	6.6	7.1	7.2
Netherlands	3.7	3.5	3.2	3.1	2.9	2.8	2.8	2.7	2.7	2.9	3.2	3.5
Austria	4.5	4.4	4.5	4.6	4.1	4.0	3.5	3.8	4.1	4.4	4.8	4.8
Poland	12.3	10.8	9.8	9.3	8.6	7.6	7.3	6.9	6.9	7.7	8.0	8.1
Portugal	8.2	8.3	8.2	8.1	7.8	7.6	7.6	7.8	8.0	8.8	9.2	9.2
Romania	7.2	6.4	6.6	6.4	6.2	5.7	5.7	5.8	5.9	6.2	6.4	:
Slovenia	5.5	5.3	4.9	4.6	4.7	4.7	4.4	4.3	4.2	4.9	5.8	5.9
Slovakia	12.4	11.4	11.2	11.3	10.7	10.2	9.8	9.1	9.1	10.1	10.9	11.7
Finland	7.4	7.1	6.9	6.9	6.6	6.3	6.2	6.4	6.7	7.4	8.2	8.5
Sweden	6.6	6.4	6.2	6.0	6.0	5.9	6.0	6.3	6.7	7.4	8.1	8.6
United Kingdom	5.5	5.5	5.3	5.3	5.1	5.1	5.3	5.8	6.3	7.0	7.7	:
Croatia	10.4	10.4	9.6	9.3	9.1	8.8	8.3	8.1	8.2	8.6	9.1	9.4
Turkey	8.1	8.2	8.5	8.7	8.8	8.9	9.0	9.9	11.2	12.5	13.2	:
Norway	2.9	2.7	2.5	2.5	2.4	2.4	2.5	2.4	2.8	3.1	3.1	:
Japan	4.0	4.0	3.8	3.8	3.8	3.9	4.0	4.0	4.0	4.5	5.2	:
United States	4.4	4.5	4.5	4.7	4.8	4.9	5.4	6.1	6.9	8.1	9.3	9.6

Source: Eurostat (une_rt_q)

3.4 The impact of the recession – statistical implications of the financial and economic crisis

The financial and economic crisis generated a number of challenges for statisticians. Statisticians working in national statistical institutes, European institutions, and international organisations have been confronted with an increased number of requests from economic actors and policymakers to improve the provision of relevant statistical indicators in a timely and reliable fashion. The worldwide nature of the crisis underlined the global dimension of economic and financial phenomena, the integration of financial markets, and the rapidity of circulation of information. This has resulted in calls for a thorough assessment of the role that official statistics played in the period up to the beginning of the crisis, and the role that statistics will play in the future.

Reactions of the European Statistical System

The reaction of statistical authorities was placed under scrutiny, while the capacity of these authorities to face the challenges of the crisis was also examined. The European Statistical System (ESS) acknowledged such challenges and promptly reacted to meet new and urgent demands both at a national level, an EU level, and at a global level.

The exceptional evolution of the financial markets and its consequences on the real economy required the ESS to deliver a prompt and coherent reaction, addressing in particular the following dimensions:

- statistical consequences on key selected statistical domains with special relevance at a European level for administrative purposes (for example, the appropriate recording of bank and other market rescue operations in the context of public finance);
- prompt availability of key short-term economic indicators for monitoring the impact of the crisis and the impact of measures to offset it;
- international coordination;
- enhanced communication at different levels among users and stakeholders.

The ESS's reaction to the crisis had, therefore, to be multi-faceted and its overall framework for action was fixed around three axes:

- the ESS action plan on the accounting consequences of the financial crisis;
- the regular production of key short-term economic indicators;
- a critical analysis of methodological and practical aspects relating to the statistical production process.

Accounting consequences in the area of public finance

One key aspect of the ESS's reaction has been to ensure the appropriate and proper consideration of the statistical consequences of the financial crisis on key statistics used in the EU for administrative purposes and for the assessment of public finance.

As the financial crisis escalated from late summer 2008, governments and central banks in European countries intervened through various operations in an effort to restore confidence in the financial system, at first to rescue individual financial institutions in distress, and then through coordinated interventions broadly targeting financial institutions regardless of whether they were in distress or not, recognising the systemic aspect of the situation.

All these operations required an appropriate recording and treatment in statistical terms, notably in the framework of public finance statistics. A key requirement for the ESS in this area was to ensure the consistency across time and across countries of the statistical treatment of public interventions in full respect of the ESA95 rules.

The ESS action plan on the accounting consequences of the financial crisis ([10]) was created and implemented to achieve this target and to support it by strengthening coordination among European statistical authorities, while also enhancing communication with users and stakeholders.

In this sense, the activation of the ESS action plan:

- streamlined the reaction of the ESS to the financial crisis;
- created awareness of the statistical consequences;
- strengthened coordination and communication;
- supported ESS actions to handle the response to the crisis.

The recording and treatment in national accounts of public interventions has clearly been the key methodological topic for official statisticians. In this field, Eurostat, in cooperation with ESS partners, has closely monitored the public interventions and their implications for national accounts data, notably for the government deficit and debt statistics used for the excessive deficit procedure (EDP).

The outcome of this methodological analysis provided the background information for defining the methodological treatment in national accounts, of these types of operations. On 15 July 2009, Eurostat published a decision on 'the statistical recording of public interventions to support financial institutions and financial markets during the financial crisis' ([11]).

International cooperation

In addition, the worldwide nature of the crisis highlighted some limits of official statistics (international comparability, timeliness, and specific indicators in key areas – for example, the housing market). The response of international official statisticians was threefold:

- enhancing the communication of available statistics;
- starting an in-depth analysis to identify the ideal statistical tools for policymakers/analysts/economic operators;
- enhancing the international comparability of key indicators.

Two initiatives are particularly important in this area:

- the work of the inter-agency group on economic and financial statistics – IAG (IMF, BIS, Eurostat, ECB, World Bank, UNSC) on the statistical consequences of the financial and economic crisis;

([10]) http://epp.eurostat.ec.europa.eu/portal/page/portal/financial_turmoil/introduction.

([11]) Eurostat news release 103/2009 - 15 July 2009.

- a set of three international seminars jointly organised by United Nations Statistical Division, Eurostat and some national statistical institutes (NSIs); two of these seminars already took place;

The first of these was an international seminar on timeliness, methodology and comparability of rapid estimates of economic trends jointly organised by Statistics Canada, UNSD and Eurostat, held in Ottawa in May 2009 [12] and the second was an international seminar on early warning and business cycle indicators jointly organised by the CBS, UNSD and Eurostat, held in Scheveningen (the Netherlands) in December 2009 [13].

Both of these groups focused their efforts on trying to identify which official economic and financial indicators should be regularly produced by national statistical authorities to monitor the evolution of the economy. The Interagency Group set up the 'Principal Global Indicators' website, offering the available indicators regularly collected by international agencies for different countries and in different relevant statistical domains – see Box 3 under Point 4.

The work of all these groups will be used to help prepare answers to the requirements expressed by the G-20 Finance Ministers and Central Bank Governors with respect to statistics in relation to the financial and economic crisis.

4. The future – challenges and constraints in relation to national accounts

One of the enduring challenges for European statistics, including macro-economic statistics, is to maintain or improve quality. The quality of data can be assessed against a number of criteria – for example, accuracy, timeliness or coherence. In recent years improvements have been made in many areas of European statistics concerning several quality criteria, including macro-economic statistics. For example, accessibility has improved through an increase in the availability of data for the EU and the euro area, along with investments that have been made in data dissemination and documentation. Timeliness has also improved through a number of actions, including: greater coordination in the delivery of data by Member States; the development and implementation of estimation methods for late data; shortening of the deadlines for the provision of data; and the development of flash (early) estimates. International comparability has improved through the development and implementation of a growing range of guidelines, rules and recommendations.

Policy developments, changes in the economic phenomena to be observed, and developments in data production techniques result in a dynamic environment for statistics. At the same time, user demands for data grow, notably in terms

[12] http://unstats.un.org/unsd/nationalaccount/workshops/2009/ottawa/ac188-2.asp.

[13] http://unstats.un.org/unsd/nationalaccount/workshops/2009/netherlands/ac202-2.asp.

of wanting more data: in relation to its speed of delivery, its frequency of delivery, or its level of detail. Given the long time lag involved to develop or improve statistics, user needs are rarely fully satisfied. As a result there is continuous work to develop, refine and maintain the statistical system. However, increases in user requirements may lead to an increase in the burden on respondents.

Attempts to make improvements in one area may lead to weaknesses in other areas. A major challenge for national accounts, and more widely for short-term macro-economic statistics such as the Principal European Economic Indicators (PEEIs) is to balance the timeliness of data with its level of accuracy and the extent of any subsequent revisions.

Beyond this basic challenge to try to improve simultaneously timeliness and accuracy there are other challenges to face. Whereas within the EU macro-economic analysis of the business cycle has already gone beyond national accounts with the development and refinement of PEEIs, the need for international comparability has led to the expansion of this towards principal global indicators – see Box 3.

Box 3: inter-agency group on economic and financial statistics – G-20 statistical website

The inter-agency group on economic and financial statistics launched a website covering economic and financial data for the group of 20 industrialised and emerging market economies (G-20), at: http://financialdatalink.sharepointsite.net/default.aspx.

The website aims to facilitate the monitoring of economic and financial developments across these countries. It presents data from the participating international agencies for a list of principal global indicators: these indicators cover the financial, government, real and external sectors of the G-20 countries, as well as a host of other macro-economic indicators such as inflation, unemployment and interest rates.

The inter-agency group on economic and financial statistics was created at the end of 2008, and comprises representatives of the Bank for International Settlements, the European Central Bank, Eurostat, the International Monetary Fund (IMF), the Organisation for Economic Co-operation and Development (OECD), the United Nations (UN), and the World Bank. The inter-agency group is chaired by the IMF who hosts the website.

4.1 Globalisation

International comparisons of national accounts have been made for a long time, although the development of international guidelines, rules and recommendations has intensified in recent decades – the first United Nations system of national accounts (SNA) was published in 1958. The international harmonisation of the system of national accounts has developed in parallel to a number of economic and political developments, for example, the single European market and a wider expansion of economic relationships – globalisation. One impact of globalisation has been the increased interest of being able to access comparable measures of economies, with the possibility of making comparisons within the EU, with other developed economies, with rapidly developing nations, and with neighbouring countries that are candidates or prospective candidate countries.

Globalisation can be defined in a relatively narrow way as describing the increasing levels of exchanges between economies, for example, of goods, services, information (including technology), capital and labour; more broadly it can be considered to include other exchanges of a social or cultural nature. These economic exchanges lead to a greater level of integration and interdependence for the economies concerned, for example, between financial markets and within production chains. The increased pace of economic globalisation during recent decades can be attributed, in part, to the removal of barriers (for example, trade in goods and services as well as capital movements) and lower costs of transportation and communication.

Globalisation is of interest for various types of analysis, including monetary and economic policies. Increased flows in and out of an economy directly affect domestic issues such as inflation and the money supply and also the extent to which these can be influenced by national policies. The knock-on effects of developments in one economy through other economies may not be immediately obvious as they pass from market to market, and from economy to economy. The challenge for statistics is to be able to provide information on these interdependencies that have increased through globalisation.

As well as requiring statisticians to think again about the range of indicators necessary to measure the economy, the evolving global economy renders the analysis of long time-series of data less useful: to what extent is the experience from a less globalised world relevant to current and future developments? This question highlights the problems for analysts developing models or interpreting forecasts.

4.2 Updating the SNA

In 2003 the United Nations statistical commission (UNSC) initiated the updating of the 1993 SNA. This was undertaken through a working group composed of representatives of the United Nations statistics division, the International Monetary Fund, the World Bank, the Organisation for Economic Cooperation and Development, the Statistical Office of the European Communities (Eurostat) and the United Nations regional commissions. The resulting 2008 SNA is the fifth version of the SNA and was adopted in two volumes, the last by the UNSC at its 40th session in February 2009. At the time of writing the final version of the 2008 SNA is available in English as a single volume (^{14}) comprising a full set of chapters representing the framework in terms of accounting conventions, the accounts, and the integration of the accounts, as well as interpretations of the accounts and extensions such as satellite accounts.

The report on national accounts to the 38th session of the UNSC identified the main changes that were recommended for the update. The updates aimed to address issues that had become more important since the previous update, to remove inconsistencies, to harmonise the SNA with other manuals, and to implement progress made in research since the previous update. The majority of the recommendations:

- were related to units and transactions that represent characteristics of an increasingly globalised economy;
- came from increased interest in the sources of wealth and debt;
- recognised the increasing role of intangible non-financial assets;
- took into account further innovation in financial markets;
- reflected the interest in better measures of the impact of pension liabilities in the context of an ageing population, and;
- recognised the need for better measures of government and public-sector debt and deficit.

There was close coordination between updating the 1993 SNA and the revision of the balance of payments manual. Attention was also paid to further harmonisation with the IMF's government finance statistics manual and the monetary and financial statistics manual, as well as with

integrated environmental and economic accounting. Among the major changes were the following:

- research and development expenditure is to be treated as fixed capital formation rather than consumption, as will military expenditure of a capital nature;
- a comprehensive accounting of pension obligations of corporations and government accruing to all individuals is to be compiled regardless of the type of pension scheme;
- goods for processing are to be recorded on the basis of a change of ownership and so, for example, outward processing in foreign countries will not impact on import and export figures.

4.3 The revision of the ESA

In June 2007, directors of national accounts from across Europe set out the basis for a revision of the ESA:

- it would start from the consolidated text of the existing Regulation and subsequent Regulations, such as that concerning the recording of taxes and social contributions unlikely to be collected;
- it would cover all the recommendations and clarifications agreed at international level, such as the capitalisation of research and development expenditure;
- it should result in a more integrated system; many linked statistical areas are likely to be impacted, such as research and development, environmental, agricultural and tourism accounts, population, labour and social protection statistics, and balance of payments.

(^{14}) For more information: http://unstats.un.org/unsd/nationalaccount/SNA2008.pdf.

Changes to ESA95 are based on the various recommendations made in the context of the SNA update. For most of the existing chapters, the structure has been kept or only slightly amended. Three existing chapters have been extended in the new ESA, namely Chapter 9 on the input-output framework, Chapter 12 on quarterly economic accounts, and Chapter 13 on regional accounts. A number of new chapters have also been drafted:

- Chapter 19 on **European accounts** outlines the objective, scope and specifics of the compilation of European accounts, including EU institutions, treatment of the rest of the world, the aggregation and balancing issue and consistency with sources and other European macro-economic statistics.
- Chapter 20 on **government accounts** presents the basic principles concerning delimitation of the government sector, relations with public corporations, the accounting issues related to government and corporations, government net lending/borrowing and its relationship with government debt.
- Chapter 21 concerns the links between **business** and national accounts.
- Chapter 22 presents a common framework for functionally oriented **satellite accounts**, with a focus on research and development which is to be included in the core accounts in the

medium or long-term. It also briefly presents satellite accounts for which a fairly complete, agreed and operational methodological framework has already been developed: economic accounts for agriculture, economic and environmental accounts, and social protection.

At the time of writing the revised ESA has been drafted and the text is in the process of being finalised. The key points in the future timetable are as follows:

- adoption of the European Commission's proposal in June 2010;
- adoption of a Regulation by the European Parliament and the Council in 2012;
- implementation of the new ESA methodology and transmission programme in 2014; it is likely that the Regulation will have two annexes, one on methodology and one on the transmission programme.

The issue of consistency of the new ESA is essential. In particular, this is being addressed by an ESA review group which brings together members of the national accounts working group and the financial accounts working group. Each draft chapter for the new ESA has been discussed by the ESA review group, while a Eurostat/ECB group has also been formed to look at the question of consistency.

4.4 GDP and beyond: measuring progress in a changing world

A number of criticisms have been levelled at national accounts, in terms of their coverage or their relevance for particular types of analysis. In some cases the solution may involve the development of supplementary tables outside of the core accounts, or even of satellite accounts. By design and purpose, national accounts in general, and GDP in particular, can not be relied upon to inform policy debates on all issues. For example, GDP has been criticised for not measuring welfare, a concept that involves many social concepts and one to which economic statistics such as those in national accounts can contribute only a partial solution. Another example is that GDP does not measure environmental sustainability.

In such cases it may be appropriate to develop indicators to complement GDP, as for example was done with the development of sustainable development indicators to monitor the objectives of the EU Sustainable Development Strategy. Initiatives to complement GDP are not new: the United Nations Development Programme (UNDP) developed a Human Development Index (HDI) to benchmark countries based on the combined measurement of GDP, health and education. The World Bank with its calculation of genuine savings has pioneered the inclusion of social and environmental aspects when assessing the wealth of nations. The OECD is running a Global Project on Measuring the Progress of Societies fostering the use of novel indicators in a participatory way. The Commission on the measurement of economic performance and social progress (Stiglitz-Sen-Fitoussi report) put in place by the French president concluded with 12 recommendations for better measures of well-being and sustainability. Several NGOs measure the 'ecological footprint' – a measurement that has been formally recognised as a target for environmental progress by some public authorities. Furthermore, numerous researchers have published pilot indices of well-being and life satisfaction.

In its Communication 'GDP and beyond, measuring progress in a changing world', the European Commission noted that there is a clear case for complementing GDP with statistics covering other economic, social and environmental issues, on which people's well-being critically depends. Work to complement GDP has been going on for years, at both national and international level and the European Commission intends to step up its efforts and communication in this field. The aim is to provide indicators that measure progress in delivering social, economic and environmental goals in a sustainable manner. The Communication proposed five actions for better measurement of progress in a changing world.

1. Complementing GDP with environmental and social indicators

The Communication notes that existing economic headline indicators such as GDP, the unemployment rate and inflation rate are not meant to reflect issues concerning environment or social inequalities: a comprehensive environmental index should be developed and quality-of-life indicators improved. Indeed, there is currently no comprehensive environmental indicator that can be used in policy debates alongside GDP. Close candidates for such a purpose are the ecological and carbon footprints, but both are limited in scope. As methodologies for composite indices and data are now sufficiently mature it is intended to present a pilot version of an index on environmental pressure in 2010. This index will reflect pollution and other harm to the environment within the EU to assess the results of environmental protection efforts. It will comprise the major strands of environmental policy:

• climate change and energy use;
• nature and biodiversity;
• air pollution and health impacts;
• water use and pollution;
• waste generation and use of resources.

Publishing this indicator with GDP and social indicators, it should be possible to analyse the level of environmental protection and whether progress is achieved in a balanced way towards social, economic and environmental goals. In addition to this comprehensive index on harm to or pressure on the environment, there is potential to develop a comprehensive indicator of environmental quality, for example, showing the numbers of European citizens living in a healthy environment.

Income, public services, health, leisure, wealth, mobility and a clean environment are means to achieve and sustain quality of life and well-being. Indicators on these inputs are therefore important for national governments and the EU. In addition, social sciences are developing increasingly robust direct measurements of quality of life and well-being as outcome indicators; for example, the European Foundation for the Improvement of Living and Working Conditions is working on this issue. In

addition, the European Commission has launched studies on the feasibility of well-being indicators and on consumer empowerment and, with the OECD, on people's perception of well-being.

2. Near real-time information for decision-making

Currently, there are considerable differences in the timeliness of statistics in different areas. For example, GDP and unemployment figures are published frequently within a few weeks of the period they are assessing and this can allow near real-time decision making. In contrast, environmental and social data in many cases are too old to provide operational information. The European Commission will therefore aim to increase the timeliness of environmental and social data to better inform policymakers across the EU.

Satellites, automatic measurement stations and the Internet make it increasingly possible to monitor the environment in real-time. The European Commission is stepping up efforts to realise this potential, for example, through the INSPIRE Directive and the global monitoring for environment and security (GMES). The European Commission has already presented the shared environmental information system (SEIS), a vision of how to link traditional and novel data sources online and make them publicly available as fast as possible. More timely data can also be produced by statistical "now-casting" techniques: for instance, the European Environment Agency (EEA) intends to produce short-term estimates of greenhouse gas emissions based on existing short-term energy statistics, and Eurostat intends to use similar techniques to produce more timely environmental accounts.

The European Commission, together with Member States, has been working to streamline and improve social surveys and reduce the time lag between data collection and publication. Whenever possible and cost-effective, the timeliness of social data will be improved.

3. More accurate reporting on distribution and inequalities

Far-reaching reforms such as those required to fight climate change or to promote new patterns of consumption can be more easily accepted if efforts and benefits are felt to be equitably shared among countries, regions, economic and social groups. This is why distributional issues attract increasing attention. For example, even if the GDP per capita figure is rising, the number of people living at-risk-of-poverty may be increasing. Existing data from national accounts such as household income or from social surveys such as the EU's survey on income and living conditions (EU-SILC) already allow for an analysis of key distributional issues. Policies affecting social cohesion need to use measures of disparity as well as aggregates such as GDP per capita.

The European Commission regularly reports on a set of indicators to inform policymakers about income disparities and particularly about the situation at the lower end of the income scale. The analysis of situations in Member States also looks at education, health, life expectancy, and various non-monetary aspects of social exclusion. Indicators of equal access to quality housing, transport and other services and infrastructure that are essential to participate fully in society

(and hence to contribute to economic and social progress) are being developed. In addition, the link between social exclusion and environmental deprivation has been gaining attention and analysis of this issue will be regularly undertaken.

4. Developing a European sustainable development scoreboard

The EU's sustainable development indicators (SDIs) have been developed together with Member States to monitor progress on the multitude of objectives of the EU's Sustainable Development Strategy and are reflected in the European Commission's biennial progress report. However, this monitoring tool does not fully capture recent developments in important areas that are not yet well covered by official statistics, such as sustainable production/consumption or governance issues. For several reasons, SDIs cannot always be based on the most recent data. Consequently, they may not fully reflect the efforts that businesses, civil society or governments at local or national levels are making to meet these challenges.

To stimulate the exchange of experience between Member States and among stakeholders on policy responses, more concise and timely data are needed. The European Commission is therefore exploring the possibilities to develop, together with Member States, a sustainable development scoreboard. The sustainable development scoreboard, based on the EU's sustainable development indicators, could also include other quantitative and qualitative publicly available information, for instance, on business and policy measures.

Thresholds for environmental sustainability

One key objective of the EU Sustainable Development Strategy is to respect the limits of the planet's natural resources. These include nature's limited capacity to provide renewable resources and absorb pollutants.

Scientists are seeking to identify related physical environmental threshold values and highlight the potential long-term or irreversible consequences of crossing them. For policymaking it is important to know these 'danger zones' before the actual tipping points are reached, thereby identifying alert levels. The cooperation of research and official statistics will be stepped up in order to identify – and regularly update – such threshold values for key pollutants and renewable resources in order to inform policy debate and support target setting and policy assessment.

5. Extending national accounts to environmental and social issues

The ESA is the main basis for economic statistics and indicators within the EU. In its June 2006 conclusions, the European Council called on the EU and its Member States to extend national accounts to key aspects of sustainable development. National accounts will therefore be complemented with integrated environmental economic accounting that provides data that are fully consistent. As methods are agreed and the data becomes available this will be complemented, in the longer-term, with additional accounts on social aspects.

This will provide an integrated basis to underpin policy analysis, helping to identify synergies and trade-offs between different policy objectives, feeding, for example, into ex-ante impact assessment of policy proposals.

In the longer-term, it is expected that more integrated environmental, social and economic accounting will provide the basis for new top-level indicators. The services of the European Commission will continue to explore through collaboration with international organisations, dialogue with civil society and research projects how such macro-indicators could best be designed and used.

Integrated environmental-economic accounting

The European Commission presented its first strategy on 'green accounting' in 1994. Accounting methods have been developed and tested to the point where several Member States now regularly provide data sets from environmental accounts. Most common are physical flow accounts on air emissions (including greenhouse gases) and on material use, as well as monetary accounts on environmental protection expenditure and taxes. The European Commission plans to extend data collection in these areas to all Member States.

As a subsequent step, physical environmental accounts will be set up for energy use and supply, waste generation and treatment, water use and supply and monetary accounts for environment-related subsidies, and the environmental goods and services sector (eco-industries). The European Commission aims to have these accounts fully available for policy analysis by 2013. A legal framework for environmental accounting will be proposed to ensure that these accounts are comparable.

A second strand of environmental accounts relates to natural capital, in particular changes in stocks, the most advanced of which are accounts on forest and fishery stocks, where the European Commission will contribute to the work currently being undertaken within the United Nations.

A further challenge in the development of environmental accounting is complementing physical environmental accounts with monetary figures, based on valuations of the damage caused and prevented, changes in the stock of natural resources and in eco-system goods and services. Monetising the costs of environmental damage and the benefits of environmental protection can help to focus policy debate on the extent that our prosperity and well-being depend on goods and services provided by nature. At a micro level such valuation is conceptually sound: it is covered by several studies, notably the economics of ecosystems and biodiversity (TEEB) initiative, an on-going wide ranging valuation of ecosystem services, jointly undertaken by the United Nations Environment Programme (UNEP), several countries and the European Commission. The European Environment Agency plans to continue its work on the valuation of and accounting for ecosystem goods and services, with a view to establishing internationally accepted methods. However, translating such studies to the macro level in a meaningful way needs further research and testing. The European Commission intends to step up work on monetary valuation and the further development of conceptual frameworks in this area.

Increasing use of existing social indicators from national accounting

The existing ESA already includes indicators that highlight socially relevant issues, such as the disposable income of households and an adjusted disposable income figure that takes into account the differences in social protection regimes of different countries. Those figures reflect better what people can consume and save than the headline GDP per capita figures. The European Commission's services intend to increase the use of these indicators.

Economy

1

The EU is active in a wide range of policy areas, but economic policies have traditionally played a dominant role (^{1}). Starting from a rather narrow focus on introducing common policies for coal and steel, atomic energy and agriculture as well as the creation of a custom union over 50 years ago, European economic policies progressively extended their scope to a multitude of domains.

Since 1993 the European Single Market has strongly enhanced the possibilities for people, goods, services and money to move around the EU as freely as within a single country. These freedoms, foreseen from the outset of the EC in the Treaty establishing the European Economic Community of 1957 have been designed: to allow individuals the right to live, work, study or retire in another Member State; to increase competition leading to lower prices, provide a wider choice of products to buy, while ensuring higher levels of protection for consumers; and to make it easier and cheaper for businesses to interact across borders.

The start of economic and monetary union (EMU) in 1999 has given economic and market integration further stimulus. The elimination of exchange risk for a large number of cross-border transactions and the associated increase in price transparency resulted not only in a substantial increase of intra-area trade flows but also intra-area foreign direct investment (^{2}). The euro has also become a symbol for Europe, and the number of countries that adopted it increased from the original 11 to 16 countries at the beginning of 2010.

Fostering economic and social progress, with constant improvements in living and working conditions has been a key objective of

(^{1}) For more information: http://ec.europa.eu/policies/index_en.htm.

(^{2}) For more information: http://ec.europa.eu/economy_finance/emu10/emu10report_en.pdf.

European policies. While the stated goal of the Lisbon Strategy in 2000 was to make the EU the 'most competitive (…) economy in the world', its re-launch after a 2005 mid-term review focused more specifically on growth and employment. Reforms agreed in the context of Lisbon delivered tangible benefits, including increased employment, a more dynamic business environment, and more choice for consumers ([3]). However, the global financial and economic crisis that hit the EU in 2008, caused a severe economic downturn and job losses in most EU Member States.

In response to the crisis, EU Member States agreed on a joint recovery plan to boost demand and restore confidence ([4]). Its measures specifically aim to keep people in work and support public investment in areas such as infrastructure, innovation, new skills for the workforce, energy efficiency and clean technologies. The new EU 2020 Strategy will not only be designed to support a full recovery from the crisis but also to address Europe's structural challenges – globalisation, climate change and an ageing population – by helping it move towards a greener, more sustainable, and more innovative economy.

As the design, implementation and monitoring of EU policies require indicators to analyse the current economic situation, this chapter comments upon key indicators from various areas, such as national accounts, government finance, exchange rates and interest rates, consumer prices, the balance of payments with respect to the current account and foreign direct investment, as well development aid.

1.1 National accounts

Introduction

National accounts are the source for a multitude of well-known economic indicators which are presented in this section after a brief description of methodological concepts (for more details on different types of national accounts, their uses and further improvements see the Spotlight chapter).

Gross domestic product (GDP) is the most frequently used measure for the overall size of an economy, while derived indicators such as GDP per capita – for example, in euro or adjusted for differences in price levels – are widely used for a rough comparison of living standards, or to monitor the process of convergence across the EU.

Moreover, the evolution of specific GDP components and related indicators, such as those for economic output, imports and exports, domestic (private and public) consumption or investments, as well as data on the distribution of income and savings, can give valuable insights into the driving forces in an economy and thus be the basis for the design, monitoring and evaluation of specific EU policies.

Definitions and data availability

The European system of national and regional accounts provides the methodology for national accounts in the EU. The current version, **ESA 95**, is fully consistent with worldwide guidelines for national accounts, the 1993 SNA. At the time

---

([3]) For more information: http://ec.europa.eu/growthandjobs/pdf/lisbon_strategy_evaluation_en.pdf.

([4]) For more information: http://ec.europa.eu/financial-crisis/index_en.htm.

of writing, the ESA is under revision to bring it into line with the updated 2008 SNA – see the Spotlight chapter at the start of this publication for more information. The main aggregates of national accounts are compiled from institutional units, namely non-financial or financial corporations, general government, households, and non-profit institutions serving households (NPISH).

Data within the national accounts domain encompasses information on GDP and its components, employment, final consumption aggregates, income, and savings. Many of these variables are calculated on an annual and on a quarterly basis. Breakdowns exist for certain variables by economic activity (industries, as defined by NACE), investment products, final consumption purpose (as defined by COICOP) and institutional sectors.

GDP is a central measure of national accounts, which summarises the economic position of a country (or region). GDP can be calculated using different approaches:

* **the output approach**, which sums the gross value added of various sectors, plus taxes and less subsidies on products;
* **the expenditure approach**, which sums the final use of goods and services (final consumption and gross capital formation), plus exports and minus imports of goods and services, and;
* **the income approach**, which sums the compensation of employees, net taxes on production and imports, gross operating surplus and mixed income.

An analysis of **GDP per capita** removes the influence of the absolute size of the population, making comparisons be-

tween different countries easier. GDP per capita is a broad economic indicator of living standards. GDP data in national currencies can be converted into purchasing power standards (PPS) using purchasing power parities that reflect the purchasing power of each currency, rather than using market exchange rates. In this way differences in price levels between countries are eliminated. The **volume index of GDP per capita in PPS** is expressed in relation to the EU average (set to equal 100). If the index of a country is higher/lower than 100, this country's level of GDP per head is above/below the EU-27 average; this index is intended for cross-country comparisons rather than temporal comparisons.

The calculation of the annual **growth rate of GDP at constant prices**, in other words the change of GDP in volume terms, is intended to allow comparisons of the dynamics of economic development both over time and between economies of different sizes, irrespective of price levels.

A further set of national accounts data is used within the context of competitiveness analyses, namely indicators relating to the productivity of the workforce, such as labour productivity measures. Productivity measures expressed in PPS, which eliminates differences in price levels between countries, are particularly useful for cross-country comparisons. **GDP in PPS per person employed** is intended to give an overall impression of the productivity of national economies. It should be kept in mind, though, that this measure depends on the structure of total employment and may, for instance, be lowered by a shift from full-time to part-time work. **GDP in PPS per hour worked** gives a clearer picture of productivity as the incidence of part-time employment varies greatly between countries and activities. The data are presented in the form of an index in relation to the EU average: if the index rises above 100, then labour productivity is above the EU average.

The output approach

The output of the economy is measured using gross value added. **Gross value added** is defined as the value of all newly generated goods and services less the value of all goods and services consumed in their creation; the depreciation of fixed assets is not included. When calculating value added, output is valued at basic prices and intermediate consumption at purchasers' prices. Taxes less subsidies on products have to be added to value added to obtain GDP at market prices.

Economic output can be analysed by activity: at the most aggregated level of analysis six NACE Rev. 1.1 headings are identified: agriculture, hunting and fishing; industry; construction; trade, transport and communication services; business activities and financial services; and other services.

An analysis of output over time can be facilitated by using a volume measure of output – in other words, by deflating the value of output to remove the impact of price changes; each activity is deflated individually to reflect the changes in the prices of its associated products.

Various measures of **labour productivity** are available, for example, based on value added or GDP relative to the number of persons employed or to the number of hours worked. Productivity indicators provide confirmation of the most labour-intensive areas of the EU economy, as well as an insight into the apparent productivity growth of particular economic activities.

The expenditure approach

National accounts aggregates from the expenditure approach are used by the European Central Bank (ECB) and European Commission services as important tools for economic analysis and policy decisions. The quarterly series are central to business-cycle analysis and subsequent policy decisions. These series are also widely employed for supporting business decisions in the private sector, in particular within financial markets.

The expenditure approach of GDP is defined as private final consumption expenditure + government final consumption expenditure + gross capital formation + exports - imports.

In the system of national accounts, only households, NPISH and government have final consumption, whereas corporations have intermediate consumption. **Private final consumption expenditure**, or that performed by households and NPISH, is defined as expenditure on goods and services for the direct satisfaction of individual needs, whereas **government consumption expenditure** includes goods and services produced by government, as well as purchases of goods and services by government that are supplied to households as social transfers in kind. **NPISHs** are private, non-market producers which are separate legal entities.

Their principal resources, apart from those derived from occasional sales, are derived from voluntary contributions in cash or in kind from households in their capacity as consumers, from payments made by general governments, and from property income. Examples of NPISHs include churches, trade unions or political parties.

Statistics on the final consumption expenditure of households cover expenditure incurred on goods or services used for the satisfaction of individual needs, either through purchase, the consumption of own production (such as garden produce), or the imputed rent of owner-occupied dwellings. Data on consumption expenditure may be broken down according to the classification of individual consumption according to purpose (CO-ICOP), which identifies 12 different headings at its most aggregated level. Housing, energy costs, transport, and food and non-alcoholic beverages account for a high proportion of the total expenditure made by most European households.

Annual information on household expenditure is available from national accounts compiled through a macro-economic approach. An alternative source for analysing household expenditure is the household budget survey (HBS): this information is obtained by asking households to keep a diary of their purchases and is much more detailed in its coverage of goods and services as well as the types of socio-economic breakdown that are made available. HBS is only carried out and published every five years – the

latest reference year currently available is 2005.

Gross capital formation is the sum of gross fixed capital formation and the change in inventories (stocks). **Gross fixed capital formation** consists of resident producers' acquisitions, less disposals, of fixed tangible and intangible assets; certain additions to the value of non-produced assets realised by productive activity are also included. **Fixed assets** are produced as outputs from processes of production that are themselves used repeatedly, or continuously, in processes of production for more than one year; such assets may be outputs from production processes or imports. Investment may be made by public or private institutions. **Changes in inventories** are measured by the value of the entries into inventories less the value of withdrawals and the value of any recurrent losses of goods held in inventories.

The external balance is the difference between exports and imports of goods and services. Depending on the size of exports and imports, it can be positive (a surplus) or negative (a deficit).

The income approach

Eurostat data on income from input factors are crucial to economic analysis in a number of contexts inside and outside the European Commission. Typical examples are studies of competitiveness, of income distribution inequalities, or of long-term economic developments.

Production requires 'input factors' such as the work of employees and capital; these input factors have to be paid for.

The income-side approach shows how GDP is distributed among different participants in the production process, as the sum of:

- **compensation of employees**: the total remuneration, in cash or in kind, payable by an employer to an employee in return for work done by the latter during the accounting period; the compensation of employees is broken down into: wages and salaries (in cash and in kind); employers' social contributions (employers' actual social contributions and employers' imputed social contributions);
- **gross operating surplus**: this is the surplus (or deficit) on production activities before account has been taken of the interest, rents or charges paid or received for the use of assets;
- **mixed income**: this is the remuneration for the work carried out by the owner (or by members of his/her family) of an unincorporated enterprise; this is referred to as 'mixed income' since it cannot be distinguished from the entrepreneurial profit of the owner;
- **taxes on production and imports less subsidies**: these consist of compulsory (in the case of taxes) unrequited payments to or from general government or institutions of the EU, in respect of the production or import of goods and services, the employment of labour, and the ownership or use of land, buildings or other assets used in production.

Household saving is the main domestic source of funds to finance capital investment; savings rates can be measured on either a gross or net basis. **Net saving rates** are measured after deducting consumption of fixed capital (depreciation). The system of accounts also provides for both disposable income and saving to be shown on a gross basis, in other words, with both aggregates including the consumption of fixed capital. In this respect, household savings may be estimated by subtracting consumption expenditure and the adjustment for the change in net equity of households in pension funds reserves from disposable income. The latter consists essentially of income from employment and from the operation of unincorporated enterprises, plus receipts of interest, dividends and social benefits minus payments of income taxes, interest and social security contributions.

Main findings

The GDP of the EU-27 was broadly EUR 12 500 000 million in 2008, with the countries of the euro area accounting for a little under three quarters (74.1 %) of this total. The sum of the four largest EU economies (Germany, the United Kingdom, France and Italy) accounted for more than three fifths (62.6 %) of the EU-27's GDP in 2008. Cross-country comparisons should be made with caution and it is necessary to consider the effect of exchange rate fluctuations when analysing data. For example, the apparent fluctuation of GDP in the United States is, to a large degree, a reflection of the dollar strengthening against the euro up to 2001, since when it has weakened, rather than any change in the level of GDP in dollar terms (which rose steadily during this period).

In order to look at standards of living, one of the most frequently cited statistics is that of GDP per capita accounting for differences in price levels (by converting from EUR to PPS). Across the EU-27, GDP per capita averaged EUR 25 100 in 2008. The highest value among EU Member States was recorded for Luxembourg, where GDP per capita in PPS was 2.5 times the EU-27 average in 2008; these high values are partly explained by the importance of cross-border workers from Belgium, France and Germany. At the other end of the range, GDP per capita in PPS terms was less than half the EU-27 average in Bulgaria and Romania.

Even if PPS figures should, in principle, be used for cross-country comparisons in a single year rather than for temporal comparisons, they also illustrate an overall convergence process in EU living standards over the past decade, with gains and losses in the position of Member States relative to the EU-27 average. For instance, Italy recorded the same average GDP per capita in PPS terms as the EU-27 average in 2008, having been 20 % above the EU-27 average ten years earlier. Over the same period of time, Spain moved from 5 % below the EU-27 average to 4 % above it. All of the Member States that joined the EU since 2004 remained below the EU-27 average in 2008, but (with the exception of Malta) moved much closer to the EU average during the last ten years: the Baltic Member States, Slovakia and Romania (1999 to 2008) all moved 20 percentage points or more closer to the EU-27 average.

Having grown at an average rate of around 3 % per annum during the late 1990s, real GDP growth slowed considerably after the turn of the millennium, to just above 1 % per annum in both 2002 and 2003, before rebounding and reaching about 3 % per annum again in 2006 and 2007. In 2008

the rate of increase again slowed to just less than 1 %; for more details concerning the evolution since the onset of the financial crisis/recession please refer to the Spotlight chapter at the start of this publication.

There has been a considerable shift in the economic structure of the EU economy in the last few decades, with the proportion of gross value added accounted for by agriculture and industry falling, while that for most services rose. This change is, at least in part, a result of phenomena such as technological change, the evolution of relative prices, and globalisation, often resulting in manufacturing bases being moved to lower labour-cost regions, both within and outside the EU. More than one quarter (28.1 %) of the EU-27's gross value added was accounted for by business activities and financial services in 2008. There were three other branches that also contributed significant shares of just over one fifth of total value added, namely other services (largely made-up of public administrations, education and health systems, as well as other community, social and personal service activities (22.5 %)); trade, transport and communication services (21.0 %); and industry (20.1 %); the remainder of the economy was divided between construction (6.5 %) and agriculture, hunting, forestry and fishing (1.8 %). As such, the three groups of services identified above accounted for 71.6 % of total gross value added in the EU-27 in 2008. The relative importance of services was particularly high in Luxembourg, Cyprus, France, Greece, Malta, Belgium and the United Kingdom, as services accounted for more than three quarters of total value added in each of these countries.

In real terms these six broad activities all recorded growth in the 10 years from 1998 to 2008, although the growth for agriculture, hunting, forestry and fishing was much lower than that for the other activities. Trade, transport and communication services, as well as business activities and financial services recorded the strongest growth in the EU-27 over the period considered.

An analysis of the change in labour productivity per person employed over the same ten-year period shows that all sectors recorded growth. Labour productivity increased most (in percentage terms) in construction, increasing by over 50 % in current prices between 1998 and 2008. Labour productivity in industry recorded the second highest growth, while, in relative terms, the lowest labour productivity growth in current prices over this period was for business activities and financial services. To eliminate inflation effects, labour productivity per person can also be derived using constant price output figures.

Over the past decade labour productivity among most of the Member States that joined the EU since 2004 has converged towards the EU-27 average. In PPS terms, labour productivity per person employed in Romania moved from 24 % of the EU-27 average in 2000 to 48 % of the EU-27 average by 2008; Estonia, Slovakia and Lithuania also recorded substantial progress towards the EU-27 average.

Final consumption expenditure across the EU-27 rose by 23.9 % in volume (constant price) terms between 1998 and 2008. This was slightly lower than the growth in GDP during the same period (25.4 %). Growth in gross capital formation outstripped both, increasing by 31.0 %.

Consumption by households and non-profit institutions serving households rose by just over 50 % in current prices between 1998 and 2008, and represented 57.6 % of the EU-27's GDP in 2008. The share of total GDP resulting from general government expenditure was 21.2 % in the EU-27 in 2008, while gross fixed capital formation represented 20.9 %; the external balance of goods and services was just 0.3 % of EU-27's GDP in 2008.

The vast majority of investment was made by the private sector: in 2008 private investment accounted for 18.4 % of the EU-27's GDP, whereas the equivalent figure for public sector investment was 2.7 %. Public investment exceeded 5 % of GDP in Bulgaria, Estonia, Ireland and Romania in 2008, while private investment exceeded 25 % of GDP in Romania, Bulgaria, Spain and Latvia. There was a wide variation in the overall investment intensity (public and private combined) that may, in part, reflect the different stages of economic development as well as growth dynamics among Member States over recent years. Gross fixed capital formation as a share of GDP ranged from more than 30 % in Bulgaria, Romania and Latvia (with Spain just below this level), to 19 % of GDP or less in Germany, the United Kingdom and Malta.

Within the EU-27, the distribution between the production factors of income resulting from the production process was dominated by the compensation of employees, which was 48.4 % of GDP in 2008, while gross operating surplus and mixed income accounted for 39.7 % of GDP and taxes on production and imports less subsidies the remaining 11.8 %.

In some countries, gross national saving as a proportion of national disposable income fell considerably between 1998 and 2008. This was particularly the case in Portugal (down 9.4 percentage points) and Ireland (down 7.2 percentage points), while Romania recorded an increase of 12.5 percentage points. The highest national savings rates in 2008 were in Sweden, Austria, Slovenia, Germany and the Netherlands, all over 25 %.

Gross household savings represented 11.3 % of gross household disposable income in 2008 in the EU-27. In 2007, Germany, Slovenia and Austria reported savings rates of more than 16 % of their gross household disposable income. In contrast, Latvia reported a negative rate (-4.3 %)

indicating that households were spending more money than they earned (and therefore were borrowers rather than savers), while Estonia and Lithuania reported rates under 1 %.

The consumption expenditure of households was at least half of GDP in the majority of Member States in 2008; this share was highest in Cyprus (76.6 %, 2007) and also exceeded 70 % in Greece (2007), Bulgaria (2006) and Malta, while it was below 40 % in Luxembourg (37.4 %, 2007); nevertheless, average household consumption expenditure per capita was, by far, highest in Luxembourg (PPS 24 900, 2007).

A little over one fifth (21.9 %) of total household consumption expenditure in the EU-27 in 2006 was devoted to housing, water, electricity, gas and other housing fuels. Transport expenditure (13.6 %) and expenditure on food and non-alcoholic beverages (12.7 %), together accounted for a little more than a quarter of the total.

Figure 1.1: GDP per capita at current market prices, 2008 (EU-27=100)

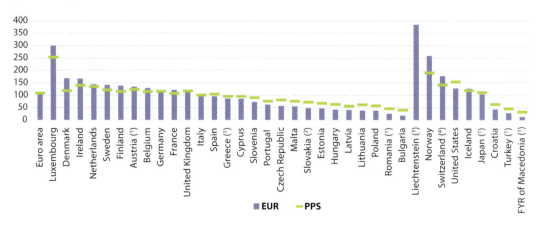

(¹) Forecast.
(²) Estimate.
(³) 2006. PPS, not available.
(⁴) Provisional.

Source: Eurostat (nama_gdp_c and tec00001)

Figure 1.2: GDP at current market prices
(EUR 1 000 million)

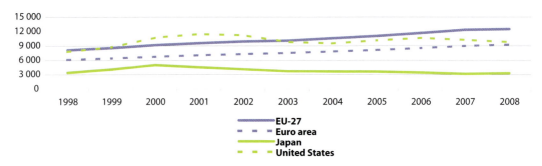

Source: Eurostat (tec00001)

Figure 1.3: Real GDP growth
(% change compared with the previous year)

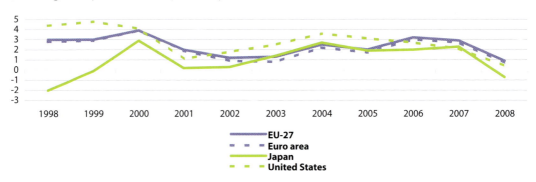

Source: Eurostat (tsieb020)

Table 1.1: GDP per capita at current market prices

	(PPS, EU-27=100)											(EUR)
	1998	1999	2000	2001	2002	2003	2004	2005	2006	2007	2008	2008 (¹)
EU-27	100	100	100	100	100	100	100	100	100	100	100	25 100
Euro area	113	113	113	112	111	111	109	110	109	109	108	28 300
Belgium	123	123	126	124	125	123	121	119	118	118	115	32 200
Bulgaria	27	27	28	29	31	33	34	35	37	37	40	4 500
Czech Republic	71	70	69	70	70	73	75	76	78	80	80	14 200
Denmark	132	131	132	128	128	124	126	124	123	120	118	42 400
Germany	122	122	119	117	115	117	116	117	116	115	116	30 400
Estonia	42	42	45	46	50	54	57	61	65	68	67	12 000
Ireland	121	126	131	133	138	141	142	144	147	150	139	40 900
Greece	83	83	84	87	90	92	94	93	94	95	95	21 300
Spain	95	96	97	98	101	101	101	102	104	105	104	23 900
France	115	115	115	116	116	112	110	111	109	109	107	30 400
Italy	120	118	117	118	112	111	107	105	104	102	100	26 300
Cyprus	87	87	89	91	89	89	90	91	90	91	95	21 700
Latvia	36	36	37	39	41	43	46	49	53	58	56	10 200
Lithuania	40	39	39	42	44	49	51	53	56	60	61	9 600
Luxembourg	217	237	244	234	240	248	253	254	267	267	253	80 500
Hungary	53	54	56	59	61	63	63	63	64	63	63	10 500
Malta	81	81	84	78	80	78	77	78	77	78	76	13 800
Netherlands	129	131	134	134	133	129	129	131	131	131	135	36 200
Austria	132	131	131	125	126	127	127	124	124	124	123	33 800
Poland	48	49	48	48	48	49	51	51	52	54	58	9 500
Portugal	77	78	78	77	77	77	75	77	76	76	75	15 700
Romania	:	26	26	28	29	31	34	35	38	42	46	6 500
Slovenia	79	81	80	80	82	83	86	87	88	89	90	18 400
Slovakia	52	51	50	52	54	56	57	60	64	67	72	12 000
Finland	114	115	117	116	115	113	116	114	115	116	115	34 800
Sweden	123	125	127	121	121	123	125	120	121	122	121	35 400
United Kingdom	118	118	119	120	121	122	124	122	121	118	117	29 600
Croatia	52	50	49	50	52	54	56	57	58	61	63	10 800
FYR of Macedonia	27	27	27	25	25	26	27	29	29	31	33	3 200
Turkey	43	39	40	36	34	34	37	40	43	45	46	7 000
Iceland	140	139	132	132	130	126	131	130	124	121	119	32 100
Norway	138	145	165	161	155	156	164	176	184	178	190	64 900
Switzerland	149	146	145	141	141	137	136	133	136	139	141	44 600
Japan	121	118	117	114	112	112	113	113	113	112	111	25 900
United States	161	163	161	157	154	156	157	159	158	156	154	32 200

(¹) Data extracted on 14 January 2010.

Source: Eurostat (tsieb010, tec00001 and nama_gdp_c)

Table 1.2: GDP at current market prices
(EUR 1 000 million)

	1998	1999	2000	2001	2002	2003	2004	2005	2006	2007	2008
EU-27	8 162	8 584	9 202	9 580	9 942	10 108	10 606	11 063	11 684	12 360	12 512
Euro area	6 160	6 441	6 779	7 075	7 324	7 544	7 854	8 148	8 556	9 001	9 276
Belgium	228	238	252	259	268	275	290	302	318	335	344
Bulgaria	11	12	14	15	17	18	20	22	25	29	34
Czech Republic	55	56	61	69	80	81	88	100	114	127	149
Denmark	155	163	174	179	185	189	197	207	218	227	232
Germany	1 952	2 012	2 063	2 113	2 143	2 164	2 211	2 242	2 325	2 428	2 496
Estonia	5	5	6	7	8	9	10	11	13	15	16
Ireland	79	91	105	117	130	139	149	162	177	191	186
Greece	122	132	138	146	157	171	186	198	213	228	243
Spain	537	580	630	681	729	783	841	909	982	1 051	1 095
France	1 315	1 368	1 441	1 497	1 549	1 595	1 660	1 726	1 806	1 895	1 950
Italy	1 087	1 127	1 191	1 249	1 295	1 335	1 392	1 429	1 485	1 545	1 572
Cyprus	9	9	10	11	11	12	13	14	15	16	17
Latvia	6	7	8	9	10	10	11	13	16	21	23
Lithuania	10	10	12	14	15	16	18	21	24	28	32
Luxembourg	17	20	22	23	24	26	28	30	34	36	37
Hungary	42	45	52	59	71	75	82	89	90	101	106
Malta	3	4	4	4	4	4	5	5	5	5	6
Netherlands	360	386	418	448	465	477	491	513	540	569	596
Austria	190	198	208	212	219	223	233	244	256	271	282
Poland	153	157	186	212	210	192	204	244	272	311	362
Portugal	106	114	122	129	135	139	144	149	155	163	166
Romania	37	34	41	45	49	53	61	80	98	124	137
Slovenia	19	21	21	23	25	26	27	29	31	34	37
Slovakia	20	19	22	24	26	29	34	38	45	55	65
Finland	116	123	132	140	144	146	152	157	167	180	185
Sweden	226	241	266	251	264	276	288	295	313	331	328
United Kingdom	1 300	1 410	1 602	1 643	1 710	1 647	1 773	1 834	1 945	2 044	1 816
Croatia	23	22	23	26	28	30	33	36	39	43	47
FYR of Macedonia	3	3	4	4	4	4	4	5	5	6	7
Turkey	239	234	290	218	243	268	315	387	419	472	498
Iceland	7	8	9	9	9	10	11	13	13	15	10
Liechtenstein	:	3	3	3	3	3	3	3	3	:	:
Norway	135	149	183	191	204	199	208	243	268	284	310
Switzerland	244	252	271	285	296	288	292	300	312	317	341
Japan	3 448	4 102	5 057	4 580	4 162	3 744	3 707	3 666	3 475	3 199	3 329
United States	7 844	8 776	10 775	11 485	11 255	9 850	9 541	10 159	10 671	10 272	9 819

Source: Eurostat (tec00001), CH: Secrétariat de l'Etat à l'Economie, JP: Bureau of Economic Analysis, US: Economic and Social Research Institute

Table 1.3: GDP at current market prices
(PPS 1 000 million)

	1998	1999	2000	2001	2002	2003	2004	2005	2006	2007	2008
EU-27	8 162	8 584	9 202	9 580	9 942	10 108	10 606	11 063	11 684	12 360	12 512
Euro area	5 976	6 280	6 716	6 983	7 216	7 299	7 597	7 945	8 370	8 848	8 918
Belgium	213	224	246	251	264	264	272	281	295	312	306
Bulgaria	38	39	43	46	50	53	57	60	66	71	77
Czech Republic	123	127	134	142	147	155	166	175	188	206	210
Denmark	119	124	134	135	141	139	147	151	158	163	163
Germany	1 704	1 786	1 855	1 900	1 945	1 994	2 078	2 166	2 257	2 356	2 391
Estonia	10	10	12	12	14	15	17	19	21	23	23
Ireland	76	84	95	101	111	116	125	134	148	163	155
Greece	153	160	175	187	203	210	225	232	248	264	269
Spain	643	685	747	790	850	879	934	995	1 084	1 178	1 189
France	1 173	1 233	1 335	1 400	1 463	1 437	1 488	1 566	1 634	1 729	1 728
Italy	1 157	1 192	1 268	1 328	1 310	1 322	1 344	1 382	1 447	1 507	1 510
Cyprus	10	11	12	13	13	13	14	15	16	18	19
Latvia	15	15	17	18	20	21	23	25	28	33	32
Lithuania	24	24	26	29	31	35	38	41	45	50	52
Luxembourg	16	18	20	20	22	23	25	27	30	32	31
Hungary	92	98	109	118	128	133	138	143	151	157	158
Malta	5	6	6	6	6	6	7	7	7	8	8
Netherlands	343	369	407	424	441	435	455	480	506	535	557
Austria	178	187	201	199	209	213	224	230	242	256	258
Poland	311	331	352	360	378	387	419	441	471	510	550
Portugal	132	142	152	157	163	166	170	183	191	201	201
Romania	103	105	111	123	131	141	160	170	196	226	247
Slovenia	26	28	30	31	34	35	37	39	42	45	46
Slovakia	48	49	52	56	60	62	67	73	81	90	98
Finland	100	106	116	119	123	122	131	135	143	153	153
Sweden	184	198	214	214	221	228	243	244	261	278	281
United Kingdom	1 167	1 232	1 335	1 400	1 465	1 503	1 603	1 651	1 728	1 799	1 801
Croatia	39	39	42	44	48	50	54	57	61	67	69
FYR of Macedonia	9	10	10	10	10	11	12	13	14	16	17
Turkey	459	448	513	482	489	497	580	654	734	786	815
Iceland	7	7	7	7	8	8	8	9	9	9	10
Norway	104	115	141	144	144	148	163	183	202	209	227
Switzerland	180	186	198	201	210	208	217	223	241	261	272
Japan	2 597	2 658	2 827	2 860	2 921	2 967	3 124	3 244	3 400	3 568	3 558
United States	7 531	8 095	8 667	8 834	9 097	9 418	9 994	10 586	11 162	11 698	11 796

Source: Eurostat (tec00001), CH: Secrétariat de l'Etat à l'Economie, JP: Bureau of Economic Analysis, US: Economic and Social Research
Institute

Table 1.4: Gross value added at basic prices
(% share of total gross value added)

	Agriculture, hunting, forestry & fishing		Industry		Construction		Trade, transport & communication services		Business activities & financial services		Other services	
	1998	2008	1998	2008	1998	2008	1998	2008	1998	2008	1998	2008
EU-27	2.6	1.8	23.1	20.1	5.5	6.5	21.3	21.0	25.0	28.1	22.2	22.5
Euro area	2.7	1.8	22.8	20.0	5.6	6.5	21.0	20.8	25.3	28.4	22.4	22.6
Belgium	1.5	0.8	22.9	17.9	4.8	5.3	21.3	23.0	26.8	29.4	22.4	23.6
Bulgaria	18.8	7.3	26.7	21.9	4.8	8.6	17.5	23.5	19.4	23.5	13.2	15.1
Czech Republic	4.2	2.3	31.2	31.3	8.1	6.3	24.7	25.4	16.3	17.8	15.4	16.9
Denmark	2.7	1.1	20.4	20.5	5.3	5.8	22.5	21.4	22.0	24.4	27.5	26.8
Germany	1.2	0.9	25.3	25.6	5.6	4.2	17.8	17.7	27.1	29.4	22.6	22.1
Estonia	6.1	2.6	22.2	20.6	7.0	8.4	26.6	25.6	20.8	24.2	16.7	18.6
Ireland	4.4	2.0	34.8	25.3	6.0	8.5	18.6	17.5	19.4	27.1	17.2	19.5
Greece	:	3.3	:	13.6	:	6.1	:	33.2	:	19.9	:	23.9
Spain	4.9	2.8	21.8	17.3	7.3	11.6	26.4	24.5	18.6	22.6	21.0	21.3
France	3.2	2.0	18.4	13.8	5.0	6.7	19.1	18.7	29.5	33.6	24.7	25.3
Italy	3.1	2.0	24.5	20.8	4.9	6.2	23.9	22.1	23.0	27.9	20.3	21.0
Cyprus	4.2	2.1	13.0	10.2	7.6	9.4	29.9	26.7	22.8	27.5	22.1	24.1
Latvia	4.0	3.1	21.5	13.8	6.1	8.9	31.5	29.8	15.1	23.9	21.4	20.5
Lithuania	9.8	4.5	23.0	22.2	8.4	10.0	27.7	30.8	11.6	15.6	19.7	17.0
Luxembourg	0.9	0.4	14.6	9.7	6.3	6.2	23.1	21.4	38.2	45.5	16.9	16.7
Hungary	5.5	4.3	28.2	24.9	4.6	4.6	23.2	22.2	19.2	21.9	19.3	22.2
Malta	2.9	2.3	23.1	17.7	4.0	3.6	31.6	26.4	17.4	21.6	21.3	28.6
Netherlands	3.0	1.8	19.9	19.7	5.3	5.8	22.3	21.0	26.6	28.3	22.3	23.5
Austria	2.2	1.7	22.9	23.2	8.0	7.5	24.7	23.3	20.7	23.8	21.6	20.5
Poland	6.0	4.5	24.9	23.1	7.9	8.0	26.4	27.3	16.4	19.4	18.1	17.8
Portugal	4.3	2.4	21.5	17.6	7.3	6.4	24.2	24.3	20.0	22.7	22.7	26.6
Romania	16.0	7.2	29.1	25.6	5.6	11.8	:	26.1	12.4	14.2	11.3	15.2
Slovenia	4.0	2.3	29.8	25.1	6.6	8.9	21.7	22.6	19.0	22.4	19.4	18.9
Slovakia	5.4	3.4	27.4	28.1	7.2	8.7	26.3	26.2	16.4	17.7	16.4	15.9
Finland	3.5	3.0	28.4	24.9	5.3	6.7	21.8	21.6	19.4	21.6	21.7	22.2
Sweden	2.4	1.6	25.1	22.8	4.1	5.1	19.0	19.4	24.0	24.3	25.1	26.8
United Kingdom	1.2	0.8	23.4	17.6	5.1	6.1	21.9	20.4	26.3	32.2	21.3	22.8
Croatia	8.9	6.4	23.0	20.2	6.6	8.3	25.6	25.2	17.3	22.9	19.4	16.9
FYR of Macedonia (¹)	13.2	11.0	27.1	25.7	6.7	7.0	22.2	27.4	9.8	11.3	19.8	17.8
Turkey	12.9	8.6	27.7	21.7	6.0	5.2	34.2	31.9	15.6	21.1	9.4	11.4
Iceland (¹)	10.2	5.6	19.6	14.3	8.4	12.2	22.0	19.4	16.6	27.2	23.1	20.9
Norway	2.7	1.2	27.5	41.3	5.1	4.8	21.4	15.7	18.2	17.3	23.7	19.6
Switzerland	1.7	1.2	22.5	22.6	5.4	5.3	22.0	22.2	22.7	23.3	25.5	25.1
Japan	1.5	:	24.8	:	7.4	:	17.6	:	17.4	:	28.1	:
United States	1.3	:	20.0	:	4.6	:	:	:	30.7	:	23.5	:

(¹) 2007 instead of 2008.

Source: Eurostat (tec00003, tec00004, tec00005, tec00006, tec00007 and tec00008)

Figure 1.4: Gross value added, EU-27
(2000=100)

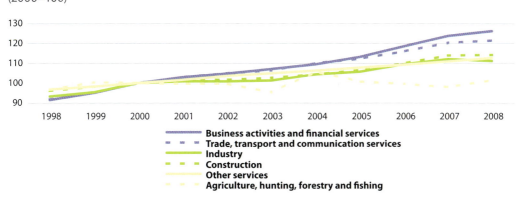

Business activities and financial services
Trade, transport and communication services
Industry
Construction
Other services
Agriculture, hunting, forestry and fishing

Source: Eurostat (nama_nace06_k)

Figure 1.5: Labour productivity, EU-27
(EUR 1 000 per person employed)

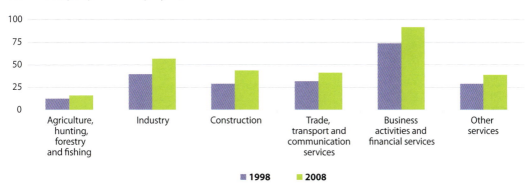

■ 1998   ■ 2008

Source: Eurostat (nama_nace06_c and nama_nace06_e)

Economy

Table 1.5: Labour productivity (based on PPS)

	Per person employed (EU-27=100)						Per hour worked (EU-15=100)					
	1998	2000	2002	2004	2006	2008	1998	2000	2002	2004	2006	2007
EU-27	100	100	100	100	100	100	:	:	87	88	89	89
Euro area	115	113	111	109	109	109	:	101	101	100	101	101
Belgium	134	137	136	132	130	125	:	:	:	:	:	:
Bulgaria	27	30	33	34	35	36	25	28	30	30	31	31
Czech Republic	60	62	63	68	70	72	44	45	48	52	53	55
Denmark	109	110	108	109	105	101	106	105	103	104	100	96
Germany	112	108	106	108	109	107	111	109	109	112	113	112
Estonia	41	46	51	57	61	64	:	35	38	43	46	48
Ireland	125	127	133	135	137	134	95	98	104	107	108	111
Greece	91	94	99	101	101	102	:	:	:	:	:	:
Spain	108	104	105	102	102	105	92	89	90	90	92	94
France	126	125	125	121	121	121	115	117	121	115	117	117
Italy	130	126	118	112	110	108	103	100	95	91	90	89
Cyprus	82	85	84	83	83	86	64	65	65	66	66	67
Latvia	37	40	43	46	50	51	:	:	:	:	:	:
Lithuania	41	43	48	53	56	61	34	34	39	44	45	47
Luxembourg	165	176	163	170	176	161	:	:	150	160	168	166
Hungary	63	65	71	72	73	74	45	46	52	54	55	55
Malta	:	97	92	90	90	88	:	:	:	:	:	:
Netherlands	111	114	113	112	114	115	114	118	119	119	121	121
Austria	121	121	117	118	115	113	104	104	101	102	101	102
Poland (¹)	51	55	59	62	61	63	:	41	43	51	53	44
Portugal	68	69	68	67	70	71	:	53	52	52	55	:
Romania	:	24	29	34	40	48	:	19	23	28	31	:
Slovenia	75	76	78	82	84	84	:	:	:	:	:	:
Slovakia	56	58	63	66	72	79	46	47	53	56	60	63
Finland	114	115	111	112	110	110	96	97	95	97	96	97
Sweden	112	113	108	113	111	112	100	103	100	105	103	103
United Kingdom	109	111	112	114	112	111	:	:	:	:	:	:
Croatia	64	61	67	70	74	77	:	:	:	:	:	:
FYR of Macedonia	46	48	46	51	55	58	:	:	:	:	:	:
Turkey	53	53	49	54	62	64	:	:	:	:	:	:
Iceland	110	103	104	108	99	99	:	:	:	:	:	:
Norway	114	139	131	142	156	157	115	141	138	149	164	157
Switzerland	112	110	107	105	106	112	100	97	98	94	95	97
Japan	98	99	98	99	100	100	:	:	:	:	:	:
United States	141	142	140	143	143	145	112	114	114	119	:	:

(¹) 2005, break in series for per person employed; 2007, break in series for per hour worked.

Source: Eurostat (tsieb030 and tsieb040), OECD

Figure 1.6: Consumption expenditure and gross capital formation at constant prices, EU-27
(2000=100)

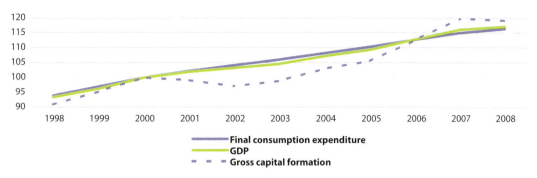

Final consumption expenditure
GDP
Gross capital formation

Source: Eurostat (nama_gdp_k)

Figure 1.7: Expenditure components of GDP, EU-27
(EUR 1 000 million)

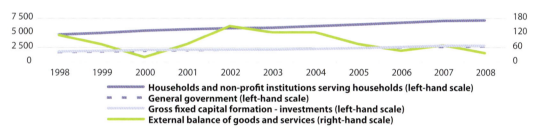

Households and non-profit institutions serving households (left-hand scale)
General government (left-hand scale)
Gross fixed capital formation - investments (left-hand scale)
External balance of goods and services (right-hand scale)

Source: Eurostat (tec00009, tec00010, tec00011 and tec00110)

Figure 1.8: Expenditure components of GDP, EU-27, 2008
(% share of GDP)

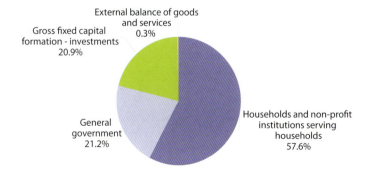

External balance of goods
and services
0.3%

Gross fixed capital
formation - investments
20.9%

General
government
21.2%

Households and non-profit
institutions serving
households
57.6%

Source: Eurostat (tec00009, tec00011, tec00010 and tec00110)

Table 1.6: Investment
(% share of GDP)

	Total investment			Public investment			Business investment		
	1998	2003	2008	1998	2003	2008	1998	2003	2008
EU-27	20.0	19.4	21.1	2.3	2.4	2.7	17.8	17.0	18.4
Euro area	20.4	20.1	21.6	2.4	2.5	2.5	18.0	17.6	19.1
Belgium	20.2	18.8	22.7	1.7	1.7	1.6	18.5	17.1	21.1
Bulgaria	13.0	19.3	33.4	3.2	2.7	5.6	9.8	16.6	27.8
Czech Republic	28.2	26.7	24.0	4.2	4.5	4.8	24.0	22.1	19.1
Denmark	20.4	19.3	21.0	1.7	1.6	1.8	18.8	17.7	19.2
Germany	21.1	17.9	19.0	1.8	1.6	1.5	19.3	16.3	17.5
Estonia	30.4	31.6	29.3	4.9	4.4	5.6	25.5	27.2	23.8
Ireland	21.4	22.3	21.1	2.7	3.7	5.4	18.8	18.7	15.7
Greece	:	23.7	19.3	3.2	3.6	2.9	:	20.1	16.4
Spain	23.0	27.2	29.4	3.3	3.6	3.8	19.8	23.6	25.6
France	17.9	18.8	21.9	2.8	3.1	3.2	15.1	15.8	18.7
Italy	19.3	20.4	20.9	2.3	2.5	2.2	17.0	17.9	18.7
Cyprus	18.7	17.6	23.3	2.9	3.4	3.0	15.8	14.2	20.3
Latvia	24.7	24.4	30.2	1.4	2.4	4.9	23.3	22.0	25.3
Lithuania	24.0	21.1	24.8	2.5	3.0	4.9	21.4	18.1	19.9
Luxembourg	21.8	22.2	20.1	4.5	4.6	3.9	17.3	17.6	16.2
Hungary	23.6	22.0	20.1	3.4	3.5	2.8	20.2	18.5	17.3
Malta	22.9	19.6	15.8	4.6	4.7	2.7	18.4	14.9	13.2
Netherlands	22.2	19.5	20.4	3.0	3.6	3.3	19.3	15.9	17.2
Austria	24.0	22.4	21.8	1.8	1.2	1.0	22.2	21.3	20.8
Poland	24.1	18.2	22.0	3.9	3.3	4.6	20.2	14.9	17.3
Portugal	26.5	22.9	21.7	4.0	3.1	2.1	22.5	19.8	19.6
Romania	18.2	21.5	33.3	1.8	3.5	5.4	16.4	18.0	27.9
Slovenia	24.9	24.0	28.9	2.9	3.2	4.2	21.2	20.6	24.8
Slovakia	35.7	24.8	25.9	4.0	2.6	1.8	32.7	22.9	24.2
Finland	19.0	18.1	20.6	2.9	2.9	2.5	16.2	15.2	18.1
Sweden	16.3	16.3	19.5	3.1	2.9	3.3	13.2	13.3	16.2
United Kingdom	17.7	16.4	16.9	1.3	1.5	2.3	16.5	14.9	14.6
Croatia	20.0	25.0	27.6	:	:	:	:	:	:
FYR of Macedonia	17.4	16.7	23.7	:	:	:	:	:	:
Turkey	22.9	17.0	20.3	:	:	:	:	:	:
Iceland	24.0	20.0	24.4	4.4	3.6	4.5	19.6	16.3	19.9
Norway	25.0	17.3	20.8	3.6	3.0	3.1	21.3	14.3	17.7
Switzerland (¹)	22.2	20.5	21.3	2.7	2.5	1.9	19.4	18.1	19.6

(¹) 2007 instead of 2008 for public and business investment.

Source: Eurostat (nama_gdp_c, tsdec210, tec00022 and tsier140)

Figure 1.9: Gross fixed capital formation, 2007
(% share of GDP)

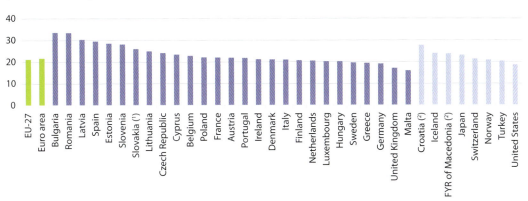

(¹) Estimate.
(²) Forecast.

Source: Eurostat (tec00011)

Figure 1.10: Distribution of income, EU-27
(1998=100)

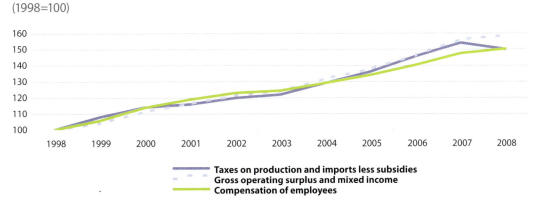

Source: Eurostat (tec00016, tec00015 and tec00013)

Figure 1.11: Distribution of income, 2008
(% share of GDP)

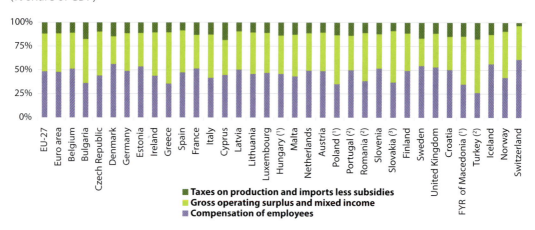

(¹) 2007.
(²) 2006.
(³) Estimates.

Source: Eurostat (tec00016, tec00015 and tec00013)

Figure 1.12: Gross national savings (¹)
(% of gross national disposable income)

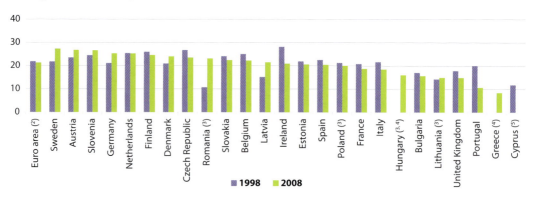

(¹) EU-27, Luxembourg and Malta, not available.
(²) EA-13 instead of EA-16.
(³) Forecast.
(⁴) 1998, not available.
(⁵) 2008, not available.

Source: Eurostat (nama_inc_c)

Table 1.7: Gross household savings (^{1})
(% of gross household disposable income)

	1998	1999	2000	2001	2002	2003	2004	2005	2006	2007	2008
EU-27	:	12.1	11.5	12.3	12.3	12.2	11.7	11.5	10.9	10.8	11.3
Belgium	17.0	17.2	15.4	16.4	15.8	14.7	13.3	12.6	12.9	13.7	:
Bulgaria	:	:	:	:	:	:	:	-22.7	-29.2	:	:
Czech Republic	9.2	8.6	8.5	7.4	8.1	7.4	5.7	8.1	9.1	8.8	:
Denmark	6.3	3.8	4.9	8.8	8.8	9.4	6.3	4.5	6.4	5.1	:
Germany	15.9	15.3	15.1	15.2	15.7	16.0	16.1	16.3	16.2	16.7	:
Estonia	4.5	2.6	4.1	3.1	0.5	-1.6	-4.8	-3.8	-3.0	0.8	:
Ireland	:	:	:	:	10.3	10.6	13.7	11.6	10.3	9.2	:
Greece	:	:	2.5	1.7	1.1	1.6	1.5	0.7	1.2	:	:
Spain	:	:	11.1	11.1	11.4	12.0	11.3	11.3	11.2	10.2	:
France	15.4	15.1	14.9	15.6	16.7	15.6	15.6	14.7	14.8	15.3	15.1
Italy	16.8	15.8	14.2	16.0	16.8	16.0	16.0	15.8	15.2	14.5	15.1
Cyprus	:	:	:	:	:	:	:	:	:	:	:
Latvia	0.7	-0.7	2.9	-0.4	1.5	3.0	4.7	1.2	-3.7	-4.3	:
Lithuania	7.2	7.8	6.5	4.9	4.7	3.0	1.3	1.3	1.2	0.1	:
Luxembourg	:	:	14.1	13.5	11.4	9.3	11.8	11.0	12.4	9.9	:
Hungary	:	:	:	:	:	:	:	:	:	:	:
Malta	:	:	:	:	:	:	:	:	:	:	:
Netherlands	16.6	13.8	12.0	14.5	13.7	13.0	13.0	12.2	11.5	13.4	:
Austria	13.3	14.5	13.9	13.0	12.9	14.0	14.1	14.5	15.4	16.3	:
Poland	14.4	13.3	12.4	14.2	10.4	10.0	10.1	9.8	8.6	8.8	:
Portugal	10.5	9.8	10.2	10.9	10.6	10.6	9.7	9.2	8.1	6.7	:
Romania	:	:	1.2	1.6	-1.4	-9.6	-6.6	-12.1	-14.0	:	:
Slovenia	:	:	14.0	15.5	16.1	13.9	15.4	17.0	17.1	16.4	:
Slovakia	12.4	11.2	11.1	9.1	8.9	7.1	6.3	6.9	6.1	7.7	:
Finland	7.9	9.3	7.5	7.7	7.8	8.3	9.2	7.8	6.1	6.4	6.8
Sweden	6.4	6.0	7.4	11.8	11.6	11.4	10.3	9.5	10.5	11.7	14.7
United Kingdom	7.4	5.2	4.7	6.0	4.8	5.1	4.0	5.1	4.2	2.5	:
Norway	10.5	9.5	9.2	8.2	12.8	13.3	11.8	14.5	5.6	4.6	:
Switzerland	15.8	16.0	16.9	17.1	16.1	14.8	14.4	15.4	16.6	17.8	:

(^{1}) Including net adjustment for the change in net equity of households in pension funds reserves.

Source: Eurostat (tsdec240)

Table 1.8: Consumption expenditure of households (domestic concept)

	As a proportion of GDP (%)			Per capita (PPS)		
	1998	2003	2008	1998	2003	2008
Belgium (¹)	51.9	51.5	50.2	10 800	13 100	14 700
Bulgaria (²)	70.8	73.2	73.5	3 200	4 900	6 300
Czech Republic (¹)	54.7	53.0	49.5	6 500	8 100	9 900
Denmark	49.9	46.9	48.2	11 200	12 100	14 300
Germany (¹)	55.0	56.1	53.7	11 400	13 600	15 400
Estonia (¹)	63.7	58.1	54.6	4 600	6 600	9 400
Ireland (¹)	48.4	43.9	43.6	10 000	12 800	16 300
Greece (¹)	:	74.3	74.1	:	14 200	17 500
Spain (¹)	62.8	60.4	59.4	10 200	12 600	15 600
France	55.1	55.8	56.1	10 800	12 900	15 100
Italy (¹)	60.2	59.8	59.3	12 200	13 700	15 000
Cyprus (¹)	81.0	77.6	76.6	11 900	14 300	17 300
Latvia (¹)	62.1	61.1	60.6	3 800	5 500	8 700
Lithuania (¹)	63.0	65.3	64.0	4 300	6 600	9 500
Luxembourg (¹)	49.3	44.3	37.4	18 200	22 800	24 900
Hungary	54.7	56.0	53.5	4 900	7 300	8 500
Malta	79.4	74.9	70.6	10 900	12 200	13 400
Netherlands	49.3	48.7	44.8	10 800	13 000	15 200
Austria (¹)	56.2	55.9	54.1	12 500	14 700	16 700
Poland (¹)	62.5	65.1	60.4	5 100	6 600	8 100
Portugal (²)	64.3	64.1	65.9	8 400	10 200	11 900
Romania (²)	74.8	65.4	67.7	:	4 200	6 100
Slovenia	59.2	57.4	55.8	7 900	9 900	12 700
Slovakia (¹)	54.3	56.0	55.0	4 800	6 400	9 200
Finland	48.2	49.6	49.6	9 400	11 600	14 300
Sweden (¹)	47.8	47.4	45.5	9 900	12 000	13 900
United Kingdom	61.9	61.6	60.6	12 400	15 600	17 800
FYR of Macedonia (¹)	72.9	77.4	78.7	3 300	4 100	6 100
Turkey	70.8	76.0	73.0	5 100	5 300	8 300
Iceland	53.7	53.1	49.2	12 800	13 800	14 700
Norway	47.5	44.5	37.3	11 100	14 400	17 800
Switzerland (¹)	59.0	59.2	55.7	15 000	16 800	19 200

(¹) 2007 instead of 2008.
(²) 2006 instead of 2008.

Source: Eurostat (nama_fcs_c)

1

Figure 1.13: Consumption expenditure of households, EU-27, 2006
(% of total household consumption expenditure)

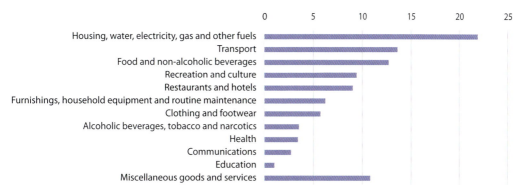

Source: Eurostat (nama_co2_c)

1.2 Government finances

Introduction

The disciplines of the stability and growth pact (SGP) keep economic developments in the EU and in the euro area countries (in particular), broadly synchronised (⁵). They prevent Member States from taking policy measures which would unduly benefit their own economies at the expense of others. There are two key principles to the pact: the deficit (planned or actual) must not exceed 3 % of GDP and that the debt-to-GDP ratio should not be more than 60 %.

A revision in March 2005 based on the first five years of experience left these principles unchanged, but introduced greater flexibility in exceeding the deficit threshold in hard economic times or to finance investment in structural improvements. It also gave Member States

a longer period to reverse their excessive deficits – although, if they do not bring their economies back into line, corrective measures, or even fines, can be imposed.

Each year, Member States provide the European Commission with detailed information on their economic policies and the state of their public finances. Euro area countries provide this information in the context of 'stability programmes', while other Member States do so in the form of 'convergence programmes'. If a Member State exceeds the deficit ceiling, an excessive deficit procedure (EDP) is triggered; this entails several steps to encourage the Member State concerned to take measures to rectify the situation. The Spotlight chapter at the start of this publication provides more information on the implementation of the EDP during the financial and economic crisis.

(⁵) For more information: http://ec.europa.eu/economy_finance/sg_pact_fiscal_policy/fiscal_policy528_en.htm.

Definitions and data availability

Under the rules on budgetary discipline within the EU's stability and growth pact (Amsterdam, 1997), Member States are to avoid situations of 'excessive government deficits'. The Member States should notify their **government deficit and debt statistics** to the European Commission before 1 April and 1 October of each year under the 'excessive deficit procedure'. In addition, Eurostat collects the data and ensures that Member States comply with the relevant Regulations. The main aggregates of general government are provided by the Member States to Eurostat twice a year, according to the ESA 95 transmission programme.

The data presented in this section correspond to the main revenue and expenditure items of the general government sector, which are compiled on a national accounts (ESA 95) basis. The difference between total revenue and total expenditure – including capital expenditure (in particular, gross fixed capital formation) – equals net lending/net borrowing of general government, which is also the balancing item of the government non-financial accounts.

The **general government sector** includes all institutional units whose output is intended for individual and collective consumption, and mainly financed by compulsory payments made by units belonging to other sectors, and/or all institutional units principally engaged in the redistribution of national income and wealth. The general government sector is subdivided into four subsectors:

- **Central government** covers all administrative departments of the state and other central agencies whose responsibilities extend over the whole economic territory, except for the administration of the social security funds.
- **State government** covers separate institutional units exercising some of the functions of government at a level below that of central government and above that of the governmental institutional units existing at local level, except for the administration of social security funds.
- **Local government** concerns all types of public administration whose competence extends to only a local part of the economic territory apart from local agencies of social security funds.
- **Social security funds** comprise all central, state and local institutional units whose principal activity is to provide social benefits, and which fulfil each of the two following criteria: (i) by law or regulation (except regulations concerning government employees), certain groups of the population are obliged to participate in the scheme or to pay contributions, and (ii) general government is responsible for the management of the institution in respect of settlement or approval of the contributions and benefits independently of its role as a supervisory body or employer.

The main **revenue of general government** consists of taxes, social contributions, sales and property income. It is defined in ESA 95 by reference to a list of categories: market output, output for own final use, payments for the other non-market output, taxes on production and imports, other subsidies on production, receivable property income, current taxes on income, wealth, etc., social contributions, other current transfers and capital transfers.

The main expenditure items consist of the compensation of civil servants, social benefits, interest on the public debt, subsidies, and gross fixed capital formation. Total **general government expenditure** is defined in ESA 95 by reference to a list of categories: intermediate consumption, gross capital formation, compensation of employees, other taxes on production, subsidies, payable property income, current taxes on income, wealth, social benefits, some social transfers, other current transfers, capital transfers and transactions on non-produced assets.

The **public balance** is defined as general government net borrowing/net lending reported for the excessive deficit procedure and is expressed in relation to GDP. Under the convergence criteria, the ratio of planned or actual government deficit (net borrowing) to GDP should be no more than 3 %.

General government consolidated gross debt is also expressed as a percentage of GDP. It refers to the consolidated stock of gross debt at nominal value at the end of the year. Under the convergence criteria, the ratio of general government consolidated gross debt to GDP should generally be no more than 60 % (unless the ratio is sufficiently diminishing and approaching the reference value at a satisfactory pace).

Taxes and social contributions correspond to revenues which are levied (in cash or in kind) by central, state and local governments, and social security funds. These levies (generally referred to as tax

revenue) are organised into three main areas, covered by the following headings:

* **taxes on income and wealth**, including all compulsory payments levied periodically by general government on the income and wealth of enterprises and households;
* **taxes on production and imports**, including all compulsory payments levied by general government with respect to the production and importation of goods and services, the employment of labour, the ownership or use of land, buildings or other assets used in production;
* **social contributions**, including all employers' and employees' social contributions, as well as imputed social contributions that represent the counterpart to social benefits paid directly by employers.

Data on public procurement are based on information contained in the calls for competition and contract award notices submitted for publication in the Official Journal of the European Communities (the S series). The numerator is the value of public procurement, which is openly advertised. For each of the sectors – works, supplies and services – the number of calls for competition published is multiplied by an average based, in general, on all the prices provided in the contract award notices published in the Official Journal during the relevant year. The value of public procurement is then expressed relative to GDP.

State aid is made up of sectoral State aid (given to specific activities of the economy such as agriculture, fisheries, manufacturing, mining, transport, services), ad-hoc State aid (given to individual undertakings), and State aid for cross-cutting or horizontal objectives (of common interest) such as research and development, safeguarding the environment, support to small and medium-sized enterprises, employment or training, including aid for regional development. The first two of these (sectoral and ad-hoc State aid) are considered potentially more distortive to competition.

Main findings

The government deficit to GDP ratio for the EU-27 fell from 3.1 % in 2003 to 0.8 % in 2007, but in 2008 the trend was reversed as it grew rapidly to 2.3 %. Four Member States recorded a reduced deficit or increased surplus relative to GDP in 2008 compared with 2007, namely Bulgaria, Hungary, the Netherlands and Austria. However, three Member States recorded large swings from surplus to deficit, namely a fall of 7.5 percentage points in Ireland, 6.0 percentage points in Spain, and 5.3 percentage points in Estonia. In 2008 the deficit ratios exceeded the target reference value of the stability and growth pact in 11 Member States, which could be compared with the situation in 2007 when only two Member States exceeded the limit of 3 % of GDP. In 2008, the largest government deficits as a percentage of GDP were recorded by Greece (-7.7 %) and Ireland (-7.2 %), while eight Member States registered a surplus in 2008, the largest being in Finland (4.5 %).

The government debt to GDP ratio in the EU-27 fell from 66.5 % at the end of 1998 to 58.7 % at the end of 2007, however, it increased to 61.5 % at the end of 2008. The lowest ratios of government debt to

GDP at the end of 2008 were recorded in Estonia (4.6 %), Luxembourg (13.5 %), Romania (13.6 %) and Bulgaria (14.1 %). A total of 18 Member States had government debt ratios under 60 % of GDP in 2008, one less than in 2007 as Austria moved back above this target. The highest government debt ratios were recorded in Italy (105.8 %), Greece (99.2 %) and Belgium (89.8 %). In 2008, the government debt ratio decreased for seven Member States, most notably Cyprus – where it fell by 9.9 percentage points. The highest increases of the debt ratio from 2007 to 2008 were observed in Ireland (up 19.0 percentage points of GDP), the Netherlands (12.7 points) and Latvia (10.5 points).

General government expenditure may be analysed by using the classification of the functions of government (COFOG). Social protection measures accounted for the highest proportion of government expenditure in 2007 in all of the Member States (except for Cyprus). Their share ranged from close to or more than 22 % of GDP in France, Denmark and Sweden to less than 10 % in Latvia, Estonia, Romania and Cyprus. Government expenditure devoted to social protection amounted to 18 % of GDP in the EU-27. The next COFOG functions in order of their relative importance across the whole of the EU were health (6.6 % of GDP), general public services (6.1 %) and education (5.1 %), while spending on economic affairs in the EU-27 was close to 4 % of GDP, and less than 2 % was of GDP was devoted to each of the following COFOG functions: defence, public order and safety, environmental protection, housing and community affairs, recreation, religion and culture.

The importance of the general government sector in the economy may be measured in terms of total general government revenue and expenditure as a percentage of GDP. In the EU-27, total government revenue in 2008 amounted to 44.6 % of GDP, and expenditure to 46.8 % of GDP. The level of general government expenditure and revenue varies considerably between the Member States. Those with the highest levels of combined government expenditure and revenue as a proportion of GDP in 2008 were Sweden, Denmark, Finland and France, for which this combined ratio was more than 100 %. Nine Member States reported relatively low combined ratios of below 80 %: out of these, the government sector was smallest in Slovakia, Romania and Lithuania (under 72 %).

The main types of government revenue are taxes on income and wealth, taxes on production and imports, and social contributions. The structure of tax revenue within the EU-27 shows that receipts from these three main headings were roughly equal in 2008, with receipts from social contributions slightly higher than the receipts from the other two categories. 2008 marked a change in the development of the revenue from these three categories of taxes. Between 2004 and 2007 the ratio of taxes on income and wealth to GDP increased in the EU-27 from 12.3 % to 13.4 %, before dropping back to 13.1 % in 2008. Taxes on production and imports relative to GDP grew steadily and smoothly from 13.1 % in 2001 to 13.5 % in 2007 (with a stable period between 2006 and 2007), before also dropping back to 13.0 % in 2008. In contrast, social contributions had fallen from 14.0 % of GDP

in 2003 to 13.5 % in 2007, before picking up to 13.7 % in 2008. However, there was considerable variation in the structure of tax revenue across the Member States. As may be expected, those countries that reported relatively high levels of expenditure tended to be those that also raised more taxes (as a proportion of GDP). For example, the highest return from these taxes and social contributions was 48.8 % of GDP recorded in Denmark, with Sweden recording the next highest share (47.5 %), while the proportion of GDP accounted for by tax revenue was below 30 % in Slovakia, Romania and Latvia.

The value of public procurement which is openly advertised reached 12.3 % of GDP in Latvia, four times as high as the 3.1 % average for the EU-27. Malta was the only Member States that joined the EU since 2004 where this indicator was below the EU-27 average in 2007. Among the EU-15 Member States, Spain and the United Kingdom recorded the highest ratio of openly advertised public procurement to GDP, while Germany and Luxembourg reported the lowest.

In total, state aid in the EU-27 amounted to 0.5 % of GDP in 2006. This average masks significant disparities between Member States: the ratio of total state aid to GDP ranged from less than 0.4 % in Luxembourg, Estonia, the United Kingdom, Spain, Italy and Belgium to 1.3 % or more in Portugal, Bulgaria and Hungary. The relatively high importance of state aid in some of the Member States that joined the EU since 2004 may be largely attributed to pre-accession measures that are either being phased-out under transitional arrangements or are limited in time.

Figure 1.14: Public balance (^{1})
(net borrowing/lending of consolidated general government sector, % of GDP)

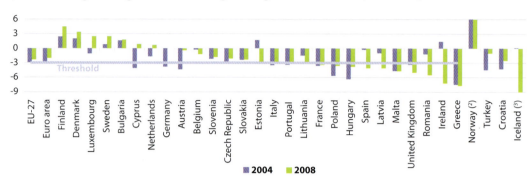

(^{1}) Data extracted on 22 October 2009.
(^{2}) Broken y-axis; value for 2004 is 11.1 %; value for 2008 is 18.8 %.
(^{3}) Broken y-axis; value for 2008 is -14.3 %.

Source: Eurostat (tsieb080)

Table 1.9: Public balance and general government debt ([1])

	Public balance (net borrowing/lending of consolidated general government sector, % of GDP)					General government debt (general government consolidated gross debt, % of GDP)				
	1998	2003	2006	2007	2008	1998	2003	2006	2007	2008
EU-27	-1.9	-3.1	-1.4	-0.8	-2.3	66.5	61.8	61.3	58.7	61.5
Euro area	-2.3	-3.1	-1.3	-0.6	-2.0	73.1	69.1	68.3	66.0	69.3
Belgium	-0.9	-0.1	0.3	-0.2	-1.2	117.1	98.7	88.1	84.2	89.8
Bulgaria	:	-0.3	3.0	0.1	1.8	79.6	45.9	22.7	18.2	14.1
Czech Republic	-5.0	-6.6	-2.6	-0.7	-2.1	15.0	30.1	29.4	29.0	30.0
Denmark	0.1	0.1	5.2	4.5	3.4	60.8	45.8	31.3	26.8	33.5
Germany	-2.2	-4.0	-1.6	0.2	0.0	60.3	63.8	67.6	65.0	65.9
Estonia	-0.7	1.7	2.3	2.6	-2.7	5.5	5.6	4.5	3.8	4.6
Ireland	2.4	0.4	3.0	0.3	-7.2	53.6	31.1	25.0	25.1	44.1
Greece	:	-5.7	-2.9	-3.7	-7.7	105.8	98.0	97.1	95.6	99.2
Spain	-3.2	-0.2	2.0	1.9	-4.1	64.1	48.7	39.6	36.1	39.7
France	-2.6	-4.1	-2.3	-2.7	-3.4	59.4	62.9	63.7	63.8	67.4
Italy	-2.8	-3.5	-3.3	-1.5	-2.7	114.9	104.4	106.5	103.5	105.8
Cyprus	-4.1	-6.5	-1.2	3.4	0.9	58.6	68.9	64.6	58.3	48.4
Latvia	0.0	-1.6	-0.5	-0.3	-4.1	9.6	14.6	10.7	9.0	19.5
Lithuania	-3.1	-1.3	-0.4	-1.0	-3.2	16.6	21.1	18.0	16.9	15.6
Luxembourg	3.4	0.5	1.3	3.7	2.5	7.1	6.1	6.6	6.6	13.5
Hungary	-8.2	-7.2	-9.3	-5.0	-3.8	62.0	58.1	65.6	65.9	72.9
Malta	-9.9	-9.9	-2.6	-2.2	-4.7	53.4	69.3	63.6	62.0	63.8
Netherlands	-0.9	-3.1	0.5	0.2	0.7	65.7	52.0	47.4	45.5	58.2
Austria	-2.4	-1.4	-1.6	-0.6	-0.4	64.8	65.5	62.2	59.5	62.6
Poland	-4.3	-6.3	-3.6	-1.9	-3.6	38.9	47.1	47.7	45.0	47.2
Portugal	-3.4	-2.9	-3.9	-2.6	-2.7	52.1	56.9	64.7	63.6	66.3
Romania	-3.2	-1.5	-2.2	-2.5	-5.5	16.6	21.5	12.4	12.6	13.6
Slovenia	-2.4	-2.7	-1.3	0.0	-1.8	:	27.5	26.7	23.3	22.5
Slovakia	-5.3	-2.8	-3.5	-1.9	-2.3	34.5	42.4	30.5	29.3	27.7
Finland	1.6	2.6	4.0	5.2	4.5	48.2	44.4	39.3	35.2	34.1
Sweden	1.1	-0.9	2.5	3.8	2.5	69.1	52.3	45.9	40.5	38.0
United Kingdom	-0.1	-3.3	-2.7	-2.7	-5.0	46.7	38.7	43.2	44.2	52.0
Croatia	:	-4.5	-3.0	-2.5	-1.4	:	40.9	35.7	33.1	33.5
Turkey	:	-11.3	0.8	-1.0	-2.2	:	85.1	46.1	39.4	39.5
Iceland	0.5	-1.6	6.3	5.4	-14.3	49.3	41.4	30.1	28.7	70.6
Norway	:	7.3	18.5	17.7	18.8	:	44.3	55.3	52.3	50.0

([1]) Data extracted on 22 October 2009.

Source: Eurostat (tsieb080 and tsieb090)

Figure 1.15: General government debt (¹)
(general government consolidated gross debt, % of GDP)

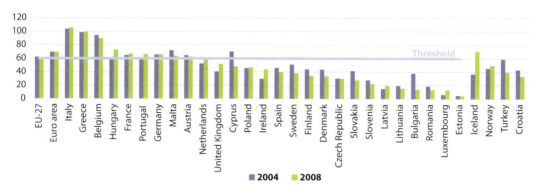

(¹) Data extracted on 22 October 2009.

Source: Eurostat (tsieb090)

Figure 1.16: General government expenditure by COFOG function, 2007 (¹)
(% of GDP)

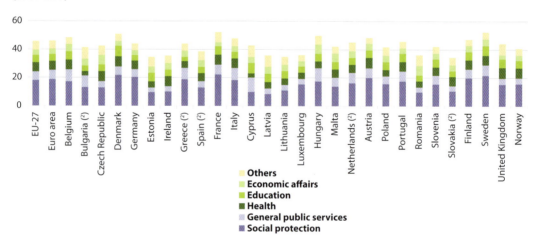

(¹) COFOG: classification of the functions of government.
(²) Forecast.

Source: Eurostat (gov_a_exp)

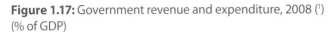

Figure 1.17: Government revenue and expenditure, 2008 (¹)
(% of GDP)

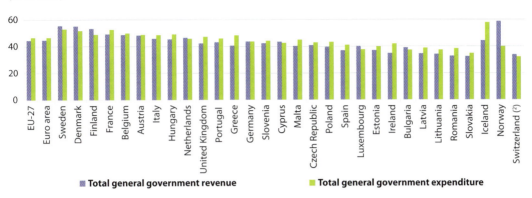

■ **Total general government revenue**　　■ **Total general government expenditure**

(¹) The figure is ranked on the average of revenue and expenditure.
(²) 2007.

Source: Eurostat (tec00021 and tec00023)

Figure 1.18: Taxes and social contributions, EU-27
(% of GDP)

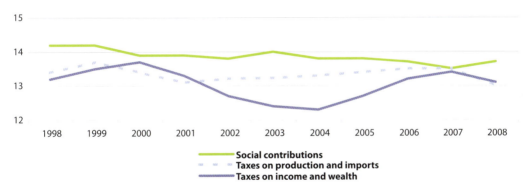

Social contributions
Taxes on production and imports
Taxes on income and wealth

Source: Eurostat (tec00019, tec00020 and tec00018)

Figure 1.19: Taxes and social contributions, 2008
(% of GDP)

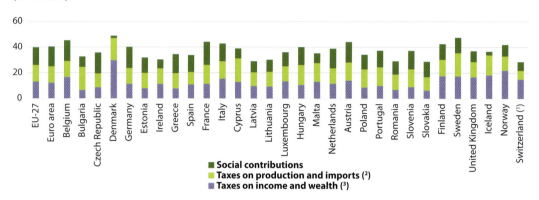

(¹) 2007.
(²) Denmark, includes taxes on production and imports paid to the Institutions of the European Union.
(³) Sweden, provisional.

Source: Eurostat (tec00019, tec00020 and tec00018)

Figure 1.20: Public procurement
(value of public procurement which is openly advertised, as % of GDP)

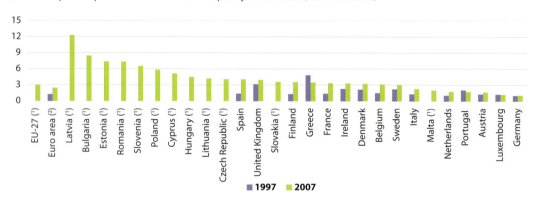

(¹) 1997, not available.
(²) EA-12 in 1997; EA-15 in 2007.

Source: Eurostat (tsier090), Commission services

Figure 1.21: State aid, 2007 (¹)
(% of GDP)

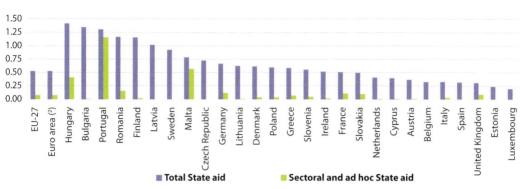

(¹) The figure is ranked on total State aid.
(²) EA-15 instead of EA-16.

Source: Eurostat (tsier100), Commission services

1.3 Exchange and interest rates

Introduction

From 1 January 2002, around 7 800 million notes and 40 400 million coins entered circulation, as 12 Member States – Belgium, Germany, Ireland, Greece, Spain, France, Italy, Luxembourg, the Netherlands, Austria, Portugal and Finland – introduced euro banknotes and coins, Slovenia subsequently joined the euro area at the start of 2007, as did Cyprus and Malta on 1 January 2008 and Slovakia on 1 January 2009, bringing the total number of Member States using the euro to 16 in total.

All economic and monetary union participants are eligible to adopt the euro. The entry criteria for the euro include two years of prior exchange rate stability via membership of the exchange rate mecha-

nism (ERM), as well as criteria relating to interest rates, budget deficits, inflation rates, and debt-to-GDP ratios.

Through using a common currency the countries of the euro area have removed exchange rates and therefore benefit from lower transaction costs. The size of the euro area market is also likely to promote investment and trade. Those countries joining the euro area have agreed to allow the European Central Bank (ECB) to be responsible for maintaining price stability, through the definition and implementation of monetary policy. When the euro was launched in 1999, the ECB took over full responsibility for monetary policy throughout the euro area, including setting benchmark interest rates and managing the euro area's foreign exchange reserves. The ECB has defined price stability as a year-on-year increase in the harmonised index of consumer prices (HICP) for the euro area below, but close to, 2 % over the medium-term (see Subchapter 1.4 for more details in relation to consumer prices). Monetary policy decisions are taken by the ECB's governing council which meets every month to analyse and assess economic developments and the risks to price stability and to decide on the appropriate level of interest rates.

Definitions and data availability

Exchange rates are the price or value of one country's currency in relation to another. Eurostat disseminates a number of different data sets concerning exchange rates. Three main ones can be distinguished, containing data on:

- bilateral exchange rates between currencies, including some special conversion factors for the countries that have adopted the euro;
- fluctuations in the exchange rate mechanism (ERM and ERM II) of the EU;
- effective exchange rate indices.

Bilateral exchange rates are available with reference to the euro, although before 1999 they were given in relation to the ecu (European currency unit). The ecu ceased to exist on 1 January 1999, when it was replaced by the euro at an exchange rate of 1:1. From that date, the currencies of the euro area became subdivisions of the euro at irrevocably fixed rates of conversion. **Daily exchange rates** are available from 1974 onwards against a large number of currencies. These daily

values are used to construct monthly and annual averages, which are based on business day rates. Alternatively, month-end and year-end rates are also provided for the daily rate of the last business day of the month/year.

An **interest rate** is defined as the cost or price of borrowing, or the gain from lending; interest rates are traditionally expressed in annual percentage terms. Interest rates are distinguished either by the period of lending/borrowing, or by the parties involved in the transaction (businesses, consumers, governments or interbank operations).

Long-term interest rates are one of the convergence criteria (or Maastricht criteria) for European economic and monetary union. Compliance with this criterion means that a Member State should have an average nominal long-term interest rate that does not exceed by more than 2 percentage points that of, at most, the three best performing Member States. Interest rates are based upon central government bond yields (or comparable securities), taking into account differences in national definitions, on the secondary market, gross of tax, with a residual maturity of around 10 years.

Eurostat publishes a number of **short-term interest rates**, with different maturities (overnight, 1 to 12 months): three-month interbank rates are shown in this publication. Other rates published include **retail bank interest rates** which are lending and deposit rates for commercial banks (non-harmonised and historical series), and harmonised monetary financial institutions (MFI) interest rates.

Main findings

It is important to note that nearly all of the information presented in this publication has been converted into euro (EUR). As such, when making comparisons between countries it is necessary to bear in mind the possible effect of currency fluctuations on the evolution of particular series. The value of the euro against the yen depreciated considerably in 1999 and 2000 and against the dollar also in 2001. However, the following years saw a marked appreciation in the value of the euro, causing it to reach a high against the yen of JPY 169.75 in July 2008 before falling back to JPY 113.65 in January 2009 and then appreciating again. Against the

dollar a high was also reached in July 2008 (EUR 1=USD 1.59), dropping back to USD 1.246 in October 2008 and then appreciating again.

Interest rates set by the central banks of the major world currencies were relatively stable from 2001 to the middle of the decade: in Japan, official lending rates were close to zero. In more recent years, interest rates rose, for example, euro area interest rates rose from 2.0 % at the beginning of December 2005 to 4.0 % in June 2007 and then 4.25 % in July 2008. Rate cuts between October 2008 and May 2009 brought euro area interest rates down to 1.0 %, in response to the financial and economic crisis.

Figure 1.22: Exchange rates against the euro (^{1})
(1998=100)

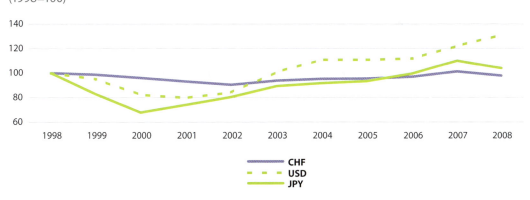

(^{1}) CHF, Swiss franc; JPY, Japanese Yen; USD, United States Dollar; a reduction in the value of the index shows an appreciation in the value of the foreign currency and a depreciation in the value of the euro.

Source: Eurostat (tec00033), ECB

Table 1.10: Exchange rates against the euro (¹)
(1 EUR=… national currency)

	2000	2001	2002	2003	2004	2005	2006	2007	2008
Bulgaria	1.9522	1.9482	1.9492	1.9490	1.9533	1.9558	1.9558	1.9558	1.9558
Czech Republic	35 599	34 068	30 804	31 846	31 891	29 782	28 342	27 766	24 946
Denmark	7.4538	7.4521	7.4305	7.4307	7.4399	7.4518	7.4591	7.4506	7.4560
Estonia	15 647	15 647	15 647	15 647	15 647	15 647	15 647	15 647	15 647
Latvia	0.5592	0.5601	0.5810	0.6407	0.6652	0.6962	0.6962	0.7001	0.7027
Lithuania	3.6952	3.5823	3.4594	3.4527	3.4529	3.4528	3.4528	3.4528	3.4528
Hungary	260.04	256.59	242.96	253.62	251.66	248.05	264.26	251.35	251.51
Poland	4.0082	3.6721	3.8574	4.3996	4.5268	4.0230	3.8959	3.7837	3.5121
Romania	1.9922	2.6004	3.1270	3.7551	4.0510	3.6209	3.5258	3.3328	3.6776
Sweden	8.4452	9.2551	9.1611	9.1242	9.1243	9.2822	9.2544	9.2501	9.6152
United Kingdom	0.65874	0.60948	0.62187	0.62883	0.69199	0.67866	0.68380	0.68173	0.68434
Croatia	7.6432	7.4820	7.4130	7.5688	7.4967	7.4008	7.3247	7.3376	7.2239
Turkey	0.5748	1.1024	1.4397	1.6949	1.7771	1.6771	1.8090	1.7865	1.9064
Iceland	72 580	87 420	86 180	86 650	87 140	78 230	87 760	87 630	143 830
Norway	8.1129	8.0484	7.5086	8.0033	8.3697	8.0092	8.0472	8.0165	8.2237
Switzerland	1.5579	1.5105	1.4670	1.5212	1.5438	1.5483	1.5729	1.6427	1.5874
Japan	99 470	108 680	118 060	130 970	134 440	136 850	146 020	161 250	152 450
United States	0.9236	0.8956	0.9456	1.1312	1.2439	1.2441	1.2556	1.3705	1.4708

(¹) The euro replaced the ecu on 1 January 1999; on 1 January 2002, it also replaced the notes and coins of 12 Community currencies; on 1 January 2007, the euro came into circulation in Slovenia; on 1 January 2008, the euro came into circulation in Cyprus and Malta ; on 1 January 2009, the euro came into circulation in Slovakia.

Source: Eurostat (tec00033 and ert_bil_eur_a), ECB

Table 1.11: Interest rates
(%)

	EMU convergence criterion bond yields (Maastricht criterion) (¹)			Short-term interest rates: three-month interbank rates (annual average)		
	1999	2004	2008	1999	2004	2008
EU-27	:	:	4.55	:	2.86	4.96
Euro area	4.66	4.12	4.30	2.96	2.11	4.63
Belgium	4.76	4.15	4.42	-	-	-
Bulgaria	:	5.36	5.38	5.88	3.74	7.14
Czech Republic	:	4.82	4.63	6.85	2.36	4.04
Denmark	4.93	4.30	4.30	3.44	2.20	5.26
Germany	4.51	4.04	4.00	-	-	-
Estonia (²)	11.39	4.39	8.16	7.81	2.50	6.67
Ireland	4.72	4.08	4.53	-	-	-
Greece	6.31	4.25	4.81	10.09	-	-
Spain	4.74	4.10	4.37	-	-	-
France	4.62	4.10	4.24	-	-	-
Italy	4.74	4.26	4.69	-	-	-
Cyprus	:	5.80	4.60	6.25	4.74	-
Latvia	:	4.86	6.43	8.44	4.23	8.00
Lithuania	:	4.50	5.61	13.89	2.68	6.04
Luxembourg	4.68	4.18	4.61	-	-	-
Hungary	:	8.19	8.24	15.07	11.53	8.79
Malta	:	4.69	4.81	5.15	2.94	-
Netherlands	4.65	4.09	4.23	-	-	-
Austria	4.69	4.15	4.27	-	-	-
Poland	:	6.90	6.07	14.73	6.20	6.36
Portugal	4.79	4.14	4.53	-	-	-
Romania	:	:	7.70	79.63	19.14	12.26
Slovenia	:	4.68	4.61	8.64	4.66	-
Slovakia	:	5.03	4.72	15.67	4.68	4.15
Finland	4.74	4.11	4.30	-	-	-
Sweden	5.00	4.42	3.90	3.33	2.31	4.74
United Kingdom	5.02	4.93	4.51	5.55	4.64	5.51
Japan	-	-	-	0.22	0.05	0.92
United States	-	-	-	5.41	1.62	2.91

(¹) The indicator for Estonia represents interest rates on new EEK-denominated loans to non-financial corporations and households with maturity over 5 years; however, a large part of the underlying claims are linked to variable interest rates. The indicator for Luxembourg is based on a basket of long-term bonds, which have an average residual maturity close to ten years; the bonds are issued by a private credit institution.
(²) Break in series for EMU convergence, 2005.

Source: Eurostat (tec00097 and tec00035), ECB, national central banks

1.4 Consumer prices: inflation and comparative price levels

Introduction

Changes in the price of consumer goods and services are usually referred to as the inflation rate. Such changes measure the loss of living standards due to price inflation and are some of the most well-known economic statistics.

Price stability is the main objective of the European Central Bank (ECB), with the inflation rate used as the prime indicator for monetary policy management in the euro area. The ECB has defined price stability as a year-on-year increase in the harmonised index of consumer prices (HICP) for the euro area of below, but close to, 2 % over the medium-term. HICPs are economic indicators constructed to measure, over time, the change in prices of consumer goods and services that are acquired by households. HICPs give comparable measures of inflation in the euro area, the EU, the European Economic Area (EEA), as well as for individual countries. They are calculated according to a harmonised approach and a single set of definitions, providing an official measure of consumer price inflation for the purposes of monetary policy and assessing inflation convergence as required under the Maastricht criteria.

A comparison of price changes between countries depends not only on movements in price levels, but also exchange rates – together, these two forces impact upon the price and cost competitiveness of individual Member States. With the introduction of the euro, prices within those Member States that share a common currency are said to be more transparent, as it is relatively simple for consumers to compare the price of items across borders. Such comparisons that provide an economic case for purchasing a good or service from another country have led to an increase in cross-border trade. From an economic point of view, the price of a given good within the Single Market should not differ significantly depending on geographic location, beyond differences that may be explained by transport costs or tax differences. However, not all goods and services converge at the same pace. For example, price convergence in housing does not necessarily follow the same pace as for tradable, consumer goods. Indeed, even within individual countries there are differences in prices between regions.

Definitions and data availability

Inflation

Harmonised indices of consumer prices (HICPs) are presented with a common reference year (currently 2005=100). Normally the indices are used to create percentage changes that show price increases/decreases for the period in question. Although the rates of change shown in this publication are annual averages, the basic indices are compiled on a monthly basis and are published at this frequency by Eurostat. Eurostat publishes HICPs some 14 to 16 days after the end of the reporting month, with these series starting in the mid-1990s. The **inflation rate** is calculated from HICPs – it equates to the all-items HICP.

HICPs cover practically every good and service that may be purchased by households in the form of final monetary consumption expenditure; owner occupied housing is, however, not yet reflected in HICPs. Goods and services are classified according to an international classification of individual consumption by purpose known as COICOP/HICP. At its most disaggregated level, Eurostat publishes around 100 sub-indices, which can be aggregated to broad categories of goods and services. In order to improve the comparability and reliability of HICPs, sampling, replacement and quality adjustment procedures are periodically reviewed, the latest changes being set out in Commission Regulation (EC) No 1334/2007 of 14 November 2007. Furthermore, minimum standards for the treatment of seasonal products (which are problematic as comparable prices of such products can not easily be observed on a monthly basis) have recently been established through Commission Regulation (EC) No 330/2009 of 22 April 2009. Detailed information on the legal requirements concerning HICPs can be found on Eurostat's website (⁶).

There are three key HICP aggregate indices: the monetary union index of consumer prices (MUICP) covers the euro area countries and Eurostat also publishes the European index of consumer prices (EICP) covering all Member States; and the European Economic Area index of consumer prices (EEAICP), which additionally covers Iceland and Norway. Note that these aggregates reflect changes over time in their country composition

through the use of a chain index formula – for example, the MUICP includes Slovenia only from 2007 onwards, Cyprus and Malta only from 2008 onwards and Slovakia only from 2009 onwards, while the EICP index only includes Bulgaria and Romania from 2007 onwards.

Comparative price levels

Purchasing power parities (PPPs) estimate price-level differences between countries. They make it possible to produce meaningful volume and price level indicators required for cross-country comparisons. PPPs are aggregated price ratios calculated from price comparisons of a large number of goods and services. PPPs are employed either:

- as **currency converters** to generate volume measures with which to compare levels of economic performance;
- or as **price level indicators** which can be used to compare relative price levels across countries, and to monitor price convergence.

Eurostat produces three sets of data using PPPs:

- levels and indices of real final expenditure are measures of volume; they indicate the relative magnitude of the aggregates being compared; at the level of GDP, they are used to compare the relative size of economies;
- levels and indices of real final expenditure per inhabitant are standardised measures of volume; they indicate the relative levels of the aggregates being compared after adjusting for differences in the size of populations between countries; at the level of GDP, they are often used as an indicator

(⁶) For more information: http://epp.eurostat.ec.europa.eu/portal/page/portal/hicp/legislation.

of the standard of living in different countries;

- **comparative price levels** are the ratios of PPPs to exchange rates; these indices provide a comparison of each country's price level relative to the EU average – if the price level index is higher than 100, the country concerned is relatively expensive compared with the EU average and vice versa; at the level of GDP, they provide a measure of the differences in the overall price levels of countries.

The **coefficient of variation of comparative price levels** is applied as an indicator of price convergence among Member States – if the coefficient of variation for comparative price levels for the EU decreases/increases over time, the national price levels in the Member States are converging/diverging.

Real effective exchange rate

The **real effective exchange rate** is deflated by nominal unit labour costs. This relative price and cost indicator aims to assess a country's competitiveness relative to its principal competitors in international markets, with changes in cost and price competitiveness depending not only on exchange rate movements but also on price trends. Double export weights are used to calculate the index, reflecting not only competition in the home markets of the various competitors, but also competition in export markets elsewhere. A rise in the index means a loss of competitiveness.

Main findings

Inflation

Compared with historical trends, consumer price indices rose only at a moderate pace during the last two decades. The EU inflation rate decreased during the 1990s, reaching 1.2 % by 1999, after which the pace of price increases settled at around 2 % per annum during the period 2000 to 2007. In 2008, an annual average inflation rate of 3.7 % was recorded for the EU. The highest annual average inflation rates among the Member States were recorded for Latvia, Bulgaria, Lithuania and Estonia, all above 10 % in 2008; the lowest rates were recorded for the Netherlands, Portugal and Germany, all below 3 %.

The sharp rise of price inflation in 2008 within the EU can be largely explained by steep increases in energy and food prices between the autumn of 2007 and the autumn of 2008: indeed, consumer prices for food recorded historically high inflation rates in 2008 with prices rising by an average of 6.4 % per annum in the EU; this increase may be particularly associated with steep price rises for dairy products, oils and fats. In the second half of 2008 a substantial decline of these rates was recorded which continued in 2009; the annual inflation rates even turned negative in June 2009.

Comparative price levels

The relative price levels of private household consumption vary significantly across the Member States. In 2008, with the average for the EU-27 being defined as 100, comparative price levels within the Member States ranged from 51 in Bulgaria to 141 in Denmark. Over the ten years from 1998 to 2008, several countries recorded substantial changes in their comparative price levels, notably Bulgaria, the Czech Republic, Estonia, Ireland, Latvia, Lithuania, Hungary, Romania, Slovakia and Sweden. Over the same ten-year period (1998 to 2008) there was a convergence of price levels within the EU-27 as a whole: the coefficient of variation of comparative price levels declined from 35 % in 1998 to 24 % by 2008. The pace at which price levels converged within the euro area was slower, but there was already a higher degree of convergence (lower coefficient of variation).

Figure 1.23: HICP all-items, annual average inflation rates (%)

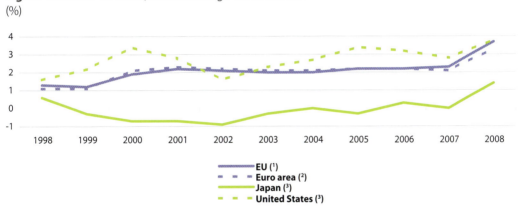

(¹) The data refer to the official EU aggregate, its country coverage changes in line with the addition of new EU Member States and integrates them using a chain index formula.
(²) The data refer to the official euro area aggregate, its country coverage changes in line with the addition of new EA Member States and integrates them using a chain index formula.
(³) National CPI: not strictly comparable with the HICP.

Source: Eurostat (tsieb060)

Table 1.12: HICP all-items, annual average inflation rates
(%)

	1998	1999	2000	2001	2002	2003	2004	2005	2006	2007	2008
EU (¹)	1.3	1.2	1.9	2.2	2.1	2.0	2.0	2.2	2.2	2.3	3.7
Euro area (²)	1.1	1.1	2.1	2.3	2.2	2.1	2.1	2.2	2.2	2.1	3.3
Belgium	0.9	1.1	2.7	2.4	1.6	1.5	1.9	2.5	2.3	1.8	4.5
Bulgaria	18.7	2.6	10.3	7.4	5.8	2.3	6.1	6.0	7.4	7.6	12.0
Czech Republic	9.7	1.8	3.9	4.5	1.4	-0.1	2.6	1.6	2.1	3.0	6.3
Denmark	1.3	2.1	2.7	2.3	2.4	2.0	0.9	1.7	1.9	1.7	3.6
Germany	0.6	0.6	1.4	1.9	1.4	1.0	1.8	1.9	1.8	2.3	2.8
Estonia	8.8	3.1	3.9	5.6	3.6	1.4	3.0	4.1	4.4	6.7	10.6
Ireland	2.1	2.5	5.3	4.0	4.7	4.0	2.3	2.2	2.7	2.9	3.1
Greece	4.5	2.1	2.9	3.7	3.9	3.4	3.0	3.5	3.3	3.0	4.2
Spain	1.8	2.2	3.5	2.8	3.6	3.1	3.1	3.4	3.6	2.8	4.1
France	0.7	0.6	1.8	1.8	1.9	2.2	2.3	1.9	1.9	1.6	3.2
Italy	2.0	1.7	2.6	2.3	2.6	2.8	2.3	2.2	2.2	2.0	3.5
Cyprus	2.3	1.1	4.9	2.0	2.8	4.0	1.9	2.0	2.2	2.2	4.4
Latvia	4.3	2.1	2.6	2.5	2.0	2.9	6.2	6.9	6.6	10.1	15.3
Lithuania	5.4	1.5	1.1	1.6	0.3	-1.1	1.2	2.7	3.8	5.8	11.1
Luxembourg	1.0	1.0	3.8	2.4	2.1	2.5	3.2	3.8	3.0	2.7	4.1
Hungary	14.2	10.0	10.0	9.1	5.2	4.7	6.8	3.5	4.0	7.9	6.0
Malta	3.7	2.3	3.0	2.5	2.6	1.9	2.7	2.5	2.6	0.7	4.7
Netherlands	1.8	2.0	2.3	5.1	3.9	2.2	1.4	1.5	1.7	1.6	2.2
Austria	0.8	0.5	2.0	2.3	1.7	1.3	2.0	2.1	1.7	2.2	3.2
Poland	11.8	7.2	10.1	5.3	1.9	0.7	3.6	2.2	1.3	2.6	4.2
Portugal	2.2	2.2	2.8	4.4	3.7	3.3	2.5	2.1	3.0	2.4	2.7
Romania	59.1	45.8	45.7	34.5	22.5	15.3	11.9	9.1	6.6	4.9	7.9
Slovenia	7.9	6.1	8.9	8.6	7.5	5.7	3.7	2.5	2.5	3.8	5.5
Slovakia	6.7	10.4	12.2	7.2	3.5	8.4	7.5	2.8	4.3	1.9	3.9
Finland	1.3	1.3	2.9	2.7	2.0	1.3	0.1	0.8	1.3	1.6	3.9
Sweden	1.0	0.5	1.3	2.7	1.9	2.3	1.0	0.8	1.5	1.7	3.3
United Kingdom	1.6	1.3	0.8	1.2	1.3	1.4	1.3	2.1	2.3	2.3	3.6
Turkey	82.1	61.4	53.2	56.8	47.0	25.3	10.1	8.1	9.3	8.8	10.4
Iceland	1.3	2.1	4.4	6.6	5.3	1.4	2.3	1.4	4.6	3.6	12.8
Norway	2.0	2.1	3.0	2.7	0.8	2.0	0.6	1.5	2.5	0.7	3.4
Switzerland	:	:	:	:	:	:	:	:	1.0	0.8	2.3
Japan (³)	0.6	-0.3	-0.7	-0.7	-0.9	-0.3	0.0	-0.3	0.3	0.0	1.4
United States (³)	1.6	2.2	3.4	2.8	1.6	2.3	2.7	3.4	3.2	2.8	3.8

(¹) The data refer to the official EU aggregate, its country coverage changes in line with the addition of new EU Member States and integrates them using a chain index formula.
(²) The data refer to the official euro area aggregate, its country coverage changes in line with the addition of new EA Member States and integrates them using a chain index formula.
(³) National CPI: not strictly comparable with the HICP.

Source: Eurostat (tsieb060)

Figure 1.24: HICP main headings, annual average inflation rates, EU, 2008
(%)

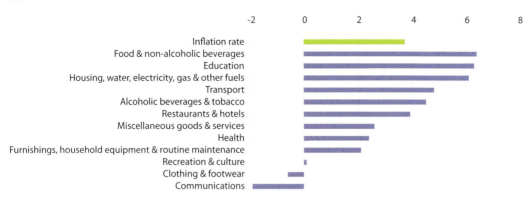

Source: Eurostat (prc_hicp_aind)

Figure 1.25: Price convergence between EU Member States
(%, coefficient of variation of comparative price levels of final
consumption by private households including indirect taxes)

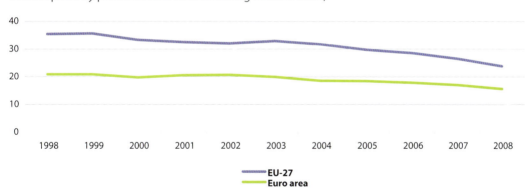

Source: Eurostat (tsier020)

Table 1.13: Comparative price levels
(final consumption by private households including indirect taxes, EU-27=100)

	1998	1999	2000	2001	2002	2003	2004	2005	2006	2007	2008
EU-27	100	100	100	100	100	100	100	100	100	100	100
Euro area	102	102	100	101	101	103	103	102	102	102	104
Belgium	108	107	102	103	102	107	107	106	107	106	111
Bulgaria	38	38	39	41	41	41	42	43	45	47	51
Czech Republic	47	46	48	50	57	55	55	58	61	62	72
Denmark	129	131	130	135	134	141	140	140	138	138	141
Germany	109	107	107	107	107	106	105	103	103	103	104
Estonia	54	57	57	61	61	62	63	65	67	72	77
Ireland	108	112	115	119	125	126	126	123	124	125	127
Greece	86	88	85	82	80	86	88	88	89	89	94
Spain	86	86	85	85	85	88	91	91	92	92	96
France	111	109	106	104	104	110	110	108	109	108	111
Italy	98	98	98	100	103	104	105	105	104	104	105
Cyprus	87	87	88	89	89	91	91	90	91	89	90
Latvia	49	52	59	59	57	54	56	57	61	66	75
Lithuania	46	47	53	54	54	52	54	55	57	60	67
Luxembourg	104	103	101	104	102	103	103	112	112	112	116
Hungary	46	47	49	53	57	58	62	63	60	66	70
Malta	69	71	73	75	75	72	73	73	75	73	78
Netherlands	102	103	100	103	103	108	106	105	104	103	103
Austria	105	105	102	105	103	103	103	103	102	101	105
Poland	54	52	58	65	61	54	53	61	62	64	69
Portugal	84	83	83	84	86	86	87	85	85	85	87
Romania	43	38	43	42	43	43	43	54	57	62	62
Slovenia	74	74	73	74	74	76	76	76	77	78	83
Slovakia	42	41	44	43	45	51	55	55	57	64	70
Finland	123	122	121	125	124	127	124	124	123	123	125
Sweden	127	126	128	120	122	124	121	119	119	117	114
United Kingdom	112	116	120	117	117	108	109	110	110	110	99
Croatia	:	:	:	:	:	65	67	69	70	70	75
FYR of Macedonia	:	:	:	:	:	44	44	43	43	43	47
Turkey	55	56	63	48	52	57	59	67	66	72	73
Iceland	125	127	144	128	135	139	138	153	144	148	117
Norway	131	134	138	142	151	142	135	141	140	139	139
Switzerland	136	140	143	146	147	144	141	138	134	126	130
Japan	147	173	198	178	156	137	130	120	110	97	101
United States	101	106	121	126	120	101	93	93	92	85	80

Source: Eurostat (tsier010)

1.5 Current and financial account

Introduction

The EU is a major player in the global economy for international trade in goods and services, as well as foreign investment. Balance of payments statistics give a full overview of all external transactions of the EU and its individual Member States. They may be used as a tool to study the international exposure of different parts of the EU's economy, indicating its comparative advantages and disadvantages with the rest of the world. Note that additional information from the balance of payments is provided in the following subchapter that covers direct investment and in Subchapter 9.2 which covers trade in services.

Definitions and data availability

The balance of payments (BoP) is a statistical statement that summarises the transactions of an economy with the rest of the world. Transactions are organised in two different accounts, the current account (goods, services, income, current transfers), the capital account and the financial account, whose sum, in principle, should be zero, as for each credit transaction there is a corresponding one on the debit side. Thus, the current account balance determines the exposure of an economy vis-à-vis the rest of the world, whereas the capital and financial account explain how it is financed.

Current account

The current account of the BoP provides information not only on international trade in goods (generally the largest category), but also on international transactions in services, income and current transfers. For all these transactions, the BoP registers the value of credits (exports) and debits (imports). A negative balance – a current account deficit – shows that a country is spending more abroad than it is earning from transactions with other economies, and is therefore a net debtor towards the rest of the world.

The **current account** gauges a country's economic position in the world, covering all transactions that occur between resident and non-resident entities and refers to trade in goods and services, income and current transfers. More specifically, the four main components of the current account are defined as follows:

- **Trade in goods** covers general merchandise, goods for processing, repairs on goods, goods procured in ports by carriers, and non-monetary gold. Exports and imports of goods are recorded on a fob/fob basis – in other words, at market value at the customs frontiers of exporting economies, including charges for insurance and transport services up to the frontier of the exporting country.

- **Trade in services** consists of the following items: transport services performed by EU residents for non-EU residents, or vice versa, involving the carriage of passengers, the movement of goods, rentals of carriers with crew and related supporting and auxiliary services; travel, which includes primarily the goods and services EU travellers acquire from non-EU residents, or vice versa; and other services, which include communications services, construction services, insurance services, financial services, computer and information services, royalties and licence fees, other business services (which comprise merchanting and other trade-related services, operational leasing services and miscellaneous business, professional and technical services), personal, cultural and recreational services, and government services not included elsewhere.
- **Income** covers two types of transactions: compensation of employees paid to non-resident workers or received from non-resident employers, and investment income accrued on external financial assets and liabilities.
- **Current transfers** include general government current transfers, for example transfers related to international cooperation between governments, payments of current taxes on income and wealth, etc., and other current transfers, for example workers' remittances, insurance premiums (less service charges), and claims on non-life insurance companies.

Under the BoP conventions, transactions which represent an inflow of real resources, an increase in assets, or a decrease in liabilities (such as, exports of goods) are recorded as credits, and transactions representing an outflow of real resources, a decrease in assets or an increase in liabilities (such as, imports of goods) are recorded as debits. Net is the balance (credits minus debits) of all transactions with each partner.

Financial account

The financial account of the BoP covers all transactions associated with changes of ownership in the foreign financial assets and liabilities of an economy. The financial account is broken down into five basic components: direct investment, portfolio investment, financial derivatives, other investment, and official reserve assets.

Direct investment implies that a resident investor in one economy has a lasting interest in, and a degree of influence over the management of, a business enterprise resident in another economy. Direct investment is classified primarily on a directional basis: resident direct investment abroad and non-resident direct investment in the reporting economy. Within this classification three main components are distinguished: equity capital, reinvested earnings, and other capital; these are discussed in detail in Subchapter 1.6.

Portfolio investment records the transactions in negotiable securities with the exception of the transactions which fall within the definition of direct investment or reserve assets. Several components are identified: equity securities, bonds and notes, money market instruments.

Financial derivatives are financial instruments that are linked to, and whose value is contingent to, a specific financial instrument, indicator or commodity, and through which specific financial risks can be traded in financial markets in their own right. Transactions in financial derivatives are treated as separate transactions, rather than integral parts of the value of underlying transactions to which they may be linked.

Reserve assets are foreign financial assets available to, and controlled by, monetary authorities; they are used for financing and regulating payments imbalances or for other purposes.

Other investment is a residual category, which is not recorded under the other headings of the financial account (direct investment, portfolio investment, financial derivatives or reserve assets). It also encompasses the offsetting entries for accrued income on instruments classified under other investment. Four types of instruments are identified: currency and deposits (in general, the most significant item), trade credits, loans, other assets and liabilities.

Main findings

The current account deficit of the EU-27 was EUR 255 000 million in 2008 (corresponding to 2.0 % of GDP), while the deficit in 2007 equalled about 1.1 %. The 2008 deficit confirmed the move away from relatively small surpluses recorded for the period between 2002 and 2004. The overall deficit for 2008 comprised deficits in the current account for goods (-1.6 % of GDP), for current transfers (-0.5 %), and for the income account (-0.5 %), alongside a positive balance for services (0.6 %).

There were a total of 20 Member States that reported current account deficits in 2008: the largest of these (relative to GDP) was in Bulgaria (-25.3 %); Sweden (7.9 %) and the Netherlands (7.3 %) reported the largest current account surpluses. Ireland, Germany, Slovakia and Italy were the only Member States to report a deficit for services in 2008, whereas 19 Member States reported a deficit for goods, and 20 Members States a deficit for income.

A positive value for the financial account indicates that inward investment flows (inward foreign direct investment (FDI) and investment liabilities) exceeds outward investment flows (outward FDI and investment assets). This was the case for the euro area in 2008, where the financial account was equivalent to 3.3 % of GDP. Three types of investment (FDI, portfolio and other) make-up the financial account, along with financial derivatives and official reserve assets.

The EU-27 was a net direct investor vis-à-vis the rest of the world in 2008. Inward flows of FDI represented 1.4 % of GDP, while outward flows of FDI represented 2.8 % of GDP, making it the main form of outward investment from the EU-27 in 2008. Luxembourg and Hungary recorded the highest levels of both inward and outward FDI (in relation to GDP) with the rest of the world, while Ireland recorded the largest disinvestment in inward FDI.

The EU-27 recorded disinvestment for portfolio investment assets equivalent to 1.8 % of GDP in 2008. EU-27 portfolio investment liabilities were valued at 5.5 % of GDP, four times the level of inward FDI, and approximately eight times the level of other investment liabilities.

More than half of the Member States recorded disinvestment for portfolio assets, with the United Kingdom recording relatively large flows (8.6 % of GDP), second only to the particular case of Luxembourg (home to a large fund management activity). Disinvestment in portfolio liabilities was also relatively common, as negative flows were reported for 11 of the Member States in 2008, with Ireland recording the biggest of these (relative to GDP) – apart from the special case of Luxembourg.

Investment in other assets (such as currency and deposits) was equivalent to 1.9 % of the EU-27's GDP in 2008, with the most important shares recorded in Ireland, Cyprus, Luxembourg and Malta. Seven of the Member States recorded an outward disinvestment for other assets, most notably the United Kingdom and Belgium. Inward investment of other liabilities was substantial in Cyprus, Luxembourg and Ireland, being negative (disinvestment) in several Member States, notably the United Kingdom and Belgium.

Figure 1.26: Current account transactions, EU-27 (¹)
(EUR 1 000 million)

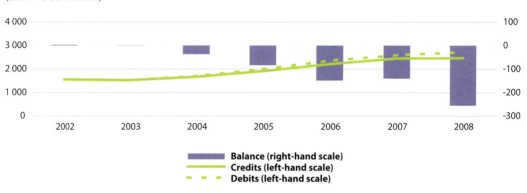

(¹) EU-25: for 2002-2003.

Source: Eurostat (bop_q_eu)

Table 1.14: Current account balance for EU Member States with the rest of the world
(EUR 1 000 million)

	2004	2005	2006	2007	2008
EU-27 (¹)	-37.2	-83.8	-148.5	-140.4	-255.0
Euro area (²)	60.6	9.2	-10.5	11.1	-101.0
Belgium	19.1	7.9	6.3	5.7	-8.1
Bulgaria	-1.3	-2.7	-4.7	-7.3	-8.6
Czech Republic	-4.7	-1.3	-2.9	-4.0	-4.6
Denmark	5.9	9.0	6.3	1.6	4.6
Germany	102.9	114.7	150.9	191.3	164.9
Estonia	-1.1	-1.1	-2.2	-2.8	-1.4
Ireland	-0.9	-5.7	-6.3	-10.1	-9.4
Greece	-10.7	-14.7	-23.7	-32.4	-35.0
Spain	-44.2	-66.9	-88.3	-105.4	-104.4
France	10.0	-10.9	-10.2	-19.6	-38.7
Italy	-13.0	-23.6	-38.5	-37.4	-53.6
Cyprus	-0.6	-0.8	-1.0	-1.8	-3.1
Latvia	-1.4	-1.6	-3.6	-4.8	-2.9
Lithuania	-1.4	-1.5	-2.6	-4.1	-3.7
Luxembourg	3.3	3.3	3.5	3.6	2.0
Hungary	-7.1	-6.7	-6.9	-6.5	-9.2
Malta	-0.3	-0.4	-0.5	-0.3	-0.4
Netherlands	36.9	37.3	50.4	43.5	43.3
Austria	4.8	4.9	7.1	8.4	9.8
Poland	-8.2	-3.0	-7.4	-14.6	-19.7
Portugal	-10.9	-14.1	-15.6	-15.4	-20.2
Romania	-5.1	-6.9	-10.2	-16.7	-16.7
Slovenia	-0.7	-0.5	-0.8	-1.5	-2.1
Slovakia	-1.2	-3.2	-3.6	-3.1	-4.3
Finland	10.0	5.7	7.6	7.5	4.4
Sweden	21.1	20.4	26.4	28.6	25.8
United Kingdom	-36.9	-48.0	-64.4	-55.3	-31.2
Croatia	-1.5	-2.0	-2.7	-3.2	-4.4
Turkey	-11.5	-17.8	-25.6	-27.8	-27.8
Iceland	-1.1	-2.1	-3.4	-2.3	:
Norway	28.3	39.7	46.2	45.3	60.2
Japan	138.5	133.3	136.0	154.0	105.1
United States	-502.6	-588.5	-627.3	-534.7	-456.1

(¹) EU vis-à-vis extra-EU.
(²) Euro area vis-à-vis extra euro area.

Source: Eurostat (bop_q_eu, bop_q_euro and bop_q_c)

Table 1.15: Current account, balance by components, 2008 (¹)
(% of GDP)

	Current account	Goods	Services	Income	Current transfers
EU-27	-2.0	-1.6	0.6	-0.5	-0.5
Euro area	-1.1	-0.1	0.5	-0.4	-1.0
Belgium	-2.3	-3.2	1.2	1.1	-1.6
Bulgaria	-25.3	-25.7	2.4	-3.5	1.5
Czech Republic	-3.1	2.8	2.2	-7.8	-0.3
Denmark	2.0	-0.5	2.9	1.4	-1.8
Germany	6.6	7.2	-1.0	1.8	-1.3
Estonia	-9.1	-11.9	7.6	-6.6	1.8
Ireland	-5.1	12.8	-2.9	-14.4	-0.6
Greece	-14.4	-18.1	7.1	-4.5	1.1
Spain	-9.5	-8.0	2.4	-3.1	-0.8
France	-2.0	-3.1	0.7	1.6	-1.2
Italy	-3.4	0.0	-0.5	-1.9	-1.0
Cyprus	-18.3	-34.7	23.3	-6.5	-0.4
Latvia	-12.7	-17.0	4.0	-1.9	2.2
Lithuania	-11.6	-11.6	1.1	-3.3	2.3
Luxembourg	5.5	-11.7	52.8	-30.1	-5.5
Hungary	-8.7	0.1	0.9	-8.4	-1.2
Malta	-6.2	-20.9	17.2	-3.0	0.6
Netherlands	7.3	6.4	1.5	0.8	-1.5
Austria	3.5	-0.1	4.8	-0.8	-0.4
Poland	-5.4	-4.6	1.0	-3.3	1.5
Portugal	-12.1	-12.9	3.9	-4.7	1.5
Romania	-12.2	-13.4	0.6	-3.8	4.4
Slovenia	-5.5	-7.1	4.8	-2.8	-0.5
Slovakia	-6.6	-1.1	-0.7	-3.4	-1.3
Finland	2.4	3.2	0.9	-0.9	-0.8
Sweden	7.9	3.8	3.7	1.7	-1.3
United Kingdom	-1.7	-6.4	3.1	2.5	-1.0
Croatia	-9.4	-22.9	14.7	-3.3	2.2
Turkey	-5.6	-7.2	2.4	-1.1	0.3
Norway	19.4	19.2	0.2	0.8	-0.8
Japan	-13.7	-16.7	2.8	2.6	-2.5
United States	1.1	0.3	-0.1	1.1	-0.1

(¹) EU-27, extra EU-27 flows; euro area, extra EA-16 flows; Member States and other countries, flows with the rest of the world.

Source: Eurostat (bop_q_eu, bop_q_euro, bop_q_c and tec00001)

Figure 1.27: Current account balance with selected partners, EU-27, 2007
(EUR 1 000 million)

Source: Eurostat (bop_q_eu)

Table 1.16: Selected items of the financial account balance, 2008 (¹)
(% of GDP)

	Financial account	Outward foreign direct investment	Inward foreign direct investment	Portfolio investment, assets	Portfolio investment, liabilities	Other investment, assets	Other investment, liabilities
EU-27	:	-2.8	1.4	1.8	5.5	-1.9	0.7
Euro area	3.3	-3.8	1.1	0.2	4.5	-0.1	1.8
Belgium	3.1	-14.7	12.5	0.4	9.4	20.3	-25.6
Bulgaria	30.7	-1.4	18.1	-0.5	-0.9	0.8	16.7
Czech Republic	3.0	-0.9	5.0	-0.1	-0.1	-2.3	2.9
Denmark	-2.2	-8.0	3.2	-2.3	4.5	-5.9	7.9
Germany	-8.1	-4.3	0.7	1.1	0.6	-5.4	0.2
Estonia	8.3	-4.4	8.8	4.0	-1.4	-2.3	6.4
Ireland	8.6	-5.0	-7.4	-16.1	-5.1	-36.3	81.1
Greece	12.4	-0.7	1.4	0.3	6.7	-11.5	16.4
Spain	8.7	-5.0	4.4	2.0	-1.7	-1.3	11.2
France	:	-7.6	4.0	-3.2	8.9	2.6	0.4
Italy	3.2	-2.0	0.6	5.1	2.8	-1.7	-1.8
Cyprus	18.1	-5.9	8.7	-70.8	-4.2	-59.6	149.5
Latvia	13.1	-0.6	4.0	0.4	0.3	-1.4	8.8
Lithuania	10.3	-0.7	3.8	0.0	-0.2	-1.9	6.9
Luxembourg	-5.1	-193.9	150.0	328.7	-280.8	-76.3	108.3
Hungary	9.5	-28.4	31.1	-2.4	0.1	-1.6	18.0
Malta	5.3	-3.3	10.9	3.5	3.0	-76.5	71.8
Netherlands	-2.5	-5.6	-1.2	0.1	12.7	5.8	-12.7
Austria	-4.2	-7.0	3.4	3.4	5.8	-13.5	3.8
Poland	8.4	-0.7	3.1	0.4	-1.0	1.2	4.7
Portugal	10.9	-0.9	1.5	:	15.8	7.1	-5.2
Romania	12.9	0.1	6.3	-0.4	-0.3	-0.8	8.0
Slovenia	6.2	-2.6	3.3	-0.1	1.7	-2.1	5.9
Slovakia	7.9	-0.3	3.7	0.7	1.8	-0.8	2.8
Finland	3.7	-0.6	-1.6	0.6	1.7	-3.3	6.3
Sweden	2.3	-7.8	9.2	-5.2	-2.4	-0.4	8.4
United Kingdom	1.2	-5.1	3.7	8.6	16.7	37.4	-61.3
Croatia	12.6	-0.3	7.0	-0.6	-0.7	-3.4	9.8
Turkey	4.7	-0.3	2.5	-0.2	-0.6	-1.0	4.1
Norway	-21.5	-6.1	-0.2	-29.3	4.4	8.0	3.1
Japan	-4.2	-2.8	0.5	-4.0	-2.5	3.3	1.3
United States	3.7	-2.2	2.3	1.2	4.0	0.7	-2.2

(¹) EU-27, extra EU-27 flows; euro area, extra EA-16 flows; Member States and other countries, flows with the rest of the world. Note that, according to the balance of payments sign convention, increases in assets and decreases in liabilities are shown with a negative sign, whereas decreases in assets and increases in liabilities are shown as positive.

Source: Eurostat (bop_q_eu, bop_q_euro, bop_q_c and tec00001)

1.6 Foreign direct investment

Introduction

In a world of increasing globalisation, where political, economic and technological barriers are rapidly disappearing, the ability of a country to participate in global activity is an important indicator of its performance and competitiveness. In order to remain competitive, modern day business relationships extend well beyond the traditional exchange of goods and services, as witnessed by the increasing reliance of firms on mergers, partnerships, joint ventures, licensing agreements, and other forms of business cooperation.

FDI may be seen as an alternative economic strategy, adopted by those enterprises that invest to establish a new plant/office, or alternatively, purchase existing assets of a foreign enterprise. These enterprises seek to complement or substitute external trade, by producing (and often selling) goods and services in countries other than where the enterprise was first established.

There are two kinds of FDI, namely the creation of productive assets by foreigners or the purchase of existing assets by foreigners (acquisitions, mergers, takeovers, etc.). FDI differs from portfolio investments because it is made with the purpose of having control or an effective voice in mangement and a lasting interest in the enterprise. Direct investment not only includes the initial acquisition of equity capital, but also subsequent capital transactions between the foreign investor and domestic and affiliated enterprises. FDI is a type of international investment where an entity that is resident in one economy (the direct investor) acquires a lasting interest (at least

10 % of the voting power) in an enterprise operating in another economy. The lasting interest implies the existence of a long-term relationship between the direct investor and the enterprise, and a significant degree of influence by the investor on the management of the enterprise.

Conventional trade is less important for services than for goods and while trade in services has been growing, the share of services in total intra-EU trade has changed little during the last decade. However, FDI is expanding more rapidly for services than for goods, as FDI in services has increased at a more rapid pace than conventional trade in services. As a result, the share of services in total FDI flows and positions has increased substantially, with European services becoming increasingly international.

Definitions and data availability

FDI statistics for the EU give a detailed presentation of FDI flows and stocks, showing which Member States invest in which countries and sectors. Eurostat collects FDI statistics for quarterly and annual flows, as well as for stocks at the end of the year. FDI stocks (assets and liabilities) are part of the international investment position of an economy at the end of the year.

A **direct investment enterprise** is an unincorporated or incorporated enterprise in which a direct investor owns 10 % or more of the ordinary shares or voting power (for an incorporated enterprise) or the equivalent (for an unincorporated enterprise).

FDI flows are new investment made during the reference period, whereas FDI stocks provide information on the position, in terms of value, of all previous investments at the end of the reference period.

Outward flows and stocks of FDI (FDI abroad) report investment by entities resident in the reporting economy in an affiliated enterprise abroad. **Inward flows and stocks** report investment by foreigners in enterprises resident in the reporting economy.

The **intensity of FDI** can be measured by averaging the value of inward and outward flows during a particular reference period and expressing this in relation to GDP.

The sign convention adopted for the data shown in this section, for both flows and stocks, is that investment is always recorded with a positive sign, and a disinvestment with a negative sign.

Main findings

Flows of FDI fluctuate considerably from one year to the next – partly as a function of economic developments, with FDI flows generally increasing during times of rapid growth, while disinvestment is more likely during periods of recession, as businesses focus on core activities in their domestic market. Inflows of FDI from non-member countries into the EU-27 were valued at EUR 198 701 million in 2008, while outflows from the EU-27 to non-member countries were valued at EUR 347 667 million. EU investments abroad were higher than inward FDI to the EU, and as such, the EU was a net investor abroad with net outflows of EUR 148 966 million. Large net outward investments were recorded for Germany, France and the United Kingdom.

Inward flows of FDI were equivalent of 1.6 % of the EU-27's GDP and outward flows of FDI were equivalent to 2.8 %, combining to give an FDI intensity of 2.2 % – this latter ratio indicates the relative importance of both inward and outward FDI flows during the course of a single year in relation to the size of the national economy. Luxembourg recorded the highest rate of FDI intensity among the individual Member States (234.0 % of GDP), but this should be interpreted with caution as the relatively high importance of FDI in Luxembourg results mainly from the role of Luxembourg-based holding companies.

FDI stocks show the value of all previous investments at the end of the reference period. At the end of 2007, the EU-27 held net outward stocks of FDI that were valued at EUR 3 151 000 million; inward FDI stocks for foreign investors in the EU-27 were valued at EUR 2 352 000 million. As such, outward stocks of FDI accounted for 25.5 % of EU-27 GDP at the end of 2007, while inward FDI stocks were valued at 19.0 %. A more detailed analysis by partner reveals that stocks of EU-27 FDI abroad were largely concentrated in North America (37.2 % of the extra EU-27 total at the end of 2007). Asia remained the second biggest partner for outward stocks of FDI, accounting for 13.2 % of the EU-27 total with non-member countries. North America was an even more important partner in terms of inward stocks, accounting for 48.8 % of the EU-27's FDI coming from non-member countries. Central America was the second most important investor in the EU-27 at the end of 2007 (with a 14.2 % share of the EU-27's inward stocks of FDI).

Table 1.17: Foreign direct investment, 2008 (¹)

	FDI flows (EUR million)			FDI flows (% of GDP)			FDI intensity: average value of inward and outward FDI flows (% of GDP)
	Inward	Outward	Net outflows	Inward	Outward	Net outflows	
EU-27	198 701	347 667	148 966	1.6	2.8	1.2	2.2
Belgium	70 231	82 383	12 152	20.4	23.9	3.5	22.1
Bulgaria	6 549	485	-6 064	19.2	1.4	-17.8	10.3
Czech Republic	7 328	1 297	-6 031	5.0	0.9	-4.1	2.9
Denmark	1 858	9 485	7 627	0.8	4.1	3.3	2.4
Germany	14 526	106 813	92 287	0.6	4.3	3.7	2.4
Estonia	1 317	722	-595	8.2	4.5	-3.7	6.3
Ireland	-13 674	9 217	22 891	-7.5	5.1	12.6	-1.2
Greece	3 070	1 646	-1 424	1.3	0.7	-0.6	1.0
Spain	47 749	54 662	6 913	4.4	5.0	0.6	4.7
France	66 341	136 775	70 434	3.4	7.0	3.6	5.2
Italy	11 626	29 928	18 302	0.7	1.9	1.2	1.3
Cyprus	2 741	2 657	-84	15.9	15.4	-0.5	15.6
Latvia	862	167	-695	3.7	0.7	-3.0	2.2
Lithuania	1 245	229	-1 016	3.9	0.7	-3.2	2.3
Luxembourg	81 332	102 774	21 442	206.7	261.2	54.5	234.0
Hungary (²)	3 149	536	-2 613	3.0	0.5	-2.5	1.7
Malta	600	189	-411	10.6	3.3	-7.3	6.9
Netherlands (²)	-5 203	13 696	18 899	-0.9	2.3	3.2	0.7
Austria (²)	9 478	20 018	10 540	3.4	7.1	3.7	5.2
Poland	9 952	1 971	-7 981	2.7	0.5	-2.2	1.6
Portugal	2 411	1 437	-974	1.4	0.9	-0.5	1.2
Romania	9 509	189	-9 320	6.9	0.1	-6.8	3.5
Slovenia	1 313	932	-381	3.5	2.5	-1.0	3.0
Slovakia	2 331	176	-2 155	3.6	0.3	-3.3	1.9
Finland	-4 895	2 284	7 179	-2.6	1.2	3.8	-0.7
Sweden	28 132	19 008	-9 124	8.6	5.8	-2.8	7.2
United Kingdom	62 498	107 703	45 205	3.4	5.9	2.5	4.7
Croatia (³)	3 626	181	-3 445	8.5	0.4	-8.1	4.4
Turkey (³)	16 268	1 537	-14 731	3.4	0.3	-3.1	1.9
Norway (³)	3 578	9 162	5 584	1.3	3.2	1.9	2.2
Switzerland (³)	35 985	36 289	304	11.3	11.4	0.1	11.4
Japan (³)	16 466	53 710	37 244	0.5	1.7	1.2	1.1
United States (⁴)	139 689	172 518	32 829	1.3	1.6	0.3	1.5

(¹) EU-27, FDI with extra-EU-27 partners; all other countries, FDI with the rest of the world; including special purpose entities; data extracted on 8 January 2010.
(²) Excluding special purpose entities.
(³) 2007.
(⁴) 2006.

Source: Eurostat (tec00049, tec00053, tec00046 and tsier130), Bank of Japan, Bureau of Economic Analysis

Economy

Figure 1.28: Foreign direct investment inward stocks by main extra-EU investor, EU-27, end-2007 (¹) (% of extra EU-27 FDI stocks)

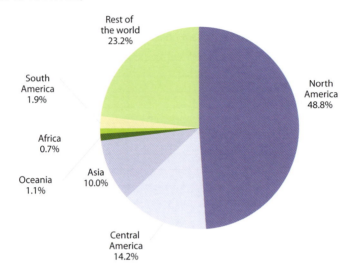

(¹) Figures do not sum to 100 % due to rounding; data extracted on 8 January 2010.

Source: Eurostat (bop_fdi_pos)

Figure 1.29: Foreign direct investment outward stocks in main extra-EU partners, EU-27, end-2007 (¹) (% of extra EU-27 FDI stocks)

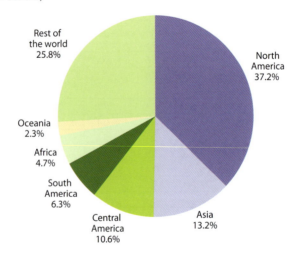

(¹) Figures do not sum to 100 % due to rounding; data extracted on 8 January 2010.

Source: Eurostat (bop_fdi_pos)

Table 1.18: Foreign direct investment stocks for selected partner countries, end-2007 ([1])
(EUR 1 000 million)

	Outward				Inward				Net assets abroad			
	Total	EU-27	JP	US	Total	EU-27	JP	US	Total	EU-27	JP	US
EU-27	3 151	–	74	1 006	2 352	–	120	1 042	799	–	-46	-37
Belgium	:	:	:	:	:	:	:	:	:	:	:	:
Bulgaria	1	0	0	0	27	23	0	1	-26	-23	0	-1
Czech Republic	6	5	0	0	76	67	1	3	-71	-62	-1	-3
Denmark	123	70	1	12	110	75	0	9	13	-5	0	3
Germany	823	529	6	142	634	464	12	72	189	65	-6	70
Estonia	4	4	0	0	11	10	0	0	-7	-7	0	0
Ireland	102	68	:	15	138	90	1	20	-36	-22	:	-5
Greece	23	14	0	1	35	29	0	3	-12	-15	0	-2
Spain	399	233	0	27	399	320	2	46	-1	-87	-2	-19
France	957	634	22	143	682	514	8	74	276	120	14	69
Italy	353	277	1	20	248	195	3	21	105	83	-2	0
Cyprus	6	4	0	0	12	7	0	0	-6	-3	0	0
Latvia	1	0	0	0	8	6	0	0	-7	-5	0	0
Lithuania	1	1	0	0	10	8	0	0	-9	-7	0	0
Luxembourg ([2])	51	37	0	3	55	46	0	6	-4	-9	0	-3
Hungary ([2])	12	7	0	0	68	46	1	3	-56	-38	-1	-3
Malta	1	0	0	0	6	3	0	0	-5	-3	0	0
Netherlands ([2])	604	:	3	57	495	:	8	90	110	:	-5	-33
Austria ([2])	101	65	0	3	110	72	2	13	-9	-7	-2	-10
Poland	14	9	0	0	121	102	1	8	-106	-94	-1	-8
Portugal	46	30	0	1	78	60	0	1	-32	-31	0	0
Romania	1	0	0	0	43	37	0	1	-42	-36	0	-1
Slovenia	5	1	0	0	10	8	0	0	-5	-7	0	0
Slovakia	1	1	0	0	29	26	0	1	-28	-25	0	-1
Finland	80	64	0	4	62	56	0	1	18	7	0	2
Sweden	223	144	1	34	199	138	2	26	25	6	-1	9
United Kingdom	1 249	562	1	276	846	421	35	228	403	140	-34	48
Croatia	2	1	:	0	30	29	0	0	-28	-28	:	0
Turkey	8	5	0	0	107	76	1	8	-98	-71	-1	-8
Iceland	:	:	0	2	:	:	:	1	:	:	:	2
Norway ([3])	93	51	0	10	71	49	0	13	22	2	0	-4
Switzerland	447	176	8	69	230	164	1	42	218	12	8	27
Japan	375	100	–	119	92	38	–	31	283	62	–	89
United States ([3])	1 810	:	70	–	1 358	:	160	–	452	:	-91	–

([1]) EU-27, FDI stocks in extra EU-27 partners; all other countries, FDI stocks in the rest of the world; data extracted on 8 January 2010.
([2]) Excluding special purpose entities.
([3]) 2006.

Source: Eurostat (tec00052 and tec00051)

1.7 Development aid

Introduction

More than half the money spent throughout the world on helping developing countries comes from the EU and its Member States. The aims of this development aid were laid out in a December 2005 document agreed by the European Parliament, Council and European Commission titled 'European consensus on development' ([7]), which seeks, in particular, to reduce poverty, to develop democratic values, and to support national strategies and procedures. The ultimate objective of the EU is to enable disadvantaged people to take control of their own development, through attacking the main sources of their vulnerability, such as access to food, clean water, education, health, employment, land and social services.

The EU's development strategy focuses on financial and technical assistance to improve basic, physical and social infrastructures and the productive potential of poor nations, including their administrative and institutional capacities. This support has the potential to help countries benefit from international trade opportunities and secure more inward investment to broaden their economic bases.

The EU's activities also extend to external trade policy, which is used to drive development through the opening-up of markets. Since the 1970s, the EU has reduced or removed tariffs and eliminated quotas on imports from developing countries, a policy that was further extended in 2001 to a generalised system of preferences (GSP). This trade scheme, renewed in 2008, covers preferential access to

imports into the EU market from 176 developing countries, a special incentive arrangement for sustainable development and good governance (GSP+) and the complete removal of tariffs on all imports (everything but arms – EBA) from the 49 least-developed countries (LDCs) ([8]).

The EU promotes self-help and poverty eradication through policies that focus on consolidating the democratic process, expanding social programmes, strengthening institutional frameworks, and reinforcing the respect for human rights, including equality between men and women. Indeed, all trade or cooperation agreements with developing countries include a human rights clause as a matter of routine, and failure to comply gives rise to automatic penalties, frozen or cancelled aid.

Aside from long-term, strategic, development aid, the EU also plays an important role in rapidly alleviating human suffering – as a result of natural disaster or military conflict. The EU's relief activities are global and are handled by ECHO, its humanitarian aid office. The initial annual budget of this office in 2008 was about EUR 750 million, reinforced on several occasions in order to respond to new crises and natural disasters, such that EUR 937 million was ultimately channelled to over 60 countries, and brought relief to around 143 million people, with close to three fifths of the assistance allocated to African, Caribbean and Pacific (ACP) states; most of this aid is in the form of non-repayable grants.

During the first half of 2008, the price of food and raw materials shot up,

([7]) For more information: http://ec.europa.eu/development/policies/consensus_en.cfm.

([8]) For more information: http://ec.europa.eu/trade/wider-agenda/development.

plunging 75 million more people into the vicious cycle of food insecurity and the EU almost doubled its emergency food aid budget. There was also an increase in the number of natural disasters in 2008, and they were more intense than in the past. European humanitarian aid helped people from Asia to Central America and Africa to deal with the devastating consequences of cyclones, floods and droughts. Civilians also continued to pay a heavy price in crises brought about solely by the actions of human beings.

Definitions and data availability

Official development assistance (ODA) consists of grants or loans that are undertaken by the official sector with the promotion of economic development and welfare in the recipient countries as the main objective. The net disbursements for ODA to development assistance committee (DAC) countries are expressed as a percentage of gross national income (GNI) at market prices.

In addition to ODA, **total financing** for development refers to net disbursements, other official flows, and private flows. **Other official flows** are transactions which do not meet the conditions for eligibility as ODA (or official aid), either because they are not primarily aimed at development, or because they have a grant element of less than 25 %.

Private flows include private export credits, direct investment and financing to multilateral institutions. Foreign direct investment includes significant investment by foreign businesses of production facilities or ownership stakes taken in the national businesses.

Commitments include both bilateral commitments and commitments to regional banks. Bilateral commitments are recorded as the full amount of the expected transfer, irrespective of the time required for the completion of disbursements. **Disbursements** are the release of funds to, or the purchase of goods or services for a recipient. Disbursements record the actual international transfer of financial resources, or of goods or services valued at the cost of the donor.

DAC countries refer to 'developing countries and territories' on Part I of the OECD DAC list of aid recipients for which there is a long-standing United Nations target of aid reaching 0.7 % of donors' gross national product.

Main findings

The EU-15 Member States paid almost EUR 45 000 million in official development assistance to DAC countries in 2007, considerably less than the further EUR 128 000 million coming in the form of private flows which increased greatly in the four most recent years.

There is a long-standing United Nations target of reaching a level of aid equivalent to 0.7 % of donors' GNI. While EU Member States, like other industrialised countries, have accepted this 0.7 % target for spending, only Sweden, Luxembourg, Denmark and the Netherlands reached or exceeded this goal in 2008. EU ministers agreed in May 2005 to set a collective target of 0.56 % of GNI by 2010, on the way to achieving the UN target of 0.7 % by 2015. The earlier commitment to reach an EU average of 0.39 % by 2006 was met, and by 2008 the EU-27 average was 0.40 %.

Table 1.19: Official development assistance

	Official development assistance (% of GNI)					Official development assistance per capita (EUR)				
	1998	2005	2006	2007	2008	1998	2004	2005	2006	2007
EU-27 (¹)	:	0.41	0.41	0.37	0.40	63.00	89.00	115.30	120.30	114.30
Belgium	0.35	0.52	0.49	0.43	0.47	66.10	112.90	150.60	149.30	134.10
Bulgaria	:	0.01	0.00	0.06	0.04	:	:	0.30	0.10	2.10
Czech Republic	0.03	0.11	0.12	0.11	0.11	:	8.50	10.60	12.50	12.60
Denmark	0.99	0.81	0.80	0.81	0.82	273.10	303.00	312.80	327.50	342.30
Germany	0.26	0.36	0.35	0.37	0.38	63.00	73.40	98.30	100.90	109.00
Estonia	:	0.07	0.09	0.12	0.09	:	3.00	5.90	8.90	11.90
Ireland	0.30	0.42	0.53	0.55	0.58	44.90	120.00	138.90	191.00	199.70
Greece	0.15	0.16	0.16	0.16	0.20	14.10	23.30	27.80	30.30	32.60
Spain	0.24	0.27	0.31	0.37	0.43	27.50	45.90	55.90	68.80	83.60
France	0.38	0.47	0.46	0.38	0.39	92.90	109.10	128.30	133.60	113.40
Italy	0.20	0.29	0.20	0.19	0.20	19.60	34.00	69.80	49.20	48.80
Cyprus	:	0.09	0.15	0.12	0.17	:	5.40	15.80	27.20	23.00
Latvia	:	0.07	0.06	0.06	0.06	:	3.00	3.50	4.40	5.30
Lithuania	:	0.06	0.08	0.11	0.13	:	2.30	3.50	5.30	8.90
Luxembourg	0.65	0.82	0.90	0.91	0.92	198.70	413.40	443.00	489.90	570.90
Hungary	:	0.10	0.14	0.08	0.07	:	5.60	8.00	11.80	7.50
Malta	:	0.18	0.15	0.15	0.11	:	19.90	19.80	17.20	19.60
Netherlands	0.80	0.80	0.78	0.81	0.80	166.50	207.60	251.90	265.60	277.20
Austria	0.22	0.52	0.47	0.50	0.42	54.80	66.70	153.50	144.10	158.70
Poland	0.01	0.07	0.09	0.10	0.08	:	2.50	4.30	6.20	6.90
Portugal	0.24	0.21	0.21	0.22	0.27	21.90	78.90	28.70	29.80	32.40
Romania	:	:	0.00	0.07	0.07	:	:	:	0.10	3.70
Slovenia	:	0.10	0.11	0.11	0.14	:	12.50	14.50	17.40	18.80
Slovakia	:	0.12	0.10	0.09	0.10	:	4.20	8.40	8.10	9.10
Finland	0.31	0.46	0.39	0.39	0.43	65.00	104.50	138.20	126.20	135.40
Sweden	0.72	0.92	0.99	0.93	0.98	172.50	243.30	299.20	346.90	346.10
United Kingdom	0.27	0.47	0.51	0.35	0.43	51.90	106.10	143.70	163.70	117.80
Turkey	0.03	0.17	0.18	0.09	:	1.10	3.80	6.70	8.00	6.30
Iceland	:	0.18	0.27	0.27	:	25.40	58.50	73.80	108.80	113.40
Norway	0.89	0.94	0.89	0.95	0.88	261.50	384.90	484.40	504.80	577.60
Switzerland	0.32	0.44	0.39	0.37	0.41	113.30	168.10	191.50	175.20	162.80

(¹) EU-15 for ODA per capita.

Source: Eurostat (tsdgp100 and tsdgp520), OECD (DAC database)

Figure 1.30: Total financing for developing countries, EU-15
(EUR million)

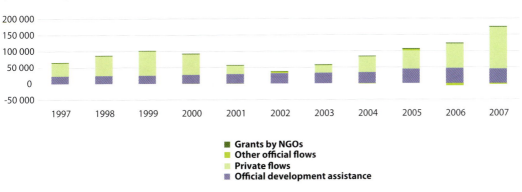

- Grants by NGOs
- Other official flows
- Private flows
- Official development assistance

Source: Eurostat (tsdgp310), OECD (DAC database)

Figure 1.31: Official development assistance, EU
(% share of GNI)

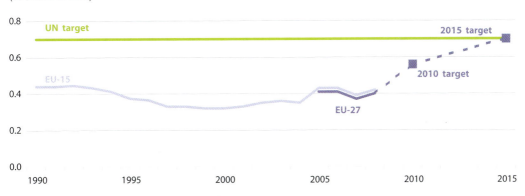

Source: Eurostat (tsdgp100), OECD (DAC database)

Population

2

The EU will, in the coming decades, face a number of challenges associated with an ageing society. There are three main factors that explain this trend: persistently low fertility rates, increasing life expectancy, and a baby-boom generation that will soon start to reach retirement age. This has led to a debate on how European countries will cope with population ageing and the impact it will have on, among others, labour markets, pensions and provisions for healthcare, housing, or social services.

In order to address these challenges, the European Commission released a Green Paper in March 2005 (COM(2005) 94) titled 'Confronting demographic change: a new solidarity between the generations' ([1]), which recognised that there will be increasing demands to support a growing number of dependent elderly people (many living alone), while a rising proportion of young adults will likely continue living with their parents well into their twenties. The Directorate-General for Employment, Social Affairs and Equal Opportunities released a Communication titled 'Dealing with the impact of an ageing population in the EU (2009 Ageing Report)' ([2]). This drew on work conducted by the Directorate-General for Economic and Financial Affairs analysing the impact of ageing populations on public expenditures, through a set of projections (for categories such as pensions, healthcare or long-term care), in order to assess the long-term sustainability of public finances based on a 'no-policy change' scenario. The Communication re-iterated five key areas for policy responses to demographic change:

- promoting demographic renewal;
- promoting employment (more jobs and longer working lives of better quality);

[1] For more information:
http://eur-lex.europa.eu/LexUriServ/site/en/com/2005/com2005_0094en01.pdf.

[2] COM(2009) 180 final; for more information: http://eur-lex.europa.eu/LexUriServ/LexUriServ.do?uri=COM:2009:0180:FIN:EN:PDF.

- a more productive and dynamic Europe;
- receiving and integrating migrants;
- sustainable public finances to guarantee adequate social protection and equity between the generations.

2.1 European population compared with other regions of the world

Introduction

Europe's ageing society and its relatively static number of inhabitants may be contrasted against a rapid expansion in the world's population, driven largely by population growth in developing countries. United Nations' population projections show that the situation in Europe is by no means unique, and that most developed, and indeed some emerging economies, will undergo changes in their demographic composition in the next half century, with shrinking working-age populations, a higher proportion of elderly persons, and increasing dependency rates.

The projected ageing of populations could lead to labour shortages in some countries, which may provide opportunities for economic development in developing economies. Much will depend upon whether the increasing pool of labour in developing countries attracts inward investment or whether labour shortages in other global regions result in migratory flows that may have repercussions for both destination and departure countries.

Definitions and data availability

All of the data in this subchapter is provided by the Population Division of the Department of Economic and Social Affairs of the United Nations (UN) Secretariat ([3]). Note that the geographical coverage relates to the whole of Europe, as opposed to the political and economic union of the 27 Member States (see the next subchapter for information relating to the EU-27 and its Member States). For this subchapter, Europe is defined as an aggregate composed of the 27 Member States, together with Albania, Andorra, Belarus, Bosnia and Herzegovina, Croatia, the Faeroe Islands, Iceland, Liechtenstein, the former Yugoslav Republic of Macedonia, the Republic of Moldova, Montenegro, Norway, the Russian Federation, Serbia, Switzerland and the Ukraine.

Since the 1970s, the UN has been involved in several multi-national survey programmes whose results provide key information about fertility, mortality, maternal and child health. The UN data reflects demographic information produced by other UN agencies or bodies, such as, the Economic and Social Commissions, the High Commissioner for Refugees (UNHCR), the United Nations Children's Fund (UNICEF), and the World Health Organization (WHO). Data from other organisations, such as Eurostat, is also consulted and used when elaborating population projections. Note the data collection made by the UN is only revised every five years, and as such the UN data reported in this edition of the Eurostat Yearbook is the same as that found in the last edition.

([3]) For more information: http://esa.un.org/unpp.

UN population data is often based on registers or estimates of population on a date close to 1 July (mid-year population); this may be contrasted with Eurostat's data that generally reflect the situation as of 1 January in each reference year.

The preparation of **population estimates and projections** by the UN involves two distinct processes: the incorporation of new and relevant information regarding past demographic dynamics; and the formulation of assumptions about the future paths of fertility, mortality and international migration. The population projections are 'what-if' scenarios that aim to provide information about the likely future size and structure of the population for a specific set of assumptions; for the purpose of this publication, the medium variant has been selected. Under this variant, total fertility in all countries is assumed to converge towards 1.85 children per woman, although not all countries reach this level during the projection period. Mortality is projected on the basis of models concerning changes in life expectancy; these produce smaller gains the higher the life expectancy that has already been reached and are based on recent trends in life expectancy by gender.

Main findings

The world's population more than doubled between 1960 and 2005, rising from 3 023 million to 6 512 million inhabitants. In its entirety, Europe had 729 million inhabitants in 2005, equivalent to 11.2 % of the global population. Asia had by far the largest share of the world's population in 2005, with 3 937 million inhabitants, equivalent to around three fifths (60.4 %) of the total. Africa accounted for the second highest share (14.1 %), while Latin America and the Caribbean (8.5 %), Northern America (5.1 %) and Oceania (0.5 %) each reported shares that were below that recorded for Europe.

Europe's share of the world's population fell considerably, from one fifth (20.0 %) of the total in 1960 to 11.2 % by 2005; the North American share also fell, although to a lesser extent (down 1.6 percentage points). The increase in global population between 1960 and 2005 can be largely attributed to Africa and Asia, their relative contributions to the world's population rose by 4.7 and 4.1 percentage points respectively.

Despite Europe's relative share of the world's population falling, the number of inhabitants continued to grow between 1960 and 2005, albeit very slowly from 1995 onwards. The fastest population expansion over the period 1960 to 2005 was reported in Africa (an overall increase of 223.1 %), while the populations of Latin America and the Caribbean (153.4 %), Asia (132.4 %) and Oceania (111.3 %) more than doubled.

The United Nations (UN) forecasts that the rate of population growth will slow considerably in the period through to 2050, by which time the global population is projected to reach 9 150 million inhabitants; this would, nevertheless, mark an overall increase of 41.1 % between 2005 and 2050, with the largest contribution to population growth (some 95 % of the total) likely to come from developing countries (in particular those in Africa). According to the same set of UN forecasts, India is likely to become the most populous nation on the planet by 2030, and its population is projected to continue growing through to 2050 when it will reach 1 614 million. These projections are in contrast to those made for China, where the population is expected to peak by 2030, after which a gradual decline in the number of inhabitants is foreseen.

One of the main reasons behind Europe's ageing population is the decline experienced in the average number of births per year, which fell from a high of 11.9 million during the period 1960 to 1965 to 7.4 million for the period 2000 to 2005. In contrast, the overall number of births in every other continent continued to rise, except in North America (where there was growth from 1980 onwards). Crude birth rates express the number of births in relation to the whole population: the European crude birth rate (10.2 births per 1 000 (‰) inhabitants) was the lowest across the continents and approximately half the world average of 21.2 ‰ during the period 2000 to 2005. By far the highest crude birth rate was reported for Africa, at 37.2 ‰, nearly twice the rate of any other continent.

The fertility rate of women in Europe fell at a relatively fast pace between the early 1960s and late 1990s, from an average of 2.6 children per woman to 1.4, and stabilised at this rate during the period 2000 to 2005. This downward trend was reflected across most of the continents, with fertility rates for the whole world falling from

an average of 4.9 children per woman to 2.7. One of the main drivers of the reduction in fertility rates was China: indeed, crude birth rates and average fertility rates were reduced considerably in China, as the former fell from 38.0 ‰ between 1960 and 1965 to 14.0 ‰ by 2000 to 2005 and the latter from an average of 5.6 children per woman between 1960 and 1965 to 1.8 children by 2000 to 2005. Average fertility rates remained relatively high in Africa, at close to five children (4.9) per woman during the period 2000 to 2005.

The relative importance of the young and the elderly in the total population varies considerably between continents. Children aged less than 15 years old accounted for 15.9 % of Europe's population in 2005, which was, coincidentally, the same share as that recorded for people aged 65 and over. The young accounted for at least 20 % of the population in the remaining continents, a share that peaked at 41.2 % in Africa. At the other end of the age spectrum, persons aged 65 years or more accounted for just 3.4 % of the total population in Africa in 2005, approximately half the value recorded for Asia and for Latin America and the Caribbean, while the elderly made up more than 10 % of the population in Northern America and Oceania.

A set of dependency ratios can be calculated to help analyse the relationship between the working-age population (generally considered to be those aged 15 to 64 years old) and dependents either under the age of 15 or aged 65 and over. As a result of declining birth and fertility rates, young-age dependency ratios in Europe were almost halved from 41 %

in 1960 to 23 % by 2005. This trend was, in part, counterbalanced by the increasing numbers of elderly persons within the European population and it is likely that elder generations will continue to account for a growing share of the European population in the coming decades. The European old-age dependency ratio rose from 14 % in 1960 to 23 % by 2005. As such, some 46 % of the European population was not of a working age in 2005.

This total dependency ratio (young-age and old-age dependency) was generally between 50 % and 57 % in the remaining continents, although in contrast to the European figures, the relative importance of young persons was consistently higher than that of the older generations. The situation in Africa was quite different, as the total dependency ratio rose as high as 80 % in 2005, almost entirely as a result of the high proportion of young persons.

Figure 2.1: World population
(% of total)

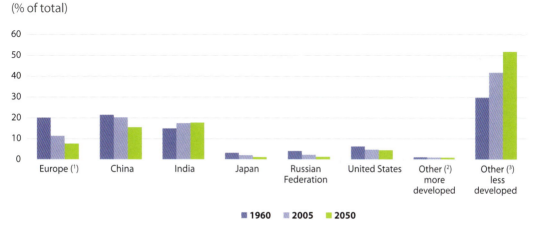

(¹) EU-27, Albania, Andorra, Belarus, Bosnia and Herzegovina, Croatia, Faeroe Islands, Iceland, Liechtenstein, the former Yugoslav Republic of Macedonia, Republic of Moldova, Montenegro, Norway, the Russian Federation, Serbia, Switzerland and the Ukraine.
(²) Excluding Europe, Japan and the United States.
(³) Excluding China, India and the Russian Federation.

Source: United Nations, Population Division of the Department of Economic and Social Affairs

2

Table 2.1: World population
(million)

	1960	1965	1970	1975	1980	1985	1990	1995	2000	2005
World	3 023	3 332	3 686	4 061	4 438	4 846	5 290	5 713	6 115	6 512
Europe (¹)	604	634	656	676	693	707	721	727	727	729
Africa	285	322	367	419	482	556	639	726	819	921
Asia	1 694	1 886	2 125	2 379	2 623	2 890	3 179	3 448	3 698	3 937
Latin America and the Caribbean	220	252	286	323	363	402	442	482	521	557
Northern America	204	219	231	242	254	267	283	300	319	335
Oceania	16	18	20	21	23	25	27	29	31	34
	1960	**1965**	**1970**	**1975**	**1980**	**1985**	**1990**	**1995**	**2000**	**2005**
China	646	716	816	911	981	1 053	1 142	1 211	1 267	1 312
India	448	497	553	617	693	775	862	953	1 043	1 131
Japan	93	98	104	112	117	121	123	125	127	127
Russian Federation	120	127	130	134	139	144	148	148	147	143
United States	186	199	209	219	229	241	255	271	288	303

(¹) EU-27, Albania, Andorra, Belarus, Bosnia and Herzegovina, Croatia, Faeroe Islands, Iceland, Liechtenstein, the former Yugoslav Republic of Macedonia, Republic of Moldova, Montenegro, Norway, the Russian Federation, Serbia, Switzerland and the Ukraine.

Source: United Nations, Population Division of the Department of Economic and Social Affairs

Table 2.2: World population
(% of total)

	1960	1965	1970	1975	1980	1985	1990	1995	2000	2005
Europe (¹)	20.0	19.0	17.8	16.6	15.6	14.6	13.6	12.7	11.9	11.2
Africa	9.4	9.7	10.0	10.3	10.9	11.5	12.1	12.7	13.4	14.1
Asia	56.0	56.6	57.7	58.6	59.1	59.6	60.1	60.4	60.5	60.4
Latin America and the Caribbean	7.3	7.6	7.8	8.0	8.2	8.3	8.4	8.4	8.5	8.5
Northern America	6.8	6.6	6.3	6.0	5.7	5.5	5.3	5.3	5.2	5.1
Oceania	0.5	0.5	0.5	0.5	0.5	0.5	0.5	0.5	0.5	0.5
	1960	**1965**	**1970**	**1975**	**1980**	**1985**	**1990**	**1995**	**2000**	**2005**
China	21.4	21.5	22.1	22.4	22.1	21.7	21.6	21.2	20.7	20.2
India	14.8	14.9	15.0	15.2	15.6	16.0	16.3	16.7	17.0	17.4
Japan	3.1	2.9	2.8	2.7	2.6	2.5	2.3	2.2	2.1	2.0
Russian Federation	4.0	3.8	3.5	3.3	3.1	3.0	2.8	2.6	2.4	2.2
United States	6.2	6.0	5.7	5.4	5.2	5.0	4.8	4.7	4.7	4.6

(¹) EU-27, Albania, Andorra, Belarus, Bosnia and Herzegovina, Croatia, Faeroe Islands, Iceland, Liechtenstein, the former Yugoslav Republic of Macedonia, Republic of Moldova, Montenegro, Norway, the Russian Federation, Serbia, Switzerland and the Ukraine.

Source: United Nations, Population Division of the Department of Economic and Social Affairs

Figure 2.2: Population change
(average annual change, million)

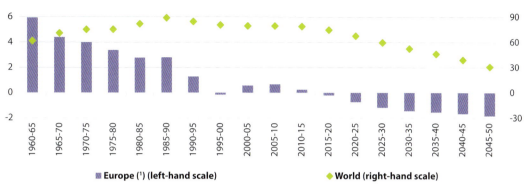

■ **Europe (¹) (left-hand scale)**   ◆ **World (right-hand scale)**

(¹) EU-27, Albania, Andorra, Belarus, Bosnia and Herzegovina, Croatia, Faeroe Islands, Iceland, Liechtenstein, the former Yugoslav Republic
  of Macedonia, Republic of Moldova, Montenegro, Norway, the Russian Federation, Serbia, Switzerland and the Ukraine.

Source: United Nations, Population Division of the Department of Economic and Social Affairs

Table 2.3: Population and population projections
(million)

	2005	2010	2015	2020	2025	2030	2035	2040	2045	2050
World	6 512	6 909	7 302	7 675	8 012	8 309	8 571	8 801	8 996	9 150
Europe (¹)	729	733	734	733	729	723	716	708	700	691
Africa	921	1 033	1 153	1 276	1 400	1 524	1 648	1 770	1 887	1 998
Asia	3 937	4 167	4 391	4 596	4 773	4 917	5 032	5 125	5 193	5 231
Latin America and the Caribbean	557	589	618	646	670	690	706	718	726	729
Northern America	335	352	368	383	398	410	421	431	440	448
Oceania	34	36	38	40	43	45	46	48	50	51
	2005	**2010**	**2015**	**2020**	**2025**	**2030**	**2035**	**2040**	**2045**	**2050**
China	1 312	1 354	1 396	1 431	1 453	1 462	1 462	1 455	1 440	1 417
India	1 131	1 214	1 294	1 367	1 431	1 485	1 528	1 565	1 594	1 614
Japan	127	127	126	124	121	117	114	110	106	102
Russian Federation	143	140	138	135	132	129	125	122	119	116
United States	303	318	332	346	359	370	380	389	397	404

(¹) EU-27, Albania, Andorra, Belarus, Bosnia and Herzegovina, Croatia, Faeroe Islands, Iceland, Liechtenstein, the former Yugoslav Republic
  of Macedonia, Republic of Moldova, Montenegro, Norway, the Russian Federation, Serbia, Switzerland and the Ukraine.

Source: United Nations, Population Division of the Department of Economic and Social Affairs

Table 2.4: Average number of live births per year
(million)

	1960-65	65-70	70-75	75-80	80-85	85-90	90-95	95-00	00-05
World	111.0	117.3	119.4	120.8	129.3	138.2	136.0	133.2	133.9
Europe (¹)	11.9	10.8	10.4	10.1	10.1	9.8	8.3	7.4	7.4
Africa	14.4	16.1	18.2	20.6	23.2	25.8	27.7	29.8	32.4
Asia	69.9	75.7	75.8	74.5	79.8	86.0	83.2	79.4	77.6
Latin America and the Caribbean	9.7	10.2	10.7	11.3	11.7	11.8	11.7	11.6	11.4
Northern America	4.7	4.0	3.7	3.7	4.0	4.3	4.5	4.4	4.5
Oceania	0.4	0.5	0.5	0.5	0.5	0.5	0.6	0.6	0.6
	1960-65	**65-70**	**70-75**	**75-80**	**80-85**	**85-90**	**90-95**	**95-00**	**00-05**
China	25.8	28.3	24.7	20.4	21.9	26.0	22.3	19.7	18.0
India	19.1	20.4	21.8	23.7	25.3	26.6	27.8	27.7	27.6
Japan	1.6	1.8	2.1	1.7	1.5	1.4	1.2	1.2	1.1
Russian Federation	2.6	1.9	2.0	2.2	2.4	2.4	1.6	1.3	1.4
United States	4.2	3.6	3.4	3.4	3.7	3.9	4.1	4.0	4.2

(¹) EU-27, Albania, Andorra, Belarus, Bosnia and Herzegovina, Croatia, Faeroe Islands, Iceland, Liechtenstein, the former Yugoslav Republic of Macedonia, Republic of Moldova, Montenegro, Norway, the Russian Federation, Serbia, Switzerland and the Ukraine.

Source: United Nations, Population Division of the Department of Economic and Social Affairs

Table 2.5: Crude birth rate
(per 1 000 population)

	1960-65	65-70	70-75	75-80	80-85	85-90	90-95	95-00	00-05
World	34.9	33.4	30.8	28.4	27.9	27.3	24.7	22.5	21.2
Europe (¹)	19.1	16.8	15.7	14.8	14.4	13.7	11.5	10.2	10.2
Africa	47.6	46.8	46.2	45.8	44.8	43.1	40.6	38.5	37.2
Asia	39.0	37.7	33.7	29.8	28.9	28.4	25.1	22.2	20.3
Latin America and the Caribbean	41.0	37.8	35.2	33.0	30.7	27.8	25.3	23.2	21.2
Northern America	22.0	17.7	15.7	15.1	15.5	15.7	15.5	14.2	13.8
Oceania	26.7	24.5	24.0	21.0	20.2	20.0	19.8	18.8	17.8
	1960-65	**65-70**	**70-75**	**75-80**	**80-85**	**85-90**	**90-95**	**95-00**	**00-05**
China	38.0	36.9	28.6	21.5	21.5	23.7	18.9	15.9	14.0
India	40.5	38.8	37.3	36.2	34.4	32.5	30.7	27.7	25.4
Japan	17.1	17.8	19.0	15.2	12.8	11.2	9.9	9.4	8.9
Russian Federation	21.0	14.4	15.3	15.9	16.8	16.1	10.9	8.9	9.9
United States	21.8	17.7	15.7	15.1	15.5	15.9	15.7	14.5	14.2

(¹) EU-27, Albania, Andorra, Belarus, Bosnia and Herzegovina, Croatia, Faeroe Islands, Iceland, Liechtenstein, the former Yugoslav Republic of Macedonia, Republic of Moldova, Montenegro, Norway, the Russian Federation, Serbia, Switzerland and the Ukraine.

Source: United Nations, Population Division of the Department of Economic and Social Affairs

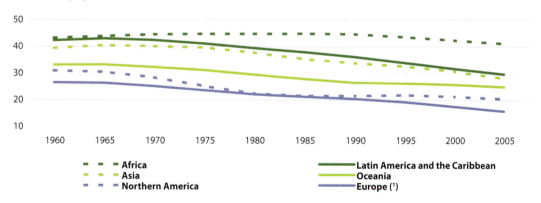

Table 2.6: Average fertility rates
(average number of children per woman)

	1960-65	65-70	70-75	75-80	80-85	85-90	90-95	95-00	00-05
World	4.9	4.8	4.3	3.8	3.6	3.4	3.1	2.8	2.7
Europe (^{1})	2.6	2.4	2.2	2.0	1.9	1.8	1.6	1.4	1.4
Africa	6.8	6.7	6.7	6.6	6.4	6.1	5.7	5.2	4.9
Asia	5.6	5.5	4.8	4.0	3.7	3.5	3.0	2.7	2.5
Latin America and the Caribbean	6.0	5.5	5.0	4.5	3.9	3.4	3.0	2.7	2.5
Northern America	3.4	2.6	2.1	1.8	1.8	1.9	2.0	2.0	2.0
Oceania	4.0	3.6	3.3	2.7	2.6	2.5	2.5	2.5	2.4
	1960-65	65-70	70-75	75-80	80-85	85-90	90-95	95-00	00-05
China	5.6	5.9	4.8	2.9	2.6	2.6	2.0	1.8	1.8
India	5.8	5.6	5.3	4.9	4.5	4.2	3.9	3.5	3.1
Japan	2.0	2.0	2.1	1.8	1.8	1.7	1.5	1.4	1.3
Russian Federation	2.6	2.0	2.0	1.9	2.0	2.1	1.6	1.3	1.3
United States	3.3	2.6	2.0	1.8	1.8	1.9	2.0	2.0	2.0

(^{1}) EU-27, Albania, Andorra, Belarus, Bosnia and Herzegovina, Croatia, Faeroe Islands, Iceland, Liechtenstein, the former Yugoslav Republic of Macedonia, Republic of Moldova, Montenegro, Norway, the Russian Federation, Serbia, Switzerland and the Ukraine.

Source: United Nations, Population Division of the Department of Economic and Social Affairs

Figure 2.3: Proportion of the population aged under 15
(% of total population)

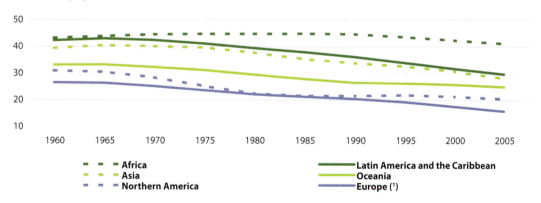

(^{1}) EU-27, Albania, Andorra, Belarus, Bosnia and Herzegovina, Croatia, Faeroe Islands, Iceland, Liechtenstein, the former Yugoslav Republic of Macedonia, Republic of Moldova, Montenegro, Norway, the Russian Federation, Serbia, Switzerland and the Ukraine.

Source: United Nations, Population Division of the Department of Economic and Social Affairs

Figure 2.4: Proportion of the population aged 65 and over
(% of total population)

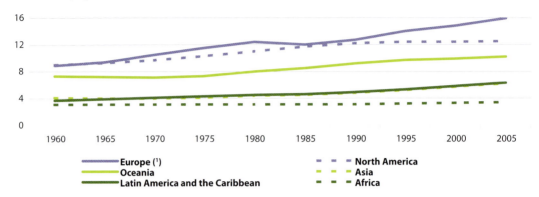

(¹) EU-27, Albania, Andorra, Belarus, Bosnia and Herzegovina, Croatia, Faeroe Islands, Iceland, Liechtenstein, the former Yugoslav Republic of Macedonia, Republic of Moldova, Montenegro, Norway, the Russian Federation, Serbia, Switzerland and the Ukraine.

Source: United Nations, Population Division of the Department of Economic and Social Affairs

Figure 2.5: Young-age dependency ratio
(%)

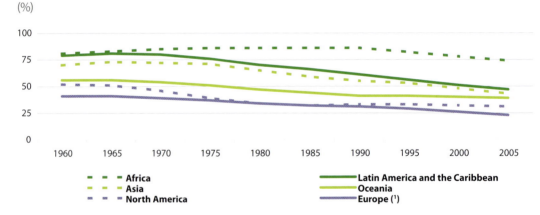

(¹) EU-27, Albania, Andorra, Belarus, Bosnia and Herzegovina, Croatia, Faeroe Islands, Iceland, Liechtenstein, the former Yugoslav Republic of Macedonia, Republic of Moldova, Montenegro, Norway, the Russian Federation, Serbia, Switzerland and the Ukraine.

Source: United Nations, Population Division of the Department of Economic and Social Affairs

Figure 2.6: Old-age dependency ratio
(%)

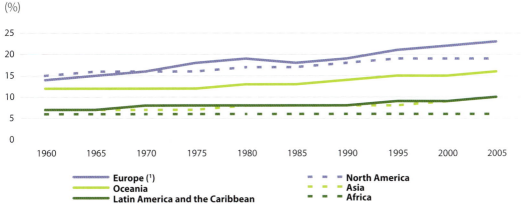

(¹) EU-27, Albania, Andorra, Belarus, Bosnia and Herzegovina, Croatia, Faeroe Islands, Iceland, Liechtenstein, the former Yugoslav Republic of Macedonia, Republic of Moldova, Montenegro, Norway, the Russian Federation, Serbia, Switzerland and the Ukraine.

Source: United Nations, Population Division of the Department of Economic and Social Affairs

2.2 EU-27 population

Introduction

The impact of demographic ageing within the EU is likely to be of major significance in the coming decades. Consistently low birth rates and higher life expectancy will transform the shape of the EU-27's age pyramid; probably the most important change will be the marked transition towards a much older population and this trend is already becoming apparent in several Member States. As a result, the proportion of people of a working age in the EU-27 is shrinking at the same time as those who are considering retirement expands. The share of older persons in the total population will increase significantly from 2010 onwards, as the post-war baby-boom generation starts to reach retirement.

Policies that are designed to increase labour force participation may play a role in reconciling demographic developments and the social expenditure burden, while pension reforms are also on-going across many Member States. In addition, policy-makers have considered ways of creating more flexible working opportunities that may encourage elderly persons to remain within the labour market, while increased longevity and healthy life years have led some administrations to consider raising statutory retirement ages.

Furthermore, the gradual break-up of the traditional family unit within the EU means that an increasing proportion of elderly people are likely to live on their own in the future; this change will likely result in a considerable increase in the

need for professional care, especially as population projections suggest that the fastest growing age group in the EU-27 will be those aged over 80 years. As a result, major challenges will include providing social services and healthcare, as well as adapted housing, transport/mobility facilities and other public infrastructure for this population age group.

Definitions and data availability

Eurostat produces a large range of demographic data, including statistics on national and regional levels of population (population estimates based on annual data collections from Member States and other European countries, census data and population projections). These are supplemented by information on a range of demographic events (births, deaths, marriages and divorces, immigration and emigration) that influence the size, structure and characteristics of population groups. A number of important European Commission policies, notably in social and economic fields, use demographic data – for example, fertility rates and life expectancy figures are used when planning social policies for retirement schemes, or regional population data are used for calculating GDP per inhabitant, which is part of the decision-making criteria for the allocation of structural funds to economically less advantaged regions.

Total population figures published by Eurostat, as well as those broken down by age or by gender, refer to the population as of 1 January. The population concept used refers to the usual residence. Countries may provide the legal or registered population instead of the usually resident population. Data are usually based on the

most recent census information, adjusted by the components of population change, or are alternatively based on population registers. Note that there is a break in series in 1998 for the EU-27, euro area and France, as prior to this date information for France was collected on the basis of metropolitan France (in other words, excluding the French overseas departments), while from 1998 onwards these regions are included.

Population density is the ratio of average population, defined as the number of inhabitants, relative to the size of the territory in square kilometres (km²); the land area concept (excluding inland waters like lakes or rivers) is used wherever available.

Age dependency ratios are important demographic indicators that relate the young and old-age populations (those generally inactive) to the population of working age. In this publication the following terminology is used:

- **young-age dependency ratio**: the population aged up to and including 14 years related to the population aged between 15 and 64 years;
- **old-age dependency ratio**: the population aged 65 years or older related to the population aged between 15 and 64 years;
- **total dependency ratio**: the population aged up to and including 14 years and aged 65 years or older related to the population aged between 15 and 64 years.

Every three to four years, Eurostat produces **population projections**, which are 'what-if' scenarios that aim to provide information about the likely future size and structure of the population. Eurostat's latest population projections scenario (EUROPOP2008 convergence scenario) is one of several possible population change scenarios based on the population as of 1 January 2008 and assumptions developed in a conceptual framework whereby socio-economic and cultural differences between Member States would fade away in the long-run.

Main findings

The number of inhabitants in the EU-27 grew from 402.6 million in 1960 to 497.4 million by 2008. Population growth was strongest at the beginning of this period in the 1960s, when average annual increases were generally over 3 million persons per year. The rate of population change slowed significantly in the 1970s, and by the 1980s the average increase was around one and a quarter million persons per annum. This level of population growth continued during much of the next 20 years, with a modest upturn in population growth from 2003 onwards, as the number of inhabitants in the EU-27 rose by approximately 2 million persons a year through to 2008.

Germany had the largest population among the Member States in 2008, accounting for 16.5 % of the EU-27 total. Together with France, the United Kingdom and Italy, who had similar sized populations, these four countries comprised almost 54 % of the total population of the EU-27 in 2008. The twelve Member States that joined the EU since 2004 had a combined population of 103.3 million persons, representing just over a fifth (almost 21 %) of the EU-27's population.

In a majority of EU-27 Member States, populations continued to grow during the period 2000 to 2008, fuelled in particular by increased net migration in Spain, France, Italy and the United Kingdom; in relative terms, Ireland, Cyprus, Spain and Luxembourg recorded the highest population growth rates (overall growth in excess of 10 % between 2000 and 2008). Romania, Bulgaria, Poland, Hungary, Lithuania and Latvia were the only Member States to record a contraction in their respective number of inhabitants between 2000 and 2008, with the largest overall decline in Romania (-4.1 %).

Eurostat projects that, under the EUROPOP2008 convergence scenario, the EU-27's population will grow gradually through to 2035, after which the number of inhabitants will start to fall. The latest projections foresee an EU-27 population of 505.7 million inhabitants by 2060, some 1.7 % higher than in 2008.

The projections for a relatively unchanged level of population in the EU-27 between 2008 and 2060 hide considerable differences across Member States. Population levels are projected to increase for most of the EU-15 Member States, whereas among most of those Member States that joined the EU since 2004 the number of inhabitants is projected to fall. In absolute terms, the largest expansions between 2008 and 2060 are projected for the United Kingdom (14.7 million additional inhabitants), metropolitan France (9.7 million) and Spain (5.2 million), while the highest growth rates are projected for Cyprus, Ireland and Luxembourg, where the population is likely to increase by more than 50 % during the period under

consideration. In contrast, the number of inhabitants in Germany is projected to fall by 11.5 million persons between 2008 and 2060, with considerable population reductions also projected for Poland (7.0 million), Romania (4.6 million) and Bulgaria (2.2 million).

Aside from country differences, the projections also highlight what is likely to be a considerable shift in the age structure of the EU-27's population. Low birth rates and rising life expectancy will likely result in a much older population structure, such that the ratio of the number of working-age people to those aged over 65 will be reduced from 4:1 in 2008 to less than 2:1 by 2060. The high number of ageing baby-boomers will swell the number of elderly persons across the EU-27, as shown by a set of

population pyramids for the EU-27, with the baby-boomer bulge moving through to older generations, while the middle parts of the age distribution and the base of the pyramids become progressively narrower.

Age dependency ratios show the relationship between the working-age population and dependents at either end of the age spectrum; they are expressed in terms of the relative size of the young or the old-age population to the working age population. These ratios suggest that persons aged 65 or over will account for 30.0 % of the EU-27's population by 2060, compared with a 17.0 % share in 2008. The importance of the very old (80 years or more) will be considerable by 2060, when this age group is likely to account for 12.0 % of the EU-27's population.

Table 2.7: Total population and population projections (¹)
(at 1 January, million)

	1960	1970	1980	1990	2000	2008	2010	2020	2030	2040	2050	2060
EU-27 (²)	402.6	435.5	457.1	470.4	482.8	497.4	499.4	513.8	519.9	520.1	515.3	505.7
Euro area (²)	257.1	278.7	292.5	300.9	312.7	326.9	328.3	339.5	344.4	345.5	342.2	335.1
Belgium	9.1	9.7	9.9	9.9	10.2	10.7	10.8	11.3	11.7	12.0	12.2	12.3
Bulgaria	7.8	8.5	8.8	8.8	8.2	7.6	7.6	7.2	6.8	6.3	5.9	5.5
Czech Republic	9.6	9.9	10.3	10.4	10.3	10.4	10.4	10.5	10.4	10.2	9.9	9.5
Denmark	4.6	4.9	5.1	5.1	5.3	5.5	5.5	5.7	5.8	5.9	5.9	5.9
Germany	72.5	78.3	78.2	79.1	82.2	82.2	82.1	81.5	80.2	77.8	74.5	70.8
Estonia	1.2	1.4	1.5	1.6	1.4	1.3	1.3	1.3	1.3	1.2	1.2	1.1
Ireland	2.8	2.9	3.4	3.5	3.8	4.4	4.6	5.4	5.9	6.2	6.5	6.8
Greece	8.3	8.8	9.6	10.1	10.9	11.2	11.3	11.6	11.6	11.6	11.4	11.1
Spain	30.3	33.6	37.2	38.8	40.0	45.3	46.7	51.1	52.7	53.3	53.2	51.9
France (²)	45.5	50.5	53.7	56.6	60.5	63.8	62.6	65.6	68.0	69.9	71.0	71.8
Italy	50.0	53.7	56.4	56.7	56.9	59.6	60.0	61.4	61.9	62.0	61.2	59.4
Cyprus	0.6	0.6	0.5	0.6	0.7	0.8	0.8	1.0	1.1	1.2	1.3	1.3
Latvia	2.1	2.4	2.5	2.7	2.4	2.3	2.2	2.2	2.0	1.9	1.8	1.7
Lithuania	2.8	3.1	3.4	3.7	3.5	3.4	3.3	3.2	3.1	2.9	2.7	2.5
Luxembourg	0.3	0.3	0.4	0.4	0.4	0.5	0.5	0.6	0.6	0.7	0.7	0.7
Hungary	10.0	10.3	10.7	10.4	10.2	10.0	10.0	9.9	9.7	9.4	9.1	8.7
Malta	0.3	0.3	0.3	0.4	0.4	0.4	0.4	0.4	0.4	0.4	0.4	0.4
Netherlands	11.4	13.0	14.1	14.9	15.9	16.4	16.5	16.9	17.2	17.2	16.9	16.6
Austria	7.0	7.5	7.5	7.6	8.0	8.3	8.4	8.7	9.0	9.1	9.1	9.0
Poland	29.5	32.7	35.4	38.0	38.7	38.1	38.1	38.0	37.0	35.2	33.3	31.1
Portugal	8.8	8.7	9.7	10.0	10.2	10.6	10.7	11.1	11.3	11.5	11.4	11.3
Romania	18.3	20.1	22.1	23.2	22.5	21.5	21.3	20.8	20.0	19.2	18.1	16.9
Slovenia	1.6	1.7	1.9	2.0	2.0	2.0	2.0	2.1	2.0	2.0	1.9	1.8
Slovakia	4.0	4.5	5.0	5.3	5.4	5.4	5.4	5.4	5.3	5.1	4.9	4.5
Finland	4.4	4.6	4.8	5.0	5.2	5.3	5.3	5.5	5.6	5.5	5.4	5.4
Sweden	7.5	8.0	8.3	8.5	8.9	9.2	9.3	9.9	10.3	10.5	10.7	10.9
United Kingdom	52.2	55.5	56.3	57.2	58.8	61.2	62.0	65.7	69.2	72.0	74.5	76.7
Croatia	4.1	4.4	4.6	4.8	4.5	4.4	:	:	:	:	:	:
FYR of Macedonia	1.4	1.6	1.9	1.9	2.0	2.0	:	:	:	:	:	:
Turkey	27.1	34.9	44.0	55.5	66.9	70.6	:	:	:	:	:	:
Iceland	0.2	0.2	0.2	0.3	0.3	0.3	:	:	:	:	:	:
Liechtenstein (³)	16.8	20.9	25.8	28.4	32.4	35.4	:	:	:	:	:	:
Norway	3.6	3.9	4.1	4.2	4.5	4.7	4.8	5.2	5.5	5.7	5.9	6.0
Switzerland	5.3	6.2	6.3	6.7	7.2	7.6	7.7	8.2	8.6	8.9	9.1	9.2

(¹) From 2010 onwards the data refer to projections (EUROPOP2008 convergence scenario).
(²) Excluding the four French overseas departments (French Guyana, Guadeloupe, Martinique and Réunion) for 1960 to 1990 and from 2010 onwards.
(³) Thousand instead of million.

Source: Eurostat (demo_pjan and proj_08c2150p)

Figure 2.7: Population density, 2007 (¹)
(inhabitants per km²)

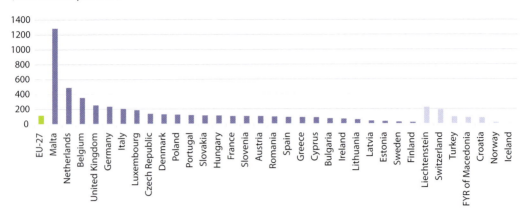

(¹) Spain, France, Cyprus, Luxembourg, Malta, Austria, Poland, Croatia, Turkey, Liechtenstein and Norway, 2006; EU-27 and the United
Kingdom, 2005.

Source: Eurostat (tps00003)

Figure 2.8: Population by age class, EU-27
(1998=100)

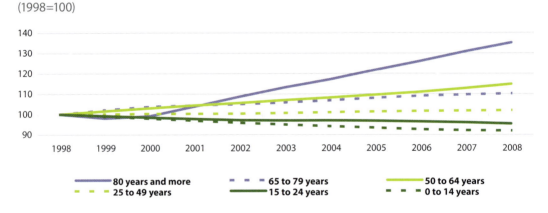

Source: Eurostat (demo_pjan)

Figure 2.9: Age pyramid, EU-27, 2008
(% of total population)

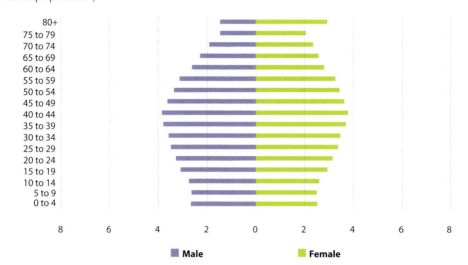

Source: Eurostat (demo_pjan)

2

Table 2.8: Population by age class, 2008
(% of total population)

	0 to 14 years	15 to 24 years	25 to 49 years	50 to 64 years	65 to 79 years	80 years and more
EU-27	15.7	12.5	36.2	18.6	12.7	4.3
Euro area	15.5	11.7	36.5	18.4	13.2	4.6
Belgium	16.9	12.1	35.1	18.8	12.4	4.7
Bulgaria	13.4	13.1	35.7	20.5	13.7	3.6
Czech Republic	14.2	13.0	37.0	21.2	11.2	3.4
Denmark	18.4	11.7	34.4	19.9	11.5	4.1
Germany	13.7	11.6	36.0	18.6	15.3	4.6
Estonia	14.8	15.2	34.8	18.0	13.5	3.7
Ireland	20.6	14.1	38.9	15.5	8.2	2.7
Greece	14.3	11.2	37.6	18.3	14.6	4.1
Spain	14.6	11.2	40.6	16.9	12.0	4.6
France	18.5	12.8	33.7	18.6	11.5	4.9
Italy	14.0	10.2	37.2	18.6	14.6	5.5
Cyprus	17.4	15.4	37.4	17.3	9.7	2.8
Latvia	13.8	15.6	35.7	17.8	13.7	3.5
Lithuania	15.4	15.9	36.1	16.8	12.6	3.3
Luxembourg	18.2	11.8	38.7	17.3	10.6	3.4
Hungary	15.0	12.7	35.7	20.4	12.5	3.7
Malta	16.2	14.1	34.5	21.3	10.7	2.8
Netherlands	17.9	12.1	35.6	19.7	11.0	3.8
Austria	15.4	12.3	37.4	17.8	12.6	4.6
Poland	15.5	15.5	36.0	19.6	10.5	3.0
Portugal	15.3	11.6	37.4	18.2	13.2	2.5
Romania	15.2	14.6	37.0	18.2	12.1	2.8
Slovenia	13.9	12.2	37.6	19.9	12.7	3.6
Slovakia	15.8	15.3	38.1	18.8	9.4	2.6
Finland	16.9	12.4	32.7	21.5	12.2	4.3
Sweden	16.8	13.0	33.0	19.6	12.2	5.3
United Kingdom	17.6	13.4	34.9	18.0	11.6	4.5
Croatia	15.4	12.6	35.0	19.4	13.9	3.2
FYR of Macedonia	18.5	15.9	37.0	17.3	9.7	1.7
Turkey	26.4	17.6	37.0	11.9	5.9	1.1
Iceland	20.9	14.7	36.4	16.5	8.4	3.2
Liechtenstein	16.8	12.2	38.6	20.1	9.3	3.1
Norway	19.2	12.7	34.9	18.6	10.0	4.6
Switzerland	15.5	11.9	37.2	19.0	11.7	4.7

Source: Eurostat (tps00010)

Figure 2.10: Moving age pyramids, EU-27 (¹)
(% of total population)

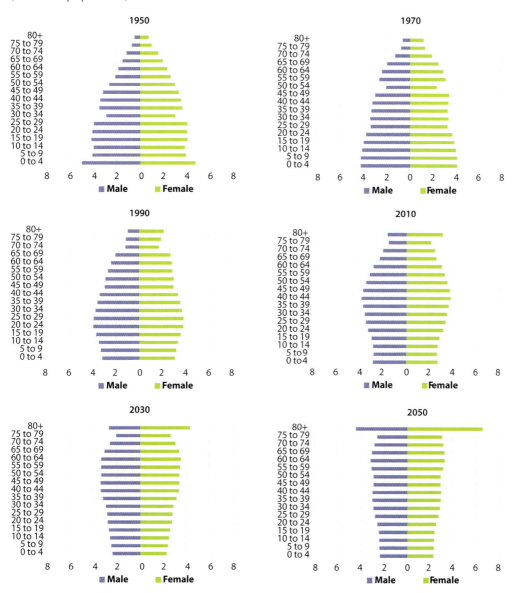

(¹) Limited data availability for 1950 and 1970, based on those Member States for which data are available; from 2010 onwards the data refer to projections (EUROPOP2008 convergence scenario).

Source: Eurostat (demo_pjan and proj_08c2150p)

Figure 2.11: Proportion of the population aged 0-14 and 65 years and more, EU-27 (¹)
(% of total population)

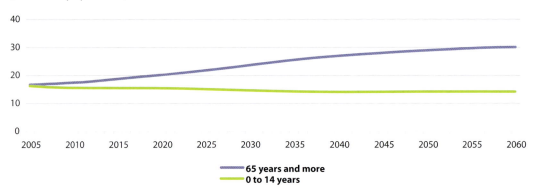

(¹) From 2008 onwards the data refer to projections (EUROPOP2008 convergence scenario).

Source: Eurostat (tps00010 and proj_08c2150p)

Figure 2.12: Proportion of the population aged 80 years and more, EU-27 (¹)
(% of total population)

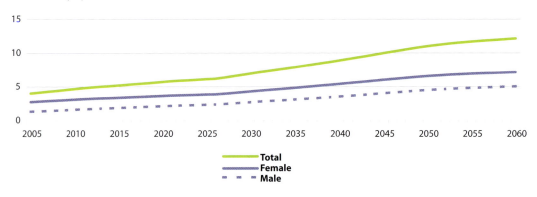

(¹) From 2008 onwards the data refer to projections (EUROPOP2008 convergence scenario).

Source: Eurostat (demo_pjan and proj_08c2150p)

Table 2.9: Age-related dependency ratios
(%)

	Young-age dependency ratio						Old-age dependency ratio					
	1960	1970	1980	1990	2000	2008	1960	1970	1980	1990	2000	2008
EU-27	:	:	:	29.2	25.7	23.3	:	:	:	20.6	23.2	25.3
Euro area	:	:	:	27.2	24.5	23.2	:	:	:	20.9	24.1	26.9
Belgium	36.2	37.5	31.0	27.0	26.9	25.6	18.5	21.2	21.9	22.1	25.5	25.8
Bulgaria	39.4	33.9	33.5	30.9	23.4	19.3	11.2	14.0	17.8	19.5	23.8	25.0
Czech Republic	39.5	32.0	37.0	33.0	23.9	20.0	14.6	17.9	21.6	19.0	19.8	20.5
Denmark	39.8	36.4	32.7	25.5	27.6	28.0	16.4	18.9	22.2	23.2	22.2	23.6
Germany	31.1	36.8	28.6	23.1	23.1	20.7	17.0	21.4	23.9	21.6	23.9	30.4
Estonia	:	33.3	32.8	33.7	27.3	21.8	:	17.7	19.0	17.5	22.4	25.3
Ireland	53.2	54.2	51.8	44.7	32.8	30.0	19.2	19.3	18.2	18.6	16.8	15.9
Greece	37.6	37.5	36.2	29.3	22.9	21.3	14.2	17.2	20.6	20.4	24.2	27.8
Spain	42.6	44.2	41.2	30.5	21.8	21.3	12.7	15.2	17.1	20.2	24.5	24.1
France (¹)	42.2	40.0	35.4	30.5	29.3	28.4	18.7	20.6	22.1	21.1	24.3	25.0
Italy	37.4	38.1	35.1	24.5	21.2	21.3	14.0	16.7	20.3	21.5	26.8	30.4
Cyprus	:	:	:	41.2	34.5	24.9	:	:	:	17.2	17.0	17.8
Latvia	:	32.8	30.7	32.1	26.7	19.9	:	18.0	19.6	17.7	22.1	24.9
Lithuania	:	43.2	36.2	33.9	30.6	22.3	:	15.9	17.4	16.2	20.8	23.0
Luxembourg	31.5	33.8	28.1	24.9	28.3	26.8	15.9	19.1	20.3	19.3	21.4	20.6
Hungary	38.7	31.3	33.8	31.0	24.8	21.8	13.6	17.0	20.9	20.0	22.0	23.5
Malta	:	:	36.1	35.8	30.2	23.2	:	:	12.5	15.7	17.9	19.8
Netherlands	49.1	43.8	34.3	26.4	27.4	26.6	14.6	16.2	17.4	18.6	20.0	21.8
Austria	33.0	39.5	32.4	26.0	25.4	22.7	18.4	22.7	24.3	22.1	22.9	25.4
Poland	54.5	42.0	36.8	39.0	28.6	21.8	9.5	12.6	15.5	15.4	17.6	18.9
Portugal	46.8	46.8	41.6	31.6	24.0	22.8	12.4	14.9	17.8	20.0	23.7	25.9
Romania	:	39.8	42.1	36.0	27.7	21.8	:	13.0	16.3	15.6	19.7	21.3
Slovenia	:	37.7	34.6	30.6	23.0	19.8	:	14.8	16.4	15.5	19.8	23.1
Slovakia	51.1	43.4	41.2	39.6	28.8	21.8	11.1	14.4	16.7	16.0	16.6	16.6
Finland	49.4	37.7	30.2	28.7	27.2	25.3	11.6	13.6	17.6	19.8	22.2	24.8
Sweden	34.5	31.8	30.9	27.7	28.8	25.6	17.8	20.7	25.3	27.7	26.9	26.7
United Kingdom	35.9	38.2	33.2	29.0	29.4	26.5	18.0	20.5	23.3	24.1	24.3	24.3
Croatia	:	:	:	29.0	24.4	23.0	:	:	:	17.0	24.4	25.6
FYR of Macedonia	:	:	:	:	33.3	26.3	:	:	:	:	14.6	16.2
Turkey	74.7	77.7	69.7	57.6	46.6	39.7	6.4	8.2	8.4	7.1	8.3	10.7
Iceland	60.9	56.4	44.3	38.8	35.8	31.0	14.0	15.0	15.7	16.4	17.8	17.1
Liechtenstein	44.7	43.5	33.1	27.4	26.3	23.7	12.3	12.3	12.9	14.2	14.8	17.5
Norway	41.3	39.1	35.5	29.2	30.8	28.9	17.3	20.4	23.3	25.2	23.5	22.1
Switzerland	36.8	36.5	30.2	24.9	25.9	22.8	15.5	17.3	20.9	21.3	22.7	24.1

(¹) Excluding the four French overseas departments (French Guyana, Guadeloupe, Martinique and Réunion) for 1960 to 1990.

Source: Eurostat (demo_pjanind)

2.3 Components of population change

Introduction

There are two components of population change:

- **natural population change:** the difference between the number of births and the number of deaths (births are covered in more detail within the next subchapter, while life expectancy and deaths are treated in Subchapter 2.5.);
- **net migration:** the difference between immigration and emigration (immigration, emigration and citizenship are covered in more detail in Subchapter 2.6).

Political, economic and sociological interest in demographic changes has risen considerably in recent years, particularly in relation to population ageing and migration. As many EU-27 Member States are currently at a point in the demographic cycle where natural population change is close to being balanced, the relative importance of migration in terms of explaining the overall changes in population has increased. This pattern could be reversed to some degree in the coming years, as the EU's population ages, such that natural population change will become increasingly negative.

Most Member States have agreed to develop a common immigration policy (⁴) in order to better manage migratory flows through a coordinated approach which takes into account the economic and demographic situation in the EU. The relative economic prosperity of the EU exerts a considerable pull effect on im-

migrants and while immigration in itself is not a solution to demographic ageing, more sustained flows could increasingly be required to meet the needs of the EU's labour market in the coming decades. These changes highlight the importance attached to ensuring that economic migrants entering the EU have already secured a job, based upon which they will be granted a legal status and a guaranteed set of rights to assist their integration.

Definitions and data availability

Population change is the difference in population between two reference dates and is equal to the sum of natural population change and net migration.

Natural population change is defined as the difference between the number of live births and the number of deaths. The natural increase is negative (in other words, a natural decrease) when the number of deaths exceeds the number of live births.

Net migration is defined as the difference between immigration and emigration (net migration is therefore negative when the number of emigrants exceeds the number of immigrants). Eurostat produces corrected net migration figures by taking the difference between total and natural population increases; this concept is referred to as net migration (including corrections). Net migration gives no indication of the relative scale of the separate immigration and emigration flows to and from a country; a country may report low net migration but experience very high immigration and emigration flows.

(⁴) The legislative provisions relating to the development of a common immigration policy do not fully apply throughout the EU: Denmark has an opt-out regarding Title IV of the Treaty establishing the European Community, while Ireland and the United Kingdom both decide upon their involvement on a case-by-case basis.

Main findings

Population growth in the EU-27 amounted to 2.1 million persons in 2008, comprising a 1.5 million net increase from migration and a 0.6 million increase from natural change. These latest figures are in keeping with recent developments, as net migration has been the main driver of population change in the EU-27 during the past decade, in particular since 2002.

Natural change to the EU-27's population remained relatively modest and stable from 1998 to 2003, rising by as much as 296 000 persons in 2000, while the lowest natural increase was 104 000 persons registered at the end of the period. There was subsequently a gradual increase in natural change through to 2008, largely attributable to an increase in the number of births in the Czech Republic, Spain, France, Italy, Poland and the United Kingdom; the highest natural increases in 2008 were recorded in France (291 000 persons), the United Kingdom (215 000 persons) and Spain (131 000 persons). There were eight Member States that reported more deaths than births in 2008. Among these, by far the largest natural decrease was recorded in Germany (161 000 persons), followed by Bulgaria, Romania and Hungary, where deaths outnumbered births by just over 30 000 persons (in each country).

The relative importance of migration in explaining population changes within the EU-27 has in recent years increased, due to natural change being almost balanced. Aggregating migratory flows between 1998 and 2008, the EU-27's population rose overall by 15.5 million persons as a result of net migration (including corrections). The evolution of net migration displays a far more volatile pattern from one year to the next when compared with the relatively smooth development of natural change. EU-27 net migration rose more than threefold between 2001 and 2002, to reach 1.85 million persons. Thereafter, net migration lay within the range of 1.64 million to 2.10 million persons through to 2007, while in 2008 the biggest single reduction in net migration flows during the past decade was reported (607 000 persons). Net migration stood at 1.49 million persons in the EU-27 in 2008; when expressed in relation to the total population this equated to a 0.30 % share.

The highest levels of net migration (including corrections) were generally recorded in the largest EU-27 Member States during the period 1998 to 2008; this was particularly the case in Spain and Italy, where the population rose by 5.5 million and 3.3 million persons as a direct result of migratory flows. In 2008, the same two countries, Spain and Italy, recorded the highest increases in net migration, 414 000 persons and 438 000 persons, while the United Kingdom was the only other Member State to record a figure in excess of 100 000 persons. Only five of the Member States reported a negative net migration (including corrections) in 2008; net migration (including corrections) was negative in Germany (-53 600 persons), Poland (-14 900 persons), Lithuania (-7 700 persons), Latvia (-2 500 persons) and Bulgaria (-900 persons).

Patterns of population change vary considerably between the Member States: in some cases, natural changes are compensated for by changes in net migration, whereas in others, the two components of population change move in the same direction, increasing the momentum with which population levels change. In the period 2003 to 2008 this was the particularly the case in Ireland, Spain, Cyprus and Luxembourg, where the population was growing by more than 2 % per annum on average.

Table 2.10: Natural population change
(1 000)

	1998	1999	2000	2001	2002	2003	2004	2005	2006	2007	2008
EU-27	168.8	162.3	296.4	231.8	152.1	104.0	391.9	292.0	475.9	483.5	592.8
Euro area	231.4	255.3	350.2	318.8	274.5	204.8	403.2	291.9	406.0	376.1	411.5
Belgium	9.7	9.3	10.0	10.7	5.6	5.1	13.7	14.7	19.8	20.0	23.4
Bulgaria	-52.8	-39.5	-41.4	-44.2	-46.1	-44.6	-40.2	-42.3	-39.5	-37.7	-32.8
Czech Republic	-19.0	-20.3	-18.1	-17.0	-15.5	-17.6	-9.5	-5.7	1.4	10.0	14.6
Denmark	7.7	7.1	9.1	7.1	5.5	7.1	8.8	9.3	9.5	8.5	10.4
Germany	-67.3	-75.6	-71.8	-94.1	-122.4	-147.2	-112.6	-144.4	-148.9	-142.3	-161.9
Estonia	-7.3	-6.0	-5.3	-5.9	-5.4	-5.1	-3.7	-3.0	-2.4	-1.6	-0.6
Ireland	22.4	21.3	23.4	27.6	31.1	32.7	33.8	33.6	36.8	42.6	46.3
Greece	-1.8	-2.7	-2.0	-0.3	-0.3	-1.1	0.7	2.5	6.6	2.0	8.5
Spain	4.7	9.0	37.2	46.2	50.2	57.1	82.7	79.0	111.5	108.6	131.1
France	225.1	229.2	267.5	262.9	248.3	231.3	280.7	269.6	303.3	288.3	291.0
Italy	-51.0	-20.5	-12.4	-16.8	-17.5	-44.8	17.5	-34.9	2.1	-9.1	-3.7
Cyprus	3.4	3.4	3.1	3.3	2.7	2.9	3.1	2.8	3.6	3.2	4.1
Latvia	-15.8	-13.4	-12.0	-13.3	-12.5	-11.4	-11.7	-11.3	-10.8	-9.8	-7.1
Lithuania	-3.7	-3.6	-4.8	-8.9	-11.1	-10.4	-10.9	-13.3	-13.5	-13.3	-8.8
Luxembourg	1.5	1.8	2.0	1.7	1.6	1.3	1.9	1.8	1.7	1.6	2.0
Hungary	-43.6	-48.6	-38.0	-35.1	-36.0	-41.2	-37.4	-38.2	-31.7	-35.3	-30.8
Malta	1.7	1.3	1.5	1.1	0.9	0.9	0.9	0.7	0.7	0.8	0.9
Netherlands	61.9	60.0	66.1	62.2	59.7	58.4	57.5	51.5	49.7	48.3	49.7
Austria	2.9	-0.1	1.5	0.7	2.3	-0.3	4.7	3.0	3.6	1.6	2.7
Poland	20.3	0.6	10.3	5.0	-5.7	-14.2	-7.4	-3.9	4.6	10.6	35.1
Portugal	7.3	8.1	14.6	7.7	8.1	3.7	7.3	1.9	3.5	-1.0	0.3
Romania	-31.9	-30.6	-21.3	-39.2	-59.1	-54.1	-42.6	-41.1	-38.6	-37.2	-31.3
Slovenia	-1.2	-1.4	-0.4	-1.0	-1.2	-2.1	-0.6	-0.7	0.8	1.2	2.6
Slovakia	4.4	3.8	2.4	-0.8	-0.7	-0.5	1.9	1.0	0.6	0.6	4.2
Finland	7.8	8.2	7.4	7.6	6.1	7.6	10.2	9.8	10.8	9.7	10.4
Sweden	-4.2	-6.6	-3.0	-2.3	0.8	6.2	10.4	9.6	14.7	15.7	17.9
United Kingdom	87.7	67.9	70.7	66.9	62.6	84.4	132.9	139.9	176.3	197.6	214.7
Croatia	-5.2	-6.8	-6.5	-8.6	-10.5	-12.9	-9.4	-9.3	-8.9	-10.5	-8.4
FYR of Macedonia	12.4	10.5	12.1	10.1	9.8	9.0	5.4	4.1	4.0	3.1	4.0
Turkey	1 046.0	1 024.0	948.0	940.0	933.0	925.0	917.0	911.0	906.0	897.0	818.0
Iceland	2.4	2.2	2.5	2.4	2.2	2.3	2.4	2.4	2.5	2.6	2.8
Liechtenstein	0.2	0.2	0.2	0.2	0.2	0.1	0.2	0.2	0.1	0.1	0.1
Norway	14.2	14.1	15.2	12.7	11.0	14.0	15.8	15.5	17.3	16.5	18.8
Switzerland	16.4	15.9	15.9	11.1	10.6	8.8	12.9	11.8	13.1	13.4	15.2

Source: Eurostat (tps00007)

Table 2.11: Net migration (including corrections)
(1 000)

	1998	1999	2000	2001	2002	2003	2004	2005	2006	2007	2008
EU-27	528.8	980.4	715.7	600.1	1 851.8	2 035.3	1 875.0	1 659.7	1 639.2	2 101.6	*1 494.6*
Euro area	436.1	843.7	961.9	1 245.7	1 667.4	1 819.3	1 698.0	1 475.1	1 320.4	1 564.9	*1 105.7*
Belgium	11.8	16.1	14.3	35.6	40.5	35.5	35.8	50.8	53.4	62.3	64.3
Bulgaria (¹)	0.0	0.0	0.0	-214.2	0.9	0.0	0.0	0.0	0.0	-1.4	-0.9
Czech Republic	9.5	8.8	6.5	-43.1	12.3	25.8	18.6	36.2	34.7	83.9	71.8
Denmark	11.0	9.4	10.1	12.0	9.6	7.0	5.0	6.7	10.1	16.5	28.9
Germany	47.0	202.1	167.9	274.8	218.8	142.2	81.8	81.6	25.8	45.2	-53.6
Estonia	-6.6	-1.1	0.2	0.2	0.2	0.1	0.1	0.1	0.2	0.2	0.1
Ireland	16.2	24.2	31.8	39.3	32.7	31.4	47.6	66.2	66.7	46.2	17.9
Greece	54.8	45.0	29.4	37.8	38.0	35.4	41.4	40.0	40.0	40.0	35.0
Spain	158.8	237.9	389.8	441.3	649.2	624.6	610.0	641.2	604.9	700.0	413.8
France	-1.4	150.3	158.3	172.7	184.2	188.7	105.1	91.6	90.1	302.5	77.0
Italy	55.8	34.9	49.5	49.9	344.8	612.0	556.6	324.2	377.5	497.1	437.9
Cyprus	4.2	4.2	4.0	4.7	6.9	12.3	15.7	14.4	8.7	7.4	0.6
Latvia	-5.8	-4.1	-5.5	-5.2	-1.8	-0.8	-1.1	-0.6	-2.5	-0.6	-2.5
Lithuania	-22.1	-20.7	-20.3	-2.6	-2.0	-6.3	-9.6	-8.8	-4.9	-5.2	-7.7
Luxembourg	3.8	4.5	3.4	3.3	2.6	5.4	4.4	6.1	5.4	6.0	7.7
Hungary	17.3	16.8	16.7	9.7	3.5	15.6	18.2	17.3	21.3	14.6	16.6
Malta	0.4	0.4	0.9	2.2	1.7	1.7	1.9	1.6	2.1	1.7	2.5
Netherlands	44.1	43.8	57.0	56.0	27.6	7.1	-10.0	-22.8	-25.9	-0.9	31.5
Austria	8.5	19.8	17.3	43.5	34.8	38.2	61.7	56.4	29.4	18.0	34.0
Poland	-13.3	-14.0	-409.9	-16.7	-17.9	-13.8	-9.4	-12.9	-36.1	-20.5	-14.9
Portugal	31.9	38.0	47.0	65.0	70.0	63.5	47.3	38.4	26.0	19.5	9.4
Romania	-5.6	-2.5	-3.7	-557.7	-1.6	-7.4	-10.1	-7.2	-6.5	0.7	1.3
Slovenia (²)	-5.4	10.8	2.7	5.0	2.2	3.5	1.7	6.4	6.3	14.3	19.5
Slovakia	1.3	1.5	-22.3	1.0	0.9	1.4	2.9	3.4	3.9	6.8	7.1
Finland	4.5	3.4	2.4	6.1	5.3	5.8	6.7	9.2	10.6	13.9	15.4
Sweden	10.9	13.7	24.4	28.6	30.9	28.7	25.3	26.7	50.8	54.0	55.6
United Kingdom	97.4	137.6	143.9	151.0	157.6	177.7	227.2	193.3	247.3	179.3	226.4
Croatia	-4.1	-23.0	-52.4	14.3	8.6	11.9	11.6	8.3	7.3	5.6	7.1
FYR of Macedonia	-2.0	-1.6	-2.5	-2.6	-24.8	-2.8	-0.1	-0.8	-0.5	0.1	-0.5
Turkey (¹)	98.9	78.9	58.2	2.5	-1.0	-3.0	1.0	-1.0	-3.0	0.0	112.8
Iceland	1.0	1.1	1.8	0.8	-0.3	-0.2	0.6	3.9	5.3	5.2	1.1
Liechtenstein	0.5	0.2	0.3	0.5	0.2	0.3	0.1	0.1	0.1	0.1	0.1
Norway	13.5	19.0	9.7	7.9	17.2	11.2	13.2	18.3	23.6	39.5	43.3
Switzerland	10.7	25.0	23.7	40.5	47.6	41.5	38.1	32.2	36.5	71.4	91.5

(¹) Due to lack of data on migration, the population figures for Bulgaria for 1998-2006 and for Turkey for 2007 are based exclusively on the natural change; data on net migration including corrections are therefore zero, or just the necessary correction of the demographic balance.
(²) Break in series, 2008.

Source: Eurostat (tsdde230)

Figure 2.13: Population change, net migration (including corrections) and natural population change, EU-27 (¹)
(million)

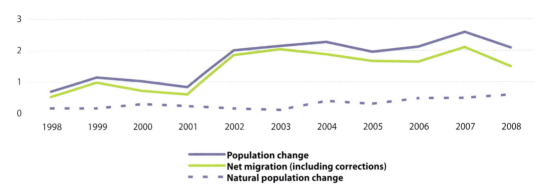

(¹) Provisional data for 2008.

Source: Eurostat (tps00006, tsdde230 and tps00007)

Figure 2.14: Net migration (including corrections) and natural population change, 2003-2008
(average annual change, %)

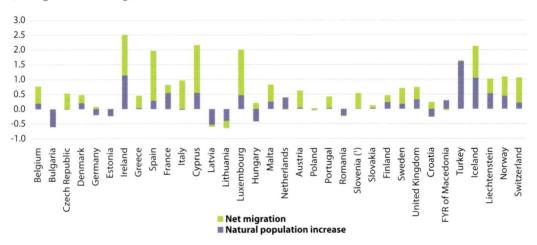

(¹) Break in series, 2008.

Source: Eurostat (demo_gind)

2.4 Families and births

Introduction

The EU's social policy does not include a specific strand for family issues. Rather, policy in this area remains the exclusive responsibility of Member States, reflecting different family structures, historical developments, social attitudes and traditions from one Member State to another.

There are, however, a number of common demographic themes apparent across the whole of the EU, including: a reduction in the number of births; a reduction in the number of marriages; an increase in the average age at which people marry; and an increase in the number of divorces. These trends have resulted in a greater number of households and in households of a smaller average size, as a higher proportion of people live alone.

There is a significant gender gap in terms of labour market participation and earnings which underlines the difficulties faced by women when trying to combine family life with a working career. At the spring European Council held in Brussels on 8 and 9 March 2007, European leaders decided to establish an alliance for families, with the aim of encouraging family-friendly policies and fostering cooperation across the EU. On 10 May 2007, the European Commission adopted a Communication titled, 'Promoting solidarity between the generations' [5]. This highlighted three areas where Member States, social partners and civil society, as well as the EU, could play an important role:

- financial support to cope with the costs of raising a family;
- quality care services, both for children and for the dependent elderly;
- flexible working times, with appropriate schedules and holiday arrangements.

Relatively high fertility rates across the EU tend to be recorded in those Member States which have implemented a range of family-friendly policies, including the introduction of accessible and affordable childcare and/or more flexible working patterns (France, the Nordic countries, or the Netherlands). Some experts consider that fertility will increase if there are stimuli, such as higher economic growth, more childcare facilities, fiscal measures that support families, family benefit income, a stock of suitable housing, or a range of policies designed to reconcile work and family life (such as part-time or telework opportunities). While a conventional analysis of declining fertility rates might suggest that the decline in fertility rates could be related to increased female participation in the labour market, there is clear evidence of a positive relationship in many countries, for example, in the Nordic Member States or Spain, where tertiary-educated women in employment tend to have more children.

[5] COM (2007) 244 final; for more information: http://eur-lex.europa.eu/LexUriServ/LexUriServ.do?uri=COM:2007:0244:FIN:EN:PDF.

Definitions and data availability

Eurostat collects a wide range of demographic data covering fertility, marriage and divorce, on an annual basis, including information at a regional level.

Live births are defined as the total number of births excluding still births. **Stillbirths** are defined as the expulsion or extraction from the mother of a dead foetus after the time at which it would normally be presumed capable of independent extra-uterine existence (commonly taken to be after 24 or 28 weeks of gestation). The **crude birth rate** is the ratio of the number of births to the average population in a particular reference year (the result is generally expressed per 1 000 inhabitants). **Live births outside of marriage** are those where the mother's marital status at the time of birth is other than married.

The **total fertility rate** is the mean number of children that would be born to a woman during her lifetime if she were to pass through her childbearing years conforming to the age-specific fertility rates of a given year. The **mean age of women at childbearing** can be calculated using fertility rates broken down by age (in general, the reproductive period is considered to be between 15 and 49 years of age).

A **marriage** is the act, ceremony or process by which the legal relationship of husband and wife is constituted. The relationship between a civil marriage and a religious marriage is not the same in all countries: the legality of a union may be established by civil, religious or other means as recognised by the laws of each country.

Divorce is defined as the final legal dissolution of a marriage, that is, a separation of husband and wife which confers on the parties the right to remarry under civil, religious and/or other provisions, according to the laws of each country. Divorce is possible in all of the Member States, except Malta; in almost all countries divorces are registered at a court.

Crude marriage and divorce rates measure the number of marriages/divorces in relation to the average population; these rates are expressed per 1 000 inhabitants.

Main findings

From the 1960s up to the beginning of the 21st century, the number of births in the EU-27 declined sharply, to reach a relative low of just under 5 million by 2002. Since this date, there has been a steady rebound, such that the total number of live births in the EU-27 had reached 5.4 million by 2008.

This overall trend was reflected in the developments for many of the Member States. However, the number of births continued to decline in Germany, the Netherlands and Portugal, while the number of births remained relatively unchanged in Denmark and Austria. At the other end of the range, the largest increase in live births between 2002 and 2008 was recorded in the United Kingdom (125 600 additional births), while Spain was the only other Member State to record growth in excess of 100 000 births. In absolute terms, the highest number of live births in 2008 was recorded in France (835 000 live births), followed by the United Kingdom (794 400 live births); among those Member States that joined the EU since 2004, Poland recorded the highest number of births (414 500 live

births). There were 1.27 million live births in Turkey in 2008, equivalent to almost a quarter of the total number of live births in the EU-27 in the same year.

The upturn in the number of live births since 2002 was reflected in the crude birth rate for the EU-27, which rose from a relative low of 10.3 ‰ in 2002 to 10.9 ‰ by 2008. Across the Member States, Ireland had the highest crude birth rate (16.9 ‰), followed by France and the United Kingdom (both close to 13.0 ‰). There were four Member States (Italy, Hungary, Austria and Portugal) where the crude birth rate was between 9.0 ‰ and 10.0 ‰, while the lowest overall rate (8.3 ‰) was registered in Germany.

In developed countries, a fertility rate of about 2.1 children per woman is considered necessary to maintain a stable population in the long-run, under a hypothetical situation with zero net migration. Fertility rates have been below this natural replacement level in each of the Member States for more than a decade.

The slowdown in the EU-27's population growth can be partly attributed to people having fewer children. The total fertility rate of the EU-27 declined from almost 2.6 children per woman in the first half of the 1960s to around 1.5 children per woman during the last decade. Fertility rates in the majority of the Member States continued to decline, with only Ireland and France reporting rates anywhere near natural replacement levels (both averaging around 2.0 children per woman in recent years). In contrast, the lowest fertility rates in the EU-27 tended to be registered in southern and eastern Member States, with the minimum value

recorded in Slovakia (1.25 children per woman in 2007).

While fertility rates of women aged less than 30 have declined since the 1970s, fertility rates of those aged 30 or more have risen. As such, part of the decline in fertility within the EU-27 is likely to have resulted from the postponement of childbearing. The mean age of women giving birth in 2006 was over 30 in five of the Member States (Spain, Ireland, the Netherlands, Sweden and Denmark) as well as in Italy in 2005, and was between 29 and 30 years in ten other Member States.

Besides low birth and fertility rates and the postponement of childbearing, another factor characterising fertility trends in the EU-27 is the growing percentage of live births outside marriage. This phenomenon has been rising quite rapidly in some Member States, and the majority of live births in Bulgaria, Estonia, France, Slovenia and Sweden in 2007 were outside marriage; at the other end of the range, the number of births outside marriage in Greece and Cyprus was less than one in ten.

The number of marriages across the EU-27 has generally followed a downward trend since the early 1970s. Nevertheless, marriages per 1 000 persons reached a relative peak of 5.2 ‰ at the turn of the millennium, after which the marriage rate fell to 4.9 ‰, where it remained through to 2007. The highest marriage rates in 2008 were recorded in Cyprus (2007), Lithuania, Romania, Poland and Denmark – at least 6.8 ‰. The marriage rate fell in 16 of the Member States (over the period 1998 to 2007/2008). Among the ten Member States reporting an upward trend, the number of marriages per 1 000 persons

2 Population

rose at a relatively rapid pace in Estonia, Ireland, Latvia, Lithuania, Poland, Finland and Sweden.

Although marriage is a form of commitment of union between partners, irreparable differences can lead to divorce. The number of divorces in the EU-27 has grown steadily and reached 2.0 ‰ by 2005. In 2008 the divorce rate peaked

at 3.1 ‰ in Lithuania, while the Czech Republic was the only other country to record at least 3 divorces per 1 000 persons. The most substantial increases in divorce rates between 1998 and 2008 were registered in Spain, Portugal and Cyprus (to 2007), while the biggest reduction was posted in Estonia.

Table 2.12: Number of live births
(1 000)

	1998	1999	2000	2001	2002	2003	2004	2005	2006	2007	2008
EU-27	5 074.8	5 073.4	5 121.6	5 022.1	4 993.3	5 040.8	5 117.0	5 134.6	5 223.1	5 281.6	5 428.2
Euro area	3 249.0	3 277.8	3 342.5	3 287.7	3 281.1	3 297.5	3 335.7	3 323.9	3 361.9	3 376.3	3 451.6
Belgium	114.2	114.2	114.9	114.2	111.2	112.1	115.6	118.0	121.4	120.7	125.0
Bulgaria	65.4	72.3	73.7	68.2	66.5	67.4	69.9	71.1	74.0	75.3	77.7
Czech Republic	90.5	89.5	90.9	90.7	92.8	93.7	97.7	102.2	105.8	114.6	119.6
Denmark	66.2	66.2	67.1	65.5	64.1	64.7	64.6	64.3	65.0	64.1	65.0
Germany	785.0	770.7	767.0	734.5	719.3	706.7	705.6	685.8	672.7	684.9	682.5
Estonia	12.2	12.4	13.1	12.6	13.0	13.0	14.0	14.4	14.9	15.8	16.0
Ireland	54.0	53.9	54.8	57.9	60.5	61.5	62.0	61.0	64.2	70.6	74.8
Greece	100.9	100.6	103.3	102.3	103.6	104.4	105.7	107.5	112.0	111.9	115.5
Spain	365.2	380.1	397.6	406.4	418.8	441.9	454.6	466.4	483.0	493.7	518.9
France	768.6	776.5	808.2	804.1	793.6	793.9	800.2	807.8	830.3	819.6	835.0
Italy	515.4	537.2	543.1	535.3	538.2	544.1	562.6	554.0	560.0	563.9	575.8
Cyprus	8.9	8.5	8.4	8.2	7.9	8.1	8.3	8.2	8.7	8.6	9.2
Latvia	18.4	19.4	20.2	19.7	20.0	21.0	20.3	21.5	22.3	23.3	23.9
Lithuania	37.0	36.4	34.1	31.5	30.0	30.6	30.4	30.5	31.3	32.3	35.1
Luxembourg	5.4	5.6	5.7	5.5	5.3	5.3	5.5	5.4	5.5	5.5	5.6
Hungary	97.3	94.6	97.6	97.0	96.8	94.6	95.1	97.5	99.9	97.6	99.2
Malta	4.7	4.4	4.4	4.0	3.9	4.1	3.9	3.9	3.9	3.9	4.1
Netherlands	199.4	200.4	206.6	202.6	202.1	200.3	194.0	187.9	185.1	181.3	184.7
Austria	81.2	78.1	78.3	75.5	78.4	76.9	79.0	78.2	77.9	76.3	77.8
Poland	395.6	382.0	378.3	368.2	353.8	351.1	356.1	364.4	374.2	387.9	414.5
Portugal	113.5	116.0	120.0	112.8	114.4	112.5	109.3	109.4	105.4	102.5	104.6
Romania	237.3	234.6	234.5	220.4	210.5	212.5	216.3	221.0	219.5	214.7	221.9

Table 2.12: Number of live births (continued)
(1 000)

	1998	1999	2000	2001	2002	2003	2004	2005	2006	2007	2008
Slovenia (¹)	17.9	17.5	18.2	17.5	17.5	17.3	18.0	18.2	18.9	19.8	*21.2*
Slovakia	57.6	56.2	55.2	51.1	50.8	51.7	53.7	54.4	53.9	54.4	57.4
Finland	57.1	57.6	56.7	56.2	55.6	56.6	57.8	57.7	58.8	58.7	59.5
Sweden	89.0	88.2	90.4	91.5	95.8	99.2	100.9	101.3	105.9	107.4	109.3
United Kingdom	716.9	700.0	679.0	669.1	668.8	695.5	716.0	722.5	748.6	772.2	*794.4*
Croatia	47.1	45.2	43.7	41.0	40.1	39.7	40.3	42.5	41.4	41.9	43.8
FYR of Macedonia	29.2	27.3	29.3	27.0	27.8	27.0	23.4	22.5	22.6	22.7	*22.9*
Turkey	1 472.0	1 451.0	1 363.0	1 362.0	1 362.0	1 361.0	1 360.0	1 361.0	1 362.0	1 361.0	*1 272.0*
Iceland	4.2	4.1	4.3	4.1	4.0	4.1	4.2	4.3	4.4	4.6	4.8
Liechtenstein	0.4	0.4	0.4	0.4	0.4	0.3	0.4	0.4	0.4	0.4	0.4
Norway	58.4	59.3	59.2	56.7	55.4	56.5	57.0	56.8	58.5	58.5	60.5
Switzerland	78.9	78.4	78.5	72.3	72.4	71.8	73.1	72.9	73.4	74.5	*76.9*

(¹) Break in series, 2008.

Source: Eurostat (tps00111)

Figure 2.15: Live births outside marriage and crude birth rate, EU-27

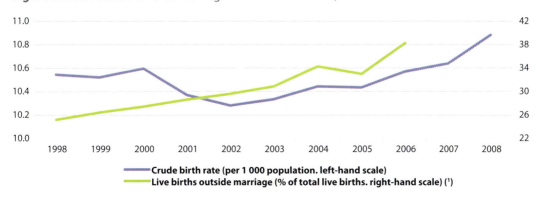

Crude birth rate (per 1 000 population. left-hand scale)
Live births outside marriage (% of total live births. right-hand scale) (¹)

(¹) 2007 and 2008, not available; excluding Belgium; excluding Italy for 2004.

Source: Eurostat (tps00112 and demo_fagec)

Table 2.13: Crude birth rate
(per 1 000 population)

	1998	1999	2000	2001	2002	2003	2004	2005	2006	2007	2008
EU-27	10.5	10.5	10.6	10.4	10.3	10.3	10.4	10.4	10.6	10.6	10.9
Euro area	10.5	10.5	10.7	10.4	10.4	10.4	10.4	10.3	10.4	10.4	10.5
Belgium	11.2	11.2	11.2	11.1	10.8	10.8	11.1	11.3	11.5	11.4	11.7
Bulgaria	7.9	8.8	9.0	8.5	8.5	8.6	9.0	9.2	9.6	9.8	10.2
Czech Republic	8.8	8.7	8.9	8.9	9.1	9.2	9.6	10.0	10.3	11.1	11.5
Denmark	12.5	12.4	12.6	12.2	11.9	12.0	12.0	11.9	12.0	11.7	11.8
Germany	9.6	9.4	9.3	8.9	8.7	8.6	8.6	8.3	8.2	8.3	*8.3*
Estonia	8.8	9.0	9.5	9.3	9.6	9.6	10.4	10.7	11.1	11.8	12.0
Ireland	14.5	14.4	14.4	15.0	15.4	15.4	15.2	14.7	15.1	16.2	16.9
Greece	9.3	9.2	9.5	9.3	9.4	9.5	9.6	9.7	10.1	10.0	10.3
Spain	9.2	9.5	9.9	10.0	10.1	10.5	10.6	10.7	10.9	11.0	11.4
France	12.8	12.9	13.3	13.1	12.9	12.8	12.8	12.9	13.1	12.9	13.0
Italy	9.1	9.4	9.5	9.4	9.4	9.4	9.7	9.5	9.5	9.5	9.6
Cyprus	13.1	12.4	12.2	11.6	11.1	11.2	11.2	10.9	11.3	10.9	11.6
Latvia	7.6	8.1	8.5	8.4	8.6	9.0	8.8	9.3	9.7	10.2	10.6
Lithuania	10.4	10.3	9.8	9.1	8.7	8.9	8.9	8.9	9.2	9.6	10.4
Luxembourg	12.7	13.0	13.1	12.4	12.0	11.7	11.9	11.5	11.7	11.4	11.5
Hungary	9.5	9.2	9.6	9.5	9.5	9.3	9.4	9.7	9.9	9.7	9.9
Malta	12.4	11.6	11.6	10.1	9.9	10.2	9.7	9.6	9.6	9.5	10.0
Netherlands	12.7	12.7	13.0	12.6	12.5	12.3	11.9	11.5	11.3	11.1	11.2
Austria	10.2	9.8	9.8	9.4	9.7	9.5	9.7	9.5	9.4	9.2	9.3
Poland	10.2	9.9	9.8	9.6	9.3	9.2	9.3	9.5	9.8	10.2	10.9
Portugal	11.2	11.4	11.7	11.0	11.0	10.8	10.4	10.4	10.0	9.7	9.8
Romania	10.5	10.4	10.5	10.0	9.7	9.8	10.0	10.2	10.2	10.0	10.3
Slovenia (¹)	9.0	8.8	9.1	8.8	8.8	8.7	9.0	9.1	9.4	9.8	10.5
Slovakia	10.7	10.4	10.2	9.5	9.5	9.6	10.0	10.1	10.0	10.1	10.6
Finland	11.1	11.1	11.0	10.8	10.7	10.9	11.0	11.0	11.2	11.1	11.2
Sweden	10.1	10.0	10.2	10.3	10.7	11.1	11.2	11.2	11.7	11.7	11.9
United Kingdom	12.3	11.9	11.5	11.3	11.3	11.7	12.0	12.0	12.4	12.7	12.9
Croatia	10.4	10.0	9.8	9.2	9.0	8.9	9.1	9.6	9.3	9.4	9.9
FYR of Macedonia	14.6	13.5	14.5	13.3	13.7	13.3	11.5	11.0	11.1	11.1	11.2
Turkey	22.6	21.9	20.2	19.9	19.7	19.4	19.1	18.9	*18.7*	19.4	17.9
Iceland	15.2	14.8	15.3	14.4	14.1	14.3	14.5	14.4	14.5	14.6	15.2
Liechtenstein	12.6	12.4	12.9	12.1	11.7	10.2	10.8	11.0	10.3	10.0	9.9
Norway	13.2	13.3	13.2	12.6	12.2	12.4	12.4	12.3	12.6	12.4	12.7
Switzerland	11.1	11.0	10.9	10.0	9.9	9.8	9.9	9.8	9.8	9.9	10.1

(¹) Break in series, 2008.

Source: Eurostat (tps00112)

Table 2.14: Total fertility rate
(average number of children per woman)

	1997	1998	1999	2000	2001	2002	2003	2004	2005	2006	2007
EU-27	:	:	:	:	:	1.45	1.47	1.49	1.50	1.53	1.55
Belgium	1.60	1.60	1.62	:	:	:	:	:	:	:	:
Bulgaria	1.09	1.11	1.23	1.26	1.21	1.21	1.23	1.29	1.32	1.38	1.42
Czech Republic	1.17	1.16	1.13	1.14	1.14	1.17	1.18	1.23	1.28	1.33	1.44
Denmark	1.76	1.73	1.74	1.78	1.76	1.72	1.76	1.78	1.80	1.85	1.84
Germany	:	:	:	1.38	1.35	1.34	1.34	1.36	1.34	1.33	1.37
Estonia	1.32	1.28	1.32	1.38	1.34	1.37	1.37	1.47	1.50	1.55	1.63
Ireland	1.93	1.94	1.90	1.89	1.94	1.97	1.96	1.94	1.86	1.89	2.01
Greece	1.28	1.26	1.24	1.26	1.25	1.27	1.28	1.30	1.33	1.40	1.41
Spain	1.18	1.16	1.19	1.23	1.24	1.26	1.31	1.33	1.35	1.38	1.40
France	:	1.78	1.81	1.89	1.89	1.88	1.89	1.92	1.94	2.00	1.98
Italy	1.21	1.21	1.23	1.26	1.25	1.27	1.29	1.33	1.32	1.35	1.37
Cyprus	1.86	1.76	1.67	1.64	1.57	1.49	1.50	1.49	1.42	1.45	1.39
Latvia	:	:	:	:	:	1.23	1.29	1.24	1.31	1.35	1.41
Lithuania	1.47	1.46	1.46	1.39	1.30	1.24	1.26	1.26	1.27	1.31	1.35
Luxembourg	1.71	1.68	1.74	1.76	1.66	1.63	1.62	1.66	1.63	1.65	1.61
Hungary	1.37	1.32	1.28	1.32	1.31	1.30	1.27	1.28	1.31	1.34	1.32
Malta	1.98	1.88	1.77	1.70	1.48	1.45	1.48	1.40	1.38	1.39	1.37
Netherlands	1.56	1.63	1.65	1.72	1.71	1.73	1.75	1.72	1.71	1.72	1.72
Austria	1.39	1.37	1.34	1.36	1.33	1.39	1.38	1.42	1.40	1.40	1.38
Poland	1.51	1.44	1.37	1.35	1.31	1.25	1.22	1.23	1.24	1.27	1.31
Portugal	1.47	1.48	1.50	1.55	1.45	1.47	1.44	1.40	1.40	1.36	1.33
Romania	1.32	1.32	1.30	1.31	1.27	1.25	1.27	1.29	1.32	1.32	1.30
Slovenia	1.25	1.23	1.21	1.26	1.21	1.21	1.20	1.25	1.26	1.31	1.38
Slovakia	1.43	1.37	1.33	1.30	1.20	1.19	1.20	1.24	1.25	1.24	1.25
Finland	1.75	1.70	1.73	1.73	1.73	1.72	1.77	1.80	1.80	1.84	1.83
Sweden	1.52	1.50	1.50	1.54	1.57	1.65	1.71	1.75	1.77	1.85	1.88
United Kingdom	1.72	1.71	1.68	1.64	1.63	1.64	1.71	1.76	1.78	1.84	1.90
Croatia	:	:	:	:	:	1.34	1.32	1.34	1.41	1.38	1.40
FYR of Macedonia	1.93	1.90	1.76	1.88	1.73	1.80	1.77	1.52	1.46	1.46	1.46
Iceland	2.04	2.05	1.99	2.08	1.95	1.93	1.99	2.04	2.05	2.08	2.09
Liechtenstein	:	:	:	1.57	1.52	1.47	1.36	1.44	1.49	1.43	1.42
Norway	1.86	1.81	1.85	1.85	1.78	1.75	1.80	1.83	1.84	1.90	1.90
Switzerland	1.48	1.47	1.48	1.50	1.38	1.39	1.39	1.42	1.42	1.44	1.46

Source: Eurostat (tsdde220)

Figure 2.16: Mean age of women at childbearing ([1])
(years)

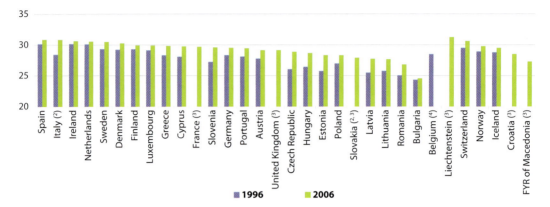

([1]) Malta, not available.
([2]) 2005 instead of 2006.
([3]) 1996, not available.
([4]) 2006, not available.

Source: Eurostat (tps00017)

Table 2.15: Marriages
(per 1 000 population)

	1998	1999	2000	2001	2002	2003	2004	2005	2006	2007	2008
EU-27	5.1	5.2	5.2	4.9	4.9	4.9	4.9	4.9	:	4.9	:
Euro area	5.0	5.0	5.1	4.8	4.8	4.7	4.7	4.6	4.5	4.5	:
Belgium	4.4	4.3	4.4	4.1	3.9	4.0	4.2	4.1	4.3	4.3	4.4
Bulgaria	4.3	4.3	4.3	4.0	3.7	3.9	4.0	4.3	4.3	3.9	3.6
Czech Republic	5.4	5.2	5.4	5.1	5.2	4.8	5.0	5.1	5.2	5.5	5.0
Denmark	6.6	6.7	7.2	6.8	6.9	6.5	7.0	6.7	6.7	6.7	6.8
Germany	5.1	5.3	5.1	4.7	4.8	4.6	4.8	4.7	4.5	4.5	4.6
Estonia	3.9	4.1	4.0	4.1	4.3	4.2	4.5	4.6	5.2	5.2	4.6
Ireland	4.5	4.9	5.0	5.0	5.2	5.1	5.1	5.1	5.1	5.2	:
Greece	5.1	5.6	4.5	5.2	5.3	5.5	4.6	5.5	5.2	5.5	4.6
Spain	5.2	5.2	5.4	5.1	5.1	5.1	5.1	4.8	4.6	4.5	:
France	4.6	4.9	5.0	4.8	4.7	4.6	4.5	4.5	4.3	4.3	4.3
Italy	4.9	4.9	5.0	4.6	4.7	4.5	4.3	4.2	4.1	4.2	4.1
Cyprus (¹)	11.4	13.2	14.1	15.1	14.5	7.7	7.2	7.8	6.8	7.5	:
Latvia	4.0	3.9	3.9	3.9	4.2	4.3	4.5	5.5	6.4	6.8	5.7
Lithuania	5.2	5.1	4.8	4.5	4.7	4.9	5.6	5.8	6.3	6.8	7.2
Luxembourg	4.8	4.9	4.9	4.5	4.5	4.4	4.4	4.4	4.2	4.1	3.9
Hungary	4.4	4.4	4.7	4.3	4.5	4.5	4.3	4.4	4.4	4.1	4.0
Malta	6.5	6.4	6.6	5.6	5.7	5.9	6.0	5.9	6.3	6.1	6.0
Netherlands	5.5	5.7	5.5	5.0	5.2	4.9	4.5	4.5	4.4	4.3	4.6
Austria	4.9	4.9	4.9	4.3	4.5	4.6	4.7	4.8	4.5	4.3	4.2
Poland	5.4	5.7	5.5	5.1	5.0	5.1	5.0	5.4	5.9	6.5	6.8
Portugal	6.6	6.8	6.2	5.7	5.5	5.2	4.7	4.6	4.5	4.4	4.1
Romania	6.5	6.2	6.1	5.9	5.9	6.2	6.6	6.6	6.8	8.8	7.0
Slovenia	3.8	3.9	3.6	3.5	3.5	3.4	3.3	2.9	3.2	3.2	3.1
Slovakia	5.1	5.1	4.8	4.4	4.7	4.8	5.2	4.9	4.8	5.1	5.2
Finland	4.7	4.7	5.1	4.8	5.2	5.0	5.6	5.6	5.4	5.6	5.8
Sweden	3.6	4.0	4.5	4.0	4.3	4.4	4.8	4.9	5.0	5.2	5.5
United Kingdom	5.2	5.1	5.2	4.8	4.9	5.1	5.2	5.2	:	4.4	:
Croatia	5.4	5.3	4.9	5.0	5.1	5.0	5.1	5.0	5.0	5.2	5.3
FYR of Macedonia	7.0	7.0	7.0	:	7.2	7.1	6.9	7.1	7.3	7.6	7.2
Turkey	:	:	:	:	:	6.8	8.8	9.1	8.9	9.1	9.0
Iceland	5.6	5.6	6.3	5.2	5.8	5.3	5.2	5.4	5.5	5.5	5.1
Liechtenstein	:	:	7.2	6.0	5.2	4.4	4.8	5.4	4.3	5.2	5.8
Norway	5.3	5.3	5.7	5.1	5.3	4.9	4.1	4.8	4.7	5.0	5.3
Switzerland	5.4	5.7	5.5	5.0	5.5	5.5	5.3	5.4	5.3	5.3	5.4

(¹) Break in series, 2003.

Source: Eurostat (tps00012)

Table 2.16: Divorces
(per 1 000 population)

	1998	1999	2000	2001	2002	2003	2004	2005	2006	2007	2008
EU-27	1.8	1.8	1.8	1.9	1.9	2.0	2.0	2.0	:	:	:
Euro area	1.6	1.7	1.7	1.7	1.8	1.8	1.9	2.0	:	:	:
Belgium	2.6	2.6	2.6	2.8	3.0	3.0	3.0	2.9	2.8	2.8	2.8
Bulgaria	1.3	1.2	1.3	1.3	1.3	1.5	1.9	1.9	1.9	2.1	1.9
Czech Republic	3.1	2.3	2.9	3.1	3.1	3.8	3.2	3.1	3.1	3.0	3.0
Denmark	2.5	2.5	2.7	2.7	2.8	2.9	2.9	2.8	2.6	2.6	2.7
Germany	2.3	2.3	2.4	2.4	2.5	2.6	2.6	2.4	2.3	2.3	2.3
Estonia	3.2	3.3	3.1	3.2	3.0	2.9	3.1	3.0	2.8	2.8	2.6
Ireland	0.4	0.6	0.7	0.7	0.7	0.7	0.8	0.8	0.9	0.8	:
Greece	0.7	0.9	1.0	1.1	1.0	1.1	1.1	1.2	1.3	1.2	:
Spain	0.9	0.9	0.9	1.0	1.0	1.1	1.2	1.7	:	2.8	:
France	2.0	2.0	1.9	1.9	1.9	2.1	2.2	2.5	2.2	:	:
Italy	0.6	0.6	0.7	0.7	0.7	0.8	0.8	0.8	0.8	0.8	0.9
Cyprus	1.3	1.7	1.7	1.7	1.9	2.0	2.2	2.0	2.3	2.1	:
Latvia	2.6	2.5	2.6	2.4	2.5	2.1	2.3	2.8	3.2	3.3	2.7
Lithuania	3.3	3.2	3.1	3.2	3.0	3.1	3.2	3.3	3.3	3.4	3.1
Luxembourg	2.4	2.4	2.4	2.3	2.4	2.3	2.3	2.3	2.5	2.3	2.0
Hungary	2.5	2.5	2.3	2.4	2.5	2.5	2.4	2.5	2.5	2.5	2.5
Malta	-	-	-	-	-	-	-	-	-	-	-
Netherlands	2.1	2.1	2.2	2.3	2.1	1.9	1.9	2.0	1.9	2.0	2.0
Austria	2.2	2.3	2.4	2.6	2.4	2.3	2.4	2.4	2.5	2.5	:
Poland	1.2	1.1	1.1	1.2	1.2	1.3	1.5	1.8	1.9	1.7	1.7
Portugal	1.5	1.7	1.9	1.8	2.7	2.2	2.2	2.2	2.3	2.4	:
Romania	1.8	1.6	1.4	1.4	1.5	1.5	1.6	1.5	1.5	1.7	1.7
Slovenia	1.0	1.0	1.1	1.1	1.2	1.2	1.2	1.3	1.2	1.3	1.1
Slovakia	1.7	1.8	1.7	1.8	2.0	2.0	2.0	2.1	2.4	2.3	2.3
Finland	2.7	2.7	2.7	2.6	2.6	2.6	2.5	2.6	2.5	2.5	2.5
Sweden	2.3	2.4	2.4	2.4	2.4	2.4	2.2	2.2	2.2	2.3	2.3
United Kingdom	2.7	2.7	2.6	2.7	2.7	2.8	2.8	2.6	2.4	2.4	:
Croatia	0.9	0.8	1.0	1.1	1.0	1.1	1.1	1.1	1.1	1.1	1.1
FYR of Macedonia	0.5	0.5	0.7	0.7	0.6	0.7	0.8	0.8	0.7	0.7	0.6
Turkey	:	:	:	:	:	0.7	1.3	1.3	1.3	1.3	1.4
Iceland	1.8	1.7	1.9	1.9	1.8	1.8	1.9	1.9	1.6	1.7	1.7
Liechtenstein	:	:	3.9	2.5	2.9	2.5	2.9	2.7	2.3	2.8	2.8
Norway	2.1	2.0	2.2	2.3	2.3	2.4	2.4	2.4	2.3	2.2	2.1
Switzerland	2.5	2.9	1.5	2.2	2.2	2.3	2.4	2.9	2.8	2.6	2.6

Source: Eurostat (tps00013)

2.5 Life expectancy

Introduction

One of the contributing factors to the ageing of the EU's population is the gradual increase in life expectancy. This may, at least in part, be attributed to higher standards of living, advances in medicine, better healthcare, as well as more general awareness of health issues.

Gender differences in life expectancy were, in the 1960s, associated with much higher mortality rates for men than for women. In the 1980s the gender gap closed in north western Europe, followed by southern Europe in the 1990s. The difference between life expectancies of men and women has further narrowed in recent years, as the speed at which female life expectancy rises has slowed. The convergence may also be a consequence of men and women leading more similar lifestyles – as considerably fewer men work in areas where high degrees of physical effort are required throughout the working day (such as agriculture, mining, or the manufacture of iron and steel).

Policymakers are increasingly considering the personal and social benefits that the increased longevity of the European population may bring. So-called health expectancy indicators extend the concept of life expectancy through the use of morbidity and disability statistics, in order to assess the quality of life. These composite indicators measure the number of remaining years that a person of a specific age is expected to live in a healthy condition – for more information, see the start of Chapter 3. From a policy perspective,

if people live longer free from disability and disease, then they could potentially continue to be active, as part of the workforce or contributing in some other way to social or community projects. On the other hand, an elderly population that is characterised by disability and disease is likely to require additional healthcare and social services.

Definitions and data availability

Statistics on life expectancy at birth refer to the mean number of years that a newborn child can expect to live if subjected throughout his/her life to current mortality conditions. A similar indicator can be analysed for persons aged 65, reflecting the mean number of years still to be lived by these persons (following current mortality conditions).

Life expectancy increases as people age, as a result of surviving and/or avoiding potential causes of death (for example, infectious diseases when young, smoking-related illness, car or occupational accidents).

Main findings

EU-27 life expectancy of a boy at birth was 75.8 years in 2006, while the life expectancy of a newborn girl was just over six years higher at 82.0 years. Although many Europeans enjoy a longer and healthier life than previous generations, major inequalities still exist between countries and regions; for example, life expectancy at birth for men varied by 14.2 years between Member States in 2007, while the

corresponding figure among women was 8.3 years. The lowest male life expectancy was recorded in Lithuania (64.9 years) and the highest in Sweden (79.0 years), while for women, the range varied between a low of 76.5 years in Latvia and a high of 84.8 years in France.

As people live longer there has been a growing interest in the older generations: firstly, in terms of their potential for filling shortages in labour markets, and secondly, from the perspective of a growing consumer segment (as it is likely that a range of new goods and services will be required to cater, in particular, for the very old); as such, a relatively healthy ageing population could provide a stimulus for economic growth. The life expectancy of persons aged 65 in the EU-27 shows that the average man could expect to live an additional 16.8 years in 2006, while the corresponding figure for women was 20.4 years. Life expectancy among men aged 65 varied by 5.6 years across Member States in 2007, from a high of 18.4 years in France to a low of 12.8 years in Latvia. The range for women was slightly greater at 6.6 years, from 23.0 years in France to 16.4 years in Bulgaria.

Figure 2.17: Life expectancy at birth, 2007 (¹)
(years)

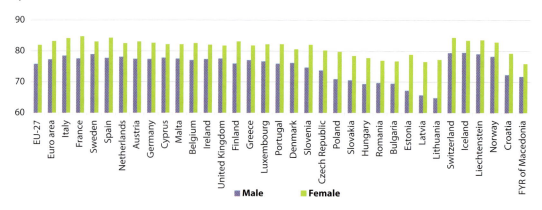

(¹) EU-27, euro area and Italy, 2006; the figure is ranked on the average of male and female.

Source: Eurostat (tps00025)

Table 2.17: Life expectancy at birth
(years)

	Male						Female					
	1997	1999	2001	2003	2005	2007	1997	1999	2001	2003	2005	2007
EU-27	:	:	:	74.6	75.4	:	:	:	:	80.8	81.5	:
Euro area	74.6	75.0	75.7	75.9	76.8	:	81.3	81.6	82.1	82.0	82.7	:
Belgium	74.2	74.4	75.0	75.3	76.2	77.1	80.7	81.0	81.2	81.1	81.9	82.6
Bulgaria	67.0	68.3	68.6	68.9	69.0	69.5	73.8	75.0	75.4	75.9	76.2	76.7
Czech Republic	70.5	71.5	72.1	72.0	72.9	73.8	77.6	78.3	78.6	78.6	79.3	80.2
Denmark	73.6	74.2	74.7	75.0	76.0	76.2	78.6	79.0	79.3	79.8	80.5	80.6
Germany	74.1	74.8	75.6	75.8	76.7	77.4	80.5	81.0	81.5	81.3	82.0	82.7
Estonia	64.2	64.7	64.8	66.1	67.3	67.2	75.9	76.0	76.4	77.1	78.1	78.8
Ireland	73.4	73.4	74.5	75.9	77.3	77.4	78.7	78.9	79.9	80.8	81.8	82.1
Greece	75.4	75.5	76.0	76.5	76.8	77.1	80.4	80.5	81.0	81.2	81.6	81.8
Spain	75.2	75.3	76.2	76.3	77.0	77.8	82.3	82.4	83.2	83.0	83.7	84.3
France	:	75.0	75.5	75.8	76.8	77.6	:	82.7	83.0	82.7	83.7	84.8
Italy	75.8	76.5	77.1	77.1	78.0	:	82.0	82.6	83.1	82.8	83.6	:
Cyprus	74.9	76.0	76.6	76.9	76.8	77.8	80.0	79.9	81.4	81.3	80.9	82.2
Latvia	:	:	:	65.6	65.4	65.8	:	:	:	75.9	76.5	76.5
Lithuania	65.5	66.3	65.9	66.4	65.3	64.9	76.6	77.0	77.6	77.8	77.3	77.2
Luxembourg	74.0	74.4	75.1	74.8	76.7	76.7	80.0	81.4	80.7	80.9	82.3	82.2
Hungary	66.7	66.7	68.2	68.4	68.7	69.4	75.5	75.6	76.7	76.7	77.2	77.8
Malta	75.2	75.3	76.6	76.4	77.3	77.5	80.1	79.4	81.2	80.8	81.4	82.2
Netherlands	75.2	75.4	75.8	76.3	77.3	78.1	80.7	80.5	80.8	81.0	81.7	82.5
Austria	74.1	74.9	75.7	75.9	76.7	77.5	80.7	81.0	81.7	81.5	82.3	83.1
Poland	68.5	68.8	70.0	70.5	70.8	71.0	77.0	77.5	78.4	78.8	79.3	79.8
Portugal	72.2	72.6	73.5	74.2	74.9	75.9	79.3	79.7	80.5	80.6	81.3	82.2
Romania	65.2	67.1	67.5	67.7	68.7	69.7	73.3	74.2	74.9	75.0	75.7	76.9
Slovenia	71.1	71.8	72.3	72.5	73.9	74.7	79.1	79.5	80.4	80.3	80.9	82.0
Slovakia	68.9	69.0	69.5	69.8	70.2	70.6	76.9	77.4	77.7	77.7	78.1	78.4
Finland	73.5	73.8	74.6	75.2	75.6	76.0	80.7	81.2	81.7	81.9	82.5	83.1
Sweden	76.8	77.1	77.6	78.0	78.5	79.0	82.0	82.0	82.2	82.5	82.9	83.1
United Kingdom	74.7	75.0	75.8	76.2	77.1	77.6	79.7	79.9	80.5	80.5	81.2	81.8
Croatia	:	:	:	71.1	71.8	72.3	:	:	:	78.2	78.8	79.3
FYR of Macedonia	70.3	70.4	70.9	70.9	71.6	71.8	74.7	75.3	76.1	75.7	75.9	75.9
Iceland	76.3	77.4	78.3	79.5	79.6	79.6	81.6	81.4	83.2	82.5	83.5	83.4
Liechtenstein	71.9	75.5	76.3	78.4	77.4	79.1	80.4	82.9	82.5	81.6	84.1	83.6
Norway	75.5	75.6	76.2	77.1	77.8	78.3	81.1	81.2	81.7	82.1	82.7	82.9
Switzerland	76.3	76.9	77.5	78.0	78.7	79.5	82.2	82.7	83.2	83.2	84.0	84.4

Source: Eurostat (tps00025)

Figure 2.18: Life expectancy at age 65, 2007 (¹)
(years)

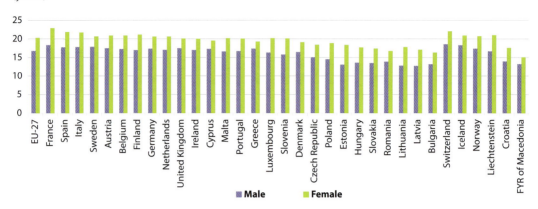

(¹) EU-27 and Italy, 2006; the figure is ranked on the average of male and female.

Source: Eurostat (tsdde210)

2.6 Citizenship and migration

Introduction

EU citizens can decide freely upon where in the European Union they live, work or retire. The Maastricht Treaty states, '*every person holding the nationality of a Member State of the European Union is, as a result, a citizen of the Union. Citizenship of the Union supplements national citizenship without replacing it. It is made up of a set of fundamental rights and obligations enshrined in the EC Treaty among which it is worth underlining the right not to be discriminated on the basis of the nationality'.*

Member States differ with regard to policies on the migration and residence of third-country nationals (persons who

are not EU citizens). Similarly, national policies differ concerning the granting of citizenship to resident foreign nationals. A European Commission Communication (⁶) in 2007 laid the foundations for a common policy on immigration.

Some of the most important legal texts adopted in this area include:

- Council Directive 2003/86/EC on the right to family reunification (⁷);
- Council Directive 2003/109/EC on a long-term resident status for third-country nationals (⁸);
- Council Directive 2004/1 14/EC on the admission of students (⁹);

(⁶) 'Towards a common immigration policy'; COM(2007) 780; for more information: http://eur-lex.europa.eu/LexUriServ/LexUriServ.do?uri=COM:2007:0780:FIN:EN:PDF. Note this does not fully apply throughout the EU: Denmark has an opt-out regarding Title IV of the Treaty establishing the European Community, while Ireland and the United Kingdom both decide upon their involvement on a case-by-case basis (possibility to opt-out or opt-in).

(⁷) For more information: http://eur-lex.europa.eu/LexUriServ/site/en/oj/2003/l_251/l_25120031003en00120018.pdf.

(⁸) For more information: http://eur-lex.europa.eu/LexUriServ/site/en/oj/2004/l_016/l_01620040123en00440053.pdf.

(⁹) For more information: http://eur-lex.europa.eu/LexUriServ/site/en/oj/2004/l_375/l_37520041223en00120018.pdf.

- Council Directive 2005/71/EC for the facilitation of the admission of researchers into the EU ([10]), and;
- Council Directive 2009/50/EC on the conditions of entry and residence for the purposes of highly qualified employment ([11]).

The 'Stockholm programme', adopted by Member State governments at the December 2009 European Council, sets a framework and series of principles for the on-going development of European policies on justice and home affairs for the period 2010-2014. Migration-related issues are a central part of this programme, which can be seen as a continuation of the efforts that have been made since the Amsterdam Treaty came into force in 1999. European policies on migration and asylum have evolved through the implementation of the Tampere programme (1999-2004) and the Hague programme (2004-2009).

The European Commission re-launched in 2005 a debate on the need for a common set of rules for the admission of economic migrants with a Green Paper on an EU approach to managing economic migration ([12]), which led to the adoption of a 'policy plan on legal migration' at the end of 2005 ([13]). In July 2006 the European Commission adopted a Communication on policy priorities in the fight against illegal immigration of third-country nationals ([14]) which aims to strike a balance between security and basic rights of individuals during all stages of the illegal immigration process. In June 2007, Council conclusions on the strengthening of integration policies in the EU by promoting unity in diversity were adopted, while in September 2007, the European Commission presented its third annual report on migration and integration ([15]).

The EU-27's population grew by 2.1 million inhabitants in 2008, with the majority of this increase – more than seven out of ten persons (72 %) – composed of migrants; the remaining population growth resulted from natural increase as births exceeded deaths (see Subchapter 2.3 for more details relating to population change). These net migration figures include flows between Member States (an increasing phenomenon, as the freedom of movement for workers is secured across the Single Market), as well as migrants from non-member countries.

Migratory flows can result from a range of economic, social or political factors, such as the search for work, family reunification, or flight from persecution (see Subchapter 2.7 for more details relating to asylum). These factors may occur in a migrant's country of origin (push factors) or in the country of destination (pull factors). Some 21 Member States reported a net inflow of migrants in 2008; this may be due to the relative economic prosperity and political stability of most Member States (thought to exert a considerable pull effect). From the perspective of the destination country, migrant flows can be seen as an instrument to resolve labour market shortages; however, most commentators agree that it is unlikely that

([10]) For more information: http://eur-lex.europa.eu/LexUriServ/site/en/oj/2005/l_289/l_28920051103en00150022.pdf.

([11]) For more information: http://eur-lex.europa.eu/LexUriServ/LexUriServ.do?uri=OJ:L:2009:155:0017:0029:EN:PDF.

([12]) COM(2004) 811; for more information: http://ec.europa.eu/justice_home/doc_centre/immigration/work/doc/com_2004_811_en.pdf.

([13]) COM(2005) 669; for more information: http://eur-lex.europa.eu/LexUriServ/site/en/com/2005/com2005_0669en01.pdf.

([14]) COM(2006) 402; for more information: http://eur-lex.europa.eu/LexUriServ/site/en/com/2006/com2006_0402en01.pdf.

([15]) COM(2007) 512; for more information: http://ec.europa.eu/justice_home/fsj/immigration/docs/com_2007_512_en.pdf.

migration alone will be enough to reverse the on-going trend of population ageing within Europe.

There are a range of economic benefits that may potentially occur as a result of the inflow of immigrant workers. Within the context of the labour market, these include alleviating labour shortages or broadening the skills base. More generally, immigrants in work are likely to contribute to overall economic development, for example, through paying taxes, financing pension schemes, consuming local goods and services, or establishing themselves as entrepreneurs. Policies relating to legal immigration of non-EU citizens increasingly underline the need to match immigrant profiles with labour market opportunities. Immigration policies relating to non-EU citizens may be based on a range of criteria: for example, language proficiency, work experience, education, age, or alternatively the selection task may be carried out directly by employers (ensuring that immigrants have a job upon their arrival in the EU). Policymakers are increasingly addressing the issue of 'brain waste', whereby immigrants are employed in jobs for which they are over-qualified.

Another way that governments assess the impact of their immigration policies is with respect to the economic development of third countries. Immigration can potentially result in a 'brain drain' from the country of origin, where a loss of talent could slow the potential for economic development. One way of addressing this issue is to encourage what has become known as 'circular migration', systems that help migrants move more easily back-

wards and forwards between their country of origin and foreign place of work. By doing so, it is hoped that the temporary or permanent return of migrant workers can result in a 'brain gain', as migrants transfer the skills they have acquired abroad back to their local communities.

Besides policies to encourage labour recruitment, immigration policy is often focused on two other areas:

- preventing unauthorised migration ([16]) and the illegal employment of migrants who are not permitted to work;
- promoting the integration of immigrants into society.

Significant resources have been mobilised in relation to the prevention and reduction of illegal immigration (people smuggling, trafficking networks, as well as illegal employment). At the end of 2010 a new set of rules will come into force concerning migrant removal and return, covering areas such as expulsion measures, detention, appeal procedures and the treatment of vulnerable people. As such, the EU aims to 'promote a dynamic and fair immigration policy, with a flexible admission system', such that the positive effects of legal immigration can be shared between host countries, employers, migrants and countries of origin alike.

When migrants fail to integrate into society there may well be socio-economic costs, as witnessed through lower employment rates (especially for women), higher exposure to undeclared work, or higher youth unemployment rates and lower educational attainment for the children of migrants.

([16]) Directive 2008/115/EC of the European Parliament and of the Council of 16 December 2008 on common standards and procedures in Member States for returning illegally staying third-country nationals. For more information: http://eur-lex.europa.eu/LexUriServ/LexUriServ.do?uri=OJ:L:2008:348:0098:0107:EN:PDF.

Definitions and data availability

Eurostat produces statistics on a range of issues related to international migration and citizenship, including the flows of immigrants and emigrants, population stocks broken down by country of citizenship or country of birth, and information relating to the acquisition of citizenship.

Data are supplied on an annual basis by national statistical institutes. Whereas some Member States base their migration flow and migrant population stock statistics on population registers or registers of resident foreign citizens, others may use sample surveys or data extracted from administrative systems such as the issuing of residence permits.

A **national citizen** is defined as a person who is a citizen of the country in which they are usually resident. **Non-nationals (foreigners)** are persons who are not citizens of the country in which they are usually resident. The statistics collected by Eurostat allow the population of foreigners to be broken down into those who are citizens of other Member States and those who are citizens of non-member countries.

The **acquisition of citizenship** is sometimes viewed as an indicator for the formal integration of migrants into their host country. The granting of citizenship usually requires a period of legal residence, together with other factors (for example, language proficiency). Citizenship may be granted to persons who have previously been citizens of another country, or to persons who have been stateless.

Immigrants are those persons arriving or returning from abroad to take-up residence in a country for a certain period, having previously been resident elsewhere. **Emigrants** are people leaving their country of usual residence and effectively taking-up residence in another country. As with the statistics on citizenship, it is possible to break down the information on migrant flows into those concerning nationals, those from other Member States, and those from non-member countries.

In the summer of 2007, a Regulation on Community statistics on migration and international protection was adopted by the European Parliament and the Council ([17]); the Regulation also repealed a previous Council Regulation ((EEC) No 311/76) relating to the compilation of statistics on foreign workers. The focus of the Regulation is to provide harmonised statistical definitions based on existing international standards (in particular, UN recommendations for migration statistics) and European legislation relating to immigration, asylum and border control issues. Although these definitions must be applied, Member States remain free to use any appropriate data sources, according to national availability and practice. The Regulation specifies the collection of statistics relating to international migration flows, foreign population stocks, the acquisition of citizenship, asylum applications and decisions, measures taken against illegal entry and stay, returns of unauthorised migrants, and residence permits issued to third-country citizens.

A further aspect of the Regulation is that most of the statistics to be collected will include a disaggregation by age and gender. This is of particular interest when trying to monitor policies aimed at preventing the trafficking of women and/or children.

([17]) Regulation (EC) No 862/2007 of the European Parliament and of the Council of 11 July 2007; for more information: http://eur-lex.europa.eu/LexUriServ/site/en/oj/2007/l_199/l_19920070731en00230029.pdf.

The first data collected under this Regulation on international migration flows, foreign population stocks, the acquisition of citizenship, measures against illegal entry and stay, returns of unauthorised migrants, and residence permits issued to third-country citizens will be published in 2010. The asylum applications and decisions data covered by the Regulation are already published.

Main findings

The population of the EU-27 was 497.4 million persons in 2008; of these, the vast majority (93.8 %) were national citizens. The 30.8 million foreigners living in the EU accounted for 6.2 % of the total population: almost two thirds (63.3 % or 19.5 million) of these were citizens from a non-member country, while just over one third (36.7 % or 11.3 million) were citizens of another Member State. In addition, a European Commission Communication (COM(2009) 262 final) cites an estimate of about eight million illegal immigrants living in the EU.

When compounded over a number of years, trends in immigration can have a considerable influence on the citizenship structure of populations. For example, in those Member States that are characterised by a long-standing period of net migration (more immigrants than emigrants), the foreign population can be considerable. However, migrants that integrate into local communities often have the possibility to acquire the citizenship of their host country (although rules differ between the Member States); if this occurs then the relative importance of national citizens can

increase. Available data suggest that more than 700 000 persons acquired the citizenship of one of the Member States in 2007, with new citizens in the United Kingdom, France and Germany totalling 410 000.

In absolute terms, the largest numbers of foreign citizens in 2008 resided in Germany (7.3 million), Spain (5.3 million), the United Kingdom (4.0 million), France (3.7 million) and Italy (3.4 million) – together these five countries accounted for more than three quarters of all foreign citizens in the EU, and they were the only Member States where the number of foreign citizens stood above one million.

In relative terms, the foreign populations of the Member States varied from less than 1 % of the total population in Romania, Poland, Bulgaria and Slovakia to 42.6 % in Luxembourg in 2008. The proportion of non-nationals in the total population was also higher than one in ten in Austria (10.3 %), Spain (11.6 %), Ireland (12.6 %), Cyprus (15.9 %), Estonia (17.1 %) and Latvia (18.3 %). Note that for the latter two countries, the figures include persons who have been resident in the country since before the break-up of the Soviet Union but have not acquired host country citizenship.

The most significant numbers of third-country nationals residing in the EU are citizens of Turkey, Morocco, Albania and China. Citizenship structures of foreign populations vary considerably across Member States; reflecting – among others – geographical proximity, recent political developments, historical ties, or a common language.

In most of the Member States, non-EU citizens formed the majority of the foreign population in 2008. In the Baltic Member States and in Slovenia, upwards of nine out of every ten foreigners were citizens from non-member countries. In contrast, the number of citizens from other Member States exceeded the number of non-EU citizens in Belgium, Ireland, Cyprus, Luxembourg, Hungary, Malta and Slovakia. This trend peaked in Luxembourg, where 86 % of the foreign population was a citizen of another Member State.

Net migration for the EU-27 peaked at 2.1 million in 2007. Although data coverage is only partial (with notably some information missing for France and Greece), more than 1.8 million persons emigrated from the EU Member States in 2007. By far the highest number of emigrants left Germany (637 000), which alone accounted for more emigrants than Spain and the United Kingdom together. Based on information that is available for 21 of the Member States, 36 % of the emigrants leaving a Member State in 2007 were citizens of a non-member country, while the same proportion were nationals leaving their own Member State, such that citizens from other EU Member States made up the remaining 28 %.

More than 3 million immigrants arrived in the Member States in 2007, with more than 2 million arriving in Spain, Germany and the United Kingdom combined. Among the 22 Member States for which data are available, some 48 % of immigrants were citizens of a non-member country, while 40 % were citizens of another EU Member State, and 12 % were nationals returning to their Member State of citizenship. Note this does not imply that all immigrants with non-EU citizenship were new arrivals in the EU, as the figures include non-EU citizens moving between Member States. Returning nationals accounted for the highest proportion of immigrants in Bulgaria, Denmark, Estonia, Lithuania and Poland (permanent stays only) in 2007. In Belgium, Germany, Ireland, Latvia, Luxembourg, Malta, the Netherlands, Austria and Slovakia, the highest proportion of immigrants were citizens from other EU Member States, while in the remaining Member States, non-EU citizens accounted for the largest share of immigrants.

In most of the Member States for which data are available for 2007, the majority of immigrants were relatively young (within the working age range of 15 to 39 years). Indeed, this age group accounted for more than seven out of ten immigrants in Denmark and the Czech Republic. Bulgaria, Latvia and Greece were the only Member States where the 15-39 year old age group did not account for at least 50 % of all immigrants.

Table 2.18: Population by group of citizenship, 1 January 2008; acquisition of citizenship, 2007 (persons)

	Nationals (¹)	Foreigners (¹)	of which: Other EU-27 countries	of which: Non EU-27 countries	Acquisition of citizenship (²)
EU-27	*466 652 667*	*30 778 489*	*11 302 401*	*19 476 088*	:
Belgium	9 695 418	971 448	659 423	312 025	36 063
Bulgaria	7 615 836	24 402	3 608	20 794	5 966
Czech Republic	10 033 481	347 649	131 516	216 133	2 371
Denmark	5 177 301	298 450	93 166	205 284	3 648
Germany	74 962 442	7 255 395	2 515 508	4 739 887	113 030
Estonia	*1 111 600*	*229 300*	*8 300*	*221 000*	4 242
Ireland	3 847 645	553 690	392 068	161 622	4 649
Greece	*10 307 400*	*906 400*	*158 300*	*748 100*	3 921
Spain	40 021 164	5 262 095	2 112 623	3 149 472	71 936
France	*60 079 000*	*3 674 000*	*1 283 000*	*2 391 000*	132 002
Italy	56 186 639	3 432 651	934 435	2 498 216	35 266
Cyprus	*664 000*	*125 300*	*81 300*	*44 000*	2 780
Latvia	1 855 401	415 493	7 933	407 560	8 322
Lithuania	3 323 423	42 934	2 669	40 265	371
Luxembourg	277 910	205 889	177 018	28 871	1 236
Hungary	9 868 821	176 580	100 806	75 774	*8 442*
Malta	394 830	15 460	8 188	7 272	553
Netherlands	15 717 024	688 375	262 964	425 411	30 653
Austria	7 483 410	835 182	289 742	545 440	14 010
Poland	38 057 799	57 842	25 032	32 810	1 542
Portugal	10 171 242	446 333	115 832	330 501	3 627
Romania	21 502 527	26 100	5 971	20 129	*31*
Slovenia	1 957 245	68 621	4 112	64 509	1 551
Slovakia	5 360 094	40 904	25 909	14 995	1 478
Finland	5 167 776	132 708	47 193	85 515	4 824
Sweden	8 658 439	524 488	240 985	283 503	33 629
United Kingdom	*57 154 800*	*4 020 800*	*1 614 800*	*2 406 000*	*164 540*
Croatia	*4 399 300*	*37 100*	*7 800*	*29 300*	13 240
FYR of Macedonia	:	:	:	:	1 713
Turkey	72 228 000	292 000	:	:	4 807
Iceland	286 113	13 778	8 061	5 717	647
Norway	4 470 911	266 260	137 891	128 369	14 877
Switzerland	5 991 401	1 602 093	968 270	633 823	43 889

(¹) Turkey and Iceland, 2006.
(²) Italy and Portugal, 2006.

Source: Eurostat (migr_st_popctz and tps00024)

Table 2.19: Emigration by group of citizenship, 2007
(persons)

	Nationals	Foreigners (¹)	of which:	
			Other EU-27 countries	Non EU-27 countries
Belgium	45 615	45 437	19 849	25 588
Bulgaria	2 923	35	6	29
Czech Republic	2 076	18 424	2 221	16 203
Denmark	23 771	17 795	8 708	9 087
Germany	161 105	475 749	278 428	197 321
Estonia	3 940	444	123	321
Ireland	:	:	:	:
Greece	:	:	:	:
Spain	28 091	198 974	23 383	175 591
France	:	:	:	:
Italy	:	11 940	:	:
Cyprus	816	10 573	1 594	8 979
Latvia	1 881	2 302	165	2 137
Lithuania	11 422	2 431	476	1 955
Luxembourg	2 033	8 641	7 506	1 135
Hungary	367	4 133	3 037	1 096
Malta	1 350	3 679	3 129	550
Netherlands	62 250	29 037	15 199	13 838
Austria	19 324	52 604	26 623	25 981
Poland	35 301	179	90	89
Portugal	:	:	:	:
Romania	8 830	0	:	:
Slovenia	3 178	11 765	1 516	10 249
Slovakia	1 574	1 996	956	1 040
Finland	9 330	3 113	1 866	1 247
Sweden	24 990	20 428	10 607	9 821
United Kingdom	159 339	158 247	64 958	93 289
Croatia	8 084	273	33	240
FYR of Macedonia	224	16	7	9
Norway	8 798	13 324	8 466	4 858
Switzerland	29 487	60 688	40 986	19 702

(¹) Italy, 2005.

Source: Eurostat (migr_emictz)

Table 2.20: Immigration by group of citizenship, 2007
(persons)

| | Nationals | Foreigners (¹) | of which: | |
			Other EU-27 countries	Non EU-27 countries
Belgium	36 483	109 926	58 025	51 901
Bulgaria	1 498	60	6	54
Czech Republic	1 934	102 511	23 026	79 485
Denmark	22 033	42 623	21 381	21 242
Germany	106 014	574 752	343 851	230 901
Estonia	1 789	1 952	1 089	863
Ireland	17 136	71 643	52 259	19 384
Greece	:	133 185	:	:
Spain	37 732	920 534	389 203	531 331
France	:	182 390	:	:
Italy	:	267 634	:	:
Cyprus	953	18 064	8 680	9 384
Latvia	986	2 555	1 642	913
Lithuania	6 141	2 468	315	2 153
Luxembourg	909	15 766	12 859	2 907
Hungary	1 754	22 607	9 059	13 548
Malta	1 1/1	5 559	3 767	1 792
Netherlands	36 561	80 258	43 228	37 030
Austria	14 911	91 748	52 251	39 497
Poland	13 384	1 611	196	1 415
Portugal	:	27 703	:	:
Romania	:	9 575	:	:
Slovenia	1 689	27 504	2 646	24 858
Slovakia	1 417	14 848	9 183	5 665
Finland	8 525	17 504	6 803	10 701
Sweden	15 949	83 536	31 352	52 184
United Kingdom	71 424	455 290	171 863	283 427
Croatia	13 704	915	251	664
FYR of Macedonia	366	954	147	807
Turkey	:	178 964	:	:
Iceland	3 130	7 304	6 224	1 080
Norway	8 276	53 498	33 426	20 072
Switzerland	21 779	143 855	99 054	44 801

(¹) France and Portugal, 2006; Italy and Turkey, 2005.

Source: Eurostat (migr_immictz)

Figure 2.19: Immigration by broad group of citizenship, 2007 (¹)
(% of total immigrants)

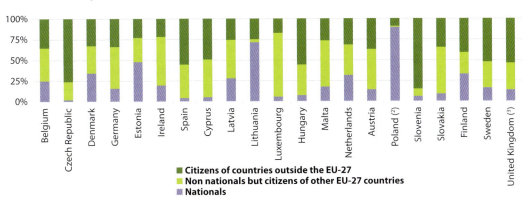

(¹) Bulgaria, Greece, France, Italy, Portugal and Romania, not available.
(²) Immigrants for permanent stay only.
(³) Excluding immigrants from Ireland, whatever their citizenship.

Source: Eurostat (migr_immictz)

Figure 2.20: Immigration by age, 2007 (¹)
(%)

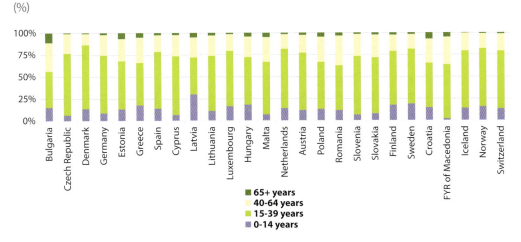

(¹) Belgium, Ireland, France, Italy, Portugal and the United Kingdom, not available.

Source: Eurostat (migr_immictz)

2.7 Asylum

Introduction

The 1951 Geneva Convention relating to the status of refugees (as amended by the 1967 New York Protocol) has for almost 60 years defined who is a refugee, and laid down a common approach towards refugees that has been one of the cornerstones for the development of a common asylum system within the EU.

Asylum is a form of protection given by a state on its territory. It is granted to a person who is unable to seek protection in his/her country of citizenship and/or residence, in particular for fear of being persecuted for reasons of race, religion, nationality, membership of a particular social group, or political opinion.

Since 1999, the EU has worked towards creating a common European asylum system (CEAS) in accordance with the Geneva Convention and other applicable international instruments. A number of Directives in this area were developed during the first phase of the CAES, the four main legal instruments on asylum including:

- the Reception Conditions Directive ([18]);
- the Asylum Procedures Directive ([19]);
- the Qualification Directive ([20]), and;
- the Dublin Regulation ([21]).

The Hague programme, adopted by heads of state and government in November 2004, took forward the idea of further developing the CAES by calling for a second phase, which would lead, among others, to common procedures and a uniform status for those granted asylum or subsidiary protection. The European Commission presented its ideas on how the second phase of the CEAS should be developed in a policy plan on asylum ([22]) adopted in 2008, proposing to move forward through further harmonisation of legislation, increasing practical cooperation, and fostering solidarity (both within the EU and between the EU and third countries).

The ideas presented by the European Commission in the policy plan on asylum led to a number of concrete proposals, presented between November 2008 and October 2009, namely:

- amendments to the Reception Conditions, Asylum Procedures and Qualification Directives;
- amendments to the Dublin Regulation;
- the establishment of a European asylum support office to support practical cooperation, and;
- the establishment of a joint European resettlement scheme to support third countries hosting large refugee populations.

([18]) Council Directive 2003/9/EC of 27 January 2003; for more information:
http://eur-lex.europa.eu/LexUriServ/site/en/oj/2003/l_031/l_03120030206en00180025.pdf.

([19]) Council Directive 2005/85/EC of 1 December 2005; for more information:
http://eur-lex.europa.eu/LexUriServ/site/en/oj/2005/l_326/l32620051213en00130034.pdf.

([20]) Council Directive 2004/83/EC of 29 April 2004 on minimum standards for the qualification and status of third country nationals or stateless persons as refugees or as persons who otherwise need international protection and the content of the protection granted; for more information: http://eur-lex.europa.eu/LexUriServ/LexUriServ.do?uri=CELEX:32004L0083:EN:HTML.

([21]) Council Regulation (EC) No 343/2003 of 18 February 2003 establishing the criteria and mechanisms for determining the Member State responsible for examining an asylum application lodged in one of the Member States by a third-country national; for more information: http://eur-lex.europa.eu/LexUriServ/site/en/oj/2003/l050/l_05020030225en00010010.pdf.

([22]) COM(2008) 360; for more information: http://eur-lex.europa.eu/LexUriServ/LexUriServ.do?uri=COM:2008:0360:FIN:EN:PDF.

Definitions and data availability

The Hague programme called for an improvement in practical cooperation and the exchange of information on migration and asylum issues. On 11 July 2007, a Regulation of the European Parliament and of the Council on Community statistics on migration and international protection was adopted. As a result, statistics on asylum applications and the subsequent decisions to grant or refuse refugee status or other types of international protection have recently been adapted. For example, asylum applications statistics are now available with a monthly frequency, in order to allow a continuous monitoring of short-term variations in the origin and numbers of asylum-seekers.

Asylum applications refer to all persons who apply on an individual basis for asylum or similar protection, irrespective of whether they lodge their application on arrival or from inside the country, and irrespective of whether they entered the country legally or illegally. **An asylum applicant** is a person who has requested protection under: either Article 1 of the Geneva Convention relating to the status of refugees of 28 July 1951, as amended by the New York Protocol of 31 January 1967; or within the remit of the United Nations convention against torture and other forms of cruel or inhuman treatment (UNCAT); or the European convention on human rights; or other relevant instruments of protection. An **asylum-seeker** is an asylum applicant awaiting a decision on an application for refugee status or another form of international protection. A **refugee** is a person with a well-founded

fear of being persecuted for reasons of race, religion, nationality, membership of a particular social group or political opinion (according to Article 1 of the 1951 Convention). It should be noted that some asylum applicants may remain in a country on a temporary or permanent basis even if they are not deemed to be refugees under the 1951 Convention definition – for example, asylum applicants may be granted subsidiary protection or humanitarian protection statuses.

Main findings

There are two different categories of person which should be taken into account when analysing asylum statistics. The first includes asylum-seekers who have lodged a claim and whose claim is under consideration by a relevant authority ('asylum applications'); those who have made an application may generally remain within the territory of the Member State concerned during consideration of their claim. The second is composed of persons who have been recognised, after consideration, as refugees or have been granted another kind of international protection ('positive decisions').

In recent years there has been a sharp decrease in the number of asylum-seekers. Having peaked in 1992 (670 000 applications in the EU-15) and again in 2001 (424 500 applications in the EU-27), there were an estimated 222 600 asylum applications received in the EU-27 in 2007. This figure did, nevertheless, constitute an increase of 25 000 when compared with the year before, in part due to an increased number of applications from Iraq.

Numbers of asylum applications and their relative importance (for example, as a percentage of the total population) vary considerably between Member States. The highest number of applications for asylum in 2007 was lodged in Sweden, with France, the United Kingdom, Greece and Germany being the other main recipients of applications. The rapid increase in applications made to Greece in recent years results from its geographical location in the south east of Europe: hence, it is frequently seen as a gateway to Europe for persons fleeing conflict in Iraq or Afghanistan. The high number of applications in Sweden was also closely linked to the Iraq conflict, as Iraqis made up the second largest group of non-nationals in Sweden – 7.6 % of the population of foreigners in 2008 – which was higher than the share recorded for either Norway or Denmark, and only less than that for Finland.

In 2006, almost a quarter (23.2 %) of EU-27 asylum decisions resulted in the granting of refugee status or subsidiary protection, while more than half (57.8 %) of all decisions resulted in a rejection. In absolute numbers, just over 55 000 persons were granted refugee status or subsidiary protection in the EU-27 in 2006; equivalent to 0.01 % of the total population.

There remains a wide diversity in the handling of asylum applications between Member States, as more than half of the decisions made in 2007 in Latvia, Luxembourg, Denmark, Italy (2006) and Malta were positive, while Sweden (48.2 %) also recorded a relatively high proportion of positive decisions. In contrast, less than one in ten decisions were positive in Ireland, Hungary, Spain, Slovakia, Cyprus, Slovenia and Greece – where the lowest positive acceptance rate was recorded (0.8 %).

In absolute terms, the highest number of positive asylum decisions in 2007 was recorded in Sweden (15 640), which was almost double the number for Germany (7 870). The United Kingdom (6 805), Italy (5 215 in 2006) and Austria (5 195) recorded the next highest number of positive decisions, while the Netherlands (2006), France, Poland and Belgium (2006) were the only other countries where more than a thousand positive decisions were made during the course of 2007.

Positive asylum applications in 2007 in Sweden represented 0.17 % of the total population in 2007, with Malta (0.15 %) and Luxembourg (0.11 %) the only other Member States to report shares above 0.1 %. Positive asylum decisions accounted for less than 0.001 % of the population in Romania, Spain, Slovenia, Latvia, Estonia and Portugal in 2007; note this could be a reflection of a low number of applications, rather than a relatively low positive acceptance rate.

Table 2.21: Asylum applications
(persons)

	1997	1998	1999	2000	2001	2002	2003	2004	2005	2006	2007
EU-27	:	313 645	380 450	406 585	424 180	421 470	344 800	276 675	234 675	197 410	222 635
Belgium	11 790	21 965	35 780	42 690	24 505	18 800	13 585	12 400	12 575	8 870	11 575
Bulgaria	370	835	1 350	1 755	2 430	2 890	1 320	985	700	500	815
Czech Republic	2 110	4 085	7 355	8 790	18 095	8 485	11 400	5 300	3 590	2 730	1 585
Denmark	5 100	5 700	6 530	10 345	12 510	5 945	4 390	3 235	2 280	1 960	2 225
Germany	104 355	98 645	94 775	78 565	88 285	71 125	50 565	35 605	28 915	21 030	19 165
Estonia	0	25	25	5	10	10	15	10	10	5	15
Ireland	3 880	4 625	7 725	10 940	10 325	11 635	7 485	4 265	4 305	4 240	3 935
Greece	4 375	2 950	1 530	3 085	5 500	5 665	8 180	4 470	9 050	12 265	25 115
Spain	4 975	4 935	8 405	7 925	9 490	6 310	5 765	5 365	5 050	5 295	7 195
France	21 415	22 375	30 905	38 745	47 290	51 085	59 770	58 545	49 735	30 750	29 160
Italy	1 890	13 100	18 450	15 195	17 400	16 015	13 705	9 630	9 345	10 350	14 055
Cyprus	:	225	790	650	1 620	950	4 405	9 675	7 715	4 540	6 780
Latvia	:	35	20	5	15	25	5	5	20	10	35
Lithuania	240	160	145	305	425	365	395	165	100	145	125
Luxembourg	435	1 710	2 930	625	685	1 040	1 550	1 575	800	525	425
Hungary	:	7 120	11 500	7 800	9 555	6 410	2 400	1 600	1 610	2 115	3 420
Malta	70	160	255	160	155	350	455	995	1 165	1 270	1 380
Netherlands	34 445	45 215	39 275	43 895	32 580	18 665	13 400	9 780	12 345	14 465	7 100
Austria	6 720	13 805	20 130	18 285	30 125	39 355	32 360	24 635	22 460	13 350	11 920
Poland	3 580	3 425	3 060	4 660	4 480	5 170	6 810	7 925	5 240	4 225	7 205
Portugal	250	355	305	225	235	245	115	115	115	130	225
Romania	1 425	1 235	1 665	1 365	2 280	1 000	885	545	485	380	660
Slovenia	70	335	745	9 245	1 510	650	1 050	1 090	1 550	500	370
Slovakia	645	505	1 320	1 555	8 150	9 745	10 300	11 395	3 550	2 850	2 640
Finland	970	1 270	3 105	3 170	1 650	3 445	3 090	3 575	3 595	2 275	1 405
Sweden	9 680	12 840	11 220	16 285	23 500	33 015	31 355	23 160	17 530	24 320	36 205
United Kingdom	32 500	46 015	71 160	80 315	71 365	103 080	60 045	40 625	30 840	28 320	27 905
Iceland	:	:	:	:	:	:	:	:	85	40	:
Norway	2 270	8 375	10 160	10 845	14 770	17 480	16 020	7 950	5 400	5 320	:
Switzerland	23 185	39 735	43 935	15 780	18 720	24 255	18 920	12 730	8 650	8 580	:

Source: Eurostat (tps00021)

Figure 2.21: Asylum applications, 2007 (¹)
(persons)

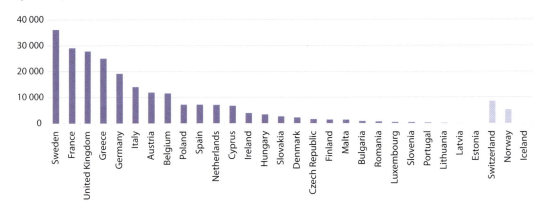

(¹) Provisional figures; EU-27, 222 635 asylum applications in 2007; Iceland, Norway and Switzerland, 2006.

Source: Eurostat (tps00021)

Table 2.22: Asylum decisions

	Number of decisions (persons)		of which, positive (%)		of which, rejections (%)	
	2002	2007	2002	2007	2002	2007
EU-27 ([1])	:	237 970	:	23.2	:	57.8
Belgium ([1])	:	8 345	:	29.2	:	70.8
Bulgaria	2 235	770	32.2	43.5	33.8	31.8
Czech Republic	12 065	2 280	1.0	17.1	42.6	68.9
Denmark	:	850	:	55.9	:	44.1
Germany	130 130	28 570	6.2	27.5	60.6	44.6
Estonia	:	15	:	33.3	:	66.7
Ireland	:	3 810	:	9.8	:	90.0
Greece	:	20 990	:	0.8	:	98.5
Spain	6 235	5 400	4.4	4.5	95.6	95.5
France	49 960	29 150	12.5	11.5	87.5	88.5
Italy ([1])	16 875	9 260	7.4	56.3	92.6	39.7
Cyprus	:	7 170	:	2.9	:	32.3
Latvia	25	20	0.0	50.0	100.0	50.0
Lithuania	385	145	74.0	41.4	11.7	34.5
Luxembourg	1 050	1 035	7.6	52.2	92.4	41.5
Hungary	9 200	2 805	17.2	8.9	27.9	49.0
Malta	:	955	:	65.4	:	34.6
Netherlands ([1])	34 255	14 180	10.4	30.6	77.3	53.0
Austria	29 880	16 045	3.6	32.4	14.3	41.4
Poland	5 415	6 185	4.7	49.1	86.2	29.7
Portugal	230	110	13.0	22.7	71.7	77.3
Romania	1 160	590	11.2	22.9	81.9	57.6
Slovenia	740	540	0.7	1.9	16.2	50.0
Slovakia	:	2 970	:	3.2	:	39.7
Finland	3 035	2 020	19.6	41.6	74.6	51.7
Sweden	27 115	32 470	20.3	48.2	68.2	37.5
United Kingdom	103 450	27 630	32.3	24.6	67.7	70.5
Iceland ([1])	:	30	:	0.0	:	66.7
Norway ([1])	:	4 215	:	40.0	:	48.0

([1]) 2006 instead of 2007.

Source: Eurostat (tps00163, migr_asydctzy and tps00164)

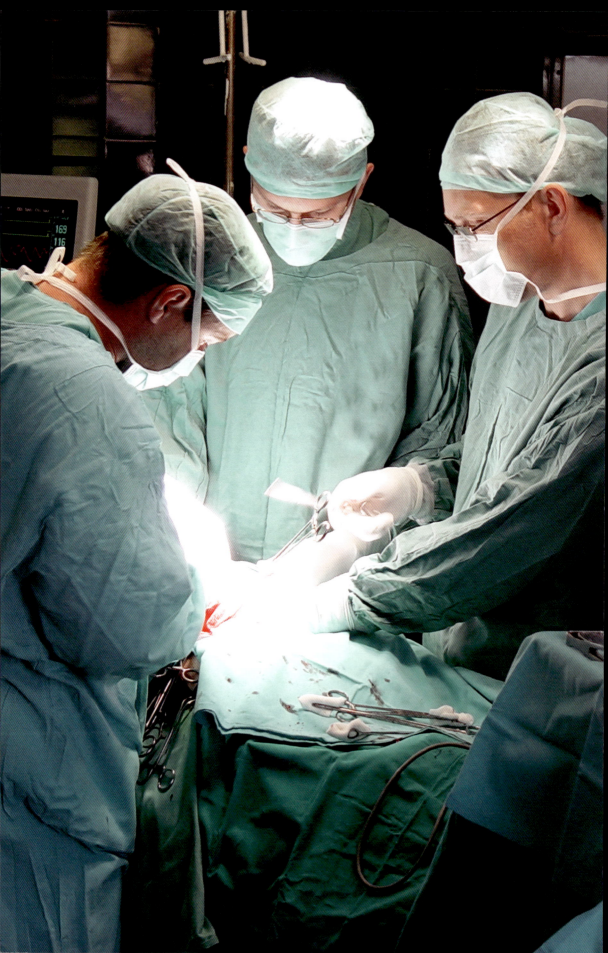

Health

3

Health is an important priority for Europeans, who expect to be protected against illness and disease – at home, in the workplace and when travelling. Health issues cut across a range of topics – including consumer protection (food safety issues), workplace safety, environmental or social policies – and thus have a considerable impact on the EU's revised Lisbon Strategy and the EU 2020 Strategy. The policy areas covered within this chapter are under the remit of the Directorate-General for Health and Consumers and of the Directorate-General for Employment, Social Affairs and Equal Opportunities.

The competence for the organisation and delivery of health services and healthcare is largely held by the Member States, while the EU complements the Member States' health policies through launching actions such as those in relation to cross-border health threats and patient mobility. Gathering and assessing accurate, detailed information on health issues is vital for the EU to effectively design policies and target future actions.

A first programme for Community action in the field of public health covered the period 2003 to 2008. On 23 October 2007 the European Commission adopted a new strategy 'Together for health: a strategic approach for the EU 2008-2013' ([1]). In order to bring about the changes sought within the sector and identified within the new strategy, the second programme of Community action in the field of health ([2]) came into force from 1 January 2008. It puts in place an overarching, strategic framework for work on health in the coming years and encompasses work not only in the health sector but across

[1] For more information: http://ec.europa.eu/health/ph_overview/strategy/health_strategy_en.htm.

[2] Decision No 1350/2007/EC of the European Parliament and of the Council of 23 October 2007 establishing a second programme of Community action in the field of health (2008-2013) (OJ L 301/3, 20.11.2007); for more information: http://eur-lex.europa.eu/LexUriServ/LexUriServ.do?uri=OJ:L:2007:301:0003:0013:EN:PDF.

all policy areas. It has four main principles and three strategic themes for improving health in the EU. The principles include taking a value-driven approach, recognising the links between health and economic prosperity, integrating health in all policies, and strengthening the EU's voice in global health issues. The strategic themes include fostering good health in an ageing Europe, protecting citizens from health threats, and dynamic health systems and new technologies. The programme is valued at EUR 321.5 million and will be implemented by means of annual work plans which will set out priority areas and funding criteria.

Set up at the Lisbon European Council of March 2000, the open method of coordination (OMC) on social protection and social inclusion provides a framework of political coordination without legal constraints. Member States agree to identify and promote their most effective policies in the fields of social protection and social inclusion with the aim of learning from each others' experiences. The health and long-term care strand of the OMC is structured according to three objectives: access to care and inequalities in outcomes, quality of care, and long-term sustainability of systems.

Concerning health and safety at work, the EC Treaty states that 'the Community shall support and complement the activities of the Member States in the improvement in particular of the working environment to protect workers' health and safety.' In 2007 the Council adopted a Resolution (2007/C 145/01 of 25 June 2007) on a new Community strategy on health and safety at work (2007-2012) [3].

In December 2008 the European Parliament and the Council adopted a Regulation on Community statistics on public health and health and safety at work [4].

3.1 Healthy life years

Introduction

Life expectancy at birth remains one of the most frequently quoted indicators of health status and economic development. While most people are aware that successive generations are living longer, less is known about the health conditions of Europe's ageing population. Life expectancy at birth has risen rapidly in the last century due to a number of important factors, including reductions in infant mortality, increased living standards, improved lifestyles and better education, as well as advances in healthcare and medicine.

The health status of a population is difficult to measure because it is hard to define among individuals, populations, cultures, or even across time. As a result, the demographic measure of life expectancy has often been used as a measure of a nation's health status because it is based on a simple and easy to understand characteristic – namely, that of death.

Indicators on healthy life years introduce the concept of the quality of life, by focusing on those years that may be enjoyed by individuals free from the limitations of illness or disability. Chronic disease, frailty, mental disorders and physical disability tend to become more prevalent in older age, and the burden of these

[3] Council Resolution 2007/C 145/01 of 25 June 2007 on a new Community strategy on health and safety at work (2007-2012); for more information:
http://eur-lex.europa.eu/LexUriServ/site/en/oj/2007/c_145/c_14520070630en00010004.pdf.

[4] Regulation (EC) No 1338/2008 or the European Parliament and of the Council of 16 December 2008 on Community statistics on public health and health and safety at work; for more information:
http://eur-lex.europa.eu/LexUriServ/LexUriServ.do?uri=OJ:L:2008:354:0070:0081:EN:PDF.

conditions may impact on healthcare and pension provisions, while resulting in a low quality of life for those who suffer from such conditions.

Healthy life years also monitor health as a productive or economic factor: these indicators form part of the structural indicators that are used to analyse progress being made in the EU with respect to the revised Lisbon criteria. An increase in healthy life years is one of the main goals for European health policy, given that this would not only improve the situation of individuals (as good health and a long life are fundamental objectives of human activity) but would also result in lower levels of public healthcare expenditure. If healthy life years are increasing more rapidly than life expectancy, then not only are people living longer, but they are also living a greater proportion of their lives free from health problems. Any loss in health will, nonetheless, have important effects: including an altered pattern of resource allocation within the healthcare system, as well as wider ranging effects on consumption and production throughout the economy.

Definitions and data availability

The indicator on **healthy life years** (also called **disability-free life expectancy**) measures the number of remaining years that a person of a specific age is expected to live without any severe or moderate health problems or acquired disabilities; in other words, this is a health expectancy indicator. The indicator is calculated separately for males and females.

There are two components to the calculation of healthy life years, namely, mortality statistics and data on self-perceived disability. Mortality data comes from Eurostat's demographic database, while self-perceived disability data comes from European Union statistics on income and living conditions (EU-SILC). The EU-SILC question is [5]: 'For at least the past 6 months, to what extent have you been limited because of a health problem in activities people usually do? Would you say you have been:

* strongly limited?
* limited?
* not limited at all?'

Main findings

As life expectancy has risen, political attention has been re-focused on healthy life years. One measure that can be used to study the relative health of Europe's population is the relationship between healthy life years and total life expectancy, in other words, what percentage of each person's life can be expected to be lived free from disability and disease. Men were likely to spend the largest proportion of their lives free from disability. Women could expect to live a slightly lower proportion of their lives free from disability; although their overall life expectancy at birth was higher than for men. Indeed, in 2007 the male population consistently reported a higher proportion of healthy life years in total life expectancy when compared with rates for women, with differences of 7 percentage points or more in Lithuania, Slovakia, Latvia and Portugal.

The indicators concerning healthy life years are calculated at two ages: birth and the age of 65. The indicator at age 65 is of particular interest in relation to the possible future demand for healthcare

---

[5] The disability prevalence data used in the calculation of the Healthy life years (HLY) indicator are provided by the GALI (Global Activity Limitation Instrument) question from EU-SILC. The way this question was implemented by the EU Member States in EU-SILC hampers cross-country comparisons for the data up to 2008. Therefore, before 2008, SILC health data should be used with caution and only the evolution in time for each country should be followed.

and social services, or the potential for older persons to remain within the workforce. For both men and women, Estonia, Slovakia and Latvia were the Member States where, in 2007, people could expect to spend the shortest period after the age of 65 without a disability. The data for Slovakia, Lithuania, Romania, Germany, the Czech Republic and Greece showed almost identical figures for men and women in terms of additional healthy life years they may expect to live at the age of 65. The highest differences between the sexes were recorded in Luxembourg, Cyprus and Portugal: in Portugal and Cyprus men aged 65 were expected to have approximately 1.5 years of healthy life more than women, while in Luxembourg the opposite situation was found, as women could expect to have 1.7 additional years of healthy life compared with men.

Figure 3.1: Healthy life years at birth, 2007 (¹)
(% of total life expectancy)

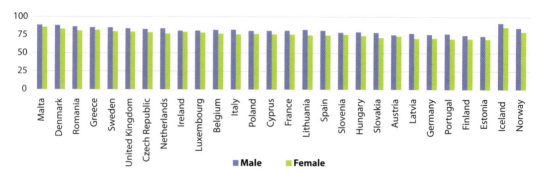

(¹) Bulgaria, not available; the figure is ranked on the average of male and female.

Source: Eurostat (tsdph100 and tps00025)

Figure 3.2: Healthy life years at age 65, 2007 (¹)
(years)

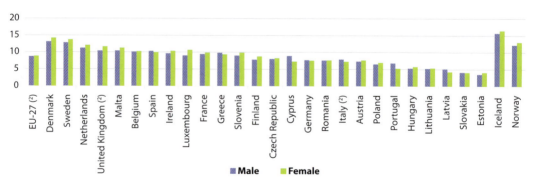

(¹) Bulgaria, not available; the figure is ranked on the average of male and female.
(²) Estimates.

Source: Eurostat)

3.2 Causes of death and infant mortality

Introduction

Broadly speaking, the EU has witnessed a very significant reduction in mortality during the last century or so – both in terms of reduced infant mortality and as a result of general declines in infectious and degenerative diseases. Non-communicable diseases are largely preventable and are linked by common risk factors, underlying determinants and opportunities for intervention. Among these, cancer and cardiovascular diseases are currently by far the most important causes of death in the EU for both men and women.

Mortality during the first year of life has decreased considerably in all Member States, with current levels among the world's lowest. However, there are still persistent differences in rates across different social groups or geographical regions.

Definitions and data availability

Eurostat began collecting and disseminating **mortality data** in 1994, broken down by:

- a shortlist of 65 causes of death;
- gender;
- age;
- geographical region (NUTS level 2).

The **infant mortality rate** represents the ratio between deaths of children under one year and the number of live births in a given year; the value is expressed per 1 000 live births.

Causes of death are classified according to the international statistical classification of diseases and related health problems (ICD), that is developed and maintained by the World Health Organisation (WHO). Causes of death statistics are based on information derived from medical certificates; the medical certification of death is an obligation in all Member States. They target the underlying cause of death, in other words, the disease or injury which initiated the train of morbid events leading directly to death, or the circumstances of the accident or violence which produced the fatal injury (a definition adopted by the World Health Assembly). Although definitions are harmonised, the statistics may not be fully comparable as classifications may vary when the cause of death is multiple or difficult to evaluate and because of different notification procedures. Annual data are provided in absolute numbers, as crude death rates and as standardised death rates.

The **standardised death rate (SDR)** is a weighted average of the age-specific mortality rates. The weights are the age distribution of the population whose mortality experience is being observed. Since most causes of death vary significantly by age and sex, the use of standardised death rates improves comparability over time and between countries. In order to facilitate the analysis of the development over time the series has been converted to indices with a fixed reference period (2000=100).

Main findings

In the EU-27 the total number of people that died in 2007 was 4.78 million. This figure was split almost equally between men and women, with about 12 000 more men dying than women. Looking at the number of deaths by each year of age, more men died than women at every year of age up to the age of 80. As a proportion of all deaths, 41 % of women who died were aged less than 80, whereas for men the proportion at the same age was much higher, at 66 %. Furthermore, 80 was the age of the peak number of deaths for men, whereas the number of deaths among women continued to rise and peaked at the age of 85.

The progress made in medical healthcare services is reflected in a decreasing infant mortality rate. In the course of the last four decades the infant mortality rate in the EU fell from 28.6 deaths per 1 000 live births in 1965 to 4.7 deaths per 1 000 live births in 2006. As a result of declining infant mortality rates, most Member States have among the world's lowest infant mortality rates, for example, 1.8 deaths per 1 000 live births in Luxembourg or less than 3 deaths per 1 000 live births in Slovenia, Sweden, Finland or the Czech Republic. Infant mortality rates have levelled-off in some countries in recent years, and actually increased in Cyprus and Malta, although the relatively small population in these two countries may lead to volatility in this rate. Reversals in infant mortality rates may, partly, be due to factors such as: an increasing number of women deferring childbirth into their forties; or a higher number of multiple births as a result of the more common use of fertility treatments.

Non-communicable diseases – a group of conditions that includes cardiovascular disease, cancer, mental health problems, diabetes mellitus, chronic respiratory disease, and musculoskeletal conditions – cause more than 85 % of deaths in Europe. Among these, cancer (malignant neoplasm) and cardiovascular diseases (characterised by a reduced blood supply to the heart muscle, often as a result of coronary artery disease) were by far the most important causes of death in the EU-27 for both men and women in 2007; there were, however, large differences between standardised death rates for men and women.

Standardised death rates were higher for men for all the main causes of death, with rates up to four to five times as high as those recorded for women for drug dependence and alcohol abuse. The rates of AIDS/HIV and suicide and intentional self-harm were also three or four times as high for men as for women.

An analysis of death rates for men and women between 2000 and 2007 shows falling rates for all of the main causes of death. Death rates from cancer fell more slowly than for ischaemic heart diseases; for both of these causes the rates fell more quickly for men than for women. Among the major causes of death studied, the death rate for pneumonia fell most strongly (for both men and women), mainly as a result of reductions between 1999 and 2001.

Deaths from cancer among men had an incidence of 229 per 100 000, while the corresponding rate for women was 132. The difference in cancer deaths between the sexes was often particularly high among those Member States that joined the EU since 2004, although France and Spain also recorded considerable disparities.

Standardised death rates for ischaemic heart diseases in 2007 were about twice as high for men (at 120 per 100 000) as for women (61) in the EU-27. Heart disease was particularly prevalent among men and women in the Baltic Member States, Slovakia, Hungary and Romania. There was a higher incidence of death from heart disease than from cancer for both men and women in five of these countries (Hungary was the exception) and this was also the case in Romania, while in Finland there were more deaths from heart disease than from cancer among the male population. Countries reporting the lowest incidence of death from heart disease included France, Portugal, Spain and the Netherlands.

Figure 3.3: Mortality, EU-27, 2006 (¹)
(number, based on age at last birthday)

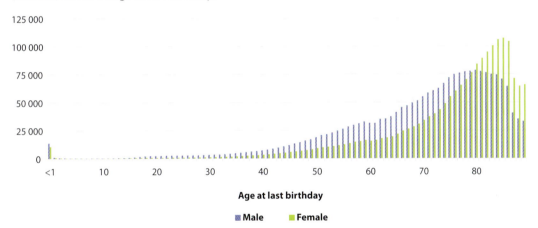

(¹) The number of deaths in the EU-27 for persons aged 90 or more in 2006 was: male – 185 508; female – 501 965.

Source: Eurostat (demo_magec)

Table 3.1: Infant mortality
(per 1 000 live births)

	1965	1970	1975	1980	1985	1990	1995	2000	2005	2008
EU-27 ([1])	28.6	25.5	20.8	15.8	12.8	10.3	7.5	5.9	4.9	4.7
Euro area ([1])	28.5	23.8	19.0	13.0	9.8	7.7	5.7	4.7	3.9	3.8
Belgium	23.7	21.1	16.1	12.1	9.8	8.0	6.0	4.8	3.7	3.4
Bulgaria	30.8	27.3	23.1	20.2	15.4	14.8	14.8	13.3	10.4	8.6
Czech Republic	23.7	20.2	19.4	16.9	12.5	10.8	7.7	4.1	3.4	2.8
Denmark	18.7	14.2	10.4	8.4	7.9	7.5	5.1	5.3	4.4	4.0
Germany	24.1	22.5	18.9	12.4	9.1	7.0	5.3	4.4	3.9	3.5
Estonia	20.3	17.7	18.2	17.1	14.1	12.3	14.9	8.4	5.4	5.0
Ireland ([2])	25.2	19.5	17.5	11.1	8.8	8.2	6.4	6.2	4.0	3.1
Greece	34.3	29.6	24.0	17.9	14.1	9.7	8.1	5.9	3.8	3.5
Spain	29.4	20.7	18.9	12.3	8.9	7.6	5.5	4.4	3.8	3.5
France ([3])	22.4	18.2	13.8	10.0	8.3	7.3	4.9	4.5	3.8	3.7
Italy	35.0	:	20.8	14.6	10.5	8.2	6.2	4.5	3.8	3.7
Cyprus	32.0	26.0	18.2	14.4	14.4	12.9	9.7	5.6	4.6	5.3
Latvia	18.9	17.7	20.3	15.3	13.0	13.7	18.8	10.4	7.8	6.7
Lithuania	24.7	19.3	19.6	14.5	14.2	10.2	12.5	8.6	6.8	4.9
Luxembourg	24.0	24.9	14.8	11.5	9.0	7.3	5.5	5.1	2.6	1.8
Hungary	38.8	35.9	32.8	23.2	20.4	14.8	10.7	9.2	6.2	5.6
Malta	34.8	27.9	18.3	15.2	14.5	9.1	8.9	5.9	6.0	9.9
Netherlands	14.4	12.7	10.6	8.6	8.0	7.1	5.5	5.1	4.9	3.8
Austria	28.3	25.9	20.5	14.3	11.2	7.8	5.4	4.8	4.2	3.7
Poland	41.6	36.4	24.8	25.4	22.1	19.4	13.6	8.1	6.4	5.6
Portugal	64.9	55.5	38.9	24.2	17.8	11.0	7.5	5.5	3.5	3.3
Romania	44.1	49.4	34.7	29.3	25.6	26.9	21.2	18.6	15.0	11.0
Slovenia	29.6	24.5	17.3	15.3	13.0	8.4	5.5	4.9	4.1	2.1
Slovakia	28.5	25.7	23.7	20.9	16.3	12.0	11.0	8.6	7.2	5.9
Finland	17.6	13.2	9.6	7.6	6.3	5.6	3.9	3.8	3.0	2.6
Sweden	13.3	11.0	8.6	6.9	6.8	6.0	4.1	3.4	2.4	2.5
United Kingdom	19.6	18.5	18.9	13.9	11.1	7.9	6.2	5.6	5.1	4.7
Croatia	49.5	34.2	23.0	20.6	16.6	10.7	8.9	7.4	5.7	4.5
FYR of Macedonia	105.8	87.9	65.1	54.2	43.4	31.6	22.7	11.8	12.8	9.7
Turkey	:	:	:	:	:	:	:	28.9	23.6	16.0
Iceland	15.0	13.2	12.5	7.7	5.7	5.9	6.1	3.0	2.3	2.5
Liechtenstein ([1])	22.8	11.8	6.5	7.6	10.7	:	:	9.5	2.6	5.5
Norway	14.6	11.3	9.5	8.1	8.5	6.9	4.0	3.8	3.1	2.7
Switzerland	17.8	15.1	10.7	9.1	6.9	6.8	5.0	4.9	4.2	4.0

([1]) 2006 instead of 2008.
([2]) 2007 instead of 2008.
([3]) 2007 instead of 2008; break in series in 2000 when French overseas departments are included.

Source: Eurostat (demo_minfind)

Table 3.2: Causes of death – standardised death rate, 2007 (^{1})
(per 100 000 inhabitants)

	Cancer (^{2})	Heart disease (^{3})	Nervous system	Pneumonia	Chronic liver disease	Diabetes mellitus	Accidents	Suicide (^{4})	Alc. abuse	Homicide, assault	AIDS (HIV)	Drug dependence
EU-27	*172.7*	*87.4*	*12.4*	*14.9*	*13.9*	*12.9*	*25.0*	*9.8*	*2.7*	*1.0*	*1.0*	*0.6*
Belgium	173.9	71.2	20.3	21.9	9.3	10.1	28.1	17.5	2.6	1.7	0.6	0.4
Bulgaria	170.3	135.4	9.7	17.6	17.8	18.0	29.8	9.5	0.3	1.7	0.0	0.0
Czech Republic	203.9	185.5	9.6	20.4	16.8	17.1	34.0	11.9	1.3	1.0	0.0	0.0
Denmark	208.0	71.6	18.4	18.3	14.5	16.3	24.5	10.6	12.6	0.7	0.5	0.7
Germany	162.1	92.6	13.2	13.7	13.3	14.4	16.0	9.4	4.7	0.6	0.5	0.9
Estonia	192.9	236.3	16.4	9.5	25.7	13.0	73.2	16.8	15.5	6.8	3.1	0.0
Ireland	184.8	109.2	15.7	41.4	5.8	11.4	18.2	9.1	2.1	0.8	0.1	2.0
Greece	157.9	73.3	8.4	5.8	4.9	7.3	27.4	2.6	0.3	1.0	0.2	0.0
Spain	157.1	50.4	21.2	10.5	9.0	12.7	20.8	6.1	0.5	0.7	2.7	0.1
France	169.2	35.7	25.3	8.6	10.7	10.7	27.3	14.6	4.4	0.7	1.2	0.3
Italy	164.9	64.1	16.9	5.5	9.6	16.6	21.8	5.2	0.3	0.9	1.5	0.7
Cyprus	122.4	85.8	14.3	9.3	4.7	36.1	31.4	2.2	0.5	1.3	0.5	0.9
Latvia	193.6	298.6	14.4	15.2	21.5	11.5	86.3	17.8	3.5	8.0	1.8	0.0
Lithuania	196.5	338.2	15.4	19.6	43.3	6.9	99.2	28.4	1.2	6.9	0.3	0.6
Luxembourg	161.1	77.0	20.8	12.2	16.5	9.2	31.4	13.2	3.1	1.4	1.0	0.2
Hungary	240.9	226.6	13.9	5.3	45.3	20.8	37.9	21.4	3.7	1.7	0.1	0.0
Malta	155.0	119.9	12.5	11.3	5.9	21.0	21.9	6.0	0.2	0.7	0.2	0.0
Netherlands	183.6	50.2	16.2	20.1	4.3	13.6	14.9	7.7	1.0	0.9	0.4	0.0
Austria	157.7	103.3	15.6	8.6	15.5	21.8	23.0	13.2	3.9	0.6	0.7	2.3
Poland	208.6	104.2	10.9	19.2	16.9	13.5	38.0	12.9	5.0	1.3	0.3	0.0
Portugal	149.4	46.2	14.5	28.9	10.8	21.4	18.6	6.8	0.8	1.5	6.3	0.1
Romania	178.1	200.9	8.3	24.5	40.9	8.5	39.6	10.5	2.2	2.0	0.8	0.0
Slovenia	202.7	67.2	8.7	18.0	26.7	9.1	40.4	18.4	2.6	0.9	0.1	0.0
Slovakia	204.4	268.6	13.3	32.1	26.8	10.7	35.6	8.8	0.0	1.2	0.0	0.0
Finland	138.3	134.2	39.7	7.1	19.9	6.8	45.3	17.6	2.4	2.1	0.2	0.4
Sweden	149.1	93.0	18.4	10.2	5.3	11.4	21.4	11.4	2.8	1.2	0.3	0.2
United Kingdom	178.1	93.0	19.3	27.7	11.4	6.4	16.6	6.1	1.3	0.4	0.4	1.8
Croatia	209.0	154.2	11.9	16.3	23.4	19.9	39.3	15.0	4.9	1.4	0.0	0.3
FYR of Macedonia	172.3	97.8	6.5	5.4	7.9	34.9	26.9	7.8	0.6	2.2	0.0	0.0
Iceland	165.5	89.0	37.6	9.5	2.9	6.6	16.3	11.5	1.5	0.6	0.0	0.3
Norway	163.7	73.3	19.0	19.6	3.7	10.5	27.9	10.0	2.8	0.7	0.2	0.5
Switzerland	146.1	66.1	20.7	9.1	7.1	10.7	20.8	15.1	2.3	0.6	0.7	0.5

(^{1}) Denmark, Ireland, Italy, Luxembourg and Portugal, 2006; Belgium, 2004.
(^{2}) Malignant neoplasms.
(^{3}) Ischaemic heart diseases.
(^{4}) Suicide and intentional self-harm.

Source: Eurostat (tps00116, tps00119, tps00134, tps00128, tps00131, tps00137, tps00125, tps00122, tps00140, tps00146, tps00143 and tps00149)

Figure 3.4: Causes of death – standardised death rate, EU-27, 2007 (¹)
(per 100 000 inhabitants)

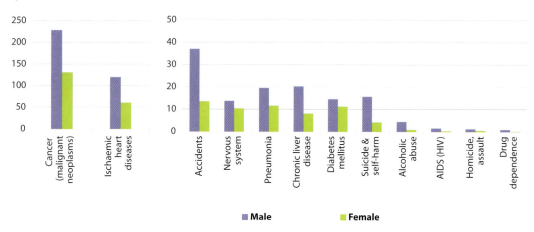

(¹) Note the differences in the scales employed between the two parts of the figure; the figure is ranked on the average of male and female; EU-27 averages calculated on the basis of the latest year available for each Member State.

Source: Eurostat (tps00116, tps00119, tps00125, tps00134, tps00128, tps00131, tps00137, tps00122, tps00140, tps00143, tps00146 and tps00149)

Figure 3.5: Causes of death – standardised death rate per 100 000 inhabitants, males, EU-27 (¹)
(2000=100)

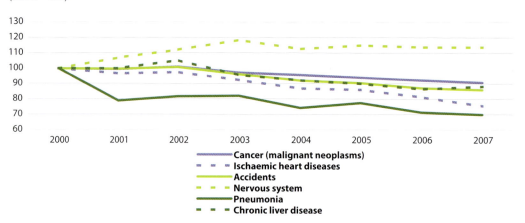

(¹) Provisional.

Source: Eurostat (hlth_cd_asdr)

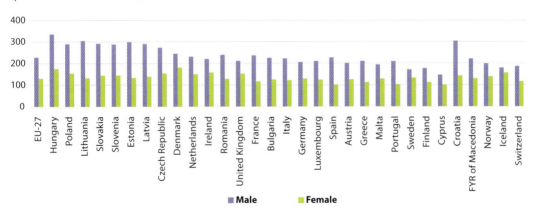

Figure 3.6: Causes of death - standardised death rate per 100 000 inhabitants, females, EU-27 (¹) (2000=100)

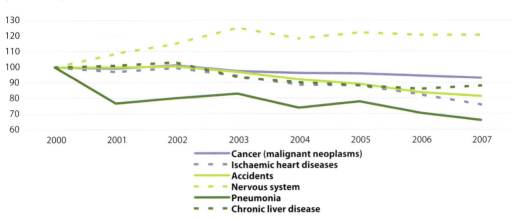

(¹) Provisional.

Source: Eurostat (hlth_cd_asdr)

Figure 3.7: Deaths from cancer (malignant neoplasms) - standardised death rate, 2007 (¹) (per 100 000 inhabitants)

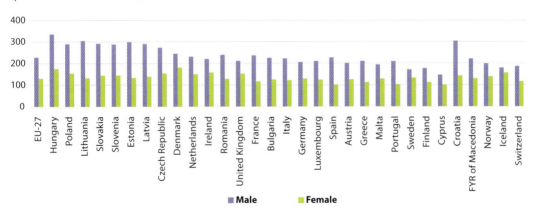

(¹) Denmark, Ireland, Italy, Luxembourg and Portugal, 2006; the figure is ranked on the average of male and female.

Source: Eurostat (tps00116)

Figure 3.8: Deaths from ischaemic heart diseases - standardised death rate, 2007 (¹)
(per 100 000 inhabitants)

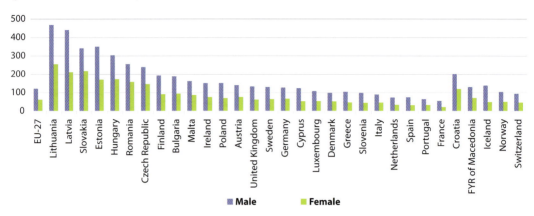

(¹) Denmark, Ireland, Italy, Luxembourg and Portugal, 2006; the figure is ranked on the average of male and female; EU-27, provisional;
Belgium, not available.

Source: Eurostat (tps00119)

Figure 3.9: Deaths from suicide - standardised death rate, 2007 (¹)
(per 100 000 inhabitants)

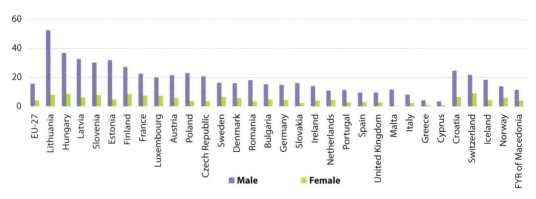

(¹) Denmark, Ireland, Italy, Luxembourg and Portugal, 2006; the figure is ranked on the average of male and female; EU-27, provisional;
Belgium, not available.

Source: Eurostat (tps00122)

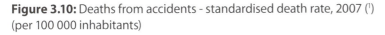

Figure 3.10: Deaths from accidents - standardised death rate, 2007 (¹)
(per 100 000 inhabitants)

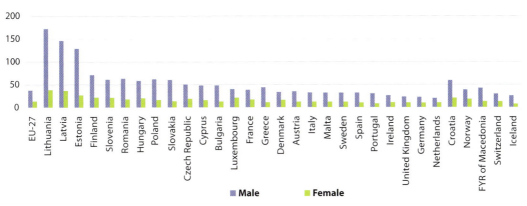

■ **Male**   ■ **Female**

(¹) Denmark, Ireland, Italy, Luxembourg and Portugal, 2006; the figure is ranked on the average of male and female; EU-27, provisional; Belgium, not available.

Source: Eurostat (tps00125)

3.3 Healthcare

Introduction

A new health strategy 'Together for health: a strategic approach for the EU 2008-2013' was adopted on 23 October 2007, putting in place a framework to improve health in the EU through a value-driven approach, recognising the links between health and economic prosperity, integrating health in all policies, and strengthening the EU's voice in global health.

The provision of healthcare varies considerably within the EU, although widespread use is made of public provision and comprehensive healthcare insurance. Healthcare schemes generally cover all residents; nevertheless, an increasing proportion of individuals choose to adhere to private insurance schemes (usually on top of the national provision for care).

Public regulation of the healthcare sector is a complex task, as the healthcare market is characterised by numerous market imperfections. Member States generally aim to balance the efficient use of resources ensuring that healthcare provisions are available to all. There is no easy answer to the question of how much a country should spend on healthcare, as the Member States face a different disease burden, while populations have different expectations of what services their national healthcare systems should offer. Indeed, the amount of money needed to fund a healthcare system is a function of several variables, the most obvious being the burden of disease requiring treatment. However, there is no simple linear relationship between the burden of disease and the need for resources, as some conditions can be treated without complications and at a relatively low cost while others may require complex and expensive care.

The main consumers of healthcare are older people – a section of the European population that is growing rapidly, partly as a result of ageing baby-boomers, but also because of continued increases in life expectancy. The increasing number of elderly persons in the coming years will probably drive demand for more healthcare provision, particularly for long-term care (nursing and convalescence homes). Medical advances are also likely to result in more and better treatments being made available.

An increasing number of Europeans (and persons from non-member countries) are travelling across borders to receive health treatment, to avoid waiting lists or to seek specialist treatment that may only be available abroad. The EU works towards ensuring that its citizens who move across borders have access to healthcare anywhere within the EU and healthcare systems and policies are becoming more interconnected. This is not only a result of the movement of patients and professionals between countries, but may also be attributed to a set of common public expectations of health services across Europe, as well as more rapid dissemination of new medical technologies and techniques. On 2 July 2008, as part of a renewed social agenda, the European Commission adopted a draft Directive on the application of patients' rights to cross-border healthcare (⁶).

Definitions and data availability

Healthcare expenditure

According to the system of health accounts (SHA), **healthcare expenditure** data can be analysed by type of provider, by function (goods and services) and by financing agent. Healthcare data on expenditure are based on various information sources including surveys and administrative data sources. The country-specific way of organising and financing healthcare, existing departures from SHA definitions, and information gaps, may explain why data are not always completely comparable between countries. To collect data on healthcare expenditure, the system of health accounts (SHA) and its related set of international classification for health accounts (ICHA) is used. The SHA is organised around a tri-axial system for recording health expenditure, defining healthcare financing agents, functions and service providers.

Mechanisms of **healthcare financing** are becoming increasingly complex in many countries with a wide range of institutions involved; at least a basic subdivision of public and private financing is reported in many cases. A detailed breakdown of expenditure on health by financing agents is an essential component of a comprehensive SHA.

Healthcare in a country comprises the sum of activities performed either by institutions or individuals pursuing, through the application of medical, paramedical and nursing knowledge and technology, the **purposes/core functions** of:

• promoting health and preventing disease;

(⁶) For more information: http://ec.europa.eu/health/ph_overview/co_operation/healthcare/docs/COM_en.pdf.

- curing illness and reducing premature mortality;
- caring for persons affected by chronic illness who require nursing care;
- caring for persons with health-related impairment, disability, and handicaps who require nursing care;
- assisting patients to die with dignity;
- providing and administering public health; and
- providing and administering health programs, health insurance and other funding arrangements.

Health-related functions such as the education and training of the health workforce, research and development in health, and environmental health should be distinguished from the core functions; as far as possible they should be excluded when measuring activities belonging to core healthcare functions.

The way of organising healthcare services reflects the country-specific division of labour between providers of healthcare services which is becoming increasingly complex in many countries. A classification of **healthcare providers** organises the country-specific institutions into common, internationally applicable categories and provides tools for linking data on personnel and other resource inputs as well as output measurement.

Non-expenditure data on healthcare

Information on healthcare can be divided into two broad groups of data: resource-related data on human and technical resources; and output-related data that focus on hospital patients and the treatment(s) they receive. Healthcare data are largely based on administrative data sources, and, to a large degree, they

reflect country-specific ways of organising healthcare; as such, the information collected may not always be completely comparable.

Hospitals are defined according to the classification of healthcare providers of the SHA; all public and private hospitals should be covered.

Data on **healthcare staff**, in the form of human resources available for providing healthcare services, is provided irrespective of the sector of employment (whether the personnel are independent, employed by a hospital, or any other healthcare provider). These statistics cover healthcare professionals such as physicians, dentists, nurses, pharmacists and physiotherapists. Physicians may be counted as licensed, professionally active or practising; data for two or more of these concepts are available in the majority of Member States. In the context of comparing healthcare services across Member States, Eurostat gives preference to the concept of '**practising professionals**', as this best describes the availability of healthcare resources. Practising physicians are defined as those providing services directly to patients. Their tasks include: conducting medical examinations and making diagnosis; prescribing medication and giving treatment for diagnosed illnesses, disorders or injuries; giving specialised medical or surgical treatment for particular types of illnesses, disorders or injuries; giving advice on and applying preventive medicine methods and treatments. The number of physicians may be used as a proxy for access to the healthcare system.

Hospital bed numbers provide information on healthcare capacities, in other words on the maximum number of patients who can be treated by hospitals. Hospital beds are those which are regularly maintained and staffed and immediately available for the care of admitted patients. These include: beds in all hospitals, including general hospitals, mental health and substance abuse hospitals, and other specialty hospitals; occupied and unoccupied beds are covered. The statistics exclude surgical tables, recovery trolleys, emergency stretchers, beds for same-day care, cots for healthy infants, beds in wards which were closed for any reason, provisional and temporary beds, or beds in nursing and residential care facilities. They cover beds accommodating patients who are formally admitted (or hospitalised) to an institution for treatment and/or care and who stay for a minimum of one night in the hospital or other institution providing in-patient care. Curative care (or acute care) beds in hospitals are beds that are available for curative care; these form a subgroup of total hospital beds.

Output-related indicators focus on hospital patients and cover the interaction between patients and healthcare systems, in the form of the treatment received. Data in this domain are available for a range of indicators including hospital discharges of in-patients and day cases by age, sex, and selected (groups of) diseases; the average length of stay of in-patients; or the medical procedures performed in hospitals; the number of hospital discharges is the most commonly used measure of the utilisation of hospital services.

Discharges, rather than admissions, are used because hospital abstracts for in-patient care are based on information gathered at the time of discharge. A hospital discharge is defined as the formal release of a patient from a hospital after a procedure or course of treatment. A discharge occurs whenever a patient leaves because of finalisation of treatment, signs out against medical advice, transfers to another healthcare institution or if a patient dies. Healthy newborn babies should be included, while patient transfers to another department within the same institution are excluded.

Main findings

Healthcare expenditure

Current expenditure on healthcare in 2006 ranged from PPS 403 per inhabitant in Romania to more than PPS 2 700 per inhabitant in Germany, France, Belgium, the Netherlands, Austria (2004), Denmark and Sweden; note that no data is available for six of the Member States. In nearly all of the Member States expenditure was greatest for care provided by hospitals, while a significant proportion of healthcare expenditure was for providers of ambulatory healthcare, as well as for retail sale and other providers of medical goods.

An analysis of the functions of healthcare expenditure show that curative care generally accounted for around half of all healthcare expenditure. Medical goods for outpatients was generally the second largest function, with around one quarter of total expenditure, although it exceeded one third in Slovakia, Bulgaria, Hungary and Lithuania. Rehabilitative care was generally 4 % or less of the total, with the 11 % share in Cyprus an exception among those Member States with data available. Long-term nursing care accounted for less than 10 % of expenditure in the majority of the Member States, but reached 22 % in Denmark.

Sources of financing varied considerably, reflecting the variety of health systems in place across the Member States. In several countries, three fifths or more of healthcare expenditure is financed from social security funds: the highest shares were in the Czech Republic (81 %) and the Netherlands (77 %). Other government financing was the main source in Denmark and Sweden at more than four fifths of the total, while more than half of the financing in Portugal, Spain, Finland and Latvia also came from this source. The other major source of funds was direct payments, referred to as 'out-of-pocket' expenditure, which ranged from less than 10 % of the total in the Netherlands and France, to over two fifths in Bulgaria and Latvia (2004), and nearly half the total in Cyprus. Private insurance enterprises generally contributed a small share of healthcare finance, only surpassing 10 % of the total in Slovenia (13.8 %) and France (13.1 %).

Non-expenditure data on healthcare

Among the Member States with recent data available, the highest number of physicians per 100 000 inhabitants was recorded in Belgium (405 practising physicians in 2008) followed by Austria (374 practising physicians in 2008); note, however, that methodological differences occur between the various types of physicians reported in some countries. Between 1997 and 2007 the number of physicians per 100 000 inhabitants increased in the

majority of Member States, although reductions were recorded in Italy, Hungary, Poland and Lithuania; the slight fall in Estonia may be due to methodological reasons.

The number of hospital beds per 100 000 inhabitants in 2007 ranged from 288 in Sweden to 829 in Germany. During the ten years between 1997 and 2007, the number of hospital beds per 100 000 inhabitants fell in every Member State for which data is available, except in Malta. The largest reductions in the availability of hospital beds were recorded in Luxembourg, Bulgaria, Sweden, the Baltic Member States and Italy. A more detailed breakdown shows that reductions in bed numbers were spread across different categories, with an average of 390 curative care beds available per 100 000 inhabitants in the EU-27 in 2007, while there were 55 psychiatric beds in hospitals per 100 000 inhabitants; when compared with 1998, these latest figures represent overall reductions in bed numbers of 22.3 % and 26.8 % respectively.

The general reduction in hospital bed numbers may result from a more efficient use of resources, with an increasing number of operations conducted as outpatient treatment, and shorter periods spent in hospital following an operation. Nevertheless, the output of each health system, as measured by the number of inpatient discharges, will usually (at least to some degree), reflect the number of physicians and hospital beds available. The highest number of hospital discharges in 2007 was recorded in Austria (more than 27 000 per 100 000 inhabitants), which was almost 25 % more than the

next highest figure (22 100 discharges in Lithuania). At the other end of the range, the number of hospital discharges of in-patients was relatively low in both Malta (2004) and Cyprus (2007), both below 8 000 per 100 000 inhabitants.

Circulatory system diseases were the most common type of diagnosis of in-patients and these accounted for around one quarter of hospital discharges in 2007 in the vast majority of Member States for which data are available, often with upwards of 3 000 discharges per 100 000 inhabitants. However, in Romania higher numbers of discharges were recorded for respiratory system diseases, while in Ireland and Spain there were more discharges from pregnancies and related diagnosis, and in Cyprus the highest number of discharges resulted from injury or poisoning. Cyprus had a particularly low level of hospital discharges, which may in part be due to patients travelling abroad for specialist treatment; indeed, this trend may also be significant for other Member States.

The average length of hospital stays was generally longest for those patients suffering from circulatory system problems, cancer, injury/poisoning, or respiratory problems. The average time spent in hospital is a function of hospital efficiency, as well as the type of treatments available.

Table 3.3: Healthcare expenditure by provider, 2006
(PPS per inhabitant)

	All providers of healthcare	Hospitals	Nursing and residential care facilities	Providers of ambulatory healthcare	Retail sale & other providers of medical goods	Provision of administration and prevention
Belgium	2 763.9	843.7	299.5	828.2	495.4	105.9
Bulgaria	611.7	234.4	4.2	109.3	234.8	7.8
Czech Republic	1 219.8	561.9	18.3	287.6	263.7	2.8
Denmark	2 680.6	1200.3	546.2	538.6	354.5	4.7
Germany	2 780.7	839.9	221.4	836.0	591.3	23.0
Estonia	778.3	338.6	18.7	164.7	216.7	17.6
Ireland	:	:	:	:	:	:
Greece	:	:	:	:	:	:
Spain	1 981.9	769.2	96.1	573.8	449.6	19.5
France	2 769.8	988.5	173.1	762.8	604.2	17.0
Italy	:	:	:	:	:	:
Cyprus	1 291.8	530.4	32.0	422.1	238.7	1.8
Latvia (¹)	675.2	273.1	18.5	172.1	187.0	1.3
Lithuania	761.5	285.1	11.0	155.4	272.5	4.3
Luxembourg (¹)	4 300.5	1437.9	518.3	1072.8	432.2	1.2
Hungary	1 203.7	397.5	27.4	250.1	436.4	58.4
Malta	:	:	:	:	:	:
Netherlands	2 743.6	1016.1	328.7	655.2	449.2	46.6
Austria (²)	2 733.9	1045.0	206.9	704.5	458.8	19.1
Poland	723.7	223.3	12.7	196.0	226.0	10.6
Portugal	1 702.7	636.9	31.5	565.1	423.0	0.1
Romania	403.0	174.5	3.2	50.0	130.5	14.0
Slovenia	1 626.3	635.6	84.9	404.5	384.2	10.0
Slovakia	1 052.3	284.7	:	259.5	411.1	19.7
Finland	2 111.7	770.0	183.5	639.7	395.0	26.9
Sweden	2 530.6	1154.1	:	533.9	426.0	29.9
United Kingdom	:	:	:	:	:	:
Iceland	2 676.1	1108.5	317.6	695.8	433.4	74.6
Norway (¹)	4 475.8	1280.0	580.7	916.3	474.6	56.5
Switzerland	3 470.0	1218.1	592.1	1120.0	321.4	0.0
Japan (¹)	2 024.5	988.0	68.0	574.1	307.2	39.2
United States	5 639.5	1859.3	358.3	2044.7	791.8	168.4

(¹) 2005.
(²) 2004.

Source: Eurostat (hlth_sha_hp)

Table 3.4: Healthcare expenditure by function, 2006
(PPS per inhabitant)

	Current healthcare expenditure	Curative care	Rehabili-tative care	Long- term nursing care	Medical goods dispensed to out-patients	Prevention and public health services
Belgium	2 763.9	1266.5	106.9	455.3	520.8	97.6
Bulgaria	611.7	309.6	8.1	1.7	234.8	21.5
Czech Republic	1 219.8	658.0	42.0	45.4	333.9	26.5
Denmark	2 680.6	:	:	602.8	354.5	63.8
Germany	2 780.7	1407.2	91.5	347.3	553.2	96.2
Estonia	778.3	413.9	9.0	27.8	216.7	20.0
Ireland	:	:	:	:	:	:
Greece	:	:	:	:	:	:
Spain	1 981.9	1112.2	0.0	167.7	488.2	47.4
France	2 769.8	1411.7	82.2	282.5	584.6	62.0
Italy	:	:	:	:	:	:
Cyprus	1 291.8	618.0	139.8	32.0	298.5	8.2
Latvia (¹)	675.2	357.9	5.3	20.8	196.6	1.8
Lithuania	761.5	364.9	30.0	30.8	273.4	9.7
Luxembourg (¹)	4 300.5	2286.4	108.3	751.4	476.9	48.4
Hungary	1 203.7	550.1	25.4	33.7	436.4	85.1
Malta	:	:	:	:	:	:
Netherlands	2 743.6	1367.5	129.5	380.9	469.5	134.3
Austria (²)	2 733.9	1564.0	111.3	351.1	459.2	59.1
Poland	723.7	366.6	21.9	50.0	228.4	17.7
Portugal	1 702.7	:	:	25.1	423.1	32.3
Romania	403.0	194.9	2.5	3.5	130.5	23.8
Slovenia	1 626.3	873.8	36.3	137.6	392.8	66.3
Slovakia	1 052.3	463.6	6.7	4.5	411.1	47.3
Finland	2 111.7	1163.5	65.0	267.7	383.7	113.4
Sweden	2 530.6	:	:	198.7	428.3	91.4
United Kingdom	:	:	:	:	:	:
Iceland	2 676.1	1411.5	139.9	548.7	433.4	40.6
Norway (¹)	3 374.9	1649.1	49.7	872.8	486.2	69.0
Switzerland	3 470.0	1950.2	55.6	667.1	431.4	75.1
Japan (¹)	2 024.5	1133.5	19.6	339.1	430.1	39.2
United States	5 295.0	:	:	344.9	735.1	189.2

(¹) 2005.
(²) 2004.

Source: Eurostat (hlth_sha_hc)

Table 3.5: Healthcare expenditure by financing agent, 2006
(PPS per inhabitant)

	All financing agents	Social security funds	Other government	Private insurance enterprises	Out-of-pocket expenditure	Rest of the world
Belgium	2 763.9	1 634.0	369.4	142.0	601.1	:
Bulgaria	611.7	240.6	102.4	2.2	260.9	0.0
Czech Republic	1 219.8	988.6	80.2	2.7	144.2	:
Denmark	2 680.6	:	2 235.9	42.5	400.6	:
Germany	2 780.7	1 945.6	203.4	263.9	346.0	:
Estonia	778.3	491.5	81.9	8.3	187.3	3.2
Ireland	:	:	:	:	:	:
Greece	:	:	:	:	:	:
Spain	1 981.9	102.2	1 300.1	123.6	440.8	:
France	2 769.8	2 046.3	145.9	363.9	191.9	:
Italy	:	:	:	:	:	:
Cyprus	1 291.8	1.4	523.3	89.7	621.2	0.0
Latvia (¹)	675.2	0.0	376.1	15.4	281.5	2.1
Lithuania	761.5	473.7	44.8	3.3	238.9	0.1
Luxembourg (¹)	4 300.5	3 115.5	776.2	:	287.7	:
Hungary	1 203.7	747.3	99.1	16.4	280.3	:
Malta	:	:	:	:	:	:
Netherlands	2 743.6	2 123.4	114.6	166.3	169.1	0.0
Austria (²)	2 733.9	1 270.0	806.9	146.3	475.8	:
Poland	723.7	449.2	51.9	4.3	196.2	:
Portugal	1 702.7	15.3	1 186.6	73.8	417.2	:
Romania	403.0	266.3	43.6	1.6	91.4	0.0
Slovenia	1 626.3	1 148.7	29.6	224.3	202.6	0.3
Slovakia	1 052.3	669.1	67.3	:	279.8	:
Finland	2 111.7	329.9	1 249.9	48.7	412.7	:
Sweden	2 530.6	:	2 075.6	:	423.8	:
United Kingdom	:	:	:	:	:	:
Iceland	2 676.1	734.5	1 458.7	:	444.4	:
Norway (¹)	3 374.9	495.9	2 307.0	:	564.1	0.0
Switzerland	3 470.0	1 490.3	561.3	228.1	1 068.5	:
Japan (¹)	2 024.5	1 331.4	334.5	51.2	295.7	:
United States	5 295.0	:	2 401.2	1 958.5	705.9	:

(¹) 2005.
(²) 2004.

Source: Eurostat (hlth_sha_hf)

Table 3.6: Healthcare indicators
(per 100 000 inhabitants)

	Practising physicians (¹)		Hospital beds		Hospital discharges of in-patients (excluding healthy new born babies)	
	1997 (²)	2007 (³)	1997 (⁴)	2007 (⁵)	2001 (⁶)	2007 (⁷)
Belgium	367.4	405.1	794.8	660.1	16 162	15 741
Bulgaria	345.9	364.9	1 031.1	638.1	:	20 015
Czech Republic	311.3	355.7	804.3	727.3	22 065	20 624
Denmark	262.0	314.4	461.5	340.8	16 326	16 498
Germany	312.7	345.5	938.0	829.1	20 060	22 138
Estonia	325.4	323.4	774.8	557.3	:	:
Ireland	213.4	298.6	670.8	519.9	14 025	13 743
Greece	398.1	:	512.4	473.8	:	:
Spain	293.5	352.2	382.9	330.2	10 904	10 659
France	325.0	335.5	847.7	700.3	17 937	16 146
Italy	400.9	363.5	588.3	386.3	:	14 417
Cyprus	249.6	271.5	467.3	375.5	7 031	6 536
Latvia	288.1	306.7	975.1	744.5	:	19 970
Lithuania	377.2	371.1	1 023.0	816.2	23 454	22 100
Luxembourg	225.5	348.3	1 066.8	569.4	18 172	16 468
Hungary	307.9	280.6	817.9	713.3	:	19 838
Malta	245.7	334.9	562.0	737.3	:	7 337
Netherlands	189.9	:	520.1	481.5	9 088	10 634
Austria	293.0	374.2	918.6	777.9	:	27 363
Poland	235.7	218.0	757.4	647.5	:	13 965
Portugal	261.0	:	394.4	:	:	9 127
Romania	:	222.0	738.7	641.1	:	21 274
Slovenia	219.1	237.6	565.3	473.2	:	16 168
Slovakia	239.8	315.9	813.8	674.9	20 534	19 290
Finland	229.9	269.5	790.8	673.6	21 045	19 620
Sweden	291.5	356.6	522.1	287.7	14 997	14 910
United Kingdom	:	248.5	:	341.8	12 698	12 248
Croatia	227.7	266.0	606.0	548.3	12 268	14 151
FYR of Macedonia	224.3	253.5	517.1	463.1	:	9 876
Turkey	:	:	252.4	:	:	:
Iceland	324.5	366.8	:	:	16 789	15 018
Norway	251.7	387.8	395.9	382.3	15 999	17 160
Switzerland	326.1	382.6	664.0	539.3	:	16 223

(¹) Greece, France, Italy, the former Yugoslav Republic of Macedonia and Switzerland, professionally active physicians; Ireland and Malta, licensed physicians; Estonia, break in series, 1998.
(²) Slovenia, 1998.
(³) Belgium, Spain, Latvia, Malta and Austria, 2008; the Czech Republic, Germany, France, Poland, Slovakia and Sweden, 2006.
(⁴) France and Switzerland, 1998.
(⁵) Belgium, France, Latvia, Malta and Slovenia, 2008; Germany, Luxembourg, Poland, Sweden and the former Yugoslav Republic of Macedonia, 2006; Greece, 2005.
(⁶) The Czech Republic, the Netherlands, Finland and the United Kingdom, 2002.
(⁷) Bulgaria, Italy, Cyprus, Slovakia, Finland, Sweden, Croatia, the former Yugoslav Republic of Macedonia and Iceland, 2006; Latvia and Portugal, 2005.

Source: Eurostat (tps00044, tps00046 and hlth_co_disch2t)

Figure 3.11: Number of hospital beds, EU-27
(per 100 000 inhabitants)

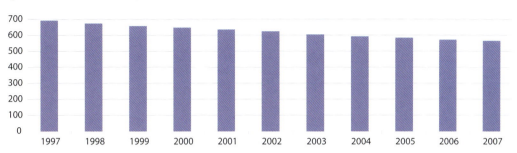

Source: Eurostat (tps00046)

Table 3.7: Hospital beds
(per 100 000 inhabitants)

	Curative care beds in hospitals			Psychiatric care beds in hospitals		
	1998	2003	2007 ([1])	1998	2003 ([2])	2007 ([3])
EU-27	476.7	418.3	389.6	75.3	62.4	55.1
Belgium	485.8	451.7	425.2	259.6	248.0	180.3
Bulgaria	:	484.3	490.6	72.8	64.4	67.2
Czech Republic	610.3	556.4	515.2	113.3	112.6	106.4
Denmark	372.2	328.6	289.9	78.9	70.4	51.0
Germany	696.6	656.6	619.6	:	:	:
Estonia	587.1	440.4	380.4	89.5	58.7	56.2
Ireland	285.1	282.2	267.4	150.5	109.3	86.3
Greece	391.7	382.2	386.9	107.7	88.1	86.9
Spain	292.6	265.2	255.5	53.2	49.0	41.7
France	434.1	385.8	355.3	118.9	99.9	89.3
Italy	501.7	352.9	314.2	33.1	13.6	11.6
Cyprus	400.2	398.7	349.1	55.7	32.4	26.5
Latvia	660.1	555.7	516.1	180.6	137.4	137.3
Lithuania	700.1	582.8	510.7	125.7	108.0	102.6
Luxembourg	596.6	553.4	450.2	124.9	110.1	92.1
Hungary	569.5	553.4	413.9	96.1	40.1	30.5
Malta	383.9	338.6	278.1	175.9	142.0	169.1
Netherlands	323.4	295.1	320.8	166.7	128.0	136.9
Austria	663.0	615.6	610.5	52.8	51.0	58.7
Poland	552.8	486.4	465.4	77.4	71.5	68.0
Portugal	:	:	:	:	:	:
Romania	525.1	452.3	448.1	88.6	76.3	79.4
Slovenia	461.6	401.3	382.5	79.8	73.7	69.0
Slovakia	588.9	509.1	491.5	92.6	89.8	82.4
Finland	260.6	230.5	211.2	109.0	98.3	88.5
Sweden	257.1	222.7	211.3	66.4	51.3	49.1
United Kingdom	:	304.6	268.8	:	83.1	66.0
Croatia	373.6	346.2	342.2	100.3	95.5	96.3
FYR of Macedonia	335.7	318.1	319.1	73.4	67.1	58.5
Turkey	181.2	223.1	:	12.6	11.9	:
Norway	324.7	292.0	275.9	68.7	113.3	94.8
Switzerland	442.3	386.5	348.7	119.8	107.8	102.5

([1]) Belgium, France, Latvia, Malta and Slovenia, 2008; Germany, Luxembourg, Poland, Sweden and the former Yugoslav Republic of Macedonia, 2006; Greece, 2005.
([2]) Luxembourg, 2004.
([3]) Belgium, France, Latvia, Malta and Slovenia, 2008; Luxembourg, Poland, Sweden and the former Yugoslav Republic of Macedonia, 2006; Greece, 2005.

Source: Eurostat (tps00168 and tps00047)

Table 3.8: Hospital discharges of in-patients by diagnosis (ISHMT – international shortlist for hospital morbidity tabulation), 2007
(per 100 000 inhabitants)

	Neoplasms (cancers)	Diseases of the circulatory system	Diseases of the respiratory system	Diseases of the digestive system	Pregnancy, childbirth & the puerperium	Injury, poisoning & certain other consequences of external causes
Belgium	1 183.9	2 068.1	1 359.1	1 649.9	1 369.7	1 634.7
Bulgaria	1 417.6	3 341.8	2 964.0	1 937.2	1 910.3	1 257.6
Czech Republic	1 775.4	3 086.8	1 397.8	1 811.3	1 596.2	1 677.8
Denmark	1 396.1	2 068.8	1 468.5	1 352.4	1 220.8	1 502.9
Germany	2 412.8	3 391.8	1 396.0	2 102.2	1 095.8	2 128.2
Estonia	1 798.9	3 371.7	1 841.2	1 612.8	1 900.8	1 210.9
Ireland	856.0	1 197.2	1 338.3	1 229.4	2 669.0	1 360.2
Greece	:	:	:	:	:	:
Spain	918.9	1 322.8	1 167.8	1 255.9	1 392.8	897.9
France	1 214.0	1 951.5	965.8	1 624.4	1 566.4	1 396.7
Italy (¹)	1 311.7	2 427.5	1 173.9	1 408.9	1 298.2	1 286.8
Cyprus	518.6	869.9	763.0	730.8	408.9	1 019.9
Latvia (²)	1 799.7	3 538.9	2 221.7	1 831.8	1 619.2	2 243.1
Lithuania	1 716.1	4 485.3	2 371.2	1 802.8	1 625.1	1 857.3
Luxembourg	1 560.0	2 172.3	1 347.7	1 509.6	1 397.5	1 234.2
Hungary	:	:	:	:	:	:
Malta	:	:	:	:	:	:
Netherlands	1 052.2	1 543.9	762.3	939.5	910.1	902.8
Austria	2 890.8	3 755.3	1 688.6	2 502.0	1 303.1	2 905.1
Poland	1 403.1	2 329.2	1 288.8	1 269.3	1 377.8	1 048.6
Portugal (²)	920.3	1 206.2	955.9	1 061.9	1 089.3	684.7
Romania	1 508.3	2 824.4	2 856.6	2 153.7	1 783.2	1 271.5
Slovenia	1 776.1	1 948.1	1 328.4	1 402.9	1 285.3	1 516.8
Slovakia (¹)	1 752.9	3 075.6	1 677.2	1 939.8	1 596.7	1 614.7
Finland (¹)	1 769.3	3 032.6	1 411.9	1 414.9	1 316.9	1 932.3
Sweden (¹)	1 376.2	2 370.6	964.4	1 174.6	1 306.2	1 421.2
United Kingdom	936.3	1 275.3	1 134.0	1 144.9	1 381.5	1 208.1
Croatia (¹)	2 022.6	1 945.9	1 108.4	1 223.5	264.7	1 073.3
FYR of Macedonia (¹)	849.5	1 669.5	1 494.6	1 104.9	494.5	624.9
Iceland (¹)	1 282.8	1 547.5	900.0	1 322.3	1 970.8	1 051.4
Norway	1 733.2	2 448.7	1 486.0	1 240.2	1 507.5	1 875.1
Switzerland	1 098.2	1 743.9	877.3	1 373.7	1 187.5	1 949.3

(¹) 2006.
(²) 2005.

Source: Eurostat (hlth_co_disch2)

Table 3.9: Hospital discharges of in-patients by diagnosis (ISHMT – international shortlist for hospital morbidity tabulation), average length of stay, 2007 (days)

	Neoplasms (cancers)	Diseases of the circulatory system	Diseases of the respiratory system	Diseases of the digestive system	Pregnancy, childbirth & the puerperium	Injury, poisoning & certain other consequences of external causes
Belgium	9.3	8.2	8.1	5.9	4.8	8.6
Bulgaria	7.4	6.0	7.5	5.8	4.6	5.8
Czech Republic	9.9	13.8	9.1	7.6	5.3	10.4
Denmark	6.4	5.4	5.4	5.0	3.4	5.1
Germany	10.3	10.4	9.0	7.4	4.8	9.3
Estonia	8.0	11.0	5.2	5.3	3.1	8.8
Ireland	11.4	10.1	7.1	6.4	2.9	5.7
Greece	:	:	:	:	:	:
Spain	9.5	8.3	7.2	5.9	3.1	8.5
France	7.6	6.9	7.0	5.3	4.8	5.6
Italy (¹)	9.5	8.8	8.4	6.8	4.0	8.1
Cyprus	8.9	6.4	5.2	5.1	5.4	5.8
Latvia (²)	9.3	9.2	7.9	6.2	5.6	7.5
Lithuania	10.3	13.2	7.6	6.7	4.5	8.7
Luxembourg	9.3	7.9	6.3	5.8	4.8	7.9
Hungary	6.2	8.5	6.8	6.5	4.9	6.7
Malta	7.5	6.5	4.9	3.9	3.5	5.9
Netherlands	7.7	7.3	7.3	6.4	3.5	7.2
Austria	7.7	10.9	8.3	6.8	5.5	8.9
Poland	7.6	7.9	8.3	6.0	5.2	6.5
Portugal (²)	8.7	7.9	8.2	5.9	3.3	9.3
Romania	7.1	8.1	7.2	6.6	5.0	6.1
Slovenia	7.9	8.3	7.0	6.2	4.6	7.0
Slovakia (¹)	9.1	8.8	8.3	6.4	5.8	6.8
Finland (¹)	9.0	16.3	13.4	6.0	3.7	11.1
Sweden (¹)	7.9	6.5	5.6	4.9	2.9	6.2
United Kingdom	8.9	10.6	7.7	6.3	2.5	8.6
Croatia (¹)	10.0	10.3	8.9	8.6	8.5	8.7
FYR of Macedonia (¹)	10.2	7.3	7.6	5.9	3.4	8.1
Iceland (¹)	7.3	6.9	6.4	4.0	2.6	6.7
Norway	7.1	5.4	6.2	4.8	3.6	4.8
Switzerland	10.7	8.7	8.5	7.2	6.0	7.6

(¹) 2007.
(²) 2005.

Source: Eurostat (hlth_co_inpst)

3.4 Health problems

Introduction

The promotion of health and healthy life-style choices can play an important role in reducing disease and early death ([7]). On average, Europeans with better jobs, more education or higher incomes live healthier and longer lives. Actions to reduce health inequalities aim to:

- improve everyone's level of health closer to that of the most advantaged;
- ensure that the health needs of the most disadvantaged are fully addressed;
- help improve faster the health of people in countries and regions with lower levels of health.

Health problems linked to lifestyle-related health determinants can be age specific (in childhood or in old-age), as well as resulting from socio-economic factors. Health promotion in various settings, such as schools, workplaces, families or local communities has proven to be efficient in addressing health issues across communities, focusing on specific diseases or target groups.

The seven most important risk factors for premature death in the EU (smoking, blood pressure, cholesterol, body mass index, inadequate fruit and vegetable intake, physical inactivity, excessive alcohol consumption) relate, at least to some extent, to consumption and exercise. As such, a balanced diet and regular physical activity, along with avoiding both smoking and excessive drinking, are important factors for promoting and maintaining good health.

Smoking is widely acknowledged as a leading cause of health problems, with legislation adopted in a majority of Member States restricting or forbidding smoking in public places and/or workplaces, as well as offering protection to passive smokers. Indirect taxes, health warnings, and restrictions on advertising have also targeted smokers. Smoking is the single largest cause of avoidable death in the EU accounting for over half a million deaths each year. The Directorate-General for Health and Consumers estimates that 25 % of all cancer deaths and 15 % of all deaths in the EU can be attributed to smoking. The European Commission is developing a tobacco control policy, focused on:

- legislative measures;
- support for Europe-wide smoking prevention and cessation activities;
- mainstreaming tobacco control into a range of other EU policies (such as agricultural, taxation or development policy);
- making sure that the pioneering role played by the EU in many tobacco control areas has an impact at a global level.

Weight problems and obesity are increasing at an alarming rate in Europe, especially among children. Obesity is a serious public health problem, as it significantly increases the risk of chronic diseases such as cardiovascular disease, type 2 diabetes and certain cancers. Lifestyle factors, including diet, eating habits and levels of physical activity (and inactivity) are often adopted during the early years of life; as

---

([7]) For more information: http://ec.europa.eu/health/ph_determinants/healthdeterminants_en.htm.

such, childhood obesity is strongly linked to adult obesity. However, maintaining a 'normal weight' can be a challenging exercise, given the abundance of energy-rich foods and lifestyle pressures that reduce the opportunities for physical activity both at work and during leisure time.

Definitions and data availability

Health interview surveys (HIS) are the source of information for describing the health status and the health-related behaviours of the European population. The following topics are usually covered in such surveys:

- height and weight which form the basis for the calculation of the body mass index (BMI);
- self-perceived health;
- activities that have been reduced because of health problems;
- long-standing illnesses or health problems;
- smoking behaviour;
- alcohol consumption.

Many health-related indicators are expressed as percentages within different population cohorts on the basis of background variables covering gender, age, activity status, and educational level. Note that the information comes from non-harmonised national surveys and that the Member States were asked to post-harmonise the data according to a set of common guidelines; Member States have since joined efforts on a harmonised EU survey (EHIS).

The **body mass index (BMI)** is a measure of a person's weight relative to their height that correlates fairly well with body fat. The BMI is accepted as the most

useful measure of obesity for adults when only weight and height data are available. It is calculated as the result of dividing body weight (in kilograms) by body height (in metres) squared. The following subdivisions are used to categorise the BMI: underweight people have a BMI less than 18.5, normal weight people have a BMI from 18.5 to less than 25, overweight people have a BMI greater than or equal to 25, while the threshold for obesity is a BMI of 30; note that the BMI is not calculated for children.

For perceptions concerning long-standing illness or health problems the data presented comes from European Union statistics on income and living conditions (EU-SILC). A long-standing illness or health problem is anything that has troubled the respondent or that is likely to affect the respondent over a period of time.

Workplace health is a special health issue: the 2007 labour force survey (LFS) included an ad-hoc module surveying work-related accidents, health problems and work-related factors affecting mental well-being or physical health – see Subchapter 3.5.

Main findings

Obesity is a serious public health problem that increases the risk of death and disability; it is primarily associated with poor dietary habits and a lack of physical activity. The proportion of the population that is overweight has increased considerably in most Member States over the last decade, resulting in approximately half the EU population being overweight or obese. In 2003 [8] the highest rates were recorded in the

---

[8] Data are collected in different years depending on the country (ranging from 1996 to 2003).

United Kingdom (61.0 %, England only) and Germany (59.7 %) ([9]), while Italy and France were the only Member States to report less than 40 % of their population as either overweight or obese.

In 2003 ([10]) the proportion of daily smokers was close to 50 % of the male population in Latvia and Estonia, while Sweden (16.5 %) reported the lowest proportion of male smokers. Daily smoking rates were lower among women (compared with men) in each of the Member States, with the exception of Sweden which reported a slightly higher proportion of female daily smokers. Austria and Denmark recorded the highest incidence of daily smoking among women, at just over 30 % of the female population, while Portugal (6.8 %) was the only Member State where the proportion of female daily smokers was under one in 10. The largest absolute differences in smoking habits between the sexes were reported for the Baltic States, where the proportion of men smoking daily was 30 percentage points or more above the rate for women. In relative terms, the proportion of men who smoked on a daily basis was four times as high as the proportion recorded among women in Portugal, while the rate for men was more than three times as high as that for women in Cyprus, Lithuania, Romania and Latvia.

There appears to be a shift in smoking patterns across Europe between the sexes. Among the population group aged 15 to 24, there was a much smaller difference between the proportion of men

and women smoking. Young females in Sweden and the United Kingdom were more likely to smoke than young males. Furthermore, in the majority of Member States the proportion of young women smoking often exceeded the corresponding average for women of all ages; this was particularly the case in the United Kingdom, Spain, Ireland and Germany.

Results from a 2007 survey of European Union statistics on income and living conditions (EU-SILC) provide information on the difficulties Europeans faced in their daily lives and the amount of assistance they might need; note that the survey data represents people's perceptions and does not specifically measure disability levels. Within the EU-27, some 29.1 % of men and 33.4 % of women (aged 18 or more) said they had a long-standing illness or health problem. In each Member State, the proportion of women that reported that they had such a long-standing problem was higher than the corresponding proportion for men, although in the United Kingdom the proportion of men was less than 1 percentage point lower than that for women. This difference between the sexes rose to over 9 percentage points in Latvia and Slovakia. Overall, the highest proportions of people reporting long-standing illnesses or health problems were in Finland and Estonia, where the proportions for both men and women were around two fifths, while the lowest proportions were recorded in Romania, Italy and Greece.

([9]) Data for Germany and England relate to valid height and weight measurements, while for the other countries the data correspond to self-declared height and weight.

([10]) Data are collected in different years depending on the country (ranging from 1996 to 2003).

Figure 3.12: Overweight people, 2003 (¹)
(% of total population)

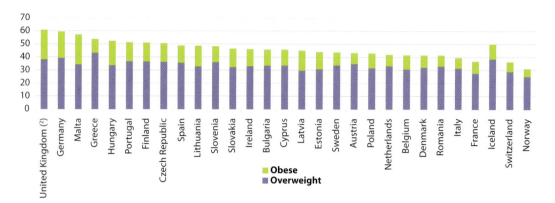

(¹) National health interview survey (HIS) data, 1996-2003 depending on the country; note that data for Germany and for England relate to valid height and weight measurements, while for the other countries the data correspond to self-declared height and weight; Luxembourg, not available.
(²) Only England.

Source: Eurostat (hlth_ls_bmia)

Figure 3.13: Daily smokers, 2003 (¹)
(% of male/female population)

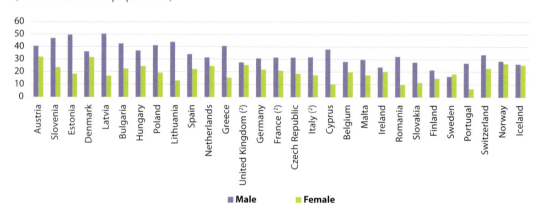

(¹) National health interview survey (HIS) data, 1996-2003 depending on the country; Luxembourg, not available; the figure is ranked on the average of male and female.
(²) No distinction between daily and occasional smoking.

Source: Eurostat (tps00169)

Figure 3.14: Daily smokers among the population aged 15-24, 2003 (¹)
(% of male/female population aged 15-24)

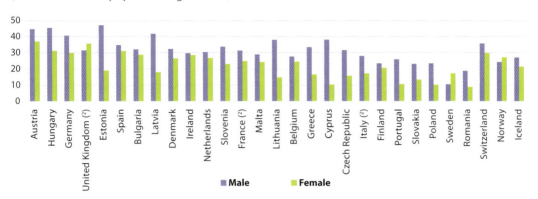

■ **Male**   ■ **Female**

(¹) National health interview survey (HIS) data, 1996-2003 depending on the country; Luxembourg, not available; the figure is ranked on the average of male and female.
(²) No distinction between daily and occasional smoking.

Source: Eurostat (tps00170)

Figure 3.15: People having a long-standing illness or health problem, 2007 (¹)
(% of male/female population aged 18 or more)

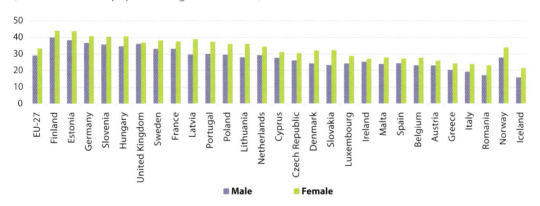

■ **Male**   ■ **Female**

(¹) Long-standing refers to any illnesses or health problems which have lasted, or are expected to last, for 6 months or more; Bulgaria, not available; graph is ranked on the average of male and female.

Source: Eurostat (hlth_silc_11)

3.5 Health and safety at work

Introduction

A relatively high proportion of people spend around eight hours a day, five days a week at work. Many aspects of work have the potential to bring about illness (or death) and these are not restricted to safety issues and accidents. Working conditions change over time, and health and safety in the workplace has been redefined in order to take account of the move from traditional, industrial, heavy industries, to focus on the modern-day world of work, which is characterised more by issues such as stress and psychological risks, musculoskeletal disorders, noise, or the abuse of tobacco, alcohol, or dangerous substances related to work.

Health at work also involves physical, moral and social well-being (issues such as intimidation and violence in the workplace), which are considered especially important determinants regarding the quality of work and the productivity of the workforce. A strategic health and safety policy is therefore not just crucial to ensuring the well-being of Europe's workers; it is also a key issue in relation to the EU's competitiveness.

The adoption and application in recent decades of a large body of Community laws has aimed to improve working conditions in the Member States and has reduced the incidence of work-related accidents and illnesses. The new strategy on health and safety at work for 2007-2012 ([11]) aims to achieve a sustained reduction of occupational accidents and diseases in the EU, which as well as having direct ef-

fects on employees, will also play a role in contributing towards the success of the revised Lisbon growth and jobs strategy.

Definitions and data availability

European statistics on **accidents at work** and occupational diseases respond to the requirements of the strategy on health and safety at work for 2007-2012. Harmonised data on accidents at work are collected in the framework of European statistics on accidents at work (ESAW). The ESAW methodology is in accordance with the International Labour Organisation (ILO) Resolution of 1998 concerning 'statistics of occupational injuries: resulting from occupational accidents'. National sources are typically declarations of accidents at work, either to the public (social security) or private insurance systems, or to other relevant national authorities. Data are presented in numbers or as incidence rates. **Incidence rates** are calculated as follows: number of persons involved in (fatal) accidents at work / number of persons in employment in the reference population x 100 000.

An **accident at work** is a discrete occurrence during the course of work which leads to physical or mental harm. This includes accidents in the course of work outside the premises of a person's business, even if caused by a third party (on clients' premises, on another company's premises, in a public place or during transport, including road traffic accidents) and cases of acute poisoning. The information presented excludes accidents on the way to or from work (commuting accidents), occurrences having only a

[11] Council Resolution 2007/C 145/01 of 25 June 2007 on a new Community strategy on health and safety at work (2007-2012) (OJ C 145, 30.6.2007, p. 1); for more information: http://eur-lex.europa.eu/LexUriServ/site/en/oj/2007/c_145/c_14520070630en00010004.pdf.

medical origin (such as a heart attack at work) and occupational diseases. The data on **serious accidents at work** refer to accidents that result in more than three days absence from work.

A **fatal accident at work** is defined as an accident which leads to the death of a victim generally within one year of the accident. In practice the notification of an accident as fatal ranges from national registration procedures where the accident is registered as fatal when the victim died the same day (the Netherlands) to cases where no time limits are laid down (Belgium, Greece, France, Italy, Luxemburg, Austria, Sweden and Norway).

The 2007 labour force survey (LFS) included an ad-hoc module consisting of four variables on accidents at work (using the standard definition), five variables on work-related health problems, and two variables on factors that can adversely affect mental well-being or physical health.

Work-related health problems include illnesses, disabilities or other physical or psychic health problems, apart from accidental injuries. The main inclusion criterion is that the person considers this health problem as caused or made worse by work (past or current). This means that the surveyed problems are not restricted to cases reported or recognised by the authorities. The onset of the problem could have been more than a year before the interview, but the person must have suffered from the problem during the 12-month reference period. The analysis is limited to persons aged 15-64 (16-64 for Spain and the United Kingdom) who are or have been employed or self-employed.

Factors that can adversely affect mental or physical well-being concern workplace exposure to a number of mentioned factors that a person is clearly exposed to more frequently or more intensively than people experience in general day-to-day life. The factors relating to mental well-being include: harassment and bullying; violence or the threat of violence; time pressure or being overloaded with work. The factors relating to physical well-being include: chemicals, dusts, fumes, smoke or gases; noise or vibration; difficult work postures, work movements or handling of heavy loads; risk of accident.

Main findings

In recent years the incidence rate of serious accidents at work in the EU-27 has fallen, such that by 2006 it had decreased by 24 % in relation to 1998. During the same period there was a 19 % reduction in fatal accidents at work in the EU-27. In 2006, 5 785 lives were lost due to accidents at work in the EU-27. The incidence of fatal accidents may, in part, reflect the structural shift of the European economy towards services, where the risks of accident and death at work are usually less than within agriculture, industry or construction.

There were only three Member States that reported a higher incidence of serious accidents at work in 2006 when compared with 1998: Estonia (20 % higher), Ireland (7 % higher) and Lithuania (1 % higher). At the other end of the scale, the incidence of serious accidents in Greece, Bulgaria and Belgium was at least 40 % lower in 2006 than in 1998. The majority of the Member States also reported a reduction in the incidence of fatal accidents at work, although this was not the case in six Member States, most notably in Slovenia (49 % increase), Lithuania (17 % increase) and Sweden (15 % increase). France (provisional data) halved its incidence of fatal accidents at work by 2006.

Men are considerably more likely to have an accident or to die at work. This is due, at least in part, to a higher proportion of men working in 'higher risk' sectors and occupations, while men are also more likely to work on a full-time basis. Structural changes, as well as changes in working practices, may also explain why the incidence of accidents tended to fall at a more rapid pace for men than for women. For example, the incidence of serious accidents for men fell by 23 % between 1998 and 2006, while the corresponding reduction for women was 18 %.

In 2007 accidents at work were most common in the sectors of agriculture, hunting and forestry, manufacturing, and construction. However, there is a clear gender difference, as the sectors with the highest likelihood of accidents for women were health and social work, and hotels and restaurants.

According to the 2007 labour force survey, some 8.6 % of persons employed (aged 15-64) in the EU-27 experienced one or more work-related health problems during the previous 12 months; two or more work-related health problems were reported by 2.1% of persons employed. Among persons with a work-related health problem, back problems (28 %), neck, shoulder, arm or hand problems (19 %), and stress, depression or anxiety (14 %) were most often reported: men were more likely to report back problems than women, whereas women were more likely to report neck, shoulder, arm or hand problems.

A recent study, in which the European Agency for Safety and Health at Work ([12]) took part, refers to figures from the International Labour Organisation (ILO) estimating that in 2006, some 159 500 workers died from occupational diseases in the EU-27.

([12]) For more information: http://osha.europa.eu/en.

Figure 3.16: Incidence of accidents at work, 2006
(1998=100, based on the number of accidents per 100 000 persons employed)

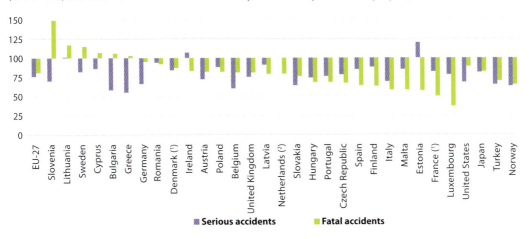

(¹) Fatal accidents, provisional.
(²) Break in series for serious accidents (re-based, 2005=100).

Source: Eurostat (tsiem090 and tsiem100)

Figure 3.17: Incidence of serious accidents at work, by gender, 2006 (¹)
(1998=100, based on the number of serious accidents per 100 000 persons employed)

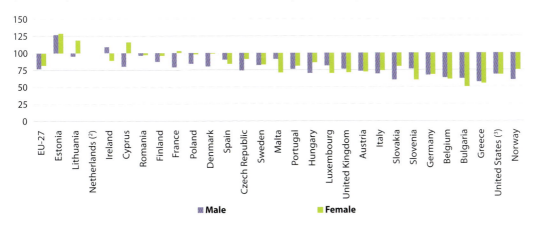

(¹) Latvia, not available; the figure is ranked on the average of male and female.
(²) Break in series, re-based, 2005=100.
(³) 2005.

Source: Eurostat (tsiem090)

Figure 3.18: Workers reporting one or more accidents in the past 12 months, EU-27, 2007 (¹) (% of male/female persons employed aged 15-64 years old)

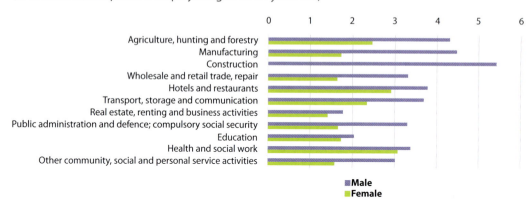

(¹) The following activities are not included since their reliability cannot be guaranteed due to small sample sizes: fishing; mining and quarrying; electricity, gas and water supply; construction (female); financial intermediation; private households with employed persons; extra-territorial organisations and bodies; the figure is ranked on the average of male and female.

Source: Eurostat (LFS)

Figure 3.19: Work-related health problems experienced in the past 12 months, EU-27, 2007 (¹) (% of male/female persons employed aged 15-64 years old)

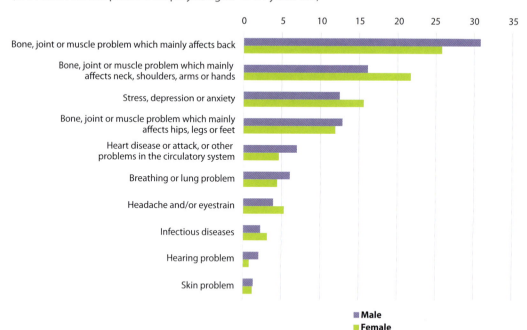

(¹) Excluding France; the figure is ranked on the average of male and female.

Source: Eurostat (LFS)

Education

Education, vocational training and more generally lifelong learning play a vital role in both an economic and social context. The opportunities which the EU offers its citizens for living, studying and working in other countries make a major contribution to cross-cultural understanding, personal development and the realisation of the EU's full economic potential. Each year, well over a million EU citizens of all ages benefit from EU-funded educational, vocational and citizenship-building programmes.

The Treaty establishing the European Community ([1]) acknowledged the importance of these areas by stating that '*the Community shall contribute to the development of quality education by encouraging co-operation between Member States and, if necessary, by supporting and supplementing their action ... The Community shall implement a vocational training policy which shall support and supplement the action of the Member States*'. As such, the European Commission follows up on policy cooperation and work with the Member States, while funding programmes such as the lifelong learning programme (LLP).

Political cooperation within the EU has been strengthened through the education and training 2010 work programme which integrated previous actions in the fields of education and training. The follow-up to this programme is the strategic framework for European co-operation in education and training ([2]) which was adopted by the Council in May 2009. Benchmarks for 2010 have been set as:

- the share of low achieving 15-year-olds in reading should decrease by at least 20 %;

([1]) Consolidated version of the Treaty establishing the European Community, Chapter 3, Articles 149([1]) and 150([1]) OJ C 352, 24.12.2002, p. 33); for more information: http://eur-lex.europa.eu/en/treaties/dat/12002E/pdf/12002E_EN.pdf.

([2]) For more information: http://eur-lex.europa.eu/LexUriServ/LexUriServ.do?uri=OJ:C:2009:119:0002:0010:EN:PDF.

- the average rate of early school leavers should be no more than 10 %;
- 85 % of 22-year-olds should complete upper secondary education;
- the total number of graduates in mathematics, science and technology should increase by at least 15 %, while the gender imbalance in these subjects should be reduced;
- the average participation of persons aged 25 to 64 in lifelong learning should reach at least 12.5 %.

The benchmarks to be achieved by 2020 are:

- at least 95 % of children between 4 years old and the age for starting compulsory primary education should participate in early childhood education;
- the share of low-achieving 15-years-olds in reading, mathematics and science should be less than 15 %;
- the share of early leavers from education and training should be less than 10 %;
- the share of 30 to 34-year-olds with tertiary educational attainment should be at least 40 %;
- an average of at least 15 % of persons aged 25 to 64 should participate in lifelong learning.

As of 2007, the lifelong learning programme became the European Commission's flagship programme in the field of education and training, covering all learning opportunities from childhood to old age. Over the period 2007 to 2013, this programme has a budget of nearly EUR 7 000 million in order to support projects that foster interchange, cooperation and mobility between education and training systems within the EU. It is made up of four sub-programmes that focus on the different stages of education and training, each with quantified targets:

- Comenius for schools should involve at least 3 million pupils in joint educational activities over the period of the programme;
- Erasmus for higher education should reach a total of 3 million individual participants in student mobility actions since the action began;
- Leonardo da Vinci for vocational education and training should increase placements in enterprises to 80 000 persons per year by the end of the programme;
- Grundtvig for adult education should support the mobility of 7 000 individuals involved in adult education each year by 2013.

The measurement of progress towards these objectives within the field of education policy requires a range of comparable statistics on enrolment in education and training, numbers of graduates and teachers, language learning, student and researcher mobility, educational expenditure, as well as data on educational attainment and adult learning.

Education statistics cover a range of subjects, including: expenditure, personnel, participation rates, and attainment. The standards for international statistics on education are set by three international organisations:

- the United Nations Educational, Scientific, and Cultural Organisation (UNESCO) institute for statistics (UIS);

- the Organisation for Economic Co-operation and Development (OECD), and;
- the statistical office of the European Union (Eurostat).

The main source of data is a joint UNESCO/OECD/Eurostat (UOE) questionnaire on education statistics and this is the basis for the core components of the Eurostat database on education statistics; Eurostat also collects data on regional enrolments and foreign language learning. Data on educational attainment and adult learning are mainly provided by household surveys, in particular the EU labour force survey (LFS), which is complemented by an adult education survey (3), while the continuous vocational training survey (CVTS) provides information on training participation, volume and costs for enterprises.

4.1 Participation in education and educational attainment of young people

Introduction

School helps young people acquire the basic life skills and competences necessary for their personal development. The quality of a pupil's school experience affects not only personal development, but also his or her place in society, educational attainment, and employment opportunities. The quality of the education experienced by pupils is directly linked to the quality of teaching, which in turn is linked to the demands placed upon teachers, the training they receive, and the roles they are asked to fill. With this in mind, several

Member States are revising their school curricula in line with the changing needs of society and the economy, as well as reflecting on how to improve teacher training and evaluation.

Demographic trends in the last three decades reflect reductions in birth rates, that have resulted in the structure of the EU's population ageing and the proportion of those aged under 30 decreasing in the majority of Member States. These changes can have a significant impact on human and material resources required for the sound functioning of education systems – such as average class sizes or teacher recruitment strategies.

Most Europeans spend significantly longer in education than the legal minimum requirement. This reflects the choice to enrol in higher education, as well as increased enrolment in pre-primary education and wider participation in lifelong learning initiatives, such as mature (adult) students returning to education – often in order to retrain or equip themselves for a career change.

At the age of four, a high proportion of children in the EU are already enrolled in pre-primary educational institutions. The general objectives for pre-primary education are fairly similar across countries, focusing on the development of children's independence, well-being, self-confidence, and preparation for life and learning at school.

On average, compulsory education lasts nine or ten years in most of the EU: lasting longest in Hungary, the Netherlands and the United Kingdom. Compulsory primary education starts at the age of five

---

(3) For more information: http://epp.eurostat.ec.europa.eu/cache/ITY_OFFPUB/KS-CC-05-005/EN/KS-CC-05-005-EN.PDF.

or six in most Member States, although some Member States have a compulsory starting age of seven (⁴).

While national curricula include broadly the same subjects across the Member States, the amount of time allocated to each subject varies considerably. In addition, there are wide-ranging differences in the freedoms that teachers have to shape the content of their classes or follow a strict curriculum. The most significant differences between countries tend to relate to the degree of instruction given in foreign languages, information and communication technology, or religion. In contrast, all countries allocate a considerable amount of time to teach their mother tongue and mathematics.

Teaching time tends to be more evenly spread across subjects in compulsory secondary education, with more emphasis given to natural and social sciences, as well as foreign languages. Pupils from a particular country follow the same common curriculum throughout their full-time compulsory education in most Member States, although in Germany, Luxembourg, the Netherlands and Austria parents have to choose a particular type of education for their child at the end of primary school.

The Comenius programme addresses developments in education and school policy and aims to:

- improve and increase the mobility of pupils and educational staff;
- enhance and increase partnerships between schools in different Member States, with at least three million pupils taking part in joint educational activities by 2010;

- encourage language learning, innovative ICT-based content, services and better teaching techniques and practices;
- enhance the quality and European dimension of teacher training;
- improve pedagogical approaches and school management.

Member States have themselves set a number of other benchmarks for improving education. These include reading proficiency, attainment in mathematics, science and technology, early school leaving, and the completion of secondary school.

Definitions and data availability

The **international standard classification of education (ISCED)** is the basic tool for classifying education statistics, describing different levels of education, as well as fields of education and training (⁵). The current version, ISCED 97 distinguishes seven levels of education:

- ISCED level 0: **pre-primary education** – defined as the initial stage of organised instruction; it is school- or centre-based and is designed for children aged at least 3 years;
- ISCED level 1: **primary education** – begins between 5 and 7 years of age, is compulsory in all countries and generally lasts from four to six years;
- ISCED level 2: **lower secondary education** – continues the basic programmes of the primary level, although teaching is typically more subject-focused; usually, the end of this level coincides with the end of compulsory education;
- ISCED level 3: **upper secondary education** – generally begins at the end of compulsory education; the entrance

(⁴) For more information: http://eacea.ec.europa.eu/education/eurydice/documents/compulsory_education/106EN.pdf.

(⁵) For more information: http://www.unesco.org/education/information/nfsunesco/doc/isced_1997.htm.

age is typically 15 or 16 years and entrance qualifications and other minimum entry requirements are usually needed; instruction is often more subject-oriented and typical duration varies from two to five years;

- ISCED level 4: **post-secondary non-tertiary education** – straddles the boundary between upper secondary and tertiary education; typical examples are programmes designed to prepare pupils for studies at level 5 or programmes designed to prepare pupils for direct entry to the labour market;
- ISCED level 5: **tertiary education (first stage)** – entry normally requires the successful completion of level 3 or 4; includes tertiary programmes with academic orientation which are largely theoretically based and occupation orientation which are typically shorter and geared for entry into the labour market;
- ISCED level 6: **tertiary education (second stage)** – leads to an advanced research qualification (Ph.D. or doctorate).

The indicator for **four-year-olds in education** presents the percentage of four-year-olds who are enrolled in education-oriented pre-primary institutions. These institutions provide education-oriented care for young children. They must recruit staff with specialised qualifications in education. Day nurseries, playgroups and day-care centres, where the staff are not required to hold a qualification in education, are not included. The indicator for **18-year-olds** who are still in any kind of school (all ISCED levels) provides an indication of the number of young people who have not abandoned their efforts to improve their skills through initial education and includes both those who had a regular education career without any delays, as well as those who are continuing even if they had to repeat some steps in the past. The indicator of **school expectancy** corresponds to how many years, on average, a child starting in school can expect to stay at school (calculated by adding the single-year enrolment rates for all ages).

Pupil-teacher ratios are calculated by dividing the number of full-time-equivalent pupils and students in each level of education by the number of full-time-equivalent teachers at the same level; all institutions, both public and private, are included. This ratio should not be confused with average class-size. There can be a difference between the number of hours of teaching provided by individual teachers and the number of hours of instruction prescribed for pupils; more than one teacher can be teaching in a class at the same time; or teachers for special education needs can work with small groups or on a one-to-one basis.

The indicator for the **youth education attainment level** is defined as the proportion of the population aged 20 to 24 having completed at least an upper secondary education (minimum of ISCED level 3a, 3b or 3c long). The denominator consists of the total population of the same age group, excluding non-response.

The indicator for **early school leavers** is defined as the proportion of the population aged 18 to 24 with at most a lower secondary level of education (ISCED levels 1, 2 or 3c short), who are no longer in further education or training (respondents

declared not having received any education or training in the four weeks preceding the survey). The denominator consists of the total population of the same age group, excluding non-response.

Main findings

In 2007, there were about 93.2 million pupils and students enrolled in educational establishments in the EU-27. The highest share of pupils and students in the EU-27 total was accounted for by Germany, where 14.3 million pupils and students attended educational establishments in 2007; this figure was 1.6 million higher than the next largest student population – in the United Kingdom – and 2.0 million higher than in France.

The proportion of students found in each level of education varied somewhat between the Member States, most notably for primary and lower secondary levels of education. The variation reflects, to some degree, the demographic structure of each population. The high proportion of pupils in primary education in Luxembourg (47.1 % in 2007), for example, reflects the lack of a developed tertiary education sector in this country. At the other end of the spectrum, Greece, Slovenia, the Baltic Member States, Poland, Finland and Romania all had relatively high proportions (around one quarter or more) of their student populations within the tertiary education sector.

The figures above exclude pre-primary education – where 88.6 % of all four-year-olds in the EU-27 attended establishments in 2007. Enrolment rates in pre-primary education ranged from 100 % in France

and Sweden, to less than one child in two across Ireland and Poland.

More than three quarters (76.8 %) of all 18-year-olds within the EU-27 remained within the education system in 2007. However, this ratio rose to above 90 % in five Member States, while less than half of all 18-year-olds were still attending an educational establishment in Cyprus and the United Kingdom. These figures may reflect a number of factors, in particular the need for students to go abroad to continue their (tertiary) education, or the practise of making students re-take a whole year if their performance at the end of each academic year is deemed to be unsatisfactory.

School expectancy is a related indicator, as Member States with longer school expectancy generally have a higher proportion of 18-year-olds in education. Nevertheless, Ireland had the second highest proportion of 18-year-olds in education, but a relatively average length of school expectancy, while Denmark had the reverse situation, with a slightly above average proportion of 18-year-olds in education, and the fourth longest school expectancy.

Pupil/teacher ratios within primary education ranged from an average of less than 11 pupils per teacher in Lithuania, Greece, Hungary and Italy in 2007, to almost double that rate in France and the United Kingdom (both above 19 pupils per teacher). Between 2002 and 2007 there was a general reduction in the average number of pupils per teacher within primary education establishments in most of the Member States.

The average number of pupils per teacher was generally lower for secondary education than for primary education, with an average of less than ten pupils for every teacher in upper secondary education in Greece, Spain, Portugal, Luxembourg, Lithuania and France. Finland, the Netherlands and Romania had the highest average number of pupils per teacher (all over 15 pupils per teacher).

Data on educational attainment show that, in 2008, just over three quarters (78.5 %) of the EU-27's population aged 20 to 24 had completed at least an upper secondary level, a figure that reached 81.4 % for women. However, in 2008, 14.9 % of those aged 18 to 24 (16.9 % of men and 12.9 % of women) were early school leavers, with at most a lower secondary education.

Table 4.1: Pupils and students (excluding pre-primary education) (¹)

| | Total (ISCED 1-6) (1 000) | | Breakdown of total number of pupils and students (% of total) | | | | | | | |
| | | | Primary level of education (ISCED 1) | | Lower secondary level of education (ISCED 2) | | Upper and post-secondary non-tertiary education (ISCED 3-4) | | Tertiary education (ISCED 5-6) | |
	2002	2007	2002	2007	2002	2007	2002	2007	2002	2007
EU-27	97 266	93 247	30.2	30.4	24.6	23.9	27.5	25.3	17.6	20.3
Belgium	2 333	2 418	32.9	30.3	17.4	17.6	33.9	35.8	15.7	16.3
Bulgaria	1 275	1 175	27.4	22.8	28.1	23.9	26.5	31.3	17.9	22.0
Czech Republic	1 935	1 856	31.2	24.9	26.5	24.7	27.6	30.8	14.7	19.5
Denmark	1 046	1 155	39.7	36.0	20.3	20.9	21.3	23.0	18.7	20.1
Germany	14 511	14 251	23.2	23.2	39.2	35.9	22.2	24.3	14.9	16.0
Estonia	304	268	35.7	28.3	21.6	19.9	22.7	26.1	20.0	25.6
Ireland	992	1 054	44.9	45.1	18.0	16.5	19.3	20.3	17.8	18.1
Greece	1 975	1 964	32.7	32.5	17.7	17.6	22.7	19.2	26.8	30.7
Spain	7 461	7 556	33.4	35.7	26.3	26.0	15.8	14.7	24.6	23.5
France	11 791	12 296	32.3	33.4	27.9	26.5	21.9	22.3	17.2	17.7
Italy	9 199	9 500	30.3	30.0	19.9	18.5	29.6	30.1	20.2	21.4
Cyprus	142	146	45.0	39.6	23.1	22.2	22.0	22.9	9.8	15.2
Latvia	510	450	22.3	27.0	34.8	20.3	21.2	24.0	21.7	28.8
Lithuania	797	760	24.8	18.9	42.2	38.5	14.3	16.2	18.7	26.3
Luxembourg	72	76	47.2	47.1	22.7	24.9	26.0	28.1	4.1	:
Hungary	1 946	1 916	24.6	20.9	25.9	24.3	31.3	32.4	18.2	22.5
Malta	77	75	42.4	37.1	36.9	34.1	11.3	15.7	9.4	13.1
Netherlands	3 208	3 346	40.1	38.3	24.6	23.3	19.2	20.8	16.1	17.6
Austria	1 422	1 457	27.2	23.8	27.3	26.6	29.8	31.6	15.7	17.9
Poland	9 153	8 416	33.9	29.5	19.1	18.4	26.1	26.6	20.8	25.5
Portugal	1 964	1 881	39.2	40.2	20.4	21.2	20.2	19.1	20.2	19.5
Romania	3 939	3 839	26.1	23.9	32.8	24.0	26.3	27.8	14.8	24.2
Slovenia	407	395	21.1	24.2	23.8	18.3	30.7	28.2	24.4	29.4
Slovakia	1 109	1 079	25.6	21.4	35.3	30.3	25.3	28.1	13.7	20.2
Finland	1 179	1 251	33.4	29.2	16.3	16.2	26.3	29.9	24.1	24.7
Sweden	2 115	2 061	37.2	32.9	17.9	19.9	26.8	27.1	18.1	20.1
United Kingdom	16 407	12 607	27.6	35.0	14.2	17.6	44.5	28.6	13.7	18.7
Croatia	:	728	:	26.2	:	28.2	:	26.4	:	19.2
FYR of Macedonia	385	369	31.5	27.4	32.6	30.6	24.3	26.2	11.6	15.8
Turkey	15 389	16 687	68.6	65.0	-	-	20.5	20.3	10.9	14.7
Iceland	77	85	41.0	35.4	16.5	16.2	27.5	29.8	15.1	18.6
Liechtenstein	:	6	:	35.6	:	27.1	:	25.1	:	10.7
Norway	1 005	1 079	42.7	39.9	16.7	17.5	21.0	22.7	19.6	19.9
Switzerland	1 294	1 350	41.5	37.8	21.6	22.1	23.1	23.4	13.1	15.8
Japan	19 956	18 885	36.7	38.2	20.1	19.2	22.0	20.2	19.9	21.4
United States	64 440	67 429	38.6	36.3	19.5	19.3	17.2	18.1	24.7	26.3

(¹) Refer to the Internet metadata file (http://epp.eurostat.ec.europa.eu/cache/ITY_SDDS/en/educ_esms.htm).

Source: Eurostat (tps00051 and educ_enrl1tl)

Figure 4.1: Four-year-olds in education, 2007 (¹)
(% of all four-year-olds)

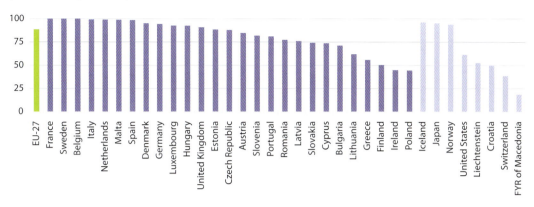

(¹) Refer to the Internet metadata file (http://epp.eurostat.ec.europa.eu/cache/ITY_SDDS/en/educ_esms.htm).

Source: Eurostat (tps00053)

Figure 4.2: 18-year-olds in education, 2007 (¹)
(% of all 18-year-olds)

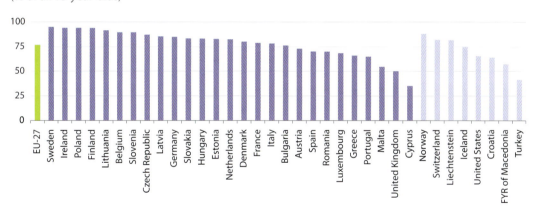

(¹) Refer to the Internet metadata file (http://epp.eurostat.ec.europa.eu/cache/ITY_SDDS/en/educ_esms.htm).

Source: Eurostat (tps00060)

Figure 4.3: School expectancy, 2007 (¹)
(years)

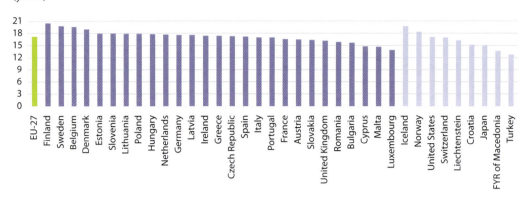

(¹) School expectancy corresponds to the expected years of education over a lifetime and has been calculated adding the single-year enrolment rates for all ages.

Source: Eurostat (tps00052)

Table 4.2: Pupil/teacher ratio in primary, lower and upper secondary education ([1])
(average number of pupils per teacher)

	Primary education (ISCED 1)		Lower secondary/second stage of basic education (ISCED 2)		Upper secondary education (ISCED 3)	
	2002	2007	2002	2007	2002	2007
Belgium	13.1	12.6	:	9.2	9.3	10.2
Bulgaria	16.8	16.0	12.8	12.1	11.7	11.6
Czech Republic	18.9	18.7	14.4	12.3	12.5	12.3
Denmark	10.9	11.2	:	:	14.2	:
Germany	18.9	18.3	15.7	15.2	13.6	14.3
Estonia ([2])	14.7	14.4	11.2	11.4	10.3	12.2
Ireland	19.5	17.9	14.6	:	14.6	13.2
Greece	12.5	10.1	9.3	7.7	9.3	7.3
Spain	14.6	13.6	13.7	11.7	8.3	7.7
France	19.4	19.7	13.7	14.3	10.6	9.6
Italy	10.6	10.5	9.9	9.4	10.3	10.8
Cyprus	19.4	15.9	13.0	11.2	11.7	11.1
Latvia	16.9	11.4	13.5	9.9	12.7	11.2
Lithuania	12.4	10.0	8.5	7.9	8.3	9.4
Luxembourg	11.6	11.2	9.0	:	9.0	9.0
Hungary	10.8	10.2	10.7	10.2	13.1	12.1
Malta ([3])	19.1	13.7	9.7	9.3	10.1	14.3
Netherlands	17.0	15.6	:	:	15.9	15.7
Austria	14.4	13.6	9.8	10.3	10.3	11.0
Poland	12.8	11.0	14.1	12.4	13.7	12.2
Portugal	11.0	11.8	9.3	7.9	7.5	8.4
Romania	17.7	16.9	13.3	12.2	14.4	15.3
Slovenia	12.6	15.2	13.1	9.5	13.5	13.7
Slovakia	20.1	17.9	14.0	13.9	13.3	14.1
Finland	15.8	15.0	10.6	9.9	16.0	15.9
Sweden	12.5	12.3	12.2	11.5	14.1	13.6
United Kingdom	19.9	19.4	17.6	16.7	21.6	11.2
Croatia	:	17.3	:	12.6	:	11.6
FYR of Macedonia	21.2	18.4	16.6	13.6	18.5	16.3
Turkey	27.5	26.2	:	:	17.7	16.2
Iceland	11.4	10.4	:	:	10.6	10.2
Liechtenstein	:	9.6	:	6.9	:	8.6
Norway	:	11.0	10.9	10.2	9.0	9.8
Japan	20.3	19.0	16.2	14.8	13.7	12.5
United States	15.5	14.6	15.5	14.7	15.6	15.6

([1]) Refer to the Internet metadata file (http://epp.eurostat.ec.europa.eu/cache/ITY_SDDS/en/educ_esms.htm).
([2]) 2001 instead of 2002.
([3]) 2006 instead of 2007.

Source: Eurostat (tps00054 and educ_iste)

Table 4.3: Youth education attainment level and early school leavers ([1])

	Youth education attainment level (%)				Early school leavers (%)			
	Total		Male	Female	Total		Male	Female
	2003	2008	2008	2008	2003	2008	2008	2008
EU-27 ([2])	76.9	78.5	75.7	81.4	16.6	14.9	16.9	12.9
Euro area	73.4	75.5	72.1	79.1	18.5	16.8	19.1	13.9
Belgium ([3])	81.2	82.2	80.5	83.9	14.3	12.0	13.4	10.6
Bulgaria	76.3	83.7	84.0	83.4	21.9	14.8	14.1	15.5
Czech Republic ([2])	92.1	91.6	91.0	92.2	6.5	5.6	5.8	5.4
Denmark ([4])	76.2	71.0	63.6	78.6	10.4	11.5	13.7	9.2
Germany ([5])	72.5	74.1	71.9	76.4	12.8	11.8	12.4	11.2
Estonia ([6])	81.5	82.2	76.0	88.3	12.9	14.0	19.8	8.2
Ireland ([2])	85.1	87.4	83.9	91.0	13.1	11.3	14.6	8.0
Greece ([2])	81.7	82.1	78.0	86.6	16.0	14.8	18.5	10.9
Spain ([7])	62.2	60.0	52.7	67.6	31.6	31.9	38.0	25.7
France ([8])	81.3	83.7	81.4	86.0	13.2	11.8	13.8	9.8
Italy ([3])	71.0	76.5	73.5	79.7	23.0	19.7	22.6	16.7
Cyprus ([2])	79.5	85.1	80.1	89.5	17.3	13.7	19.0	9.5
Latvia	75.4	80.0	74.3	86.0	18.0	15.5	20.2	10.7
Lithuania ([3, 9])	84.2	89.1	85.9	92.3	11.4	7.4	10.0	4.7
Luxembourg ([6, 8])	72.7	72.8	68.3	77.4	12.3	13.4	15.8	10.9
Hungary ([8])	84.7	83.6	81.7	85.5	12.0	11.7	12.5	10.9
Malta ([8])	45.1	54.2	50.5	58.3	49.9	39.0	41.7	36.1
Netherlands ([2])	75.0	76.2	71.9	80.6	14.3	11.4	14.0	8.8
Austria ([2])	84.2	84.5	84.2	84.8	9.0	10.1	10.4	9.8
Poland ([3])	90.3	91.3	89.3	93.3	6.0	5.0	6.1	3.9
Portugal ([3, 10])	47.9	54.3	47.1	61.9	41.2	35.4	41.9	28.6
Romania ([3])	75.0	78.3	77.9	78.6	22.5	15.9	15.9	16.0
Slovenia ([2, 11])	90.8	90.2	87.4	93.6	4.6	5.1	7.2	2.6
Slovakia ([2])	94.1	92.3	91.0	93.6	5.3	6.0	7.1	4.9
Finland ([2])	85.3	*86.2*	*84.6*	*87.6*	10.1	9.8	12.1	7.7
Sweden ([2, 5, 12])	85.8	87.9	86.2	89.7	9.2	11.1	12.3	9.9
United Kingdom ([2])	78.6	78.2	76.4	80.0	12.1	17.0	18.3	15.6
Croatia ([13])	91.0	95.4	94.6	96.3	7.9	3.7	4.1	3.3
FYR of Macedonia	:	79.7	81.7	77.6	:	19.6	17.6	21.7
Turkey	44.2	47.8	56.4	40.9	53.0	46.6	38.5	53.7
Iceland ([2])	51.2	53.6	47.9	59.8	20.3	24.4	26.2	22.4
Norway ([2, 14])	93.7	70.0	65.4	74.7	6.3	17.0	21.0	12.9
Switzerland ([2])	77.5	82.6	81.4	83.8	9.7	7.7	7.8	7.5

([1]) Refer to the Internet metadata file (http://epp.eurostat.ec.europa.eu/cache/ITY_SDDS/en/lfsi_edu_a_esms.htm); early school leavers: based on annual averages of quarterly data, data extracted on 20 November 2009. ([2]) Early school leavers: break in series, 2003. ([3]) Early school leavers: break in series, 2004. ([4]) Breaks in series, 2003 and 2007. ([5]) Break in series, 2005. ([6]) Female early school leavers: unreliable or uncertain data. ([7]) Early school leavers: break in series, 2005. ([8]) Break in series, 2003. ([9]) Male and female early school leavers: unreliable or uncertain data. ([10]) Provisional. ([11]) Early school leavers: unreliable or uncertain data. ([12]) Provisional for 2008; early school leavers: break in series, 2007. ([13]) Early school leavers: unreliable or uncertain data for 2008. ([14]) Break in series, 2006.

Source: Eurostat (tsiir110 and tsisc060)

4.2 Foreign language learning

Introduction

Since the latest amendment in 2007, there are 23 official languages recognised within the EU, in addition to which there are regional, minority languages, and languages spoken by migrant populations. School is the main opportunity for the vast majority of people to learn these languages – as linguistic diversity is actively encouraged within schools, universities, adult education centres and the workplace.

For several decades it has been mandatory for most European children to learn at least one foreign language during their compulsory education, with the time devoted to foreign language instruction generally increasing in recent years. In 2002, the Barcelona European Council recommended that at least two foreign languages should be taught to all pupils from a very early age. This recommendation has been implemented to varying degrees, usually for compulsory secondary education, either by making it mandatory to teach a second language, or ensuring that pupils have the possibility to study a second foreign language as part of their curriculum.

In September 2008 the European Commission adopted a Communication ([6]) titled 'Multilingualism: an asset for Europe and a shared commitment', which was followed in November 2008 by a Council Resolution on a European strategy for multilingualism ([7]). The Communication addresses languages in the wider context of social cohesion and prosperity and fo-

cuses on actions to encourage and assist citizens in acquiring language skills. It explores issues such as:

- the role languages play in developing mutual understanding in a multicultural society;
- how language skills improve employability and ensure a competitive edge for European businesses;
- what to do to encourage European citizens to speak two languages in addition to their mother tongue;
- how the media and new technologies can serve as a bridge between speakers of different languages.

Definitions and data availability

Data on the **number of pupils studying foreign languages** are related to the corresponding numbers of students enrolled; mentally handicapped students enrolled in special schools are excluded.

The **average number of foreign languages learned per pupil** is collected for different ISCED levels. The data refer to all pupils, even if teaching languages does not start in the first years of instruction for the particular ISCED level considered. This indicator is defined as the sum of language students divided by the total number of students enrolled in the educational level considered. Each student studying a foreign language is counted once for each language he or she is studying, i.e. students studying more than one language are counted as many times as the number of languages studied. Irish, Luxembourgish and regional languages

---

([6]) For more information: http://ec.europa.eu/education/languages/pdf/com/2008_0566_en.pdf.

([7]) For more information:. http://eur-lex.europa.eu/LexUriServ/LexUriServ.do?uri=OJ:C:2008:320:0001:01:EN:HTML.

are excluded, although provision may be made for them in certain Member States. Allowing for exceptions, when one of the national languages is taught in schools where it is not the teaching language, it is not considered a foreign language.

Main findings

Within primary education, there is a clear prominence in terms of the proportion of pupils that (choose to) study English. Learning English is mandatory in several countries within secondary education institutions, and so a number of Member States have close to 100 % shares of pupils learning this language in primary education. The highest shares of primary education pupils studying English were recorded in Greece, Spain, Italy, Malta and Austria, where over nine out of every ten children were studying English. The relative importance of English as a foreign language may be further magnified because pupils tend to receive more instruction in their first foreign language than they do for any subsequent languages they (choose to) study.

The central and eastern Member States that joined the EU since 2004 have a distinctive position in relation to language teaching, as in the past learning Russian was compulsory for many pupils. This situation has changed rapidly and these days most pupils have more choice concerning the language(s) they wish to study, for example, in most countries there has also been a marked increase in the proportion of pupils learning English, often above 40 % of all students and in some cases over 60 %. Luxembourg is also of particular interest, insofar as there are three official languages, with most pupils receiving instruction in Luxembourgish, German and French at primary level, while English is introduced as a foreign language at secondary school.

Turning to language learning in upper secondary education, some 83.5 % of all EU-27 students at ISCED level 3 were studying English as a foreign language in 2007, compared with around one fifth studying French (21.8 %) or German (22.5 %). Luxembourg and the Netherlands stood out as the countries with the highest proportion of secondary education students (at ISCED levels 2 or 3) learning three or more languages in 2007; note this indicator includes all foreign languages, not just German, English and French.

Figure 4.4: Proportion of pupils learning foreign languages in primary education, by language, 2007 (¹)

(%)

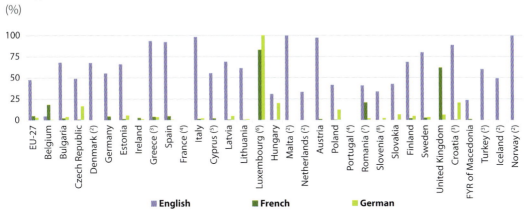

(¹) Refer to the Internet metadata file (http://epp.eurostat.ec.europa.eu/cache/ITY_SDDS/en/educ_esms.htm).
(²) French and German, not available.
(³) 2006.
(⁴) Not available.
(⁵) German, not available.
(⁶) English, not available.
(⁷) German, 2006.
(⁸) French, not available.

Source: Eurostat (educ_ilang), Unesco, OECD

Table 4.4: Foreign languages learnt per pupil in secondary education (¹)
(%)

	Proportion of students learning 3 or more languages (at ISCED level 2 or 3)		Upper secondary education (ISCED 3)					
			Pupils learning English in general programmes		Pupils learning French in general programmes		Pupils learning German in general programmes	
	2002	2007	2002	2007	2002	2007	2002	2007
EU-27	4.7	2.8	69.7	83.5	17.7	21.8	17.7	22.5
Belgium	15.2	14.5	94.1	94.1	47.7	48.1	30.1	28.5
Bulgaria	0.7	0.5	80.8	86.2	18.7	15.0	39.3	38.5
Czech Republic	:	1.0	98.9	100.0	17.3	24.5	73.5	65.8
Denmark	:	2.3	94.2	91.8	23.6	10.7	71.8	35.6
Germany	:	:	90.9	91.0	27.1	27.4	-	-
Estonia	28.6	18.9	91.2	95.0	4.7	6.7	45.6	41.6
Ireland	0.3	0.3	-	-	65.7	59.6	18.7	18.3
Greece (²)	:	:	95.2	94.0	10.3	8.6	2.1	2.9
Spain	0.0	0.2	95.9	95.3	27.7	27.7	1.1	1.1
France	3.4	:	99.4	99.4	-	-	30.5	21.8
Italy	3.1	2.1	85.9	95.3	27.2	20.5	8.2	7.2
Cyprus	:	:	100.0	78.5	60.4	32.2	1.0	2.4
Latvia	3.8	4.6	89.3	96.0	3.1	4.1	48.1	32.2
Lithuania	1.5	0.8	76.5	85.1	6.8	4.9	35.1	25.4
Luxembourg	60.7	61.9	96.3	96.5	96.3	96.5	96.3	96.5
Hungary	:	0.2	57.6	76.4	6.3	6.5	49.3	50.1
Malta	13.4	20.0	78.5	70.2	8.3	9.6	0.8	2.2
Netherlands (³)	20.4	56.7	99.9	100.0	22.7	70.3	23.3	86.3
Austria	2.1	2.4	96.9	96.9	42.8	54.1	-	-
Poland	:	0.7	90.6	91.2	14.1	9.8	61.5	62.7
Portugal (²)	:	:	:	50.7	:	15.1	:	1.6
Romania (⁴)	:	1.1	87.8	95.9	85.1	83.0	10.7	11.6
Slovenia	2.2	3.2	98.2	98.3	9.1	10.8	83.0	76.0
Slovakia	0.1	0.7	96.0	97.9	12.4	16.0	78.2	71.2
Finland	44.4	34.6	99.7	99.3	21.9	19.3	41.5	33.2
Sweden	4.5	3.3	99.8	99.9	25.8	21.1	48.9	29.6
United Kingdom	:	:	-	-	:	32.0	:	11.7
Croatia (²)	:	1.2	:	98.3	:	3.4	:	65.6
Turkey (²)	:	-	:	67.3	:	0.7	:	6.5
Iceland (²)	15.8	19.7	66.2	76.1	14.7	17.1	32.1	30.7
Norway (²)	:	:	:	100.0	:	20.3	:	31.3

(¹) Refer to the Internet metadata file (http://epp.eurostat.ec.europa.eu/cache/ITY_SDDS/en/educ_esms.htm).
(²) 2006 instead of 2007.
(³) Proportion of students learning 2 or more languages: break in series, 2004.
(⁴) Pupils learning German: 2006 instead of 2007.

Source: Eurostat (educ_thfrlan, tps00057, tps00058 and tps00059), Unesco, OECD

4.3 Educational expenditure

Introduction

Expenditure on education may help foster economic growth, enhance productivity, contribute to personal and social development, and reduce social inequalities. The proportion of total financial resources devoted to education is one of the key choices made in each country by governments, enterprises and individual students and their families.

There is an on-going debate in many Member States as to how to increase education funding and efficiency, while promoting fairness. Possible approaches include charging tuition fees, administrative/examination charges, introducing grants or income-contingent loans to stimulate enrolment rates in higher education (in particular, among the less well-off), as well as raising funds through promoting partnerships between business and higher educational establishments.

Education accounts for a significant proportion of public expenditure in all of the Member States – the most important budget item being expenditure on staff. The cost of teaching increases significantly as a child moves through the education system, with expenditure per pupil/student considerably higher in universities than primary schools. Although tertiary education costs more per head, the highest proportion of total education spending is devoted to secondary education systems, as these teach a larger proportion of the total number of pupils/students.

Definitions and data availability

Indicators on education expenditure cover schools, universities and other public and private institutions involved in delivering or supporting educational services. Expenditure on institutions is not limited to expenditure on instructional services but also includes public and private expenditure on ancillary services for students and families, where these services are provided through educational institutions. At the tertiary level, spending on research and development can also be significant and is included, to the extent that the research is performed by educational institutions.

Total public expenditure on education includes direct public funding for educational institutions and transfers to households and enterprises. In general the public sector finances education either by assuming direct responsibility for the current and capital expenses of schools (direct expenditure for educational institutions) or by providing financial support to students and their families through scholarships and public loans; furthermore, the public sector may subsidise the education or training activities of the private business sector or non-profit organisations (transfers to households and enterprises).

Expenditure on educational institutions from private sources comprises school fees; materials (such as textbooks and teaching equipment); transport to school (if organised by the school); meals (if provided by the school); boarding fees; and expenditure by employers on initial vocational training.

4 Education

Public schools/institutions are defined as those which are directly or indirectly administered by a public education authority. Private schools/institutions are directly or indirectly administered by a non-governmental organisation (such as a church, trade union, a private business concern or another body) and are considered to be independent if they get less than 50 % of their funding from any level of government (local, regional or national). Expenditure per pupil/student in public and private institutions measures how much central, regional and local government, private households, religious institutions and enterprises spend per pupil/student; it includes expenditure for personnel, as well as other current and capital expenditure.

Main findings

Public expenditure on education in the EU-27 in 2006 was equivalent to 5.1 % of GDP, while the expenditure of both public and private sources of funds on educational institutions amounted to 5.7 % of GDP.

The highest public spending on education was observed in Denmark (8.0 % of GDP), while Cyprus (7.0 %), Sweden (6.9 %) and Malta (6.8 %) also recorded relatively high proportions. Most Member States reported that public expenditure on education accounted for between 4 % and 6 % of their GDP, although this share fell to below 4 % of GDP in Slovakia and Romania. It should also be noted that GDP growth can mask significant increases that have been made in terms of education spending over the last decade within some Member States. Furthermore, declining birth rates will result in reduced school age populations, which will have an effect on ratios such as the average expenditure per pupil (given that expenditure is held constant).

Annual expenditure on public and private educational institutions shows that an average of PPS 6 003 was spent per pupil/student in 2006 in the EU-27, with the average approximately ten times higher in Denmark than in Romania (2005).

Figure 4.5: Public expenditure on education, 2006 (¹)
(% of GDP)

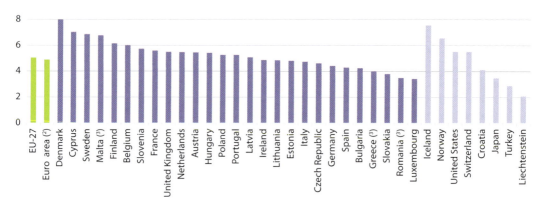

(¹) Refer to the Internet metadata file (http://epp.eurostat.ec.europa.eu/cache/ITY_SDDS/en/tsiir010_esms.htm).
(²) EA-15 instead of EA-16.
(³) 2005.

Source: Eurostat (tsiir010)

Table 4.5: Expenditure on educational institutions (¹)

	Public expenditure (% of GDP)		Private expenditure (% of GDP)		Expenditure on public and private educational institutions per pupil/student (PPS for full-time equivalents)	
	2001	2006	2001	2006	2001	2006
EU-27	4.99	5.05	0.60	0.67	5 081	6 003
Euro area (²)	4.98	4.89	0.60	0.55	5 665	6 459
Belgium	6.00	6.00	0.44	0.34	6 322	7 013
Bulgaria	3.78	4.24	0.70	0.65	1 326	2 139
Czech Republic	4.09	4.61	0.40	0.56	2 787	4 442
Denmark	8.44	7.98	0.27	0.59	7 306	14 308
Germany	4.49	4.41	0.96	0.71	5 815	6 481
Estonia	5.28	4.80	:	0.34	:	3 217
Ireland	4.27	4.86	0.34	0.28	4 637	6 740
Greece (³)	3.50	4.00	0.21	0.25	3 238	4 485
Spain	4.23	4.28	0.57	0.52	4 527	6 141
France	5.94	5.58	0.56	0.54	5 931	6 510
Italy	4.86	4.73	0.31	0.38	6 385	6 465
Cyprus	5.93	7.02	1.24	1.21	4 953	7 101
Latvia	5.64	5.07	0.75	0.66	1 995	3 126
Lithuania	5.89	4.84	:	0.46	1 860	2 761
Luxembourg	3.74	3.41	:	:	:	:
Hungary	5.01	5.41	0.55	0.54	:	4 008
Malta (⁴)	4.46	6.76	0.85	0.38	3 307	5 914
Netherlands	5.06	5.46	0.84	0.88	6 266	7 477
Austria	5.79	5.44	0.32	0.59	7 002	8 583
Poland	5.42	5.25	:	0.54	2 184	3 062
Portugal	5.61	5.25	0.08	0.44	4 037	5 007
Romania (³)	3.25	3.48	0.21	0.40	:	1 438
Slovenia	5.89	5.72	0.82	0.78	4 648	6 323
Slovakia	4.00	3.79	0.11	0.62	1 846	2 940
Finland	6.04	6.14	0.12	0.15	5 286	6 389
Sweden	7.12	6.85	0.20	0.17	6 096	7 411
United Kingdom	4.57	5.48	0.82	1.44	5 152	7 937
Croatia	:	4.11	:	0.38	:	:
Turkey	2.71	2.86	0.03	:	:	:
Iceland	6.24	7.55	0.53	0.81	6 713	7 966
Liechtenstein	:	2.06	:	:	:	7 677
Norway	7.18	6.55	0.25	:	8 153	9 290
Switzerland	5.42	5.50	0.67	0.56	:	:
Japan	3.63	3.47	1.18	1.66	6 160	7 421
United States	5.63	5.51	2.26	2.39	9 212	11 085

(¹) Refer to the Internet metadata file (http://epp.eurostat.ec.europa.eu/cache/ITY_SDDS/en/educ_esms.htm).
(²) EA-15 instead of EA-16.
(³) 2005 instead of 2006.
(⁴) 2005 instead of 2006; break in series, 2005.

Source: Eurostat (educ_figdp, tps00068 and tps00067), Unesco, OECD

4

4.4 Tertiary education

Introduction

Higher education plays a central role in the development of human beings and modern societies, enhancing social, cultural and economic development, as well as active citizenship and ethical values. The EU has around 18 million tertiary education students and approximately 1.3 million tertiary education staff; some European universities are among the most respected in the world.

The European Commission has published a modernisation agenda for universities as part of the revised Lisbon Strategy for growth and jobs. The main fields for reform were identified as:

- **curricular reform**: a three-cycle system (bachelor-master-doctorate), competence based learning, flexible learning paths, recognition, mobility;
- **governance reform**: university autonomy, strategic partnerships, including with enterprises, quality assurance;
- **funding reform**: diversified sources of university income better linked to performance, promoting equity, access and efficiency, including the possible role of tuition fees, grants and loans.

Curricular reforms are also promoted through the Bologna process ([8]), which sets out plans to create a European higher education area by 2010, facilitating student mobility, the transparency and rec-

ognition of qualifications, while promoting a European dimension within higher education and the attractiveness of European institutions to non-Community students; this initiative has been extended to 46 European countries.

The Erasmus programme is one of the most well-known European programmes. Around 90 % of European universities take part in it and some 2 million students have already participated in exchanges since it started in 1987. Erasmus became part of the EU's lifelong learning programme in 2007 and was expanded to cover student placements in enterprises, university staff training and teaching for enterprise staff. The programme seeks to expand its mobility actions in the coming years, with a target of 3 million Erasmus students by 2012.

Some of the most recent policy initiatives in this area include efforts to develop links between universities and businesses. In April 2009, the European Commission presented a Communication titled 'A new partnership for the modernisation of universities: the EU forum for university-business dialogue' ([9]). The Communication includes proposals to establish a university-business forum as a European platform for dialogue, to enable and stimulate the exchange of good practice, discuss common problems, and work together on possible solutions.

([8]) For more information: http://ec.europa.eu/education/policies/educ/bologna/bologna_en.html.

([9]) For more information: http://ec.europa.eu/education/higher-education/doc1261_en.htm.

Definitions and data availability

The international standard classification of education (ISCED) is used to define levels of education: **tertiary education** includes both programmes which are largely theoretical and designed to provide qualifications for entry to advanced research programmes and professions with high skills requirements, as well as programmes which are classified at the same level of competencies, but are more occupationally-oriented and lead to direct labour market access.

Student and teacher mobility are both seen as important tools for increasing innovation, productivity and competitiveness. Historically, it has been rare for countries to have precise details concerning the number of students that study abroad. Instead, these statistics have usually been collected by summing the numbers of students studying in receiving countries. This method has a downside: as a lack of information on the distribution of students according to their nationality is likely to lead to underestimation (for example, the number of students studying abroad may be a count of students enrolled on a certain day, whereas the actual number of foreign students could be higher, as many students stay abroad for just a few months). The number of foreign students may be defined as all students with a foreign nationality – however, this means that permanent residents with a foreign nationality are included in the numerator, even though they have not changed country for their studies. The statistics presented on student mobility are based on **actual numbers of foreign students studying in the host country** and exclude foreigners who are resident.

Main findings

There were 18.9 million students active within tertiary education in the EU-27 in 2007. Five Member States reported more than 2 million tertiary students in 2007, namely the United Kingdom, Germany, France, Poland and Italy; together with Spain these six countries accounted for just over two thirds of all EU-27 students in tertiary education. The median age of students in tertiary education ranges from 20.6 in Belgium and France to 22.7 in Latvia and the United Kingdom, with five Member States above this range, the Nordic countries of Denmark, Sweden and Finland, as well as Germany and Austria. The age of students in tertiary education can be influenced by a number of factors: whether students postpone starting tertiary education either by choice (for example, by taking a break or a gap year between secondary and tertiary education) or obligation (for example, for military service); the length of the tertiary education courses studied; the extent to which mature students return to tertiary education later in life.

Just under one quarter of the population aged 25 to 64 in the EU-27 had a tertiary education in 2008, rising to over one third in Finland, Cyprus, Estonia and Denmark. In contrast, less than 15 % of the population in this age range had a tertiary education in Slovakia, the Czech Republic, Italy, Portugal, Malta and Romania.

Around 4.1 million students graduated from tertiary education in the EU in 2007. An analysis of the number of graduates by field of education shows that 35.0 % had studied social sciences, business and law;

this share was higher than the equivalent share (33.9 %) of tertiary education students still in the process of studying within this field, suggesting that less students had started this type of study in recent years, or that drop-out rates were higher in other fields. A similar situation was observed in health and welfare fields, which made up 14.8 % of graduates from 12.6 % of the tertiary student population. The reverse situation was observed in engineering, manufacturing and construction, as well as agriculture and veterinary fields, where the proportion of graduates was lower

than corresponding shares of the current student population.

Female graduates outnumbered male graduates by a ratio of approximately three to two. This ratio reached three to one in health and welfare fields of education. Male graduates outnumbered female graduates slightly in agriculture and veterinary fields, more so in science, mathematics and computing fields, and by close to three to one in engineering, manufacturing and construction fields.

Table 4.6: Students in tertiary education, 2007 (¹)

	Total number of students in tertiary education (1 000)	of which, studying (%)						
		Human-ities & arts	Social sciences, business & law	Science, math. & com-puting	Engin., manuf. & con-struction	Agricul. & vet-erinary	Health & welfare	Services
EU-27	18 877	13.1	33.9	10.5	14.0	1.9	12.6	4.1
Belgium	394	10.9	29.5	6.5	9.5	2.5	19.4	1.9
Bulgaria	259	7.9	44.0	5.1	19.7	2.5	6.2	8.0
Czech Republic	363	8.7	28.6	8.7	14.2	3.7	11.9	4.1
Denmark	232	15.3	29.0	8.7	10.1	1.5	22.0	2.2
Germany	2 279	15.5	27.4	15.3	15.5	1.5	14.5	3.1
Estonia	69	11.4	39.8	9.9	13.1	2.4	8.3	8.1
Ireland	190	14.7	22.0	11.0	10.3	1.2	13.1	4.9
Greece	603	13.5	31.8	13.6	17.0	5.8	9.6	3.1
Spain	1 777	10.3	31.6	10.5	17.6	2.0	11.7	5.6
France	2 180	16.0	35.6	12.4	12.8	1.1	15.1	3.4
Italy	2 034	15.3	35.6	7.9	15.6	2.3	12.9	2.7
Cyprus	22	9.5	49.9	11.9	6.8	0.1	6.1	6.1
Latvia	129	7.2	53.7	5.1	10.4	1.1	6.3	5.6
Lithuania	200	7.1	42.8	5.9	18.2	2.2	8.4	3.1
Luxembourg (²)	3	8.2	45.2	8.4	15.0	0.0	0.4	0.0
Hungary	432	8.6	40.6	6.9	11.5	2.7	8.8	9.1
Malta	10	16.2	35.4	10.3	7.9	0.1	17.6	1.9
Netherlands	583	8.5	37.5	6.5	8.1	1.2	16.9	6.2
Austria	261	15.4	36.5	12.0	12.7	1.1	7.9	1.8
Poland	2 147	10.2	40.3	9.5	12.6	2.2	6.1	5.6
Portugal	367	8.5	32.0	7.3	22.3	1.9	16.5	5.7
Romania	928	9.9	51.0	6.2	17.2	2.7	5.6	4.3
Slovenia	116	7.8	41.7	5.6	16.7	3.2	7.2	9.5
Slovakia	218	6.2	29.4	8.9	15.7	2.6	16.2	5.5
Finland	309	14.6	22.7	11.2	25.4	2.2	13.7	4.9
Sweden	414	12.5	26.3	9.4	16.1	0.9	17.7	2.0
United Kingdom	2 363	17.1	26.9	13.4	8.4	0.9	16.0	3.1
Croatia	140	9.7	41.7	7.7	15.7	3.8	7.0	10.2
FYR of Macedonia	58	11.2	38.0	9.4	14.8	3.2	9.0	4.3
Turkey	2 454	6.2	48.7	7.5	13.1	3.7	5.6	3.8
Iceland	16	14.6	38.5	7.9	7.7	0.6	12.7	1.5
Liechtenstein	1	0.7	74.3	0.0	22.9	0.0	2.1	0.0
Norway	215	11.6	32.3	8.8	7.0	0.8	19.8	4.0
Switzerland	213	12.7	37.0	10.5	13.2	1.1	11.0	3.5
Japan	4 033	15.7	29.1	2.9	15.8	2.2	12.5	5.7
United States	17 759	10.6	27.3	8.9	6.7	0.6	13.9	5.1

(¹) Refer to the Internet metadata file (http://epp.eurostat.ec.europa.eu/cache/ITY_SDDS/en/educ_esms.htm).
(²) 2006.

Source: Eurostat (tps00062 and educ_enrl5)

Figure 4.6: Proportion of the population having a tertiary educational attainment, 2008 (¹)
(%)

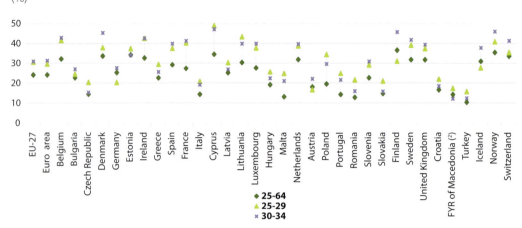

(¹) Refer to the Internet metadata file (http://epp.eurostat.ec.europa.eu/cache/ITY_SDDS/en/educ_esms.htm).
(²) 2007.

Source: Eurostat (lfsa_pgaed)

Figure 4.7: Median age in tertiary education, 2007 (¹)
(years)

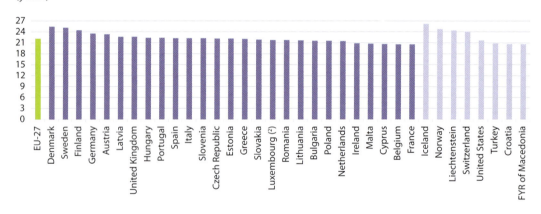

(¹) Refer to the Internet metadata file (http://epp.eurostat.ec.europa.eu/cache/ITY_SDDS/en/educ_esms.htm).
(²) 2006.

Source: Eurostat (tps00061)

Figure 4.8: Graduates from tertiary education, by field of education and gender, EU-27, 2007 (¹)
(1 000)

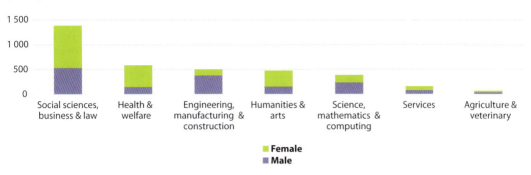

(¹) Refer to the Internet metadata file (http://epp.eurostat.ec.europa.eu/cache/ITY_SDDS/en/educ_esms.htm).

Source: Eurostat (educ_grad5)

Table 4.7: Graduates from tertiary education, by field of education, 2007 (¹)

	Total number of graduates from tertiary education (1 000)	of which, studying (%)							
		Human- ities & arts	Teach- ing & training	Social sciences, business & law	Science, math. & com- puting	Engin., manuf. & con- struction	Agricul. & vet- erinary	Health & welfare	Services
EU-27	4 101	12.1	5.9	35.0	9.7	12.6	1.7	14.8	4.0
Belgium	104	11.7	10.8	29.5	7.3	10.4	2.7	18.0	2.0
Bulgaria	49	6.9	5.4	51.4	4.1	14.8	1.8	6.2	7.8
Czech Republic	78	8.0	13.2	29.3	7.6	16.0	3.7	10.4	4.3
Denmark	51	13.4	6.2	31.9	7.3	12.6	2.2	21.7	2.9
Germany	439	16.1	3.8	24.2	12.3	13.2	1.7	18.9	3.6
Estonia	13	10.4	9.4	35.8	10.5	10.6	2.1	10.9	8.9
Ireland	59	25.2	:	28.4	15.1	8.5	0.7	12.5	2.4
Greece	60	15.6	7.5	25.5	9.3	12.2	4.2	15.9	9.8
Spain	279	8.7	11.0	27.0	9.4	16.8	1.8	14.5	7.6
France	623	10.9	0.8	40.9	11.1	15.6	1.5	14.0	4.1
Italy	402	15.4	5.8	32.7	6.7	13.9	1.8	15.1	2.5
Cyprus	4	7.6	9.1	47.7	8.6	3.7	0.2	7.5	14.1
Latvia	27	6.2	10.8	55.7	4.7	7.1	0.8	5.8	6.0
Lithuania	43	7.0	11.9	42.7	5.8	15.0	1.7	9.8	3.6
Luxembourg	:	:	:	:	:	:	:	:	:
Hungary	67	7.7	15.5	41.2	6.4	7.5	2.7	10.0	8.3
Malta	3	16.0	10.1	47.1	8.0	7.4	0.0	10.5	0.9
Netherlands	123	8.7	12.5	38.0	6.5	7.7	1.5	17.2	4.7
Austria	36	8.9	11.5	30.5	12.1	19.8	2.2	9.7	3.1
Poland	533	8.6	4.7	43.0	8.1	8.7	1.7	8.2	5.4
Portugal	83	9.9	7.2	33.0	12.4	19.6	1.8	22.3	6.8
Romania	206	11.0	0.6	49.0	5.2	14.4	2.3	11.9	3.4
Slovenia	17	5.9	8.9	49.7	4.4	12.6	2.4	7.9	8.2
Slovakia	46	5.1	12.6	28.1	8.7	14.7	3.4	18.9	6.1
Finland	43	14.7	4.8	22.7	8.8	19.9	2.1	19.3	5.5
Sweden	60	6.1	16.2	25.3	7.4	17.2	1.2	25.7	2.3
United Kingdom	651	15.9	6.9	30.3	13.2	8.4	0.9	18.3	0.8
Croatia	22	8.1	6.9	37.7	7.0	11.7	3.1	9.5	15.6
FYR of Macedonia	9	11.3	20.9	31.8	6.5	10.5	3.8	10.7	4.4
Turkey	416	6.3	15.1	40.2	8.0	13.6	4.3	6.0	5.8
Iceland	4	10.8	20.1	38.7	6.9	6.0	0.8	12.8	1.1
Liechtenstein	0	2.7	0.0	65.8	0.0	31.5	0.0	0.0	0.0
Norway	35	9.8	10.5	27.5	7.5	7.4	1.1	24.5	4.1
Switzerland	76	7.0	9.3	37.9	8.5	13.2	2.1	14.1	6.4
Japan	1 062	15.1	0.9	26.9	3.0	17.8	2.2	12.9	9.5
United States	2 704	13.1	:	38.0	8.7	7.0	1.1	14.2	6.7

(¹) Refer to the Internet metadata file (http://epp.eurostat.ec.europa.eu/cache/ITY_SDDS/en/educ_esms.htm).

Source: Eurostat (educ_grad5)

4.5 Lifelong learning and vocational training

Introduction

The European Commission has integrated its various educational and training initiatives under a single umbrella, the lifelong learning programme (LLP). This new programme replaces previous education, vocational training and e-learning programmes, which ended in 2006.

Lifelong learning is defined as encompassing learning for personal, civic and social purposes, as well as for employment-related purposes. It can take place in a variety of environments, both inside and outside formal education and training systems. Lifelong learning implies raising investment in people and knowledge; promoting the acquisition of basic skills, including digital literacy and broadening opportunities for innovative, more flexible forms of learning. The aim is to provide people of all ages with equal and open access to high-quality learning opportunities, and to a variety of learning experiences throughout Europe.

The EC Treaty recognised the importance of vocational training in Article 150 by stating that 'Community action shall aim to … facilitate access to vocational training …; stimulate cooperation on training between educational or training establishments and firms' ([10]).

A European Commission Communication of November 2001 titled 'making a European area of lifelong learning a reality' ([11]) underlines in paragraph 1.1 that the 'Lisbon European Council confirmed lifelong learning as a basic component of the European social model'. As such, learning is no longer given weight only in the area of education; it is also seen as a critical factor in areas such as employment and social security policy, economic performance and competitiveness.

The European Employment Strategy (EES) ([12]), agreed on 22 July 2003, introduced two guidelines to tackle the need for improved skills levels through lifelong learning. These guidelines called upon the Member States to address labour shortages and skills' bottlenecks and also encouraged them to implement comprehensive lifelong learning strategies in order to equip all individuals with the skills required of a modern workforce. The guidelines stated that policies should aim to increase investment in human resources, in particular through the training of adults by enterprises. In 2005, the Lisbon Strategy was revised and employment guidelines integrated with macro-economic and micro-economic guidelines, and in 2008 these integrated guidelines were further revised.

([10]) Consolidated version of the Treaty establishing the European Community, Chapter 3, Article 150([2]) (OJ C 352, 24.12.2002, p. 33); for more information: http://eur-lex.europa.eu/en/treaties/dat/12002E/pdf/12002E_EN.pdf.

([11]) 'Making a European area of lifelong learning a reality', COM(2001) 678 final of 21 November 2001; for more information: http://ec.europa.eu/education/policies/lll/life/communication/com_en.pdf.

([12]) For more information: http://ec.europa.eu/employment_social/employment_strategy/index_en.htm.

The Leonardo da Vinci programme in the field of vocational education and training (VET) is designed to encourage projects which give individuals the chance to improve their competences, knowledge and skills through a period spent abroad, as well as to encourage Europe-wide cooperation between training organisations.

The Grundtvig programme was launched in 2000 and now forms part of the lifelong learning programme. It aims to provide adults with ways of improving their knowledge and skills, keeping them mentally fit and potentially more employable. It not only covers learners in adult education, but also the teachers, trainers, education staff and facilities that provide these services.

Definitions and data availability

Lifelong learning encompasses all purposeful learning activity undertaken on an on-going basis with the aim of improving knowledge, skills and competence. The intention or aim to learn is the critical point that distinguishes these learning activities from non-learning activities such as cultural activities or sports activities. The information collected relates to all subjects whether they are relevant or not for the respondent's current or possible future job.

Within the domain of lifelong learning statistics, formal education corresponds to education and training in the regular system of schools, universities and colleges. Non-formal education and training includes all types of taught learning activities which are not part of a formal education programme. Note that the statistics presented do not cover informal learning, which corresponds to self-learning (through the use of printed material, computer-based learning/training, on-line Internet-based web education, visiting libraries, etc).

The target population for lifelong learning statistics refers to all persons in private households aged between 25 and 64 years old. Data are collected through the EU labour force survey. The denominator used in this subchapter consists of the total population of the same age group, excluding those who did not answer the question concerning participation in education and training.

Additional information is available from two other surveys:

- the third European survey of continuing vocational training in enterprises (CVTS3) which was implemented with 2005 as reference year in the Member States and Norway, and;
- an adult education survey (AES) which was carried out by EU, EFTA and candidate countries between 2005 and 2008.

Continuing vocational training (CVT) concerns persons employed by enterprises; the qualifying criteria are: the training must be planned in advance; the training must be organised or supported with the specific goal of learning; the training must be financed at least partly by the enterprise.

The **adult education survey** is included as part of the EU's statistics on lifelong learning. Surveys have been carried out between 2005 and 2008 as a pilot exercise with a standard questionnaire, covering participation in education and lifelong learning activities whether formal, non-formal or informal, and included job-related activities. The survey also collects information on learning activities, self-reported skills, as well as modules on social and cultural participation. Learning includes activities with the intention to improve an individual's knowledge, skills, and competences. Intentional learning (as opposed to random learning) is defined as a deliberate search for knowledge, skills, competences, or attitudes of lasting value. Organised learning is defined as learning planned in a pattern or sequence with explicit or implicit aims.

Formal education is defined as education provided in the system of schools, colleges, universities and other formal educational institutions that normally constitute a continuous 'ladder' of full-time education for children and young people (up to 20 or 25 years of age). **Non-formal education** is defined as any organised and sustained educational activities that do not correspond to the definition of formal education. Non-formal education may or may not take place in educational institutions and cater to persons of all ages. It may cover educational programmes to impart adult literacy, basic education for out-of-school children, life skills, work skills, and general culture.

Main findings

In 2008, the proportion of persons aged 25 to 64 receiving some form of lifelong learning in the four weeks preceding the labour force survey was 9.6 % within the EU-27; this figure was only 1.1 percentage points higher than the corresponding share for 2003. The proportion of the population who had participated in life-long learning activities was higher among women (10.4 % in 2008) than among men (8.7 %). Sweden, Denmark, and to a lesser extent Finland and the United Kingdom stood out as they reported considerably higher proportions of their respective populations participating in lifelong learning, between one fifth and one third; in contrast, Bulgaria and Romania reported lifelong learning participation rates of less than 2 %.

In 2007, more than one third of the EU-27's population aged 25 to 64 participated in formal or non-formal education and training during the last 12 months, according to results from the first adult education survey. A large majority of these participated in non-formal education and training, while most of the education and training undertaken was job-related. Indeed, the main reason given by respondents for their participation in non-formal education and training was to do their job better/improve their career prospects (64 % of those undertaking education or training), while getting knowledge or skills relating to interesting subjects (51 %) and getting useful skills/knowledge for everyday life (30 %) were also common reasons.

Nearly two thirds of the population in the EU-27 did not participate in formal or non-formal education and training in 2007. The three most commonly cited obstacles to participation in education and training among those who wanted to participate but did not do so were family responsibilities (40.2 % of those not participating), conflict with work schedules (38.7 %) and cost (31.2 %).

Employers were the most common providers of non-formal education and training activities, providing close to two fifths of such activities. Employers provided more than two thirds of non-formal education and training in Bulgaria, and half of such activities in the United Kingdom. Among the less common providers used across the EU-27 as a whole, the importance of employers' organisations and chambers of commerce was particularly high in Hungary (32.8 %) and Slovenia (20.8 %), non-commercial institutions (such as libraries) in Finland (29.5 %) and Cyprus (15.5 %), and trade unions in Hungary (13.1 %).

As regards vocational training, the proportion of all enterprises that provided training to their employees in 2005 ranged from 21 % in Greece to 90 % in the United Kingdom, and averaged 60 % across the EU.

Combining information on the proportion of training enterprises and the intensity of continuing vocational training (the latter measured by the average number of training hours per employee) several groups of countries could be clearly distinguished. Finland, Sweden, Austria, Denmark, Luxembourg, the Czech Republic, Germany and Estonia had high proportions of training enterprises and high intensity in CVT courses; the United Kingdom, the Netherlands, France, Slovenia, Ireland, Belgium and Slovakia had high rates of training enterprises and relatively low intensity in CVT courses; Greece, Italy, Poland, Latvia, Portugal, Malta and Spain had low rates of training enterprises and relatively high intensity in CVT courses; the remaining Member States had relatively low proportions of training enterprises and low intensity in CVT courses.

Table 4.8: Lifelong learning ([1])
(% of the population aged 25 to 64 participating in education and training)

	Total		Male		Female	
	2003	2008	2003	2008	2003	2008
EU-27	8.5	*9.6*	*7.9*	*8.7*	*9.1*	*10.4*
Euro area ([2])	6.5	*8.5*	6.4	*8.1*	6.6	*8.8*
Belgium	7.0	6.8	7.0	6.4	6.9	7.2
Bulgaria	1.3	1.4	1.1	1.3	1.4	1.5
Czech Republic	5.1	*7.8*	4.8	*7.7*	5.4	*7.9*
Denmark	24.2	30.2	21.0	25.0	27.4	35.5
Germany	6.0	7.9	6.4	8.0	5.6	7.8
Estonia	6.7	*9.8*	5.0	*6.6*	8.2	*12.6*
Ireland	5.9	10.2	5.1	8.7	6.8	11.7
Greece	2.6	2.9	2.6	2.8	2.7	3.1
Spain	4.7	10.4	4.3	9.5	5.1	11.3
France	7.1	7.2	7.0	6.9	7.2	7.5
Italy	4.5	6.3	4.2	6.1	4.8	6.6
Cyprus	7.9	8.5	7.1	8.1	8.5	8.9
Latvia	7.8	6.8	5.4	4.3	10.0	9.0
Lithuania	3.8	4.9	2.8	3.7	4.7	6.1
Luxembourg	6.5	8.5	6.8	7.6	6.1	9.5
Hungary	4.5	3.1	4.0	2.7	4.9	3.5
Malta	4.2	6.2	4.7	6.1	3.6	6.2
Netherlands	16.4	17.0	16.1	16.8	16.8	17.2
Austria	8.6	13.2	8.6	12.2	8.6	14.2
Poland	4.4	4.7	3.9	4.2	4.9	5.2
Portugal	3.2	*5.3*	3.0	*5.0*	3.4	*5.6*
Romania	1.1	1.5	1.1	1.3	1.2	1.6
Slovenia	13.3	13.9	12.0	12.5	14.7	15.4
Slovakia	3.7	3.3	3.5	2.6	3.9	4.0
Finland	22.4	23.1	18.6	19.3	26.2	26.9
Sweden ([3])	31.8	*32.4*	28.4	*25.8*	35.4	*39.3*
United Kingdom ([4])	27.2	19.9	23.4	16.6	31.1	23.2
Croatia	1.8	2.2	1.8	2.1	1.9	2.3
Turkey	1.2	1.8	1.7	2.1	0.7	1.6
Iceland	29.5	25.1	25.0	20.1	34.1	30.5
Norway	17.1	19.3	16.2	18.2	18.0	20.5
Switzerland ([3])	24.7	26.8	25.3	26.2	24.0	27.5

([1]) Refer to the Internet metadata file (http://epp.eurostat.ec.europa.eu/cache/ITY_SDDS/en/lfsi_edu_a_esms.htm).
([2]) EA-15 instead of EA-16.
([3]) 2007 instead of 2008.
([4]) Break in series, 2007.

Source: Eurostat (tsiem080)

Table 4.9: Reasons for participation in non-formal education and training, 2007 (¹)
(%)

	To get knowledge/ skills relating to interesting subjects	To get knowledge/ skills useful for everyday life	To increase possibility of getting a job/ changing job	To be obliged to participate	To be less likely to lose job	Do job better/ improve career prospects	Meet new people, for fun	Obtain qualification	Start own business	Other/ no resp.
EU	51.0	30.0	17.0	22.0	13.0	64.0	15.0	16.0	4.0	5.0
Belgium	38.7	29.8	9.2	24.1	3.3	64.4	11.8	8.1	2.6	1.9
Bulgaria	38.5	40.0	20.8	22.1	22.0	77.3	9.2	34.3	1.8	1.2
Czech Republic	46.2	33.7	16.8	7.4	13.3	54.6	10.4	20.8	4.5	0.5
Denmark	:	:	:	:	:	:	:	:	:	:
Germany	45.9	14.3	15.6	25.0	20.0	68.0	10.5	11.6	3.8	5.4
Estonia	21.1	17.6	5.8	24.9	15.1	80.2	2.4	8.8	1.6	5.5
Ireland	:	:	:	:	:	:	:	:	:	:
Greece	76.7	52.4	25.5	18.1	16.0	74.8	20.6	48.6	7.9	4.3
Spain	66.6	50.8	28.4	11.8	12.7	68.4	11.8	25.0	4.8	5.0
France	:	:	:	:	:	:	:	:	:	:
Italy	43.9	20.9	10.9	13.8	2.5	47.6	13.3	13.5	2.6	3.9
Cyprus	64.3	38.2	8.7	16.9	2.1	53.6	14.7	13.3	1.6	4.4
Latvia	43.8	58.6	17.8	33.7	27.7	74.7	24.3	37.8	4.4	1.8
Lithuania	50.6	42.3	17.5	26.2	31.3	77.5	11.8	41.4	3.4	3.2
Luxembourg	:	:	:	:	:	:	:	:	:	:
Hungary	56.0	52.0	33.3	51.4	38.3	67.8	13.2	35.2	7.5	1.3
Malta	:	:	:	:	:	:	:	:	:	:
Netherlands	42.4	40.2	12.8	35.9	6.6	66.4	19.2	23.7	4.2	10.1
Austria	57.4	57.1	16.2	23.7	10.5	67.1	20.9	10.7	4.6	5.1
Poland	7.6	7.2	7.2	5.2	6.6	67.1	0.5	7.2	1.5	2.8
Portugal	80.5	81.6	31.8	12.2	16.0	69.9	23.7	47.4	6.6	6.2
Romania	:	:	:	:	:	:	:	:	:	:
Slovenia	12.5	21.2	1.7	13.1	1.0	54.4	1.8	2.3	0.3	2.5
Slovakia	34.6	30.2	23.1	66.1	26.6	63.1	8.8	19.2	4.6	1.8
Finland	62.1	41.1	16.1	35.3	14.3	69.1	30.0	13.5	3.7	9.4
Sweden	59.3	41.8	6.5	36.4	8.0	61.8	20.8	8.9	1.5	5.5
United Kingdom	82.0	44.8	18.1	57.7	2.8	55.0	9.7	33.9	9.3	86.1
Croatia	44.7	35.2	16.9	31.1	17.2	76.9	8.2	15.0	4.8	1.4
Norway	67.9	33.2	9.6	43.1	12.7	71.8	16.0	18.3	1.5	7.2

(¹) Multiple answers allowed; Denmark, Ireland, Greece, France, Luxembourg, Malta, Romania and the United Kingdom are not included in the EU average; Bulgaria, the Czech Republic, Greece, Spain, Cyprus, Portugal, Finland and the United Kingdom did not interview participants taking part in guided on the job training; refer to the Internet metadata file (http://epp.eurostat.ec.europa.eu/cache/ITY_SDDS/en/trng_aes_esms.htm).

Source: Eurostat (trng_aes_142)

Table 4.10: Obstacles to participation in education and training, 2007 (¹)
(%)

	Health or age	None within reachable distance	No time due to family	Did not have the pre-requisites	Too expensive, could not afford	Did not like idea of going back to school	Lack of employer support	Conflict with work schedule	Other/ no resp.
EU	14.8	20.8	40.2	15.6	31.2	14.9	18.4	38.7	26.8
Belgium	21.8	13.1	38.4	9.5	17.9	4.8	14.7	33.1	10.6
Bulgaria	11.5	29.7	28.8	16.3	56.7	6.2	11.6	24.1	7.7
Czech Republic	11.9	16.1	38.5	7.8	19.7	2.1	22.5	36.8	3.6
Denmark	:	:	:	:	:	:	:	:	:
Germany	12.1	24.9	33.9	24.1	43.7	11.1	32.8	36.9	13.3
Estonia	18.2	34.5	38.8	2.9	53.1	8.5	8.8	32.6	42.6
Ireland	:	:	:	:	:	:	:	:	:
Greece	10.5	19.1	48.3	7.5	33.4	9.7	9.7	43.0	19.0
Spain	5.8	8.5	41.2	7.5	13.4	2.7	4.7	32.5	27.7
France	:	:	:	:	:	:	:	:	:
Italy	19.7	16.8	49.5	19.2	26.2	16.6	15.2	44.1	12.4
Cyprus	9.3	12.0	67.9	5.2	16.2	4.8	5.2	42.1	12.3
Latvia	11.9	24.1	40.1	11.2	50.8	11.9	29.7	36.8	11.4
Lithuania	13.2	19.6	34.3	3.2	45.6	4.9	16.2	48.4	13.5
Luxembourg	:	:	:	:	:	:	:	:	:
Hungary	12.5	32.4	37.5	13.9	42.3	18.9	39.9	53.2	15.0
Malta	:	:	:	:	:	:	:	:	:
Netherlands	23.8	13.0	29.9	4.2	25.1	13.5	20.1	17.6	22.8
Austria	6.3	22.4	42.3	7.1	34.6	2.8	16.1	39.5	15.8
Poland	9.1	31.0	29.2	9.2	61.3	17.5	20.4	31.4	11.5
Portugal	6.8	34.2	34.5	11.8	22.7	4.1	20.0	26.5	18.9
Romania	:	:	:	:	:	:	:	:	:
Slovenia	15.5	30.2	37.7	7.6	48.5	7.3	22.3	55.5	8.8
Slovakia	10.8	30.9	35.5	56.5	39.3	3.0	25.2	40.7	3.7
Finland	17.1	25.6	31.0	11.6	22.2	7.2	24.0	43.7	21.4
Sweden	23.7	22.0	23.0	5.8	32.5	6.9	19.1	32.4	20.5
United Kingdom	17.0	25.9	42.5	20.8	33.8	24.1	22.6	43.9	56.5
Croatia	11.0	26.7	48.7	14.9	53.8	4.2	17.1	28.8	8.6
Norway	19.5	13.6	25.8	4.3	17.6	9.2	21.1	32.2	15.7

(¹) Multiple answers allowed; Denmark, Ireland, France, Luxembourg, Malta and Romania are not included in the EU average; refer to the Internet metadata file (http://epp.eurostat.ec.europa.eu/cache/ITY_SDDS/en/trng_aes_esms.htm).

Source: Eurostat (trng_aes_176)

Table 4.11: Providers of non-formal education and training activities, 2007 (¹)
(%)

	Employer	Non-formal educ. & training instit.	Formal educ. instit.	Comm. Instit. where educ. & training is not main activity	Employers' org., chamber of commerce	Non-comm. instit. (e.g. library)	Non-profit assoc.	Individ.	Trade union	Other/ no resp.
EU	38.4	16.4	10.3	8.9	5.0	4.5	4.3	4.3	1.4	4.0
Belgium	41.7	7.3	15.2	8.9	2.8	7.1	7.4	5.6	0.7	0.6
Bulgaria	68.8	14.1	3.1	3.1	3.0	5.8	0.7	1.1	0.2	0.2
Czech Republic	42.9	27.9	10.7	7.6	1.8	2.1	1.5	3.2	0.6	1.1
Denmark	:	:	:	:	:	:	:	:	:	:
Germany	42.4	14.7	4.8	13.8	4.8	6.2	5.3	5.8	1.1	0.5
Estonia	29.2	34.4	10.0	9.4	1.2	3.9	2.1	2.5	5.5	1.7
Ireland	:	:	:	:	:	:	:	:	:	:
Greece	36.0	12.1	14.6	13.6	3.3	5.2	3.2	1.4	2.3	4.8
Spain	19.9	26.2	9.7	5.0	6.7	4.5	5.4	2.9	4.2	11.5
France	:	:	:	:	:	:	:	:	:	:
Italy	27.6	8.5	12.9	8.0	12.9	2.2	4.4	6.3	1.3	11.3
Cyprus	27.1	19.3	5.4	10.1	1.3	15.5	7.1	12.9	0.9	0.3
Latvia	42.6	21.3	13.4	6.8	2.7	1.6	2.2	2.1	0.2	5.2
Lithuania	14.5	28.7	20.8	15.0	9.2	:	1.4	8.7	0.4	:
Luxembourg	:	:	:	:	:	:	:	:	:	:
Hungary	0.6	32.0	7.0	3.5	32.8	6.2	0.1	1.9	13.1	2.7
Malta	:	:	:	:	:	:	:	:	:	:
Netherlands	38.6	:	38.2	:	:	:	4.7	2.1	1.9	11.8
Austria	27.7	21.8	6.7	12.4	4.6	1.4	4.9	4.5	0.3	14.2
Poland	20.8	49.9	13.1	6.1	1.7	:	2.2	3.8	0.2	2.1
Portugal	40.7	20.9	9.1	8.4	2.3	4.5	5.5	1.4	1.4	5.8
Romania	:	:	:	:	:	:	:	:	:	:
Slovenia	*11.8*	*44.6*	*8.7*	*8.0*	*20.8*	:	*3.9*	*1.9*	*0.3*	:
Slovakia	40.0	28.2	17.0	7.5	2.8	:	0.7	1.8	0.1	1.1
Finland	36.0	10.1	8.8	1.1	6.7	29.5	0.8	3.0	3.0	:
Sweden	45.5	14.6	4.2	17.1	3.9	3.4	5.6	2.5	2.0	0.5
United Kingdom	50.2	8.2	11.1	:	7.0	1.8	1.9	4.3	0.1	5.4
Croatia	22.0	24.2	15.6	12.8	5.0	1.6	3.3	0.8	0.4	7.7

(¹) Denmark, Ireland, France, Luxembourg, Malta and Romania are not included in the EU average; refer to the Internet metadata file (http://epp.eurostat.ec.europa.eu/cache/ITY_SDDS/en/trng_aes_esms.htm).

Source: Eurostat (trng_aes_170)

Table 4.12: Continuous vocational training, 2005 (¹)

	Training enterprises (% of all enterprises)	Cost of CVT courses (% of total labour cost)	Average time spent in CVT courses per employee (hours)	Enterprises where there was an impact of public measures on CVT plans (% of all training enterprises) (²)
EU-27	60	2	9	36
Belgium	63	2	12	60
Bulgaria	29	1	4	32
Czech Republic	72	2	14	21
Denmark	85	3	10	33
Germany	69	1	9	18
Estonia	67	2	7	20
Ireland	67	2	12	:
Greece	21	1	3	59
Spain	47	1	9	38
France	74	2	13	56
Italy	32	1	7	38
Cyprus	51	1	7	72
Latvia	36	1	4	24
Lithuania	46	1	5	15
Luxembourg	72	2	16	22
Hungary	49	2	6	24
Malta	46	2	11	32
Netherlands	75	2	12	52
Austria	81	1	9	43
Poland	35	1	6	25
Portugal	44	1	7	54
Romania	40	1	5	8
Slovenia	73	2	14	30
Slovakia	60	2	12	21
Finland	77	2	10	25
Sweden	78	2	15	37
United Kingdom	90	1	7	45
Norway	86	1	9	5

(¹) Refer to the Internet metadata file (http://epp.eurostat.ec.europa.eu/cache/ITY_SDDS/en/trng_cvts3_esms.htm).
(²) EU-27 calculated on the basis of the available country data (i.e. excluding Ireland).

Source: Eurostat (trng_cvts3_01, trng_cvts3_53, trng_cvts3_71 and trng_cvts3_29)

Labour market

5

Labour market statistics are at the heart of many EU policies following the introduction of an employment chapter into the Amsterdam Treaty in 1997. The European Employment Strategy (EES) was launched at the Luxembourg jobs summit in November 1997 and was revamped in 2005 to align the employment strategy more closely to the revised Lisbon objectives. The EU has set itself the ambitious targets of a 70 % total employment rate and 60 % female employment rate by 2010, while in the spring of 2001 a 50 % target rate was added for the employment rate of persons aged between 55 and 64 years.

In July 2008, the Council decided on updated employment policy guidelines for the period 2008 to 2010. To meet the objectives of full employment, improved quality and productivity at work, and strengthening economic, social and territorial cohesion, it was decided that actions should continue to concentrate on the priorities established in the 2005 review, namely to:

- attract and retain more people in employment, increase labour supply and modernise social protection systems;
- improve adaptability of workers and enterprises;
- increase investment in human capital through better education and skills.

These guidelines for the period 2008 to 2010 ([1]) form part of an integrated approach based on three pillars: macro-economic policies, micro-economic reforms and employment policies. The integrated employment guidelines for 2008-2010 encourage Member States to:

- work with renewed endeavour to build employment pathways for young people and reduce youth unemployment, in particular,

([1]) For more information: http://register.consilium.europa.eu/pdf/en/08/st10/st10614-re02.en08.pdf.

through adapting education and training systems in order to raise quality, broaden supply, diversify access, ensure flexibility, respond to new occupational needs and skills requirements;

- take action to increase female participation and reduce gender gaps in employment, unemployment and pay, through better reconciliation of work and private life and the provision of accessible and affordable childcare facilities and care for other dependants;
- give support to active ageing, including initiatives for appropriate working conditions, improved health and incentives to work and discouragement of early retirement;
- develop modern social protection systems, including pensions and healthcare, ensuring their social adequacy, financial sustainability and responsiveness to changing needs, so as to support participation, better retention in employment and longer working lives.

5.1 People in the labour market – employment

Introduction

EU citizens have the right to work in any Member State without the need for work permits. While some temporary restrictions apply for some workers from the Member States that joined the EU since 2004, the freedom of movement is designed to help create a single market for jobs and could potentially provide a boost to the economy while helping thousands of people to achieve their career and lifestyle aspirations.

All EU citizens that move to work in another Member State must be treated in the same way as nationals in terms of employment rights that cover work-related issues like pay and dismissal.

Flexible working conditions – for example, part-time work or work from home – are thought to stimulate employment and activity rates, by encouraging more persons into the labour force. Other initiatives that may encourage a higher proportion of persons into the labour market include improvements in the availability of childcare facilities, or providing opportunities for lifelong learning.

'Flexicurity' is a way of looking at flexibility and security within the labour market. Flexicurity involves policies that simultaneously address the flexibility of labour markets, work organisation and labour relations, while also taking into account employment and income security. The flexicurity model includes a strong emphasis on active labour market policies, and motivating lifelong learning and training, improving customised support to job-seekers, supporting equal opportunities for all and equality between women and men.

Definitions and data availability

The indicators presented here are derived from the EU labour force survey (LFS). Given the considerable interest in labour market policies, the LFS has grown in importance and has become a key tool for observing labour market developments. The LFS is a quarterly household sample survey carried out in the Member States of the EU, candidate countries and EFTA countries (except Liechtenstein). It is the main source of information concerning the situation and trends within the labour market of the EU. The LFS primarily reports on the EU's population of working age (15 years and more) which is composed of persons in employment, unemployed persons and economically inactive persons. It provides comprehensive information on these three categories, describing the employment situation of employed persons by reporting on, for example, their education level, the branches in which they work, their occupations, as well as their propensity to engage in part-time work, the duration of their work contracts, and their search for new jobs. Note that coverage in terms of labour force status is restricted to those aged 16 and over in Spain and the United Kingdom. In Denmark, Estonia, Latvia, Hungary, Finland, Sweden (from 2001 onwards) and Norway, the coverage relates to those aged 15 to 74, while in Sweden (prior to 2001) and Iceland, coverage refers to those aged 16 to 74. The sample size amounts approximately to 1.5 million individuals each quarter, with quarterly sampling rates of between 0.2 % and 3.3 % in each country. During the period from 1998 to 2005, the survey underwent a transition towards a continuous quarterly survey; all Member States now provide quarterly results.

The economically **active population** (labour force) comprises employed and unemployed persons. The total **employment rate** is calculated by dividing the number of persons aged 15 to 64 in employment by the total population of the same age group. The employment rate of older workers is calculated by restricting the population to persons aged 55 to 64. **Employed persons** are defined as persons

aged 15 and over who during the reference week of the (EU labour force) survey performed some work, even for just one hour per week, for pay, profit or family gain or were not at work but had a job or business from which they were temporarily absent because of, for example, illness, holidays, industrial dispute and education or training. The data include family workers.

Self-employed persons work in their own business, farm or professional practice. A self-employed person is considered to be working if she/he meets one of the following criteria: works for the purpose of earning profit; spends time on the operation of a business, or; is in the process of setting-up a business.

Employees are defined as persons who work for a public or private employer and who receive compensation in the form of wages, salaries, payment by results or payment in kind; non-conscript members of the armed forces are also included.

Annual employment growth gives the change in percentage terms from one year to another of the total number of persons employed in resident producer units. The indicator is based on national accounts data; EU labour force survey breakdowns are applied to provide results by gender.

The population considered for atypical employment consists of persons aged 15 to 64. Persons with **temporary** contracts are those who have a job for which the employer and employee agree that its end is determined by objective conditions, such as a specific date, the completion of an assignment, or the return of an employee who was temporarily replaced; this can be contrasted with those in permanent employment, for whom no fixed end date is foreseen. Typical cases include: persons with seasonal employment; persons engaged by an agency or employment exchange and hired to a third party to perform a specific task (unless there is a written work contract of unlimited duration); persons with specific training contracts. In the labour force survey, the distinction between **full-time** and **part-time** employment is left to the respondent, since working hours differ from one Member State to the next and between economic activities; exceptions are in Germany, Ireland and the Netherlands, where thresholds for usual hours worked are used. The indicator on **persons with a second job** refers only to persons with more than one job running in parallel; persons having changed job during the reference week are not counted as having two jobs.

The **dispersion of regional (NUTS level 2) employment rates** shows regional differences in employment within countries and groups of countries (EU-27, euro area). It is zero when the employment rates in all regions are identical, and will rise if there is an increase in the differences between employment rates among regions. The indicator is not applicable for several countries as these comprise only one or a handful of NUTS level 2 regions. However, the employment rates of these countries are used to compute the indicator at a European level.

Main findings

The employment rate among the EU-27's population aged between 15 and 64 years old was 65.9 % in 2008. Although this represented the sixth successive annual increase in the employment rate, it remains below the target of 70 % that the Lisbon European Council set for 2010. Employment rates above 70 % were achieved in eight of the Member States (Denmark, the Netherlands, Sweden, Austria, the United Kingdom, Finland, Cyprus and Germany). In contrast, employment rates were below 60 % in Poland, Romania, Italy, Hungary and Malta.

Employment rates within the Member States often varied considerably according to regional patterns (see also Chapter 13 where regional employment rates are presented), with a relatively high dispersion (16.3 %) observed across Italy (as measured by the coefficient of variation for regions at NUTS level 2). In contrast, there was relatively little divergence in employment rates across the regions of Austria, Greece, Portugal, Sweden or the Netherlands (all below 4 %). The dispersion of regional employment across the whole of the EU-27 was seen to be converging, as the coefficient of variation declined from 13.2 % to 11.1 % between 2002 and 2007.

The Lisbon European Council set a target employment rate for women of 60 %. In 2008, the employment rate for women was 59.1 % in the EU-27, a significantly higher rate than that recorded five years earlier (54.9 %), although considerably lower than the corresponding rate for men (72.8 %). Some 15 of the Member States recorded employment rates for women above the target of 60 % in 2007, with female employment rates in Denmark, Sweden and the Netherlands exceeding 70 %.

Employment rates are generally lower among older workers and higher among persons having achieved higher levels of education. The Stockholm European Council of 2001 set a target employment rate for older workers (aged between 55 and 64 years) of 50 % by 2010. The employment rate for older workers across the EU-27 was 45.6 % in 2008, higher than the corresponding rate (40.0 %) recorded in 2003. The employment rate for older workers was higher than 50 % in 12 of the Member States, with the highest rates recorded in Sweden (70.1 %).

There were considerable differences between employment rates, according to the level of educational attainment. The employment rate of those aged 25 to 64 ([2]) who had completed tertiary education was 83.9 % across the EU-27 in 2008, much higher than the rate (48.1 %) for those who had only attained a low educational level (primary or lower secondary education).

The proportion of the workforce working part-time in the EU-27 increased from 15.9 % in 1998 to 18.2 % by 2008. The highest proportion of people working part-time was found in the Netherlands (47.3 % in 2008), followed at some distance by Sweden, Germany, the United Kingdom and Denmark, where part-time work accounted in each case for about a quarter of those in employment. In contrast, part-time employment was relatively uncommon in Bulgaria (2.3 % of those in employment) and Slovakia (2.7 %).

A little less than one third (31.1 %) of the women employed in the EU-27 did so on a part-time basis in 2008, a much higher proportion than the corresponding figure (7.9 %) for men. Three quarters (75.3 %) of all women employed in the Netherlands worked on a part-time basis in 2008, by far the highest rate among the Member States ([3]).

More than one quarter of employees were employed on a temporary basis in 2008 in Spain and Poland, as were more than one fifth of the workforce in Portugal. There was a considerable range in the propensity to use limited duration contracts between Member States that may, at least to some degree, reflect national practices, the supply and demand of labour and the ease with which employers can hire or fire. Among the remaining Member States, the proportion of employees working on a contract of limited duration ranged from 18.2 % in the Netherlands down to just 1.3 % in Romania.

([2]) For statistics on education level attainment, the age group 25 to 64 is used instead of 15 to 64.

([3]) Anyone working fewer than 35 hours a week is considered as working part-time in the Netherlands.

Figure 5.1: Employment rate, 2008
(%)

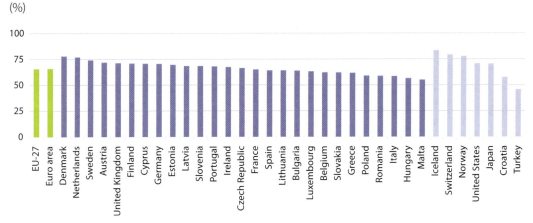

Source: Eurostat (tsiem010)

Table 5.1: Employment rate
(%)

	1998	1999	2000	2001	2002	2003	2004	2005	2006	2007	2008
EU-27	61.2	61.8	62.2	62.6	62.4	62.6	63.0	63.6	64.5	65.4	65.9
Euro area	59.3	60.4	61.4	62.1	62.3	62.6	63.1	63.7	64.7	65.6	66.1
Belgium	57.4	59.3	60.5	59.9	59.9	59.6	60.3	61.1	61.0	62.0	62.4
Bulgaria	:	:	50.4	49.7	50.6	52.5	54.2	55.8	58.6	61.7	64.0
Czech Republic	67.3	65.6	65.0	65.0	65.4	64.7	64.2	64.8	65.3	66.1	66.6
Denmark	75.1	76.0	76.3	76.2	75.9	75.1	75.7	75.9	77.4	77.1	78.1
Germany (¹)	63.9	65.2	65.6	65.8	65.4	65.0	65.0	66.0	67.5	69.4	70.7
Estonia	64.6	61.5	60.4	61.0	62.0	62.9	63.0	64.4	68.1	69.4	69.8
Ireland	60.6	63.3	65.2	65.8	65.5	65.5	66.3	67.6	68.6	69.1	67.6
Greece	56.0	55.9	56.5	56.3	57.5	58.7	59.4	60.1	61.0	61.4	61.9
Spain (¹)	51.3	53.8	56.3	57.8	58.5	59.8	61.1	63.3	64.8	65.6	64.3
France	60.2	60.9	62.1	62.8	63.0	64.0	63.7	63.9	63.8	64.6	65.2
Italy (²)	51.9	52.7	53.7	54.8	55.5	56.1	57.6	57.6	58.4	58.7	58.7
Cyprus	:	:	65.7	67.8	68.6	69.2	68.9	68.5	69.6	71.0	70.9
Latvia	59.9	58.8	57.5	58.6	60.4	61.8	62.3	63.3	66.3	68.3	68.6
Lithuania	62.3	61.7	59.1	57.5	59.9	61.1	61.2	62.6	63.6	64.9	64.3
Luxembourg	60.5	61.7	62.7	63.1	63.4	62.2	62.5	63.6	63.6	64.2	63.4
Hungary	53.7	55.6	56.3	56.2	56.2	57.0	56.8	56.9	57.3	57.3	56.7
Malta	:	:	54.2	54.3	54.4	54.2	54.0	53.9	53.6	54.6	55.2
Netherlands	70.2	71.7	72.9	74.1	74.4	73.6	73.1	73.2	74.3	76.0	77.2
Austria (²)	67.9	68.6	68.5	68.5	68.7	68.9	67.8	68.6	70.2	71.4	72.1
Poland	59.0	57.6	55.0	53.4	51.5	51.2	51.7	52.8	54.5	57.0	59.2
Portugal	66.8	67.4	68.4	69.0	68.8	68.1	67.8	67.5	67.9	67.8	68.2
Romania (³)	64.2	63.2	63.0	62.4	57.6	57.6	57.7	57.6	58.8	58.8	59.0
Slovenia	62.9	62.2	62.8	63.8	63.4	62.6	65.3	66.0	66.6	67.8	68.6
Slovakia	60.6	58.1	56.8	56.8	56.8	57.7	57.0	57.7	59.4	60.7	62.3
Finland	64.6	66.4	67.2	68.1	68.1	67.7	67.6	68.4	69.3	70.3	71.1
Sweden (¹)	70.3	71.7	73.0	74.0	73.6	72.9	72.1	72.5	73.1	74.2	74.3
United Kingdom (⁴)	70.5	71.0	71.2	71.4	71.4	71.5	71.7	71.7	71.6	71.5	71.5
Croatia	:	:	:	:	53.4	53.4	54.7	55.0	55.6	57.1	57.8
Turkey	:	:	:	:	:	:	:	:	45.9	45.8	45.9
Iceland	:	:	:	:	:	83.3	82.3	83.8	84.6	85.1	83.6
Norway	:	:	77.5	77.2	76.8	75.5	75.1	74.8	75.4	76.8	78.0
Switzerland	78.0	78.4	78.3	79.1	78.9	77.9	77.4	77.2	77.9	78.6	79.5
Japan	69.5	68.9	68.9	68.8	68.2	68.4	68.7	69.3	70.0	70.7	70.7
United States	73.8	73.9	74.1	73.1	71.9	71.2	71.2	71.5	72.0	71.8	70.9

(¹) Break in series, 2005.
(²) Break in series, 2004.
(³) Break in series, 2002.
(⁴) Break in series, 1999.

Source: Eurostat (tsieb090)

Table 5.2: Employment rates for selected population groups
(%)

	Male			Female			Older workers (55-64)		
	1998	2003	2008	1998	2003	2008	1998	2003	2008
EU-27	70.3	70.3	72.8	52.0	54.9	59.1	36.2	40.0	45.6
Euro area	69.8	71.5	73.3	48.7	53.8	58.8	33.3	37.7	44.3
Belgium	67.1	67.3	68.6	47.6	51.8	56.2	22.9	28.1	34.5
Bulgaria	:	56.0	68.5	:	49.0	59.5	:	30.0	46.0
Czech Republic	76.0	73.1	75.4	58.7	56.3	57.6	37.1	42.3	47.6
Denmark	79.9	79.6	81.9	70.2	70.5	74.3	52.0	60.2	57.0
Germany	71.9	70.9	75.9	55.8	58.9	65.4	37.7	39.9	53.8
Estonia	69.6	67.2	73.6	60.3	59.0	66.3	50.2	52.3	62.4
Ireland	72.1	75.2	74.9	49.0	55.7	60.2	41.7	49.0	53.6
Greece	71.7	73.4	75.0	40.5	44.3	48.7	39.0	41.3	42.8
Spain	66.8	73.2	73.5	35.8	46.3	54.9	35.1	40.7	45.6
France	67.4	69.9	69.8	53.1	58.2	60.7	28.3	37.0	38.3
Italy	66.8	69.6	70.3	37.3	42.7	47.2	27.7	30.3	34.4
Cyprus	:	78.8	79.2	:	60.4	62.9	:	50.4	54.8
Latvia	65.1	66.1	72.1	55.1	57.9	65.4	36.3	44.1	59.4
Lithuania	66.2	64.0	67.1	58.6	58.4	61.8	39.5	44.7	53.1
Luxembourg	74.5	73.3	71.5	46.2	50.9	55.1	25.1	30.3	34.1
Hungary	60.5	63.5	63.0	47.2	50.9	50.6	17.3	28.9	31.4
Malta	:	74.5	72.5	:	33.6	37.4	:	32.5	29.1
Netherlands	80.2	81.1	83.2	60.1	66.0	71.1	33.9	44.3	53.0
Austria	77.0	76.4	78.5	58.8	61.6	65.8	28.4	30.3	41.0
Poland	66.5	56.5	66.3	51.7	46.0	52.4	32.1	26.9	31.6
Portugal	75.9	75.0	74.0	58.2	61.4	62.5	49.6	51.6	50.8
Romania (¹)	70.4	63.8	65.7	58.2	51.5	52.5	51.5	38.1	43.1
Slovenia	67.2	67.4	72.7	58.6	57.6	64.2	23.9	23.5	32.8
Slovakia	67.8	63.3	70.0	53.5	52.2	54.6	22.8	24.6	39.2
Finland	67.8	69.7	73.1	61.2	65.7	69.0	36.2	49.6	56.5
Sweden	72.8	74.2	76.7	67.9	71.5	71.8	63.0	68.6	70.1
United Kingdom	77.3	77.8	77.3	63.6	65.3	65.8	49.0	55.4	58.0
Croatia	:	60.3	64.9	:	46.7	50.7	:	28.4	36.6
FYR of Macedonia	:	:	:	:	:	:	:	:	:
Turkey	:	:	67.7	:	:	24.3	:	:	29.5
Iceland	:	86.3	87.3	:	80.1	79.6	:	83.0	82.9
Norway	:	78.3	80.5	:	72.6	75.4	:	66.9	69.2
Switzerland	87.2	85.1	85.4	68.8	70.7	73.5	64.5	65.8	68.4
Japan	81.7	79.8	81.6	57.2	56.8	59.7	63.8	62.1	66.3
United States	80.5	76.9	76.4	67.4	65.7	65.5	57.7	59.9	62.1

(¹) Break in series, 2002.

Source: Eurostat (tsiem010 and tsiem020)

5

Figure 5.2: Dispersion of regional employment rates (¹)
(coefficient of variation of employment rates (of the age group 15-64) across regions
(NUTS 2 level))

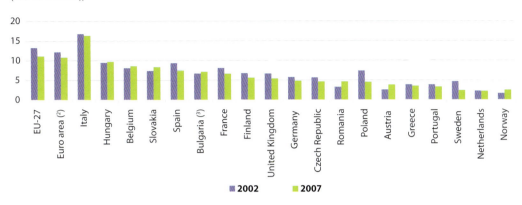

(¹) At the NUTS 2 level: Estonia, Cyprus, Latvia, Lithuania, Luxembourg and Malta are treated as one region.
(²) EA-13 instead of EA-16.
(³) 2003 instead of 2002.

Source: Eurostat (tsisc050)

Figure 5.3: Employment rate of older workers (55-64 years), 2008 (¹)
(%)

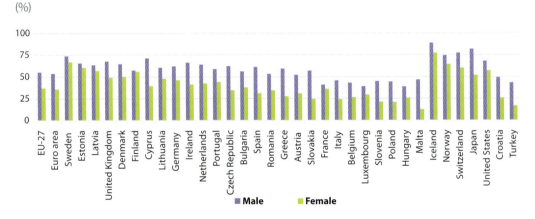

(¹) The figure is ranked on the average of male and female.

Source: Eurostat (tsiem020)

Table 5.3: Employment rate, by highest level of education, 2008
(% of age group 25-64 years)

	Pre-primary, primary & lower secondary - ISCED levels 0-2	Upper secondary & post-secondary non-tertiary - ISCED levels 3-4	Tertiary - ISCED levels 5-6
EU-27	48.1	70.6	83.9
Belgium	39.7	67.0	83.0
Bulgaria	32.9	72.7	86.1
Czech Republic	24.1	73.1	83.2
Denmark	64.6	81.5	88.8
Germany	45.9	74.7	86.4
Estonia	34.9	75.4	85.2
Ireland	46.9	71.9	84.4
Greece	52.4	61.2	82.1
Spain	55.5	67.4	81.7
France	47.2	69.6	81.0
Italy	46.0	67.9	78.5
Cyprus	50.9	74.0	86.5
Latvia	37.1	74.5	86.9
Lithuania	20.7	68.1	87.7
Luxembourg	48.4	65.3	83.6
Hungary	27.2	63.3	79.5
Malta	46.0	72.5	85.6
Netherlands	62.8	80.9	87.9
Austria	51.0	77.1	86.1
Poland	25.5	63.3	83.7
Portugal	65.8	65.8	84.7
Romania	41.0	63.5	85.7
Slovenia	42.9	72.0	87.5
Slovakia	15.9	70.1	83.8
Finland	46.4	75.1	85.6
Sweden	52.6	80.7	88.1
United Kingdom	56.2	75.1	85.3
Croatia	35.1	62.3	81.9
FYR of Macedonia (¹)	24.8	47.4	69.8
Turkey	41.2	50.8	72.4
Iceland	79.2	84.1	90.9
Norway	60.6	82.0	90.4
Switzerland	61.7	80.8	89.9

(¹) 2007.

Source: Eurostat (tsdec430)

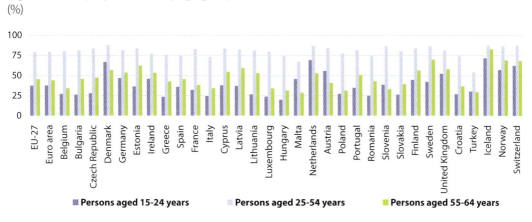

Figure 5.4: Employment rate by age group, 2008
(%)

■ **Persons aged 15-24 years**   ■ **Persons aged 25-54 years**   ■ **Persons aged 55-64 years**

Source: Eurostat (lfsi_emp_a)

Figure 5.5: Annual employment growth
(% change compared with previous year)

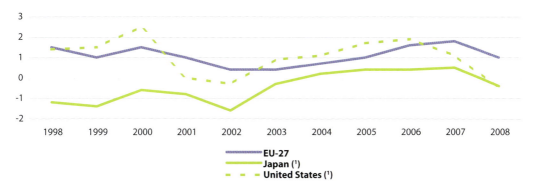

━━ **EU-27**
━━ **Japan** (¹)
╍╍╍ **United States** (¹)

(¹) Forecast, 2007 and 2008.

Source: Eurostat (tsieb050)

Table 5.4: Annual employment growth
(% change compared with previous year)

	Total			Male			Female		
	1998	2003	2008	1998	2003	2008	1998	2003	2008
EU-27	1.5	0.4	1.0	1.0	0.1	0.6	2.1	0.7	1.5
Euro area	1.9	0.4	0.8	1.2	-0.1	0.2	2.8	1.2	1.6
Belgium	1.6	0.0	1.6	0.6	-0.9	0.8	3.0	1.3	2.7
Bulgaria	-1.0	3.0	3.3	:	3.7	3.5	:	2.1	3.0
Czech Republic	-1.5	-1.3	1.5	:	-1.2	1.9	:	-1.6	1.0
Denmark	1.4	-1.1	0.9	0.6	-0.4	0.6	2.4	-1.9	1.1
Germany	1.2	-0.9	1.4	0.8	-1.4	1.2	1.8	-0.3	1.7
Estonia	-1.9	1.4	0.2	:	1.6	0.3	:	1.2	0.1
Ireland	8.6	2.0	-0.8	7.5	1.5	-2.2	10.3	2.7	1.0
Greece	*2.9*	1.0	1.2	*3.6*	0.5	0.7	*1.8*	1.8	2.1
Spain	4.5	3.1	-0.5	4.0	1.9	-2.2	5.4	5.1	2.0
France	1.5	0.1	0.5	1.1	-0.7	0.3	2.0	1.2	0.8
Italy	1.0	1.5	0.3	0.4	1.2	-0.4	2.0	2.0	1.4
Cyprus	1.6	3.8	2.6	:	2.8	2.6	:	5.1	2.6
Latvia	-0.3	1.0	0.8	:	1.6	0.1	:	0.5	1.6
Lithuania	-0.8	2.2	-0.5	:	2.5	-0.7	:	1.9	-0.2
Luxembourg	4.5	1.8	4.7	3.0	-2.7	6.6	7.1	9.2	2.2
Hungary	1.8	1.3	-1.2	0.8	0.6	-1.5	2.9	2.1	-0.8
Malta	:	1.0	2.5	:	1.0	0.6	:	1.0	6.6
Netherlands	2.6	-0.5	1.5	1.8	-1.2	0.9	3.7	0.4	2.2
Austria	1.0	0.3	1.9	0.8	0.6	0.9	1.3	0.0	3.0
Poland	1.3	-1.2	*4.0*	0.9	-1.3	*4.1*	1.9	-1.1	*3.9*
Portugal	2.8	-0.6	0.4	2.3	-1.3	0.2	3.5	0.2	0.7
Romania	:	0.0	*0.3*	:	1.0	*0.9*	:	-1.3	*-0.5*
Slovenia	-0.2	-0.4	2.9	:	0.1	2.4	:	-1.0	3.5
Slovakia	-0.5	1.1	*2.8*	:	1.1	*2.7*	:	1.1	*2.8*
Finland	2.0	0.1	1.6	2.4	0.3	2.0	1.5	-0.1	1.2
Sweden	1.7	-0.6	0.9	2.0	-0.6	1.1	1.4	-0.5	0.7
United Kingdom	0.9	1.0	0.1	1.0	1.1	-0.2	0.8	0.9	0.4
Croatia	-3.0	0.6	*1.1*	:	0.9	*0.6*	:	0.2	*1.7*
Turkey	2.8	*-1.0*	*1.8*	:	:	*1.1*	:	:	*3.7*
Norway	2.7	-1.0	3.1	:	-1.3	3.1	:	-0.7	3.1
Japan	-1.2	-0.3	*-0.4*	:	:	:	:	:	:
United States	1.4	0.9	*-0.5*	:	:	:	:	:	:

Source: Eurostat (tsieb050)

Table 5.5: Persons working part-time and persons with a second job
(% of total employment)

	Persons employed working part-time			Persons in employment with second job		
	1998	2003	2008	1998	2003	2008
EU-27	15.9	16.5	18.2	:	3.5	3.8
Euro area	15.1	16.4	19.5	:	2.7	3.4
Belgium	16.5	20.5	22.6	2.9	3.7	3.8
Bulgaria	:	2.3	2.3	:	0.7	0.8
Czech Republic	5.7	5.0	4.9	3.4	2.6	1.8
Denmark	22.3	21.3	24.6	7.3	10.1	9.5
Germany	18.4	21.7	25.9	2.8	2.5	3.7
Estonia	8.6	8.5	7.2	8.3	4.1	3.3
Ireland	16.5	16.9	:	0.8	1.8	2.6
Greece	5.6	4.3	5.6	4.8	2.9	3.4
Spain	7.8	8.2	12.0	1.6	1.8	2.5
France	17.3	16.5	16.9	3.5	2.7	3.2
Italy	7.3	8.5	14.3	1.3	1.2	1.9
Cyprus	:	8.9	7.8	:	6.9	4.2
Latvia	12.8	10.3	6.3	5.0	7.5	6.0
Lithuania	:	9.6	6.7	6.0	7.4	5.1
Luxembourg	9.1	13.4	18.0	1.2	1.1	2.1
Hungary	3.8	4.4	4.6	2.3	1.9	1.6
Malta	:	9.2	11.5	:	4.9	5.1
Netherlands	38.9	45.0	47.3	5.9	5.9	7.3
Austria	15.7	18.7	23.3	5.5	3.6	4.4
Poland	10.4	10.5	8.5	8.6	7.4	7.5
Portugal	11.0	11.7	11.9	6.0	6.7	6.5
Romania (¹)	15.8	11.5	9.9	6.2	4.1	3.1
Slovenia	:	6.2	9.0	2.7	1.8	3.7
Slovakia	2.3	2.4	2.7	1.1	0.9	1.1
Finland	11.4	13.0	13.3	4.5	3.7	4.4
Sweden	19.8	22.9	26.6	8.7	9.4	8.2
United Kingdom	24.5	25.6	25.3	4.5	4.1	3.8
Croatia	:	8.5	8.9	:	3.0	3.1
Turkey	:	:	9.6	:	:	2.9
Iceland	:	22.1	20.5	16.6	11.8	9.6
Norway	:	28.8	28.2	8.2	8.4	8.5
Switzerland	29.6	32.7	34.3	5.2	6.0	7.4

(¹) 2002, break in series.

Source: Eurostat (tps00159, tps00074 and lfsi_emp_a)

Figure 5.6: Persons employed part-time, 2008 (¹)
(% of total employment)

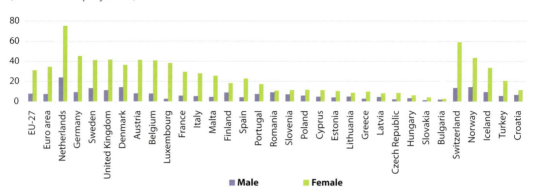

(¹) The figure is ranked on the average of male and female; Ireland, not available.

Source: Eurostat (tps00159)

Figure 5.7: Proportion of employees with a contract of limited duration, 2008
(% of total employees)

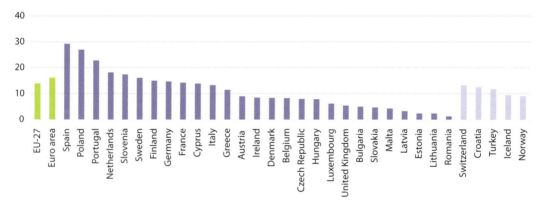

Source: Eurostat (tps00073)

5.2 People in the labour market - unemployment

Introduction

Male, youth and long-term unemployment appear to be more susceptible to cyclical economic changes than overall unemployment. Indeed, social policymakers are challenged to remedy these situations by designing ways to increase the employment opportunities open to various (disadvantaged) groups of society, those working in particular economic activities, or those living in specific regions.

Globalisation and technological progress have an ever-increasing effect on many daily lives, and the demand for different types of labour and skills is evolving at a rapid pace. While enterprises need to be increasingly innovative and productive, some of their risk may be passed on to the labour force, as increased flexibility is demanded both from those in employment as well as those searching for a new job.

Within the context of the European Employment Strategy, there are a number of measures that are designed to help encourage people to remain in work or find a new job, including: the promotion of a lifecycle approach to work, encouraging lifelong learning, improving support to those seeking a job, as well as ensuring equal opportunities.

The integrated employment guidelines for 2008-2010 set a number of additional benchmarks, whereby Member States are encouraged:

- to ensure that by 2010 every unemployed person is offered a job, appren-

ticeship, additional training or another employability measure (for young persons leaving school within four months, and for adults within no more than 12 months);
- to work towards 25 % of the long-term unemployed participating in training, retraining, work practice, or other employability measures by 2010;
- to guarantee that job-seekers throughout the EU are able to consult all job vacancies advertised in the national employment services of each Member State.

Definitions and data availability

Unemployed persons are defined as those persons aged 15-74 ([4]) who were not employed during the reference week of the labour force survey, were available for work and were either actively seeking work in the four weeks prior to the survey, or had already found a job to start within the next three months. For the purposes of this final point, the following are considered as specific steps in the search for a job: having been in contact with a public employment office to find work, whoever took the initiative (renewing registration for administrative reasons only is not an active step); having been in contact with a private agency (temporary work agency, firm specialising in recruitment, etc.) to find work; applying to employers directly; asking among friends, relatives, unions, etc., to find work; placing or answering job advertisements; studying job advertisements; taking a recruitment test or

---

([4]) In Spain and the United Kingdom this is restricted to persons aged 16 to 74 years old.

examination or being interviewed; looking for land, premises or equipment; applying for permits, licences or financial resources. This definition is in accordance with the International Labour Organisation (ILO) standards and Commission Regulation (EC) No 1897/2000.

Unemployment data are generally presented as rates. The **unemployment rate** is the share of unemployed persons over the total number of active persons in the labour market; active persons are those who are either employed or unemployed. Please note that at the end of this publication, Chapter 13 presents regional data for unemployment rates.

The unemployment rate can be broken down into a number of more detailed groups – for example, **unemployment according to educational attainment**, where the indicator provides a measure of the difficulties that people with different levels of education face in the labour market, offering some information on the impact of education on the chances of being unemployed.

The duration of unemployment is defined as the duration of a search for a job, or as the period since the last job was held (if this period is shorter than the duration of the search for a job). The **long-term unemployment rate** is the proportion of active persons in the labour market who have been unemployed for 12 months or more; the **very long-term unemployment rate** represents the number of persons who have been unemployed for at least 24 months, again expressed as a share of the total number of active persons in the labour market.

Main findings

The unemployment rate is considered to be a lagging indicator. When there is a downturn in the economy, it usually takes several months before the unemployment rate begins to rise. Once the economy starts picking up again, employers are usually cautious and it can take several months before the unemployment rate starts to fall again.

The average unemployment rate across the EU-27 in 2008 was 7.0 %, which represented a further fall from the relative peak of 9.0 % that was recorded in 2003 and 2004. This latest annual figure represented a reduction of just 0.1 percentage points in comparison with 2007, which was a marked slowdown when compared with the 1.1 and 0.7 percentage point reductions for the two previous years.

There remain considerable differences in unemployment rates between Member States. Spain's rate of 11.3 % in 2008 was the only double-digit unemployment rate, with Slovakia (9.5 %) recording the next highest share of persons out of work. Most of the remaining Member States recorded unemployment rates in the range of 7.8 % (France and Hungary) to 3.7 % (Cyprus), with Denmark (3.3 %) and the Netherlands (2.8 %) below this. The distribution of unemployment rates across the EU narrowed considerably between 2001 and 2007, as the range between the highest and lowest unemployment rates across the Member States fell from 17.6 percentage points to 7.9 percentage points; in 2008 the range rose to 8.5 percentage points as the Spanish unemployment rate reversed its declining trend, while the Dutch unemployment rate continued to fall.

Long-term unemployment is one of the main concerns of governments and social planners/policymakers. Besides its effects on personal life, long-term unemployment limits social cohesion and, ultimately, hinders economic growth. Some 2.6 % of the labour force in the EU-27 in 2008 had been unemployed for more than one year; slightly more than half of these, 1.5 % of the labour force, had been unemployed for more than two years.

The unemployment rate for women (7.5 %) in the EU-27 in 2008 remained higher than that for men (6.6 %); this pattern was reflected in the majority of Member States, with exceptions limited to the Baltic Member States, Romania, Ireland, the United Kingdom and Germany. Higher unemployment rates for women were particularly marked in Greece, Italy and Spain.

Unemployment rates by age group show that persons under the age of 25 tend to face the most difficulty in securing a job. The average unemployment rate among

15 to 24 year olds was 15.4 % across the EU-27 in 2008. The highest youth unemployment rates among the Member States were in Spain (24.6 %), Greece (22.1 %), Italy (21.3 %) and Sweden (20.0 %) and the same countries reported the largest difference between unemployment rates for those aged 25 or more and those aged less than 25. In contrast, youth unemployment rates were closest to (but not lower than) the overall unemployment rate in Germany and the Netherlands.

A lack of qualifications can be another discriminating factor for job-seekers, as unemployment rates tend to decrease according to the level of education attained. This was a characteristic noted in almost every Member State in 2008, as the average unemployment rate in the EU-27 for those having attained at most a lower secondary education was 9.8 % in 2008, almost three times the rate of unemployment (3.4 %) for those that had a tertiary education.

Table 5.6: Unemployment rate
(%)

	1998	1999	2000	2001	2002	2003	2004	2005	2006	2007	2008
EU-27	:	:	8.7	8.5	8.9	9.0	9.0	8.9	8.2	7.1	7.0
Euro area	10.1	9.3	8.5	8.0	8.4	8.8	9.0	9.0	8.3	7.5	7.5
Belgium	9.3	8.5	6.9	6.6	7.5	8.2	8.4	8.5	8.3	7.5	7.0
Bulgaria	:	:	16.4	19.5	18.2	13.7	12.1	10.1	9.0	6.9	5.6
Czech Republic	6.4	8.6	8.7	8.0	7.3	7.8	8.3	7.9	7.2	5.3	4.4
Denmark	4.9	5.2	4.3	4.5	4.6	5.4	5.5	4.8	3.9	3.8	3.3
Germany	9.1	8.2	7.5	7.6	8.4	9.3	9.8	10.7	9.8	8.4	7.3
Estonia	9.2	11.3	12.8	12.4	10.3	10.0	9.7	7.9	5.9	4.7	5.5
Ireland	7.5	5.7	4.3	3.9	4.5	4.8	4.6	4.4	4.5	4.6	6.0
Greece	10.8	12.0	11.2	10.7	10.3	9.7	10.5	9.9	8.9	8.3	7.7
Spain	15.0	12.5	11.1	10.3	11.1	11.1	10.6	9.2	8.5	8.3	11.3
France	11.0	10.4	9.0	8.3	8.6	9.0	9.3	9.3	9.2	8.4	7.8
Italy	11.4	11.0	10.1	9.1	8.6	8.5	8.1	7.7	6.8	6.1	6.8
Cyprus	:	:	4.9	3.8	3.6	4.1	4.7	5.3	4.6	4.0	3.7
Latvia	14.3	14.0	13.7	12.9	12.2	10.5	10.4	8.9	6.8	6.0	7.5
Lithuania	13.2	13.7	16.4	16.5	13.5	12.5	11.4	8.3	5.6	4.3	5.8
Luxembourg	2.7	2.4	2.2	1.9	2.6	3.8	5.0	4.6	4.6	4.2	4.9
Hungary	8.4	6.9	6.4	5.7	5.8	5.9	6.1	7.2	7.5	7.4	7.8
Malta	:	:	6.7	7.6	7.5	7.6	7.4	7.2	7.1	6.4	6.0
Netherlands	3.8	3.2	2.8	2.2	2.8	3.7	4.6	4.7	3.9	3.2	2.8
Austria	4.5	3.9	3.6	3.6	4.2	4.3	4.9	5.2	4.8	4.4	3.8
Poland	10.2	13.4	16.1	18.3	20.0	19.7	19.0	17.8	13.9	9.6	7.1
Portugal	5.0	4.5	4.0	4.1	5.1	6.4	6.7	7.7	7.8	8.1	7.7
Romania	:	7.1	7.3	6.8	8.6	7.0	8.1	7.2	7.3	6.4	5.8
Slovenia	7.4	7.3	6.7	6.2	6.3	6.7	6.3	6.5	6.0	4.9	4.4
Slovakia	12.6	16.4	18.8	19.3	18.7	17.6	18.2	16.3	13.4	11.1	9.5
Finland	11.4	10.2	9.8	9.1	9.1	9.0	8.8	8.4	7.7	6.9	6.4
Sweden (¹)	8.2	6.7	5.6	4.9	4.9	5.6	6.3	7.4	7.0	6.1	6.2
United Kingdom	6.1	5.9	5.4	5.0	5.1	5.0	4.7	4.8	5.4	5.3	5.6
Croatia	:	:	:	:	14.8	14.2	13.7	12.7	11.2	9.6	8.4
Turkey	:	:	:	:	:	:	:	:	8.4	8.5	9.8
Norway	3.1	3.0	3.2	3.4	3.7	4.2	4.3	4.5	3.4	2.5	2.5
Japan	4.1	4.7	4.7	5.0	5.4	5.3	4.7	4.4	4.1	3.9	4.0
United States	4.5	4.2	4.0	4.8	5.8	6.0	5.5	5.1	4.6	4.6	5.8

(¹) Break in series, 2005.

Source: Eurostat (tsiem110)

5

Figure 5.8: Unemployment rate, 2008 (^{1})
(%)

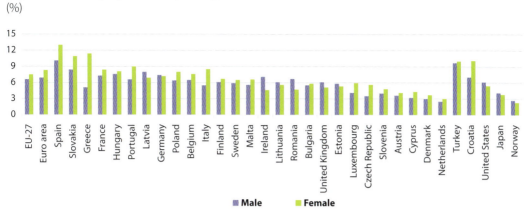

(^{1}) The figure is ranked on the average of male and female.

Source: Eurostat (tsiem110)

Figure 5.9: Unemployment rate by duration, 2008
(%)

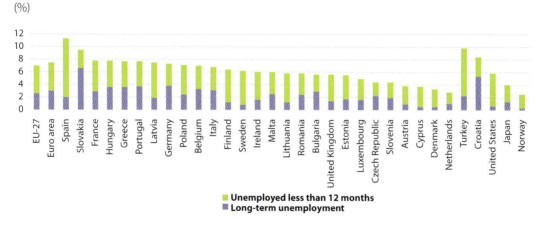

Source: Eurostat (tsiem110 and tsisc070)

Table 5.7: Unemployment rate by gender and by age
(%)

	Male		Female		< 25 years	25-74 years
	2003	2008	2003	2008	2008	2008
EU-27	8.4	6.6	9.7	7.5	15.4	5.9
Euro area	7.9	6.9	10.0	8.3	15.4	6.6
Belgium	7.7	6.5	8.9	7.6	18.0	5.9
Bulgaria	14.1	5.5	13.2	5.8	12.7	5.0
Czech Republic	6.2	3.5	9.9	5.6	9.9	3.9
Denmark	4.8	3.0	6.1	3.7	7.6	2.5
Germany	9.8	7.4	8.7	7.2	9.9	6.9
Estonia	10.2	5.8	9.9	5.3	12.0	4.6
Ireland	5.0	7.1	4.4	4.6	12.6	4.9
Greece	6.2	5.1	15.0	11.4	22.1	6.6
Spain	8.2	10.1	15.3	13.0	24.6	9.8
France	8.1	7.3	9.9	8.4	19.1	6.5
Italy	6.5	5.5	11.4	8.5	21.3	5.6
Cyprus	3.6	3.2	4.8	4.3	9.0	3.1
Latvia	10.6	8.0	10.4	6.9	13.1	6.6
Lithuania	12.7	6.1	12.2	5.6	13.4	5.0
Luxembourg	3.0	4.1	4.9	5.9	16.9	4.0
Hungary	6.1	7.6	5.6	8.1	19.9	6.9
Malta	6.9	5.6	9.1	6.6	11.9	4.7
Netherlands	3.5	2.5	3.9	3.0	5.3	2.3
Austria	4.0	3.6	4.7	4.1	8.0	3.1
Poland	19.0	6.4	20.5	8.0	17.3	5.9
Portugal	5.6	6.6	7.3	9.0	16.4	6.8
Romania	7.6	6.7	6.4	4.7	18.6	4.4
Slovenia	6.3	4.0	7.1	4.8	10.4	3.7
Slovakia	17.4	8.4	17.8	10.9	19.0	8.4
Finland	9.2	6.1	8.9	6.7	16.5	4.9
Sweden	6.0	5.9	5.2	6.5	20.0	4.1
United Kingdom	5.5	6.1	4.3	5.1	15.0	3.9
Croatia	12.9	7.0	15.8	10.1	21.9	6.9
Turkey	:	9.7	:	10.0	18.5	7.8
Norway	4.5	2.7	3.9	2.3	7.2	1.7
Japan	5.5	4.1	4.9	3.8	7.3	3.7
United States	6.3	6.1	5.7	5.4	12.8	4.6

Source: Eurostat (tsiem110 and une_rt_a)

Table 5.8: Unemployment rate, EU-27
(%)

	2000	2001	2002	2003	2004	2005	2006	2007	2008
Male	7.8	7.7	8.3	8.4	8.5	8.3	7.6	6.6	6.6
Female	9.8	9.4	9.7	9.7	9.8	9.6	8.9	7.8	7.5
Less than 25 years	17.4	17.3	17.9	18.0	18.4	18.3	17.1	15.3	15.4
Between 25 and 74 years	7.4	7.2	7.6	7.7	7.8	7.6	7.0	6.1	5.9
Long-term unemployment rate	4.0	3.9	4.0	4.1	4.2	:	3.7	3.0	2.6
Male	3.5	3.5	3.6	3.8	3.8	:	3.5	2.8	2.4
Female	4.6	4.4	4.5	4.5	4.6	:	4.0	3.3	2.8
Very long-term unemployment rate	2.4	2.3	2.3	2.3	2.4	:	2.2	1.8	1.5

Source: Eurostat (tsiem110, une_rt_a, tsisc070 and une_ltu_a)

Figure 5.10: Unemployment rate (among persons aged 25-64 years) by level of educational attainment, 2008 ([1])
(%)

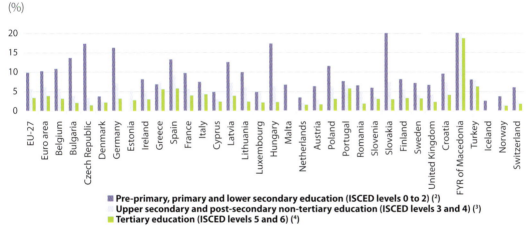

- ■ **Pre-primary, primary and lower secondary education (ISCED levels 0 to 2) ([2])**
- ☐ **Upper secondary and post-secondary non-tertiary education (ISCED levels 3 and 4) ([3])**
- ■ **Tertiary education (ISCED levels 5 and 6) ([4])**

([1]) Former Yugoslav Republic of Macedonia, 2007.
([2]) Estonia, not available; Lithuania, Slovenia and Croatia, unreliable data; Slovakia, y-axis has been cut, 35.9 %; former Yugoslav Republic of Macedonia, y-axis has been cut, 41.2 %.
([3]) Malta and Iceland, not available; former Yugoslav Republic of Macedonia, y-axis has been cut, 31.2 %.
([4]) Malta and Iceland, not available; Estonia, Lithuania, Slovenia and Croatia, unreliable data.

Source: Eurostat (tps00066)

5.3 Wages and labour costs

Introduction

The structure and evolution of earnings are important features of any labour market, reflecting labour supply from individuals and labour demand by enterprises. At the same time, the level and structure of earnings and labour costs are among the key macro-economic indicators used by policymakers, employers and trade unions.

The European employment guidelines include two that are related to wages and labour cost, namely to ensure:

- that wage developments contribute to macro-economic stability and growth;
- employment-friendly labour cost developments and wage-setting mechanisms by encouraging social partners within their own responsibilities to set the right framework for wage-bargaining in order to reflect productivity and labour market challenges at all relevant levels and to avoid gender pay gaps, by reviewing the impact on employment of non-wage labour costs and where appropriate adjust their structure and level, especially to reduce the tax burden on the low-paid.

Article 141(1) of the EC Treaty sets out the principle of equal pay for male and female workers for equal work or work of equal value, and Article 141(3) provides the legal basis for legislation on the equal treatment of men and women in employment matters. The European Commission in March 2006 set a roadmap [5] for equality between women and men during the period 2006-2010, which was subject to a mid-term progress report in 2008 [6]. Particular attention is given to the gender pay gap, the difference between male and female pay, which is a multidimensional phenomenon: some underlying factors that may, in part, explain gender pay gaps include sectoral and occupational segregation, education and training, awareness and transparency. The EU seeks to promote equal opportunities implying progressive elimination of the gender pay gap.

Gender differences are not restricted to pay, and the principle of equal treatment has been extended to cover a range of employment aspects, including equal access to self-employment, working conditions and vocational training. Policy measures within this area are designed to take account of differences in male and female labour market participation rates and career structures, wage structures, promotion policies, as well as the concentration of women in low pay sectors and occupations.

[5] COM(2006) 92 final; for more information: http://eur-lex.europa.eu/LexUriServ/LexUriServ.do?uri=COM:2006:0092:FIN:EN:PDF.

[6] COM(2008) 760 final; for more information: http://eur-lex.europa.eu/LexUriServ/LexUriServ.do?uri=COM:2008:0760:FIN:EN:PDF.

Definitions and data availability

Labour costs refer to the expenditure incurred by employers in order to employ personnel. They include employee compensation (including wages, salaries in cash and in kind, employers' social security contributions), vocational training costs, other expenditure such as recruitment costs, spending on working clothes and employment taxes regarded as labour costs minus any subsidies received. These labour cost components and their elements are defined in Commission Regulation (EC) 1737/2005 of 21 October 2005 amending Regulation (EC) No 1726/1999 as regards the definition and transmission of information on labour costs implementing Council Regulation (EC) No 530/1999 concerning structural statistics on earnings and labour costs. Data relate to three core indicators:

* **average monthly labour costs**, defined as total labour costs per month divided by the corresponding number of employees, expressed as full-time units;
* **average hourly labour costs**, defined as total labour costs divided by the corresponding number of hours worked;
* the **structure of labour costs** (wages and salaries; employers' social security contributions; other labour costs), expressed as a percentage of total labour costs.

Gross earnings are the most important part of labour costs – information is provided on average annual gross earnings. The main definitions relating to earnings are detailed in a European Commission Regulation [7] concerning structural statistics on earnings and labour costs. Gross earnings cover remuneration in cash paid directly by the employer, before tax deductions and social security contributions payable by wage earners and retained by the employer. All bonuses, whether or not regularly paid, are included (13th or 14th month, holiday bonuses, profit-sharing, allowances for leave not taken, occasional commissions, etc.). The information is presented for full-time employees working in industry and services (as covered by NACE Rev. 1.1 Sections C to K). The statistical unit is the enterprise or local unit. The population consists of all units having employees, although it is at present still confined to enterprises with at least 10 employees in most countries.

Information on **median earnings** are based on gross monthly earnings, and represent the median earnings of full-time employees in enterprises with 10 or more employees. **Low wage earners** are full-time employees that earn less than two thirds of the median gross monthly earnings.

Net earnings are derived from gross earnings and represent the part of remuneration that employees can actually spend. Compared with gross earnings, net earnings do not include social security contributions and taxes, but do include family allowances.

---

[7] European Commission Regulation (EC) 1738/2005 of 21 October 2005 amending Regulation (EC) No 1916/2000 as regards the definition and transmission of information on the structure of earnings implementing Council Regulation (EC) No 530/1999 concerning structural statistics on earnings and labour costs.

Minimum wages are enforced by law and apply nationwide to the majority of full-time employees in each country. Minimum wages are expressed as gross amounts, that is, before the deduction of income tax and social security contributions. For most countries, the minimum wage is agreed in terms of an hourly or monthly rate, with the following exceptions for those countries where the minimum wage is fixed at an hourly rate:

- France: minimum wage per hour * 35 hours per week * 52/12;
- Ireland: minimum wage per hour * 39 hours per week * 52/12;
- United Kingdom: minimum wage per hour * 38.1 hours per week * 52.14/12;
- In the case of Greece, Spain and Portugal, where 14 monthly minimum wages are paid per year, the minimum monthly wage is multiplied by 14/12;
- United States: minimum wage per hour * 40 hours per week * 52/12.

Data on minimum wages are transmitted by national ministries responsible for areas such as social affairs, labour or employment.

The **gender pay gap** in unadjusted form is defined as the difference between average gross hourly earnings of male and female paid employees, and is shown as a percentage of men's earnings. Gross earnings are remuneration (wages and salaries) paid directly to an employee, before any deductions for income tax and social security contributions paid by employees. The population consists of all paid employees in enterprises with 10 or more employees in NACE Rev. 1.1 Sections C to K and M to O, in other words, excluding agriculture, fishing, public administration, private households

and extra-territorial organisations. The methodology for the compilation of the indicator has recently changed and is now based on data collected from the structure of earnings survey rather than on non-harmonised sources (as was previously the case).

The **tax wedge** on labour costs is defined as income tax plus the employee and the employer's social security contributions, expressed as a percentage of the total labour costs (gross earnings plus the employer's social security contributions plus payroll taxes where applicable). This indicator is for single persons without children, earning 67 % of the earnings of an average worker (AW) in NACE Rev. 1.1 Sections C to K (the business economy).

The **unemployment trap** measures the percentage of gross earnings which is taxed away through higher tax and social security contributions and the withdrawal of unemployment and other benefits when an unemployed person returns to employment; it is defined as the difference between gross earnings and the increase of the net income when moving from unemployment to employment, expressed as percentage of the gross earnings. This indicator is also available for single persons without children, earning 67 % of the earnings of an AW when in work.

The **low wage trap** measures the percentage of gross earnings which is taxed away through the combined effects of income taxes, social security contributions and any withdrawal of benefits when gross earnings increase from 33 % to 67 % of the earnings of an AW. This indicator is available for single persons without children and for one-earner couples with two children between 6 and 11 years old.

Main findings

The mean (average) gross annual earnings of full-time employees in enterprises with 10 or more employees was EUR 31 302 in the EU-27 in 2006. Among the Member States, mean earnings were highest in Denmark (EUR 53 165) in 2007, followed by the United Kingdom, Luxembourg, Germany (2006) and Ireland (2005) – all above EUR 40 000 – and lowest in Romania (EUR 4 828) and Bulgaria (EUR 2 626). Median earnings, as opposed to mean earnings, show a broadly similar ranking of countries, with mean earnings higher than median earnings in all countries except Malta. The proportion of employees considered to be low wage earners in 2006 was highest in Latvia, at 30.9 %, while more than one in four employees were also on low wages in Lithuania, Bulgaria and Romania.

Statutory minimum wages also vary considerably between Member States, and reflect to some degree the price levels in each economy, with the highest minimum wage in 2009 being recorded in Luxembourg (EUR 1 642 per month) and the lowest in Bulgaria and Romania (EUR 123 and EUR 153 respectively).

Despite some progress, there remains an important gap between the earnings of men and women in the EU-27. Women were paid, on average, 17.5 % less than men in 2007. The pay gap was below 10 % in Belgium, Portugal, Slovenia, Poland, Malta and Italy (where it was 4.4 %), but was wider than 25 % in Estonia and Austria. Various effects may contribute to these gender pay gaps, such as: differences in labour force participation rates, differences in the occupations and activities that tend to be male or female dominated, differences in the degrees to which men and women work on a part-time basis, as well as the attitudes of personnel departments within private and public bodies towards career development and unpaid/maternity leave.

Tax wedge data for 2002 and 2007 show little overall change in the EU-27, however the tax wedge has fallen in 18 of the Member States and remained relatively unchanged in three others. The tax wedge only increased between these two years in six of the Member States, most notably by around 2 to 3 percentage points in the United Kingdom, Greece and Luxembourg, although the tax wedge in all three of these Member States remained below the EU-27 average.

There were quite large differences in the structure of labour costs within the Member States in 2007; the relative importance of wages and salaries ranged from less than 70 % of total labour costs in Belgium, France and Sweden to more than 85 % in Denmark and Malta (2006).

Figure 5.11: Median earnings, 2006 (¹)
(median gross monthly earnings of full-time employees)

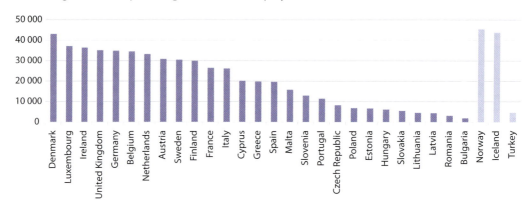

(¹) Enterprises employing 10 or more employees; excluding agriculture, fishing, public administration, private households and extra-
territorial organizations.

Source: Eurostat (Structure of earnings survey 2006)

Figure 5.12: Low wage earners - full-time employees earning less than two thirds of the median
gross monthly earnings, 2006 (¹)
(% of employees)

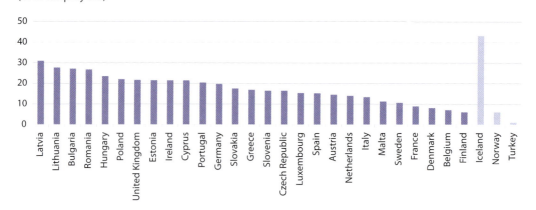

(¹) Enterprises employing 10 or more employees; excluding agriculture, fishing, public administration, private households and extra-
territorial organizations.

Source: Eurostat (Structure of earnings survey 2006)

Table 5.9: Earnings in industry and services (average gross annual earnings full-time employees) (¹)
(EUR)

	1997	1998	1999	2000	2001	2002	2003	2004	2005	2006	2007
EU-27	:	:	:	:	27 947	30 140	30 347	28 226	29 114	31 302	:
Belgium	28 901	29 616	30 701	31 644	33 109	34 330	34 643	35 704	36 673	37 674	:
Bulgaria	896	1 216	1 330	1 436	1 518	1 588	1 678	1 784	1 978	2 195	2 626
Czech Republic	:	:	:	:	:	6 016	6 137	6 569	7 405	8 284	:
Denmark	36 235	37 209	39 515	40 962	41 661	43 577	44 692	46 122	47 529	48 307	53 165
Germany	35 093	35 432	36 228	37 319	38 204	39 153	40 056	40 954	41 694	42 382	:
Estonia	:	:	:	:	:	:	:	:	:	:	:
Ireland	:	:	:	:	:	:	:	:	40 462	:	:
Greece	12 605	13 210	13 926	14 721	15 431	16 278	16 739	:	:	:	:
Spain	16 192	16 528	17 038	17 432	17 768	18 462	19 220	19 828	20 439	21 150	:
France	25 545	25 777	26 339	26 712	27 418	28 185	28 847	29 608	30 521	31 369	:
Italy	:	:	:	:	:	:	:	:	:	:	:
Cyprus	14 021	14 709	15 161	16 335	16 948	17 740	18 406	19 290	20 549	21 310	:
Latvia	:	:	:	:	:	:	:	3 806	4 246	5 211	6 690
Lithuania	2 286	2 799	3 017	:	:	:	:	:	:	:	:
Luxembourg	32 600	33 337	34 462	35 875	37 745	38 442	39 587	40 575	42 135	43 621	45 284
Hungary	3 543	3 686	3 770	4 173	4 898	5 846	6 196	7 100	7 798	7 840	8 952
Malta (²)	10 144	10 745	11 608	11 658	11 974	12 096	11 886	11 926	11 180	11 669	:
Netherlands	28 061	29 189	30 426	31 901	33 900	35 200	36 600	37 900	38 700	:	:
Austria	:	:	:	:	:	:	:	34 995	36 032	36 673	:
Poland	:	4 156	5 310	:	7 510	:	:	6 230	6 270	:	:
Portugal	:	:	:	12 620	13 338	13 322	13 871	14 253	14 715	15 930	:
Romania	:	:	:	:	:	:	:	2 414	3 155	3 713	4 828
Slovenia	:	:	:	:	:	:	:	:	:	:	:
Slovakia	3 179	3 292	3 125	3 583	3 837	4 582	4 945	5 706	6 374	7 040	8 400
Finland	24 005	24 944	25 739	27 398	28 555	29 916	30 978	31 988	33 290	34 080	36 126
Sweden	:	:	:	31 621	30 467	31 164	32 177	33 620	34 049	35 084	36 871
United Kingdom	:	29 370	32 269	37 677	39 233	40 553	38 793	41 253	42 866	44 496	46 051
Croatia	:	:	:	:	:	:	8 491	9 036	9 634	:	:
Iceland	:	:	32 311	37 639	34 101	36 764	:	:	:	:	:
Norway	:	31 456	33 741	36 202	38 604	43 736	42 882	42 224	45 485	47 221	:
Switzerland	:	40 727	:	43 683	:	48 498	:	45 760	:	46 058	:

(¹) Enterprises employing 10 or more employees; excluding agriculture, fishing, public administration, private households and extra-
territorial organisations.
(²) Break in series, 2000.

Source: Eurostat (tps00175)

Table 5.10: Minimum wage
(per month, as of 1 January)

	National currency (¹)			EUR			PPS
	1999	2004	2009	1999	2004	2009	2009
Belgium	1 074	1 186	1 388	1 074	1 186	1 388	1 254
Bulgaria	64	120	240	33	61	123	240
Czech Republic	3 250	6 700	8 000	93	207	306	443
Denmark	-	-	-	-	-	-	-
Germany	-	-	-	-	-	-	-
Estonia	:	2 480	4 350	:	159	278	362
Ireland	:	1 037	1 462	:	1 073	1 462	1 153
Greece	505	631	:	505	631	:	:
Spain	416	537	728	416	537	728	760
France	1 036	1 113	1 321	1 036	1 113	1 321	1 189
Italy	-	-	-	-	-	-	-
Cyprus	-	-	-	-	-	-	-
Latvia	50	80	180	75	121	254	343
Lithuania	430	430	800	92	125	232	347
Luxembourg	1 162	1 403	1 642	1 162	1 403	1 642	1 413
Hungary	22 500	53 000	71 500	89	200	270	408
Malta	475	543	635	462	541	635	810
Netherlands	1 064	1 265	1 382	1 064	1 265	1 382	1 336
Austria	-	-	-	-	-	-	-
Poland	650	824	1 126	159	177	281	468
Portugal	357	426	525	357	426	525	606
Romania	35	280	600	28	69	153	263
Slovenia	285	465	589	363	471	589	710
Slovakia	:	202	296	:	148	296	409
Finland	-	-	-	-	-	-	-
Sweden	-	-	-	-	-	-	-
United Kingdom	608	761	914	866	1 084	1 010	1 154
Turkey	78	423	666	217	240	319	480
United States	893	893	1 135	762	727	844	961

(¹) Including 'euro fixed' series for euro area countries.

Source: Eurostat (earn_minw_cur)

Figure 5.13: Gender pay gap, 2007 (¹)
(% difference between average gross hourly earnings of male and female employees, as % of male gross earnings, unadjusted form)

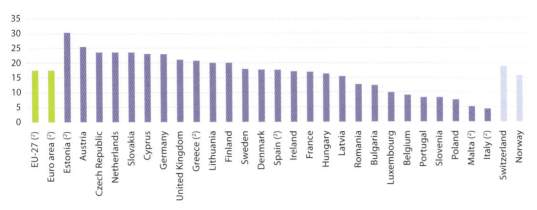

(¹) Enterprises employing 10 or more employees; excluding agriculture, fishing, public administration, private households and extra-territorial organisations.
(²) Provisional.

Source: Eurostat (tsiem040)

Figure 5.14: Tax rate on low wage earners: tax wedge on labour cost, 2007
(%)

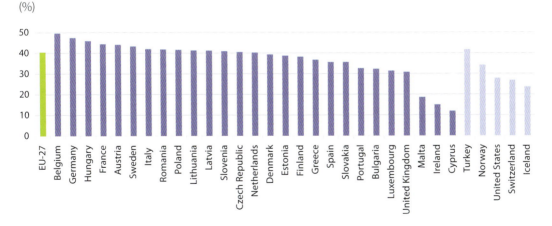

Source: Eurostat (tsiem050), OECD, Commission services

Table 5.11: Tax rate indicators on low wage earners
(%)

	Tax wedge on labour cost		Unemployment trap		Low wage trap - single person without children		Low wage trap - one earner couple with two children	
	2002	2007	2002	2007	2002	2007	2002	2007
EU-27	40	41	73	75	73	75	56	63
Belgium	51	50	87	83	87	83	48	47
Bulgaria	36	32	76	76	76	76	54	19
Czech Republic	42	41	67	72	67	72	72	43
Denmark	40	39	91	90	91	90	93	91
Germany	48	47	75	74	75	74	66	84
Estonia	40	39	50	63	50	63	74	22
Ireland	17	15	73	78	73	78	76	87
Greece	34	37	56	59	56	59	16	16
Spain	36	36	80	82	80	82	16	14
France	47	44	80	77	80	77	59	62
Italy	43	42	60	72	60	72	-14	-13
Cyprus	17	12	55	61	55	61	74	115
Latvia	42	41	87	87	87	87	100	67
Lithuania	43	41	59	80	59	80	94	58
Luxembourg	29	31	87	88	87	88	110	110
Hungary	48	46	68	81	68	81	60	55
Malta	18	19	59	62	59	62	11	30
Netherlands	39	40	70	81	70	81	77	84
Austria	43	44	67	68	67	68	83	65
Poland	42	42	82	79	82	79	79	74
Portugal	32	33	81	82	81	82	66	64
Romania	45	42	61	71	61	71	29	24
Slovenia	43	41	84	81	84	81	96	67
Slovakia	41	36	71	43	71	43	124	30
Finland	41	38	82	75	82	75	100	100
Sweden	47	43	87	82	87	82	93	80
United Kingdom	28	31	68	68	68	68	66	85
Turkey	42	42	:	:	:	:	:	:
Iceland	23	24	72	82	72	82	79	56
Norway	35	34	75	76	75	76	91	93
Switzerland	27	27	:	:	:	:	:	:
Japan	23	:	59	60	59	60	98	93
United States	27	28	71	71	71	71	59	51

Source: Eurostat (tsiem050, earn_nt_unemtrp and tsiem060)

Figure 5.15: Average hourly labour costs in industry and services of full-time employees, 2007 (¹)
(EUR)

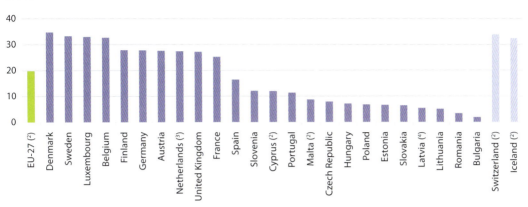

(¹) Enterprises employing 10 or more employees; excluding agriculture, fishing, public administration, private households and extra-territorial organisations; Ireland, Greece and Italy, not available.
(²) 2006.
(³) 2005.
(⁴) 2008.

Source: Eurostat (tps00173)

Figure 5.16: Breakdown of labour costs in industry and services, 2007 (¹)
(% share of total labour costs)

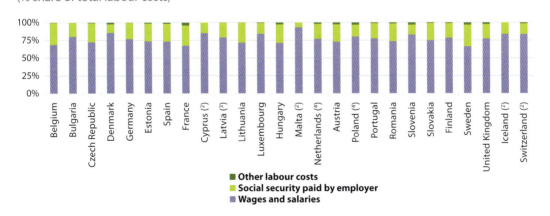

■ **Other labour costs**
■ **Social security paid by employer**
■ **Wages and salaries**

(¹) Enterprises employing 10 or more employees; excluding agriculture, fishing, public administration, private households and extra-territorial organisations; Ireland, Greece and Italy, not available.
(²) 2006.
(³) 2008.
(⁴) 2005.

Source: Eurostat (tps00115, tps00114 and tps00113)

5.4 Job vacancies

Introduction

Policy developments in this area have principally focused on trying to improve the labour market by more closely matching supply and demand, through: the modernisation and strengthening of labour market institutions, notably employment services; removing obstacles to mobility for workers across Europe; better anticipating skill needs, labour market shortages and bottlenecks; providing appropriate management of economic migration; and improving the adaptability of workers and enterprises so that there is a greater capacity to anticipate, trigger and absorb economic and social change.

Job-seekers throughout the EU should be able to consult all job vacancies advertised in each of the Member States' employment services. With this goal in mind, the EU set up EURES, the European jobs and mobility portal, which can be found at: www.eures.europa.eu. This website provides access to a range of job vacancies for 31 European countries (each of the Member States, as well as Iceland, Liechtenstein, Norway and Switzerland).

Definitions and data availability

A **job vacancy** is defined as a post (newly created, unoccupied or about to become vacant):

- for which the employer is taking active steps to find a suitable candidate from outside the enterprise concerned and is prepared to take more steps; and

- which the employer intends to fill either immediately or in the near future.

A vacant post that is open only to internal candidates should not be treated as a job vacancy. The **job vacancy rate (JVR)** measures the percentage of posts that are vacant. It is calculated as the proportion of the number of job vacancies relative to the total number of posts, where the latter is composed of the number of occupied posts plus the number of job vacancies. It is expressed as follows: JVR = number of job vacancies / (number of occupied posts + number of job vacancies) * 100. An occupied post is a post within an organisation to which an employee has been assigned.

Eurostat publishes quarterly and annual data on job vacancies. Quarterly data is broken down by economic activity and enterprise size while annual data is additionally broken down by region and occupation making it more suitable for structural analysis. The national institutions responsible for compiling job vacancy statistics send aggregated statistics to Eurostat. These data are then used to compile the job vacancy rate for the EU-27 and the euro area. At present, job vacancy statistics of the Member States do not provide complete coverage and as a result there are currently no EU totals for the absolute numbers of job vacancies or occupied posts. The EU job vacancy rate is calculated simply on the basis of the information available; no estimates are made for any country not participating in the data collection exercise.

Main findings

The job vacancy rate, in part, reflects the unmet demand for labour, as well as a potential mismatch between the skills and availability of those who are unemployed and those sought by employers. Job vacancy statistics are used by the European Commission and the European Central Bank (ECB) to analyse and monitor the evolution of the labour market at national and European level. These statistics are also a key indicator used for the assess-

ment of the business cycle and for structural analysis.

There was a broad upward development in the job vacancy rate in the EU, reaching 2.2 % in 2007, before falling back to 1.9 % in 2008. Among the Member States for which data are available, the job vacancy rate in 2008 was highest in Cyprus (4.1 %) and lowest in Spain, Luxembourg and Portugal (0.6 %), while the remaining Member States recorded rates within the range of 0.9 % to 3.2 %.

Figure 5.17: Job vacancy rate
(%)

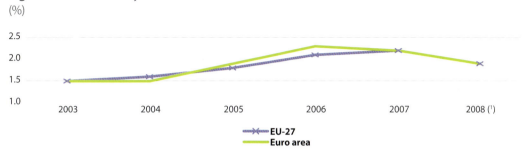

(¹) Provisional.

Source: Eurostat (jvs_a_nace1)

Figure 5.18: Job vacancy rate, 2008 (¹)
(%)

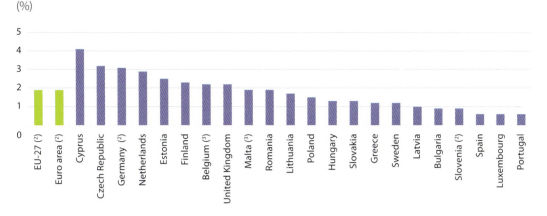

(¹) Denmark, Ireland, France, Italy and Austria, not available.
(²) Provisional.
(³) 2007.

Source: Eurostat (jvs_a_nace1)

5.5 Labour market policy interventions

Introduction

Labour market policy (LMP) interventions are generally targeted at providing assistance to the unemployed and other groups of people with particular difficulties to enter the labour market. The primary target groups in most countries remain those people that are registered as unemployed by national public employment services (PES). However, policy objectives are increasingly focused on a broader range of inactive persons within society. As such, LMP interventions are increasingly being targeted at women, the young, the elderly, or other groups of society that may face disadvantages and barriers that prevent them from joining the labour force.

Definitions and data availability

The **LMP methodology** provides guidelines for the collection of data on labour market policy interventions: which interventions to cover and how to classify interventions by type of action, how to measure expenditure associated with each intervention and how to calculate the numbers of participants in these interventions (stocks, entrants and exits).

LMP statistics cover all labour market interventions which can be described as 'public interventions in the labour market aimed at reaching its efficient functioning and correcting disequilibria and which can be distinguished from other general employment policy interventions in that they act selectively to favour particular groups in the labour market'.

The scope of LMP statistics is limited to public interventions which are explicitly targeted at groups of persons with difficulties in the labour market: the unemployed, persons employed but at risk of involuntary job loss and inactive persons who would like to enter the labour market.

LMP interventions are classified into three main types:

- **LMP services** refer to labour market interventions where the main activity of participants is job-search related and where participation usually does not result in a change of labour market status.
- **LMP measures** refer to labour market interventions where the main activity of participants is other than job-search related and where participation usually results in a change in labour market status. An activity that does not result in a change of labour market status may still be considered as a measure if the intervention fulfils the following criteria: 1) the activities undertaken are not job-search related, are supervised and constitute a full-time or significant part-time activity of participants during a significant period of time, and 2) the aim is to improve the vocational qualifications of participants, or 3) the intervention provides incentives to take-up or to provide employment (including self-employment).
- **LMP supports** refer to interventions that provide financial assistance, directly or indirectly, to individuals for labour market reasons, or which compensate individuals for disadvantage caused by labour market circumstances.

These main types are further broken down into nine detailed categories according to the type of action.

- **LMP services:** labour market services.
- **LMP measures:** training; job rotation and job sharing; employment incentives; supported employment and rehabilitation; direct job creation; start-up incentives.
- **LMP supports** out-of-work income maintenance and support; early retirement.

Main findings

The breakdown of expenditure and participants for different labour market policy interventions across the Member States varies greatly, reflecting the different characteristics and problems faced within individual labour markets, as well as the political convictions of different governments. Within the EU-27, the highest level of relative expenditure on labour market policy interventions in 2007 was reported in Belgium (over 3 % of GDP), while the lowest shares were recorded in the United Kingdom, the Czech Republic, Latvia, Lithuania, Romania and Estonia (all below 0.5 % of GDP). There was also a wide range of expenditure patterns in terms of spending on labour market policy services, with the Netherlands reporting the highest relative expenditure (more than twice the EU-27 average).

The largest share of expenditure in 2007 on active labour market policy measures in the EU-27 went on training (38.3 %) to improve the employability of the unemployed and other target groups. Over one quarter (25.8 %) of the EU-27's expenditure was accounted for by employment incentives, with a slightly larger share (28.1 %) being relatively equally shared between programmes developed to promote labour market integration among persons with reduced working capacity and programmes to create additional jobs.

An estimate of the participation in labour market policy initiatives suggests that an average of 11.5 million persons were engaged in different types of action across the EU-27 at any point of time throughout 2007. Of these, the most common were employment incentives (5.6 million persons) and training (3.4 million persons).

Table 5.12: Labour market policy measures, participants by type of action, 2007 (annual average stock in 1 000)

	Training (¹)	Job rotation & job sharing	Employment incentives (²)	Supported employment & rehabilita-tion (³)	Direct job creation (⁴)	Start-up incentives (⁵)
EU-27	3 446.8	111.5	5 617.3	830.6	822.3	703.9
Belgium	106.9	-	207.7	41.9	126.6	0.7
Bulgaria	8.5	-	16.3	2.1	48.8	4.2
Czech Republic	7.3	-	13.2	26.5	7.4	3.9
Denmark	53.8	-	22.3	62.7	-	-
Germany	1 240.0	0.4	126.8	23.2	372.9	279.8
Estonia	1.1	-	0.2	0.0	0.1	0.0
Ireland	33.2	-	5.5	3.0	23.7	4.8
Greece	42.3	-	14.2	0.1	:	5.2
Spain	227.7	79.4	3 538.1	50.0	222.8	258.9
France	570.6	-	525.0	139.7	358.9	101.9
Italy	:	19.7	610.3	-	26.8	8.2
Cyprus	1.0	-	1.6	0.2	-	0.1
Latvia	2.3	-	4.5	0.0	1.3	-
Lithuania	8.1	0.0	:	6.4	3.7	0.2
Luxembourg	2.1	-	9.4	0.0	1.0	-
Hungary	13.6	-	32.2	-	16.5	1.9
Malta	1.5	-	0.0	-	0.0	0.0
Netherlands	118.5	-	36.0	154.5	-	-
Austria	96.6	0.1	52.7	2.0	8.0	2.5
Poland	90.7	:	105.7	:	10.4	4.1
Portugal	45.5	:	78.0	6.0	22.7	4.4
Romania	14.7	-	47.1	-	21.2	:
Slovenia	4.6	-	1.8	-	5.6	0.3
Slovakia	0.6	-	8.5	1.2	65.2	18.3
Finland	50.2	7.8	16.1	8.4	13.8	4.5
Sweden	37.9	4.1	97.6	34.9	-	3.0
United Kingdom	20.5	-	41.8	17.7	7.2	-
Norway	31.7	-	4.8	13.7	6.8	0.4

(¹) Greece and Malta, 2006.
(²) Germany and Greece, 2006.
(³) Greece, 2006.
(⁴) Germany and Spain, 2006.
(⁵) Greece, Italy and Lithuania, 2006.

Source: Eurostat (lmp_partsumm)

Figure 5.19: Public expenditure on labour market policy interventions, 2007
(% of GDP)

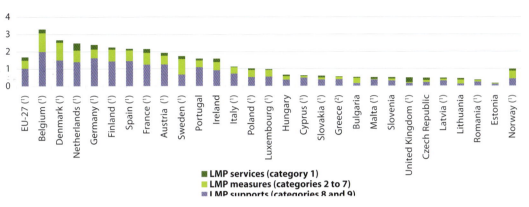

(¹) Includes estimates.
(²) 2006; includes estimates.

Source: Eurostat (lmp_expsumm)

Figure 5.20: Public expenditure on labour market policy measures, EU-27, 2007 (¹)
(% of total)

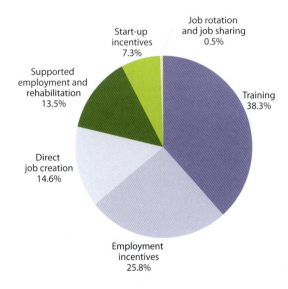

(¹) Estimates.

Source: Eurostat (tps00077)

6

Living conditions and welfare

Eurostat data on living conditions and welfare aim to show a comprehensive picture of the social situation in the EU, covering variables related to income, housing, poverty, social exclusion and other living conditions – all social exclusion and housing conditions information is collected at the household level.

The demand for statistics on living conditions and welfare received a new impetus following the social chapter of the Amsterdam Treaty (1997) which became the driving force for EU social statistics. This impetus was reinforced by successive European Councils that have kept the social dimension high on the political agenda. Moreover, the year 2010 has been designated as the European year for combating poverty and social exclusion ([1]).

Income, poverty and social exclusion are multidimensional problems. To monitor them effectively at a European level, a subset of so-called 'social cohesion indicators' has been developed within the structural indicators. Additionally, a broader portfolio of social inclusion indicators are calculated under the open method of coordination for social protection and social inclusion ([2]). Actions that are undertaken in the EU to help protect people against social risks (such as unemployment, ill health or social exclusion) or that are undertaken to help meet social needs can be evaluated by studying data on social protection expenditure and receipts.

This chapter concludes with a snapshot of indicators relating to good governance, in other words, whether political/public institutions allocate resources effectively and take decisions in an efficient and responsible manner. The public's perception of such ideals may be gauged through indicators such as voter turnout or measures of the public's confidence in these institutions.

[1] Decision No. 1098/2008/EC.
[2] For more information: http://ec.europa.eu/employment_social/soc-prot/soc-incl/indicator_en.htm.

6.1 Living conditions

Introduction

Favourable living conditions depend on a wide range of factors, which may be divided into two broad groups – those that are income-related and those that are not. The second group includes factors such as: quality healthcare services, education and training opportunities, or good transport facilities – aspects that affect everyday lives and work. Analysis of the distribution of income within a country provides a picture of inequalities: on the one hand, inequalities may create incentives for people to improve their situation through work, innovation or acquiring new skills, while on the other, crime, poverty and social exclusion are often seen as being linked to such income inequalities.

Definitions and data availability

Eurostat statistical indicators within the income and living conditions domain cover a range of topics relating to income, poverty and social exclusion. One group of indicators relate to monetary poverty analysed in various ways (for example, by age, gender and activity status). Another set relate to income distribution and income inequalities, while there are also indicators relating to non-monetary poverty and social exclusion (for example, material deprivation, or newly developed indicators describing housing conditions). A set of childcare arrangement indicators complements the information in this domain.

To calculate living condition indicators, Eurostat initially used micro-data ([3]) from the European Community household panel (ECHP) survey which was launched in 1994. However, after eight years of using this source, a new instrument was introduced in 2003, namely, data collection under a framework Regulation on **European Union statistics on income and living conditions (EU-SILC)**. One of the main reasons for this change was the need to adapt the content and timeliness of data production to reflect current political and research needs.

EU-SILC is now Eurostat's main reference source for comparative income distribution and social exclusion statistics. It comprises both a cross-sectional dimension and a longitudinal dimension. From 2005, EU-SILC covered the 25 Member States, as well as Norway and Iceland; Bulgaria, Romania, Turkey and Switzerland launched EU-SILC in 2007.

While comparisons of standards of living between countries are frequently based on GDP per capita, such figures say little about the distribution of income within a country. In this section, indicators measuring the distribution of income and relative poverty are presented. **Household disposable income** is established by summing up all monetary incomes received from any source by each member of the household (including income from work and social benefits) plus income received at the household level and deducting taxes and social contributions paid. In

---

([3]) Data gathered at the micro-level, for example, from individuals, households or enterprises, rather than aggregate data compiled at the level of the economy.

order to reflect differences in household size and composition, this total is divided by the number of '**equivalent adults**' using a standard (equivalence) scale, the so-called 'modified OECD' scale, which attributes a weight of 1 to the first adult in the household, a weight of 0.5 to each subsequent member of the household aged 14 and over, and a weight of 0.3 to household members aged less than 14. The resulting figure is called **equivalised disposable income** and is attributed to each member of the household. For the purpose of poverty indicators, the equivalised disposable income is calculated from the total disposable income of each household divided by the equivalised household size; consequently, each person in the household is considered to have the same equivalised income.

The **S80/S20 income quintile share ratio** is a measure of the inequality of income distribution and is calculated as the ratio of total income received by the 20 % of the population with the highest income (the top quintile) to that received by the 20 % of the population with the lowest income (the bottom quintile); where all incomes are compiled as equivalised disposable income.

The **relative median income ratio** is defined as the ratio of the median equivalised disposable income of persons aged above 65 to the median equivalised disposable income of persons aged below 65.

The **at-risk-of-poverty rate** is defined as the share of persons with an equivalised disposable income that is below the at-risk-of-poverty threshold, set at 60 % of the national median equivalised disposable income. This rate may be expressed before or after social transfers, with the difference measuring the hypothetical impact of national social transfers in reducing poverty risk; retirement and survivor's pensions are counted as income before transfers and not as social transfers. Various breakdowns of this indicator are calculated: by age, gender, activity status, household type, education level, etc. It should be noted that the indicator does not measure wealth, per se, but low current income (in comparison with other persons in the same country) which does not necessarily imply a low standard of living.

The **relative median at-risk-of-poverty gap** is calculated as the difference between the median equivalised disposable income of persons below the at-risk-of-poverty threshold and the at-risk-of-poverty threshold, expressed as a percentage of the at-risk-of-poverty threshold (cut-off point: 60 % of median equivalised income). The EU aggregate is a population weighted average of individual national figures. In line with decisions of the European Council, the at-risk-of-poverty rate is measured relative to the situation in each country rather than applying a common threshold to all countries.

Material deprivation, in the context of this publication, covers an economic strain and a durables strain, defined as the enforced inability (rather than the choice of not being able/having) to pay for at least three of the following nine items: unexpected expenses; one week annual holiday away from home; arrears (mortgage or rent payments, utility bills, or hire purchase instalments or other loan payments); a meal with meat or fish every other day; heating to keep the home adequately warm; a washing machine; a colour television; a telephone; or a car.

The indicators relating to the share of the population in **jobless households** are calculated as the proportion of persons of the specified age who live in households where no one is working. The indicator for children refers to the age group 0 to 17, whereas the indicator for adults refers to persons aged 18 to 59. Students aged 18 to 24 who live in households composed solely of students of the same age class are counted neither in the numerator nor the denominator of the ratio; the data comes from the EU labour force survey (LFS).

Main findings

Societies cannot combat poverty and social exclusion without analysing inequalities within society, whether they are economic in nature or social. Data on economic inequality becomes particularly important for estimating relative poverty, because the distribution of economic resources may have a direct bearing on the extent and depth of poverty.

There were wide inequalities in the distribution of income among the population of the EU-27 in 2007; the 20 % of the population with the highest equivalised disposable income received five times as much income as the 20 % of the population with the lowest equivalised disposable income. This ratio varied considerably across the Member States, from 3.3 in Slovenia and 3.4 in Sweden, through 6.0 or more in

Greece, Latvia and Portugal, to highs of 6.9 in Bulgaria and 7.8 in Romania. Relatively wide income inequalities were not confined to those countries with relatively low GDP per capita, as the distribution of income (using this measure) was noticeably more equitable in Slovakia and the Czech Republic, by way of example, than it was in the United Kingdom or Italy.

There is policy interest in the inequalities felt by many different groups in society: one group of particular interest is that of the elderly, in part reflecting the growing proportion of the EU's population aged over 65 years. Pension systems can play an important role in addressing poverty amongst the elderly. In this respect, it is interesting to compare the incomes of the elderly with the rest of the population.

Poland was the only Member State where the median equivalised disposable income of the elderly was similar or slightly higher than it was for persons under 65; in France, Austria, Luxembourg, and Hungary, the median income of the elderly was more than 90 % of that recorded for people under 65. In contrast, the elderly in Cyprus had a median income that was around 57 % of that recorded for people under 65, with shares between 65 % and 70 % in Ireland, Lithuania, Estonia, Latvia and Denmark. These relatively low proportions may broadly reflect pension entitlements, as well as fast economic growth through to 2007, which mainly benefited people of an active age.

The depth of poverty, which helps to quantify just how poor the poor are, can be measured by the relative median at-risk-of poverty gap. The median income of persons at-risk-of-poverty in the EU-27 was, on average, 23 % below the 60 % poverty threshold in 2007. Among the Member States, the national at-risk-of-poverty gap was widest in Romania and Bulgaria in 2007, but also relatively wide in Greece, Lithuania and Latvia; this gap was narrowest in Finland.

Social protection measures can be used as a means for reducing poverty and social exclusion. This may be achieved, for example, through the distribution of (means-tested) benefits. One way of evaluating the success of social protection measures is to compare at-risk-of-poverty indicators before and after social transfers. In 2007, social transfers reduced the at-risk-of-poverty rate among the population of the EU-27 from 26 % before transfers to 17 % after transfers, thereby lifting 35 % of those in poverty above the poverty line. The impact of social benefits was lowest in Bulgaria and a number of the Mediterranean Member States (Greece, Spain, Italy and Cyprus) in 2007. In contrast, one half or more of those persons who were at-risk-of poverty in Sweden, Hungary, Denmark, Finland, the Netherlands, Austria, the Czech Republic and France were removed as a result of social transfers.

Different groups in society are more or less vulnerable to poverty. Although there was little difference in the at-risk-of-poverty rate (after social transfers) between men and women in the EU-27 (16 % compared with 18 % respectively), there were notable differences when the population was classified according to activity status. The unemployed are a particularly vulnerable group: a little over two fifths (43 %) of the unemployed was at-risk-of-poverty in the EU-27 in 2007, with higher rates in the Baltic Member States. About one in six (17 %) retired persons in the EU-27 was at-risk-of-poverty in 2007; rates were much higher in the Baltic Member States, the United Kingdom and, in particular, Cyprus. Those in employment were far less likely to be at-risk-of-poverty (8 % in the EU-27), although there were relatively high rates in Greece (14 %) and Romania (18 %).

Across the Member States, households comprising three or more adults were typically the least likely to be at-risk-of-poverty, reflecting wider opportunities to pool resources. In a majority of Member States, households comprising two parents and two children were also less at-risk-of-poverty than the average for the whole population. In contrast, there were typically three types of household that were at much greater risk; these were single person households, single parent households with dependent children, and households comprising two adults with three or more dependent children (so-called large family households).

Income-related measures of poverty need to be analysed together with other measures –such as material deprivation – in order to have a deeper understanding of poverty. About one in every six (18 %) of the EU-27's population was materially deprived in 2007, although this reflected considerable differences between EU-15 Member States on the one hand and, on the other, those Member States that joined the EU since 2004.

Less than one in ten people in Luxembourg, the Nordic Member States and the Netherlands were materially deprived in 2007, whereas the proportion rose to a little over one third of those in Hungary and Poland, and was closer to half of the population in Latvia and Romania, reaching almost three quarters of the population in Bulgaria.

Living in a household where no adult works is likely to have a significant effect on a child's current and future living conditions and their risk of poverty. Slightly less than one in every ten children (9.4 %) in the EU-27 lived in a job-

less household in 2007, a similar proportion to that recorded for adults of working age (18 to 59 years, 9.3 %) who lived in jobless households. Among the Member States, the proportion of children in jobless households was highest in the United Kingdom (16.7 %) and Hungary (13.9 %), where it was also considerably more than the corresponding proportion of working-age adults in jobless households. In contrast, less than 4 % of children in Greece, Cyprus, Luxembourg and Slovenia were in jobless households; these figures were, by and large, much lower than the corresponding rates for adults of a working age.

Figure 6.1: Inequality of income distribution, 2007 (¹)
(S80/S20 income quintile share ratio)

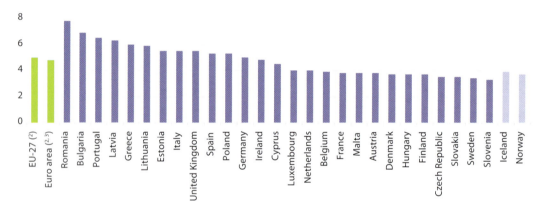

(¹) The income reference period concerns the year preceding the survey year for the majority of countries.
(²) Eurostat estimates based on population-weighted averages of national data.
(³) EA-15 instead of EA-16.

Source: Eurostat (ilc_ov2)

Figure 6.2: Relative median income ratio, 2007 (¹)
(ratio)

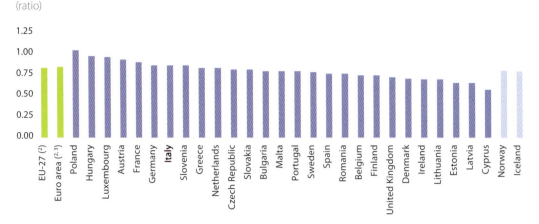

(¹) The income reference period concerns the year preceding the survey year for the majority of countries.
(²) Eurostat estimates based on population-weighted averages of national data.
(³) EA-15 instead of EA-16.

Source: Eurostat (ilc_ov7a)

Figure 6.3: Relative median at-risk-of-poverty gap, 2007 (¹)
(%)

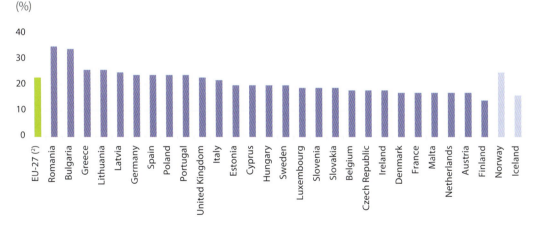

(¹) The income reference period concerns the year preceding the survey year for the majority of countries.
(²) Eurostat estimates based on population-weighted averages of national data.

Source: Eurostat (ilc_sip3)

Table 6.1: At-risk-of-poverty rate after social transfers ([1])
(%)

	Male			Female		
	2005	2006	2007	2005	2006	2007
EU-27 ([2])	15	15	16	17	17	18
Euro area ([2, 3])	14	15	15	16	16	17
Belgium	14	14	14	15	16	16
Bulgaria ([4])	13	17	21	15	19	23
Czech Republic ([5])	10	9	9	11	11	10
Denmark	12	11	11	12	12	12
Germany ([5])	11	12	14	13	13	16
Estonia	17	16	17	19	20	22
Ireland	19	17	16	21	19	19
Greece	18	20	20	21	21	21
Spain	19	18	19	21	21	21
France	12	12	12	14	14	14
Italy	17	18	18	21	21	21
Cyprus	15	14	14	18	18	17
Latvia ([5])	18	21	19	20	25	23
Lithuania ([5])	20	19	17	21	21	21
Luxembourg	13	14	13	14	14	14
Hungary	14	16	12	13	16	12
Malta	14	13	14	15	14	15
Netherlands ([5])	11	10	10	11	10	11
Austria	11	11	11	13	14	13
Poland ([5])	21	20	18	20	19	17
Portugal	19	18	17	20	19	19
Romania ([4])	18	18	24	18	19	25
Slovenia ([5])	11	10	10	14	13	13
Slovakia ([5])	13	12	10	13	12	11
Finland	11	12	12	13	13	14
Sweden	9	12	11	10	12	11
United Kingdom ([5])	19	18	18	19	20	20
Iceland	10	9	9	10	10	11
Norway	10	10	11	13	12	14

([1]) The income reference period concerns the year preceding the survey year for the majority of countries.
([2]) Eurostat estimates based on population-weighted averages of national data.
([3]) EA-15 instead of EA-16.
([4]) Break in series, 2007.
([5]) Break in series, 2005.

Source: Eurostat (ilc_ov1a1)

Table 6.2: At-risk-of-poverty rate after social transfers by most frequent activity status, 2007 ([1])
(%)

	Total population	Persons employed	Not employed	Unemployed	Retired	Inactive population, others
EU-27 ([2])	16	8	24	43	17	27
Euro area ([2, 3])	16	8	24	41	16	27
Belgium	15	4	25	34	20	27
Bulgaria ([4])	20	6	32	56	23	19
Czech Republic	8	3	13	48	6	13
Denmark	12	4	23	31	17	32
Germany	15	7	24	51	18	24
Estonia	20	8	37	62	37	32
Ireland	17	6	32	43	27	32
Greece	20	14	25	35	22	25
Spain	19	11	28	36	22	30
France	12	6	18	33	11	26
Italy	19	10	26	44	16	30
Cyprus	16	6	31	28	51	17
Latvia	21	10	38	57	38	31
Lithuania	18	8	32	57	30	29
Luxembourg	12	9	15	46	8	15
Hungary	10	6	15	46	8	23
Malta	13	4	22	39	23	20
Netherlands	9	5	15	27	9	18
Austria	11	6	17	42	12	21
Poland	15	12	19	43	6	21
Portugal	17	10	27	32	23	30
Romania ([4])	23	18	28	46	23	33
Slovenia	11	5	19	36	17	19
Slovakia	9	5	14	45	8	15
Finland	13	5	25	41	21	27
Sweden	10	7	16	26	11	31
United Kingdom	18	8	34	58	31	37
Croatia	:	7	27	36	23	29
Iceland	9	7	17	21	16	19
Norway	12	6	22	44	13	37

([1]) Persons aged 18 years and over; the income reference period concerns the year preceding the survey year for the majority of countries.
([2]) Eurostat estimates based on population-weighted averages of national data.
([3]) EA-15 instead of EA-16.
([4]) Break in series, 2007.

Source: Eurostat (ilc_sis1c)

Figure 6.4: At-risk-of-poverty rate, 2007 (¹)
(%)

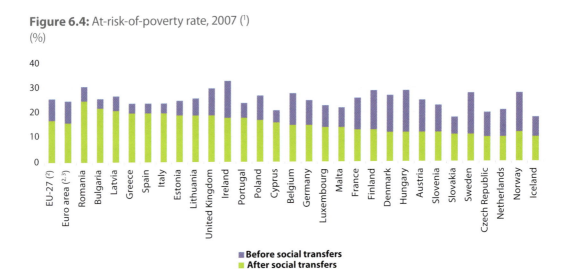

■ **Before social transfers**
■ **After social transfers**

(¹) The income reference period concerns the year preceding the survey year for the majority of countries.
(²) Eurostat estimates based on population-weighted averages of national data.
(³) EA-15 instead of EA-16.

Source: Eurostat (ilc_ov1a1 and ilc_ov251)

Figure 6.5: At-risk-of-poverty rate after social transfers, by household type, EU-27, 2007 (¹)
(%)

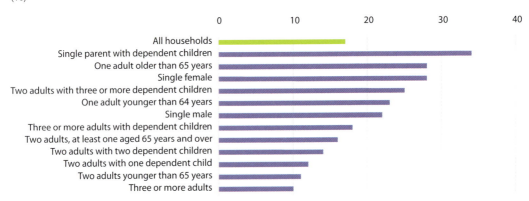

(¹) Eurostat estimates based on population-weighted averages of national data; the income reference period concerns the year preceding the survey year for the majority of countries.

Source: Eurostat (ilc_sis1a)

Figure 6.6: At-risk-of-poverty rate after social transfers, persons aged 65 years and over, 2007 (¹)
(%)

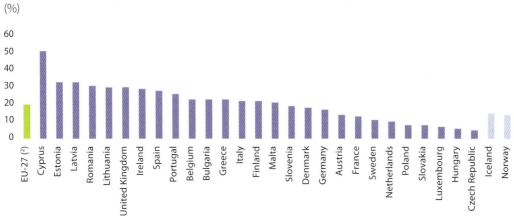

(¹) The income reference period concerns the year preceding the survey year for the majority of countries.
(²) Eurostat estimate based on population-weighted averages of national data.

Source: Eurostat (ilc_ov1a1)

Figure 6.7: Material deprivation rate – economic strain and durables dimension, 2007 (¹)
(%)

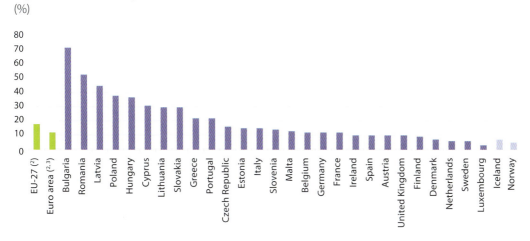

(¹) The income reference period concerns the year preceding the survey year for the majority of countries.
(²) Eurostat estimate based on population-weighted averages of national data.
(³) EA-15 instead of EA-16.

Source: Eurostat (ilc_sip8)

Figure 6.8: Persons living in jobless households, by age, 2007 (¹)
(% of respective age group living in households where no-one works)

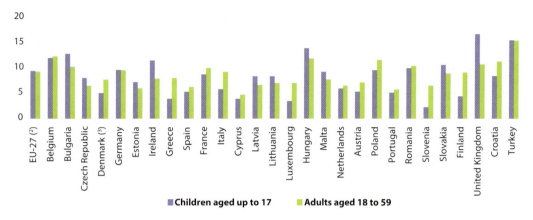

■ Children aged up to 17   ■ Adults aged 18 to 59

(¹) Sweden, not available.
(²) Estimates.
(³) 2006.

Source: Eurostat (tsdsc310)

Figure 6.9: Persons living in jobless households, by gender, 2007 (¹)
(% of respective gender aged 18-59 who are living in households where no-one works)

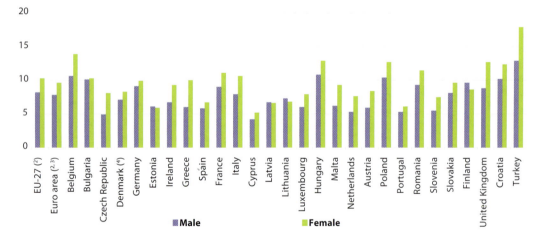

■ Male   ■ Female

(¹) Sweden, not available.
(²) Estimates.
(³) EA-15 instead of EA-16.
(⁴) 2006.

Source: Eurostat (tsisc090)

6.2 Housing

Introduction

Questions of social housing, homelessness or integration play an important role within the social policy agenda. The charter of fundamental rights stipulates in Article II-94 that 'in order to combat social exclusion and poverty, the Union recognises and respects the right to social and housing assistance so as to ensure a decent existence for all those who lack sufficient resources, in accordance with Community law and national laws and practices'.

However, the EU does not have any responsibilities in respect of housing; rather, national governments have the duty to develop their own housing policies. Many countries face similar challenges: for example, how to renew housing stocks, how to plan and combat urban sprawl, how to promote sustainable development, how to help young and disadvantage groups to get on the housing ladder, or how to promote energy efficiency among homeowners. The social and economic cost of the absence of decent housing is generally accepted to compromise the efficiency of a country or region. Indeed, decent housing, at an affordable price in a safe environment is likely to alleviate poverty and social exclusion.

Definitions and data availability

The data used in this section are primarily derived from micro-data from European Union statistics on income and living conditions (EU-SILC). The reference population is all private households and their current members residing in the territory of the Member State at the time of data collection; persons living in collective households and in institutions are generally excluded from the target population.

A **household** is defined in terms of shared household expenses. If household expenses are not shared, then the persons constitute separate households at the same address. A household may comprise either one person living alone or a group of people, not necessarily related, living at the same address with common housekeeping. The **average number of persons per private household** is the number of persons living in private households divided by the number of private households; collective households such as boarding houses, halls of residence and hospitals and the persons living in them are excluded.

Households are considered as **overcrowded** if the dwelling in which they live does not comprise a minimum number of rooms, established upon the basis of: one room for the household; one room for each couple; one room for each single person aged 18 or more; one room for two single people of the same sex between 12 and 17 years of age; one room for each single person of a different sex between 12 and 17 years of age; and one room for two people under 12 years of age.

Housing deprivation is a measure of poor amenities and is calculated by referring to those households with a leaking roof, no bath/shower and no indoor toilet, or a dwelling that is considered too dark. **Severe housing deprivation** is defined as households that are overcrowded, while also exhibiting at least one of the housing deprivation measures.

Main findings

The average number of persons living in a household in the EU-27 was 2.4 in 2007, although among the Member States this average ranged from a low of just over two persons per household in Germany to an average of three persons in Malta. Overcrowding depends not only upon the number of persons in a household, but also on the number of rooms in each dwelling; overcrowding was recorded for 17 % of all households in the EU-27 in 2007. However, it was relatively common among the central and eastern Member

States that have joined the EU since 2004 and, to a lesser extent, Greece, Italy, Portugal and Austria. Between one fifth and one third of the populations of Lithuania, Latvia, Poland and Romania lived in severe housing deprivation.

There were notable differences between Member States in housing ownership status in 2007. Less than 5 % of households in Bulgaria, Poland, Lithuania and Romania rented their own house/flat in 2007 compared with closer to one third of households in Sweden, Denmark, the Netherlands, France and Austria. It is difficult to pinpoint the reasons for such differences, as the distribution of households may be related to a range of factors, including: the degree of urbanisation, the quality of accommodation, or the supply of new or renovated housing.

Figure 6.10: Average number of persons per private household, 2007 (¹)

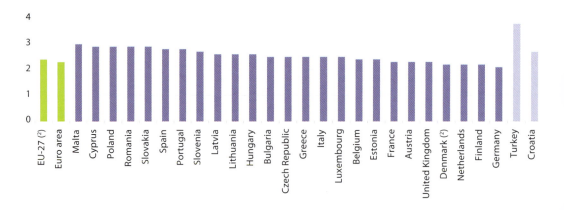

(¹) Ireland and Sweden, not available.
(²) 2006.

Source: Eurostat (lfst_hhantych)

Figure 6.11: Overcrowding, 2007
(% of all households)

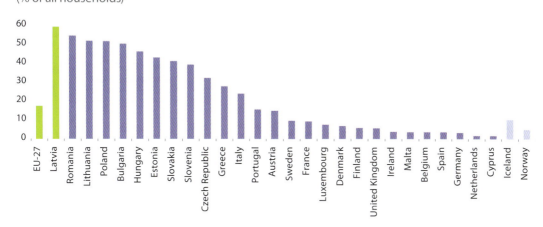

Source: Eurostat (EU-SILC)

Figure 6.12: Severe housing deprivation, 2007 (¹)
(% of population)

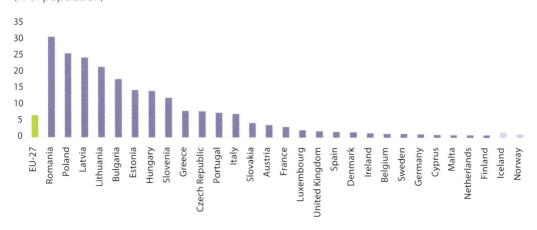

(¹) Indicator shows the percentage of persons living in a household that is overcrowded and has at least one of the following: leaking roof, no bath/shower and no indoor toilet, dwelling is considered as being too dark.

Source: Eurostat (EU-SILC)

6   Living conditions and welfare

Figure 6.13: Distribution of population by tenure status, 2007
(%)

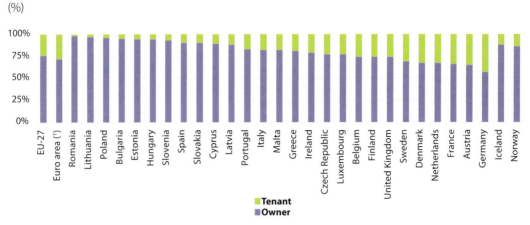

(¹) EA-15 instead of EA-16.

Source: Eurostat (ilc_lvho02)

6.3 Social protection

Introduction

Social protection systems are highly developed in the EU: they are designed to protect people against the risks and needs associated with unemployment, parental responsibilities, sickness/healthcare and invalidity, the loss of a spouse or parent, old age, housing and social exclusion (not elsewhere classified). The organisation and financing of social protection systems is the responsibility of each of the Member States. The model used in each Member State is therefore somewhat different, while the EU plays a coordinating role to ensure that people who move across borders continue to receive adequate protection. This role also promotes actions among the Member States to combat poverty and social exclusion, and to reform social protection systems on the basis of policy exchanges and mutual learning; this policy is known as the social protection and social inclusion process. The process underpinned the revised Lisbon objectives for 2010, promoting a more inclusive Europe that, it was argued, would be vital to achieve the EU's goals of sustained economic growth, more and better jobs and greater social cohesion.

Definitions and data availability

Data on expenditure and receipts of social protection are drawn up according to the **European system of integrated social protection statistics (ESSPROS)** methodology; this system has been designed to allow a comparison of social protection flows between Member States. In April 2007, a legal basis was established for the provision of ESSPROS data; this basis is provided for by Regulation (EC) No 458/2007 of the European Parliament and of the Council and was later supplemented by Commission Regulation No 1322/2007 and No 10/2008 ([4]); all this information and ESSPROS data can be found on the Eurostat website ([5]).

Social protection encompasses all interventions from public or private bodies intended to relieve households and individuals of the burden of a defined set of risks or needs, provided that there is neither a simultaneous reciprocal nor an individual arrangement involved. Social interventions are made through collectively organised schemes. **Expenditure on social protection** includes: social benefits, administration costs (which represent the costs charged to the scheme for its management and administration) and other expenditure (which consists of miscellaneous expenditure by social protection schemes, principally, payment of property income).

Social protection benefits are direct transfers, in cash or in kind, by social protection schemes to households and individuals to relieve them of the burden of one or more of the defined risks or needs. Social benefits are paid to households by social security funds, other government units, NPISHs (non-profit institutions serving households), employers administering unfunded social insurance

---

([4]) For more information: http://epp.eurostat.ec.europa.eu/portal/page/portal/living_conditions_and_social_protection/
legal_bases/social_protection_sub.
([5]) For more information: http://epp.eurostat.ec.europa.eu/portal/page/portal/living_conditions_and_social_protection/
introduction.

schemes, insurance enterprises or other institutional units administering privately funded social insurance schemes. Benefits are classified according to eight social protection functions ([6]), which represent a set of risks or needs:

- sickness/healthcare benefits – including paid sick leave, medical care and provision of pharmaceutical products;
- disability benefits – including disability pensions and the provision of goods and services (other than medical care) to the disabled;
- old age benefits – including old age pensions and the provision of goods and services (other than medical care) to the elderly;
- survivors' benefits – including income maintenance and support in connection with the death of a family member, such as survivors' pensions;
- family/children benefits – including support (except healthcare) in connection with the costs of pregnancy, childbirth, childbearing and caring for other family members;
- unemployment benefits – including vocational training financed by public agencies;
- housing benefits – including interventions by public authorities to help households meet the cost of housing;
- social exclusion benefits not elsewhere classified – including income support, rehabilitation of alcohol and drug abusers and other miscellaneous benefits (except healthcare).

The **pensions aggregate** comprises part of periodic cash benefits under the disability, old age, survivors and unemployment functions. It is defined as the sum of the following social benefits: disability pension, early-retirement benefit due to reduced capacity to work, old age pension, anticipated old age pension, partial pension, survivors' pension, early-retirement benefit for labour market reasons. **Expenditure on care for the elderly** is defined as the percentage of social protection expenditure devoted to old age care in GDP. These expenditures cover care allowance, accommodation, and assistance in carrying out daily tasks. The **aggregate replacement ratio** is defined as the median individual gross pensions of those aged 65 to 74 relative to median individual gross earnings of those aged 50 to 59, excluding other social benefits; it is expressed in percentage terms.

The schemes responsible for providing social protection are financed in different ways, their **social protection receipts** comprise social security contributions paid by employers and protected persons, contributions by general government, and other receipts from a variety of sources (for example, interest, dividends, rent and claims against third parties). **Social contributions by employers** are all costs incurred by employers to secure entitlement to social benefits for their employees, former employees and their dependants; they can be paid by resident or non-resident employers. They include all payments by employers to social protection institutions (actual contributions) and social benefits paid directly by employers to employees (imputed contributions). **Social contributions made by protected persons** comprise contributions paid by employees, by the self-employed and by pensioners and other persons.

([6]) Expenditure on education is not included in ESSPROS statistics.

Main findings

Social protection expenditure in the EU-27 averaged over one quarter (26.9 %) of GDP in 2006. Its share was highest in Sweden (30.7 %) and France (31.1 %), and was higher than 25 % in 11 of the EU-15 Member States. In contrast, social protection expenditure represented less than 20 % of GDP in all of the Member States that joined the EU since 2004, with the exception of Slovenia and Hungary, as well as being below this threshold in Ireland (18.2 %).

The use of a purchasing power standard (PPS) allows an unbiased comparison of social protection expenditure per capita between countries, taking account of differences in price levels. The highest level of expenditure on social protection per capita in 2006 was registered for Luxembourg [7] (PPS 13 458 per capita), followed some way behind by the Netherlands, Sweden, Denmark, Austria, Belgium and France where social protection per capita was between PPS 8 200 and PPS 9 100. In contrast, expenditure in the Baltic Member States, Bulgaria and Romania was less than PPS 2 000 per capita. These disparities between countries are partly related to differing levels of wealth and also reflect differences in social protection systems, demographic trends, unemployment rates and other social, institutional and economic factors.

Among social protection benefits (the largest component of total expenditure), a majority of the EU-27's expenditure was directed towards either old age (for example, pensions) or to sickness and healthcare; together these two items accounted

for close to 70 % of total EU-27 benefits in 2006. Benefits related to children, disabilities, survivors and unemployment each accounted for shares of between 5 % and 8 % of total expenditure, while housing accounted for 2.3 %.

Expenditure on pensions across the EU-27 was equivalent to 11.9 % of GDP in 2006, ranging from a high of 14.7 % in Italy to a low of 5.0 % in Ireland. Expenditure on care for the elderly in the EU-27 accounted for 0.5 % of GDP in the same year, although Sweden reported a rate that was almost five times as high; expenditure on the elderly fell to less than 0.1 % of GDP in Greece, Estonia, Belgium, Bulgaria, Romania and Cyprus.

A breakdown of social protection receipts across the EU-27 in 2006 shows that the majority of receipts could be attributed to employers' social contributions (38.2 %) and general government contributions (37.6 %). Approximately one fifth (20.6 %) of all EU-27 receipts were funded by contributions made by protected persons.

Pension systems can also play a key role in allowing retirees to maintain living standards they previously enjoyed in the later years of their working lives. The aggregate replacement ratio measures the difference between retirement benefits (excluding other social benefits) for pensioners (aged 65 to 74 years old) and salaries received by those aged 50 to 59. Average pension levels were generally lower than the earnings of those aged 50 to 59 in 2007. This was particularly the case in Cyprus (where pensions represented a little less than 30 % of the earnings among those aged 50 to 59) but also in Denmark, Latvia and Bulgaria

[7] Luxembourg is a special case insofar as a significant proportion of benefits (primarily expenditure on healthcare, pensions and family benefits) are paid to persons living outside the country.

(under 40 %). The ratio was highest in France, Luxembourg, Austria and Sweden, but even in these Member States it was only just above 60 %. It should be borne in mind that these relatively low ratios may reflect low coverage and/or low income replacement from statutory pension schemes and maturing pension systems, as well as incomplete careers or an under-declaration of earnings.

Table 6.3: Expenditure on social protection (% of GDP)

	1996	1997	1998	1999	2000	2001	2002	2003	2004	2005	2006
EU (¹)	27.8	27.4	27.0	26.9	26.5	26.7	27.0	27.3	27.2	27.1	26.9
Euro area (²)	:	:	:	:	26.7	26.8	27.4	27.8	27.7	27.8	27.5
Belgium	28.0	27.4	27.1	27.0	26.5	27.3	28.0	29.1	29.3	29.7	30.1
Bulgaria	:	:	:	:	:	:	:	:	:	16.0	15.0
Czech Republic	17.6	18.6	18.5	19.2	19.5	19.4	20.2	20.2	19.3	19.1	18.7
Denmark	31.2	30.1	30.0	29.8	28.9	29.2	29.7	30.9	30.7	30.2	29.1
Germany	29.4	28.9	28.9	29.2	29.3	29.4	30.1	30.4	29.8	29.7	28.7
Estonia	:	:	:	:	14.0	13.1	12.7	12.6	13.0	12.7	12.4
Ireland	17.6	16.4	15.2	14.6	13.9	14.9	17.5	17.9	18.2	18.2	18.2
Greece	20.5	20.8	21.7	22.7	23.5	24.3	24.0	23.6	23.5	24.3	24.2
Spain	21.5	20.8	20.2	19.8	20.3	20.0	20.4	20.6	20.7	21.1	20.9
France	30.6	30.4	30.1	29.9	29.5	29.6	30.4	30.9	31.3	31.4	31.1
Italy	24.3	24.9	24.6	24.8	24.7	24.9	25.3	25.8	26.0	26.3	26.6
Cyprus	:	:	:	:	14.8	14.9	16.3	18.4	18.1	18.4	18.4
Latvia	:	15.3	16.1	17.2	15.3	14.3	13.9	13.8	12.9	12.4	12.2
Lithuania	13.4	13.8	15.2	16.4	15.8	14.7	14.0	13.5	13.3	13.1	13.2
Luxembourg	21.2	21.5	21.2	20.5	19.6	20.9	21.6	22.1	22.2	21.7	20.4
Hungary	:	:	:	20.7	19.3	19.3	20.4	21.1	20.8	21.9	22.3
Malta	17.5	18.0	17.9	17.8	16.9	17.8	17.8	18.2	18.6	18.4	18.1
Netherlands	29.6	28.7	27.8	27.1	26.4	26.5	27.6	28.3	28.3	27.9	29.3
Austria	28.9	28.8	28.5	29.0	28.4	28.8	29.2	29.7	29.3	28.8	28.5
Poland	:	:	:	:	19.7	21.0	21.1	21.0	20.1	19.7	19.2
Portugal	20.2	20.3	20.9	21.4	21.7	22.7	23.7	24.1	24.7	25.4	25.4
Romania	:	:	:	:	13.2	13.2	13.4	12.6	15.1	14.2	14.0
Slovenia	23.8	24.2	24.5	24.4	24.2	24.5	24.4	23.7	23.4	23.0	22.8
Slovakia	19.5	19.8	20.0	20.2	19.4	19.0	19.1	18.2	17.2	16.7	15.9
Finland	31.4	29.1	27.0	26.2	25.1	24.9	25.6	26.5	26.6	26.7	26.2
Sweden	33.1	32.2	31.4	31.0	30.1	30.8	31.6	32.5	32.0	31.5	30.7
United Kingdom	27.4	26.9	26.3	25.7	26.4	26.8	25.7	25.7	25.9	26.3	26.4
Iceland	18.7	18.5	18.3	18.8	19.2	19.4	21.2	23.0	22.7	21.7	21.2
Norway	25.8	25.1	26.9	26.9	24.4	25.4	26.0	27.2	25.9	23.8	22.6
Switzerland	26.4	27.3	27.3	27.3	26.9	27.6	28.5	29.1	29.3	29.3	28.4

(¹) EU-15 for 1996-1999; EU-25 for 2000-2004; EU-27 for 2005-2006.
(²) EA-15 instead of EA-16.

Source: Eurostat (tps00098)

Figure 6.14: Expenditure on social protection per inhabitant, 2006
(PPS)

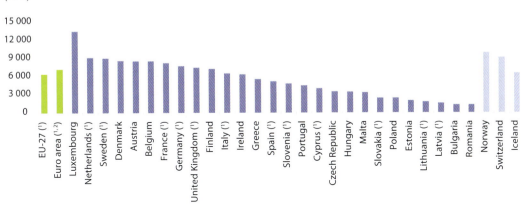

(¹) Provisional.
(²) EA-15 instead of EA-16.

Source: Eurostat (tps00100)

Figure 6.15: Social benefits, EU-27, 2006 (¹)
(%, based on PPS)

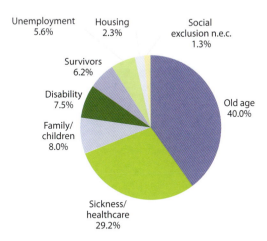

(¹) Provisional; figures do not sum to 100 % due to rounding.

Source: Eurostat (tps00107)

Figure 6.16: Expenditure on pensions, 2006
(% of GDP)

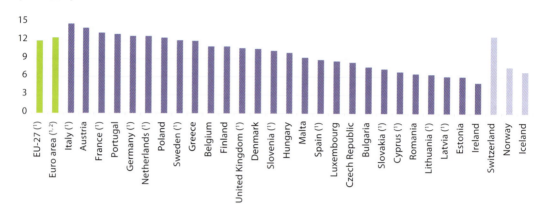

(¹) Provisional.
(²) EA-15 instead of EA-16.

Source: Eurostat (tps00103)

Figure 6.17: Expenditure on care for the elderly, 2006
(% of GDP)

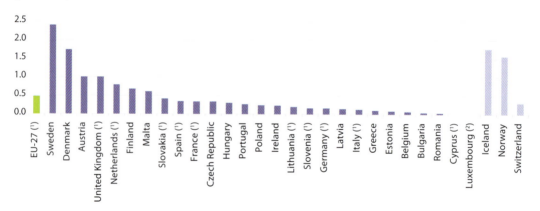

(¹) Provisional.
(²) Not available: expenditure was recorded together with similar benefits under the disability function as the split between old-age and disability was not available.

Source: Eurostat (tsdde530)

Figure 6.18: Social protection receipts, EU-27, 2006 (¹)
(% of total receipts)

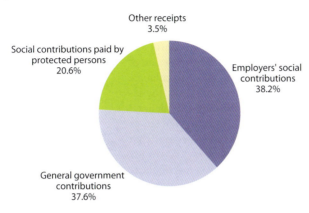

Other receipts
3.5%

Social contributions paid by
protected persons
20.6%

Employers' social
contributions
38.2%

General government
contributions
37.6%

(¹) Provisional; figures do not sum to 100 % due to rounding.

Source: Eurostat (tps00108)

Figure 6.19: Aggregate replacement ratio, 2007 (¹)
(%)

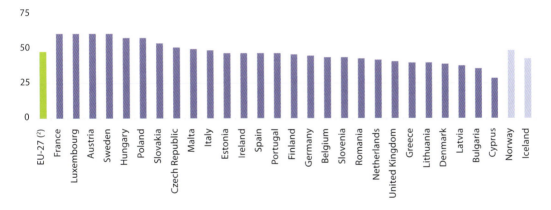

(¹) The income reference period concerns the year preceding the survey year for the majority of countries.
(²) Eurostat calculation based on population-weighted averages of national data.

Source: Eurostat (ilc_pnp3)

6.4 Good governance

Introduction

In July 2001, the European Commission adopted a White Paper on European governance. This contained a series of recommendations on how to enhance democracy in Europe and boost the legitimacy of its institutions. It defined governance in a European context as the rules, processes and behaviour that affect the way in which powers are exercised at European level, particularly as regards openness, participation, accountability, effectiveness and coherence (the 'five principles of good governance'). The White Paper aims to modernise European public action in order to increase the accountability of European executive bodies to the elected assemblies and open-up the EU's decision-making procedures to allow citizens to participate. Ultimately, it is hoped that these new forms of governance will bring the EU closer to its citizens, making it more effective, reinforcing democracy and consolidating the legitimacy of its institutions, while improving the quality of European legislation and making it clearer and more effective.

Since the adoption of the White Paper and under the label of 'better regulation' the European Commission has transposed the principles of good governance into various policies relating to reinforcing a culture of consultation and dialogue, improving the knowledge base for better policies, impact assessment (assessment of the potential economic, social and environmental consequences of new initiatives), better lawmaking, simplifying the regulatory environment, reducing administrative burdens, and monitoring of the transposition and application of EU law [8].

Definitions and data availability

Voter turnout is the percentage of persons who cast a vote or 'turn out' at an election as a share of the total population entitled to vote. It includes those who cast blank or invalid votes. In Belgium, Luxembourg and Greece, voting is compulsory. In Italy, voting is a civic obligation (no penalty).

The **level of citizens' confidence in each EU institution** (Council of the European Union, European Parliament and European Commission) is expressed as the share of positive opinions, people who declare that they 'tend to trust' each institution. Trust is not precisely defined and could leave some room for interpretation to the interviewees. The data are based on a twice-yearly Eurobarometer survey which has been used, since 1973, to monitor the evolution of public opinion in the Member States. The remaining categories, not shown in the table, include the percentage of negative opinions (people who declare that they 'tend not to trust'), as well as 'don't know' and/or 'no answer'.

---

[8] For more information: http://ec.europa.eu/governance/better_regulation/index_en.htm.

Main findings

Voter turnout at EU parliamentary elections in June 2009 ranged from 90.8 % in Luxembourg (where voting is compulsory) down to 19.6 % in Slovakia. Voter turnout in Bulgaria for their second elections to the European Parliament in 2009 was a little less than 40 %, and in Romania it was a little less than 30 %, both rates being at the lower end of the range among Member States.

According to the latest survey of public opinion in 2008, about one half (51 %) of all citizens declared that they tended to trust the European Parliament. Slightly less than half (47 %) of all respondents tended to trust the European Commission, with an even lower proportion (42 %) tending to trust the Council of the European Union.

Figure 6.20: Voter turnout
(%)

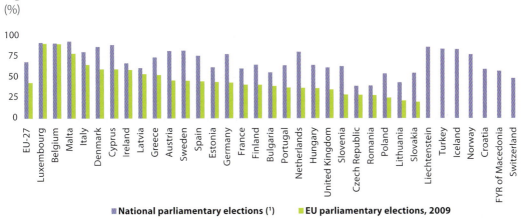

(¹) Latest elections: the Czech Republic; Spain, Italy, Lithuania, Malta, Austria, Romania, Slovenia and the former Yugoslav Republic of Macedonia, 2008; Belgium, Denmark, Estonia, Ireland, Greece, France, Poland, Finland, Croatia, Turkey, Iceland and Switzerland, 2007; Cyprus, Latvia, Hungary, the Netherlands, Slovakia and Sweden, 2006; Bulgaria, Germany, Portugal, the United Kingdom, Liechtenstein and Norway, 2005; Luxembourg, 2004; EU-27, average estimated by Eurostat on the basis of the trends observed in each of the Member States for national parliamentary elections.

Source: Eurostat (tsdgo310), International Institute for Democracy and Electoral Assistance

Table 6.4: Level of citizens' confidence in EU institutions (¹)
(%)

	European Parliament			Commission of the European Communities			Council of the European Union		
	2004	2006	2008	2004	2006	2008	2004	2006	2008
EU-27	:	:	51	:	:	47	:	:	42
Belgium	70	67	65	68	68	64	59	56	57
Bulgaria	57	55	57	50	51	51	45	46	46
Czech Republic	60	62	58	51	59	54	37	56	54
Denmark	60	62	63	53	55	53	55	41	47
Germany	55	52	47	44	42	43	39	39	38
Estonia	62	59	61	58	59	58	50	56	57
Ireland	70	66	54	66	60	50	51	50	56
Greece	66	70	59	61	68	56	57	69	50
Spain	64	51	57	57	49	52	55	44	40
France	59	50	52	54	47	45	43	41	45
Italy	63	56	53	60	52	49	55	46	46
Cyprus	64	57	55	59	55	53	56	55	54
Latvia	45	47	41	41	46	38	34	42	36
Lithuania	66	60	57	62	59	55	56	52	49
Luxembourg	71	63	64	67	63	57	62	55	49
Hungary	68	65	59	64	60	56	59	55	51
Malta	58	59	64	59	57	59	53	56	56
Netherlands	63	58	58	57	54	62	48	43	56
Austria	56	50	47	49	45	44	41	41	39
Poland	51	59	52	51	58	47	40	52	43
Portugal	64	61	57	61	60	53	53	56	51
Romania	65	64	63	59	62	55	38	57	52
Slovenia	66	73	62	64	73	61	54	68	60
Slovakia	70	71	70	61	66	63	49	63	62
Finland	63	56	59	58	54	57	53	48	48
Sweden	55	58	57	47	53	52	46	36	36
United Kingdom	39	25	27	39	25	27	26	19	21
Croatia	52	46	39	48	43	37	45	44	39
FYR of Macedonia	:	:	48	:	:	45	:	:	45
Turkey	41	34	20	39	32	19	34	32	18

(¹) The indicator presents the proportion of positive opinions ('tend to trust'); remaining answers were either 'tend not to trust', 'don't know' or 'no answer'.

Source: Eurostat (tsdgo510), European Commission - Eurobarometer survey

6.5 Crime

Introduction

The need to provide information on the development of crime in the EU was recognised in the Hague programme adopted by the European Council in 2004. The figures currently available on crime and criminal justice reflect the differing legal systems in the Member States and therefore cannot readily be compared. However, a more comparable system of crime and criminal justice statistics is being developed, as outlined in Commission Communication COM/2006/437, 'Developing a comprehensive and coherent EU strategy to measure crime and criminal justice: an EU action plan 2006-2010'.

Definitions and data availability

Total **crime** statistics include offences against the penal (or criminal) code. Less serious crimes (misdemeanours) are generally excluded.

Homicide is defined as the intentional killing of a person, including murder, manslaughter, euthanasia and infanticide. Attempted (uncompleted) homicide is excluded. Causing death by dangerous driving, abortion and help with suicide are also excluded. Unlike other offences, the counting unit for homicide is normally the victim.

Violent crime includes violence against the person such as physical assault, robbery (stealing by force or by threat of force), and sexual offences (including rape and sexual assault). **Robbery** is a subset of violent crime: it is defined as stealing from a person with force or threat of force, including muggings (bag-snatching) and theft with violence; pick-pocketing, extortion and blackmailing are generally not included.

Domestic burglary is defined as gaining access to a dwelling by the use of force to steal goods. **Theft of motor vehicles** covers all land vehicles with an engine that run on the road which are used to carry people (including cars, motorcycles, buses, lorries, construction and agricultural vehicles, etc.).

Drug trafficking includes illegal possession, cultivation, production, supplying, transportation, importing, exporting, financing etc. of drug operations which are not solely in connection with personal use.

Main findings

During the period between 2002 and 2007, there was a general decline in recorded crime in the EU, with the notable exceptions of drug trafficking offences (which remained almost unchanged) and violent crime (which rose, on average, by 1.6 % annually). Property offences, such as the theft of motor vehicles (down 6.8 % per annum) and domestic burglary (down 4.8 % per annum) declined relatively sharply during this five-year period, as did homicide (4.5 % lower per annum) and robbery (3.4 % lower per annum).

In a number of the Member States recorded crime figures for the period between 2002 and 2007 fell sharply; this was particularly the case in Poland, the United Kingdom, the Netherlands and France, where crime recorded by the police fell by between 12 % and 18 % over the five-year period considered; improved surveillance methods (such as closed-circuit cameras and alarm systems) are possible reasons for these changes. In other countries (such as Italy), crime appears to have risen noticeably, but in many cases the introduction of new recording methods makes it difficult to distinguish a definite trend.

Figure 6.21: Recorded crimes, EU, 2002-2007 (¹)
(%, average annual change)

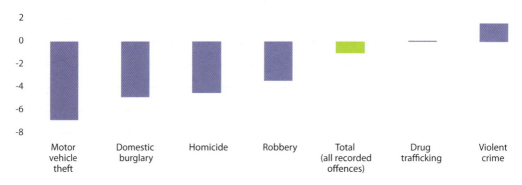

(¹) Excluding Estonia, Ireland, Cyprus and Malta.

Source: Eurostat (crim_gen)

Table 6.5: Crimes recorded by the police
(1 000)

	1997	1998	1999	2000	2001	2002	2003	2004	2005	2006	2007
Belgium	:	:	:	1 002	959	1 008	1 001	1 005	990	1 010	1 003
Bulgaria	228	159	145	149	147	147	144	142	138	136	135
Czech Republic	404	426	427	391	359	372	358	352	344	336	357
Denmark	531	499	494	504	473	492	486	474	433	425	445
Germany	6 586	6 457	6 302	6 265	6 364	6 507	6 572	6 633	6 392	6 304	6 285
Estonia	41	46	52	58	58	53	54	53	53	52	50
Ireland	91	86	81	73	87	106	103	99	102	103	:
Greece	1 823	386	374	369	440	441	442	406	456	464	423
Spain	924	1 866	1 896	1 853	2 052	2 183	2 144	2 141	2 231	2 267	2 310
France	3 493	3 566	3 568	3 772	4 062	4 114	3 975	3 825	3 776	3 726	3 589
Italy	2 441	2 426	2 374	2 206	2 164	2 232	2 457	2 418	2 579	2 771	2 933
Cyprus	4	4	4	4	5	5	7	8	7	8	8
Latvia	37	37	44	50	51	49	52	62	51	62	56
Lithuania	76	78	77	82	79	73	79	84	82	75	68
Luxembourg	24	27	27	23	23	26	26	27	25	26	28
Hungary	514	601	506	451	466	421	413	419	437	426	427
Malta	:	15	16	17	16	17	18	18	19	17	15
Netherlands	1 220	1 235	1 303	1 329	1 379	1 402	1 369	1 319	1 255	1 218	1 215
Austria	482	480	493	560	523	592	643	644	605	589	594
Poland	992	1 073	1 122	1 267	1 390	1 404	1 467	1 461	1 380	1 288	1 153
Portugal	322	341	363	363	372	392	417	416	392	399	400
Romania	361	399	364	354	340	312	277	232	208	233	281
Slovenia	37	55	62	68	75	77	77	87	84	90	88
Slovakia	92	94	94	89	93	107	112	131	124	115	111
Finland	374	383	372	386	361	365	367	354	340	325	344
Sweden	1 196	1 181	1 194	1 215	1 189	1 235	1 255	1 249	1 242	1 225	1 306
United Kingdom	5 081	5 650	5 856	5 714	6 086	6 544	6 549	6 194	6 096	5 969	5 445
Croatia	55	56	58	68	78	78	80	85	80	81	76
FYR of Macedonia	:	:	:	20	17	18	23	23	23	22	26
Turkey	357	357	339	340	414	459	499	533	674	987	963
Iceland	:	:	:	19	19	20	18	17	12	13	13
Liechtenstein	1	1	1	1	1	1	1	1	1	1	1
Norway	285	294	292	307	300	320	304	288	276	277	272
Switzerland	383	378	355	317	322	357	379	389	353	335	326
Japan	1 900	2 034	2 166	2 443	2 736	2 854	2 790	2 563	2 269	2 051	:
United States	13 195	12 486	11 634	11 608	11 877	11 879	11 827	11 679	11 565	11 402	11 252

Source: Eurostat (crim_gen)

Industry and services

7

The European Commission's enterprise policy aims to create a favourable environment for enterprises and businesses to thrive within Europe, thus creating the productivity growth, jobs and wealth that are necessary to achieve the objectives set by the revised strategy for growth and jobs that has superseded the Lisbon objectives.

While competitiveness as a macro-economic concept is understood to mean increased standards of living and employment opportunities for those who wish to work, at the level of individual enterprises or industrial sectors, competitiveness is more concerned with the issue of productivity growth. Enterprises have a variety of options to improve their performance, such as tangible investment or spending on human capital, research and development, or other intangible assets. This latter category covers non-monetary assets created over time in the form of legal assets (such as patents or copyrights, which protect intellectual property) and competitive assets (such as collaboration), which can play an important role in determining the effectiveness and productivity of an enterprise. Human capital is generally regarded as the primary source of competitiveness in relation to intangibles, re-enforcing the belief that enterprises need to constantly invest in their workforces, attracting qualified staff, improving their skills, and maintaining their motivation. Innovation is seen as a key element towards the competitiveness of enterprises, and the competitiveness and innovation framework programme (CIP) aims to support innovation including eco-innovation.

The legal basis for the European Commission's activities with respect to enterprise policy is Article 157 of the EC Treaty, which ensures that the conditions necessary for industrial competitiveness exist. It also provides for conditions to encourage entrepreneurial initiatives, par-

ticularly among small and medium-sized enterprises (SMEs). The EU seeks to:

- reduce administrative burden;
- facilitate the rapid start-up of new enterprises, and;
- create an environment more supportive of business.

In October 2007, the European Commission adopted a Communication 'small and medium-sized enterprises – key for delivering more growth and jobs: a mid-term review of modern SME policy' ([1]), which outlines progress since 2005 in SME policy and notes encouraging results in the mainstreaming of SMEs' interests in national and EU policymaking.

The business environment in which European enterprises operate plays a significant role in their potential success through factors such as access to capital markets (in particular for venture capital), or the openness of markets. Ensuring that businesses can compete openly and fairly is also important with respect to making Europe an attractive place in which to invest and work. Creating a positive climate in which entrepreneurs and businesses can flourish is considered by many as the key to generating the growth and jobs that Europe needs. This is all the more important in a globalised economy, where some businesses have considerable leeway to select where they wish to operate.

7.1 Business structures

Introduction

Despite the changing face of the business economy, manufacturing still plays a key role in Europe's prosperity. The European Commission adopted a Communication on 'fostering structural change: an industrial policy for an enlarged Europe' ([2]) which rejected the claim that Europe was experiencing a widespread process of de-industrialisation. However, the combination of a decline in the competitiveness of European industry, and increased international competition, were identified as threats that could impede the process of structural change in Europe. The Communication also examined how structural change could be brought about and fostered through better regulation, synergies between various Community policies, and strengthening the sectoral dimension of industrial policy.

Small and medium-sized enterprises (SMEs) are often referred to as the backbone of the European economy, providing a potential source for jobs and economic growth. The European Commission's strategy for SMEs aims to apply the 'think small first' principle to make the business environment easier for SMEs. Policy is concentrated in five priority areas, covering

([1]) COM(2007) 592.

([2]) COM(2004) 274 final; for more information: http://eur-lex.europa.eu/LexUriServ/site/en/com/2004/com2004_0274en01.pdf.

the promotion of entrepreneurship and skills, the improvement of SMEs' access to markets, cutting red tape, the improvement of SMEs' growth potential, and strengthening dialogue and consultation with SME stakeholders. A special SME envoy has been set-up in the European Commission Directorate-General for Enterprise and Industry with the objective of better integrating the SME dimension into EU policies. Through the European charter for small enterprises, Member States have also committed themselves to develop an SME-friendly business environment, in particular through learning from each other's experience in designing and implementing policies, so each can apply the best practice to their own situations.

Structural business statistics (SBS) describe the structure, conduct and performance of businesses within their economic activities, down to the most detailed activity level (several hundred sectors). SBS with a breakdown by size-class is the main source of data for an analysis of SMEs. SBS can provide answers to questions, such as: how much wealth and how many jobs are created in an activity?; is there a shift from the industrial sector to the services sector and in which specific activities is this shift most notable?; which countries are relatively specialised in the manufacture of aerospace equipment?; what is the average wage of an employee within the hotels and restaurants sector?; how productive is chemicals manufacturing and how does it fare in terms of profitability? Without this structural information, short-term data on the economic cycle would lack background and be hard to interpret.

It should be noted that there have been some important recent changes within this domain. The SBS Regulation (EC) No. 295/2008 of the European Parliament and of the Council of 11 March 2008 concerning structural business statistics (recast) introduces, among other items, a legal basis for data collections in relation to business services (annex VIII) and business demography (annex IX). With this new Regulation, SBS will move to the latest version of the NACE classification of economic activities, namely NACE Rev. 2. This will allow a broader and more detailed collection of information to be compiled on services, while also updating the classification to identify better new areas of activity (such as technology-producing sectors). The first reference year for which SBS data are due to be provided according to NACE Rev. 2 is 2008. The SBS data presented in this publication, therefore, are based on the NACE Rev. 1.1 version of the classification.

Definitions and data availability

SBS cover the '**business economy**' (NACE Rev. 1.1 Sections C to K), which includes industry, construction and services. Note that financial services (Section J) are treated separately because of their specific nature and the limited availability of most types of standard business statistics in this area. As such, the term '**non-financial business economy**' is generally used within business statistics to refer to economic activities covered by Sections C to I and K of NACE Rev. 1.1 and the units that carry out those activities. SBS do not cover agriculture, forestry and fishing, nor public administration and (largely) non-market services such as education and health.

SBS describe the economy through the observation of units engaged in an economic activity, which in SBS is generally the enterprise. An **enterprise** carries out one or more activities at one or more locations and may comprise one or more legal units. Note that enterprises that are active in more than one economic activity (and the value added and turnover they generate and the persons they employ, and so on) will be classified under the NACE heading which is their principal activity, normally the one that generates the largest amount of value added. An abbreviated list of the NACE Rev. 1.1 classification is provided in an annex at the end of the publication. Note that a revised classification (NACE Rev. 2) was adopted at the end of 2006, and its implementation has since begun – however, the first reference year for SBS data using this new classification will be 2008.

SBS are compiled under the legal basis provided by the Council Regulation on Structural Business Statistics (EC, EURATOM) No. 58/97 of December 1996 (and later amendments), and in accordance with the definitions, breakdowns, deadlines for data delivery, and various quality aspects specified in the Commission Regulations implementing it. Note that the breakdown of economic activities is very detailed and that the data included in the SBS domain of Eurostat's dissemination database goes into much more detail than the limited set of information which, given space constraints, can be presented in this yearbook.

The SBS data collection consists of a common module (Annex I), including a set of basic statistics for all activities, as well as six sector-specific annexes covering a more extensive list of characteristics. The sector-specific annexes are: industry (Annex II), distributive trades (Annex III), construction (Annex IV), insurance services (Annex V), credit institutions (Annex VI), and pension funds (Annex VII). There are also three newly introduced annexes: business services (Annex VIII), business demography (Annex IX) and a flexible module for ad-hoc data collections (Annex X).

SBS contain a comprehensive set of basic variables describing business demography and employment characteristics, as well as monetary variables (mainly concerning operating income and expenditure or investment). In addition, a set of derived indicators are compiled: for example, in the form of ratios of monetary characteristics or per head values. The variables presented in this section are defined as follows:

- The **number of enterprises** is a count of the number of enterprises active during at least a part of the reference period; the enterprise is the smallest combination of legal units that is an organisational unit producing goods or services, which benefits from a certain degree of autonomy in decision-making, especially for the allocation of its current resources. An enterprise carries out one or more activities at one or more locations. An enterprise may be a sole legal unit.
- **Value added** represents the difference between the value of what is produced and intermediate consumption entering the production, less subsidies on production and costs, taxes and levies. Value added can be calculated from turnover, plus capitalised production,

plus other operating income, plus or minus the changes in stocks, minus the purchases of goods and services, minus other taxes on products which are linked to turnover but not deductible, minus the duties and taxes linked to production. Alternatively it can be calculated from gross operating surplus by adding personnel costs.

- The **number of persons employed** is defined as the total number of persons who work in the observation unit (inclusive of working proprietors, partners working regularly in the unit and unpaid family workers), as well as persons who work outside the unit who belong to it and are paid by it (for example, sales representatives, delivery personnel, repair and maintenance teams); it excludes manpower supplied to the unit by other enterprises, persons carrying out repair and maintenance work in the enquiry unit on behalf of other enterprises, as well as those on compulsory military service.

- **Average personnel costs** (or unit labour costs) are defined as personnel costs divided by the number of employees (paid persons with an employment contract). Personnel costs are the total remuneration, in cash or in kind, payable by an employer to an employee (regular and temporary employees as well as home workers) in return for work done by the latter during the reference period. All remuneration paid during the reference period is included, regardless of whether it is paid on the basis of working time, output or piecework. Included are all gratuities, workplace and performance bonuses, ex gratia payments, 13th month pay (and similar fixed bonuses), payments

made to employees in consideration of dismissal, lodging, transport, cost of living and family allowances, commissions, attendance fees, overtime, night work, etc., as well as taxes, social security contributions and other amounts owed by employees and retained at source by employers. Also included are the social security costs for the employer. Payments for agency workers are not included in personnel costs.

- **Apparent labour productivity** equals value added divided by the number of persons employed.

SBS are also available broken down by region or by **enterprise size class**. In SBS, size classes are defined based on the number of persons employed, except for specific series within retail trade activities where turnover size classes can also be used. A limited set of the standard SBS variables (for example, the number of enterprises, turnover, persons employed, value added) is available mostly down to the 3-digit (group) level of NACE divided by size class. According to Commission Recommendation 2003/361/EC adopted on 6 May 2003, small and medium-sized enterprises are classified with regard to their number of employees, annual turnover, and their independence. For statistical purposes, small and medium-sized enterprises are generally defined as those enterprises employing fewer than 250 people. The number of size classes available varies according to the activity under consideration. However, the main groups used in this publication for presenting the results are:

- small and medium-sized enterprises (SMEs): with 1-249 persons employed, further divided into
- micro enterprises: with less than 10 persons employed;
- small enterprises: with 10 to 49 persons employed;
- medium-sized enterprises: with 50 to 249 persons employed;
- large enterprises: with 250 or more persons employed.

Structural business statistics also provide information on a number of special topics, of which **business demography** is one. Business demography statistics present data on the active population of enterprises, their birth, survival (followed up to five years after birth) and death. Special attention is paid to the impact of these demographic events on employment levels. Business demography variables presented in this section are defined as follows.

- An **enterprise birth** amounts to the creation of a combination of production factors with the restriction that no other enterprises are involved in the event. Births do not include entries into the population due to mergers, break-ups, split-off or restructuring of a set of enterprises, nor do the statistics include entries into a sub-population resulting only from a change of activity. A birth occurs when an enterprise starts from scratch and actually starts activity. The birth rate is the number of births relative to the stock of active enterprises.
- An **enterprise death** amounts to the dissolution of a combination of production factors with the restriction that no other enterprises are involved

in the event. An enterprise is included in the count of deaths only if it is not reactivated within two years. Equally, a reactivation within two years is not counted as a birth.

- **Survival** occurs if an enterprise is active in terms of employment and/or turnover in the year of birth and the following year(s). Two types of survival can be distinguished: an enterprise born in year x is considered to have survived in year x+1 if it is active in terms of turnover and/or employment in any part of year x+1 (survival without change); an enterprise is also considered to have survived if the linked legal unit(s) have ceased to be active, but their activity has been taken over by a new legal unit set-up specifically to take-over the factors of production of that enterprise (survival by take-over). The information presented in this publication focuses on the two-year survival rate.

Main findings

There were an estimated 20.2 million enterprises within the EU-27 non-financial business economy (defined as industry, construction, distributive trades and services, and therefore excluding financial services) in 2006. A little over three in every ten of these enterprises was active in the distributive trades sector (composed of motor trades, wholesale trade, and retail trade and repair) and generated EUR 1 099 thousand million of value added in 2006, whilst providing employment for about 31.7 million persons. Manufacturing enterprises, which represented a little over one in every ten (11.5 %) enterprises within the EU-27 non-financial business economy, generated a further EUR 1 712 thousand million of value added and provided employment for 34.4 million persons. It should be noted, though, that the employment data presented here are head counts and not, for example, full-time equivalents, and there may be a significant proportion of persons working part-time in some activities, notably distributive trades.

High rates of part-time work in many service sectors also help explain the considerable differences in average personnel costs within the non-financial business economy of the EU-27. Average personnel costs in the EU-27 electricity, gas and water supply sector were EUR 42 200 per employee in 2006, a level that was 2.7 times that for hotels and restaurants and 1.7 times that for the distributive trades. The variation in wages and salaries was even more marked between Member States. For example, average personnel costs across the manufacturing sectors (of available Member States) ranged by a factor of ten, from a high of EUR 53 000 per employee in Belgium (2007) to a low of EUR 5 300 per employee in Latvia (2006).

SBS broken down by enterprise size class (defined in terms of the number of persons employed) show that less than one enterprise in 400 within the EU-27 non-financial business economy employed 250 or more persons (and was therefore considered as large) in 2006, but these enterprises accounted for approximately one third (32.6 %) of employ-ment and more than two fifths (43.1 %) of value added. Nevertheless, small and medium-sized enterprises (SMEs, with less than 250 persons employed) generated the majority of value added (56.9 %) and employed most (67.4 %) of the workforce in the non-financial business economy. Micro enterprises (those with less than 10 persons employed) played a particularly important role, providing employment to nearly as many persons as large enterprises.

Large enterprises were particularly dominant within mining and quarrying; electricity, gas and water supply; and transport, storage and communication. These activities are characterised by relatively high minimum efficient scales of production and/or by (transmission) networks that are rarely duplicated due to their high fixed investment cost. On the other hand, small and medium-sized enterprises (SMEs) were relatively important within the activities of construction and hotels and restaurants, where enterprises with less than 250 persons employed accounted for more than three quarters of the wealth created (value added).

There are significant changes in the stock of enterprises within the business economy from one year to the next, reflecting the level of competition and entrepreneurial spirit. Newly-born enterprises accounted for at least one out of every 10 active enterprises in Estonia, Romania, Portugal, the United Kingdom, Luxembourg, Bulgaria, Spain and Germany in 2006.

Figure 7.1: Breakdown of number of enterprises within the non-financial business economy, EU-27, 2006 (¹)
(%)

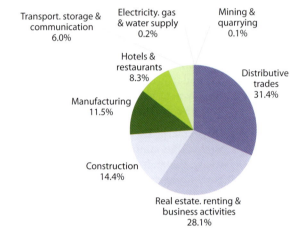

(¹) The total number of enterprises in the EU-27 non-financial business economy was estimated as 20.2 million in 2006.

Source: Eurostat (tin00050)

Table 7.1: Value added, 2006
(EUR 1 000 million)

	Mining & quarrying	Manu-facturing	Elec., gas & water supply	Construc-tion	Distrib. trades	Hotels & restaur.	Trans., storage & communi-cation	Real estate, renting & business activities
EU-27	88.55	1 711.79	203.66	510.02	1 099.04	181.91	652.93	1 202.14
Belgium (¹)	0.32	51.67	6.17	12.31	35.63	3.79	20.00	33.85
Bulgaria	0.64	3.58	1.09	1.06	:	0.33	1.89	0.95
Czech Republic	1.47	26.49	4.88	5.29	11.42	1.26	7.57	9.23
Denmark (¹)	7.16	29.23	2.54	11.08	24.09	2.54	15.35	30.55
Germany	6.47	459.39	44.23	55.44	202.96	23.23	118.70	242.11
Estonia (¹)	0.12	2.28	0.37	1.12	1.99	0.19	1.08	1.40
Ireland	1.17	35.50	2.07	9.22	16.38	3.41	7.13	16.03
Greece	0.95	15.83	2.68	6.38	22.27	3.46	9.21	8.78
Spain	2.50	132.37	15.13	94.26	106.23	25.17	58.68	102.46
France	4.61	215.48	25.78	69.55	151.49	28.53	97.27	202.55
Italy	7.32	218.77	19.79	63.26	116.04	21.99	76.09	108.07
Cyprus	0.04	1.14	0.28	1.21	1.73	0.92	1.03	1.20
Latvia	0.04	1.78	0.35	0.98	2.46	0.23	1.49	1.40
Lithuania	0.10	2.62	0.64	1.27	2.38	0.16	1.53	1.32
Luxembourg	0.03	2.76	0.27	1.62	2.60	0.49	2.57	4.08
Hungary	0.16	17.17	2.03	2.36	7.52	0.70	5.61	6.46
Malta	:	:	:	:	:	:	:	:
Netherlands	6.51	60.13	5.89	23.92	58.53	6.61	33.01	10.03
Austria (¹)	0.87	48.32	5.69	13.64	28.35	6.66	16.02	27.92
Poland	6.47	45.44	8.99	9.32	27.62	1.52	15.46	15.91
Portugal (¹)	0.69	19.78	3.84	9.46	17.00	3.36	10.12	12.54
Romania (¹)	3.02	13.81	2.61	5.26	9.67	0.75	5.94	5.30
Slovenia	0.12	6.43	0.64	1.42	3.06	0.46	1.71	1.92
Slovakia	0.19	6.94	2.67	0.99	3.19	0.17	1.91	1.99
Finland	0.42	33.23	3.32	7.01	13.47	1.81	9.42	13.81
Sweden (¹)	1.76	57.22	6.86	14.85	31.99	3.95	18.02	44.85
United Kingdom	34.98	217.89	35.65	97.62	212.38	41.71	121.86	310.46
Norway	43.65	22.60	5.43	9.98	19.72	2.45	17.88	23.39

(¹) 2007.

Source: Eurostat (tin00002)

Table 7.2: Number of persons employed, 2006
(1 000)

	Mining & quarrying	Manufac-turing	Elec., gas & water supply	Construc-tion	Distrib. trades	Hotels & restaur.	Trans., storage & communi-cation	Real estate, renting & business activities
EU-27	733	34 413	1 598	14 093	31 676	9 266	11 885	26 109
Belgium (¹)	3	611	25	272	640	172	247	570
Bulgaria	30	664	57	185	:	115	191	173
Czech Republic	44	1 354	57	393	694	158	337	501
Denmark (¹)	3	421	16	207	470	109	188	406
Germany	88	7 109	276	1 499	4 784	1 316	1 966	4 463
Estonia (¹)	5	132	8	59	101	21	47	71
Ireland	6	220	9	72	318	149	92	223
Greece	13	400	24	310	966	304	236	336
Spain	39	2 590	70	2 798	3 358	1 259	1 053	2 741
France	33	3 658	195	1 652	3 320	915	1 548	3 343
Italy	42	4 577	115	1 845	3 443	1 115	1 237	2 802
Cyprus	1	36	2	34	64	39	24	21
Latvia	3	164	15	73	181	31	83	93
Lithuania	3	268	25	125	269	39	102	101
Luxembourg	0	37	1	36	43	15	24	53
Hungary	6	778	54	240	583	127	265	483
Malta	:	:	:	:	:	:	:	:
Netherlands	7	779	24	481	1 383	345	475	1 599
Austria (¹)	6	638	31	262	625	248	243	436
Poland	185	2 591	204	700	2 240	231	761	969
Portugal (¹)	13	818	24	515	871	287	195	638
Romania (¹)	93	1 508	127	513	1 032	134	399	484
Slovenia	4	236	12	72	113	32	56	73
Slovakia	9	412	39	72	191	22	104	113
Finland	4	407	16	136	266	55	161	224
Sweden (¹)	9	806	31	298	633	139	315	640
United Kingdom	66	3 141	137	1 393	4 755	1 927	1 561	4 759
Norway	34	262	15	158	355	84	167	255

(¹) 2007.

Source: Eurostat (tin00004)

Table 7.3: Average personnel costs, 2006
(EUR 1 000 per employee)

	Mining & quarrying	Manufac- turing	Elec., gas & water supply	Construc- tion	Distrib. trades	Hotels & restaur.	Trans., storage & communi- cation	Real estate, renting & business activities
EU-27	31.3	33.3	42.2	27.9	24.2	15.6	33.0	29.7
Belgium ([1])	48.8	53.0	94.5	38.7	40.2	17.7	48.4	46.0
Bulgaria	:	:	:	2.4	:	1.6	3.9	3.1
Czech Republic	14.8	11.1	16.1	11.0	10.9	6.7	12.6	13.4
Denmark ([1])	66.1	48.2	49.9	43.0	35.8	17.4	47.2	42.1
Germany	49.4	47.2	69.5	32.6	27.2	12.6	32.8	30.5
Estonia ([1])	13.1	10.6	13.3	12.3	10.8	6.8	12.0	11.4
Ireland	52.8	43.8	92.9	49.3	29.0	18.0	46.1	41.3
Greece	42.0	26.2	49.2	17.4	18.7	14.3	31.9	22.7
Spain	33.9	31.1	52.3	26.8	23.2	17.6	31.9	23.8
France	50.6	44.2	62.1	37.7	35.2	26.9	43.2	44.3
Italy	48.1	34.4	49.9	27.7	29.1	19.5	37.6	28.0
Cyprus	29.9	20.0	41.9	24.1	20.1	17.8	26.1	23.6
Latvia	6.2	5.3	8.7	5.2	4.6	3.3	6.5	5.9
Lithuania	8.6	6.0	9.4	6.9	5.4	3.3	6.6	6.5
Luxembourg	42.5	50.3	77.8	35.2	38.4	24.6	52.6	46.3
Hungary	12.8	10.4	16.9	7.1	8.5	5.3	12.3	10.4
Malta	:	:	:	:	:	:	:	:
Netherlands	73.7	46.4	59.8	46.2	26.9	12.9	39.0	2.7
Austria ([1])	54.9	45.6	71.7	38.5	32.5	21.6	42.3	39.4
Poland	18.1	8.9	14.3	8.1	7.1	5.1	9.9	9.8
Portugal ([1])	17.9	14.8	38.3	12.6	12.8	9.1	24.4	12.3
Romania ([1])	16.5	6.4	12.5	4.9	4.3	3.4	7.1	5.5
Slovenia	26.8	17.8	25.5	15.2	17.7	12.8	20.6	20.0
Slovakia	8.5	8.6	12.1	7.8	7.9	5.2	9.4	9.6
Finland	40.5	45.5	50.5	38.3	34.1	27.1	39.9	40.4
Sweden ([1])	57.8	51.6	64.9	45.1	41.3	25.9	44.8	49.8
United Kingdom	76.1	41.9	52.4	39.0	26.1	13.5	43.9	38.5
Norway	129.9	58.6	66.5	52.8	39.1	25.1	51.6	56.6

([1]) 2007.

Source: Eurostat (tin00049)

Figure 7.2: Value added breakdown by enterprise size-class, EU-27, 2006 (¹)
(% of sectoral total)

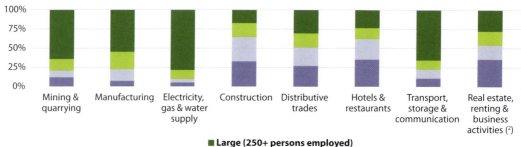

(¹) Estimates.
(²) 2005.

Source: Eurostat (tin00053)

Figure 7.3: Employment breakdown by enterprise size-class, EU-27, 2006 (¹)
(% of sectoral total)

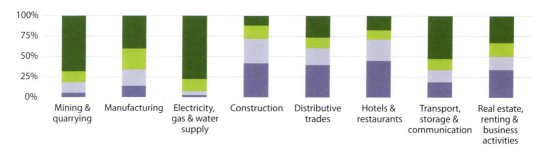

(¹) Estimates.

Source: Eurostat (tin00052)

Table 7.4: Value added by enterprise size-class, non-financial business economy, 2006

	Value added (EUR 1 000 million)	Share in total value added (%)			
		Micro (1-9 persons employed)	Small (10-49 persons employed)	Medium-sized (50-249 persons employed)	Large (250 + persons employed)
EU-27 (¹)	*5 650.2*	*20.2*	*18.8*	*17.8*	*43.1*
Belgium (²)	163.7	19.4	:	:	:
Bulgaria	:	:	:	:	:
Czech Republic	67.6	18.8	16.0	19.9	45.3
Denmark (²)	122.6	25.9	:	19.0	:
Germany	1 152.5	15.5	:	:	:
Estonia (²)	8.5	20.2	26.5	:	:
Ireland	90.9	:	:	:	:
Greece	69.6	35.1	:	17.1	:
Spain	536.8	26.5	24.1	17.3	32.1
France	795.3	21.0	18.7	15.6	44.8
Italy	631.3	32.7	23.0	16.1	28.3
Cyprus	7.6	31.3	:	:	:
Latvia	8.7	18.5	:	28.4	:
Lithuania	10.0	11.6	:	29.2	:
Luxembourg	14.4	24.3	:	:	:
Hungary	42.0	17.5	:	18.2	:
Malta	:	:	:	:	:
Netherlands	259.9	:	:	:	:
Austria (²)	147.5	18.8	19.7	:	:
Poland	130.7	18.3	11.8	21.6	48.3
Portugal (²)	76.8	:	22.8	21.4	:
Romania	35.1	13.9	15.8	19.8	50.4
Slovenia	15.8	19.9	:	:	:
Slovakia	18.0	:	:	:	:
Finland	82.4	:	:	:	:
Sweden (²)	179.6	20.3	18.2	18.1	43.5
United Kingdom	1 072.6	18.5	15.5	16.6	49.3
Norway	145.1	29.8	15.7	18.9	35.5

(¹) 2005 for the breakdown by size class.
(²) 2007.

Source: Eurostat (sbs_sc_1b_se02, sbs_sc_3ce_tr02, sbs_sc_4d_co02, sbs_sc_2d_mi02, sbs_sc_2d_dade02 and sbs_sc_2d_el02)

Table 7.5: Number of persons employed by enterprise size-class, non-financial business economy, 2006

	Number of persons employed (1 000)	Share in total employment (%)			
		Micro (1-9 persons employed)	Small (10-49 persons employed)	Medium-sized (50-249 persons employed)	Large (250 + persons employed)
EU-27	129 773	29.6	20.7	17.0	32.6
Belgium (¹)	2 541	29.1	:	:	:
Bulgaria	:	:	:	:	:
Czech Republic	3 539	29.0	18.7	19.8	32.5
Denmark (¹)	1 822	19.6	:	21.2	:
Germany	21 501	19.3	21.8	19.3	39.5
Estonia (¹)	444	24.1	27.6	:	:
Ireland	1 089	:	:	:	:
Greece	2 589	58.0	:	11.8	:
Spain	13 908	37.7	25.5	14.8	22.0
France	14 663	24.7	20.8	16.2	38.3
Italy	15 177	46.9	21.6	12.5	19.0
Cyprus	220	39.0	:	:	:
Latvia	643	21.7	28.0	26.1	24.1
Lithuania	932	22.8	:	26.5	:
Luxembourg	210	19.1	:	:	:
Hungary	2 536	35.4	:	16.4	:
Malta	:	:	:	:	:
Netherlands	5 094	29.0	:	16.7	:
Austria (¹)	2 489	24.9	23.2	:	:
Poland	7 882	38.6	11.6	18.7	31.1
Portugal (¹)	3 362	:	:	16.5	:
Romania	4 114	21.2	19.8	22.6	36.4
Slovenia	597	:	:	:	:
Slovakia	961	:	:	:	:
Finland	1 268	:	:	:	:
Sweden (¹)	2 874	24.2	21.0	18.3	36.3
United Kingdom	17 737	21.5	17.9	15.4	45.2
Norway	1 329	26.5	25.0	18.3	30.3

(¹) 2007.

Source: Eurostat (sbs_sc_1b_se02, sbs_sc_3ce_tr02, sbs_sc_4d_co02, sbs_sc_2d_mi02, sbs_sc_2d_dade02 and sbs_sc_2d_el02)

Table 7.6: Enterprise demography, business economy, 2006 ([1])

	Enterprise birth rates (% of enterprise births among active enterprises) ([2])	Enterprise death rates (% of enterprise deaths among active enterprises) ([3])	Enterprise survival (% of enterprise births of year n-2 which are still active in year n) ([4])
Belgium	:	:	:
Bulgaria	11.9	*11.2*	47.3
Czech Republic	9.3	11.3	64.1
Denmark	:	10.3	:
Germany	10.0	:	:
Estonia	15.9	10.3	64.6
Ireland	:	:	:
Greece	:	:	:
Spain	10.4	6.9	75.2
France	9.4	6.8	76.6
Italy	7.1	7.5	74.7
Cyprus	7.1	:	:
Latvia	9.9	7.9	73.0
Lithuania	:	:	:
Luxembourg	12.3	*8.3*	76.7
Hungary	8.7	12.0	63.1
Malta	:	:	:
Netherlands	9.8	8.6	73.1
Austria	8.4	6.1	:
Poland	:	:	:
Portugal	14.2	*14.8*	59.5
Romania	*14.6*	*8.9*	77.6
Slovenia	9.7	5.4	84.2
Slovakia	7.3	5.2	72.8
Finland	8.3	6.8	66.7
Sweden	6.7	5.6	87.3
United Kingdom	12.9	10.7	79.2
Norway	9.8	:	:
Switzerland	3.6	3.5	70.7

([1]) Covers the business economy (NACE Rev. 1.1 Sections C to K) excluding holdings (NACE Rev. 1.1 Class 74.15); Portugal and Romania, sole proprietorships are not covered.
([2]) Cyprus, the Netherlands, Slovakia and Finland, 2005; Germany and Switzerland, 2004.
([3]) 2005, except the Netherlands, Slovakia, Finland and Switzerland, 2004.
([4]) 2006, except the Netherlands, Slovakia, Finland and Switzerland, 2005.

Source: Eurostat (tsier150)

7.2 Industry and construction

Introduction

In its mid-term review of industrial policy (³), the European Commission identified globalisation and technological change as key challenges for European industry. Industrial policy within the EU is designed to complement measures taken by the Member States. Whether or not a business succeeds depends ultimately on the vitality and strength of the business itself, but the environment in which it operates can help or harm its prospects, in particular when faced with the challenges of globalisation and intense international competition.

A 2005 European Commission Communication on industrial policy was based for the first time on an integrated approach; addressing sector-specific as well as common issues. Since this date, the overall performance of European industry continued to develop against a background of an increasingly integrated world and the accelerating pace of technological change. The European Commission's new industrial policy includes seven new initiatives on competitiveness, energy and the environment, intellectual property rights, better regulation, industrial research and innovation, market access, skills, and managing structural change. Seven additional initiatives are targeted at key strategic sectors, including pharmaceuticals, defence-related industries, and information and communication technologies.

Definitions and data availability

For background information relating to structural business statistics (SBS), including definitions of value added and persons employed, refer to the section titled 'definitions and data availability' in the previous section (Subchapter 7.1: business structures). It is important to reiterate that in this publication, SBS data continue to be based on the NACE Rev. 1.1 classification of economic activities. Additional variables presented in this section are defined as follows.

- The **wage adjusted labour productivity ratio** is defined as the ratio of value added at factor cost divided by personnel costs (the latter having been divided by the share of employees in the number of persons employed); the result is expressed as a percentage. The ratio can also be calculated by dividing the apparent labour productivity by average personnel costs and expressing the result as a percentage.

- The **gross operating rate** is one measure of profitability that is a key factor for competitiveness and enterprise success. It is defined as the size of the gross operating surplus relative to turnover, and is expressed as a percentage. The **gross operating surplus** is the surplus generated by operating activities after the labour factor input has been recompensed (it can be calculated from value added at factor cost

(³) COM(2007) 374; for more information:
http://ec.europa.eu/enterprise/policies/industrial-competitiveness/documents/comm-policy-framework/index_en.htm.

less personnel costs); turnover is often referred to as sales; capital-intensive activities tend to report higher gross operating rates, while distributive activities often report lower rates.

PRODCOM (PRODuction COMmunautaire) is a system for the collection and dissemination of statistics on the production of industrial (mainly manufactured) goods, both in value and quantity terms. It is based on a list of products called the Prodcom List which consists of about 4 500 headings relating to industrial products. These products are detailed at an 8-digit level, with the first four digits referring to the equivalent NACE class, and the next two digits referring to subcategories within the statistical classification of products by activity (CPA). Most headings correspond to one or more combined nomenclature (CN) codes.

Aside from SBS and PRODCOM, a large proportion of the statistics presented in this section are derived from **short-term business statistics (STS)**. Among these, some of the most important indicators are a set of principal European economic indicators (PEEIs) that are essential to the European Central Bank (ECB) for reviewing monetary policy within the euro area. These short-term statistics give information on a wide range of economic activities and are now based on the NACE Rev. 2 classification (unlike the SBS statistics, which until data for 2008 are available remain based on NACE Rev 1.1); they are generally based on surveys and administrative sources. The Member States are encouraged to transmit seasonally adjusted data and trend-cycle indices: if they do not, then Eurostat calculates the seasonal adjustment. The national statis-

tical authorities are responsible for data collection and the calculation of national time series, while Eurostat is responsible for euro area and EU aggregations.

The presentation of short-term statistics may take a variety of different forms.

- The adjustment of **working days** takes account of the calendar nature of a given month in order to adjust the index. The adjustment of working days is intended to adjust calendar effects, whatever their nature. The number of working days for a given month depends on the timing of certain public holidays (Easter can fall in March or in April depending on the year), the possible overlap of certain public holidays and non-working days (1 May can fall on a Sunday), the fact that a year is a leap year or not and other reasons.

- **Seasonal adjustment**, or the adjustment of seasonal variations, aims, after adjusting for calendar effects, to take account of the impact of the known seasonal factors that have been observed in the past. For example, in the case of the production index, annual summer holidays have a negative impact on industrial production. Where necessary, Eurostat calculates the seasonal adjustment using the methods TRAMO (time-series regression with ARIMA noise, missing observations, and outliers) and SEATS (signal extraction in ARIMA time-series), referred to as TRAMO/SEATS.

- The trend is a slow variation over a long period of years, generally associated with the structural causes of the phenomenon in question. The cycle is a quasi-periodic oscillation. It is characterised by alternating periods of higher and lower rates of change possibly, but not always, involving expansion and contraction. Generally, if this irregular component of the time-series is relatively important, the trend-cycle series is a better series for the analysis of longer-term past developments. However, this advantage is less clear when analysing very recent developments. This is because trend-cycle values for recent periods may have greater revisions than the equivalent seasonally adjusted values. Hence, the latter may be more appropriate for the analysis of recent developments; this is particularly true around turning points.

Short-term business statistics are compiled within the scope of the STS Regulation ([4]). Despite major changes brought in by the STS Regulation, and improvements in the availability and timeliness of indicators that followed its implementation, strong demands for further development were voiced even as the STS Regulation was being adopted. The emergence of the ECB fundamentally changed expectations as regards STS. As a result, the STS Regulation was amended (Regulation (EC) No 1158/2005) on 6 July 2005. Among the main changes introduced were:

- new indicators for the purpose of analysis, namely the introduction of industrial import prices, services output prices, and the division of non-domestic turnover, new orders and industrial output prices between euro area and non-euro area markets;

- more timely data, by shortening data delivery deadlines for the industrial and construction production indices, the retail trade and services turnover (and volume of sales) indices, and employment indices for all activities;

- more frequent data, increasing the frequency of the index of production for construction to monthly from quarterly.

The **production index** aims to provide a measure of the volume trend in value added at factor cost over a given reference period. The index of production should take account of:

- variations in type and quality of the commodities and of the input materials;
- changes in stocks of finished goods and services and work in progress;
- changes in technical input-output relations (processing techniques);
- services such as the assembling of production units, mounting, installations, repairs, planning, engineering, creation of software.

The data necessary for the compilation of such an index are generally not available on a sub-annual basis. In practice, suitable proxy values for the compilation of the indices are needed. Within industry these may include gross production values (deflated), production quantity data, turnover (deflated), work input, raw material input, or energy input, while within construction they may include input data (consumption of typical raw materials, energy or labour) or output data (production quantities, deflated production values, or deflated sales values).

([4]) Council Regulation (EC) No 1165/98 of 19 May 1998 concerning short-term statistics.

The **building production index** and the **civil engineering production index** is a split of construction production between buildings and civil engineering works according to the classification of types of construction (CC); the aim of the indices is to show the development of value added for each of the two main parts of construction. These indices may be calculated by assigning the basic information (deflated output, hours worked, authorisations/permits) to products in the CC and then aggregating the product indices in accordance with the CC to the section level. Buildings are sub-divided into residential buildings (in methodological terms, those buildings of which at least half are used for residential purposes) and non-residential buildings. Civil engineering works are all constructions not classified under buildings: for example, railways, roads, bridges, highways, airport runways, dams.

It is particularly difficult to compile a production index for construction, given that it is problematic to measure output in physical quantities, as almost every project is unique in terms of the building being constructed and the site being used; equally, it is difficult to obtain reliable output prices to use as a deflator in the event that output is measured in value terms. As a result, a wide variety of approaches are used in different countries to provide these statistics, including the use of hours worked as a proxy.

The **output price index** (sometimes referred to as the **producer price index**) shows monthly price changes in industrial output, which can be an indicator of inflationary pressure before it reaches the consumer. The appropriate price is the basic price that excludes VAT and similar deductible taxes directly linked to turnover, as well as all duties and taxes on the goods and services invoiced by the unit, whereas subsidies on products received by the producer, if there are any, should be added. The price should refer to the moment when the order is made, not the moment when the commodities leave the factory gates. Output price indices are compiled for the total, domestic and non-domestic markets, with the latter further split between euro area and non-euro area markets (the information presented in this publication refers only to price developments within the domestic market). All price-determining characteristics should be taken into account, including the quantity of units sold, transport provided, rebates, service conditions, guarantee conditions and destination.

The **index of turnover** shows the evolution of the market for goods and services in terms of sales made. The index is not deflated, and so its objective is to measure market activity in value terms. Turnover comprises the totals invoiced by the observation unit during the reference period, and this equates to market sales of goods or services supplied to third parties. Turnover also includes all other charges (transport, packaging, etc.) passed on to the customer, even if these charges are listed separately in the invoice. Turnover excludes VAT and other similar deductible taxes directly linked to turnover as well as all duties and taxes on the goods or services invoiced by the unit. Reduction in prices, rebates and discounts as well as the value of returned packing must be deducted.

Main findings

The EU-27 construction sector generated about one fifth (20.3 %) of the combined industrial and construction sectors' value added in 2006, more than two and a half times the contribution (7.7 %) of the machinery and equipment n.e.c. sector, which was the largest manufacturing sector (at the NACE division level) in these terms. The construction sector's share of employment was even higher, more than one quarter (27.7 %) of the total. A few sectors recorded a notably lower share of employment than of value added, and these were concentrated in energy-related activities and chemicals manufacturing.

The average value added generated per person within each of the EU-27 industrial sectors as well as construction more than covered respective average personnel costs in 2006. However, there were considerable differences between the various sectors; the wage adjusted labour productivity ratio was high for many of the energy-related activities, particularly for the extraction of crude petroleum and natural gas sector (900 % in 2005) and the coke, refined petroleum products and nuclear fuel sector (357 % in 2005), but less than 150 % for the clear majority of industrial sectors as well as the construction sector.

Based on PRODCOM data, transport equipment products dominated the list of the most sold manufacturing products in value terms in the EU-27 in 2008, occupying the first two places, with a number of further products among the top 20.

The indices of industrial production and industrial output prices (based on the NACE Rev. 2 classification) for the EU-27 followed broadly similar developments during the ten-year period through until July 2009; growth through until the start of 2001 then a period of stability until mid-2003, followed by a period of sustained and relatively strong growth until an abrupt downturn during the first half of 2008. The decline in the index of industrial production for the EU-27 from the relative peak in February 2008 was particularly steep, the index level of July 2009 being lower than that of July 1999. By contrast, although the index of industrial output prices for July 2009 fell from the relative peak of July 2008, it was similar to the pre-peak level of October 2007. In part this continued to reflect the relatively high price of oil and associated energy-related and intermediate products. In this respect, it should be noted that the domestic industrial output price index was about 5 % or more higher in 2008 than in 2007 in all Member States, and between 10 % and 18 % higher in 11 of them, the highest rates of increase being in Malta and the United Kingdom.

The downturn in activity was also noted for construction. The index of production for construction declined by about 14 % between the relative peak in February 2008 and the figure for June 2009. However, there was a distinct difference between the indices for buildings and civil engineering works in this same period; the index for buildings declined by 16.1 %, whereas that for civil engineering works remained relatively unchanged (-0.7 %).

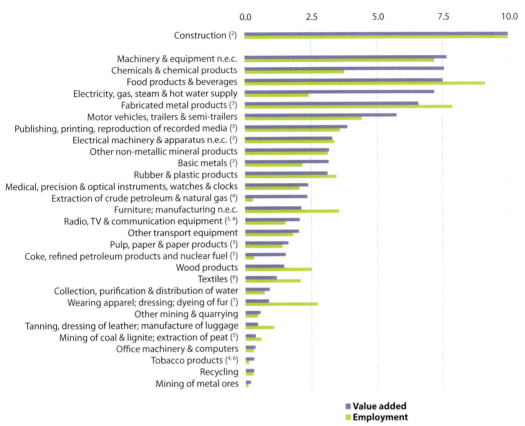

Figure 7.4: Breakdown of industrial and construction value added and employment, EU-27, 2006 ([1])
(% of industrial and construction value added and employment)

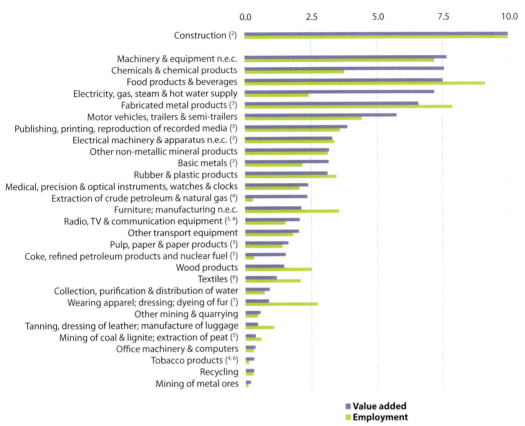

([1]) Mining of uranium and thorium ores, not available
([2]) Note that the axis is cut: value added, 20.3 %, employment, 27.7 %.
([3]) Estimates.
([4]) Employment, 2005.
([5]) Value added, 2005.
([6]) Employment, estimate.
([7]) Value added, estimate.

Source: Eurostat (ebd_all)

Figure 7.5: Wage adjusted labour productivity within industry and construction, EU-27, 2006 ([1]) (%)

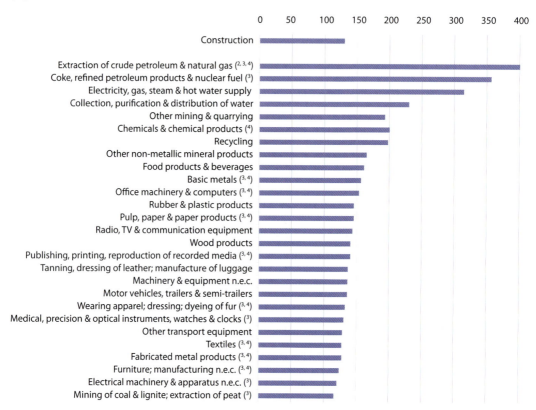

([1]) Mining of uranium and thorium ores, mining of metal ores and tobacco products, not available.
([2]) Y-axis has been cut at 400 % from 900 %.
([3]) 2005.
([4]) Estimate.

Source: Eurostat (ebd_all)

Figure 7.6: Gross operating rate within industry and construction, EU-27, 2006 ([1])
(%)

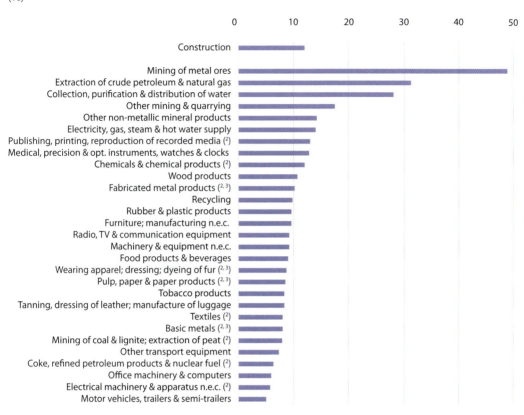

([1]) Mining of uranium and thorium ores, not available.
([2]) 2005.
([3]) Estimate.

Source: Eurostat (ebd_all)

Figure 7.7: Industrial and construction value added by enterprise size-class, EU-27, 2006 (¹)
(% of sectoral total)

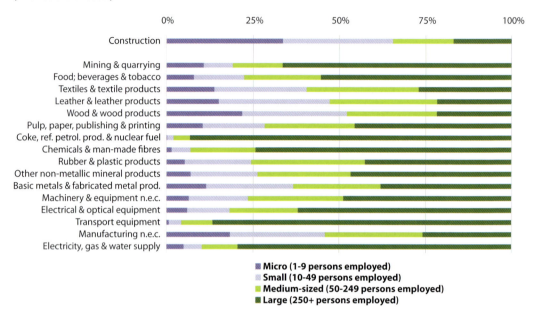

(¹) Includes rounded estimates based on non-confidential data.

Source: Eurostat (tin00053)

Table 7.7: Production sold in value terms, selected products, EU-27, 2008 (¹)

PRODCOM code	Product	Value (EUR million)	Rounding base (million) (²)
29.10.22.30	Motor vehicles with a petrol engine > 1 500 cm³ (including motor caravans of a capacity > 3 000 cm³) (excluding vehicles for transporting >= 10 persons, snowmobiles, golf cars and similar vehicles)	111 332	
29.10.23.30	Motor vehicles with a diesel or semi-diesel engine > 1 500 cm³ but <= 2 500 cm³ (excluding vehicles for transporting >= 10 persons, motor caravans, snowmobiles, golf cars and similar vehicles)	90 339	
21.20.13.80	Other medicaments of mixed or unmixed products, p.r.s., n.e.c.	61 449	
17.29.11.20	Self-adhesive printed labels of paper or paperboard	52 434	
29.32.30.90	Other parts and accessories, n.e.c., for vehicles of HS 87.01 to 87.05; parts thereof	49 400	200
25.11.23.60	Other structures of iron or steel	36 081	9
29.32.20.90	Parts and accessories of bodies (including cabs), n.e.c.	33 911	
29.10.21.00	Vehicles with spark-ignition engine of a cylinder capacity <= 1 500 cm³, new	31 969	
25.62.20.00	Metal parts (excluding turned metal parts)	31 900	50
11.05.10.00	Beer made from malt (excluding non-alcoholic beer, beer containing <= 0.5 % by volume of alcohol, alcohol duty)	30 942	
10.71.11.00	Fresh bread containing by weight in the dry matter state <= 5 % of sugars and <= 5 % of fat (excluding with added honey; eggs; cheese or fruit)	27 954	
17.21.13.00	Cartons, boxes and cases, of corrugated paper or paperboard	27 492	
23.63.10.00	Ready-mixed concrete	27 246	
10.51.40.50	Grated, powdered, blue-veined and other non-processed cheese (excluding fresh cheese, whey cheese and curd)	26 000	400
29.10.41.10	Goods vehicles with a diesel or semi-diesel engine, of a gross vehicle weight <= 5 tonnes (excluding dumpers for off-highway use)	24 223	

(¹) Data extracted on 17 December 2009.
(²) Indicates the magnitude of the rounding employed to protect confidential cell (in the case of PRODCOM code 25.11.23.60, the confidential value lies within the range +/- EUR 9 million of the reported value).

Source: Eurostat, from http://epp.eurostat.ec.europa.eu/portal/page/portal/statistics/search_database go to
Data Navigation Tree/Database by themes/Industry, trade and services/
Statistics on the production of manufactured goods (prom)/NACE Rev. 2 (prodcom_n2)/Prodcom Annual Sold (NACE Rev. 2.)
(DS056120)

Table 7.8: Production sold in volume terms, selected products, EU-27, 2008 (¹)

PRODCOM code	Product	Quantity (1 000)	Rounding base (1 000) (²)	Unit
24.10.22.10	Flat semi-finished products (slabs) (of stainless steel)	180 204		kg
23.51.12.10	Portland cement	220 699 380		kg
11.02.11.30	Champagne (important: excluding alcohol duty)	260 788		l
20.42.11.50	Perfumes	13 000	500	l
20.11.11.70	Oxygen	29 561 233		m³
16.10.10.34	Coniferous wood; sawn or chipped lengthwise, sliced or peeled, of a thickness > 6 mm, planed (excluding end-jointed or sanded)	14 980	70	m³
12.00.11.50	Cigarettes containing tobacco or mixtures of tobacco and tobacco substitutes (excluding tobacco duty)	758 642 288		p/st
27.90.52.20	Fixed electrical capacitors, tantalum or aluminium electrolytic (excluding power capacitors)	12 761 920		p/st

(¹) Data extracted on 17 December 2009.
(²) Indicates the magnitude of the rounding employed to protect confidential cell (in the case of PRODCOM code 16.10.10.34, the confidential value lies within the range +/- 70 000 m³ of the reported value).

Source: Eurostat, from http://epp.eurostat.ec.europa.eu/portal/page/portal/statistics/search_database go to
Data Navigation Tree/Database by themes/Industry, trade and services/
Statistics on the production of manufactured goods (prom)/NACE Rev. 2 (prodcom_n2)/Prodcom Annual Sold (NACE Rev. 2.)
(DS056120)

Figure 7.8: Production and domestic output price indices for industry (excluding construction), EU-27 (2005=100)

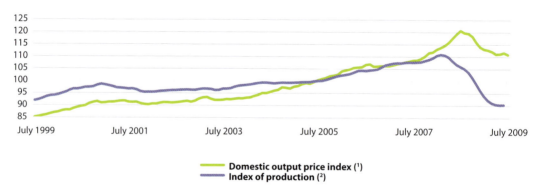

(¹) Gross series; estimates, 1999-2004.
(²) Trend-cycle; estimates.

Source: Eurostat (sts_inppd_m and sts_inpr_m)

Table 7.9: Annual growth rates for industry (excluding construction)
(%)

	Index of production (¹)					Domestic output price index (²)				
	2004	2005	2006	2007	2008	2004	2005	2006	2007	2008
EU-27	2.1	1.2	4.0	3.5	-1.8	2.9	5.0	5.6	2.8	7.6
Euro area	2.1	1.3	4.2	3.7	-1.8	2.3	4.1	5.1	2.7	6.1
Belgium	3.7	-0.9	5.0	2.9	-0.6	5.2	2.5	5.1	3.1	9.3
Bulgaria	12.7	7.2	6.0	9.5	0.6	5.4	7.3	8.7	8.0	13.2
Czech Republic	9.5	4.3	8.7	10.7	-2.2	5.6	3.1	1.5	4.1	4.5
Denmark	-1.5	2.8	4.0	-2.1	-1.1	3.8	9.2	7.9	1.6	13.2
Germany	3.1	3.5	5.7	6.0	0.0	1.7	4.4	5.4	1.3	5.4
Estonia	9.5	11.1	10.2	6.4	-6.2	3.4	1.7	4.3	9.6	9.6
Ireland	1.2	3.9	3.0	4.9	-1.5	0.5	2.2	1.8	1.6	5.3
Greece	0.7	-1.6	0.8	2.3	-4.2	3.6	5.9	7.3	4.1	10.0
Spain	1.9	0.8	3.9	2.0	-7.3	3.4	4.7	5.4	3.6	6.6
France	1.4	0.1	1.4	1.2	-2.6	2.0	3.1	3.8	2.8	5.6
Italy	-0.4	-0.8	3.6	2.1	-3.3	2.7	4.0	5.2	3.3	5.8
Cyprus	1.8	0.5	0.4	4.6	4.0	4.4	5.0	5.3	3.6	11.7
Latvia	6.2	7.4	6.5	1.0	-3.8	7.4	7.1	9.6	18.6	15.7
Lithuania	10.9	7.6	6.7	2.5	4.9	2.5	5.9	6.9	9.4	15.8
Luxembourg	4.7	2.8	2.1	-0.3	-5.4	9.1	3.6	12.8	4.4	15.1
Hungary	6.8	7.3	10.6	8.1	-1.0	8.4	6.1	8.4	6.5	11.6
Malta	0.0	0.0	0.0	0.0	0.0	:	:	21.7	-4.9	17.5
Netherlands	4.5	0.5	1.5	2.3	1.4	2.4	7.0	8.6	5.3	8.9
Austria	6.1	4.3	7.8	5.8	0.8	2.0	3.4	2.1	4.1	4.8
Poland	12.2	4.5	12.3	9.2	2.2	7.6	2.2	3.4	4.0	5.4
Portugal	-4.2	-3.5	3.2	0.1	-4.1	:	:	4.4	2.8	5.2
Romania	1.9	-2.9	9.5	10.2	3.1	19.2	10.8	10.3	8.4	12.8
Slovenia	3.9	4.1	6.1	7.2	-1.9	4.4	2.8	2.4	5.5	5.6
Slovakia	3.7	-2.6	12.2	16.1	5.0	2.7	3.7	6.3	1.8	6.2
Finland	5.4	0.4	9.9	4.2	-0.5	0.7	4.3	6.3	3.9	8.6
Sweden	4.4	2.2	3.6	3.9	-2.9	1.8	3.9	6.1	3.6	6.1
United Kingdom	-0.9	-1.6	-0.5	0.1	-3.4	4.0	11.1	8.6	1.7	16.1
Croatia	2.5	5.0	4.3	5.1	0.6	3.5	2.7	2.7	3.5	8.3
Turkey	9.7	5.7	5.8	4.4	-0.9	12.2	7.1	9.8	6.0	13.0
Norway	-1.2	-0.3	-2.2	-1.3	0.3	3.9	6.1	8.6	-0.6	15.2
Switzerland	4.4	2.7	7.8	9.5	1.2	:	:	:	:	:
Japan	4.7	1.4	4.4	2.8	-3.3	:	:	:	:	:
United States	2.5	3.3	2.2	1.7	-1.8	:	:	:	:	:

(¹) Working day adjusted.
(²) Gross series.

Source: Eurostat (sts_inprgr_a and sts_inppdgr_a)

Figure 7.9: Average annual growth rate for the industrial index of production, EU-27, 2003-2008 (¹)
(%)

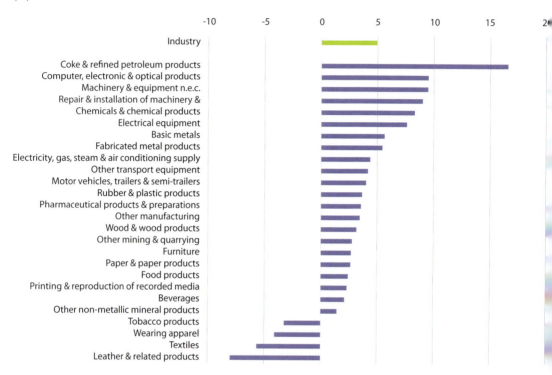

(¹) Working day adjusted.

Source: Eurostat (sts_inprgr_a)

Table 7.10: Annual growth rates for construction
(%)

	Index of production (¹)					Construction costs index (²)				
	2004	2005	2006	2007	2008	2004	2005	2006	2007	2008
EU-27	0.7	1.8	3.3	2.0	-3.1	6.6	4.1	4.7	4.5	3.5
Euro area	-0.2	2.0	3.1	1.1	-4.8	4.5	3.6	4.8	4.2	3.5
Belgium	-1.9	-3.4	3.3	2.3	-1.2	:	:	4.1	3.1	:
Bulgaria	34.8	32.2	23.9	27.8	-3.5	:	:	:	:	:
Czech Republic	8.4	5.3	6.3	7.1	-0.5	8.3	3.8	2.1	4.8	3.5
Denmark	-0.2	3.0	10.0	3.6	1.7	1.5	2.7	4.7	6.6	3.0
Germany	-5.3	-5.3	6.4	2.9	-0.8	2.4	0.8	1.5	3.3	2.4
Estonia	12.5	24.5	27.1	16.5	-15.4	5.3	6.2	10.5	12.7	3.5
Ireland	25.3	13.4	-1.7	-14.2	-30.1	12.8	8.7	9.6	1.7	:
Greece	-15.9	-38.7	3.8	15.2	2.7	3.1	3.4	4.2	4.6	5.1
Spain	2.3	10.1	2.2	-4.3	-16.3	4.7	4.6	6.9	5.0	4.7
France	-0.8	2.5	1.8	1.1	-0.6	5.8	2.3	5.3	4.6	5.5
Italy	1.6	1.3	3.9	6.4	-0.4	4.2	4.0	3.1	3.9	3.7
Cyprus	4.5	2.8	4.0	6.3	2.3	7.3	4.5	5.1	5.0	8.0
Latvia	14.1	15.3	13.2	13.8	-3.0	:	:	:	33.7	15.6
Lithuania	6.8	9.9	21.7	22.2	4.0	7.0	8.3	10.7	16.1	9.5
Luxembourg	-1.1	-0.9	2.5	2.6	-1.9	2.8	3.0	2.8	2.9	:
Hungary	4.3	15.7	-0.7	-14.0	-5.2	5.9	3.2	6.2	7.2	7.5
Malta	1.1	4.3	8.3	1.8	2.4	:	:	:	:	:
Netherlands	-2.5	3.4	2.6	5.8	5.6	2.1	1.8	3.2	4.0	4.3
Austria	5.0	4.9	5.9	3.9	-1.1	5.1	2.1	4.6	4.5	5.2
Poland	-1.1	9.4	15.9	16.2	9.6	2.6	2.8	1.4	6.6	:
Portugal	-4.4	-4.5	-6.6	-3.8	-1.4	:	:	:	:	:
Romania	1.8	6.1	15.6	33.0	27.0	25.1	14.3	11.1	10.2	16.2
Slovenia	0.7	2.0	15.7	18.5	15.5	10.4	6.1	3.4	5.1	5.1
Slovakia	6.0	14.1	15.7	5.4	11.5	6.9	4.8	4.0	4.4	:
Finland	4.1	5.3	7.5	10.2	4.1	2.4	3.4	3.8	5.9	3.9
Sweden	-1.0	2.7	8.8	7.6	6.0	3.9	3.9	5.0	6.1	4.8
United Kingdom	3.5	-0.5	1.4	2.3	-1.3	12.0	5.0	4.6	3.9	:
Croatia	1.9	-0.7	9.4	2.4	:	:	:	:	:	:
Turkey	:	:	:	:	:	14.6	9.9	16.0	8.3	13.6
Norway	7.3	8.9	6.1	5.7	2.5	3.0	3.4	3.7	7.4	5.7

(¹) Working day adjusted.
(²) Gross series for new residential buildings.

Source: Eurostat (sts_copr_a and sts_copi_a)

Figure 7.10: Index of production, construction, EU-27 (¹)
(2005=100)

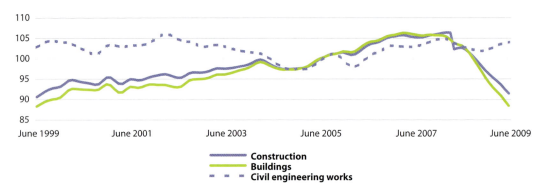

(¹) Trend-cycle; estimates.

Source: Eurostat (sts_copr_m)

7.3 Services

Introduction

The contribution of services to the European economy grows almost every year, and it is important that official statistics are able to provide information on this growing area. The knowledge-based economy and the demand for intangibles, either for consumption or investment purposes, as well as international outsourcing, has led to a major restructuring of many European economies, with a shift away from industrial activities towards services activities. This weightlessness that is inherent to many sectors of the economy provides new opportunities and with it competition both nationally and internationally. Traditionally, business statistics were concentrated on industrial

and construction activities, and to a lesser extent distributive trades and services. Since the early 1990s major developments in official statistics within the EU have seen data collection efforts focus more on services.

The internal market is one of the EU's most important and continuing priorities. The central principles governing the internal market for services are set out in the EC Treaty, which guarantees EU companies the freedom to establish themselves in other Member States, and the freedom to provide services on the territory of another Member State other than the one in which they are established. The objective of the Services Directive (⁵) is to eliminate obstacles to trade in services,

(⁵) Directive 2006/123/EC of the European Parliament and of the Council of 12 December 2006 on services in the internal market.

thus allowing the development of cross-border operations. It is intended to improve competitiveness, not just of service enterprises, but also of European industry as a whole. The Directive was adopted by the European Parliament and the Council in December 2006, with transposition by the Member States foreseen for the end of 2009. It is hoped that the Directive will help achieve potential economic growth and job creation, and it is for this reason that the Directive is seen as a central element of the renewed Lisbon Strategy for growth and jobs. Moreover, by providing for administrative simplification, it also supports the better regulation agenda.

Definitions and data availability

For background information relating to structural business statistics (SBS), refer to the section titled 'definitions and data availability' in Subchapter 7.1 (business structures), which includes definitions of value added and persons employed, while definitions of wage adjusted labour productivity and gross operating rate are presented in Subchapter 7.2 (industry and construction). Equally, a great deal of background information relating to short-term business statistics (STS) is provided in the section titled 'definitions and data availability' in Subchapter 7.2. Once again, it should be borne in mind that SBS data continue to be based on the NACE Rev. 1.1 classification of activities in this publication (the first reference year for which SBS data are due to be provided in NACE Rev. 2 is 2008), whereas the STS data are already based on the NACE Rev. 2 classification (including revised historical data).

The term 'non-financial services' is generally used within business statistics to refer to economic activities covered by Sections G to I and K of NACE Rev. 1.1 and the units that carry out those activities.

Retailing covers the resale without transformation of new and used goods to the general public for personal or household use and consumption. Retail trade has a particular importance because of its role as an interface between producers and final customers, allowing retail sales turnover and volume of sales indices to be used as a short-term indicator for final domestic demand by households.

Retail trade turnover indices are business cycle indicators which show the monthly activity of the retail sector in value and volume terms. The volume measure of the retail trade turnover index is more commonly referred to as the index of the volume of (retail) sales. Retail trade turnover indices are short-term indicators for final domestic demand. In order to eliminate the price effect on turnover in retail trade a deflator of sales is used. The deflator of sales is an index with a similar methodology to that of an output price index adapted to the particularities of retail trade but reflecting price changes in the goods retailed rather than the retail service provided. These indices may be split between food and non-food products. Food products are sold, either in non-specialised stores (hypermarkets, supermarkets) or in specialised stores (for example fruit and vegetable grocers). A greater proportion of sales in specialised stores is a sign of a more traditional pattern of retail trade.

The index of turnover for other services shows the evolution of sales in value terms. Note that prices for some services have actually been falling, perhaps due to market liberalisation and increased competition (for example, telecommunications and other technology-related activities). In such cases, the rapid growth rates observed for turnover value indices for some activities would be even greater in volume terms.

Main findings

Business services play a particularly important role in the services economy. Many of the activities covered by this sector of the economy (computer services, research and development, and other business activities such as legal, accounting, market research, advertising, industrial cleaning and security services) have grown, a likely result of the outsourcing phenomenon.

Within non-financial services, other business activities (as defined by NACE Rev. 1.1 Division 74) contributed more than one fifth (22.7 %) of the value added generated in the EU-27 in 2006. In comparison, wholesale trade (16.5 %) and retail trade and repair (13.3 %) contributed smaller shares. In terms of employment, however, retail trade activities were of a similar size to other business activities (22.1 % and 24.6 % respectively of the EU-27 workforce in the non-financial services in 2006), which in part reflects the high incidence of part-time employment in retail trade and repair activities.

The structure of EU-27 non-financial services activities varied considerably, in part reflecting differences in start-up costs and differences in market reach. Small and medium-sized enterprises (SMEs) in real estate activities generated the overwhelming majority (88.1 %) of value added in 2006 whereas they contributed a little less than one tenth (8.3 %) of the value added of post and telecommunications enterprises and a little less than one fifth (18.8 %) of the value added of air transport.

Among service activities (at the NACE Rev. 2 division level), the fastest rate of turnover growth in the five-year period between 2003 and 2008 was for employment activities (an average 9.4 % per annum), followed by legal, accounting and management consultancy activities (an average 9.0 % per annum). By contrast, growth was slowest for cinema, video and TV production activities (an average 1.3 % per annum). It should be noted, however, that the relatively steady growth in turnover came to an abrupt end in mid-2008, albeit to a less dramatic degree than the downturn for industry. In terms of the volume of sales, there was relative stability for retail trade as a whole in the year through to July 2009, with continued growth recorded for the retailing of textiles, clothing, footwear and leather in specialised stores.

Figure 7.11: Breakdown of non-financial services value added and employment, EU-27, 2006 (% of non-financial services value added and employment)

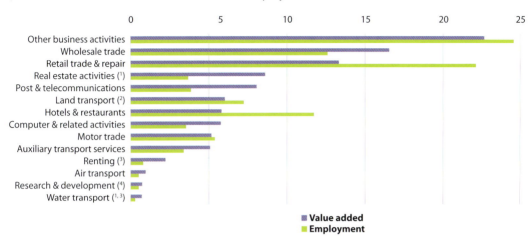

(1) Value added, estimate.
(2) Estimate, 2005.
(3) Number of persons employed, 2005.
(4) Value added, estimate, 2005.

Source: Eurostat (ebd_all)

Figure 7.12: Wage adjusted labour productivity within non-financial services, EU-27, 2006 (%)

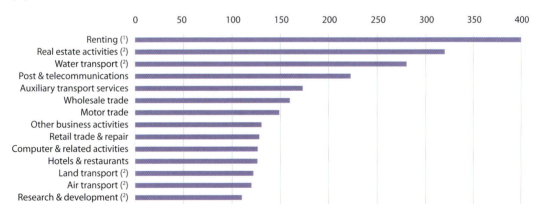

(1) 2005.
(2) Estimate, 2005.

Source: Eurostat (ebd_all)

Figure 7.13: Gross operating rate within non-financial services, EU-27, 2006 (¹)
(%)

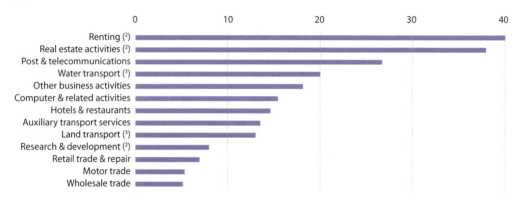

(¹) Air transport, confidential.
(²) Estimate, 2005.
(³) 2005.

Source: Eurostat (ebd_all)

Figure 7.14: Non-financial services value added by enterprise size-class, EU-27, 2006 (¹)
(% of sectoral total)

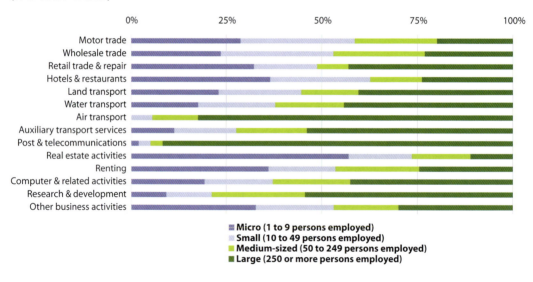

(¹) Includes rounded estimates based on non-confidential data.

Source: Eurostat (tin00053)

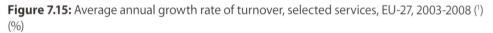

Figure 7.15: Average annual growth rate of turnover, selected services, EU-27, 2003-2008 ([1])
(%)

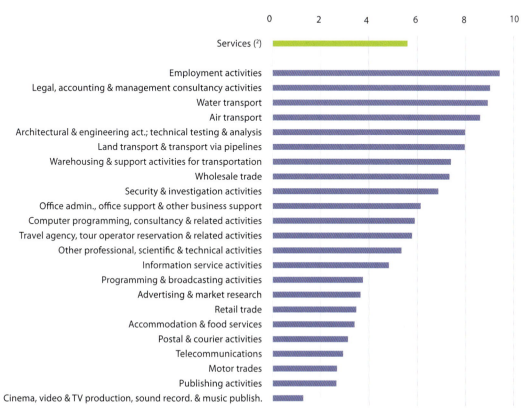

([1]) Working day adjusted.
([2]) As required by the STS Regulation.

Source: Eurostat (sts_setu_a and sts_trtu_a)

Table 7.11: Annual growth rates for the index of turnover, selected services (¹)
(%)

	Distributive trades		Transport. & storage		Accomm. & food services		Info. & comm.		Profes., scient. & technical activities (²)		Admin. & support serv. (²)	
	2007	2008	2007	2008	2007	2008	2007	2008	2007	2008	2007	2008
EU-27	5.3	5.1	10.2	5.7	3.9	1.4	5.0	2.8	8.7	7.8	10.3	4.6
Euro area	4.2	2.9	7.0	3.5	4.0	0.3	3.4	1.6	6.9	7.0	8.3	6.1
Belgium	6.9	3.2	9.7	7.9	5.3	4.1	:	:	7.6	40.8	11.3	7.3
Bulgaria	16.3	13.8	18.6	18.3	21.8	16.4	21.9	0.8	51.6	11.2	42.5	5.8
Czech Republic	9.1	3.0	12.0	1.7	6.4	-2.9	9.5	6.0	11.3	8.6	19.3	1.1
Denmark	4.0	0.0	7.7	8.9	9.6	3.3	13.9	-1.5	10.1	6.3	-8.1	9.0
Germany	0.2	4.3	8.1	3.9	-0.8	-0.2	0.5	0.9	7.5	8.6	12.7	12.5
Estonia	25.9	-4.8	11.4	-6.2	18.1	1.6	18.7	10.6	31.6	8.0	37.5	-0.4
Ireland	7.4	-4.9	3.1	-2.4	5.0	-5.2	:	:	8.3	-0.9	:	:
Greece	8.9	6.3	8.8	5.3	6.4	3.2	-2.6	0.1	9.3	6.6	16.1	6.0
Spain	5.4	-4.5	5.9	-0.8	4.7	-2.3	6.4	1.1	9.0	-4.3	6.1	-0.2
France	4.8	3.7	5.4	4.2	4.5	1.0	5.8	4.7	4.8	4.7	3.6	2.8
Italy	3.3	1.1	:	:	:	:	1.5	-1.8	:	:	:	:
Cyprus	12.0	10.9	5.9	4.5	12.6	3.5	12.0	11.4	14.0	9.4	6.2	-1.4
Latvia	25.7	-4.8	17.5	24.9	21.9	-0.4	15.0	5.0	19.9	8.8	38.9	10.0
Lithuania	21.8	12.6	31.3	8.1	10.5	15.2	14.8	11.2	30.4	20.7	28.5	19.6
Luxembourg	:	:	:	:	3.4	2.2	:	:	:	:	:	:
Hungary	1.3	0.8	-8.8	21.1	5.5	4.2	1.4	3.3	2.1	34.8	6.2	24.1
Malta	17.0	-1.0	2.7	6.1	6.4	5.2	:	:	1.6	12.2	:	:
Netherlands	7.6	7.0	:	:	5.6	0.2	7.1	1.6	6.8	6.3	12.3	6.8
Austria	3.6	4.1	5.2	4.3	5.2	4.4	3.3	0.1	4.5	3.9	7.5	4.6
Poland	12.6	7.7	14.3	13.4	12.5	11.7	9.1	11.7	16.5	30.3	20.5	21.9
Portugal	4.3	0.7	:	:	:	:	:	:	:	:	:	:
Romania	27.3	21.3	17.4	25.4	20.3	-0.4	19.0	21.7	31.8	27.8	15.8	19.8
Slovenia	14.2	15.7	16.5	-5.9	9.8	6.5	13.4	6.5	2.2	6.4	21.9	4.8
Slovakia	7.7	12.3	15.0	13.7	4.0	5.9	8.4	8.3	10.9	7.2	4.7	28.4
Finland	6.8	6.2	8.0	7.1	6.7	5.4	5.2	3.8	14.2	8.7	13.8	12.7
Sweden	:	:	6.5	2.6	8.6	4.6	5.2	1.3	7.9	-0.3	9.6	0.8
United Kingdom	6.9	13.3	20.3	9.1	1.6	3.3	7.9	4.8	11.0	6.6	14.3	0.5
Norway	:	:	:	:	12.2	5.8	:	:	:	:	:	:

(¹) Working day adjusted.
(²) As required by the STS Regulation.

Source: Eurostat (sts_trtu_a and sts_setu_a)

Figure 7.16: Index of turnover, selected service activities, EU-27 ([^1])
(2005=100)

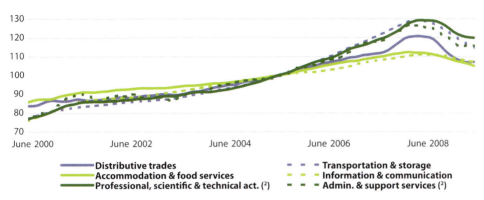

- ━━━━━ **Distributive trades**
- ━━━━━ **Accommodation & food services**
- ━━━━━ **Professional, scientific & technical act. ([^2])**
- ‐ ‐ ‐ **Transportation & storage**
- ‐ ‐ ‐ **Information & communication**
- ‐ ‐ ‐ **Admin. & support services ([^2])**

([^1]) Trend-cycle; estimates.
([^2]) As required by the STS Regulation.

Source: Eurostat (sts_trtu_m and sts_setu_m)

Figure 7.17: Breakdown of turnover, retail sales of food, beverages and tobacco, 2006 ([^1])
(% of total turnover)

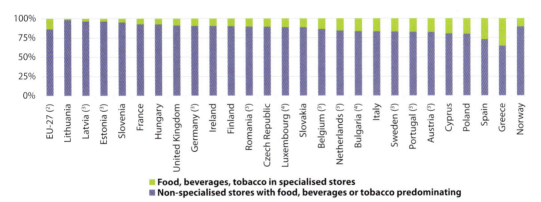

- ▪ **Food, beverages, tobacco in specialised stores**
- ▪ **Non-specialised stores with food, beverages or tobacco predominating**

([^1]) Denmark, confidential; Malta, not available.
([^2]) 2005; non-specialised stores, estimate.
([^3]) 2007.
([^4]) 2005.

Source: Eurostat (tin00007)

Table 7.12: Annual growth rates for the volume of sales index, retail trade (¹)
(%)

	1998	1999	2000	2001	2002	2003	2004	2005	2006	2007	2008
EU-27	2.8	2.4	2.4	2.2	2.0	1.7	2.6	2.3	3.2	2.5	0.3
Euro area	3.0	2.1	1.5	1.6	1.1	0.8	1.4	1.7	2.3	1.4	-0.8
Belgium	4.1	2.2	5.2	0.2	-0.9	-0.2	1.7	1.3	1.7	1.8	1.2
Bulgaria	:	:	:	2.9	5.9	15.5	16.7	14.6	13.0	19.0	3.1
Czech Republic	-6.5	3.2	-1.0	7.3	1.2	8.0	3.1	6.8	8.9	7.8	4.0
Denmark	2.2	1.1	0.8	4.4	3.3	3.2	4.5	8.9	4.7	-1.4	-3.4
Germany	0.7	-0.2	0.5	0.0	-2.3	-0.9	1.7	0.9	0.3	-3.0	-0.7
Estonia	:	2.3	14.2	12.9	13.0	-0.9	11.0	14.8	17.6	10.5	-4.5
Ireland	:	:	:	9.0	3.6	3.5	5.7	6.7	8.8	8.0	-2.3
Greece	2.6	1.8	8.8	4.3	4.9	4.3	4.5	3.0	9.0	2.2	1.3
Spain	6.0	3.4	2.7	3.5	6.4	3.2	2.5	1.3	2.3	2.7	-5.4
France	4.6	4.5	2.8	3.4	3.3	2.9	3.1	3.3	2.7	4.1	1.3
Italy	1.2	0.9	-0.6	-0.6	-0.6	-0.7	-2.5	-0.6	1.9	0.8	-2.3
Cyprus	:	:	:	9.2	2.6	-1.4	3.2	4.9	6.9	8.5	4.8
Latvia	:	5.9	20.1	5.5	10.7	12.7	10.0	20.0	19.9	15.3	-7.2
Lithuania	8.1	-5.1	14.3	2.8	10.1	11.2	9.3	11.7	7.2	13.7	3.8
Luxembourg	:	:	:	:	:	:	:	:	:	:	:
Hungary	:	6.0	3.4	3.8	8.5	7.7	6.0	4.3	4.9	-2.0	-1.9
Malta	:	:	:	8.0	-4.9	15.5	-5.4	-20.4	-6.4	17.6	-11.3
Netherlands	4.1	3.4	-0.9	2.9	1.2	-1.0	-0.3	1.8	4.6	2.7	-0.1
Austria	:	:	2.0	-1.9	-0.5	-0.1	0.1	1.4	1.8	0.8	-0.8
Poland	:	:	:	2.5	-1.2	4.7	4.7	1.4	12.5	11.0	4.4
Portugal	9.9	6.3	-0.7	2.7	0.5	-2.1	2.1	6.0	1.8	0.6	1.2
Romania	:	:	:	0.0	3.0	8.4	14.7	16.2	19.6	20.4	20.4
Slovenia	:	-15.0	30.5	10.1	2.9	3.4	3.8	8.0	2.6	6.1	12.1
Slovakia	4.6	16.7	-3.0	7.6	8.3	-2.4	8.2	10.2	8.2	5.5	9.0
Finland	7.7	5.7	5.3	5.6	3.6	4.8	5.0	4.8	4.6	5.2	1.2
Sweden	2.8	3.7	5.7	2.7	3.8	3.9	3.9	5.8	6.2	0.9	0.8
United Kingdom	:	3.5	5.9	4.4	5.9	3.3	5.7	2.5	3.3	4.3	2.4
Croatia	:	:	:	12.4	11.6	10.7	7.3	3.1	4.3	2.8	-0.4
Norway	:	:	:	1.8	5.2	2.6	3.2	3.4	5.6	6.6	1.5

(¹) Working day adjusted.

Source: Eurostat (sts_trtu_a)

Figure 7.18: Volume of sales index, selected retail trade activities, EU-27 (¹)
(2005=100)

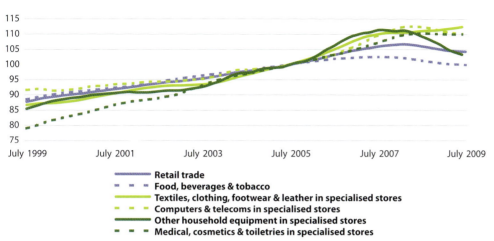

- Retail trade
- Food, beverages & tobacco
- **Textiles, clothing, footwear & leather in specialised stores**
- **Computers & telecoms in specialised stores**
- **Other household equipment in specialised stores**
- **Medical, cosmetics & toiletries in specialised stores**

(¹) Trend-cycle.

Source: Eurostat (sts_trtu_m)

7.4 Tourism

Introduction

Europe is a major tourist destination with six of the EU Member States among the world's top ten destinations for holiday-makers. As a result, tourism plays an important role in terms of its economic and employment potential, while presenting social and environmental implications; these twin characteristics drive the demand for reliable and harmonised statistics within this field.

Tourism plays an important role in terms of its economic and employment potential; infrastructure created for tourism purposes contributes to local development, while jobs that are created (often

with an emphasis on opportunities for young people) or maintained can help counteract industrial or rural decline.

However, tourism also has social and environmental implications that put into question whether tourism is developing in a sustainable way; as well as concerns about global pollution from mass tourism transport, there are localised concerns about the allocation of sometimes scarce resources, the environmental impact of tourist infrastructure, the pressure of tourism on the quality of living of local communities and the maintenance of their cultural and historical heritage. The twin characteristics of economic potential and environmental concern drive the demand for reliable and harmonised statistics within this field. 'Sustainable tourism' involves the preservation and enhancement of cultural and natural heritage, ranging from the arts, to local gastronomy, or the preservation of biodiversity.

A new policy approach for tourism is in the process of being developed. The European Commission adopted in 2006 a Communication titled 'a renewed EU tourism policy: towards a stronger partnership for European tourism'. The document addressed a range of challenges that will shape tourism in the coming years, including:

• Europe's ageing population;
• growing external competition;
• consumer demand for more specialised tourism;
• the need to develop more sustainable and environmentally-friendly tourism practices.

The document argues that a more competitive tourism industry and sustainable destinations would contribute further to the success of the renewed Lisbon Strategy, tourist satisfaction, and securing the position of Europe as the world's leading tourist destination.

This was followed by a communication from the European Commission in October 2007 – 'Agenda for a sustainable and competitive European tourism' – which outlined the future steps for promoting the sustainability of European tourism and further contributes to the implementation of the renewed Lisbon Strategy for growth and jobs and of the renewed Sustainable Development Strategy, through addressing stakeholders playing a role in

European tourism. The sustainable management of destinations, the integration of sustainability concerns by businesses, and sustainability awareness of tourists form the framework of the actions proposed.

Definitions and data availability

Eurostat publishes tourism statistics relating to capacity and occupancy of tourism accommodation establishment and tourism demand by European residents, collected and compiled by the national statistical authorities.

Statistics in this field are not only used to monitor tourism-specific policies, but also play a role in the wider context of regional policy and sustainable development. A system of tourism statistics has been laid down in Council Directive 95/57/EC of 23 November 1995 on the collection of statistical information in the field of tourism. This legal basis requires EU Member States' national governments to provide a regular set of comparable tourism statistics. A Commission Decision of December 1998 (1999/35/EC) implemented some aspects of this Directive; amendments in 2004 and 2006 concerned the enlargement of the EU and recent changes in the world market for tourism.

The system consists of two main components: on the one hand, statistics relating to capacity and occupancy in collective tourist accommodation and, on the other hand, statistics relating to tourism demand. In most Member States, the former are collected via surveys filled in by accommodation establishments, while the latter are mainly collected via traveller surveys at border crossings or via traditional household surveys.

Statistics on the **capacity of collective tourist accommodation** include the number of establishments, the number of bedrooms and the number of bed places. These statistics are available by establishment type or by region, and are compiled annually.

Statistics on the **occupancy of collective tourist accommodation** refer to the number of arrivals (at accommodation establishments) and the number of nights spent by residents and non-residents, separated into establishment type or region. Annual and monthly statistical series are available. In addition, statistics on the use of bed places (occupancy rates) are compiled.

Statistics on **tourism demand** refer to tourist participation, in other words, the number of people in the population who make at least one trip of at least four overnight stays during the reference period (quarter or year). They also look at the number of tourism trips made (and the number of nights spent on those trips), separated into tourism-related variables, such as:

- destination country;
- departure month;
- length of stay;
- type of trip organisation;
- transport mode;
- accommodation type;
- expenditure.

The statistical data is also separated into socio-demographic explanatory variables, such as age and gender.

Besides pure tourism statistics, data from other sources may be used to further explore the statistical picture of EU tourism. In the tourism accommodation sector, these additional statistics include employment data (from the labour force survey (LFS)) or information from the balance of payments (BoP):

- working time (either full- or part-time);
- working status;
- age;
- level of education;
- sex;
- permanency and seniority of work with the same employer;
- tourism receipts and expenditure.

Furthermore, transport statistics (for example, air passenger transport) and structural business statistics (SBS) can give additional indications, respectively, on tourism flows, and on the economic performance of certain tourism-related sectors.

'**Tourism**' refers to the activity of visitors taking a trip to a main destination outside their usual environment, for less than a year. It can be for any main purpose, including business, leisure or other personal reasons other than to be employed by a resident person, household or enterprise in the place visited. The statistics presented here are limited to at least an overnight stay; the possibility of including statistics relating to same-day visits is being examined.

A **tourist** is any visitor who stays at least one night in collective or private accommodation. A **night spent** is defined as each night that a guest is registered to stay in a hotel or similar establishment (his/her physical presence there is not necessary). A breakdown of nights spent is provided for **residents and non-residents,**

the former are identified as having lived for most of the past year in a country/place, or having lived in that country/place for a shorter period and intending to return within a year to live there; note that a significant proportion of tourism, using the definitions above, is accounted for by business customers.

Tourism intensity and international tourism receipts relative to GDP both give an indication of the importance of the size of tourism. Tourism intensity shows the number of nights spent by tourists relative to the population of the host country.

On the supply side, tourism relies on enterprises from a variety of sectors, which can be summarised as the provision of accommodation, food and drink, transport facilities and services, and entertainment. The term **tourist accommodation** refers to all types of collective accommodation – thus, excluding privately rented tourist accommodation. This may be broken down to cover **hotels and similar establishments** which include the provision of lodging in hotels, motels, inns and similar establishments combined with typical hotel services like bed-making and cleaning of the room and sanitary facilities, and **other collective accommodation establishments** which consist of holiday dwellings, tourist campsites and other short-stay accommodation, like youth hostels, tourist dormitories and holiday homes. The **number of bed places** in an establishment or dwelling is determined by the number of persons who can stay overnight in beds set-up in the establishments, ignoring any extra beds that may be set-up by customer request. The term 'bed place' applies to a single bed. A double bed is counted as two bed places.

Travel services carried out by enterprises that are engaged in arranging transport, accommodation and catering on behalf of travellers, are classified within NACE Rev. 1.1 Group 63.3, which encompasses the following activities: furnishing travel information, advice and planning; arranging custom-made tours, accommodation and transportation for travellers and tourists; furnishing tickets; selling package tours; tour operating; and organising tourist guides.

Main findings

In 2007, EU residents made nearly a thousand million holiday trips. They made 76 % of these trips to a destination within their own country of residence, while the remaining 24 % of trips were abroad. Slightly more than half of all trips (55 %) were short trips of one to three nights.

Large differences could be observed across the EU, as some countries reported over half of all holidays were spent abroad; this was the case for Belgium, Denmark, Ireland, Luxembourg, the Netherlands and Slovenia. However, 10 % or less of the residents in Greece, Spain, France and Portugal went abroad for their holiday trips; this pattern appeared to be influenced by both the Member State's size and its geographical location.

From the supply perspective, there were 202 353 hotels and similar establishments active in 2007 within the EU. In addition, there were 220 497 other collective tourist accommodation establishments (such as campsites and holiday dwellings, etc.). These hotels and similar establishments provided over 11.7 million bed places, of which nearly half (47 %) were in the top three countries: Italy (2.1 million bed places), Germany and Spain (both 1.7 million bed places). In 2007, non-resident (foreign) tourists spent almost 730 million nights in hotels and similar establishments in the EU-27.

In 2008, the biggest group of outbound tourists among the EU population was recorded for Germany. During that year, Germans spent more than 625 million nights in collective accommodation establishments outside of Germany, closely followed by residents from the United Kingdom (546 million nights abroad in 2007). These two Member States alone accounted for more than half of the total number of nights spent by EU residents outside their respective countries. The top 10 countries made-up slightly more than 90 % of the 2 000 million nights that Europeans spent in tourist accommodation establishments outside the Member State where they had their usual place of residence in 2008. When taking into account the country's size in terms of population, Luxembourg was the Member State where the highest proportion of residents (16 years of age or more) went abroad, followed by Cyprus and Sweden. At the other end of the spectrum, during 2008, only 1.6 % of Bulgarians spent at least four holiday nights abroad.

In 2008, Spain was the most popular tourism destination for non-residents, with 225 million nights spent in collective accommodation. This country alone accounted for more than 23 % of the total nights spent by non-residents in the EU. The top three most popular countries were Spain (224 million nights), Italy

(163 million nights in 2007) and France (107 million nights). Together these three countries accounted for 51 % of the nights spent by EU residents in collective accommodation establishments outside their own country. The least popular destinations were Luxembourg and the three Baltic Member States of Lithuania, Latvia and Estonia – in each case, the effect of the size of these countries should be considered.

Putting the number of nights spent in perspective by comparing them to the population of the Member State, tourism intensity can be ascertained. In 2008, this indicator revealed the Mediterranean island destinations of Malta and Cyprus, as well as the alpine/city destination of Austria, as the most popular destinations.

The economic importance of tourism can be measured by looking at the ratio of international tourism receipts relative to gross domestic product (GDP). In 2007, this was highest in Cyprus (11.55 %), confirming the importance of tourism to this island nation. In absolute terms, the highest international tourism receipts from personal travel were recorded in France (EUR 34 995 million), Italy (EUR 24 280 million) and the United Kingdom (EUR 20 301 million). The biggest spenders in terms of international tourism were the British with expenditure totalling over EUR 44 878 million. In 2007, when taking into account the size of each economy, Cypriot and Luxembourgish residents spent the highest amount per capita on personal travel (more than 6.5 % of GDP), well ahead of the third-placed country, Ireland (3.32 %).

Figure 7.19: Tourism destinations, 2008 (¹)
(1 000 nights spent in the country by non-residents)

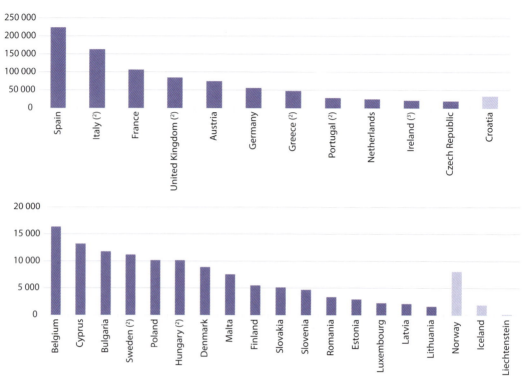

(¹) Note the differences in the scales employed between the two parts of the figure.
(²) 2007.
(³) 2006.

Source: Eurostat (tour_occ_ni)

Table 7.13: Tourism indicators

	Hotels & similar establishments (units)		Other collective accommodation establishments (units)		Bed places in hotels & similar establishments (1 000)		Nights spent in hotels & similar establishments (1 000) (¹)		Ratio of population (aged 15+) taking part in tourism	
	2003 (²)	2008 (³)	2003 (²)	2008 (³)	2003 (²)	2008 (³)	2003 (²)	2008 (⁴)	2003	2008 (⁵)
EU-27	204 457	202 353	193 275	220 497	10 895	11 715	626 802	729 871	:	:
Euro area	143 062	142 277	139 446	163 787	8 309	8 871	498 328	574 260	:	:
Belgium	1 957	2 009	1 561	1 527	122	125	10 281	11 120	0.45	0.47
Bulgaria	849	1 646	210	482	144	240	8 987	11 641	:	0.07
Czech Republic	4 377	4 483	3 549	3 222	227	258	13 688	17 741	0.50	0.54
Denmark	478	470	623	588	68	73	4 512	4 552	0.64	0.62
Germany	37 547	35 891	17 572	18 068	1 611	1 677	33 301	45 218	0.66	0.63
Estonia	230	368	313	680	18	30	2 086	2 727	0.23	0.34
Ireland	4 821	3 947	4 150	5 483	146	169	17 748	:	:	:
Greece	8 689	9 385	333	321	645	716	39 760	47 410	0.43	0.42
Spain	17 102	18 026	14 447	20 976	1 452	1 685	136 865	155 379	0.50	0.43
France	18 617	17 970	10 489	10 697	1 236	1 256	69 323	71 725	0.59	0.67
Italy	33 480	34 058	79 864	96 991	1 969	2 143	93 935	113 017	0.50	:
Cyprus	829	708	122	161	91	86	13 424	13 151	0.75	0.89
Latvia	261	387	65	104	15	24	963	1 913	:	0.20
Lithuania	270	365	218	177	14	22	766	1 544	:	0.36
Luxembourg	307	267	277	236	15	14	1 144	1 297	0.66	0.77
Hungary	2 261	2 001	1 256	923	159	155	8 046	8 635	:	0.51
Malta	194	155	4	7	40	39	7 301	7 416	:	:
Netherlands	2 908	3 196	3 795	4 072	180	200	13 798	14 962	0.69	0.69
Austria	14 708	13 756	6 206	6 682	566	580	55 200	60 462	0.53	0.61
Poland	1 547	2 642	5 569	4 215	134	211	5 450	7 939	0.35	0.36
Portugal	1 934	2 031	280	308	246	265	23 215	26 769	0.28	0.19
Romania	2 989	4 362	580	522	202	238	2 688	3 251	:	0.29
Slovenia	381	410	422	440	29	34	3 166	3 659	0.57	0.60
Slovakia	838	1 313	1 246	1 454	55	70	3 560	3 978	:	0.52
Finland	992	901	472	448	120	121	3 758	4 768	0.56	0.58
Sweden	1 765	1 893	2 048	2 083	185	207	4 833	5 842	:	:
United Kingdom	44 126	39 860	37 604	41 988	1 204	1 245	49 003	64 253	0.64	0.58
Croatia	832	835	509	1 150	194	164	16 830	17 605	:	0.35
FYR of Macedonia	150	:	175	:	16	:	249	:	:	:
Turkey	9 877	:	:	:	820	:	51 118	74 192	:	:
Iceland	283	301	384	280	15	19	1 070	1 517	:	:
Liechtenstein	46	45	101	103	1	1	105	131	:	:
Norway	1 099	1 108	1 120	1 179	144	157	4 375	4 871	0.72	0.72
Switzerland	5 643	5 582	94 100	:	259	270	17 768	21 478	:	:

(¹) Nights spent by non-residents.
(²) Former Yugoslav Republic of Macedonia and Switzerland, 2002.
(³) EU-27, euro area, Italy, the Netherlands, Portugal, Sweden and the United Kingdom, 2007.
(⁴) EU-27, euro area, Greece, Italy, Hungary, Portugal, Sweden, the United Kingdom and Turkey, 2007.
(⁵) The Czech Republic, Denmark, Greece, Portugal, the United Kingdom and Norway, 2007.

Source: Eurostat (tin00039, tin00040, tin00041, tin00043, tin00045, tps00001 and tps00010)

Figure 7.20: Country of origin for outbound holidays, 2008 (¹)
(1 000 nights spent abroad)

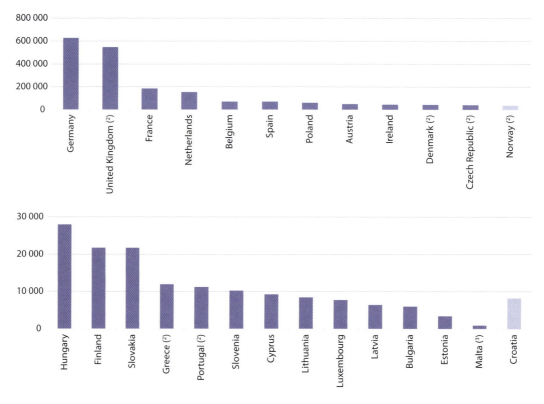

(¹) Note the differences in the scales employed between the two parts of the figure; Italy, Romania and Sweden, not available.
(²) 2007.
(³) Estimate, 2007.

Source: Eurostat (tour_dem_tnw)

Figure 7.21: Tourism intensity, 2008
(ratio of nights spent by residents and non-residents in hotels and similar establishments and other collective accommodation establishments per inhabitant)

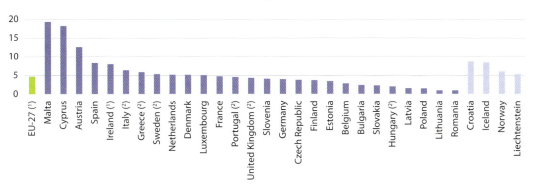

(¹) 2006.
(²) 2007.

Source: Eurostat (tour_occ_ni and tps00001)

Figure 7.22: Proportion of the population aged 15+ going on holiday abroad for at least four nights, 2008 (¹)
(%)

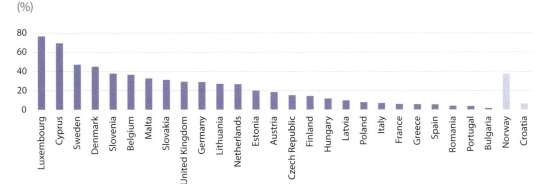

(¹) Bulgaria, the Czech Republic and Malta, estimates; Denmark, Malta and Norway, 2007; Italy and Sweden, 2006; Ireland, not available.

Source: Eurostat (tour_dem_toage, tps00001 and tps00010)

Table 7.14: Holiday trips of EU residents aged 15+, 2008

	Number of trips (1 000)			Breakdown of all trips by destination and duration (%)			
	All trips	Short trips (1-3 nights)	Long trips (4+ nights)	Short domestic trips (1-3 nights)	Long domestic trips (4+ nights)	Short outbound trips (1-3 nights)	Long outbound trips (4+ nights)
Belgium	10 712	3 609	7 103	16.5	11.3	17.2	55.0
Bulgaria	6 251	3 775	2 476	57.0	32.0	3.4	7.6
Czech Republic	24 532	14 626	9 906	53.6	20.1	6.0	20.3
Denmark (¹)	10 368	4 377	5 991	32.5	15.2	9.7	42.6
Germany	214 482	110 659	103 823	44.9	21.1	6.7	27.3
Estonia	1 241	813	428	49.5	7.7	17.0	25.8
Ireland	11 839	6 023	5 816	38.4	10.4	12.5	38.8
Greece	13 561	5 627	7 934	40.3	50.4	1.2	8.1
Spain	119 969	80 687	39 282	65.4	28.0	1.9	4.7
France	212 562	125 587	86 975	56.4	34.3	2.7	6.6
Italy (²)	78 055	36 920	41 134	43.3	39.8	4.0	12.9
Cyprus	1 704	813	891	42.2	11.4	5.5	40.9
Latvia	4 262	3 318	944	71.8	6.4	7.6	14.2
Lithuania	3 813	2 418	1 395	49.5	13.9	13.9	22.7
Luxembourg	1 199	444	755	0.5	0.3	36.6	62.7
Hungary	22 155	15 010	7 144	60.8	19.6	7.0	12.7
Malta	:	:	:	:	:	:	:
Netherlands (¹)	29 083	10 621	18 462	25.5	22.7	11.0	40.8
Austria	15 426	6 857	8 569	30.7	20.9	13.8	34.6
Poland	36 245	19 080	17 165	49.4	35.6	3.3	11.7
Portugal (²)	10 265	6 423	3 842	60.5	29.6	2.1	7.9
Romania	10 275	:	:	:	:	:	:
Slovenia	3 733	2 149	1 584	36.7	11.4	20.9	31.0
Slovakia	6 724	2 071	4 653	24.1	33.8	6.7	35.4
Finland	30 115	23 246	6 869	69.5	15.3	7.7	7.5
Sweden (²)	38 399	25 618	12 781	58.3	19.1	8.5	14.2
United Kingdom (²)	112 695	53 375	59 320	40.8	20.1	6.5	32.5
Croatia	6 721	3 557	3 164	39.5	32.3	13.4	14.7
Norway	16 800	9 650	7 150	44.9	19.9	12.6	22.6

(¹) 2007.
(²) 2006.

Source: Eurostat (tour_dem_ttmd)

Table 7.15: Tourism receipts and expenditure from personal travel

	Receipts				Expenditure			
	(EUR million)			Relative to GDP, 2007 (%)	(EUR million)			Relative to GDP, 2007 (%)
	2005	2006	2007		2005	2006	2007	
EU-27 (¹)	51 644	56 643	59 366	0.48	66 150	67 028	73 166	0.59
Belgium	6 506	6 658	6 330	1.89	10 330	10 551	10 728	3.20
Bulgaria	1 735	1 832	2 027	7.02	295	325	302	1.04
Czech Republic	2 892	3 465	3 675	2.89	1 566	1 805	2 217	1.74
Denmark	3 281	3 428	3 490	1.54	4 207	4 507	4 837	2.14
Germany	:	:	:	:	:	:	:	:
Estonia	599	629	572	3.74	213	287	308	2.02
Ireland	3 813	:	4 312	2.26	:	:	6 321	3.32
Greece	10 082	10 439	10 339	4.53	1 429	1 308	1 425	0.62
Spain	:	:	:	:	:	:	:	:
France	30 838	32 368	34 995	1.85	19 763	18 223	20 413	1.08
Italy	22 679	23 825	24 280	1.57	11 652	11 895	12 710	0.82
Cyprus	1 779	1 776	1 810	11.55	736	751	1 048	6.69
Latvia	190	270	343	1.62	345	451	564	2.67
Lithuania	594	604	579	2.04	455	510	717	2.52
Luxembourg	1 871	1 767	1 732	4.76	2 184	2 282	2 382	6.54
Hungary	2 684	2 766	2 792	2.75	1 621	1 292	1 595	1.57
Malta	:	:	:	:	:	:	:	:
Netherlands	5 639	6 149	6 564	1.15	9 847	10 256	10 519	1.85
Austria	:	:	:	:	:	:	:	:
Poland	4 008	4 618	6 160	1.98	2 555	3 545	3 109	1.00
Portugal	5 557	5 998	6 649	4.07	1 565	1 727	1 807	1.11
Romania	432	382	329	0.27	229	294	331	0.27
Slovenia	1 392	1 493	1 739	5.04	520	596	618	1.79
Slovakia	:	:	1 250	2.28	:	:	963	1.76
Finland	1 049	1 072	1 231	0.68	1 651	1 765	2 058	1.15
Sweden	:	:	:	:	5 827	6 268	6 995	2.11
United Kingdom	18 320	19 500	20 301	0.99	40 778	42 708	44 878	2.20
Croatia	5 458	5 876	6 345	14.82	337	355	450	1.05
United States	78 599	81 660	83 729	0.82	58 646	60 982	58 876	0.57

(¹) Extra-EU-27 flows.

Source: Eurostat (bop_its_det and nama_gdp_c)

7.5 Information society

Introduction

Information and communication technologies (ICT) are considered as critical for improving the competitiveness of European industry and, more generally, to meet the demands of its society and economy. ICT affects many aspects of everyday lives, at both work and in the home. EU policies in this area range from the regulation of entire industrial sectors to the protection of an individual's privacy.

The policy framework for ICT is the i2010 initiative ([6]) – 'a European information society for growth and employment' – which seeks to boost efficiency throughout the European economy by means of wider use of ICT. The initiative is designed to promote an open and competitive digital economy, research into information and communication technologies, as well as their application to improve social inclusion, public services and quality of life. Indeed, at the heart of the policy is a desire to ensure that social and geographical differences are overcome, thus creating an inclusive digital society that provides opportunities for all. The i2010 initiative has three main priorities:

- creating a single European information space, which promotes an open and competitive internal market for information society and media services;
- stimulating the information society – to strengthen investment in innovation and research in ICT;

- exploiting the benefits of ICT – to foster inclusion, better public services and quality of life through the use of ICT.

A benchmarking framework for i2010 was approved by the EU Member States and the European Commission in 2006. It defines a comprehensive set of indicators on Internet and broadband take-up and on the use of computers and on-line services by citizens and businesses. In addition, it provides for flexible modules on a specific issue to be defined each year.

After undergoing a mid-term review, an updated i2010 Strategy was presented in April 2008, addressing key challenges for the period 2008-2010. This was followed by a European Commission Communication on future networks and the Internet ([7]) which outlined the social and economic potential of the Internet in the future, based on the premise of a high-speed Internet available to all, internationally open and competitive, secure and safe to use, with transparent and effective governance. These fundamental conditions of accessibility, openness, transparency and security form the basis of the European Commission's short-term agenda for the Internet of the future, as summarised by six actions:

- the construction of high-speed Internet infrastructures that are open to competition and give consumers real choices;
- promoting access for all to a good-quality Internet connection at an affordable price;

([6]) For more information: http://ec.europa.eu/information_society/eeurope/i2010/index_en.htm.

([7]) COM(2008) 594 final; for more information: http://ec.europa.eu/information_society/eeurope/i2010/docs/future_internet/act_future_networks_internet_en.pdf.

- keeping the Internet open to competition, innovation and consumer choice;
- launching a debate on the design and development of the Internet of the future;
- providing clear guidelines on the implementation of existing rules on data protection and a coherent strategy for a secure Internet of the future;
- taking into account the crucial role played by international policy, regulatory dialogue and research cooperation in all these developments.

Broadband technologies are considered to be of major importance when measuring access and use of the Internet as they offer users the possibility to rapidly transfer large volumes of data and keep their access line open; the take-up of broadband is considered a key indicator within the domain of ICT policymaking. Widespread access to the Internet via broadband is seen as essential for the development of advanced services on the Internet, for example, in the field of e-business, e-government or e-learning. Broadband growth has continued in recent years and 49 % of all households in the EU-27 have broadband. Digital subscriber lines (DSL) remain the main form of delivery for broadband technology, although alternatives such as cable, satellite, fibre optics and wireless local loops are becoming much more widespread.

Definitions and data availability

Statisticians are well aware of the challenges posed by rapid technological change in areas related to the Internet and other new means of ICT. As such, there has been a considerable degree of evolu-

tion in this area, with statistical tools being adapted to satisfy new demands for data. Statistics within this domain are re-assessed on an annual basis in order to meet user needs and reflect the rapid pace of technological change.

It is also clear that while ICTs have become available to a wider public, in terms of accessibility and cost, there remains a gap between users and non-users, often referred to as the 'digital divide'. This may be attributed to a number of factors, including: a lack of infrastructure (particularly in remote, rural areas), or a lack of computer literacy/skills necessary to take part in the information society, or a lack of awareness or interest in what the information society can offer; tracking this divide provides important policy insight.

This approach is reflected in **Eurostat's surveys on the use of information and communication technologies in households and by individuals** as well as its **surveys on the use of information and communication technologies in enterprises**. These annual surveys on ICT use in households/by individuals and in enterprises can be used to benchmark ICT-driven developments, both by following developments for core variables over time, as well as by looking in greater depth at other aspects at a point in time. While the surveys initially concentrated on access and connectivity issues, their scope has subsequently been extended to cover a variety of subjects (including, for example, e-government, e-skills) and socio-economic breakdowns, such as regional diversity, gender specificity, age, educational differences and the individual's employment situation in the household survey or a breakdown by size

(small, medium-sized, large) in the enterprise survey. The scope of the surveys with respect to different technologies is also adapted so as to cover emerging technologies and uptake of these technologies by end-users (enterprises and households).

Households and individuals

Households in this survey are defined in terms of those households with at least one member in the age group 16 to 74 years old. **Internet access of households** refers to the percentage of households with an Internet access, so anyone in the household could use the Internet at home, if desired, even if just to send an e-mail. **Internet users** are defined as all individuals aged 16-74 who had used the Internet in the three months prior to the survey. **Regular Internet users** are individuals who used the Internet, on average, at least once a week in the three months prior to the survey (in general, during the first quarter of 2008).

The most commonly used technologies to access the Internet are distinguished according to speed of connection between broadband and narrowband access, either fixed or mobile. **Broadband includes digital subscriber lines (DSL)** or cable TV networks and uses technology that transports data at high speeds. **Broadband lines** are defined as having a capacity equal to or higher than 144 kbit/s. A **dial-up access** using a modem can be made over a normal or an ISDN telephone line. Due to its limited bandwidth it is often referred to as narrowband. The **availability of broadband** is measured as the percentage of households that are connectable to an exchange that has been converted to

support xDSL-technology, to a cable network upgraded for Internet traffic, or to other broadband technologies.

A **computer** is defined as a personal computer powered by one of the major operating systems (Mac OS, Linux or Microsoft); handheld computers or palmtops (PDAs) are also included.

The **ordering of goods and services by individuals** includes confirmed reservations for accommodation, purchasing financial investments, participation in lotteries and betting, Internet auctions, as well as information services from the Internet that are directly paid for. Goods and services that are obtained via the Internet for free are excluded. Orders made by manually written e-mails are also excluded. The indicator shows the percentage of individuals aged 16 to 74 who have used the Internet, in the 12 months prior to the survey, for ordering goods or services. Services related to travel and accommodation include using the Internet for ascertaining information or for purchasing goods and services in relation to travel and accommodation, for example, travel tickets, hotels or any other types of accommodation or websites containing information for tourists.

On the Internet people cannot only view information, buy goods or services, or obtain content-related products (for example, downloading music, films or games over the Internet). With the availability of Web 2.0 technology, individuals can also participate in social or professional networks enabling them to generate content and share it with those who have a common interest.

Enterprises

The survey on ICT usage in enterprises covers enterprises with 10 or more persons employed. Its activity coverage is restricted to those enterprises whose principal activity is within NACE Rev. 1.1 Sections D, F, G, I and K and Groups 55.1, 55.2, 92.1 and 92.2, in other words manufacturing, construction, distributive trades, hotels and other accommodation, transport, storage and communication, real estate, renting and business activities, motion picture, video, radio and television activities. A distinction is made according to the size of enterprises in terms of persons employed into small (10-49 persons employed), medium-sized (50-249) and large enterprises (250 or more persons employed).

Sharing information within the enterprise means sharing information electronically and automatically between different functions of the enterprise under any of the following aspects:

- using one single software application to support the different functions of the enterprise;
- data linking between the software applications that support the different functions of the enterprise;
- using a common database or data warehouse accessed by the software applications that support the different functions of the enterprise, or
- automated data exchange between different software systems.

The sharing of information in this survey was studied in case of receipt of a sales order with at least one of the following functions: management of inventory levels, accounting, production or services management, distribution management; in case of sending of a purchase order with at least one of the following functions: management of inventory levels or accounting.

Sharing information outside the enterprise means sharing information electronically on supply chain management under the following aspects:

- exchanging all types of information with suppliers and/or customers in order to coordinate the availability and delivery of products or services to the final consumer;
- including information on demand forecasts, inventories, production, distribution or product development;
- via computer networks, not only the Internet but also other connections between computers of different enterprises;
- excluding normal e-mail messages manually written.

Indicators relating to **interaction with public authorities** by enterprises use a concept of public authorities that is as wide as possible, referring to both public services and administration activities. Administration refers to obligations and rights in the country (so-called 'red tape'), public services referring to non-administrative tasks or competences of government bodies, for example offering a public library's catalogue on-line. **Obtaining information** refers to searches for information from public authority websites. **Obtaining forms** includes downloading official forms for any purpose of use (for example for information or for requesting a service). **Returning filled in forms** (for example provision of statistical information

to public authorities), includes filled in forms sent via Internet only. **Treating an administrative procedure completely electronically** includes only administrative procedures (for example registration, authorisation request) for which all steps can be treated electronically by means of the Internet without the need for additional paper work, including possible payments, signatures, etc. **Submitting a proposal in an electronic tender system** (e-procurement) includes the submission of proposals in Internet-based systems (either based on web interfaces or any other architecture).

E-commerce is defined as ordering or selling goods and services over computer mediated networks. On-line purchases or orders received exclude those relating to manually typed e-mail purchases or orders received. The indicator on enterprises having **received orders or made purchases on-line** covers on-line selling and EDI via Internet or via other computer networks within the year prior to the survey. Only enterprises buying/selling more than 1 % on-line are included.

Data on **information technology (IT) expenditure** covers expenditure for IT hardware, equipment, software and other services.

Main findings

During the last decade, information and communication technologies (ICTs) have become widely available to the general public, in terms of accessibility as well as cost. A boundary was crossed in 2007, when a majority (54 %) of households across the EU-27 had Internet access and this proportion grew still further in 2008

(60 %). The highest proportion (86 %) of households with Internet access in 2008 was recorded in the Netherlands, the lowest (25 %) in Bulgaria. Widespread and affordable broadband access is one of the means of promoting the knowledge-based and informed society. In almost all Member States, broadband was by far the most common form of Internet access (an average of 49 % of all EU-27 households in 2008 compared with 11 % of households that used dial-up access or ISDN access), the exception being Romania.

Two thirds (66 %) of individuals in the EU-27, aged between 16 and 74 years, used a computer in the three months before the 2008 ICT survey. A similar proportion (62 %) of individuals used the Internet. The proportion of individuals using a computer and the Internet in the three months before the 2008 survey rose to between 80 % and 90 % in Sweden, the Netherlands, Denmark, Finland and Luxembourg, but was in a minority in Bulgaria, Greece, Italy, Portugal, Cyprus and particularly in Romania. Almost one third (32 %) of individuals in the EU-27 used the Internet for services related to travel and accommodation in 2008, the spread among Member States being from less than 10 % of individuals in Bulgaria and Romania to between 50 % and 60 % of individuals in Finland, the Netherlands and Luxembourg.

Among Internet users, in other words, those EU-27 individuals using the Internet in the three months before the ICT survey, a large majority (86 %) accessed the Internet from home. By comparison, about one half of this proportion accessed it at work (42 %), around double the proportion accessing from a friend, neighbour or relative's house (22 %). While 87 % of all individuals aged 16 to 74 used a mobile phone, the proportion of individuals who used a mobile phone for browsing the Internet was only 6 % in EU-27. Finland and Sweden had the highest shares (16 %) for web browsing via a mobile phone.

Of the 62 % of individuals in the EU-27 that used the Internet in the three months before the 2008 ICT survey, seven in every ten accessed the Internet on a daily or almost daily basis. Among Internet users, the proportion of those who used the Internet on a daily basis was highest in Denmark (85 %) and Italy (84 %), the latter despite a relatively low overall rate of Internet use.

Almost two fifths (38 %) of individuals across the EU-27 used the Internet to obtain or share digital content. Looking at selected activities, 28 % of individuals downloaded music or films and 9 % downloaded computer or video games. The proportion of individuals having uploaded self-created content such as text, images, photos, videos or music to any website to be shared was 11 %.

A large minority (40 %) of enterprises in the EU-27 had some form of automated data exchange with an ICT system outside their own enterprise in 2008. For example, about one quarter (27 %) of all enterprises automatically sent payment instructions to financial institutions, similar shares exchanging data with public authorities (25 %) and with customers and/or suppliers (25 %). In motion picture, video, radio and TV activities, a small majority (53 %) of enterprises carried out automated data exchanges. In contrast, only one third (32 %) of hotels,

camping and other accommodation enterprises and of construction enterprises carried out automated data exchanges with ICT systems outside their own enterprise in 2008. Sharing information automatically within the same enterprise (for different functions) or outside on the supply chain grew with enterprise size: more than two thirds (70 %) of large enterprises (those employing at least 250 persons) shared within the enterprise and one third (32 %) had automated supply chain management systems in place, which represented more than double the rates for small enterprises (10-49 persons employed).

Around two thirds (68 %) of enterprises made use of e-government services in 2008: a majority using e-government services to obtain information and to download forms (in both cases 61 %), while 50 % of enterprises returned filled in forms. The take-up of e-government services among enterprises was particularly strong (all above 90 % of enterprises) in Finland, Ireland, Denmark and Luxembourg in 2008. Romania was the only Member State to report a minority of enterprises making use of e-government services.

About six in every ten enterprises (64 %) in the EU-27 with over ten persons employed (excluding those in the financial sector) had their own website in 2008. This share increased with enterprise size, as nine out of ten large enterprises had their own website; overall rates were highest in Denmark and Sweden.

Some 16 % of enterprises in the EU-27 received orders on-line during 2007, which was about three fifths of the proportion of enterprises (28 %) that used computer networks to place orders to purchase goods or services. The percentage of enterprises purchasing or selling on-line tends to rise with the size of the enterprise. It may be easier for large enterprises to finance investments for the introduction of e-commerce services. The general pattern across Member States is one where a considerably higher proportion of enterprises have made purchases on-line when compared with those that have received orders on-line (probably reflecting the greater complexity of setting up an on-line selling system compared with making purchases). Almost one third (32 %) of all enterprises in the United Kingdom received orders on-line

in 2008, while corresponding shares were also equal to or above one quarter in the Netherlands and Ireland. In contrast, a small majority of enterprises in Ireland, Germany and Sweden made purchases on-line in 2008, with upwards of 40 % of all enterprises in the United Kingdom and the Netherlands also making purchases on-line.

Compared with Japan or the United States, the EU has a relatively low share of ICT expenditure, expressed as a share of GDP; expenditure on information technology represented 2.7 % of GDP in the EU-27 in 2006, compared with 3.4 % in Japan and 3.3 % in the United States.

Table 7.16: Use of ICTs and use of on-line services for travel and accommodation
(% of individuals aged 16 to 74)

	Computer use			Internet use			Used Internet for services related to travel and accommodation		
	2006	**2007**	**2008**	**2006**	**2007**	**2008**	**2006**	**2007**	**2008**
EU-27	59	63	66	52	57	62	25	31	32
Euro area (¹)	60	64	66	53	59	63	25	33	34
Belgium	67	70	71	62	67	69	30	34	36
Bulgaria	30	35	40	24	31	35	4	5	6
Czech Republic	52	55	63	44	49	58	22	25	26
Denmark	86	84	86	83	81	84	45	51	47
Germany	76	78	80	69	72	75	41	45	42
Estonia	62	65	66	61	64	66	20	21	27
Ireland	58	62	67	51	57	63	37	39	41
Greece	38	40	44	29	33	38	12	16	17
Spain	54	57	61	48	52	57	16	33	35
France	55	69	71	47	64	68	15	30	38
Italy	43	43	46	36	38	42	15	18	20
Cyprus	44	47	47	34	38	39	16	23	18
Latvia	53	58	63	50	55	61	18	18	25
Lithuania	47	52	56	42	49	53	12	14	15
Luxembourg	76	80	83	71	78	81	48	55	50
Hungary	54	58	63	45	52	59	20	24	23
Malta	43	48	51	38	45	49	15	21	22
Netherlands	84	87	88	81	84	87	43	48	50
Austria	68	73	76	61	67	71	26	28	32
Poland	48	52	55	40	44	49	11	11	14
Portugal	42	46	46	36	40	42	13	14	12
Romania	30	34	35	21	24	29	4	5	7
Slovenia	57	58	60	51	53	56	24	26	26
Slovakia	61	64	72	50	56	66	21	26	29
Finland	80	81	84	77	79	83	53	57	58
Sweden	87	88	89	86	80	88	45	41	46
United Kingdom	73	78	80	66	72	76	47	46	48
Croatia	:	47	46	:	38	42	:	10	15
FYR of Macedonia	34	:	50	25	:	42	2	:	7
Iceland	90	91	92	88	90	91	61	60	62
Norway	85	90	90	81	85	89	51	55	61
Serbia	:	41	:	:	30	:	:	9	:

(¹) EA-15 instead of EA-16.

Source: Eurostat (isoc_ci_cfp_cu, isoc_ci_ifp_iu and isoc_ci_ac_i)

Figure 7.23: Internet access of households
(% of all households)

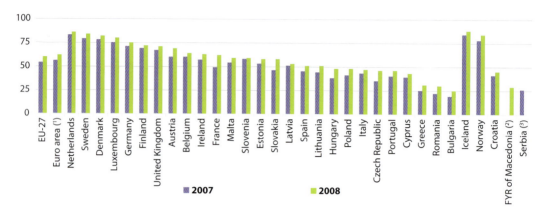

(¹) EA-13 in 2007; EA-15 in 2008.
(²) 2007, not available.
(³) 2008, not available.

Source: Eurostat (tsiir040)

Figure 7.24: Internet access of households by type of connection, 2008
(% of all households)

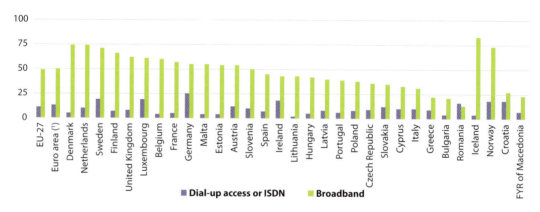

(¹) EA-15 instead of EA-16.

Source: Eurostat (tin00073)

Table 7.17: Place of Internet use, 2008
(% of individuals aged 16 to 74 who used the Internet in the three months prior to the survey)

	Home	Place of work (other than home)	Place of education	Neighbour, friend or relative's house	Other place
EU-27	86	42	13	22	12
Euro area (¹)	86	43	11	23	13
Belgium	92	34	11	8	5
Bulgaria	81	33	12	4	10
Czech Republic	83	39	17	13	5
Denmark	95	53	13	14	10
Germany	91	41	9	20	11
Estonia	87	39	13	11	5
Ireland	83	39	11	4	5
Greece	70	43	11	13	22
Spain	78	44	12	25	20
France	86	39	9	36	12
Italy	79	46	13	21	18
Cyprus	77	49	12	18	14
Latvia	82	37	17	24	15
Lithuania	86	38	20	19	10
Luxembourg	94	44	10	14	15
Hungary	81	36	20	23	10
Malta	93	36	8	12	4
Netherlands	97	51	13	19	6
Austria	80	51	10	12	10
Poland	82	30	18	19	7
Portugal	80	41	20	31	17
Romania	77	31	20	9	4
Slovenia	86	51	16	29	18
Slovakia	74	51	18	23	12
Finland	91	54	20	36	22
Sweden	94	54	14	21	15
United Kingdom	90	45	14	20	11
Croatia	80	40	17	15	5
FYR of Macedonia	62	21	18	17	36
Iceland	96	60	28	44	28
Norway	95	60	16	22	17

(¹) EA-15 instead of EA-16.

Source: Eurostat (isoc_pibi_pai)

Figure 7.25: Frequency of Internet use, 2008
(% of individuals aged 16 to 74)

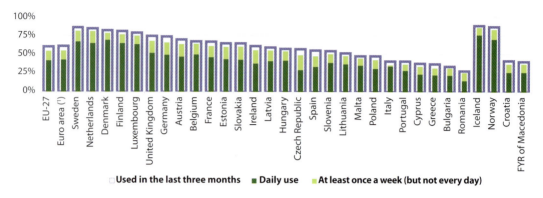

(¹) EA-15 instead of EA-16.

Source: Eurostat (isoc_ci_ifp_iu and isoc_ci_ifp_fu)

Figure 7.26: Individuals who ordered goods or services over the Internet for private use in the twelve months prior to the survey
(% of individuals aged 16 to 74)

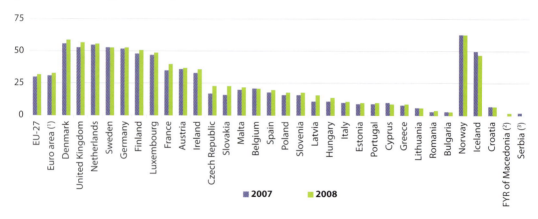

(¹) EA-13 in 2007; EA-15 in 2008. (²) 2007, not available. (³) 2008, not available.

Source: Eurostat (isoc_ec_ibuy)

Figure 7.27: Individuals using a mobile phone for browsing the Internet, 2008
(% of individuals aged 16 to 74)

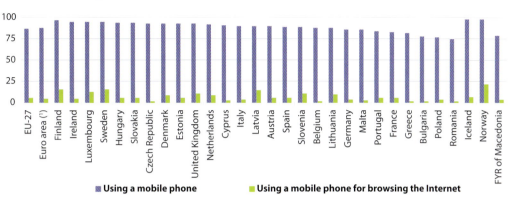

(¹) EA-15 instead of EA-16.

Source: Eurostat (isoc_cias_mph)

Table 7.18: Individuals using the Internet for obtaining and sharing content, 2008
(% of individuals aged 16 to 74)

	Using the Internet for obtaining and sharing content			Individuals using the Internet for selected content-related activities		
	Total	Male	Female	Downloading, listening or watching music and/or films	Downloading computer or video games	Uploading self-created content to any website to be shared
EU-27	38	43	32	28	9	11
Euro area (¹)	38	44	32	28	10	11
Belgium	31	34	27	23	6	5
Bulgaria	24	27	22	21	6	3
Czech Republic	26	32	20	19	5	2
Denmark	57	63	51	36	11	14
Germany	43	53	33	29	18	14
Estonia	36	42	31	25	11	21
Ireland	27	30	23	19	5	8
Greece	24	29	19	19	6	4
Spain	40	45	35	31	7	8
France	48	51	45	38	6	17
Italy	21	26	16	15	4	7
Cyprus	22	27	17	16	7	6
Latvia	42	47	37	33	13	19
Lithuania	35	40	32	32	12	8
Luxembourg	57	67	47	42	9	15
Hungary	37	40	34	30	13	17
Malta	35	38	32	29	12	5
Netherlands	61	68	54	46	15	19
Austria	31	39	23	20	6	8
Poland	31	35	28	21	7	7
Portugal	27	32	21	19	7	7
Romania	19	22	17	16	8	5
Slovenia	38	39	36	29	9	10
Slovakia	38	45	32	28	11	4
Finland	53	59	48	34	7	9
Sweden	55	62	47	34	8	15
United Kingdom	46	52	39	34	10	19
Croatia	24	31	18	18	6	6
FYR of Macedonia	34	39	29	28	9	5
Iceland	68	71	65	37	9	20
Norway	63	72	55	42	14	12

(¹) EA-15 instead of EA-16.

Source: Eurostat (isoc_cias_av)

Figure 7.28: Automated data exchange between the enterprise and ICT systems outside the own enterprise, EU-27, January 2008 (¹)
(% of enterprises)

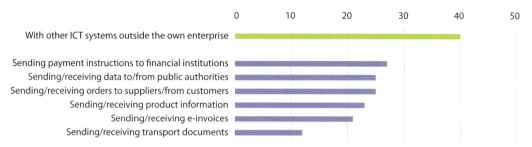

(¹) Automated data exchange between the enterprise and ICT systems outside the own enterprise covers:
– exchange of messages (e.g. orders, invoices, payment transactions or description of goods);
– via the Internet or other computer networks;
– in an agreed format which allows its automatic processing (e.g. XML, EDIFACT etc.);
– without the individual message being manually typed.
Enterprises with 10 or more persons employed; enterprises that have their main activity in NACE Rev. 1.1 Sections D, F, G, I and K or Groups 55.1, 55.2, 92.1 and 92.2.

Source: Eurostat (isoc_pibi_isc)

Figure 7.29: Automated data exchange between the enterprise and ICT systems outside the enterprise, EU-27, January 2008 (¹)
(% of enterprises)

(¹) Automated data exchange between the enterprise and ICT systems outside the own enterprise covers:
– exchange of messages (e.g. orders, invoices, payment transactions or description of goods);
– via the Internet or other computer networks;
– in an agreed format which allows its automatic processing (e.g. XML, EDIFACT etc.);
– without the individual message being manually typed.
Enterprises with 10 or more persons employed; enterprises that have their main activity in NACE Rev. 1.1 Sections D, F, G, I and K or Groups 55.1, 55.2, 92.1 and 92.2.

Source: Eurostat (isoc_pibi_isc)

Table 7.19: Enterprises using the Internet for interacting with public authorities, 2008 (¹)
(% of enterprises)

	E-government usage by enterprises	Obtaining information	Down-loading official forms	Returning filled in forms	Treating admin. procedures electronically	E-procurement
EU-27	68	61	61	50	39	9
Euro area (²)	70	62	62	52	42	9
Belgium	69	:	:	49	47	7
Bulgaria	58	53	51	43	36	8
Czech Republic	73	70	63	35	20	8
Denmark	90	86	85	65	45	8
Germany	56	47	48	45	30	10
Estonia	77	75	75	62	46	12
Ireland	91	84	85	68	63	26
Greece	83	68	66	66	53	:
Spain	64	59	60	45	40	5
France	73	67	66	67	68	13
Italy	82	74	71	42	41	9
Cyprus	65	62	55	18	26	0
Latvia	55	51	50	39	30	8
Lithuania	86	83	85	75	57	20
Luxembourg	90	82	87	41	28	7
Hungary	60	56	58	50	25	9
Malta	74	73	68	46	37	7
Netherlands	85	77	79	75	16	6
Austria	80	71	75	59	44	16
Poland	68	56	58	60	20	6
Portugal	75	67	69	68	54	14
Romania	39	37	35	23	20	10
Slovenia	88	85	82	69	60	11
Slovakia	88	82	81	51	54	7
Finland	95	90	92	81	46	0
Sweden	78	76	76	58	30	11
United Kingdom	64	60	57	51	43	9
Croatia	57	52	54	37	33	17
Iceland	91	89	85	87	73	11
Norway	76	70	70	63	40	16

(¹) Enterprises with 10 or more persons employed; enterprises that have their main activity in NACE Rev. 1.1 Sections D, F, G, I and K or Groups 55.1, 55.2, 92.1 and 92.2; the year given relates to the survey year; the e-government data relates to the year prior to the survey.
(²) EA-15 instead of EA-16.

Source: Eurostat (tsiir140 and tin00065)

Table 7.20: Enterprises having a website or a homepage by size-class, 2008 ([1])
(% of enterprises)

	All enterprises	Small	Medium	Large
EU-27	64	60	80	91
Euro area ([2])	65	61	82	92
Belgium	76	72	89	95
Bulgaria	33	28	48	69
Czech Republic	74	70	86	92
Denmark	87	85	94	96
Germany	77	73	89	94
Estonia	66	62	83	92
Ireland	65	60	83	95
Greece	60	56	76	88
Spain	54	51	72	89
France	54	50	71	85
Italy	58	55	81	91
Cyprus	48	42	77	95
Latvia	42	37	61	86
Lithuania	55	49	73	91
Luxembourg	64	60	77	94
Hungary	48	44	65	77
Malta	57	53	72	87
Netherlands	85	83	94	96
Austria	79	77	90	97
Poland	57	50	77	88
Portugal	46	42	68	92
Romania	27	25	37	61
Slovenia	71	67	84	97
Slovakia	73	72	78	84
Finland	82	79	94	94
Sweden	86	84	95	97
United Kingdom	76	71	91	98
Croatia	64	61	75	84
Iceland	77	74	:	100
Norway	73	70	87	90

([1]) Enterprises with 10 or more persons employed; enterprises that have their main activity in NACE Rev. 1.1 Sections D, F, G, I and K or Groups 55.1, 55.2, 92.1 and 92.2; small enterprises: 10-49 persons employed; medium-sized enterprises: 50-249 persons employed; large enterprises: 250 or more persons employed.
([2]) EA-15 instead of EA-16.

Source: Eurostat (isoc_pi_b3)

Figure 7.30: Enterprises sharing information automatically within the enterprise for different functions and outside the enterprise on supply chain management, by size-class, EU-27, January 2008 (¹)
(% of enterprises)

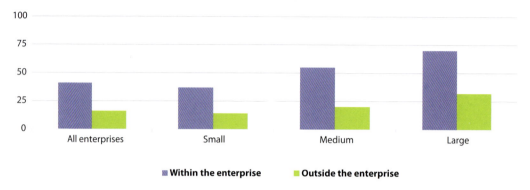

(¹) Enterprises with 10 or more persons employed; enterprises that have their main activity in NACE Rev. 1.1 Sections D, F, G, I and K or Groups 55.1, 55.2, 92.1 and 92.2; small enterprises: 10-49 persons employed; medium-sized enterprises: 50-249 persons employed; large enterprises: 250 or more persons employed.

Source: Eurostat (isoc_pibi_ibp and isoc_pibi_isc)

Figure 7.31: Enterprises sharing information automatically within the enterprise for different functions and outside the enterprise on supply chain management, by economic activity, EU-27, January 2008 (¹)
(% of enterprises)

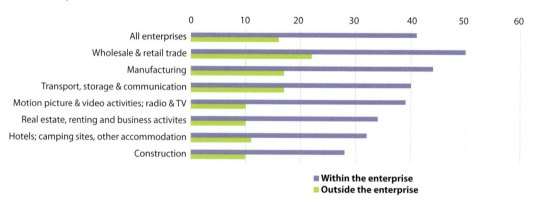

(¹) Enterprises with 10 or more persons employed; enterprises that have their main activity in NACE Rev. 1.1 Sections D, F, G, I and K or Groups 55.1, 55.2, 92.1 and 92.2; the figure is ranked on the average of within and outside the enterprise.

Source: Eurostat (isoc_pibi_ibp and isoc_pibi_isc)

Figure 7.32: E-commerce among enterprises by size-class, EU-27, 2008 (¹)

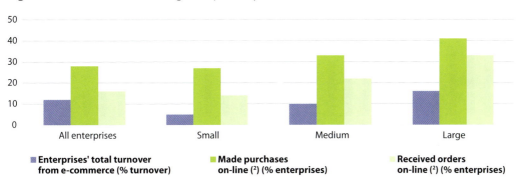

- ■ **Enterprises' total turnover from e-commerce (% turnover)**
- ■ **Made purchases on-line (²) (% enterprises)**
- ■ **Received orders on-line (²) (% enterprises)**

(¹) Enterprises with 10 or more persons employed; enterprises that have their main activity in NACE Rev. 1.1 Sections D, F, G, I and K or Groups 55.1, 55.2, 92.1 and 92.2; small enterprises: 10-49 persons employed; medium-sized enterprises: 50-249 persons employed; large enterprises: 250 or more persons employed.
(²) Only enterprises having made purchases/received orders on-line of at least 1 % of total purchases/total turnover.

Source: Eurostat (isoc_ec_eval, isoc_ec_ebuy and isoc_ec_esel)

Figure 7.33: Enterprises having received orders/made purchases on-line, 2008 (¹)
(% of enterprises)

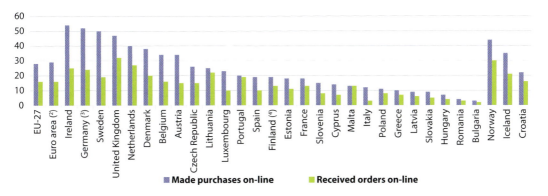

- ■ **Made purchases on-line**
- ■ **Received orders on-line**

(¹) Enterprises with 10 or more persons employed; enterprises that have their main activity in NACE Rev. 1.1 Sections D, F, G, I and K or Groups 55.1, 55.2, 92.1 and 92.2; only enterprises having made purchases/received orders on-line of at least 1 % of total purchases/total turnover.
(²) EA-15 instead of EA-16.
(³) 2007.
(⁴) Made purchases on-line, 2007.

Source: Eurostat (isoc_ec_ebuy and tin00068)

Figure 7.34: Information technology expenditure, 2006 (¹) (% of GDP)

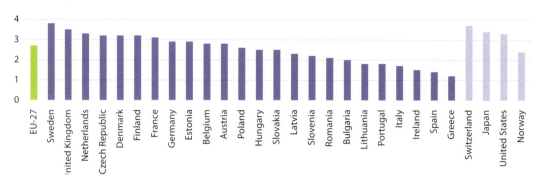

(¹) Cyprus, Luxembourg and Malta, not available.

Source: Eurostat (tsiir090), European Information Technology Observatory (EITO)

7.6 Telecommunications

Introduction

Telecommunication networks and services are the backbone of Europe's developing information society. Individuals, enterprises and public organisations alike have come to rely ever more on convenient, reliable networks and services.

The European telecommunications sector was historically characterised by public service, monopoly providers, often run in conjunction with postal services. Liberalisation moves began in the first half of the 1980s and, at first, concerned value added services or business users, while basic services were left in the hands of monopoly providers. By 1998, telecommunications were, in principle, fully liberalised across all of the Member States. The liberalisation of telecommunication markets has led to considerable reduc-

tions in prices. This may, in part, reflect the introduction of competition into a number of markets that were previously the domain of incumbent, monopoly suppliers, as well as reflecting technological changes that have increased capacity and made it possible to communicate not only by voice, but also over the Internet. Market regulation has nonetheless continued, and the European Commission oversees this to ensure that consumers benefit. Regulation continues to monitor the significant market power of former monopolies, ensure universal service and protect consumers, especially those social groups that may otherwise face exclusion.

On 30 June 2007, a new set of rules on mobile phone roaming entered into force. These foresee that people travelling within the EU are able to phone across borders at more affordable and transparent prices. The so-called roaming Regulation ([8]) put in place a set of maximum prices for phone calls made and received while abroad (Eurotariff); these maximum prices apply to all consumers unless they opt for special packages offered by operators. The European Commission and national regulators have closely monitored price developments for text messages and data services. On the basis of this monitoring, a review was conducted which came to the conclusion that competition has not encouraged mobile operators to voluntarily reduce very high roaming charges for text messages. The European Commission therefore proposed on 23 September 2008:

- to bring down prices for text messages sent while travelling in another EU Member State;
- to ensure that consumers are kept informed of the charges that apply for data roaming services;
- to introduce a Euro-SMS Tariff from 1 July 2009 so that sending an SMS from abroad would cost no more than 11 cents (excluding VAT), while receiving an SMS in another EU Member State would remain free of charge;
- to improve transparency so that customers travelling to another Member State should receive an automated message of the charges that apply for data roaming services upon arrival; while from 1 July 2010, operators should provide customers with the opportunity to determine in advance how much they want to spend before a data roaming service is 'cut-off';

- to restrict to EUR 1 per megabyte wholesale data roaming fees, so these are more predictable for operators;
- to reduce further the cost of Eurotariff voice calls, with the price for making calls decreasing from 43 cents on 1 July 2009, to 40 cents, 37 cents and 34 cents in each of the subsequent years, while the price of receiving a call would decrease from 19 cents on 1 July 2009 to 16 cents, 13 cents and 10 cents.

Definitions and data availability

Eurostat's data collection in relation to **telecommunications statistics** is conducted through the use of a predefined questionnaire (TELECOM), which is sent on annual basis to the national statistical institutes. They collect information from their relevant regulatory authorities and send the completed questionnaires back to Eurostat.

Main telephone lines are the traditional way of connecting to communication networks. They are usually used for voice telephony, but may also be used for accessing the Internet via a modem or dial-up connection. The rapid growth of more powerful means to access the Internet (broadband) and mobile communications has eroded somewhat the market for traditional fixed telecommunication networks.

Indicators presented in relation to market share refer to fixed-line telecommunications and mobile telephony. The **incumbent** for **fixed-line telephony** is defined as the enterprise active in the market just before liberalisation. The market share is calculated on the basis of retail revenues. Indicators relating to

---

([8]) Regulation (EC)No 717/2007 of the European Parliament and of the Council of 27 June 2007 on roaming on public mobile telephone networks within the Community and amending Directive 2002/21/EC; for more information: http://eur-lex.europa.eu/LexUriServ/LexUriServ.do?uri=OJ:L:2007:171:0032:0040:EN:PDF.

the **mobile market** refer to the number of subscriptions to public cellular mobile telecommunication systems and also include active pre-paid cards. Note that an increasing number of people have multiple mobile subscriptions (for example, for private and work use, or for use in different countries). **SMS** messages are short-message services, traditionally sent between mobile phones, but also between a range of other SMS-enabled devices and on-line web services.

Data on **expenditure for telecommunications** covers hardware, equipment, software and other services. The data are not collected by Eurostat; further methodological information is available at: http://www.eito.com/.

Telecommunications prices are based on the price (including VAT) in euro of a 10-minute call at 11 am on a weekday in August, based on normal rates. Three markets are presented, namely a **local call** (3 km), a **national long-distance call** (200 km) and an **international call** (to the United States). The data are not collected by Eurostat; further methodological information is available at: http://www.teligen.com/.

Main findings

Telecommunications expenditure accounted for 3.0 % of GDP in the EU-27 in 2006, compared with 2.1 % in the United States and 4.2 % in Japan. The highest

relative levels of expenditure were generally recorded in those Member State that have joined the EU since 2004 (Cyprus and Malta, not available), in particular in the Baltic Member States, Bulgaria and Romania.

Although overall expenditure on telephony has increased, the proportion accounted for by ex-monopoly providers has generally been reduced, as the share of the total telecommunication market accounted for by fixed-line voice operations has shrunk, whereas growth has been concentrated in mobile markets and other data services. The incumbents in fixed telecommunications markets across the EU-25 accounted for 72 % of local calls in 2005, 66 % of national calls and 56 % of international calls. In contrast, the share of the leading operator in the mobile market was relatively low at 39 % in 2006.

The average number of mobile subscriptions per 100 inhabitants stood at 106 in the EU-27 in 2006, and surpassed parity (100) in 17 of the Member States, where there were more subscriptions than inhabitants.

Total turnover in value terms is based on sales from all telecommunication services, including leased lines, fixed network services, cellular mobile telecommunication services, interconnection services, and Internet service provisions. In the majority of Member States (with data available) turnover from mobile services exceeded that from fixed network services in 2006.

The price of telecommunications fell between 2004 and 2006 in a large number of Member States. Price reductions were most apparent for national long-distance and international calls (defined here as calls to the United States), as on average in the EU-25 the price of a national long-distance call fell by almost 20 % between 2004 and 2006, while the price of an international call fell by almost 16 %. In comparison, there was a modest reduction in the price of a local call, which fell by less than 3 %.

The prices of local, national long-distance or international calls varied greatly across the Member States in 2006. Local and national long-distance calls were most expensive in Slovakia, while the price of international calls was highest in Latvia. The cheapest tariff for local calls was found in Spain, for national long-distance calls in Cyprus, and for calls to the United States in Germany.

Figure 7.35: Communications expenditure, 2006 (¹)
(% of GDP)

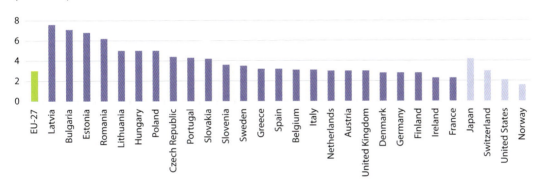

(¹) Cyprus, Luxembourg and Malta, not available.

Source: Eurostat (tsiir090), European Information Technology Observatory (EITO)

Table 7.21: Market share of incumbents in fixed telecommunications and leading operators in mobile telecommunications
(% of total market)

	Fixed telecommunications, 2005			Leading operator in mobile telecommunications, 2006 (³)
	Local calls (¹)	National long-distance calls (²)	International calls (²)	
EU-25	72	66	56	39
Belgium	68	68	58	45
Bulgaria	:	:	:	:
Czech Republic	76	63	65	41
Denmark	:	:	:	32
Germany	56	57	39	37
Estonia	:	:	:	46
Ireland	83	63	62	47
Greece	78	73	74	41
Spain	78	75	62	46
France	80	68	67	46
Italy	71	73	47	41
Cyprus	:	:	86	90
Latvia	97	98	72	35
Lithuania	97	88	76	36
Luxembourg	:	:	:	51
Hungary	92	90	87	45
Malta	99	99	98	52
Netherlands	75	75	45	48
Austria	53	59	50	39
Poland	85	70	71	34
Portugal	:	78	80	46
Romania	:	:	:	:
Slovenia	100	100	83	71
Slovakia	99	100	88	56
Finland	95	45	41	45
Sweden	:	:	:	43
United Kingdom	60	52	53	26
Norway	:	73	61	57

(¹) Austria and Finland, 2004.
(²) Finland, 2004.
(³) Norway, 2005.

Source: Eurostat (tsier070 and tsier080), National Regulatory Authorities

7

Figure 7.36: Mobile phone subscriptions and the use of SMS, 2006

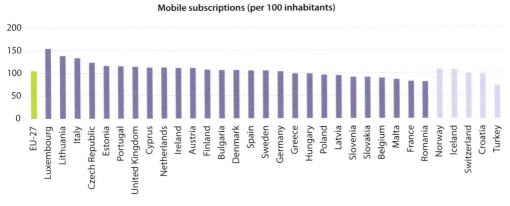

Mobile subscriptions (per 100 inhabitants)

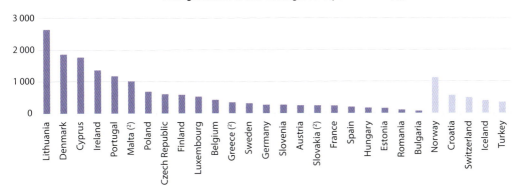

Average number of SMS messages sent (per inhabitant) (¹)

(¹) Data for SMS in Italy, Latvia, the Netherlands and the United Kingdom, not available.
(²) 2005 instead of 2006.

Source: Eurostat (tin00060, isoc_tc_sms and tps00001)

Table 7.22: Turnover from telecommunications, 2006 ([1])
(EUR million)

| | Total turnover | of which: | | |
		Fixed network services	Cellular mobile services	Internet service provision
Belgium	9 721	863	4 226	:
Bulgaria	*1 754*	399	920	73
Czech Republic	4 304	1 503	2 458	287
Denmark ([2])	5 433	1 314	1 949	214
Germany ([3])	66 200	21 900	23 100	3 400
Estonia ([4])	557	165	400	:
Ireland	4 284	2 180	1 924	:
Greece ([5])	8 034	3 284	4 305	123
Spain	42 006	7 734	13 402	2 786
France	47 448	11 420	16 771	3 739
Italy	:	:	:	:
Cyprus	303	111	158	34
Latvia	:	:	:	:
Lithuania	781	123	359	77
Luxembourg ([4])	593	238	248	29
Hungary	4 792	768	1 461	323
Malta ([5])	175	57	79	8
Netherlands	14 241	4 678	7 243	:
Austria	4 719	1 401	2 708	520
Poland	:	:	:	:
Portugal ([3])	7 781	1 601	2 112	255
Romania ([6])	4 307	848	1 510	228
Slovenia	1 049	205	406	127
Slovakia ([5])	1 492	307	898	64
Finland	4 511	573	2 260	:
Sweden	8 659	2 108	1 820	861
United Kingdom	:	:	:	:
Croatia	1 945	699	1 089	96
Turkey	9 167	3 925	5 165	597
Iceland ([5])	374	102	160	23
Norway	3 862	1 090	1 782	653
Switzerland ([3])	*10 363*	*2 951*	*3 009*	113

([1]) Possibility of double counting in the breakdown of the total turnover.
([2]) Cellular and Internet services, 2005.
([3]) Internet services, 2005.
([4]) Total turnover, 2005.
([5]) 2005.
([6]) Fixed, cellular and Internet services, 2005.

Source: Eurostat (isoc_tc_tur)

Table 7.23: Price of fixed telecommunications (¹)
(EUR per 10-minute call)

	Local calls			National long-distance calls			Calls to the United States		
	2001	2005	2006	2001	2005	2006	2001	2005	2006
EU-25	0.39	0.35	0.36	1.17	0.76	0.74	:	2.11	1.79
Belgium	0.54	0.57	0.57	0.54	0.57	0.57	1.84	1.98	1.98
Bulgaria	:	:	:	:	:	:	:	:	:
Czech Republic	0.40	0.56	0.56	2.44	1.13	0.56	:	2.02	2.02
Denmark	0.41	0.37	0.37	0.41	0.37	0.37	2.71	2.38	2.38
Germany	0.43	0.39	0.39	1.23	0.49	0.49	1.23	1.23	0.46
Estonia	0.23	0.23	0.23	0.23	0.23	0.23	:	2.10	2.13
Ireland	0.51	0.49	0.49	0.94	0.82	0.82	1.91	1.91	1.91
Greece	0.36	0.31	0.31	0.98	0.74	0.74	2.91	2.93	3.49
Spain	0.28	0.28	0.19	1.60	0.84	0.85	4.25	1.53	1.53
France	0.39	0.33	0.36	0.96	0.83	0.89	2.97	2.27	2.32
Italy	0.25	0.22	0.22	1.44	1.15	1.15	2.79	2.12	2.12
Cyprus	0.16	0.22	0.22	0.40	0.22	0.22	3.82	0.66	0.66
Latvia	0.36	0.36	0.36	1.03	1.03	1.03	5.92	5.94	5.94
Lithuania	0.35	0.39	0.39	1.20	0.79	0.79	11.96	4.07	4.07
Luxembourg	0.31	0.31	0.31	-	-	-	1.44	1.37	1.37
Hungary	0.35	0.41	0.40	1.23	1.09	1.04	4.29	2.97	2.88
Malta	:	0.25	0.25	-	-	-	:	1.77	1.64
Netherlands	0.32	0.33	0.33	0.48	0.49	0.49	0.78	0.85	0.85
Austria	0.69	0.49	0.49	0.77	0.59	0.59	4.32	1.90	1.90
Poland	0.35	0.30	0.50	1.22	1.22	1.00	10.58	3.74	1.23
Portugal	0.30	0.37	0.37	1.13	0.65	0.65	2.89	3.11	3.11
Romania	:	:	:	:	:	:	:	:	:
Slovenia	0.17	0.26	0.26	0.17	0.26	0.26	2.98	1.40	1.40
Slovakia	0.42	0.60	0.60	1.17	1.23	1.29	8.92	3.02	1.23
Finland	0.23	0.24	0.24	0.88	0.94	0.94	4.80	4.90	4.90
Sweden	0.29	0.29	0.29	0.29	0.29	0.29	1.10	1.06	1.18
United Kingdom	0.59	0.44	0.44	1.17	0.44	0.44	3.50	2.08	2.23
Norway	0.33	0.34	:	0.34	0.34	:	1.18	0.77	:
Japan	0.29	0.25	0.25	1.02	1.02	1.02	4.39	4.39	4.34
United States	0.09	0.07	0.07	0.43	1.03	1.03	-	-	-

(¹) The indicator gives the price in euro of a 10-minute call at 11 am on a weekday (including VAT) for respectively a local call (3 km), a national call (200 km) and an international call to the United States; prices refer to August 2001, August 2005 and September 2006; normal tariffs without special rates are used.

Source: Eurostat (tsier030), Teligen

Agriculture, forestry and fisheries

8

Agriculture was one of the first sectors of the economy (following coal and steel) to receive the attention of EU policymakers. Article 39 of the Treaty of Rome on the EEC (1957) set out the objectives for the first common agricultural policy (CAP); these were focused on increasing agricultural productivity as a way to ensure a fair standard of living for the agricultural community, stabilising markets, and ensuring security of supply at affordable prices to consumers.

As the primary objective of producing more food was realised, food surpluses accrued, distorting trade and raising environmental concerns. These were the principal drivers for changes in the CAP, a process that started in the early 1990s and which resulted in a change from support for production towards a market-oriented and a more environment-friendly and sustainable form of agriculture. These reforms have focused mainly on increasing the competitiveness of agriculture by reducing support prices and compensating farmers by the introduction of direct aid payments. A decisive step came in the 2003/04 CAP reforms with the decoupling of direct aids from production and a move to try to realign the CAP with consumer concerns. The scope of this latest reform of the CAP was widened with the introduction of a comprehensive rural development policy. Together these policies aim to encourage entrepreneurial behaviour so that farm managers can respond better to market signals, introduce new techniques and promote diversified activities such as rural crafts, food processing facilities on farms, tourism, or afforestation, as well as promoting sustainable farming practices and various other rural development measures.

In November 2007, the European Commission adopted a Communication 'preparing the health check of the CAP reform' with the objective of assessing the implementation of the 2003 CAP reforms, and to introduce those adjustments to the reform process that were deemed necessary. Notably, these proposals included a shift in funding from direct payments to greater rural development support.

8.1 Agricultural output, price indices and income

Introduction

One of the principal objectives of the CAP remains providing farmers with a reasonable standard of living. Although this concept is not defined explicitly, one of the measures tracked is the development of incomes from farming activities; economic accounts for agriculture (EAA) are one data source that provides such income measures. This macro-economic set of data is used to analyse the production process of the agricultural activity and the primary income generated by it. The EAA provide key insights into the economic viability of agriculture, its contribution to a Member State's wealth, the structure and composition of agricultural production and inputs, the remuneration of factors of production, relationships between prices and quantities of both inputs and outputs, and responds to the need to have internationally comparable information.

Definitions and data availability

The EAA comprise a production account, a generation of income account, an entrepreneurial income account, some elements of a capital account and agricultural labour input. For the output items of agricultural, hunting and related service activities, Member States transmit to Eurostat values at basic prices, as well as their components (the value at producer prices, subsidies on products and taxes on products). For the items of intermediate consumption, values at purchaser prices are transmitted. The data for the production account and for gross fixed capital formation are transmitted in both current prices and the prices of the previous year.

Animal and crop output are the main product categories of **agricultural output**. The output of agricultural activity includes output sold (including trade in agricultural goods and services between agricultural units), changes in stocks, output for own final use (own final consumption and own-account gross fixed capital formation), output produced for further processing by agricultural producers, as well as intra-unit consumption of livestock feed products. The output of the agricultural industry is made up of the sum of the output of agricultural products and of the goods and services produced in inseparable non-agricultural secondary activities. **Intermediate consumption** represents the value of all goods and services used as inputs in the production process, excluding fixed assets whose consumption is recorded as fixed capital consumption.

Gross value added equals the value of output less the value of intermediate consumption, and is shown here measured at producer prices (the producer price excludes subsidies less taxes on products).

Agricultural income indicators (in the EAA) are presented in the form of an index of real income of factors in agricultural activity per annual work unit (indicator A); the index of real net agricultural entrepreneurial income, per unpaid annual work unit (indicator B), and; net entrepreneurial income of agriculture (indicator C).

Eurostat also collects annual **agricultural prices** (in principle net of VAT) to compare agricultural price levels between Member States and study sales channels. Price indices for agricultural products and the means of agricultural production, on the other hand, are used principally to analyse price developments and their effect on agricultural income. EU agricultural price indices are obtained by a base-weighted Laspeyres calculation (2000=100), and are expressed both in nominal terms and deflated using an implicit HICP deflator.

Main findings

The agricultural industry of the EU-27 generated EUR 141 200 million of gross value added at producer prices in 2008, which represented a modest reduction of 2.4 % in relation to the previous year. Strong increases in both the value of crop output (up 5.7 % to a relative high of EUR 195 700 million in 2008) and animal output (up 7.6 % to a relative high of EUR 148 900 million) were countered by a larger increase in the value of intermediate consumption of goods and services (12.7 % higher in 2008).

Values comprise a volume and price component. One important strand of recent agricultural policy has been the move away from price support, so that prices more accurately reflect market forces and changes in supply and demand. Among the Member States, there were sharp contrasts in the development of deflated agricultural output prices during the period between 2002 and 2008; there were rises in the majority of Member States, the strongest increases being recorded for Malta (average growth of 3.9 % per annum) and the United Kingdom (4.8 % per annum), while reductions were posted in eight of the Member States, the largest of which was in Slovakia (-3.9 % per annum).

Across the EU-27, deflated agricultural output prices rose by an average of 0.9 % per annum in the six-year period through until 2008, although this was far less than the average rate of increase in deflated input prices for the means of agricultural production during the same period (2.4 % per annum). This characteristic was widespread among the Member States: indeed, Germany was the only Member State for whom the deflated price of the means of agricultural production was relatively unchanged over the period in question (an average rate of decline of 0.1 % per annum).

Real net value added at factor cost of agriculture per unit of full-time labour (measured in annual work units), also termed as agricultural income indicator A, declined by an average 3.7 % across the EU-27 in 2008, compared with a relative peak in 2007. There were stark contrasts among the Member States, with increases of between 15 % and 20 % in the United Kingdom and Hungary, and closer to 30 % in Romania and Bulgaria, contrasting with declines of around 20 % to 25 % in Latvia, Belgium, Estonia and Denmark.

Table 8.1: Agricultural output at producer prices
(EUR million)

	Gross value added of the agricultural industry			Crop output			Animal output		
	1998	2003	2008	1998	2003	2008	1998	2003	2008
EU-27	132 898	131 305	141 207	150 700	157 453	195 658	123 116	123 850	148 914
Belgium	2 450	2 172	1 973	3 016	3 051	3 200	3 645	3 361	4 034
Bulgaria	1 802	1 532	1 767	1 315	1 629	2 437	1 658	1 019	1 347
Czech Republic	888	829	923	1 376	1 370	2 460	1 499	1 444	1 984
Denmark	2 067	2 128	2 116	2 635	2 563	3 668	4 316	4 462	5 330
Germany	12 064	10 899	14 376	18 952	17 067	24 610	17 883	18 163	22 113
Estonia	125	140	177	113	153	235	194	203	339
Ireland	1 960	1 621	1 592	1 130	1 303	1 658	3 624	3 535	4 195
Greece	6 005	6 290	5 576	6 434	6 878	6 739	2 245	2 590	2 858
Spain	19 760	23 449	20 427	18 670	24 136	24 279	10 828	12 678	14 280
France	24 947	21 672	24 584	31 342	29 623	36 380	21 959	21 514	24 574
Italy	25 236	25 320	25 743	24 631	25 383	27 682	12 865	13 884	15 352
Cyprus	321	362	311	308	288	318	544	579	616
Latvia	173	185	236	201	246	481	222	208	395
Lithuania	497	389	512	686	662	1 102	514	498	833
Luxembourg	107	97	110	77	79	88	146	147	182
Hungary	1 970	1 727	2 737	2 241	2 652	4 566	2 041	2 224	2 453
Malta	65	55	44	52	42	47	72	69	68
Netherlands	8 824	8 253	8 048	9 130	10 517	11 418	8 259	7 400	9 630
Austria	1 948	2 044	2 669	2 192	2 294	3 002	2 357	2 403	3 082
Poland	5 084	4 036	6 740	6 295	5 646	10 034	5 627	5 500	9 910
Portugal	1 818	2 219	1 867	2 949	3 751	3 824	2 122	2 162	2 562
Romania	5 111	5 547	7 559	5 286	6 885	12 115	4 285	3 671	4 223
Slovenia	452	322	376	477	400	589	499	479	552
Slovakia	456	350	539	630	609	1 240	815	767	862
Finland	538	831	673	1 159	1 403	1 890	1 519	1 688	1 906
Sweden	1 143	1 178	1 247	1 706	1 678	1 951	2 230	2 146	2 308
United Kingdom	7 085	7 657	8 284	7 698	7 144	9 644	11 147	11 056	12 924
FYR of Macedonia	362	429	:	560	707	:	185	206	:
Norway	1 014	948	1 041	1 204	1 252	1 349	1 675	1 783	2 048
Switzerland	3 089	2 540	2 636	3 098	2 870	2 837	3 337	3 307	3 385

Source: Eurostat (aact_eaa01)

Figure 8.1: Agricultural output and gross value added at producer prices, EU-27 (2005=100)

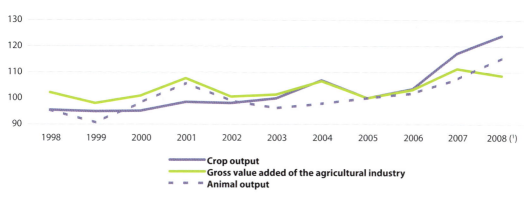

(¹) Estimates.

Source: Eurostat (aact_eaa01)

Table 8.2: Index of income from agricultural activity (indicator A)
(2005=100)

	1998	1999	2000	2001	2002	2003	2004	2005	2006	2007	2008
EU-27	:	:	94.6	103.9	99.5	101.6	109.9	100.0	103.6	112.7	108.5
Belgium	113.2	105.6	119.0	109.1	96.4	106.5	108.3	100.0	120.3	123.0	95.3
Bulgaria	:	:	102.2	114.2	91.9	86.4	84.5	100.0	96.0	98.5	127.0
Czech Republic	64.2	54.0	65.7	83.6	65.4	57.4	90.3	100.0	102.2	129.4	132.6
Denmark	85.7	82.8	106.8	129.0	91.4	89.4	100.7	100.0	107.6	115.8	87.2
Germany	70.7	70.0	90.0	112.0	82.7	76.1	110.4	100.0	104.8	125.7	116.6
Estonia	46.8	30.3	40.3	54.0	51.7	55.0	92.4	100.0	93.7	131.7	101.4
Ireland	78.3	73.1	95.4	90.3	78.9	75.7	80.0	100.0	88.0	97.6	89.1
Greece	121.1	119.2	116.7	116.5	113.1	104.1	98.2	100.0	99.7	101.6	93.5
Spain	106.4	99.8	104.2	112.4	108.9	123.1	113.2	100.0	95.6	100.5	98.0
France	117.8	112.9	111.5	112.4	108.8	106.8	105.2	100.0	110.4	122.2	109.4
Italy	117.6	123.9	117.6	115.3	113.5	113.8	114.4	100.0	96.4	93.8	95.4
Cyprus	:	141.0	106.9	119.1	120.6	111.0	100.6	100.0	102.6	113.6	113.4
Latvia	54.1	39.2	41.1	53.4	52.5	57.6	96.0	100.0	130.8	143.0	115.3
Lithuania	68.0	55.1	52.3	48.5	45.0	50.5	79.8	100.0	91.9	158.6	150.5
Luxembourg	119.8	110.2	104.3	105.4	105.5	99.2	98.9	100.0	97.2	107.0	93.6
Hungary	92.8	72.2	68.7	73.6	62.5	63.0	99.4	100.0	111.7	120.0	142.4
Malta	109.2	104.9	93.7	108.0	107.3	100.4	96.9	100.0	98.9	96.1	83.6
Netherlands	135.7	125.8	127.0	118.6	101.0	108.6	101.0	100.0	119.3	117.0	103.6
Austria	81.8	83.1	90.2	105.7	97.8	97.1	102.2	100.0	107.8	118.7	113.3
Poland	69.3	60.1	61.0	70.1	63.3	58.5	110.2	100.0	110.4	135.1	111.3
Portugal	90.9	112.2	95.3	102.3	97.6	98.5	108.9	100.0	104.4	100.1	103.8
Romania	104.6	81.6	67.1	115.0	106.9	120.8	175.3	100.0	99.3	78.8	101.2
Slovenia	65.4	64.3	71.5	62.1	81.9	64.5	99.5	100.0	97.5	106.3	96.5
Slovakia	80.9	85.6	82.5	93.7	88.6	82.9	107.3	100.0	122.1	128.9	141.3
Finland	61.5	77.0	94.0	91.1	91.7	95.5	95.1	100.0	97.5	102.2	88.7
Sweden	95.9	83.6	91.7	97.8	108.7	107.6	93.1	100.0	106.8	125.7	124.1
United Kingdom	85.6	83.4	81.0	85.1	94.7	108.0	101.3	100.0	104.0	109.7	127.9
FYR of Macedonia	99.7	83.1	77.5	51.3	74.9	87.3	121.3	100.0	112.6	99.5	:
Norway	158.7	143.1	124.2	121.1	126.8	123.3	121.8	100.0	94.0	105.5	101.8
Switzerland	103.9	99.9	103.0	95.7	102.1	94.8	105.9	100.0	97.4	103.4	103.4

Source: Eurostat (tag00057)

Figure 8.2: Evolution of deflated price indices of agricultural output and means of agricultural production, 2002-2008
(average annual growth rate, %)

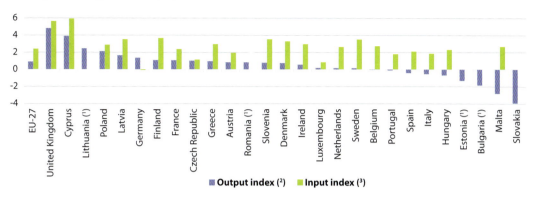

(¹) Input index, not available.
(²) Estonia and Cyprus, 2004-2008; Austria, provisional.
(³) Cyprus and Slovakia, 2004-2007; EU-27, provisional.

Source: Eurostat (tag00046 and tag00052)

Table 8.3: Price indices of agricultural output (nominal), EU-27 (2000=100)

	2000	2001	2002	2003	2004	2005	2006	2007	2008
CROP OUTPUT (including fruit and vegetables)	100.0	105.7	106.7	114.7	113.0	107.7	116.6	133.1	136.1
Cereals (including seeds)	100.0	101.2	93.9	101.0	108.2	90.7	102.6	158.4	161.4
Industrial crops	100.0	108.2	106.2	111.4	113.3	105.9	104.1	113.1	128.6
Forage plants	100.0	113.7	113.8	116.5	125.6	105.8	103.1	118.6	132.7
Vegetables and horticultural products	100.0	105.0	109.3	116.3	107.6	115.1	117.4	121.9	122.0
Potatoes (including seeds)	100.0	125.2	126.0	145.7	141.1	128.8	203.0	198.3	168.4
Fruits	100.0	109.8	115.3	129.3	124.4	120.4	122.3	134.1	144.6
Wine	100.0	95.7	96.6	100.2	102.2	92.3	92.5	98.7	106.8
Olive oil	100.0	96.9	105.4	114.3	124.7	146.3	163.0	135.3	129.8
Other crop products	100.0	103.2	101.7	106.2	103.9	104.8	107.8	125.1	133.4
ANIMAL OUTPUT	100.0	107.4	101.5	101.2	104.1	105.3	107.7	111.9	122.2
Animals	100.0	106.1	97.8	97.0	103.5	106.5	110.9	108.2	119.1
Cattle	100.0	88.5	94.2	96.6	101.4	108.5	116.7	113.8	119.9
Cattle (excluding calves)	100.0	88.6	95.8	97.0	100.4	109.3	116.9	113.0	122.0
Calves	100.0	95.2	96.2	103.4	107.1	103.7	115.4	117.4	108.6
Pigs	100.0	119.9	98.4	91.3	102.6	103.7	107.3	98.5	111.0
Equines	100.0	111.6	109.6	104.3	102.4	104.5	115.7	117.4	145.2
Sheep and goats	100.0	117.4	116.9	119.9	119.6	120.0	122.5	116.2	125.8
Poultry	100.0	107.4	101.5	104.4	104.7	103.6	104.0	117.4	128.1
Other animals	100.0	109.5	91.4	102.5	102.8	102.1	108.4	97.6	108.4
Animal products	100.0	105.8	101.6	102.0	104.8	103.7	103.2	117.2	128.1
Milk	100.0	107.8	103.6	103.1	103.7	103.4	101.5	115.3	126.5
Eggs	100.0	101.7	102.7	119.4	108.7	102.4	110.9	129.5	138.7
Other animal products	100.0	113.2	114.0	105.4	124.0	121.5	129.9	123.2	131.8
AGRICULTURAL GOODS (CROP & ANIMAL OUTPUT)	100.0	106.4	103.9	107.9	108.6	106.5	112.2	122.6	129.3

Source: Eurostat (apri_pi00_outa)

8.2 Agriculture – farm structure and land use

Introduction

The structure of agriculture in the Member States of the EU varies considerably. Among other factors, this reflects differences in geology, topography, climate and natural resources, as well as the diversity of regional activities, infrastructure and social customs. The survey on the structure of agricultural holdings, also known as the farm structure survey (FSS), helps assess the agricultural situation across the EU, monitoring trends and transitions in the structure of holdings, while providing the possibility to model the impact of external developments or policy proposals.

Rural development policy aims to improve competitiveness in agriculture and forestry, improve the environment and countryside, improve the quality of life in rural areas, and encourage the diversification of rural economies. As agriculture modernised and the importance of industry and services within the economy increased, agriculture became much less important as a source of jobs. Consequently, more and more emphasis is placed on the role farmers can play in rural development, including forestry, biodiversity, diversification of the rural economy to create alternative jobs and environmental protection in rural areas. The FSS continues to be adapted to try to provide the necessary data to help analyse and follow these types of developments.

Definitions and data availability

Data on farm structures and land use are collected through the basic farm structure survey (FSS), which is carried out by Member States every 10 years (the full scope being the agricultural census), and intermediate sample surveys that are carried out three times between these basic surveys. The Member States collect information from individual agricultural holdings and, observing strict rules of confidentiality, data are forwarded to Eurostat. The information collected covers land use, livestock numbers, rural development, management and farm labour input (including age, gender and relationship to the holder). The survey data can then be aggregated to different geographic levels (Member States, regions, and for basic surveys also districts) and can be arranged by size-class, area status, legal status of holding, objective zone and farm type.

The basic unit underlying the FSS is the **agricultural holding**. A holding is a technical-economic unit under single management engaged in agricultural production. The FSS covers all agricultural holdings with a utilised agricultural area (UAA) of at least one hectare (ha) and those holdings with a UAA of less than 1 ha if their market production exceeds certain natural thresholds.

Utilised agricultural area (UAA) is defined as the area taken up by arable land, permanent grassland, permanent crops, and kitchen gardens – it does not include wooded areas, forests or other land uses. **Arable land** is worked regularly, generally under a system of crop rotation, normally with annual crops like cereals; it also includes temporary grassland (less than five years), melons and strawberries, seedlings, and crops grown under glass or cover. **Permanent grassland** is land used (for five years or more) to grow herbaceous forage crops; it is usually used for grazing or mowed for silage or hay. **Permanent crops** are those not grown in rotation, occupying the soil for a long period and yielding harvests over several years – for example, olive groves, orchards or vineyards. **Wooded area** on agricultural holdings is land with tree crown cover of more than 5 %, where trees reach a height of at least 5 metres, or where crown cover is over 10 % (irrespective of height). **Built-up and related land** comprises residential land, industrial land, quarries, pits and mines, commercial land, land used by public services, land of mixed use, land used for transport and communications, for technical infrastructure, recreational and other open land; scattered farm buildings, yards and annexes are excluded.

Other gainful activity is any activity other than one relating to farm work, including activities carried out on the holding itself (camping sites, accommodation for tourists, etc.) or that use its resources (machinery, etc.) or products (such as processing farm products, renewable energy production), and which have an economic impact on the holding. Other gainful activity is carried out by the holder, his/her family members, or one or more partners on a group holding.

The **farm labour force** is made up of all persons having completed their compulsory education (having reached school-leaving age) who carried out farm work on the holding under survey during the 12 months up to the survey day. The figures include the holders, even when not working on the holding, whereas their spouses are counted only if they carry out farm work on the holding. The **holder** is the natural person (sole holder or group of individuals) or the legal person (e.g. a cooperative, an institution) on whose account and in whose name the holding is operated and who is legally and economically responsible for the holding, i.e. who takes the economic risks of the holding. For group holdings, only the main holder (one person) is counted. The **regular labour force** covers the family labour force (even those who were working accidentally on the holding) and permanently employed (regular) non-family workers. The **family labour force** includes the holder and the members of his/her family who carried out farm work (including all persons of retiring age who continue to work on the holding).

One **annual work unit** (AWU) corresponds to the work performed by one person who is occupied on an agricultural holding on a full-time basis. **Full-time** means the minimum hours required by the national provisions governing contracts of employment. If these do not indicate the number of hours, then 1 800 hours are taken to be the minimum (225 working days of eight hours each).

Main findings

There were 7.3 million commercial agricultural holdings in the EU-27 in 2007, with a further 6.4 million small holdings (those below a threshold of 1 ESU ([1])). Almost half (48 %) of the small holdings in the EU-27, principally being subsistence in nature, were found in Romania. A little over one third of all the EU-27's commercial agricultural holdings (of a size greater than 1 ESU) in the EU-27 were in Poland (15.4 %) and Italy (18.9 %) in 2007. A further one third of commercial holdings were located in Spain (12.9 %), Romania (11.9 %) and Greece (9.7 %).

Among most Member States and across the EU-27 as a whole, there was a further steady decline in the number of agricultural holdings during the period between 2003 and 2007. In this four-year period, the number of agricultural holdings in the EU-27 declined by 1.3 million (or 8.8 %), of which almost half were commercial holdings. There were particularly fast structural changes in Estonia, where the number of holdings declined by more than one third (-36.7 %), as well as in Bulgaria (-25.9 %), Portugal (-23.4 %) and Hungary (-19.0 %).

The total farm labour force in the EU-27 was the equivalent of 11.7 million full-time workers, of which 9.0 million worked on commercial holdings. Agriculture remains very much a family-oriented activity in the majority of Member States; almost four fifths (78 %) of the total agricultural labour force were farm holders or members of their family. The main excep-

tions were Slovakia (44 %) and the Czech Republic (27 %), where there is a different ownership structure to the majority of Member States. Just over one third (34 %) of the regular agricultural labour force in the EU-27 was female, although in the Baltic Member States this share was closer to half, reaching 50 % in Latvia. There were relatively few (6.1 %) agricultural holders in the EU-27 under the age of 35 years, but a relatively large proportion (34.1 %) over the age of 65 years.

Besides agricultural activity, other gainful activities were also conducted by about one in every ten (9.9 %) of the EU-27's agricultural holdings in 2007, this proportion being slightly higher (13.5 %) among commercial holdings. A little over one quarter (27.6 %) of all holdings in Finland reported another gainful activity in 2007, with rates above 20 % also being recorded in Austria, Germany, Sweden, the United Kingdom, Denmark and France.

Two fifths (an estimated 40.1 %) of the total land area of the EU-27 was utilised agricultural area in 2007. This proportion rose to two thirds (an estimated 66.5 %) of the land area of the United Kingdom, but was less than one tenth of the total in Sweden and Finland. Arable land (which includes cereals and other arable land) accounted for a little less than one quarter (24.2 %) of the total land area of the EU-27, with permanent grassland (which is composed of pasture, meadow and rough grazing) accounting for 13.2 % of the total land area. During the ten years through until 2007, the make-up of land use in the EU-27 did not change very much.

([1]) For each activity ('enterprise') on a holding, or farm (e.g. wheat, dairy cows or vineyard), a standard gross margin (SGM) is estimated, based on the area (or the number of heads) and a regional coefficient. The sum of all margins, for all activities of a given farm, is referred to as the economic size of that farm. The economic size is expressed in European size units (ESU), 1 ESU being equal to EUR 1 200 of SGM.

Table 8.4: Agricultural holdings

	Number of agricultural holdings (1 000)			Holdings with dairy cows (1 000)			Holdings with irrigable area (% of UAA)		
	2003	2005	2007	2003	2005	2007	2003	2005	2007
EU-27	15 021.0	14 482.0	13 700.4	:	:	:	:	:	:
Belgium	54.9	51.5	48.0	16.6	15.2	13.3	4.2	4.2	4.6
Bulgaria	665.6	534.6	493.1	195.0	152.6	120.8	20.5	14.3	14.8
Czech Republic	45.8	42.3	39.4	8.5	6.8	5.6	4.5	4.6	5.2
Denmark	48.6	51.7	44.6	8.0	6.6	5.4	19.4	17.9	15.0
Germany	412.3	389.9	370.5	121.8	110.4	101.1	:	:	:
Estonia	36.9	27.8	23.3	12.4	9.2	6.1	:	:	:
Ireland	135.6	132.7	128.2	28.1	23.8	21.3	0.0	0.0	0.0
Greece	824.5	833.6	860.2	11.6	9.8	8.0	64.0	64.8	62.3
Spain	1 140.7	1 079.4	1 043.9	51.0	42.4	37.3	47.5	46.1	45.3
France	614.0	567.1	527.4	113.9	103.9	93.1	17.3	17.8	18.0
Italy	1 963.8	1 728.5	1 679.4	67.5	61.0	62.8	36.2	37.6	40.4
Cyprus	45.2	45.2	40.1	0.3	0.2	0.2	74.5	76.8	78.0
Latvia	126.6	128.7	107.8	63.7	50.9	43.7	0.1	0.3	0.2
Lithuania	272.1	253.0	230.3	193.4	170.8	123.2	0.0	0.1	0.0
Luxembourg	2.5	2.5	2.3	1.0	1.0	1.1	0.0	:	0.0
Hungary	773.4	714.8	626.3	22.0	16.3	12.2	4.0	2.3	0.2
Malta	11.0	11.1	11.0	0.2	0.2	0.2	34.2	27.5	25.0
Netherlands	85.5	81.8	76.7	25.0	23.5	24.5	22.2	23.5	25.5
Austria	173.8	170.6	165.4	65.1	54.6	49.5	3.6	4.4	4.4
Poland	2 172.2	2 476.5	2 391.0	873.8	727.1	651.1	0.7	1.0	1.1
Portugal	359.3	323.9	275.1	27.1	15.9	13.5	62.1	62.0	62.0
Romania	4 484.9	4 256.2	3 931.4	1 204.9	1 134.4	1 012.4	5.6	3.4	2.6
Slovenia	77.2	77.2	75.3	17.2	19.7	19.2	1.5	2.3	2.3
Slovakia	71.7	68.5	69.0	14.2	13.5	11.5	5.9	10.2	2.2
Finland	75.0	70.6	68.2	19.4	16.9	14.4	10.6	8.1	8.5
Sweden	67.9	75.8	72.6	9.7	8.6	7.1	7.7	6.0	5.2
United Kingdom	280.6	286.8	299.8	28.2	26.3	28.1	1.7	1.4	13.5
Norway	58.2	53.0	49.9	17.5	15.9	13.7	16.5	16.7	17.4
Switzerland	:	63.6	:	:	:	:	:	0.0	:

Source: Eurostat (tag00001, ef_r_nuts and ef_ov_lusum)

Table 8.5: Farm labour force, 2007

	Total farm labour force (1 000 AWU) (¹)	Regular farm labour force (% of total)	Full-time regular farm labour force (% of total)	Female regular farm labour force (% of total)	Family farm labour force (% of total)	Agric. holders being a natural person (1 000)	Agric. holders <35 years old (1 000)	Agric. holders >=65 years old (1 000)
EU-27	11 693	92	34	34	78	13 441	823	4 584
Belgium	66	95	71	29	79	44	3	9
Bulgaria	491	95	38	39	85	490	15	222
Czech Republic	137	98	68	32	27	36	4	7
Denmark	56	96	70	23	61	44	3	9
Germany	609	91	50	28	69	365	28	27
Estonia	32	98	46	46	61	22	1	7
Ireland	148	98	60	21	93	128	9	32
Greece	569	86	22	29	82	860	60	321
Spain	968	82	42	20	65	988	44	361
France	805	89	67	25	47	428	34	66
Italy	1 302	90	37	30	84	1 664	49	741
Cyprus	26	94	31	32	75	40	1	12
Latvia	105	99	30	50	84	108	8	32
Lithuania	180	98	14	48	85	230	10	93
Luxembourg	4	98	63	27	85	2	0	0
Hungary	403	97	25	37	77	619	47	172
Malta	4	99	41	14	88	11	0	3
Netherlands	165	91	56	26	61	73	3	13
Austria	163	97	53	41	88	161	16	18
Poland	2 263	97	34	42	95	2 387	294	388
Portugal	338	93	35	41	82	269	5	130
Romania	2 205	93	4	42	90	3 914	167	1 762
Slovenia	84	96	21	41	92	75	3	26
Slovakia	91	96	40	32	44	67	2	22
Finland	72	94	56	30	83	67	6	4
Sweden	65	97	42	26	76	68	4	15
United Kingdom	341	93	55	23	67	283	7	92
Norway	56	94	32	25	80	50	4	4

(¹) AWU: annual work unit.

Source: Eurostat (tag00020, tag00021, ef_so_lfwtime, ef_so_lfaa, tag00029 and tag00030)

Figure 8.3: Agricultural holdings with another gainful activity, 2007
(%)

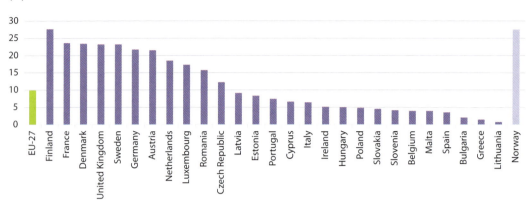

Source: Eurostat (tag00096)

Figure 8.4: Utilised agricultural area by land use, EU-27, 2007
(% share of utilised agricultural area)

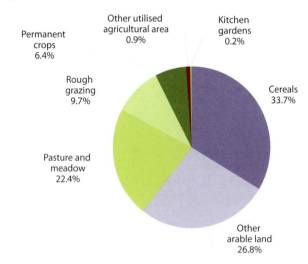

Other utilised
agricultural area
0.9%

Kitchen
gardens
0.2%

Permanent
crops
6.4%

Rough
grazing
9.7%

Cereals
33.7%

Pasture and
meadow
22.4%

Other
arable land
26.8%

Source: Eurostat (ef_lu_ovcropesu)

Table 8.6: Land use, 2007

	Total land area (km²)	Share of total land area (%)					
		Utilised agricultural area (¹)	of which:			Wooded area (²)	Built-up area, 2000
			Land under permanent crops	Permanent grassland	Arable land		
EU-27	*4 303 351*	*40.1*	*2.5*	*13.2*	*24.2*	*7.2*	*:*
Belgium	30 328	45.3	0.7	16.9	27.8	0.2	18.6
Bulgaria	111 002	27.5	0.8	2.5	24.0	8.6	:
Czech Republic	77 246	45.5	0.5	11.8	33.3	18.9	10.5
Denmark	43 098	61.8	0.2	4.7	56.9	4.8	16.9
Germany	357 108	47.4	0.6	13.5	33.3	3.8	12.8
Estonia	43 432	20.9	0.1	6.3	14.4	5.3	:
Ireland	68 394	60.5	0.0	45.8	14.7	1.9	:
Greece	130 822	31.2	8.6	6.3	16.2	0.5	:
Spain	505 987	*49.2*	8.6	*17.1*	23.5	9.6	:
France	632 834	43.4	1.7	12.8	28.9	1.5	6.7
Italy	295 114	43.2	7.9	11.7	23.5	12.9	:
Cyprus	9 250	*15.8*	*3.9*	*0.2*	*11.7*	*0.2*	2.2
Latvia	62 290	28.5	0.3	10.3	17.8	11.4	4.2
Lithuania	62 678	42.3	0.3	13.1	28.9	2.6	3.2
Luxembourg	2 586	*50.6*	*0.6*	*26.4*	*23.6*	*2.5*	8.5
Hungary	93 029	45.5	1.7	5.4	38.2	14.6	0.0
Malta	316	*32.7*	*4.2*	*0.0*	*25.4*	*0.0*	0.0
Netherlands	33 756	56.7	1.0	24.3	31.4	0.3	17.0
Austria	83 214	*38.3*	*0.8*	*20.8*	*16.7*	*32.9*	4.6
Poland	312 685	*49.5*	*1.2*	*10.5*	*37.6*	*3.8*	6.6
Portugal	92 118	37.7	6.5	19.3	11.7	7.8	17.8
Romania	229 973	59.8	1.5	19.7	37.8	4.7	4.4
Slovenia	20 141	24.3	1.3	14.3	8.6	18.8	3.9
Slovakia	49 035	39.5	0.5	11.2	27.7	21.4	7.5
Finland	304 086	7.5	0.0	0.1	7.4	10.4	*2.5*
Sweden	410 335	7.6	0.0	1.2	6.4	9.1	:
United Kingdom	242 495	*66.5*	0.1	*41.6*	24.8	*2.6*	:
Norway	304 280	3.4	0.0	1.4	2.0	7.7	:

(¹) Spain, Cyprus, Luxembourg, Malta, Austria, Poland and the United Kingdom, 2006.
(²) On agricultural holdings.

Source: Eurostat (reg_d3area, ef_lu_ovcropesu and tsdnr510)

8.3 Agricultural products

Introduction

Collecting data on agricultural products is important to understand developments in markets across the EU and Member States, both for the current period (estimated production levels for the current year) and to analyse trends. Studies of historical series help to distinguish between cycles and changing production patterns and also to analyse responses to policy actions or the testing of policy scenarios. As predominantly supply-side information, agricultural product data are important to understand corresponding price developments (which are of particular interest to agricultural commodity traders and policy analysts) but can also illustrate the consequences of policy decisions taken within agriculture.

Definitions and data availability

Annual statistics on the production of near 200 specific crops in the EU are mostly covered by Council Regulations, although the data for fresh fruit and vegetables are collected under gentlemen's agreements with the Member States.

Agricultural production of crops is harvested production (excluding losses to the harvest). The **harvested production** includes marketed quantities, as well as quantities consumed directly on the farm, losses and waste on the holding, and losses during transport, storage and packaging. **Cereals** include wheat (common wheat and spelt and durum wheat), rye, maslin, barley, oats, mixed grain other than maslin, grain maize, sorghum, triticale, other cereals, and rice (unless otherwise stated). **Vegetables** include brassicas (for example, cabbage, cauliflower and broccoli), other leafy or stalked vegetables (for example, celery, leeks, lettuce, spinach and asparagus), vegetables cultivated for fruit (for example, tomatoes, cucumbers, gherkins, melons, egg plant (aubergine), pumpkins and red pepper), root and tuber vegetables (for example, turnips, carrots, onions, garlic, beetroot and radishes), pulses (for example, peas and beans), cultivated mushrooms, wild products and other fresh vegetables. **Fruit** includes apples, pears, stoned fruits (for example, peaches or apricots), nuts (for example, walnuts or hazelnuts), other top fruits (for example, figs or kiwi), berries, citrus fruits, grapes, olives and wild fruits.

Statistics on milk, eggs and meat products are also compiled according to Community legislation. Milk production covers production on the farm of milk from cows, ewes, goats and buffaloes. A distinction should be made between **milk collected by dairies** and **milk production on the farm**. Milk collection is only a part of the total use of milk production on the farm, the remainder generally includes domestic consumption, direct sale and cattle feed. **Dairy cows** are female bovines that have calved (including any aged less than 2 years). They are cows kept exclusively or principally for the production of milk for human consumption and/or dairy produce, including cows for slaughter (fattened or not between last lactation and slaughter).

Meat production is based on the carcass weight of meat fit for human consumption. The concept of **carcass weight** varies according to the animal under consideration. For **pigs** (the species *Sus*), it is the weight of the slaughtered pig's cold body, either whole or divided in half along the mid-line, after being bled and eviscerated and after removal of the tongue, bristles, hooves, genitalia, flare fat, kidneys and diaphragm. Regarding **cattle** (the species *Bos taurus*), it is the weight of the slaughtered animal's cold body after being skinned, bled and eviscerated, and after removal of the external genitalia, the limbs, the head, the tail, the kidneys and kidney fats, and the udder. For **sheep and goats**, the carcass weight is the slaughtered animal's cold body after having been bled, skinned and eviscerated, and after removal of the head, feet, tail and genital organs; kidneys and kidney fats are included. For **poultry** (defined as

hens, chicken, ducks, turkey, guinea fowl and geese), the weight is the cold body of slaughtered farmyard poultry after being bled, plucked and eviscerated; the value includes poultry offal, with the exception of foie gras. For all other animal species, the carcass weight is considered to be the weight of the animal's cold body.

Main findings

The EU-27 produced an estimated 315 million tonnes of cereals (including rice) in 2008, of which a little under one half (47.7 %) was wheat, about one fifth (20.8 %) was barley and a further one fifth (20.1 %) was grain maize. France and Germany were the Member States who produced the most cereals, sugar beet and oilseed rape: together their production accounted for over one third (38.2 %) of the EU-27's cereals (including rice) in 2008, almost half of its sugar beet, and more than half (52.1 %) of its oilseed rape.

Despite the vagaries of the weather, cereal production for the EU-27 was relatively stable between 2000 and 2007, albeit with a notably higher harvest in 2004. The production of cereals rose again sharply in 2008, to attain a level that was close to that recorded in 2004. There was a strong rise (of almost 70 %) in the production of oilseed rape between 2003 and 2008, which could be contrasted with a relatively steady decline in the production of potatoes (down about 25 % between 2000 and 2008).

The bulk of fruit and fresh vegetable production was concentrated in a few Member States. Just over two thirds of the EU-27's apple production in 2008 was located in Poland, Italy and France,

whilst more than 80 % of oranges were produced in Spain and Italy. About two thirds of tomato production was from Italy and Spain in 2008, whilst over half of the onions were produced in the Netherlands and Spain.

The principal meat product in the EU is pig meat (22.6 million tonnes for the EU-27 in 2008), significantly more than other types of meat, such as beef/veal (8.1 million tonnes). A little over one fifth (22.6 %) of pig meat production in the EU-27 came from Germany, the next highest contributions coming from Spain (15.4 %) and France (10.1 %): the 7.6 % share of Denmark is also notable. A little under one fifth (18.8 %) of beef/veal in the EU-27 was produced in France in 2008, with further significant production originating from Germany, Italy, the United Kingdom, Spain and Ireland.

Dairy production is structured quite differently among Member States, both as a result of varying farm and dairy herd sizes as well as yields. However, milk production has been controlled under a system of milk quotas since 1984 that effectively put a limit on the amount of milk produced. Germany and France have by far the largest quotas, and the 27.5 million tonnes of milk collected in Germany in 2008 was double the third highest level that was collected in the United Kingdom. One third (33.2 %) of the milk collected in the EU-27 in 2008 was converted into cheese, with a further quarter (24.9 %) being transformed into butter. Only one tenth (9.9 %) of the milk collected across the EU-27 was used as drinking milk in 2008.

Figure 8.5: Indices of the agricultural production of crops, EU-27 (2000=100)

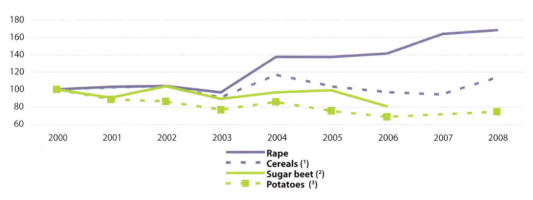

(¹) Provisional, 2008; estimate, 2004 and 2005.
(²) Estimate, 2006; not available, 2007 and 2008.
(³) Provisional, 2008; not available, 2007.

Source: Eurostat (tag00104, tag00031, tag00106 and tag00108)

Table 8.7: Agricultural production of crops, 2008
(1 000 tonnes)

	Cereals (¹)	Rape	Vegetables (²)	Potatoes	Fruit (³)	Sugar beet (⁴)
EU-27	313 759	18 936	45 160	61 614	59 271	97 299
Belgium	3 307	33	:	2 947	:	4 714
Bulgaria	6 977	231	507	353	469	0
Czech Republic	8 370	1 049	:	770	:	2 885
Denmark	9 074	637	245	1 417	72	2 011
Germany	50 105	5 155	:	11 369	:	23 003
Estonia	864	111	39	125	6	0.0
Ireland	2 384	23	:	372	:	45
Greece	4 820	-	3 445	848	5 423	902
Spain	23 286	23	8 860	2 325	11 176	3 988
France	70 142	4 719	5 638	6 808	8 579	30 306
Italy	20 459	28	13 306	1 730	20 858	44
Cyprus	7	-	132	132	207	-
Latvia	1 689	205	131	673	32	0
Lithuania	3 422	330	264	710	93	339
Luxembourg	190	16	2	22	29	0
Hungary	16 831	655	1 818	684	1 411	573
Malta	-	-	66	19	10	:
Netherlands	2 063	10	4 537	6 993	589	5 219
Austria	5 748	175	574	757	1 215	3 091
Poland	27 664	2 106	:	10 462	3 841	8 715
Portugal	1 159	-	:	567	2 289	137
Romania	16 778	673	2 666	3 649	2 189	707
Slovenia	580	11	78	100	240	262.0
Slovakia	4 137	424	118	245	127	679
Finland	4 229	89	230	684	18	468
Sweden	5 195	259	:	853	:	1 975
United Kingdom	24 282	1 973	2 503	5 999	398	7 500
Croatia	3 726	63	202	256	446	1 270
FYR of Macedonia	599	1	:	189	15 592	0
Turkey	28 533	84	27 259	4 225	32	15 488
Norway	1 347	10	:	400	32	:
Switzerland	1 008	60	:	408	:	1 508

(¹) Excluding rice.
(²) The United Kingdom, 2007; Denmark, 2006; EU-27, sum of available data.
(³) The United Kingdom, 2007; Denmark and Greece, 2006; EU-27, sum of available data.
(⁴) Estonia, 2007; Slovenia, 2006; EU-27, sum of available data.

Source: Eurostat (tag00031, tag00104, tag00097, tag00108, tag00112 and tag00106)

Figure 8.6: Production of cereals (including rice), EU-27, 2008 (^{1})
(%)

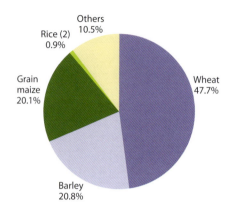

(^{1}) Provisional.
(^{2}) 2007.

Source: Eurostat (apro_cpp_crop)

Figure 8.7: Breakdown of production of fruit, EU, 2008 (^{1})
(% of total, based on tonnes)

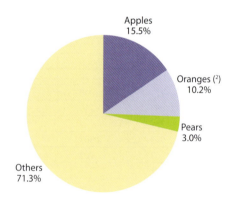

(^{1}) EU based on available data: Cyprus, Slovakia and the United Kingdom, 2007; Denmark and Greece, 2006; Spain, 2005; excluding Belgium, the Czech Republic, Germany, Estonia, Ireland, the Netherlands, Portugal, Finland and Sweden.
(^{2}) Member States not reporting any production are assumed to have negligible or no production of oranges.

Source: Eurostat (tag00036, tag00114, tag00113 and tag00112)

Figure 8.8: Utilisation of milk, EU, 2008 (¹)
(%)

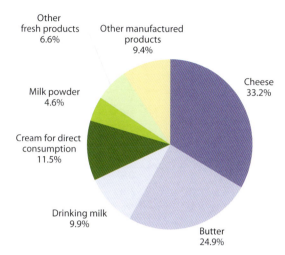

(¹) Figures do not sum to 100 % due to rounding; EU excluding Bulgaria, Ireland, Greece, Italy, Latvia, Luxembourg, Austria, Slovenia and the United Kingdom.

Source: Eurostat (apro_mk_pobta)

Table 8.8: Agricultural production related to animals, 2008
(1 000 tonnes)

	Collection of cows' milk (¹)	Butter (²)	Cheese (³)	Meat: cattle (⁴)	Meat: pigs (⁴)	Meat: sheep & goats (⁴)
EU-27	*132 856*	*2 142*	*8 529*	8 090	22 596	*1 027*
Belgium	2 849	88	70	267	1 056	1
Bulgaria	705	1	73	20	73	21
Czech Republic	2 446	37	116	80	336	2
Denmark	4 581	113	319	128	1 707	2
Germany	27 466	465	1 941	1 210	5 111	43
Estonia	606	7	36	15	40	0
Ireland	5 106	206	:	537	202	59
Greece	716	2	188	57	119	110
Spain	5 834	41	310	658	3 484	166
France	23 819	436	1 875	1 518	2 277	118
Italy	10 497	115	1 158	1 059	1 606	60
Cyprus	152	0	11	4	59	7
Latvia	634	6	34	21	41	1
Lithuania	1 376	11	106	48	76	1
Luxembourg	265	:	:	10	10	0
Hungary	1 425	8	74	32	460	1
Malta	40	0	3	1	9	0
Netherlands	11 295	182	724	378	1 318	15
Austria	2 717	33	140	221	526	8
Poland	8 893	138	594	386	1 888	2
Portugal	1 887	30	67	109	381	12
Romania	1 051	9	70	190	455	65
Slovenia	524	2	19	37	31	0
Slovakia	946	10	38	20	102	1
Finland	2 254	54	107	83	217	1
Sweden	2 987	38	114	136	271	5
United Kingdom	13 350	111	343	862	740	326
Croatia	673	:	:	55	156	8

(¹) EU-27, the Czech Republic, Greece and Croatia, 2007.
(²) EU-27 excluding Luxembourg; the Czech Republic, Greece and Italy, 2007.
(³) EU-27 excluding Ireland and Luxembourg; the Czech Republic and Greece, 2007.
(⁴) Croatia, 2007.

Source: Eurostat (tag00037, tag00038, tag00040, tag00044, tag00042 and tag00045)

8.4 Forestry

Introduction

Contrary to what is happening in some other parts of the world, forest cover in the EU is slowly increasing. Ecologically, EU forests belong to numerous vegetation zones, ranging from coastal plains to alpine zones, while socio-economic management conditions vary from small family holdings to large estates belonging to vertically integrated enterprises.

In 2006, the Commission underpinned its support for enhancing sustainable forest management and the multifunctional role of forests by adopting an EU forest action plan. This action plan provides a framework for forest-related actions and will serve as an instrument of coordination between Community actions and the forest policies of the Member States, with 18 key actions proposed by the Commission to be implemented jointly with the Member States during the period 2007 to 2011. The action plan focuses on four main objectives:

* improving long-term competitiveness;
* improving and protecting the environment;
* contributing to the quality of life;
* fostering coordination and communication.

The EU-27 has approximately 177 million hectares of forests and other wooded land, just over 42 % of its land area, and the area of land devoted to forestry is gradually increasing. About 60 % of wooded land is under private ownership.

Definitions and data availability

An inter-secretariat working group (IWG) brings together Eurostat, the Timber Committee of the United Nations Eco-

nomic Commission for Europe (UNECE), the Forestry Section of the Food and Agriculture Organisation of the United Nations (FAO) and the International Tropical Timber Organisation (ITTO) in collecting forest sector statistics; other Directorates-General of the European Commission are also represented. Within this context, the primary tool for statistical cooperation is the Eurostat/UNECE/FAO/ITTO Joint Forest Sector Questionnaire (JFSQ), which is used by all organisations; each agency collects data from the countries for which it is responsible (as such, Eurostat is responsible for data from the Member States and EFTA countries).

Forest is defined as land with a tree crown cover (or equivalent stocking level) of more than 10 % and an area of more than 0.5 hectares. The trees should be able to reach a minimum height of 5 metres at maturity in situ. **Roundwood production** is a synonym for **removals**; it comprises all quantities of wood removed from the forest and other wooded land or other felling sites during a given time period; it is reported in cubic metres underbark (i.e. excluding bark).

Sawnwood production is wood that has been produced either by sawing lengthways or by a profile-chipping process and that exceeds 6 mm in thickness; it includes, for example, planks, beams, joists, boards, rafters, scantlings, laths, boxboards and lumber in all kinds of forms, for example, unplaned, planed and end-jointed; it is reported in cubic metres (m³) of solid volume.

Paper and paperboard comprises graphic papers, sanitary and household papers, packaging materials, and other paper and paperboard. It excludes manufactured paper products such as boxes, cartons, books and magazines.

The **degree of defoliation** is the extent of visually assessed loss of leaves in trees based on a method developed by the International Cooperative Programme of the executive committee for the Convention on Long-range Transboundary Air Pollution in Europe. Damage is classed on a scale from 0 to 4:

- no defoliation (class 0) – up to and including 10 % needle/leaf loss;
- slight (warning stage) defoliation (class 1) – more than 10 % and up to 25 % needle/leaf loss;
- moderate defoliation (class 2) – more than 25 % and up to 60 % needle/leaf loss;
- severe defoliation (class 3) – more than 60 % and up to 100 % needle/leaf loss;
- dead (class 4) – 100 % defoliation.

Main findings

Since 1998, there has been a relatively steady rise in the level of roundwood production in the EU-27, both for coniferous (softwood) and non-coniferous (broad-leaved or hardwood) species. The level of EU-27 roundwood production in 2008 was approximately 80 million m³ higher than in 1998, against the backdrop of a steady increase in forest area.

The 419.7 million m³ of roundwood produced within the EU-27 in 2008 was about one tenth less than the relative peak that was recorded in 2007. This peak was due to exceptional windthrow caused by storms in many parts of Europe – notably in Sweden and Germany – after which much more wood had to be removed from forests than planned. Among the Member States,

Sweden was the largest producer of roundwood in 2008 (almost 70 million m³), followed by France, Germany and Finland (each producing between 50 million to 60 million m³ of roundwood in 2008).

A further 104.9 million m³ of sawnwood was produced in the EU-27 in 2008, one half of which came from the three largest producing Member States; Germany (22.0 %), Sweden (16.8 %) and Austria (11.4 %). The level of sawnwood production in the EU-27 in 2008 was also about one tenth (9.0 %) lower than in 2007.

There was a strong correlation between the volume of roundwood production and the value added generated by the forestry industry. However, it is worth noting that in France and to a lesser extent Portugal, the value added per cubic metre of roundwood was substantially higher, often more than double, that for the other Member States, likely reflecting the use of oak within the cooperage trade (casks and barrels) of their respective wine and port industries.

The production of paper and paperboard in the EU-27 was about 100 million tonnes in 2008, which was 2.4 % down on the level of the previous year, bucking the relatively steady upward trend in output during the previous nine years. A little less than half of the EU-27's paper and paperboard production in 2008 came from three Member States; Germany (22.9 %), Finland (13.6 %) and Sweden (12.4 %).

Between one fifth and one quarter of forest and woodland trees across the EU-27 suffered from moderate or worse defoliation in 2006. This share rose to a little over one third of all trees in France and Bulgaria, over 40 % of all trees in Luxembourg, and about half of all trees in the Czech Republic.

Table 8.9: Wood production
(1 000 m³)

	Roundwood production					Sawnwood production				
	1998	2003	2006	2007	2008	1998	2003	2006	2007	2008
EU-27	339 622	387 181	426 343	462 507	419 715	91 128	102 074	112 138	115 340	104 909
Belgium	4 435	4 765	5 075	5 015	4 700	:	1 215	1 520	1 555	1 400
Bulgaria	3 231	4 833	5 992	5 696	6 071	257	332	683	690	690
Czech Republic	13 991	15 140	17 678	18 508	16 187	3 432	3 805	5 080	5 454	4 636
Denmark	1 558	1 627	2 358	2 566	2 786	240	248	300	300	300
Germany	39 052	51 182	62 290	76 728	55 367	15 074	17 596	24 420	25 063	23 060
Estonia	6 061	10 500	5 400	4 500	4 860	853	1 954	1 958	1 584	1 300
Ireland	2 266	2 683	2 671	2 710	2 024	675	1 005	1 094	1 094	697
Greece	1 692	1 673	1 562	1 743	1 261	137	191	108	108	106
Spain	14 874	16 105	15 716	14 528	16 893	3 228	3 630	3 806	3 332	3 142
France	35 527	32 828	61 790	58 786	*58 383*	10 427	9 539	9 992	9 965	*9 630*
Italy	9 550	8 219	8 618	8 125	10 448	1 615	1 590	1 748	1 700	1 384
Cyprus	35	12	7	20	20	11	6	4	9	10
Latvia	10 030	12 916	12 845	12 173	8 806	3 200	3 951	4 320	3 459	2 545
Lithuania	4 879	6 275	5 870	6 195	5 590	1 150	1 400	1 466	1 380	1 075
Luxembourg	:	257	268	291	353	:	133	133	:	202
Hungary	4 167	5 785	5 913	5 640	5 276	349	299	186	235	207
Malta	-	-	-	-	-	-	-	-	-	-
Netherlands	1 023	1 044	1 107	1 022	1 118	350	269	265	273	243
Austria	14 033	17 055	19 135	21 317	21 795	8 737	10 473	10 507	11 816	11 990
Poland	23 107	30 836	32 384	35 935	34 447	4 320	3 360	3 607	4 417	4 068
Portugal	8 548	9 673	10 805	10 823	10 866	1 590	1 383	1 010	1 011	1 010
Romania	11 649	15 440	13 970	15 341	13 667	2 204	4 246	3 476	4 143	3 794
Slovenia	2 133	2 591	3 179	2 882	472	666	511	580	610	280
Slovakia	5 519	6 355	7 869	8 131	9 269	1 272	1 651	2 440	2 781	2 842
Finland	53 660	54 240	50 812	56 612	51 647	12 367	13 745	12 227	12 477	9 881
Sweden	60 600	67 100	64 600	78 200	69 000	15 150	16 800	18 300	18 738	17 601
United Kingdom	7 600	8 046	8 430	9 021	8 411	2 515	2 742	2 907	3 145	2 818
Croatia	3 398	3 847	4 452	4 210	4 469	678	585	669	702	721
Turkey	17 668	15 810	18 084	18 319	17 864	4 891	5 615	6 471	6 599	6 261
Iceland	-	-	-	-	-	-	-	-	-	-
Norway	8 172	8 298	9 794	10 465	10 319	2 527	2 186	2 389	2 402	2 228
Switzerland	4 276	5 120	4 557	5 520	5 096	1 425	1 345	1 392	1 541	1 540
Canada	176 942	179 642	188 193	194 098	155 533	47 185	56 892	58 709	52 284	41 548
Russia	95 000	174 000	190 600	207 000	181 400	20 534	20 155	22 127	24 258	21 613
United States	469 750	448 513	457 048	425 129	380 225	88 991	86 159	92 903	85 377	72 869

Source: Eurostat (tag00072 and tag00073), UNECE

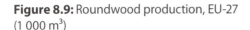

Figure 8.9: Roundwood production, EU-27
(1 000 m³)

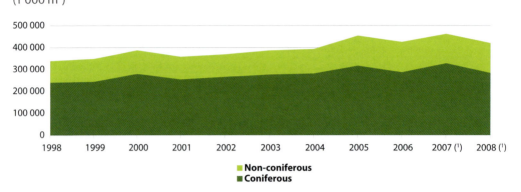

(¹) Estimates.

Source: Eurostat (for_rem41)

Figure 8.10: Roundwood production and gross value added of the forestry industry, 2005 (¹)

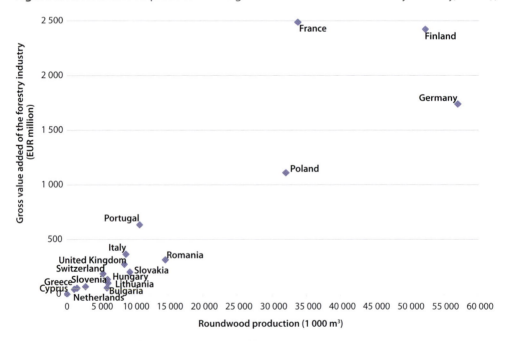

(¹) France, 2004; Member States that are not shown, not available.

Source: Eurostat (tag00072 and tag00058)

Table 8.10: Paper and paperboard production
(1 000 tonnes)

	1998	1999	2000	2001	2002	2003	2004	2005	2006	2007	2008
EU-27	80 320	84 782	89 698	88 028	90 545	92 627	97 019	97 584	101 352	102 710	99 687
Belgium	:	1 666	1 727	1 662	1 704	1 919	1 957	1 897	1 897	1 931	2 006
Bulgaria	153	126	136	171	171	171	326	326	313	443	420
Czech Republic	768	770	804	864	870	920	934	969	1 042	1 023	932
Denmark	393	397	263	389	384	388	402	423	442	417	418
Germany	16 311	16 742	18 182	17 879	18 526	19 310	20 391	21 679	22 656	23 317	22 842
Estonia	43	48	54	70	75	64	66	64	78	78	69
Ireland	42	42	43	43	44	45	45	45	:	49	48
Greece	622	352	496	495	493	493	510	510	412	409	462
Spain	3 545	4 436	4 765	5 131	5 365	5 437	5 526	5 697	6 898	6 713	7 048
France	9 161	9 603	10 006	9 625	9 809	9 939	10 255	10 332	10 006	9 871	9 420
Italy	8 254	8 568	9 129	8 926	9 317	9 491	9 667	9 999	10 008	10 112	9 467
Cyprus	-	-	-	-	-	-	-	-	-	-	-
Latvia	18	19	16	24	33	38	38	39	57	60	52
Lithuania	37	37	53	68	78	92	99	113	119	119	119
Luxembourg	:	:	:	:	:	:	:	:	:	19	31
Hungary	482	473	506	495	517	546	579	571	553	552	424
Malta	-	-	-	-	-	-	-	-	-	-	-
Netherlands	3 180	3 256	3 333	3 174	3 346	3 339	3 459	3 471	3 367	3 219	2 977
Austria	4 009	4 141	4 385	4 250	4 419	4 565	4 852	4 950	5 213	5 199	5 153
Poland	1 718	1 839	1 934	2 086	2 342	2 461	2 635	2 732	2 857	2 992	3 090
Portugal	1 136	1 163	1 290	1 419	1 537	1 530	1 664	1 570	1 644	1 644	1 669
Romania	301	289	340	395	370	443	454	371	432	536	617
Slovenia	491	417	411	633	704	417	497	763	760	794	595
Slovakia	597	803	925	988	710	674	798	858	888	915	921
Finland	12 703	12 947	13 509	12 502	12 789	13 058	14 036	12 391	14 189	14 709	13 549
Sweden	9 879	10 071	10 786	10 534	10 724	11 061	11 589	11 775	12 066	12 361	12 374
United Kingdom	6 477	6 576	6 605	6 204	6 218	6 226	6 240	6 039	5 454	5 228	4 983
Croatia	403	417	406	451	467	463	464	592	564	545	535
Turkey	1 357	1 349	1 567	1 513	1 643	1 643	1 643	1 643	1 643	1 643	1 643
Iceland	-	-	-	-	-	-	-	-	-	-	-
Norway	2 260	2 241	2 300	2 220	2 114	2 186	2 294	2 223	2 109	2 010	1 900
Switzerland	1 592	1 755	1 616	1 750	1 805	1 818	1 777	1 751	1 805	1 705	1 698
Canada	18 875	20 280	20 921	19 834	20 073	19 964	20 462	19 498	18 189	17 367	15 773
Russian Federation	3 595	4 535	5 310	5 625	5 978	6 377	6 830	7 126	7 434	7 581	7 676
United States	86 469	88 670	86 252	81 249	81 879	80 712	82 084	83 697	84 317	83 916	80 178

Source: Eurostat (tag00074), UNECE

Figure 8.11: Forest trees damaged by defoliation, 2006 (¹)
(%)

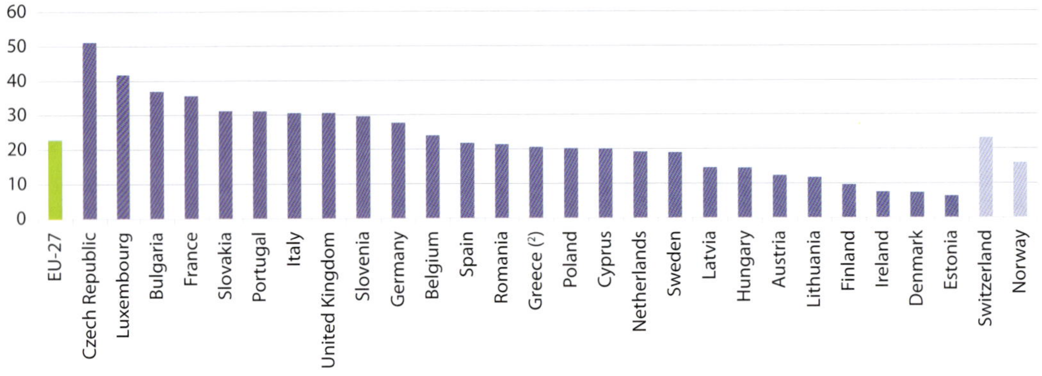

(¹) Malta, not available.
(²) 2005.

Source: Eurostat (tsdnr530)

8.5 Fisheries

Introduction

Fish are a natural, biological, mobile (sometimes over wide distances) and renewable resource. Aside from fish farming, fish can not be owned until they have been caught. For this reason, fish stocks continue to be regarded as a common resource, which therefore need to be managed collectively. This has led to policies that regulate the amount of fishing, as well as the types of fishing techniques and gear used in fish capture.

The first common European policy measures in the fishing sector date from 1970. They set rules for access to fishing grounds, markets and structures. All these measures became more significant when, in 1976, the Member States followed an international movement and agreed to extend their rights to marine resources from 12 to 200 miles from their coasts.

After years of difficult negotiations, the common fisheries policy (CFP), the EU's instrument for the management of fisheries and aquaculture, was born in 1983. The CFP sets maximum quantities of fish that can be safely caught every year: the total allowable catch (TAC). Each country's share is called a national quota. The common fisheries policy (CFP) was reformed in 2002 to deal with the environmental, economic and social dimensions of fishing. Common measures are agreed in four main areas:

- the conservation of stocks/environmental impact – to protect fish resources by regulating the amount of fish taken from the sea, by allowing young fish to reproduce, and by ensuring that measures are respected;
- structures and fleet management (such as vessels, port facilities and fish processing plants) – to help the fishing and aquaculture sectors adapt their equipment and organisations to the constraints imposed by scarce resources and the market;
- the organisation of the market for fish in the EU – to maintain a common organisation of the market in fish products and to match supply and demand for the benefit of both producers and consumers;
- and external fisheries policy – to set-up fisheries agreements and to negotiate at an international level within regional and international fisheries organisations for common conservation measures in deep-sea fisheries.

The 2002 reform of the CFP identified the need to limit fishing efforts, the level of catches, and to enforce certain technical measures. To ensure sustainable fishing, it is not only the quantity of fish taken from the sea that is important, but also their species, size, and the techniques used in catching them, as well as the areas where they are caught.

The European Fisheries Fund (EFF) has a budget of around EUR 3 800 million and covers the period 2007 to 2013. It aims to support the objectives of the CFP by:

- supporting sustainable exploitation of fisheries resources and a stable balance between these resources and the capacity of Community fishing fleet;

- strengthening the competitiveness and the viability of operators in the sector;
- promoting environmentally-friendly fishing and production methods;
- providing adequate support to people employed in the sector;
- fostering the sustainable development of fisheries areas.

Definitions and data availability

Fishery statistics are derived from official national sources either directly by Eurostat for the members of the European Economic Area (EEA) or indirectly through other international organisations for other countries. The data are collected using internationally agreed concepts and definitions developed by the coordinating working party on fishery statistics, comprising Eurostat and several other international organisations with responsibilities in fishery statistics. The flag of the fishing vessel is used as the primary indication of the nationality of the catch, though this concept may be varied in certain circumstances.

In general, the data refer to the **fishing fleet** size on 31 December of the reference year. The data are derived from the national registers of fishing vessels which are maintained pursuant to Council Regulation (EC) No 26/2004 which contains information on the vessel characteristics to be recorded on the registers – the administrative file of fishing vessels maintained by the European Commission's Directorate-General for Maritime Affairs and Fisheries. There has been a transition in measuring the tonnage of the fishing fleet from gross registered tonnage (GRT) to that of gross tonnage (GT). This change, which has taken place at different speeds within the national administrations, gives rise to the possibility of non-comparability of data over time and of non-comparability between countries.

Catches of fishery products (fish, molluscs, crustaceans and other aquatic animals, residues and aquatic plants) include items taken for all purposes (commercial, industrial, recreational and subsistence) by all types and classes of fishing units (fishermen, vessels, gear, etc.) operating both in inland, fresh and brackish water areas, and in inshore, offshore and high-seas fishing areas. The catch is normally expressed in **live weight** and derived by the application of conversion factors to the landed or product weight. As such, catch statistics exclude quantities which are caught and taken from the water (that is, before processing) but which, for a variety of reasons, are not landed; production from aquaculture (see below for definition) is excluded.

Geographical **fishing areas** are defined for a number of specific areas of water, including:

- the north-east Atlantic, which is roughly the area to the east of 42°W longitude and north of 36°N latitude, including the waters of the Baltic Sea;
- the north-west Atlantic, which is the region that is roughly the area to the west of 42°W longitude and north of 35°N latitude;

- the eastern central Atlantic, which is the region to the east of 40°W longitude between latitudes 36°N and 6°S;
- the Mediterranean, which is also known as FAO Major Fishing Area 37, comprises the Mediterranean Sea and the adjacent Black Sea.

Aquaculture is the farming of aquatic organisms including fish, molluscs, crustaceans and aquatic plants. Farming implies some form of intervention in the rearing process to enhance production, such as regular stocking, feeding and protection from predators. Farming also implies individual or corporate ownership of, or rights resulting from contractual arrangements to, the stock being cultivated.

Main findings

Among Member States, by far the largest fishing fleets in terms of power were those of Italy, France, Spain and the United Kingdom; in 2008, the fishing fleets of each of these countries had a collective power of between 0.8 million and 1.1 million kW. In terms of tonnage, however, the fishing fleet in Spain was the largest, being about two and a half times the size of those in the United Kingdom, France or Italy.

Total catches by the fishing fleets of Spain, Denmark, the United Kingdom and France accounted for almost half of all the catches made by the EU-27 in

2007. This share has declined in recent years from about 60 % in 2000, mainly as a result of the sharp reduction in the share of the Danish catch, as well as (to a lesser degree) that of Spain. Since 1997, the total EU-27 catch has fallen every year with the exception of 2001; the total catch by the EU-27 in 2007 was almost one third (31.6 %) less than in 1997. Almost three quarters of the catches made by the EU-27 in 2007 were in the northeast Atlantic, with the Mediterranean the second largest fishing area.

The level of aquaculture production in the EU-27 remained relatively stable between 1.2 million tonnes and 1.4 million tonnes during the period 1996 to 2006.

By far the largest five aquaculture Member States were Spain, France, Italy, the United Kingdom and Greece, which together accounted for a little over three quarters (77.2 %) of total aquaculture production in the EU-27 in 2006. There were strong contrasts among the Member States in the development of aquaculture production in the ten years through to 2007; production in the Netherlands almost halved from about 100 000 tonnes and that in Germany declined by about one third from 65 000 tonnes, whereas production rose by one third in the United Kingdom (albeit growth being limited through until 2004) and more than doubled in Greece.

Figure 8.12: Fishing fleet, 2008 (¹)

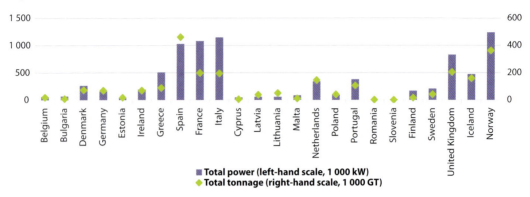

(¹) The Czech Republic, Luxembourg, Hungary, Austria and Slovakia are landlocked countries without a marine fishing fleet.

Source: Eurostat (tsdnr420 and tag00083), Directorate-General for Maritime Affairs and Fisheries

Figure 8.13: Catches by fishing region, EU-27, 2007
(%, based on tonnes)

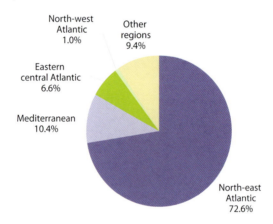

Source: Eurostat (tag00078, tag00080, tag00081, tag00079 and tag00076)

Table 8.11: Total catches in all fishing regions
(1 000 tonnes live weight)

	1997	1998	1999	2000	2001	2002	2003	2004	2005	2006	2007
EU-27	7 518	7 285	6 880	6 794	6 933	6 338	5 900	5 878	5 633	5 412	5 143
Belgium	31	31	30	30	30	29	27	27	25	23	25
Bulgaria	11	19	11	7	7	15	12	8	5	8	9
Czech Republic	3	4	4	5	5	5	5	5	4	5	4
Denmark	1 827	1 557	1 405	1 534	1 511	1 442	1 031	1 091	911	868	653
Germany	259	267	239	206	211	224	261	262	286	298	249
Estonia	124	119	112	113	105	102	80	89	100	87	99
Ireland	293	325	284	276	356	282	266	280	262	211	227
Greece	157	110	121	99	94	96	93	93	92	98	95
Spain	1 204	1 243	1 170	1 069	1 106	863	863	773	771	741	736
France	638	599	664	703	681	704	709	671	595	593	558
Italy	344	306	283	302	310	270	296	279	298	316	287
Cyprus	18	19	40	67	81	2	2	2	2	2	2
Latvia	106	102	125	136	128	114	115	125	151	140	155
Lithuania	44	67	73	79	151	150	157	162	140	155	187
Luxembourg	0	0	0	0	0	0	0	0	0	0	0
Hungary	7	7	8	7	7	7	7	7	8	8	7
Malta	1	1	1	1	1	1	1	1	1	1	1
Netherlands	452	537	515	496	518	464	526	522	549	435	413
Austria	0	0	0	0	0	0	0	0	0	0	0
Poland	348	242	236	218	225	223	180	192	155	145	152
Portugal	224	228	213	191	193	202	209	221	212	229	253
Romania	8	9	8	7	8	7	10	5	6	7	6
Slovenia	2	2	2	2	2	2	1	1	1	1	1
Slovakia	1	1	1	1	2	2	2	2	2	2	3
Finland	165	156	145	156	150	146	122	135	132	149	164
Sweden	357	411	351	339	312	295	287	270	256	269	238
United Kingdom	892	923	841	748	740	690	637	655	669	621	616
Croatia	17	22	19	21	18	21	20	30	35	38	40
FYR of Macedonia	0	0	0	0	0	0	0	0	0	0	0
Turkey	459	487	574	503	528	567	508	550	426	533	632
Iceland	2 225	1 700	1 754	2 000	2 001	2 145	2 002	1 750	1 661	1 345	1 399
Liechtenstein	0	0	0	0	0	0	0	0	0	0	0
Norway	2 863	2 861	2 628	2 700	2 687	2 740	2 549	2 525	2 393	2 256	2 379
Switzerland	2	2	2	2	2	2	2	2	1	1	1

Source: Eurostat (tag00076), FAO

Table 8.12: Fish catches from stocks outside safe biological limits, north-east Atlantic (%)

	1996	1997	1998	1999	2000	2001	2002	2003	2004	2005	2006
Total	11	14	6	8	10	40	8	22	21	10	21
Demersal	35	47	50	51	42	61	46	61	62	51	51
Pelagic	9	15	3	4	5	49	4	22	12	2	13
Benthic	40	37	38	31	49	41	36	31	29	40	42
Industrial	0	0	0	0	0	0	0	41	39	21	33

Source: Eurostat (tsdnr110)

Table 8.13: Aquaculture production (1 000 tonnes live weight)

	1997	1998	1999	2000	2001	2002	2003	2004	2005	2006	2007
EU-27	1 254	1 376	1 429	1 399	1 386	1 272	1 343	1 311	1 261	1 283	:
Belgium	1	1	2	2	2	2	1	1	0	0	0
Bulgaria	5	4	8	4	3	2	4	2	3	3	4
Czech Republic	18	17	19	19	20	19	20	19	20	20	20
Denmark	40	42	43	44	42	32	38	43	39	28	31
Germany	65	73	80	66	53	50	74	57	45	38	45
Estonia	0	0	0	0	0	0	0	0	1	1	1
Ireland	37	42	44	51	61	63	63	58	60	53	53
Greece	49	60	84	95	98	88	101	97	106	113	113
Spain	239	314	318	309	309	255	268	293	219	295	285
France	287	268	265	267	252	252	240	243	245	238	237
Italy	196	209	210	217	218	184	192	118	181	174	181
Cyprus	1	1	1	2	2	2	2	2	2	4	3
Latvia	0	0	0	0	0	0	1	1	1	1	1
Lithuania	2	2	2	2	2	2	2	3	2	2	3
Luxembourg	0	0	0	0	0	0	0	0	0	0	0
Hungary	9	10	12	13	13	12	12	13	14	15	16
Malta	2	2	2	2	1	1	1	1	1	7	9
Netherlands	98	120	109	75	57	54	67	79	71	42	53
Austria	3	3	3	3	2	2	2	2	2	3	3
Poland	29	30	34	36	35	33	35	35	38	36	:
Portugal	7	8	6	8	8	8	8	7	7	8	7
Romania	11	10	9	10	11	9	9	8	7	9	10
Slovenia	1	1	1	1	1	1	1	2	1	1	1
Slovakia	1	1	1	1	1	1	1	1	1	1	1
Finland	16	16	15	15	16	15	13	13	14	13	13
Sweden	7	5	6	5	7	6	6	6	6	8	5
United Kingdom	130	137	155	152	171	179	182	207	173	172	174

Source: Eurostat (tag00075), FAO

Table 8.13 (continued)

	1997	1998	1999	2000	2001	2002	2003	2004	2005	2006	2007
Croatia	4	6	6	7	10	9	8	10	11	14	13
FYR of Macedonia	1	1	2	2	1	1	1	1	1	1	1
Turkey	45	57	63	79	67	61	80	94	120	129	140
Iceland	4	4	4	4	4	4	6	9	8	9	5
Norway	368	411	476	491	511	551	584	637	662	709	830
Switzerland	1	1	1	1	1	1	1	1	1	1	1

Source: Eurostat (tag00075), FAO

8.6 Agriculture and the environment

Introduction

Around 40 % of the EU's land area is farmed. This fact alone highlights the importance of farming for the EU's natural environment. The links between the two, however, are complex. On the one hand, farming has contributed over the centuries to creating and maintaining a variety of valuable, semi-natural habitats and agricultural landscapes. While many of these are maintained by different farming practices and a wide range of wild species rely on this for their survival, agriculture can also have an adverse impact on natural resources. Pollution of soil, water and air, the fragmentation of habitats, and a loss of wildlife can result from agricultural practices and land use.

This complex relationship has necessitated the integration of environmental concerns and safeguards into the CAP, with particular attention paid to reducing the risks of environmental degradation through cross-compliance criteria (as a condition for benefiting from direct payments, farmers must comply with certain requirements, some related to environmental protection), incentives and targeted environmental measures, while encouraging farmers to continue to play a positive role to enhance the sustainability of agro-ecosystems.

The importance attached to assessing the interaction between agriculture and the environment is underlined by the fact that the Commission adopted a list of 28 agri-environmental indicators [2] in 2006.

Definitions and data availability

Organic farming can be defined as a method of production which places the highest emphasis on environmental protection and animal welfare considerations. In the EU, farming is only considered to be organic if it complies with Council Regulation (EEC) No 834/2007. The detailed rules for the implementation of this Council Regulation on organic products and the labelling of organic products are laid down in Commission Regulation

[2] COM(2006) 508 final; for more information: http://eur-lex.europa.eu/LexUriServ/site/en/com/2006/com2006_0508en01.pdf.

(EC) No 889/2008. Organic farming involves holistic production management systems for crops and livestock, emphasising the use of management practices in preference to the use of off-farm inputs. This is accomplished by using, where possible, cultural, biological and mechanical methods in preference to synthetic chemical units such as fertilisers, pesticides (fungicides, herbicides and insecticides), additives and medicinal products.

The **irrigable area** is that which is equipped for irrigation – the actual amount of land irrigated varies depending, for example, on meteorological conditions or the choice of crop. Over-exploitation of water can lead to the drying-out of natural areas, and to salt-water intrusion in coastal aquifers.

The **livestock density index** measures the stock of animals per hectare. It is the ratio of the livestock units (converted from the number of animals using standard coefficients) per hectare of utilised agricultural area. A **livestock unit** (LSU) is a reference unit which facilitates the aggregation of livestock from various species and ages. Eurofarm LSU coefficients are established by convention (originally, they were related to the animals' feed requirements, the reference being a dairy cow with an annual yield of 3 000 kg of milk, without additional concentrated feedingstuffs). The livestock species aggregated in the LSU total, for the purpose of the indicator in this publication are: equidae, cattle, sheep, goats, pigs, poultry and rabbits.

Main findings

As well as availability and price, many consumers make some decisions about food purchases based on environmental, welfare and health considerations. Determining influences cover a broad scope of considerations regarding the impact of farming practices on wild flora and fauna, soil and water degradation, farm animal welfare, the use of food additives and preservatives, as well as the food miles involved in getting food to market. The future strength of food production in the EU is likely to depend (to some degree) on how farming and the wider food chain responds to these varied consumer influences.

As an example of a more sustainable farming system (at least at a local level), one response appears to be the growth of certified organic production methods in the EU. An estimated 4.0 % of the utilised agricultural area of the EU-27 was classified as under organic agricultural production in 2007. The corresponding shares in Austria (15.7 %) and Sweden (9.9 %) were well above the average, in contrast to Ireland, Romania, Bulgaria and Malta – where the share of organic agriculture represented 1 % or less of the utilised agricultural area.

The use of water by the agricultural industry is also under increasing scrutiny as competing demands are made for an increasingly scarce resource. The proportion of agricultural area that is irrigable is, unsurprisingly, particularly high in the southern Member States, notably Greece, Malta, Cyprus and Italy, where irrigation is essential for many types of agriculture. In a number of other Member States, particularly the Netherlands and Denmark, supplementary irrigation is also used to improve production.

Figure 8.14: Area occupied by organic farming, 2007 (¹)
(% of UAA)

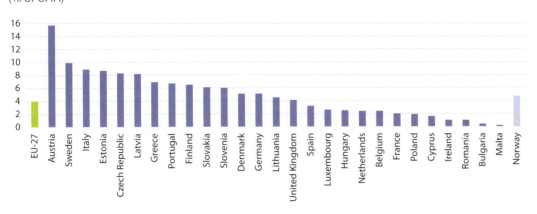

(¹) EU-27, Denmark, Malta and Romania, estimates.

Source: Eurostat (tsdpc440)

Table 8.14: Agri-environmental indicators, 2007

	Utilised agricultural area (UAA) (1 000 hectares)	Organic crop area (fully converted) (% UAA) (¹)	Total organic crop area (% UAA) (²)	Irrigable area (% UAA)	Livestock density index (livestock units per hectare)
Belgium	1 374	1.7	2.4	1.7	2.8
Bulgaria	3 051	0.3	0.4	3.4	0.4
Czech Republic	3 518	6.4	8.3	1.1	0.6
Denmark	2 663	4.9	5.1	16.4	1.7
Germany	16 932	:	5.1	:	1.1
Estonia	907	6.1	8.7	:	0.4
Ireland	4 139	0.6	1.0	0.0	1.4
Greece	4 076	4.3	6.9	38.2	0.6
Spain	24 893	2.6	3.2	14.7	0.6
France	27 477	1.8	2.0	9.7	0.8
Italy	12 744	7.0	8.9	31.0	0.8
Cyprus	146	1.0	1.6	31.4	1.7
Latvia	1 774	3.5	8.2	0.0	0.3
Lithuania	2 649	2.1	4.5	0.1	0.4
Luxembourg	131	2.1	2.6	0.0	1.2
Hungary	4 229	2.3	2.5	3.3	0.6
Malta	10	:	0.2	31.0	4.8
Netherlands	1 914	2.3	2.4	23.9	3.4
Austria	3 189	:	11.7	3.6	0.8
Poland	15 477	0.9	1.9	0.7	0.7
Portugal	3 473	3.2	6.7	16.8	0.6
Romania	13 753	0.5	1.0	4.5	0.4
Slovenia	489	4.8	6.0	0.8	1.1
Slovakia	1 937	4.1	6.1	9.5	0.4
Finland	2 292	5.8	6.5	3.3	0.5
Sweden	3 118	7.5	9.9	5.1	0.6
United Kingdom	16 130	3.2	4.1	0.9	0.9
Norway	1 032	3.9	4.7	11.0	1.2
Switzerland (³)	1 062	:	:	0.0	1.7

(¹) Romania, 2008; Denmark, 2006; Ireland and Portugal, 2005.
(²) Romania, 2008; Denmark and Malta, 2006.
(³) 2005.

Source: Eurostat (ef_lu_ovcropesu, food_in_porg1, tag00095 and tsdpc450)

Trade

9

The EU's external trade policy contributes to Europe's competitiveness in foreign markets. Being an open economy, the EU's aim is to secure improved market access for its industries, services and investments, as well as to enforce the rules of free and fair trade. Coordinated trade policy takes on even greater importance in an era of globalisation, with economies and borders opening up, leading to an increase in trade and capital movements, and the spread of information, knowledge and technology.

The EC Treaty establishes the overall aims and objectives of the EU's trade policy: Article 2 sets the general aims, including promoting the development of economic activities, high employment and competitiveness, and environmental protection. Article 131 explains how common commercial policy should operate: 'to contribute, in the common interest, to the harmonious development of world trade, the progressive abolition of restrictions on international trade and the lowering of customs barriers'. Article 133 sets out the scope, instruments and decision-making procedures. Article 300 establishes the current inter-institutional procedure for the conclusion of international agreements, principally through the European Council.

Within the EU, there are two main sources for statistics on international trade. **External trade statistics (ETS)** provide information on trade in merchandise goods, collected predominantly on the basis of customs and VAT declarations. ETS provide information on the value and volumes (quantity) of external trade in goods; there is a highly-detailed classification of different commodities. In contrast, **balance of payments statistics (BoP)** register all the transactions of an economy with the rest of the world. The current account of the BoP provides information on external trade in goods (generally the largest category), but also on external transactions in services,

income (from employment and investment) and current transfers. For all these
transactions, the BoP registers the value
of exports (credits) and imports (debits),
the difference of which is usually referred
to as the balance (surplus or deficit); for
more information on the current account,
refer to Subchapter 1.5.

Statistics on international trade are an
important data source for many public
and private sector decision-makers, as
they can be extensively used for multilateral and bilateral trade negotiations,
for example, to define and implement
anti-dumping policies, or evaluate the
progress of the Single Market.

9.1 Trade in goods

Introduction

The EU has a common trade policy whereby the European Commission negotiates trade agreements and represents the
EU's interests on behalf of its 27 Member
States. The European Commission con-
sults Member States through an advisory
committee which discusses the full range
of trade policy issues affecting the Community including multilateral, bilateral
and unilateral instruments.

Globally, multilateral trade issues are
dealt with under the auspices of the
World Trade Organisation (WTO). Its
membership covers 153 countries (as of
July 2008), with several candidate members in the process of joining. The WTO
sets the global rules for trade, provides
a forum for trade negotiations, and for
settling disputes between members. The
European Commission negotiates with

its WTO partners and participated in
the latest round of WTO multilateral
trade negotiations, known as the Doha
Development Agenda (DDA). However,
having missed deadlines to conclude
these talks in 2005 and again in 2006,
the Doha round of talks broke down
again at a WTO meeting in July 2008 ([1]).
Although world leaders included a
pledge to complete the Doha round in a
declaration at the end of the G20 summit
of world leaders in London in 2009, no
timetable was set.

Definitions and data availability

External trade statistics for goods are used
extensively by public body decision-makers at an international, EU and national
level, as well as by the private sector. In
the case of Community authorities, external trade statistics help in the preparation
of multilateral and bilateral trade negotiations, in defining and implementing
anti-dumping policies, for the purposes
of macro-economic and monetary policies and in evaluating the progress of the
Single Market, or the integration of European economies. In the private sector,
businesses can use external trade data
to carry out market research and define
their commercial strategy.

A positive balance of trade is known as a
trade surplus and consists of exporting
more than importing. On the contrary,
a negative balance of trade is known as
a trade deficit and consists of importing
more than exporting. Neither is necessarily damaging in a modern economy,
although large trade surpluses or trade
deficits may sometimes be a sign of other
economic problems.

([1]) For more information: http://ec.europa.eu/trade and http://www.wto.org.

The two main flows covered by EU trade statistics concern **extra-EU trade**, which covers the trading of goods with non-member countries, and **intra-EU trade**, which refers to trade between Member States. Whereas extra-EU trade statistics are required for a common trade and customs policy, intra-EU trade statistics measure the integration of the Member States in a common Single Market.

In extra-EU trade statistics, the data shown for the EU-27 treats this entity as a single trading block and reports exports from the whole of the EU-27 to the rest of the world and imports from the rest of the world into the EU-27. In contrast, when reporting data for individual Member States, external trade flows are generally presented in terms of world trade flows (including both intra-EU and extra-EU partners).

Statistics on trade with non-member countries (extra-EU trade) cover movable property imported and exported by the EU, using a variety of product classifications. One of the most common is the standard international trade classification of the United Nations (SITC Rev. 4); this classification allows a comparison of external trade statistics to be made on a worldwide basis. The definitions of extra-EU trade are as follows:

- **imports** are goods which enter the statistical territory of the EU from a non-member country and are placed under the customs procedure for free circulation (as a general rule goods intended for consumption), inward processing, or processing under customs control (goods for working, processing), either immediately or after a period in a customs warehouse;

- **exports** are goods which leave the statistical territory of the EU for a non-member country after being placed under the customs procedure for exports (definitive export), outward processing, or re-exportation following either inward processing or processing under customs control.

Statistics on trade with non-member countries do not, therefore, include goods in transit or those placed under a customs procedure for bonded warehousing or temporary entry (for fairs, exhibitions, tests, etc.), nor do they include re-export following entry under one of these procedures.

Statistics on trade between the Member States (intra-EU trade) cover the arrivals and dispatches of movable goods recorded by each Member State. Arrivals and dispatches are defined as follows:

- **arrivals** are goods in free circulation within the EU which enter the statistical territory of a given Member State;
- **dispatches** are goods in free circulation within the EU which leave the statistical territory of a given Member State to enter another Member State.

Intra-EU trade generally accounts for the majority of trade flows recorded for Member States. Countries that are near the centre of Europe are more likely to have a higher proportion of intra-EU trade than countries that are geographically on the periphery of the EU.

As a result of customs controls being abolished between the borders of the Member States during the creation of the Single Market, intra-EU trade statistics are collected directly from trade operators.

The statistical values of extra-EU trade and intra-EU trade are recorded at their free-on-board (FOB) value for exports/dispatches and their cost, insurance and freight (CIF) value for imports/arrivals. The values reported comprise only those subsidiary costs (freight and insurance) which relate, for exports/dispatches, to the journey within the territory of the Member State from which the goods are exported/dispatched and, for imports/arrivals, to the journey outside the territory of the Member State into which the goods are imported/enter.

Main findings

External trade forms an increasing part of the world economy, through the influence of globalisation, as well as rapidly growing exchanges with developing economies such as China and India, and some of the countries formed out of the Soviet Union – in particular those where indigenous energy supplies are of particular importance. For each of the main players in external trade, the values of both exports and imports of goods rose sharply in the ten years through until 2008, highlighting the globalisation of trade flows. The EU-27 accounted for about one fifth of the world's trade in goods in 2008.

The EU-27 exported goods to the value of EUR 1 308 600 million to non-member countries in 2008, and imported goods to the value of EUR 1 550 700 million from the rest of the world. The trade deficit of EUR 242 100 million in goods recorded for 2008 was larger than that for any other year in the period for which EU-27 data are available (since 1999), and confirmed a widening trend recorded since 2002.

The trade in goods between Member States (intra-EU trade), which was valued in terms of dispatches at EUR 2 701 700 million in 2008, was a little over twice the value of exports from the EU-27 to non-member countries. The importance of the internal market was underlined by the fact that for each of the Member States, intra-EU trade of goods was higher than extra-EU trade. The proportion of the total trade in goods accounted for by these two flows varied considerably among the Member States, reflecting to some degree historical ties and geographical location. The highest levels of intra-EU trade (about 80 %) were recorded for Luxembourg, the Czech Republic and Slovakia, with this share falling to less than 60 % in the United Kingdom, Italy, Bulgaria, Lithuania and Finland.

Germany recorded the highest trade surplus (extra and intra-EU combined) for goods in 2008, valued at EUR 175 500 million. This represented a narrowing of the surplus by almost EUR 20 000 million compared with 2007. The next highest trade surplus in 2008 (EUR 40 500 million) was recorded for the Netherlands, followed by Ireland (EUR 28 000 million). In contrast, the highest trade deficit in goods (EUR 118 000 million) was recorded by the United Kingdom, although this figure represented a considerable narrowing of the deficit compared with 2007. The trade deficits for a number of Member States widened in 2008, none more so than France (by EUR 18 600 million to EUR 67 900 million).

Exports of goods from the EU-27 to the United States were valued at EUR 249 400 million in 2008, representing a little less than one fifth (19.1 %) of all exports to non-member countries.

The value of exports to the United States was about two and a half times the size of the next largest market, namely that of Russia. However, whereas the value of exports to the United States declined to its lowest level since 2004 (in part reflecting the relative strength of the euro against the dollar), the value of exports to Russia rose sharply (up 18.0 % on their 2007 level).

Since 2006, China has become the main origin of EU-27 imports of goods; it accounted for 16.0 % of extra-EU imports in 2008, up from 7.1 % in 1999. Although growth in the value of imports from China continued in 2008, there was faster growth in a number of other countries from which energy supplies were secured; the share of extra-EU imports from Russia rose sharply to 11.2 % of the total in 2008 and that from Norway to 5.9 %.

Machinery and transport equipment accounted for the largest share (43.5 %) of exports of goods from the EU-27 to non-member countries in 2008; this latest figure represented a slightly lower proportion of EU-27 exports than five years earlier (45.0 % in 2003). Machinery and transport equipment also recorded the largest trade surplus (EUR 155 200 million) in 2008. Mineral fuels and lubricants accounted for the largest share (28.6 %) of extra EU-27 imports in 2008, which marked a considerable increase when compared with five years before (16.9 % in 2003). It should be noted that these shares are calculated on the basis of the value of transactions, and comparisons over time reflect both changes in quantity and price levels (with a significant increase in the price of most energy raw materials over the period considered).

Table 9.1: Main players for external trade
(EUR 1 000 million)

	Exports			Imports			Trade balance		
	1998	2003	2008	1998	2003	2008	1998	2003	2008
EU-27 ([1])	:	869	1 309	:	935	1 551	:	-66	-242
Norway	36	61	114	33	35	60	3	25	53
Switzerland	70	89	136	71	85	124	-1	4	12
Canada ([2])	191	241	306	180	213	277	12	28	29
China (excluding Hong Kong) ([2])	164	387	889	125	365	698	39	23	191
Japan ([2])	346	417	521	250	339	454	96	78	67
United States ([2])	607	640	848	842	1 154	1 472	-235	-514	-624

([1]) External trade flows with extra EU-27.
([2]) 2007 instead of 2008.

Source: Eurostat (ext_lt_intertrd)

9 Trade

Figure 9.1: Main players for external trade, 2008
(EUR 1 000 million)

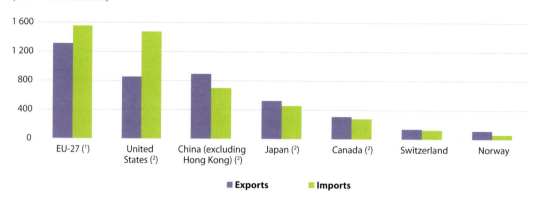

(¹) External trade flows with extra EU-27.
(²) 2007 instead of 2008.

Source: Eurostat (ext_lt_intertrd)

Figure 9.2: Shares in the world market for exports, 2007
(% share of world exports)

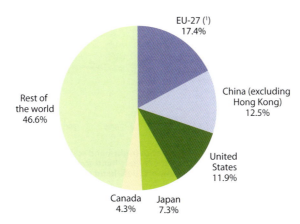

(¹) External trade flows with extra EU-27.

Source: Eurostat (ext_lt_introle)

Figure 9.3: Shares in the world market for imports, 2007
(% share of world imports)

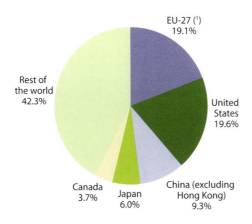

(¹) External trade flows with extra EU-27.

Source: Eurostat (ext_lt_introle)

Figure 9.4: Development of external trade, EU-27 (¹)
(EUR 1 000 million)

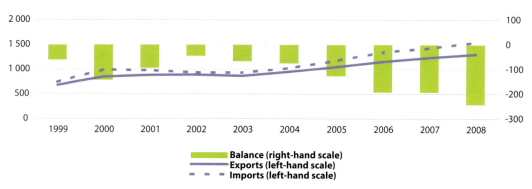

(¹) External trade flows with extra EU-27.

Source: Eurostat (ext_lt_intertrd)

Table 9.2: External trade
(EUR 1 000 million)

	Exports			Imports			Balance	
	2007	2008	2007-08 growth rate (%)	2007	2008	2007-08 growth rate (%)	2007	2008
EU-27 (¹)	1 241.6	1 308.6	5.4	1 434.1	1 550.7	8.1	-192.5	-242.1
Belgium	315.3	323.3	2.6	301.4	319.2	5.9	13.9	4.1
Bulgaria	13.5	15.3	13.1	21.9	25.3	15.9	-8.4	-10.1
Czech Republic	89.4	99.4	11.2	86.2	96.2	11.6	3.2	3.2
Denmark	74.9	79.5	6.2	71.9	75.6	5.1	3.0	3.9
Germany	964.0	993.9	3.1	769.8	818.5	6.3	194.3	175.5
Estonia	8.0	8.4	4.5	11.4	10.9	-4.8	-3.4	-2.5
Ireland	88.7	84.5	-4.8	61.2	56.4	-7.7	27.5	28.0
Greece	17.2	17.2	-0.3	55.6	52.9	-4.9	-38.4	-35.7
Spain	184.8	182.4	-1.3	284.1	272.9	-3.9	-99.2	-90.5
France	402.7	411.7	2.2	452.0	479.7	6.1	-49.3	-67.9
Italy	358.6	365.8	2.0	368.1	377.3	2.5	-9.5	-11.5
Cyprus	1.0	1.1	6.9	6.3	7.2	14.5	-5.3	-6.1
Latvia	6.1	6.9	13.2	11.2	10.9	-2.5	-5.1	-4.0
Lithuania	12.5	16.1	28.5	17.8	21.0	18.0	-5.3	-5.0
Luxembourg	16.4	17.3	5.4	20.1	21.5	6.9	-3.7	-4.2
Hungary	69.6	73.2	5.2	69.7	73.4	5.2	-0.1	-0.1
Malta	2.3	1.9	-15.6	3.5	3.1	-10.1	-1.2	-1.2
Netherlands	401.9	430.4	7.1	359.4	389.8	8.4	42.4	40.5
Austria	119.4	123.0	3.1	119.0	124.7	4.8	0.4	-1.7
Poland	102.3	114.3	11.7	120.9	138.9	14.9	-18.7	-24.6
Portugal	37.6	38.0	1.0	57.1	61.2	7.2	-19.5	-23.2
Romania	29.5	33.6	13.7	51.3	56.2	9.6	-21.8	-22.7
Slovenia	22.0	23.2	5.6	23.0	25.1	9.2	-1.1	-2.0
Slovakia	42.5	48.2	13.6	43.9	49.8	13.4	-1.5	-1.6
Finland	65.7	65.5	-0.3	59.6	61.7	3.4	6.1	3.8
Sweden	123.2	124.6	1.1	111.3	113.5	1.9	11.9	11.2
United Kingdom	320.4	311.7	-2.7	454.5	429.7	-5.4	-134.1	-118.0
Iceland	3.5	:	:	4.9	:	:	-1.4	:
Norway	99.3	113.6	14.4	58.5	60.5	3.4	40.8	53.1
Switzerland	125.5	136.3	8.6	117.6	124.4	5.8	7.9	11.9
Canada	306.4	:	:	277.3	:	:	29.1	:
China	888.6	:	:	697.5	:	:	191.0	:
Japan	521.2	:	:	454.0	:	:	67.2	:
United States	848.3	:	:	1 471.8	:	:	-623.6	:

(¹) External trade flows with extra EU-27.

Source: Eurostat (tet00002)

Table 9.3: Extra EU-27 trade, 2008

	Exports		Imports		Trade balance
	(EUR 1 000 million)	**Share of EU-27 exports (%)**	**(EUR 1 000 million)**	**Share of EU-27 imports (%)**	**(EUR 1 000 million)**
EU-27	1 308.6	100.0	1 550.7	100.0	-242.1
Belgium	74.0	5.7	94.8	6.1	-20.9
Bulgaria	6.1	0.5	11.0	0.7	-4.9
Czech Republic	15.0	1.1	22.2	1.4	-7.2
Denmark	23.9	1.8	21.0	1.4	2.9
Germany	361.0	27.6	291.7	18.8	69.2
Estonia	2.5	0.2	2.2	0.1	0.3
Ireland	30.8	2.4	16.8	1.1	14.0
Greece	6.2	0.5	19.9	1.3	-13.7
Spain	58.1	4.4	117.7	7.6	-59.7
France	152.2	11.6	155.6	10.0	-3.4
Italy	151.9	11.6	173.3	11.2	-21.4
Cyprus	0.3	0.0	2.3	0.2	-2.0
Latvia	2.2	0.2	2.7	0.2	-0.5
Lithuania	6.4	0.5	9.0	0.6	-2.6
Luxembourg	1.9	0.1	5.4	0.4	-3.5
Hungary	16.1	1.2	23.5	1.5	-7.4
Malta	1.0	0.1	0.8	0.1	0.2
Netherlands	91.7	7.0	198.8	12.8	-107.1
Austria	34.2	2.6	27.4	1.8	6.8
Poland	25.7	2.0	39.9	2.6	-14.2
Portugal	10.0	0.8	16.2	1.0	-6.2
Romania	9.9	0.8	17.3	1.1	-7.4
Slovenia	7.4	0.6	7.2	0.5	0.2
Slovakia	7.1	0.5	13.5	0.9	-6.5
Finland	28.9	2.2	23.6	1.5	5.3
Sweden	49.8	3.8	35.3	2.3	14.4
United Kingdom	134.4	10.3	201.1	13.0	-66.7

Source: Eurostat (ext_lt_intratrd)

Table 9.4: Intra EU-27 trade

	Dispatches		Arrivals		Balance	
	2003	2008	2003	2008	2003	2008
EU-27	1 914.5	2 701.7	1 824.1	2 621.9	-	-
Belgium	174.4	249.4	152.8	224.4	21.6	25.0
Bulgaria	4.2	9.2	5.6	14.3	-1.3	-5.1
Czech Republic	37.6	84.4	32.7	74.0	4.9	10.5
Denmark	41.3	55.6	37.2	54.6	4.1	1.0
Germany	431.1	633.0	353.3	526.7	77.8	106.2
Estonia	3.3	5.9	3.7	8.7	-0.4	-2.8
Ireland	51.2	53.7	29.9	39.6	21.3	14.0
Greece	7.7	11.0	23.1	33.0	-15.4	-22.0
Spain	103.9	124.4	127.9	155.2	-24.0	-30.8
France	231.1	259.5	247.6	324.1	-16.6	-64.6
Italy	165.0	213.9	166.5	204.0	-1.5	9.9
Cyprus	0.3	0.8	2.2	4.9	-1.9	-4.1
Latvia	2.0	4.7	3.5	8.2	-1.5	-3.5
Lithuania	3.9	9.7	4.8	12.1	-0.9	-2.4
Luxembourg	10.5	15.4	11.1	16.0	-0.6	-0.7
Hungary	32.1	57.1	27.3	49.8	4.8	7.3
Malta	1.0	0.9	1.9	2.3	-1.0	-1.4
Netherlands	210.4	338.7	128.4	191.0	81.9	147.6
Austria	64.7	88.8	72.0	97.3	-7.3	-8.5
Poland	38.9	88.5	42.0	99.0	-3.1	-10.5
Portugal	22.8	28.0	33.2	45.0	-10.4	-17.0
Romania	11.8	23.7	14.5	38.9	-2.7	-15.3
Slovenia	7.7	15.8	9.4	17.9	-1.7	-2.1
Slovakia	16.6	41.2	14.8	36.3	1.8	4.9
Finland	28.3	36.6	25.7	38.1	2.7	-1.4
Sweden	53.0	74.9	53.1	78.2	-0.1	-3.3
United Kingdom	160.0	177.3	200.2	228.6	-40.2	-51.3

Source: Eurostat (tet00039)

Figure 9.5: Intra and extra EU-27 trade, 2008
(imports + exports, % share of total trade)

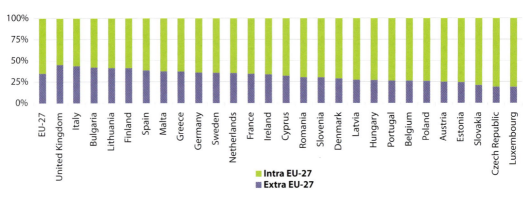

Source: Eurostat (ext_lt_intratrd)

Figure 9.6: Main trading partners for exports, EU-27, 2008
(% share of extra EU-27 exports)

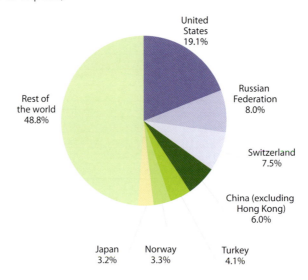

Source: Eurostat (ext_lt_maineu)

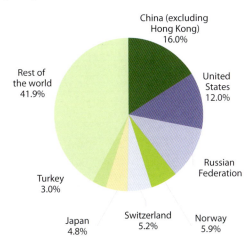

Figure 9.7: Main trading partners for imports, EU-27, 2008
(% share of extra EU-27 imports)

China (excluding
Hong Kong)
16.0%

Rest of
the world
41.9%

United
States
12.0%

Russian
Federation

Turkey
3.0%

Japan
4.8%

Switzerland
5.2%

Norway
5.9%

Source: Eurostat (ext_lt_maineu)

Table 9.5: Extra EU-27 trade by main trading partners, EU-27 ([1])
(EUR 1 000 million)

	1999	2000	2001	2002	2003	2004	2005	2006	2007	2008
EXPORTS										
Extra EU-27	683.1	849.7	884.7	891.9	869.2	953.0	1 052.7	1 159.3	1 241.6	1 308.6
United States	187.0	238.2	245.6	247.9	227.3	235.5	252.7	269.0	261.4	249.4
China (excl. Hong Kong)	19.7	25.9	30.7	35.1	41.5	48.4	51.8	63.8	71.9	78.4
Russian Federation	16.9	22.7	31.6	34.4	37.2	46.0	56.7	72.3	89.1	105.2
Switzerland	63.7	72.5	76.5	72.8	71.4	75.2	82.6	87.7	92.9	97.7
Norway	23.9	26.4	27.2	28.2	27.7	30.8	33.8	38.5	43.6	43.7
Japan	35.7	45.5	45.5	43.5	41.0	43.4	43.8	44.8	43.8	42.4
Turkey	21.6	31.9	21.9	26.6	30.9	40.1	44.6	50.0	52.7	54.3
South Korea	11.7	16.7	15.8	17.7	16.5	17.9	20.2	22.9	24.8	25.7
Brazil	14.4	16.9	18.6	15.7	12.4	14.2	16.1	17.7	21.3	26.3
India	10.6	13.7	13.0	14.3	14.6	17.2	21.3	24.4	29.5	31.5
IMPORTS										
Extra EU-27	743.3	992.7	979.1	937.0	935.3	1 027.5	1 179.6	1 351.7	1 434.1	1 550.7
United States	165.9	206.3	203.3	182.6	158.1	159.4	163.5	175.2	181.6	186.3
China (excl. Hong Kong)	52.6	74.6	82.0	90.2	106.2	128.7	160.3	194.8	232.6	247.6
Russian Federation	35.9	63.8	65.9	64.5	70.7	84.0	112.6	140.9	144.3	173.3
Switzerland	55.1	62.6	63.6	61.7	59.1	62.0	66.6	71.6	76.9	80.1
Norway	30.4	47.2	46.4	48.0	51.0	55.3	67.2	79.2	76.7	92.0
Japan	75.4	92.1	81.1	73.7	72.4	74.7	74.1	77.3	78.4	74.8
Turkey	16.0	18.7	22.1	24.6	27.3	32.7	36.1	41.7	47.0	45.9
South Korea	20.5	27.0	23.3	24.6	26.0	30.7	34.5	40.8	41.4	39.4
Brazil	14.1	18.7	19.6	18.4	19.1	21.7	24.1	27.2	32.8	35.5
India	10.5	12.9	13.5	13.7	14.1	16.4	19.1	22.6	26.6	29.4
TRADE BALANCE										
Extra EU-27	-60.2	-143.0	-94.4	-45.1	-66.0	-74.6	-126.9	-192.4	-192.5	-242.1
United States	21.1	31.9	42.3	65.3	69.2	76.1	89.2	93.8	79.8	63.1
China (excl. Hong Kong)	-32.9	-48.8	-51.3	-55.1	-64.8	-80.3	-108.5	-131.1	-160.7	-169.2
Russian Federation	-19.0	-41.0	-34.3	-30.1	-33.5	-37.9	-55.9	-68.6	-55.2	-68.2
Switzerland	8.6	10.0	12.9	11.1	12.3	13.2	16.0	16.1	16.0	17.6
Norway	-6.5	-20.8	-19.2	-19.9	-23.4	-24.5	-33.4	-40.7	-33.1	-48.3
Japan	-39.7	-46.6	-35.6	-30.2	-31.4	-31.3	-30.3	-32.5	-34.6	-32.4
Turkey	5.7	13.2	-0.2	2.0	3.6	7.4	8.5	8.3	5.7	8.4
South Korea	-8.8	-10.2	-7.4	-6.9	-9.6	-12.7	-14.2	-17.9	-16.6	-13.7
Brazil	0.3	-1.8	-1.0	-2.6	-6.7	-7.6	-8.1	-9.5	-11.5	-9.2
India	0.2	0.8	-0.5	0.7	0.5	0.8	2.2	1.8	2.9	2.1

([1]) Partners are sorted according to the sum of exports and imports in 2008.

Source: Eurostat (tet00040)

Table 9.6: Extra EU-27 trade by main products, EU-27

	1999		2003		2008	
	(EUR 1 000 million)	(%)	(EUR 1 000 million)	(%)	(EUR 1 000 million)	(%)
EXPORTS						
Total	683.1	100.0	869.2	100.0	1 308.6	100.0
Food, drinks & tobacco	41.8	6.1	48.5	5.6	68.3	5.2
Raw materials	14.5	2.1	18.3	2.1	32.4	2.5
Mineral fuels, lubricants	15.7	2.3	27.4	3.2	80.7	6.2
Chemicals & related prod.	97.4	14.3	141.1	16.2	205.2	15.7
Other manufactured goods	181.2	26.5	223.9	25.8	316.5	24.2
Machinery & transport equip.	314.6	46.0	391.6	45.0	569.0	43.5
IMPORTS						
Total	743.3	100.0	935.3	100.0	1 550.7	100.0
Food, drinks & tobacco	50.3	6.8	57.3	6.1	80.1	5.2
Raw materials	38.9	5.2	43.1	4.6	75.6	4.9
Mineral fuels, lubricants	84.1	11.3	157.9	16.9	444.0	28.6
Chemicals & related prod.	58.7	7.9	80.5	8.6	126.8	8.2
Other manufactured goods	200.3	26.9	238.5	25.5	374.3	24.1
Machinery & transport equip.	288.2	38.8	326.8	34.9	413.8	26.7
TRADE BALANCE						
Total	-60.2	-	-66.0	-	-242.1	-
Food, drinks & tobacco	-8.5	-	-8.8	-	-11.7	-
Raw materials	-24.4	-	-24.8	-	-43.2	-
Mineral fuels, lubricants	-68.5	-	-130.5	-	-363.3	-
Chemicals & related prod.	38.8	-	60.6	-	78.4	-
Other manufactured goods	-19.1	-	-14.7	-	-57.7	-
Machinery & transport equip.	26.4	-	64.8	-	155.2	-

Source: Eurostat (ext_lt_intertrd)

Figure 9.8: Main exports, EU-27
(% share of extra EU-27 exports)

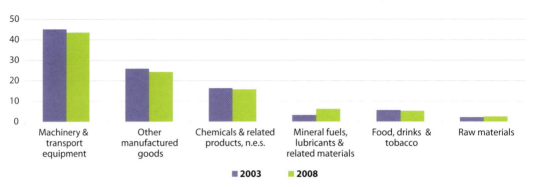

Source: Eurostat (ext_lt_intertrd)

Figure 9.9: Main imports, EU-27
(% share of extra EU-27 imports)

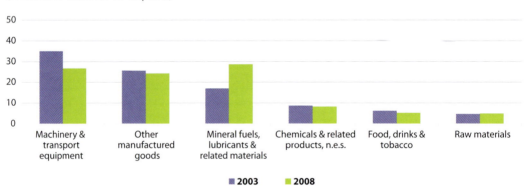

Source: Eurostat (ext_lt_intertrd)

9.2 Trade in services

Introduction

Whereas the previous subchapter described trade in goods, this subchapter focuses on trade in services. Statistics on trade in services are compiled in the balance of payments (BoP) framework. Services play a major role in all modern economies. An efficient services sector is crucial for trade and economic growth and for vibrant and resilient economies. Trade in services also plays an important role in creating wealth and jobs for all economies around the world, and is a catalyst for development. Services are the backbone of economies and trade around the world and provide vital support to the economy and industry as a whole, for example, through finance, logistics and communications. Increased trade in and availability of services may boost economic growth by improving the performance of other industries, since services can provide key intermediate inputs, especially in an increasingly interlinked globalised world. For more information on BoP statistics, refer to Subchapter 1.5.

Definitions and data availability

BoP statistics are of particular interest for analysing the services economy, as external trade statistics only cover goods. The provision of services tends to contribute an increasing share of the economic wealth of the EU, and accounts for more than 50 % of GDP in each Member State. Nevertheless, the value of exports and imports of goods is approximately three times higher than that of services. Part of this imbalance may be due to the nature of some services: for example, the provi-

sion of services of proximity that are difficult to provide over long distances or alternatively professional services that are bound by distinct national legislation. Due to its intangible nature, trade in services is more difficult to record than trade in goods. Services are also often difficult to separate from goods with which they may be associated and trade in goods may indistinguishably include the value of some services, such as insurance, maintenance contracts, transport charges or royalty/licence payments.

Trade integration of goods and services is defined as the average value of debits and credits (summed and divided by two), presented in relation to GDP. This indicator is calculated for both goods and services, based on BoP data; if the values increase over time, then the reporting territory became more integrated within the international economy. It is normal that smaller countries will display a higher degree of trade integration, as they are more likely to import a range of goods and services that are not produced within their domestic markets.

Main findings

In 2008 the EU-27 economy continued to be progressively more integrated with the international economy in terms of its level of credits and debits relative to GDP. The average value of EU-27 trade flows of goods corresponded to 11.4 % of GDP in 2008, up on the 10.7 % share of the previous year. Although the level of external trade in services is less than that for goods, the trade integration of services also rose (from 3.7 % of GDP in 2007), to reach 3.9 % in 2008.

The importance of services in the EU-27's economy is scarcely reflected in terms of external trade. Indeed, the share of services in total trade (goods and services) has remained fairly stable at around 25 % to 27 % since 2002; in 2008 services accounted for 28.3 % of exports and 22.5 % of imports. The EU-27 reported a surplus in service transactions of EUR 78 300 million with the rest of the world in 2008, reflecting credits of EUR 523 600 million and debits of EUR 445 300 million.

The United Kingdom recorded a net credit (extra and intra-EU combined) of EUR 56 900 million in service transactions in 2008, the highest net credit among the Member States and considerably more than the next highest that was recorded by Spain (EUR 26 300 million). In contrast, Germany recorded a net deficit in service transactions of EUR 25 700 million in

2008, the largest deficit by far among the Member States. It is important to underline that most trade in services by Member States involved intra-EU transactions, amounting to 57.3 % of credits and 59.2 % of debits. More than two thirds of the EU-27's credits (68.4 %) and almost three quarters of its debits (73.1 %) in the external trade of services in 2008 were accounted for by three categories: transportation, travel and other business services. The surplus of EUR 32 159 million for other business services was the highest among services, followed by a surplus of EUR 30 364 million for financial services, EUR 20 551 million for transport and EUR 16 428 million for computer and information services. In contrast, the largest deficits were EUR 22 186 million for travel and EUR 11 918 million for royalties and license fees.

Figure 9.10: Trade integration, EU-27 ([1])
(% of GDP)

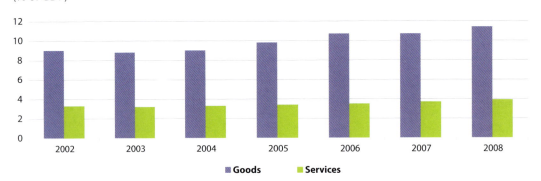

([1]) EU-25 for 2002 and 2003.

Source: Eurostat (tsier120)

Table 9.7: Share of goods and services in GDP, 2008 (¹)
(% of GDP)

	Goods			Services		
	Exports	Imports	Balance	Exports	Imports	Balance
EU-27	10.6	12.2	-1.6	4.2	3.6	0.6
Euro area	17.0	17.1	-0.1	5.5	5.0	0.5
Belgium	73.4	76.5	-3.2	17.6	16.4	1.2
Bulgaria	44.8	70.4	-25.7	15.7	13.3	2.4
Czech Republic	66.5	63.7	2.8	10.2	8.0	2.2
Denmark	33.6	34.0	-0.5	21.1	18.3	2.9
Germany	40.7	33.6	7.2	6.7	7.8	-1.0
Estonia	53.8	65.7	-11.9	22.3	14.7	7.6
Ireland	43.9	31.1	12.8	37.3	40.2	-2.9
Greece	8.2	26.3	-18.1	14.0	7.0	7.1
Spain	17.7	25.7	-8.0	8.9	6.5	2.4
France	20.9	24.0	-3.1	5.6	4.9	0.7
Italy	23.6	23.6	0.0	5.3	5.8	-0.5
Cyprus	7.7	42.3	-34.7	42.1	18.8	23.3
Latvia	28.0	45.0	-17.0	13.4	9.4	4.0
Lithuania	49.8	61.4	-11.6	10.2	9.2	1.1
Luxembourg	39.7	51.4	-11.7	128.2	75.4	52.8
Hungary	68.3	68.2	0.1	12.9	12.1	0.9
Malta	36.1	57.0	-20.9	44.1	26.9	17.2
Netherlands	60.7	54.3	6.4	12.0	10.5	1.5
Austria	45.1	45.2	-0.1	15.1	10.3	4.8
Poland	33.2	37.8	-4.6	6.7	5.7	1.0
Portugal	23.0	35.8	-12.9	10.8	6.8	3.9
Romania	24.5	37.9	-13.4	6.4	5.8	0.6
Slovenia	54.0	61.0	-7.1	14.0	9.2	4.8
Slovakia	73.5	74.6	-1.1	8.9	9.7	-0.7
Finland	35.5	32.3	3.2	10.5	9.7	0.9
Sweden	38.5	34.7	3.8	15.0	11.4	3.7
United Kingdom	17.4	23.8	-6.4	10.7	7.6	3.1
Turkey	20.6	43.5	-22.9	21.3	6.6	14.7
Norway	19.2	26.3	-7.2	4.8	2.4	2.4
Japan	38.0	18.8	19.2	10.0	9.8	0.2
United States	15.3	14.5	0.7	3.1	3.5	-0.4

(¹) EU-27, extra-EU flows; euro area, extra-euro area flows; Member States and other countries, flows with the rest of the world.

Source: Eurostat (bop_q_eu, bop_q_euro, bop_q_c and tec00001)

Table 9.8: Trade in services (¹)
(EUR 1 000 million)

	Credits			Debits			Net	
	2003	2008	2007-08 growth rate (%)	2003	2008	2007-08 growth rate (%)	2003	2008
EU-27	:	523.6	4.1	:	445.3	6.8	:	78.3
Euro area	329.8	506.5	3.3	307.3	463.8	5.1	22.5	42.8
Belgium	39.5	60.6	9.0	37.9	56.3	10.0	1.6	4.3
Bulgaria	2.8	5.4	13.3	2.3	4.5	13.9	0.5	0.8
Czech Republic	6.9	15.1	21.1	6.5	11.8	13.3	0.4	3.3
Denmark	27.8	49.1	9.5	24.7	42.5	8.2	3.1	6.6
Germany	109.2	168.0	3.3	152.9	193.7	3.1	-43.7	-25.7
Estonia	2.0	3.5	10.6	1.2	2.3	4.2	0.7	1.2
Ireland	37.1	69.2	1.8	48.2	74.6	8.0	-11.1	-5.4
Greece	21.4	34.1	8.7	9.9	16.9	14.8	11.5	17.1
Spain	65.7	97.5	4.6	42.4	71.2	1.6	23.3	26.3
France	87.3	109.8	0.4	73.3	95.7	0.0	14.0	14.1
Italy	63.4	83.7	2.6	65.8	91.5	3.3	-2.4	-7.8
Cyprus	4.7	7.1	11.4	2.0	3.2	16.5	2.8	3.9
Latvia	1.3	3.1	15.6	0.8	2.2	10.1	0.5	0.9
Lithuania	1.7	3.3	12.7	1.1	3.0	19.7	0.5	0.3
Luxembourg	22.5	47.0	-2.0	13.7	27.7	-0.5	8.8	19.4
Hungary	8.1	13.7	9.8	8.1	12.8	12.0	0.0	0.9
Malta	1.2	2.5	2.1	0.8	1.5	-6.0	0.4	1.0
Netherlands	55.9	71.3	1.2	56.5	62.3	1.3	-0.6	9.0
Austria	28.8	42.4	5.1	21.0	29.0	2.1	7.9	13.4
Poland	9.8	24.1	15.3	9.7	20.6	17.3	0.2	3.6
Portugal	10.9	17.9	5.6	7.3	11.4	8.5	3.6	6.5
Romania	2.7	8.8	26.5	2.6	7.9	22.8	0.1	0.8
Slovenia	2.5	5.2	20.8	1.9	3.4	9.7	0.5	1.8
Slovakia	2.9	5.8	12.8	2.7	6.3	31.9	0.2	-0.5
Finland	10.1	19.4	14.1	10.7	17.8	9.4	-0.6	1.6
Sweden	27.2	49.4	6.2	25.3	37.3	6.7	1.9	12.1
United Kingdom	140.3	194.7	-6.3	112.5	137.8	-6.3	27.8	56.9
Croatia	:	10.1	10.4	:	3.1	9.5	:	7.0
Turkey	15.9	23.8	13.7	6.6	11.9	6.1	9.3	11.9
Norway	25.2	31.1	5.6	23.2	30.4	8.7	2.1	0.8
Japan	68.7	101.6	7.8	98.7	115.9	5.6	-29.9	-14.3
United States	266.1	368.6	2.5	221.3	275.8	-0.1	44.8	92.8

(¹) EU-27, extra EU-27 flows; euro area, extra EA-16 flows; Member States and other countries, flows with the rest of the world.

Source: Eurostat (bop_q_eu, bop_q_euro and bop_q_c)

Table 9.9: Contribution to extra EU-27 trade in services, 2007

	Credits		Debits		Net
	(EUR 1 000 million)	Share of EU-27 credits (%)	(EUR 1 000 million)	Share of EU-27 debits (%)	(EUR 1 000 million)
EU-27 (¹)	498.5	100.0	414.4	100.0	84.1
Belgium	18.7	3.7	15.5	3.7	3.2
Bulgaria	1.3	0.3	1.0	0.2	0.4
Czech Republic	3.1	0.6	3.1	0.8	0.0
Denmark	23.1	4.6	17.6	4.2	5.5
Germany	73.9	14.8	77.8	18.8	-3.9
Estonia	0.9	0.2	0.5	0.1	0.4
Ireland	24.4	4.9	36.8	8.9	-12.5
Greece	14.7	3.0	6.6	1.6	8.2
Spain	25.9	5.2	24.3	5.9	1.5
France	50.1	10.0	46.8	11.3	3.3
Italy	30.3	6.1	33.4	8.1	-3.1
Cyprus	1.7	0.3	0.8	0.2	1.0
Latvia	1.4	0.3	0.7	0.2	0.6
Lithuania	1.2	0.2	0.9	0.2	0.3
Luxembourg	11.7	2.4	8.0	1.9	3.7
Hungary	3.8	0.8	3.9	0.9	-0.1
Malta	0.6	0.1	0.6	0.1	0.0
Netherlands	33.4	6.7	27.8	6.7	5.6
Austria	9.8	2.0	7.5	1.8	2.3
Poland	5.3	1.1	4.2	1.0	1.1
Portugal	3.9	0.8	2.8	0.7	1.1
Romania	1.7	0.3	1.9	0.5	-0.2
Slovenia	1.2	0.2	1.3	0.3	-0.1
Slovakia	1.1	0.2	0.8	0.2	0.3
Finland	9.9	2.0	5.8	1.4	4.1
Sweden	23.3	4.7	13.3	3.2	10.0
United Kingdom	122.2	24.5	70.3	17.0	51.9

(¹) Data for the EU institutions are included in the aggregate information presented for the EU-27.

Source: Eurostat (bop_its_det)

Figure 9.11: Trade in services, EU-27, 2007
(% share of extra EU-27 transactions)

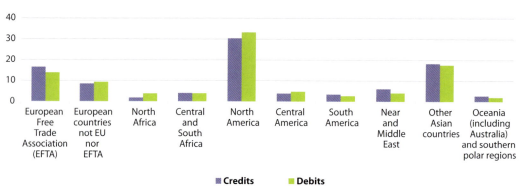

■ Credits   ■ Debits

Source: Eurostat (tec00082 and bop_its_det)

Table 9.10: Contribution to intra EU-27 trade in services, 2007

	Credits		Debits		Net
	(EUR 1 000 million)	Share of EU-27 credits (%)	(EUR 1 000 million)	Share of EU-27 debits (%)	(EUR 1 000 million)
EU-27 (¹)	679.6	100.0	622.6	100.0	57.0
Belgium	39.0	5.7	37.3	6.0	1.6
Bulgaria	3.3	0.5	2.5	0.4	0.8
Czech Republic	9.4	1.4	7.3	1.2	2.1
Denmark	21.6	3.2	21.6	3.5	0.0
Germany	84.3	12.4	110.9	17.8	-26.7
Estonia	2.3	0.3	1.7	0.3	0.5
Ireland	41.3	6.1	31.7	5.1	9.5
Greece	*16.6*	*2.4*	*8.2*	*1.3*	*8.4*
Spain	68.3	10.1	47.7	7.7	20.6
France	56.2	8.3	48.5	7.8	7.7
Italy	51.3	7.6	55.2	8.9	-3.9
Cyprus	4.7	0.7	2.0	0.3	2.7
Latvia	1.3	0.2	1.2	0.2	0.1
Lithuania	1.8	0.3	1.6	0.3	0.2
Luxembourg	35.3	5.2	19.3	3.1	16.0
Hungary	8.6	1.3	7.5	1.2	1.1
Malta	1.9	0.3	1.0	0.2	0.8
Netherlands	48.1	7.1	44.0	7.1	4.2
Austria	30.6	4.5	20.9	3.4	9.7
Poland	15.6	2.3	13.3	2.1	2.3
Portugal	12.9	1.9	7.3	1.2	5.6
Romania	6.0	0.9	5.5	0.9	0.5
Slovenia	3.1	0.5	1.8	0.3	1.3
Slovakia	4.1	0.6	4.0	0.6	0.1
Finland	7.0	1.0	10.3	1.7	-3.3
Sweden	23.0	3.4	21.6	3.5	1.4
United Kingdom	81.9	12.0	76.8	12.3	5.1

(¹) Data for the EU institutions are included in the aggregate information presented for the EU-27.

Source: Eurostat (bop_its_det)

Table 9.11: EU-27 credits for services
(%)

	2004	2005	2006	2007	2008
Extra-EU	41.5	41.8	41.9	42.3	42.7
European Free Trade Association	6.9	6.8	6.6	7.0	:
Switzerland	5.3	5.2	5.0	5.2	5.5
European countries not EU nor EFTA	3.0	3.5	3.8	3.6	:
Central and Eastern Europe	0.8	0.9	1.0	0.4	:
Community of Independent States	1.5	1.8	2.0	2.3	:
Russian Federation	1.0	1.3	1.4	1.6	1.8
Africa	2.5	2.5	2.5	2.4	:
America	16.9	16.7	16.4	15.9	:
Canada	0.9	0.9	1.0	1.0	0.9
United States	13.3	12.7	12.5	11.8	11.2
Brazil	0.4	0.5	0.5	0.5	0.7
Asia	9.3	9.8	9.6	10.2	:
China (excl. Hong Kong)	1.0	1.3	1.3	1.5	1.7
Hong Kong	0.8	0.9	0.7	0.7	0.7
India	0.4	0.6	0.7	0.8	0.7
Japan	2.1	2.0	1.7	1.6	1.5
Oceania (including Australia) and southern polar regions	1.1	1.1	1.1	1.1	:
OECD countries	83.0	81.9	81.1	80.1	:
North American Free Trade Association member countries	14.7	14.1	13.9	13.2	:
Petroleum Exporting Countries (OPEC)	2.2	2.3	2.6	3.0	:
African, Caribbean and Pacific countries, signatories of the Partnership Agreement (Cotonou agreement)	1.8	1.9	2.0	1.9	:
Association of South-East Asian Nations	1.6	1.6	1.7	1.7	:
Southern Common Market	0.6	0.7	0.7	0.8	:

Source: Eurostat (tec00080)

Table 9.12: EU-27 debits for services
(%)

	2004	2005	2006	2007	2008
Extra-EU	39.9	39.9	39.7	40.0	40.8
European Free Trade Association	5.5	5.5	5.2	5.5	:
Switzerland	4.1	4.3	4.0	4.2	4.4
European countries not EU nor EFTA	4.0	4.4	4.3	3.7	:
Central and Eastern Europe	1.2	1.3	1.3	0.7	:
Community of Independent States	1.6	1.8	1.9	1.9	:
Russian Federation	1.0	1.1	1.2	1.2	1.3
Africa	3.1	3.1	3.1	3.1	:
America	17.4	17.3	16.8	16.2	:
Canada	0.9	0.8	0.9	0.9	0.9
United States	13.5	13.4	12.8	12.3	12.1
Brazil	0.4	0.5	0.5	0.5	0.6
Asia	7.7	8.0	8.4	8.6	:
China (excl. Hong Kong)	0.9	1.1	1.2	1.3	1.3
Hong Kong	0.6	0.6	0.7	0.8	0.8
India	0.5	0.6	0.6	0.7	0.7
Japan	1.3	1.4	1.4	1.3	1.3
Oceania (including Australia) and southern polar regions	0.8	0.9	0.8	0.8	:
OECD countries	82.3	82.1	81.3	80.7	:
North American Free Trade Association member countries	14.7	14.5	14.0	13.6	:
Petroleum Exporting Countries (OPEC)	1.5	1.5	1.6	1.7	:
African, Caribbean and Pacific countries, signatories of the Partnership Agreement (Cotonou agreement)	2.1	2.1	2.0	2.0	:
Association of South-East Asian Nations	1.6	1.6	1.7	1.7	:
Southern Common Market	0.6	0.7	0.7	0.7	:

Source: Eurostat (tec00081)

Table 9.13: Development of trade in services, EU-27
(EUR 1 000 million)

	2006			2007			2008		
	Credits	Debits	Net	Credits	Debits	Net	Credits	Debits	Net
Total	447.1	378.6	68.5	498.5	414.4	84.1	520.5	445.0	75.4
United States	133.8	122.0	11.7	139.1	127.7	11.4	136.0	132.2	3.8
EFTA	70.9	50.0	20.9	81.9	57.2	24.7	:	:	:
Japan	18.6	13.2	5.4	19.4	13.8	5.6	18.7	14.0	4.7
Russia	14.7	11.0	3.7	19.2	12.0	7.2	21.6	14.0	7.6
China	13.3	11.9	1.5	17.8	13.8	4.0	20.3	14.5	5.8
Canada	10.4	8.5	1.9	11.7	9.6	2.0	11.4	9.6	1.8
India	7.3	5.8	1.5	9.6	7.0	2.5	9.0	7.4	1.5
Hong Kong	7.0	6.6	0.4	8.2	8.1	0.1	8.1	8.4	-0.3
Brazil	5.3	4.7	0.6	6.4	4.8	1.6	9.0	6.1	2.9
Other countries	165.8	145.0	20.8	185.2	160.3	24.9	:	:	:

Source: Eurostat (bop_its_det)

Figure 9.12: Trade in services, by main categories, EU-27, 2008 (¹)
(EUR 1 000 million)

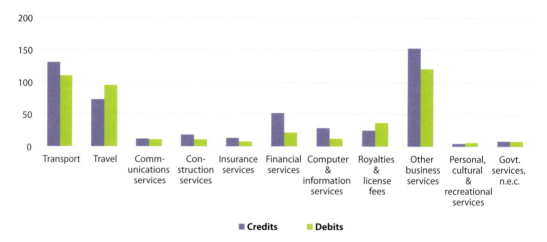

(¹) Extra EU-27 flows.

Source: Eurostat (bop_its_det)

Transport

10

Transport plays a crucial role in an economy, transferring goods between the place of production and consumption, as well as transporting passengers for work or pleasure. However, transport problems such as congestion, quality of services (such as punctuality and connectivity), affordability and environmental impact put general economic developments at risk.

Measures to address these concerns, among others, whilst maintaining the EU's competitiveness, were at the heart of an EU transport policy White Paper titled 'European transport policy for 2010: time to decide' ([1]), which was adopted in 2001. This policy document was supplemented in June 2006 by a mid-term review ([2]) 'keep Europe moving – sustainable mobility for our continent'. Some of the key conclusions of this review were that each transport mode must be optimised to help ensure competitiveness and prosperity; all modes must become more environmentally friendly (underlining commitments such as those under the Kyoto Protocol), safe and energy efficient; each mode should be used efficiently on its own and in combination to achieve an optimal and sustainable utilisation of resources.

Approaching the end of this ten-year policy remit, a further European Commission Communication ([3]) was adopted in June 2009 on 'a sustainable future for transport', which will form the basis for outlining transport policy for the decade through until 2020. The Communication is both consultative and strategic in nature, and underlines the challenges of reducing greenhouse gas emissions,

[1] COM(2001) 370 final; for more information: http://ec.europa.eu/transport/white_paper/index_en.htm.

[2] COM(2006) 314 final; for more information:
http://ec.europa.eu/transport/transport_policy_review/index_en.htm.

[3] COM(2009) 279 (final); for more information:
http://ec.europa.eu/transport/publications/doc/2009_future_of_transport_en.pdf.

the growing demand for – but increasing scarcity of – fossil fuels that is forcing oil prices up to new levels, and increasingly restrictive levels of congestion in many cities, airports and ports as the trend of urbanisation continues.

In this respect, it is worth noting that the transport sector is the fastest growing consumer of energy and producer of greenhouse gases in the EU, even if advances in transport technology and fuel have resulted in marked decreases in emissions of certain pollutants. Although issues in their own right, the environment and energy clearly come together (see Chapter 11 for more details) when looking at the subject of transport sustainability, for consumption and emissions are fairly closely linked: what goes into the fuel tank comes out of the exhaust pipe.

The European Commission also issued a Communication (4) in January 2009 in which it presented the main strategic objectives for the European maritime transport system up to 2018. In broad terms, the strategic goals and recommendations were:

- the ability of the maritime transport sector to provide cost-efficient maritime transport services adapted to the needs of sustainable economic growth of the EU and world economies, and;
- the long-term competitiveness of the EU shipping sector, enhancing its capacity to generate value and employment in the EU, both directly and indirectly, through the whole cluster of maritime industries.

Eurostat's transport statistics describe the most important features of transport, not only in terms of the quantities of freight and numbers of passengers that are moved each year, or the number of vehicles and infrastructure that are used, but also the contribution of transport services to the economy as a whole. Data collection is supported by several legal acts obliging the Member States to report statistical data, as well as voluntary agreements to supply additional data.

10.1 Modal breakdown

Introduction

Transport is defined as any movement of passengers and/or goods (freight). The demand for increased mobility from individuals and increased flexibility and timeliness of delivery from enterprises (both within the Single Market and outside it) has driven rapid growth in road transport and maritime freight transport services. Each mode of transport has its own particular advantages in relation to a set of criteria covering issues such as capacity, speed, cost, safety, flexibility, energy consumption, and environmental impact. European transport policy aims to create a transport system that allows each mode of transport to play a role in a developing transport infrastructure, resulting in more efficient, cost-effective and sustainable transport solutions.

One of the main challenges identified by successive transport policies has been the imbalance in the development of the different modes of transport. One of the key programmes to address this imbalance is the Marco Polo programme, which aims to shift freight transport from the road to short-sea shipping, rail and inland waterways. The second of these programmes (5)

(4) COM(2009) 8 final; for more information: http://ec.europa.eu/transport/strategies/2018_maritime_transport_strategy_en.htm.

(5) Revised Regulation (EC) No 923/2009; for more information:
   http://eur-lex.europa.eu/LexUriServ/LexUriServ.do?uri=OJ:L:2009:266:0001:0010:EN:PDF.

runs from 2007 to 2013 and is enlarged to cover a wider geographical scope (incorporating neighbouring non-member countries), includes new actions regarding 'motorways of the sea' and traffic avoidance, and builds on improving modal synergies and common learning actions.

Definitions and data availability

Definitions of terms used within transport statistics are available in a 'glossary for transport statistics – third edition'.

For statistical comparisons between different modes of transport, standardised units are often used:

- for measuring freight, a **tonne-kilometre** is the unit of measure representing the transport of one tonne of goods by a given mode of transport over one kilometre;
- for measuring passengers, a **passenger-kilometre** is the unit of measure representing the transport of one passenger by a given mode of transport over one kilometre.

A number of inland movements are recorded:

- **rail and inland waterways movements** are recorded in each reporting country on national territory ('territoriality principle'), regardless of the nationality of the vehicle or vessel; road statistics are based on all movements, in the registration country or abroad, of the vehicles registered in the reporting country ('nationality principle');
- **inland passenger transport** corresponds to road (buses and passenger cars) and rail (including inter-city and urban rail transport), thus excluding air and water transport;

- **inland freight transport** corresponds to road, rail, inland waterways and pipeline transport, thus excluding air and sea transport.

The **modal split** (of transport) indicates the share of each mode of transport based on passenger-kilometres (p-km) for passenger transport and tonne-kilometres (t-km) for goods (freight) transport, based on movements on national territory, regardless of the nationality of the vehicle. It should be noted that the data collection methodology is not harmonised at the EU level. As statistics on road and other inland modes are based on different principles, the figures of the smallest reporting countries (for example, Luxembourg and Slovenia) may, therefore, be misleading.

Modes of transport include train, sea, inland waterways and air (for goods and passengers), as well as passenger cars, powered two-wheelers, buses, coaches, trams and metros for passengers and pipelines for goods. In practice, an analysis of the modal split may exclude certain modes, for example, it may be limited to inland transport and therefore exclude international air and sea transport.

Passenger cars are road motor vehicles, other than motorcycles, intended for the carriage of passengers and designed to seat no more than nine persons (including the driver). The term passenger car therefore covers microcars (which need no permit to be driven), taxis, and hired passenger cars, provided that they have fewer than ten seats; this category may also include pick-ups. **Railways** are lines of communication made up by rail exclusively for the use of railway vehicles. **Inland waterways** (navigable) are stretches of water, not part of the sea, over which vessels of a carrying

capacity of not less than 50 tonnes can navigate when normally loaded; this term covers both navigable rivers and lakes and navigable canals. The length of rivers and canals is measured in mid-channel, while the length of lakes and lagoons is measured along the shortest navigable route between the most distant points to and from which transport operations are performed. A waterway forming a common frontier between two countries is reported by both.

Main findings

The vast majority of inland freight in the EU-27 was carried by road in 2007; road transport accounted for a little over three quarters (76.5 %) of total inland freight (excluding pipelines). A little less than one fifth (17.9 %) of inland freight transport across the EU-27 was by rail, with the rest (5.6 %) accounted for by inland waterways.

Among the individual Member States, road was also the dominant means of inland freight transport in the vast majority of cases. The two exceptions were Estonia and Latvia, where a majority (56.8 % and 58.1 % respectively) of inland freight transport was by rail. Rail was also used to a relatively high degree in Lithuania (a little over 41.5 % of inland freight), Sweden (36.4 %) and Austria (34.8 %). Between 10 % and 15 % of inland freight was carried by inland waterways transport in Belgium, Germany and Romania,

this share rising to one third (33.0 %) of inland freight in the Netherlands.

The main measure of the volume of passenger transport is the number of passenger-kilometres travelled within the national territory, which can be analysed by mode of transport; some caution must be applied in making comparisons because of the coverage of national data. Nonetheless, car transport accounted for a sizable majority of inland passenger transport (excluding motorcycles and other powered two-wheelers) among all the Member States for which data are available [6]. The reliance on the car for inland passenger transport was particularly strong in Lithuania, the United Kingdom and the Netherlands, where it accounted for upwards of 86 % of all inland passenger-kilometres in 2007. Between a fifth and one quarter of inland passenger-kilometres in Hungary, Bulgaria, Slovakia, Greece and Estonia were by bus. Railways (including also trams and underground railways/metros) accounted for about one tenth of all inland passenger-kilometres in Austria, France and the Netherlands, a share that rose as high as 13.1 % in Hungary.

It should be noted that the above analysis refers only to inland transport: significant proportions of international freight and passenger travel are accounted for by maritime and air transport, and in some countries national (domestic) maritime and air transport may also be important.

[6] Cyprus and Malta, not available.

Table 10.1: Modal split of inland passenger and freight transport, 2007

	(% of total inland passenger-km) [1]			(% of total inland tonne-km) [2]		
	Passenger cars	Buses	Railways, trams and metros	Railways	Roads	Inland waterways
EU-27	*83.4*	*9.5*	*7.1*	*17.9*	*76.5*	*5.6*
Belgium	80.1	13.3	6.7	13.2	71.1	15.7
Bulgaria	*71.3*	*23.6*	*5.1*	25.1	70.0	4.8
Czech Republic	*75.7*	17.0	7.3	25.3	74.7	0.1
Denmark	80.2	10.8	8.9	7.8	92.2	-
Germany	85.8	6.4	7.8	21.9	65.7	12.4
Estonia	*77.2*	*20.7*	*2.1*	56.8	43.2	0.0
Ireland	*76.3*	*18.6*	*5.1*	0.7	99.3	-
Greece	*77.0*	*21.2*	*1.9*	2.9	97.1	-
Spain	80.9	13.9	5.2	3.9	96.1	-
France	84.9	5.5	9.6	*15.2*	*81.4*	*3.4*
Italy	*82.4*	*11.9*	*5.7*	*11.6*	*88.3*	*0.0*
Cyprus	:	:	0.0	-	100.0	-
Latvia	*79.5*	*15.0*	*5.5*	58.1	41.9	0.0
Lithuania	90.7	8.4	0.9	41.5	58.5	0.0
Luxembourg	*84.9*	*11.1*	*4.1*	4.1	92.5	3.3
Hungary	61.8	25.2	13.1	21.0	74.4	4.6
Malta	:	:	0.0	-	100.0	-
Netherlands	*86.7*	*3.8*	*9.5*	5.7	61.4	33.0
Austria [3]	79.2	10.8	10.1	34.8	60.9	4.2
Poland	83.6	9.6	6.8	26.4	73.5	0.1
Portugal	*83.3*	*12.2*	*4.5*	5.3	94.7	-
Romania	*75.3*	*15.3*	*9.4*	18.9	71.3	9.8
Slovenia	85.1	11.9	3.0	20.8	79.2	-
Slovakia	72.4	21.6	6.0	25.5	71.8	2.7
Finland	84.9	10.0	5.0	25.9	73.9	0.3
Sweden	84.1	7.2	8.7	36.4	63.6	-
United Kingdom	87.3	6.3	6.4	*13.3*	*86.6*	0.1
Croatia	*82.9*	*12.1*	*5.0*	25.2	74.0	0.8
FYR of Macedonia	:	:	:	11.5	88.5	-
Turkey	*51.9*	*45.5*	*2.5*	5.1	94.9	-
Iceland	88.6	11.4	0.0	-	100.0	-
Norway	88.0	7.0	4.9	15.1	84.9	-

[1] Excluding powered two-wheelers.
[2] Excluding pipelines.
[3] The railway in Liechtenstein is owned and operated by the Austrian ÖBB and included in their statistics.

Source: Eurostat (tsdtr210 and tsdtr220)

10

10.2 Passenger transport

Introduction

The principal goal of EU transport policy is to establish a sustainable transport system that meets society's economic, social and environmental needs. People from different regions of Europe have been brought closer together through an expanded road infrastructure, the creation of an integrated high-speed rail network, as well as the expansion of air travel at affordable prices to numerous new destinations. As well as the closer reach of Europe's regions, improving the speed, connectivity and convenience of urban transport continues to be a key policy initiative. This was the subject of a Green Paper [7] in 2007 that looked to stimulate the adoption of best practices regarding transport infrastructure, norm-setting, congestion and traffic management, public transport services, infrastructure charging, urban planning, safety, security and cooperation with the surrounding region.

Against this background, a 2009 European Commission Communication on a 'sustainable future for transport' underlines that within an improvement of the overall quality of transport, a high priority must continue to be given to personal security, the reduction of accidents and of health hazards, the protection of passengers' rights and the accessibility of remote regions.

Definitions and data availability

The **volume of inland passenger transport** is defined as the ratio between passenger-km (inland modes) and GDP (gross domestic product in constant (2000) euro terms), indexed on 2000. It is based on transport movements by passenger cars, buses and coaches, and trains on the national territory, regardless of the nationality of the vehicle.

Rail transport statistics are reported on the basis of the '**territoriality principle**'. This means that each reporting country reports the loading/embarkation, unloading/disembarkation and movements of goods and passengers that take place in their national territory. For this reason, indicators that use tonne-kilometres and passenger-kilometre as units are generally considered as the best measure for comparisons between transport modes and countries, because the use of tonnes or passengers entails a high risk of double-counting, particularly in international transport. A **rail passenger** is any person, excluding members of the train crew, who makes a journey by rail. A **rail passenger-kilometre** is a unit of measure representing the transport of one rail passenger by rail over a distance of one kilometre. Rail passenger data are not available for Malta and Cyprus as they do not have railways. Annual passenger transport statistics (international and national breakdown) cover railway undertakings subject to detailed reporting only, while total annual passenger statistics may include the undertakings under simplified reporting as well. Some countries apply detailed reporting to all railway undertakings and in the case of these countries the total passenger transport is equal to the sum of international and national passenger transport.

---

[7] COM(2007) 551 final; for more information: http://ec.europa.eu/transport/clean/green_paper_urban_transport/index_en.htm.

Maritime transport data are available for most of the period from 2001 onwards, although some Member States have provided data since 1997. Maritime transport data are not transmitted to Eurostat by the Czech Republic, Luxembourg, Hungary, Austria and Slovakia as they have no maritime traffic. A **merchant ship** is a ship designed for the carriage of goods, transport of passengers, or specially fitted out for a specific commercial duty. A **sea passenger** is any person that makes a sea journey on a merchant ship. Service staff assigned to merchant ships are not regarded as passengers. Non-fare paying crew members travelling but not assigned and infants in arms are excluded.

Air transport statistics concern national and international transport. Passenger transport is measured by the number of passengers on board, passengers carried and passenger commercial air flights, in all cases separating arrivals and departures. Statistics on individual routes provide information on seats available, again separating arrivals from departures. The data are presented with monthly, quarterly and annual frequencies. Annual data are available for the Member States for most of the period from 2003 onwards. **Air passengers carried** relate to all passengers on a particular flight (with one flight number) counted once only and not repeatedly on each individual stage of that flight. This includes all revenue and non-revenue passengers whose journey begins or terminates at the reporting airport and transfer passengers joining or leaving the flight at the reporting airport; but excludes direct transit passengers.

Fatalities caused by road accidents include drivers and passengers of motorised

vehicles and pedal cycles as well as pedestrians, killed within 30 days from the day of the accident. For Member States not using this definition, corrective factors were applied.

Main findings

In the vast majority of Member States, the growth in GDP between 1997 and 2007 was greater than the growth in the volume of inland passenger transport. The most notable exception was Lithuania, where the rate of growth in the volume of inland passenger transport was about one third faster than the rate of growth in GDP, although other exceptions were also recorded for Latvia, Portugal, Poland and Greece. In contrast, the rate of GDP growth in Slovakia and Hungary was about one third faster than the rate of growth in the volume of inland passenger transport between 1997 and 2007.

The average distance travelled on railways (national and international travel) per inhabitant, was higher in France, Sweden, Denmark and Austria than elsewhere in the EU-27 in 2007, averaging 1 000 kilometres per inhabitant in each of these Member States. In terms of international travel, the average distance travelled on railways per inhabitant was highest in Luxembourg and Austria, reflecting, for example, the number of international borders, the importance of international commuters within the workforce, the relative proximity of capitals or other cities to international borders, the access to high-speed network rail links, or their position on major international transport corridors.

Almost 800 million passengers were carried by air in 2008 in the EU-27. The largest number of passengers carried (about

214 million) was reported by the United Kingdom; this was equivalent to 3.5 passengers carried per inhabitant. Relative to the size of the population, however, the largest numbers of air passengers carried were reported by the islands of Cyprus and Malta (equivalent to 9.1 and 7.6 passengers carried per inhabitant).

Within the EU, London Heathrow remained the busiest airport in terms of passenger numbers (about 67 million in 2008), followed by Paris' Charles de Gaulle airport (about 60 million), and then Frankfurt, Madrid's Barajas airport and Amsterdam's Schiphol airport (all three with between 53 million and 47 million passengers).

With the exception of Madrid's Barajas airport, the overwhelming majority (about 90 % or higher) of passengers through the other four largest airports in 2008 were on international flights. Madrid's Barajas airport stands out in that national (domestic) flights accounted for a high share (40.8 % in 2008) of the passengers carried. There were also relatively high proportions of passengers on national flights to and from Roma's Fiumicino airport, Barcelona and, in particular, Paris' Orly airport where they were in the majority (representing 55.8 % of all passengers).

Ports in the EU-27 handled 414 million ([8]) maritime passengers in 2008, a rise of 1.9 % on numbers for 2007. Greek and Italian ports handled more passengers than in any other Member State, followed by Danish ports and then, with similar numbers, ports in Sweden, the United Kingdom and Germany. Relative to the size of national populations, the largest numbers of maritime passengers were recorded in Malta (almost 20 passengers per inhabitant), followed by Denmark and Greece (both between 8 and

9 passengers per inhabitant), Estonia and then, some way behind Sweden, Finland and Italy; in the remaining Member States, the number of maritime passengers per inhabitant averaged less than one.

Road fatalities in the EU-27 fell sharply (down 29.9 %) in the decade between 1997 and 2007, from 60 267 deaths to 42 854 deaths. The road fatality rate, expressed as the number of deaths per million inhabitants, averaged 87 across the EU-27, although there were stark contrasts between Member States. The highest road fatality rates in 2007 were recorded in Lithuania (218 deaths per million inhabitants), Latvia (184), Poland and Estonia (both 146). In contrast, rates were much lower in the United Kingdom and the Netherlands (50 and 43), and particularly in Malta (29).

Around 2 900 people were the victims (seriously injured or killed) of railway accidents in the EU-27 in 2007, which represented a sharp rise of about 15 % in the number of victims compared with 2006. It should be noted that the number of victims in any particular year can be greatly influenced by a small number of major incidents and that there had been considerable declines in the number of victims in 2005 and 2006. Of the total number of victims seriously injured or killed in railway accidents in the EU-27 in 2007, a little less than one sixth (16 %) were either train passengers or railway employees. Approximately two thirds (66.5 %) of the lives lost in rail accidents were from incidents involving rolling stock in motion, with almost all others (32.5 %) from incidents at level-crossings. The highest numbers of rail fatalities within the EU-27 in 2007 occurred in Poland (359) and Germany (200).

([8]) The total number of maritime passengers includes passengers who have been double-counted, once when embarking and then when disembarking. The double counting arises when both ports of embarkation and disembarkation report data to Eurostat. This is quite common for the maritime transport of passengers, which is a short distance activity, compared with the seaborne transport of goods. Indeed, there is no significant difference between the number of passengers embarking and disembarking at an aggregated level, as most transport corresponds to main national and intra-EEA ferry connections.

Table 10.2: Volume of inland passenger transport
(index of inland passenger transport volume relative to GDP (2000=100))

	1997	1998	1999	2000	2001	2002	2003	2004	2005	2006	2007
EU-27	:	:	:	100.0	:	99.8	:	:	96.3	95.8	93.9
Belgium	102.6	104.3	102.6	100.0	101.3	101.9	102.5	101.6	97.9	96.5	96.3
Bulgaria	:	:	104.1	100.0	98.2	99.8	92.6	86.9	84.9	78.9	79.5
Czech Republic	98.2	100.0	100.6	100.0	98.6	96.9	95.5	90.5	86.6	82.6	79.6
Denmark	106.7	105.5	104.2	100.0	98.0	97.7	98.0	98.2	96.8	95.8	96.7
Germany	105.4	104.6	104.7	100.0	100.9	101.4	101.1	101.2	99.4	98.0	95.8
Estonia	:	:	:	100.0	:	:	:	:	83.3	76.6	71.3
Ireland	114.5	110.9	104.9	100.0	98.8	96.5	95.7	94.4	92.3	93.1	93.9
Greece	91.3	92.8	95.6	100.0	100.9	102.8	100.4	99.8	101.6	101.3	101.6
Spain	101.5	101.6	102.3	100.0	98.4	97.2	95.8	96.0	94.5	91.1	90.3
France	104.4	103.8	103.3	100.0	101.6	101.6	101.0	98.8	96.2	94.2	93.1
Italy (¹)	95.0	96.4	95.5	100.0	97.4	96.4	96.4	96.1	92.7	97.1	93.1
Cyprus	:	:	:	:	:	:	:	:	:	:	:
Latvia	:	:	:	100.0	:	99.8	:	:	133.0	125.0	119.4
Lithuania	:	:	:	100.0	:	93.3	98.8	120.2	145.6	151.3	137.4
Luxembourg	110.0	105.3	97.5	100.0	101.3	99.8	98.6	95.9	94.3	91.7	88.9
Hungary	111.1	106.1	103.6	100.0	96.3	93.4	89.6	85.2	80.1	77.1	69.0
Malta	:	:	:	100.0	:	:	:	:	:	:	:
Netherlands	109.4	106.0	103.8	100.0	98.5	99.8	99.5	100.8	97.3	94.1	91.6
Austria	106.6	104.1	102.3	100.0	100.0	99.6	100.0	98.5	96.9	95.4	93.4
Poland	103.0	103.8	100.3	100.0	101.5	103.1	101.3	99.6	102.2	104.5	105.6
Portugal	97.7	97.9	99.5	100.0	99.8	102.1	105.4	107.3	110.8	111.3	112.2
Romania	:	:	102.6	100.0	95.7	91.7	93.1	88.4	89.2	84.9	81.8
Slovenia	111.5	105.4	105.7	100.0	98.7	96.7	94.7	92.5	89.7	86.4	81.6
Slovakia	94.9	89.9	93.0	100.0	96.4	94.1	88.3	81.9	79.3	74.8	66.9
Finland	108.8	105.4	103.7	100.0	99.1	99.5	99.5	97.7	96.4	92.7	90.8
Sweden	107.4	104.4	102.8	100.0	99.6	99.6	99.5	95.8	93.1	89.6	89.6
United Kingdom	109.3	106.4	104.2	100.0	99.7	100.7	97.6	96.0	93.9	93.1	91.1
Croatia	:	:	:	100.0	100.8	99.4	96.9	95.3	93.3	92.9	92.6
FYR of Macedonia	:	:	:	100.0	100.0	103.6	107.8	:	104.8	101.5	98.5
Turkey	:	:	108.1	100.0	100.6	:	93.5	89.9	90.6	90.6	91.4
Iceland	90.2	89.9	89.8	100.0	103.7	106.5	107.0	102.5	101.9	102.7	88.3
Norway	103.8	102.9	102.1	100.0	99.8	100.2	101.1	98.4	97.3	95.8	95.2

(¹) Break in series, 2000.

Source: Eurostat (tsien070)

Table 10.3: Rail passenger transport

	Rail passenger transport (million passenger-km)				Rail passenger transport (passenger-km per inhabitant)				Rail accidents (number of persons)			
	National		International		National		International		Killed		Seriously injured	
	2006	2007	2006	2007	2006	2007	2006	2007	2007	2008	2007	2008
EU-27	361 305	369 137	21 149	20 175	733	746	43	41	1 512	:	1 381	:
Belgium	8 190	8 547	774	856	779	807	74	81	37	15	48	26
Bulgaria	2 366	2 342	45	62	307	305	6	8	27	44	34	38
Czech Republic	6 564	6 536	358	362	640	635	35	35	25	44	101	139
Denmark	5 531	5 554	359	425	1 019	1 020	66	78	8	12	11	9
Germany	75 263	75 528	3 472	3 587	913	918	42	44	200	:	199	:
Estonia	231	246	26	27	172	183	19	20	0	9	19	10
Ireland	1 872	1 898	:	109	445	440	:	25	1	1	1	1
Greece	1 748	1 853	63	77	157	166	6	7	18	17	38	29
Spain	20 260	19 966	714	618	463	449	16	14	75	49	34	24
France	72 359	74 473	7 476	7 517	1 149	1 175	119	119	78	93	44	39
Italy	43 712	44 707	2 726	:	744	756	46	22	71	68	49	39
Cyprus	-	-	-	-	-	-	-	-	-	-	-	-
Latvia	893	889	93	86	389	390	41	38	28	29	17	31
Lithuania	246	223	22	24	72	66	6	7	36	40	13	13
Luxembourg	219	233	79	84	467	489	168	176	0	0	0	0
Hungary	9 190	8 379	334	372	912	832	33	37	59	115	92	60
Malta	-	-	-	-	-	-	-	-	-	-	-	-
Netherlands	15 445	15 634	251	254	946	956	15	16	20	20	10	6
Austria	7 051	7 235	1 211	1 279	853	872	147	154	52	40	63	53
Poland	17 675	18 952	565	573	463	497	15	15	359	307	274	264
Portugal	3 821	3 933	55	55	362	371	5	5	58	:	34	:
Romania	7 902	7 271	164	146	366	337	8	7	186	208	185	233
Slovenia	675	690	48	49	337	343	24	24	17	9	30	41
Slovakia	2 043	1 970	170	195	379	365	32	36	57	56	36	38
Finland	3 447	3 675	93	103	656	696	18	20	18	21	3	6
Sweden	9 037	9 771	580	499	999	1 072	64	55	25	15	15	9
United Kingdom	45 565	48 633	1 472	1 537	754	800	24	25	57	59	31	20
Croatia	1 257	1 508	65	65	283	340	15	15	27	13	25	45
Turkey	5 201	5 472	76	81	2 551	2 680	37	40	108	111	204	247
Liechtenstein	:	:	:	:	:	:	:	:	0	0	0	0
Norway	2 779	2 840	41	61	599	607	9	13	0	1	5	1

Source: Eurostat (rail_pa_typepkm, tps00001 and rail_ac_catvict)

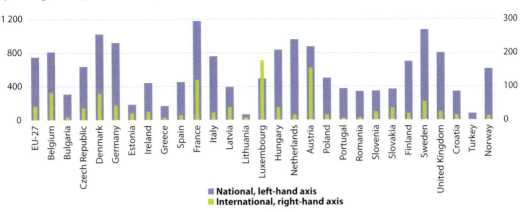

Figure 10.1: Rail passenger transport, 2007 (¹)
(passenger-km per inhabitant)

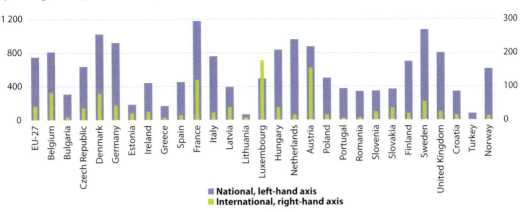

(¹) Cyprus, Malta and Liechtenstein, not applicable.

Source: Eurostat (rail_pa_typepkm and tps00001)

Figure 10.2: Top 15 airports, passengers carried (embarked and disembarked), EU-27, 2008
(million passengers)

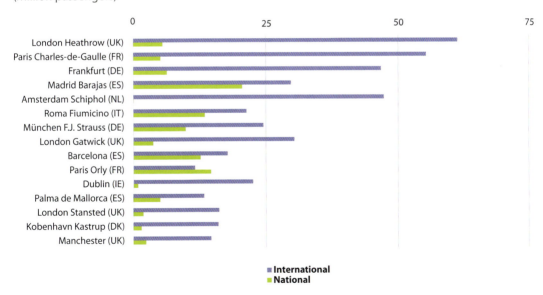

Source: Eurostat (avia_paoa)

Table 10.4: Air and sea passenger transport (¹)

	Air passengers, 2008 (²)		Maritime passengers, 2007 (³)	
	(1 000)	(passengers per inhabitant)	(1 000)	(passengers per inhabitant)
EU-27	797 892	1.6	414 232	0.8
Belgium	21 982	2.1	909	0.1
Bulgaria	6 418	0.8	10	0.0
Czech Republic	13 429	1.3	-	-
Denmark	24 629	4.5	48 409	8.9
Germany	165 822	2.0	30 200	0.4
Estonia	1 804	1.3	8 665	6.5
Ireland	30 016	6.8	3 225	0.7
Greece	34 404	3.1	92 423	8.3
Spain	161 401	3.6	23 134	0.5
France	122 724	1.9	27 048	0.4
Italy	105 236	1.8	86 970	1.5
Cyprus	7 218	9.1	174	0.2
Latvia	3 687	1.6	362	0.2
Lithuania	2 552	0.8	212	0.1
Luxembourg	1 713	3.5	-	-
Hungary	8 429	0.8	-	-
Malta	3 125	7.6	8 132	19.8
Netherlands	50 419	3.1	1 871	0.1
Austria	23 900	2.9	-	-
Poland	18 727	0.5	2 456	0.1
Portugal	25 047	2.4	735	0.1
Romania	8 031	0.4	0	0.0
Slovenia	1 649	0.8	51	0.0
Slovakia	2 596	0.5	-	-
Finland	14 851	2.8	16 450	3.1
Sweden	27 817	3.0	32 662	3.6
United Kingdom	213 888	3.5	30 465	0.5
Croatia	4 504	1.0	24 611	5.5
Iceland	2 241	7.1	433	1.4
Norway	27 717	5.9	6 447	1.4
Switzerland	36 596	4.8	-	-

(¹) For air: aggregates exclude the double-counting impact of passengers flying between countries belonging to the same aggregate. For maritime: figures refer to the number of passengers 'handled in ports' (i.e. the sum of passengers embarked and then disembarked in ports); if both the port of embarkation and disembarkation report data to Eurostat, then these passengers are counted twice.
(²) Total passengers carried (arrivals and departures for national and international).
(³) Malta, 2008; Iceland, 2006.

Source: Eurostat (ttr00012 and mar_pa_aa)

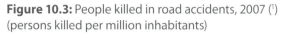

Figure 10.3: People killed in road accidents, 2007 (¹)
(persons killed per million inhabitants)

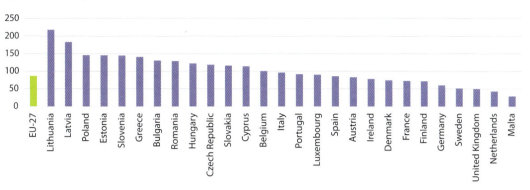

(¹) Italy, 2006.

Source: Eurostat (tsdtr420), European Commission CARE database (Community Database on Road Accidents)

Table 10.5: Rail accidents by type of victim and accident, EU-27, 2007 (¹)
(number of persons)

	Total		Passengers		Railway employees		Others	
	Killed	Seriously injured	Killed	Seriously injured	Killed	Seriously injured	Killed	Seriously injured
Total	1 512	1 381	61	259	37	102	1 414	1 020
Collisions (excluding level-crossing accidents)	12	44	2	16	5	23	5	5
Derailments	5	18	2	14	3	4	0	0
Accidents involving level-crossings	491	571	2	26	2	19	487	526
Accidents to persons caused by rolling stock in motion	1 005	680	53	168	27	40	925	472
Fire in rolling stock	0	0	0	0	0	0	0	0
Others	13	68	2	35	1	16	10	17

(¹) Slightly injured persons are not included in rail accident statistics; Cyprus and Malta, not applicable.

Source: Eurostat (rail_ac_catvict)

10.3 Freight transport

Introduction

The ability to move goods safely, quickly and cost-efficiently to market is important for national and international trade, and economic development. Strains on infrastructure, demonstrated by congestion and delays, as well as the constraints of disparate standards, technical barriers and poor interoperability all impact on economic development.

The European Commission's Communication on 'boosting the efficiency, integration and sustainability of freight transport in the EU' in October 2007 set out a number of policy initiatives and actions. These ideas have been brought up-to-date in the 2009 through a Communication on 'a sustainable future for transport', which sets out a number of policy initiatives for the period through until 2020. These revolve around the following themes:

- **infrastructure – better integrating the different transport modes**; the promotion and development of intermodal and transhipment platforms: the optimising of transport chains to reduce congestion and pollution (for which the European global navigation satellite systems, Galileo and EGNOS, will complement more traditional tools) in part through the promotion of interoperability across the individual parts of the network.
- **funding – sending the correct price signals**; external costs of transport (such as pollution, noise, global warming, congestion and accidents) should be internalised in price structures for all transport modes, in a stepwise

strategy ([9]). Furthermore, the inclusion of aviation in the EU emission trading scheme from 2012 ([10]) and the introduction of internalisation charges for heavy goods vehicles should be considered.

- **technology – accelerating the transition to a low-carbon economy**; standards and norms for new low and zero-emission vehicles to be set: the further development of e-freight and intelligent transport systems as well as alternative vehicle propulsion systems.
- **legislation and effective governance – promoting further market opening but harmonising actions at all levels**; the removal of regulatory obstacles but strong enforcement of competition rules, without sacrificing safety and security, working conditions and customer rights; development of harmonised environmental obligations; consideration of transnational infrastructure managers.
- **behaviour – inform travellers and businesses about different transport possibilities**; educate, inform and involve the public about the effects of transport behaviour and reasons for sometimes controversial transport policies.

Definitions and data availability

Road freight transport statistics are reported by Member States for vehicles registered in their country. On the basis of information on the reporting country, country of loading, and country of unloading, five types of operations are derived:

- national transport;

([9]) COM(2008) 435.

([10]) A Commission proposal on aviation activities was made in 2006 and the resulting Directive adopted in November 2008.

- international transport – goods loaded in the reporting country;
- international transport – goods unloaded in the reporting country;
- international transport – cross-trade (transport between two countries by a vehicle registered in a third country);
- international transport – cabotage (transport inside one country by a vehicle registered in another country).

Rail freight data are provided to Eurostat in line with Regulation 91/2003; this Regulation has been implemented from 2004. Whereas the quarterly data concern railway enterprises under detailed reporting (usually large ones ([1])), annual data cover all enterprises. Rail freight data are not available for Malta and Cyprus as they do not have railways. Switzerland will provide railway statistics starting from 2008 as a reference year, while Iceland has no railways.

Maritime transport data are available for most of the period from 2001 onwards, although some Member States have provided data for the period since 1997. Maritime transport data are not transmitted to Eurostat by the Czech Republic, Luxembourg, Hungary, Austria and Slovakia as they have no maritime ports.

Air freight and mail transport statistics are broken down by freight and mail on-board (arrivals, departures and total), freight and mail loaded and unloaded, and all-freight and mail commercial air flights (arrivals, departures and total). The data are presented with monthly, quarterly and annual frequencies. Annual data are available for most of the Member States for the period from 2003, with a majority also providing data for 2001 and 2002, while some Member States have provided data back to 1993.

Weight transported by rail and inland waterways is the gross-gross weight of goods. This includes the total weight of the goods, all packaging, and tare-weight of the container, swap-body and pallets containing goods. In the case of rail, it also includes road goods vehicles carried by rail. The tare-weight is the weight of a transport unit before any cargo is loaded; when the tare-weight is excluded, the weight is the gross weight (as is the case for sea and road freight transport).

Goods loaded are those goods placed on a road vehicle/railway vehicle/merchant ship and dispatched by road/rail/sea. Unlike in road and inland waterway transport, transhipments from one railway vehicle directly to another and change of tractive vehicle are not regarded as unloading/loading; however, if the goods are unloaded from one railway vehicle to another railway vehicle, this is considered as a break of the journey. **Goods unloaded** are those goods taken off a road vehicle/railway vehicle/merchant ship.

The **volume of inland freight transport** is defined as the ratio between tonne-km (inland modes) and GDP (gross domestic product in constant (2000) euro terms), indexed on 2000. Rail and inland waterways transport are based on movements on the national territory, regardless of the nationality of the vehicle or vessel. Road transport is based on all movements of vehicles registered in the reporting country.

Main findings

The volume of freight transported by road in the EU was a little over four times as high as the volume transported by rail in 2008. About two thirds of the volume of road freight transport by

---

([1]) Countries may cover all railway undertakings operating on their national territory with detailed reporting only (irrespective of the undertaking's transport performance). In this case, quarterly data are comparable with annual ones.

vehicles registered in the EU was national in 2008. However, this proportion varied greatly between Member States: national transport dominated in Cyprus (99.1 % of all road freight transport), the United Kingdom (93.6 % in 2007) and Finland (92.5 %), whereas its importance was much lower in Slovenia (16.2 %), Lithuania (12.5 %) and Luxembourg (6.6 %).

Across the whole of the EU-27, the volume of inland freight transport grew at a slightly faster pace than GDP during the ten-year period through until 2007. Relative to growth in GDP, Spain and Portugal recorded the most dramatic growth in their respective volumes of inland freight transport during this period, followed by Bulgaria, Lithuania, Ireland, Hungary and Slovenia. In contrast, there was sustained decoupling of transport growth from economic growth in a number of Member States, most notably Cyprus, the Czech Republic, Finland, Denmark and the United Kingdom.

Estonia and Latvia were the only Member States where a greater volume of freight was transported by rail than by road in 2008, while the Netherlands was the only Member State where a greater volume of freight was transported by inland water-

ways than by rail. Relative to the size of the population, the greatest volume of road freight transport was reported by Luxembourg, over 21 000 tonne-km per inhabitant, about two and a half times the next highest volume in Slovenia; in both cases, the majority of road freight was performed outside these countries, but by vehicles registered in them.

About 14 million tonnes of air freight (both national and international) was carried through airports within the EU-27. Airports in Germany dealt with 3.6 million tonnes of air freight in 2008, considerably more than in any other Member State. Some of the smaller Member States are relatively specialised in air freight, notably all of the Benelux countries, and in particular, Luxembourg.

Maritime ports in the EU-27 handled 3 934 million tonnes of goods in 2007 (about 2.5 % higher than in 2006). Ports in the United Kingdom handled 582 million tonnes of goods in 2007, more than any other Member State and about 15 % of the EU-27 total. Among the smaller Member States, the weight of goods handled in maritime ports was particularly high in Estonia, the Netherlands, Latvia, Finland, Belgium and Sweden.

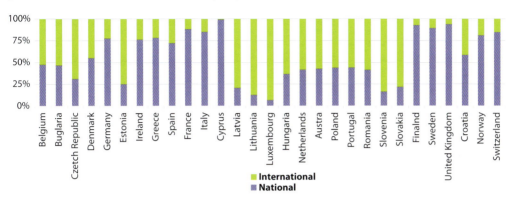

Figure 10.4: National and international road transport of goods, 2008 (¹)
(% based on million t-km of laden transport)

(¹) Greece, Italy and the United Kingdom, 2007; Malta, not available.

Source: Eurostat (road_go_ta_to)

Table 10.6: Volume of inland freight transport (^{1})
(index of inland freight transport volume relative to GDP, 2000=100)

	1997	1998	1999	2000	2001	2002	2003	2004	2005	2006	2007
EU-27	101.5	101.1	100.1	100.0	99.0	100.0	99.4	105.5	105.4	106.3	106.8
Belgium	94.2	89.0	80.3	100.0	102.2	101.2	97.0	91.2	84.7	82.3	78.3
Bulgaria	82.0	63.6	49.9	100.0	104.8	105.0	109.9	119.7	128.0	118.3	116.6
Czech Republic	117.3	100.9	101.5	100.0	99.6	103.9	105.2	98.6	88.5	94.0	86.4
Denmark	97.7	95.6	100.1	100.0	91.9	92.7	94.5	93.2	91.0	80.7	78.0
Germany	95.4	97.0	100.4	100.0	99.9	98.9	100.0	104.5	106.0	109.9	111.9
Estonia	65.4	76.4	91.3	100.0	89.4	92.7	84.9	90.2	87.3	76.7	67.1
Ireland	76.8	82.0	91.9	100.0	95.1	102.3	106.8	111.5	108.9	99.8	102.1
Greece	:	:	:	:	:	:	:	:	:	:	:
Spain	87.5	93.6	95.5	100.0	104.0	114.9	116.1	128.1	130.1	129.6	133.1
France	100.3	100.3	103.2	100.0	97.1	95.0	92.5	92.8	87.4	87.8	88.5
Italy	101.1	105.1	99.4	100.0	98.8	100.4	91.6	101.2	107.0	96.4	95.2
Cyprus	106.3	104.8	101.6	100.0	99.3	101.2	105.3	80.7	96.6	77.6	76.7
Latvia	110.7	104.3	96.7	100.0	99.9	101.9	111.0	107.2	105.0	91.6	95.2
Lithuania	91.1	85.5	97.4	100.0	89.9	107.6	109.2	106.2	116.8	118.5	121.5
Luxembourg	77.5	80.9	91.6	100.0	109.2	109.4	111.6	106.9	92.3	87.5	89.3
Hungary	100.0	110.7	102.2	100.0	93.9	89.7	86.1	93.9	105.0	118.1	132.2
Malta	:	:	:	:	:	:	:	:	:	:	:
Netherlands	103.7	106.7	106.9	100.0	97.4	95.5	96.2	105.6	98.7	95.2	88.7
Austria	91.9	93.4	98.1	100.0	104.7	105.7	105.2	104.3	98.1	101.9	97.9
Poland	118.3	112.0	103.0	100.0	97.6	98.4	98.4	108.2	108.9	115.2	121.7
Portugal	105.5	101.6	101.2	100.0	108.4	107.0	99.7	143.5	148.6	153.8	155.8
Romania	:	:	95.0	100.0	106.3	119.6	127.1	145.1	174.2	171.4	165.8
Slovenia	106.1	106.2	102.1	100.0	101.3	95.5	98.9	114.5	128.9	132.0	138.5
Slovakia	114.9	116.3	112.9	100.0	92.4	86.9	88.1	88.0	93.7	86.9	92.1
Finland	97.0	98.6	98.4	100.0	93.4	94.8	91.7	91.5	87.2	81.5	77.3
Sweden	110.4	102.9	98.0	100.0	95.4	96.9	96.7	94.4	95.3	94.4	94.4
United Kingdom	112.8	110.8	104.3	100.0	97.0	95.1	94.0	93.8	91.6	93.6	90.1
FYR of Macedonia	:	:	:	100.0	93.4	111.7	146.0	138.9	141.4	198.4	:
Turkey	92.8	96.7	99.2	100.0	98.4	92.2	89.1	84.2	82.2	81.7	:
Iceland	102.4	102.1	103.8	100.0	105.5	108.3	108.8	109.7	113.2	119.2	:
Norway	101.8	102.6	101.5	100.0	97.8	96.6	101.4	102.8	105.3	109.4	107.0

(^{1}) Excluding pipelines; breaks in series: Estonia, 1997; Bulgaria, Hungary and Slovakia, 2000; Bulgaria, 2001; EU-27, Spain, Portugal and Romania, 2004.

Source: Eurostat (tsien060)

Table 10.7: Inland freight transport, 2008

	(million t-km)			(t-km per inhabitant)			National air freight and mail transport (tonnes) (³)
	Road (¹)	Rail (²)	Inland water-ways	Road (¹)	Rail (²)	Inland water-ways	
EU-27	:	:	145 680	:	:	293	659 223
Belgium	38 356	9 258	8 746	3 596	875	820	721
Bulgaria	15 322	5 241	2 890	2 005	682	378	29
Czech Republic	50 877	16 304	28	4 901	1 585	3	1 934
Denmark	19 480	1 779	-	3 560	327	-	2 403
Germany	341 532	114 615	64 056	4 154	1 392	779	141 139
Estonia	7 354	8 430	:	5 484	6 280	:	0
Ireland	17 402	129	-	3 954	30	-	9 827
Greece	27 791	835	-	2 488	75	-	15 023
Spain	242 983	11 064	-	5 366	249	-	102 265
France	206 304	41 190	8 896	3 224	654	139	141 920
Italy	179 411	25 285	:	3 034	428	:	62 195
Cyprus	1 308	-	-	1 657	-	-	566
Latvia	12 344	18 313	:	5 436	8 027	:	0
Lithuania	20 419	14 373	:	6 066	4 246	:	7
Luxembourg	10 273	427	367	21 234	897	759	0
Hungary	35 759	10 048	2 250	3 560	998	224	0
Malta	:	-	-	:	-	-	:
Netherlands	81 457	7 216	46 024	4 965	441	2 805	0
Austria	34 327	21 371	2 359	4 127	2 575	284	854
Poland	164 930	54 253	277	4 327	1 423	7	6 914
Portugal	39 091	2 586	-	3 682	244	-	20 599
Romania	56 386	15 757	8 687	2 619	731	404	291
Slovenia	16 261	3 603	:	8 089	1 792	:	0
Slovakia	29 276	9 647	1 101	5 420	1 789	204	1
Finland	29 856	10 434	:	5 633	1 977	:	3 628
Sweden	29 075	23 250	-	3 166	2 551	-	19 314
United Kingdom	171 477	26 384	:	2 820	434	:	129 593
Croatia	11 042	3 574	79	2 489	805	18	1 590
Turkey	:	9 755	-	:	140	-	:
Iceland	:	:	-	:	:	-	:
Liechtenstein	:	18	:	:	512	:	:
Norway	20 595	3 456	-	4 348	738	-	17 095
Switzerland	11 321	:	:	1 491	:	:	4 685

(¹) Greece, Italy and the United Kingdom, 2007; road transport is based on movements all over the world of vehicles registered in the reporting country.
(²) All data refer to 2007, except France, 2006.
(³) Data based on departures; Denmark does not include data for Copenhagen/Kastrup airport; France underestimated as freight transport at Paris Charles-de-Gaulle and Paris Orly is incomplete.

Source: Eurostat (road_go_ta_tott, rail_go_typeall, ttr00007, tps00001 and avia_gooc) and Directorate-General for Energy and Transport

Figure 10.5: Air freight transport, 2008 (¹)
(1 000 tonnes)

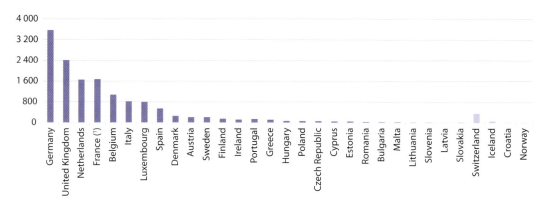

(¹) Underestimated: freight transport at Paris Charles-de-Gaulle and Paris Orly is incomplete.

Source: Eurostat (ttr00011)

Figure 10.6: Gross weight of seaborne goods handled in ports, 2008 (¹)
(million tonnes)

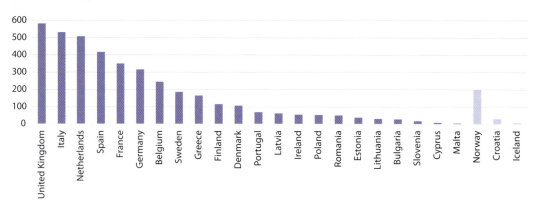

(¹) Germany, Ireland, Greece, France, Italy, Cyprus, Lithuania, the Netherlands, Poland, Portugal, Romania, Finland, Sweden, the United Kingdom and Norway, 2007; Iceland, 2006; the Czech Republic, Luxembourg, Hungary, Austria and Slovakia, not applicable.

Source: Eurostat (mar_go_aa)

Environment and energy

11

There is general international consensus that the planet is exhibiting a number of transformations that appear to be linked to climate change and scientists state that this is very likely connected to human activities. International negotiations for reaching a global agreement related to reducing greenhouse gas emissions for the period after 2012, when key provisions of the Kyoto Protocol expire, have been at the forefront of policy activity in recent months. The EU formulated a policy response to help reduce greenhouse gas emissions in the shape of an integrated energy and climate change policy, which was adopted in December 2008 and includes the following three key targets:

- cut greenhouse gases by at least 20 % of their 1990 levels (30 % if other developed countries commit to comparable cuts) by 2020;
- increase the use of renewables (wind, solar, biomass, etc.) to 20 % of total energy production by 2020, including a 10 % biofuel target for transport;
- cut energy consumption by 20 % in relation to projected 2020 levels – by improving energy efficiency.

The intention of this integrated energy and climate change policy is to move Europe towards a sustainable future with a low-carbon, energy-efficient economy. These changes will in turn contribute towards preventing the world's temperatures rising by more than 2 °C, a threshold identified by scientists, beyond which the effects of climate change may be catastrophic and irreversible.

To achieve these goals, households as well as enterprises will need to act. Changing lifestyle and consumption behaviour will be necessary – for example, by reducing consumption of goods with high levels of embedded emissions, reducing transportation-related emissions and trying to conserve energy in homes and buildings. Enterprises should also continue to reduce their use of natural resources, including energy, and switch to more renewable forms of energy. New technologies and applications of existing technologies such as capturing and storing carbon dioxide could become an important way of treating and eliminating carbon dioxide emissions from being released into the atmosphere. Reversing deforestation is also considered one of the most cost-effective ways of capturing carbon but there are many challenges connected to the protection of forests and rainforests.

Sustainable development is described as meeting the needs of present generations without jeopardising the ability of future generations to meet their own needs. In this way, today's social, economic and environmental concerns need to consider long-term, intergenerational objectives.

In July 2009, the European Commission adopted a review of its updated (2006) Sustainable Development Strategy, which highlighted the mainstreaming of sustainable development issues into a broad range of policy areas, in particular, by taking the lead internationally in the work related to climate change. Complementary to climate change and energy policy, the revised Sustainable Development Strategy also stresses the importance of education, research and public funding to achieve sustainable production and consumption patterns.

The sixth Community environment action programme (sixth EAP), laid down by the European Parliament and Council

Decision 1600/2002/EC of 22 July 2002, is the EU's ten-year (2002-2012) policy programme for the environment. It identifies four key priorities:

- **tackling climate change:** to achieve the EU's target of reducing greenhouse gas emissions by 8 % by 2008-2012;
- **nature and biodiversity:** to avert the loss of species and their habitats in Europe by completion of the Natura 2000 network and by developing new sectoral biodiversity action plans, to pay greater attention to protecting landscapes, the marine environment and soils, and to establish measures to prevent industrial and mining accidents;
- **environment and health:** to completely overhaul the EU's risk-management system for chemicals, to develop a strategy for reducing risks from pesticides, to protect water quality, to encourage noise abatement, and to develop a thematic strategy for air quality;
- **sustainable use of natural resources and the management of waste:** to increase resource efficiency and decouple resource use from economic growth, to increase recycling and waste prevention with the aid of an integrated product policy, and to encourage measures targeting specific waste streams such as hazardous waste, sludge and biodegradable waste.

In order to implement the sixth EAP, the European Commission adopted seven thematic strategies; these are air pollution (adopted in September 2005), marine environment (October 2005), the prevention and recycling of waste (December 2005), the sustainable use of natural resources (December 2005), urban environment (January 2006), soil (September 2006) and the sustainable use of pesticides (July 2006). A mid-term review of the sixth EAP was adopted by the European Commission in April 2007 ([1]).

A competitive, reliable and sustainable energy sector is essential for an economy, and this has been put under the spotlight in recent years by a number of issues, including the volatility in oil prices, interruptions to energy supply from non-member countries, blackouts aggravated by inefficient connections between national electricity networks, the difficulties of market access for suppliers in relation to gas and electricity markets, and increased attention to climate change. These issues have pushed energy towards the top of national and European political agendas.

The use of renewable energy sources is seen as a key element in energy policy, reducing the dependence on fuel from non-member countries, reducing emissions from carbon sources, and decoupling energy costs from oil prices. The second key element is constraining demand, by promoting energy efficiency both within the energy sector itself and at end-use.

As noted above, the EU has already adopted a comprehensive package of measures to reduce its contribution to greenhouse gas emissions, promote the sustainable use of natural resources and the management of waste, and ensure reliable and sufficient supplies of energy through far-reaching reforms contained within the integrated energy and climate change policy. Among others, this aims to boost the use of renewable energy and curb energy consumption, such that the EU becomes a world leader in renewable energy and low-carbon technologies.

11.1 Air pollution

Introduction

Air pollution often results from human activities, although there are also natural events which can potentially lead to air pollution – for example, volcanic eruptions; it has the potential to cause serious health problems.

Ozone (O_3) is present in small concentrations throughout the atmosphere; most (about 90 % of all ozone) exists in the stratosphere, a layer that sits between 10 and 50 km above the surface of the earth. This ozone layer performs the essential task of filtering out most of the sun's biologically harmful ultraviolet (UV-B) radiation. At ground-level, ozone is harmful: it is formed by the chemical reaction of a number of emissions arising primarily from the burning of fossil fuels such as in the production of energy and provision of transport (road, rail, air and water), industrial processes, and the use of solvents. Ground-level ozone is a secondary pollutant caused by the oxidation of nitrogen oxides and volatile organic compounds reacting in sunlight and is the primary constituent of smog. High levels of ground-level ozone interfere with the ability of plants to produce and store food making them more susceptible to diseases, insects and harsh weather. Reduced forest growth and crop yields and reducing species diversity in ecosystems can also result

([1]) Commission Communication on the mid-term review of the Sixth Community Environment Action Programme, for more information: http://eur-lex.europa.eu/lexuriserv/lexuriserv.do?uri=com:2007:0225:fin:en:pdf.

from high concentrations of ground-level ozone. People living in urban areas are most at risk from ground-level ozone, as a result of high levels of urban traffic emissions; this problem may be exacerbated by particular climatic conditions. Breathing high concentrations of ground-level ozone can have harmful effects on the respiratory tract, causing breathing difficulties (coughing, throat irritation, and congestion), damage or even scar lung tissue, or trigger asthma attacks and worsen bronchitis and emphysema.

Since the early 1970s, the EU has been working to improve air quality by controlling emissions of harmful substances into the atmosphere, improving fuel quality, and integrating environmental protection requirements into the transport and energy sectors. The EU acts at many levels: at an international level in order to reduce cross-border pollution, through work with national/regional authorities and NGOs, to work with individual industrial sectors, as well as providing funding to help support research.

Environment and health is one of four target areas within the sixth environment action programme (sixth EAP). The sixth EAP aims to achieve levels of air quality that do not give rise to unacceptable impacts on, and risks to, human health and the environment. Most of the legislation establishes health-based standards (limits) for pollutants, with action required if levels exceed these limits. In 2008, a Directive ([2]) of the European Parliament and of the Council on ambient air quality and cleaner air for Europe was adopted, setting binding limits on emissions of fine particles. These microscopic particles are principally released by cars and

trucks (diesel-engine exhaust smoke) or from the burning of wood (soot). Under the new law, which takes effect in 2011, Member States will have to reduce exposure in urban areas by an average of 20 % during the following decade (in relation to 2010 levels). In 2008 there was also a Directive ([3]) of the Council concerning integrated pollution prevention and control of stationary source emissions.

The emissions of acidifying substances that result in acid rain are to a large extent regulated by the Gothenburg Protocol under the convention on long-range transboundary air pollution – CLRTAP. Sources of acidifying substances come from agriculture (ammonia), from the combustion of fuels by industry and road traffic (nitrogen oxides) and the combustion of fuels and metal production (sulphur dioxide). Emissions of sulphur dioxide occur at the time of emission but then react in the atmosphere to form different sulphur oxides (SO_x). All of these gases may be transported over long distances so the emissions from one country may be transported by the winds and be deposited in other countries. For this reason acidification is considered a regional problem rather than a global problem since the effects are more localised, rather than influencing global climate as do greenhouse gases.

Definitions and data availability

Eurostat, in close partnership with the European Environment Agency (EEA) and the Joint Research Centre (JRC), provides statistics, indicators and meta-information on environmental pressures and the state of the environment to support the implementation and monitoring of the sixth

([2]) Directive 2008/50/EC of the European Parliament and of the Council of 21 May 2008; for more information: http://eur-lex.europa.eu/LexUriServ/LexUriServ.do?uri=CELEX:32008L0050:EN:NOT.

([3]) Directive 2008/1/EC of the Council of 15 January 2008; for more information: http://eur-lex.europa.eu/LexUriServ/LexUriServ.do?uri=CELEX:32008L0001:EN:NOT.

EAP. This is done through ten topic-specific data centres: the EEA is responsible for the European topic centre on air and climate change. The European pollutant emission register (EPER) provides public access to emissions of key air pollutants in the EU ([4]), and a near to real-time ozone information system is also available on the EEA website ([5]).

Data on air pollution is officially reported under the CLRTAP, with information on: ammonia (NH_3), sulphur oxides (SO_2 and SO_3 as SO_x), nitrogen oxides (NO and NO_2 as NO_x), non-methane volatile organic compounds (NMVOC), carbon monoxide (CO), and particulate matter.

In 1996, the Environment Council adopted framework Directive 96/62/EC on ambient air quality assessment and management, which was followed by four daughter directives detailing limits for specific pollutants. The first daughter Directive (1999/30/EC) limits values for particulate matter, the second (2000/69/EC) deals with emissions of carbon monoxide and benzene, the third (2002/3/EC) relates to ozone, while the fourth (2004/107/EC) covers polyaromatic hydrocarbons, arsenic, nickel, cadmium and mercury. Annual reporting must follow Commission Decision 2004/224/EC which lays down arrangements for the submission of information in relation to limit values for certain pollutants in ambient air.

Particulates whose diameter is less than 10 micrometres (PM10) typically come from smoke, dust, pollen, mould and spores. These enter the body through breathing and can cause inflammation and a worsening of the condition of people with heart and lung diseases. *Ozone* is a strong photochemical oxidant, which can cause serious health problems and damage to ecosystems, agricultural crops and forests. Human exposure to elevated ozone concentrations can give rise to inflammatory responses and decreases in lung function.

Two indicators are presented for **urban population exposure to air pollution** – covering particulate matter and ground-level ozone. These show the population weighted annual mean concentrations of air pollutants at urban background stations in agglomerations. In 1999 an annual limit on PM10 and other pollutants in ambient air was fixed at 40 micrograms of PM10 per cubic metre. For ozone, the indicator is based on maximum daily 8-hour mean ozone concentrations above the threshold of 70 micrograms of ozone per cubic metre.

The indicator for **weighted emissions of acidifying substances** tracks trends in anthropogenic (human-induced) atmospheric emissions of acidifying substances (sulphur dioxide, nitrogen oxides and ammonia) by source; these emissions are combined in terms of their acidifying effects, and expressed in terms of tonnes of acid equivalents.

Main findings

From 1997 to 2006 the EU-27 recorded a 28 % decline in weighted emissions of acidification gases (aggregated using acidification potentials of each gas). Of the EU-27 Member States, only Greece (1 %) and Romania (18 %) showed increases of weighted emissions of acidification gases over this period. In contrast, the Czech Republic, Luxembourg, Malta, Hungary and Slovenia all had decreases of 50 % or more. Norway, Switzerland and Turkey also showed decreases in emissions of 14 % to 15 %.

([4]) For more information: http://eper.ec.europa.eu/eper.

([5]) For more information: http://www.eea.europa.eu/maps/ozone/welcome.

For specific acidification and tropospheric ozone precursors there were substantial reductions in the past decade across the EU. For nitrogen oxides there was a reduction of 21.0 %, for carbon monoxide the reduction was 40.7 % and for sulphur oxides the reduction was 45.2 % (to 2006). These declines were spread across Member States, as between 1997 and 2006/2007 the only exceptions were: higher emissions of carbon monoxide in Romania and Finland; higher emissions of methane in Spain and Portugal; higher emissions of sulphur oxides in Greece and Romania; and higher emissions of nitrogen oxides in Bulgaria, Greece, Spain, Lithuania and Austria. The EFTA countries of Norway and Switzerland reduced emissions for all three of these air pollutants.

There was a relatively stable trend to EU-27 emissions of coarse particulate matter (PM10) within urban areas during the period 1999 to 2007, with annual mean concentrations ranging from 27.0 micrograms per m³ (2001) to 31.2 micrograms per m³ (2003); the latest figure for 2007 was 28.1 micrograms per m³. The highest concentrations of particulate

matter were recorded in Bulgaria (with values more than double the EU-27 average), Romania, Italy and Poland (more than 20 % above the EU-27 average).

There was a considerable spike in ozone concentrations in 2003 (associated with exceptionally dry and hot weather), with some of the highest concentrations being recorded in Belgium, south west Germany, central Spain, and parts of France and Italy. Exposure to ozone pollution in 2007 was highest among the urban populations of Greece and Malta (more than double the EU-27 average), while Hungary, Italy, Slovenia and Austria recorded values that were more than 50 % above the EU-27 average.

Emissions of acidifying substances contribute to acid deposition, leading, among other things, to potential changes in soil and water quality and damage to forests, crops and other vegetation. Total EU-27 emissions amounted to 727 420 tonnes of acid equivalents in 2006. Almost one third (31.3 %) of these were from agriculture, while a quarter (24.7 %) could be attributed to energy industries (in particular, coal-based activities).

Figure 11.1: Weighted emissions of acidifying substances, 2006 (1 000 tonnes acid equivalent)

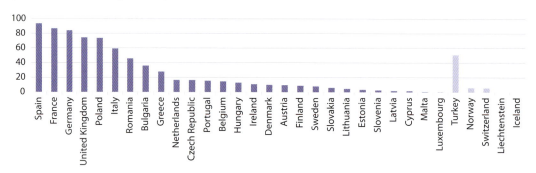

Source: Eurostat (tsdpc260), European Environment Agency, Topic Centre on Air and Climate

Table 11.1: Air pollutants

| | Weighted emissions of acidifying substances (thousand tonnes acid equivalent) | | (million tonnes) | | | | | |
| | | | Emissions of carbon monoxide | | Emissions of sulphur oxides | | Emissions of nitrogen oxides | |
	1997	2006	1997	2007	1997	2006	1997	2007
EU-27	1 012.5	727.4	47.08	27.92	14.49	7.95	13.84	10.94
Belgium	21.7	14.7	1.01	0.75	0.23	0.14	0.34	0.26
Bulgaria	48.6	36.0	0.53	0.25	1.31	0.88	0.14	0.19
Czech Republic	45.6	16.5	0.98	0.51	0.98	0.21	0.47	0.28
Denmark	15.2	10.1	0.56	0.45	0.10	0.03	0.26	0.17
Germany	117.2	84.3	6.11	3.75	1.21	0.56	1.94	1.28
Estonia	5.2	3.4	0.24	0.17	0.12	0.07	0.04	0.03
Ireland	15.1	10.9	0.31	0.17	0.17	0.06	0.13	0.12
Greece	27.6	27.9	1.36	0.73	0.52	0.54	0.33	0.37
Spain	105.8	93.7	3.49	2.55	1.74	1.17	1.35	1.48
France	107.1	87.0	8.38	4.67	0.80	0.45	1.70	1.35
Italy	97.8	59.2	6.28	3.33	1.13	0.39	1.73	1.15
Cyprus	2.2	1.8	0.03	0.02	0.05	0.04	0.02	0.02
Latvia	2.9	1.9	0.31	0.30	0.04	0.00	0.04	0.04
Lithuania	5.7	4.7	0.35	0.21	0.08	0.04	0.06	0.07
Luxembourg	0.7	0.3	0.00	0.00	0.00	0.00	0.02	0.01
Hungary	29.2	13.0	0.64	0.51	0.66	0.12	0.20	0.19
Malta	1.2	0.6	0.03	0.00	0.03	0.01	0.01	0.01
Netherlands	22.2	16.6	0.72	0.53	0.10	0.06	0.39	0.28
Austria	9.7	9.7	1.14	0.77	0.04	0.03	0.19	0.22
Poland	113.0	73.6	4.70	2.60	2.18	1.20	1.11	0.88
Portugal	19.5	15.6	0.81	0.60	0.29	0.19	0.25	0.23
Romania	38.9	45.8	1.43	1.49	0.59	0.86	0.38	0.33
Slovenia	6.4	2.7	0.24	0.10	0.12	0.02	0.06	0.04
Slovakia	11.3	6.2	0.36	0.28	0.20	0.09	0.13	0.08
Finland	10.9	9.0	0.48	0.50	0.10	0.09	0.26	0.18
Sweden	11.1	8.1	0.79	0.57	0.06	0.04	0.24	0.17
United Kingdom	120.8	74.3	5.80	2.11	1.66	0.68	2.07	1.49
Croatia	:	:	:	0.36	0.00	0.00	:	0.08
Turkey	59.6	50.9	:	:	1.26	0.88	:	:
Iceland	0.0	0.0	:	:	:	:	:	:
Liechtenstein	0.0	0.0	:	:	:	:	:	:
Norway	7.2	6.1	0.67	0.40	0.03	0.02	0.22	0.19
Switzerland	6.8	5.8	0.45	0.29	0.03	0.02	0.11	0.08

Source: Eurostat (tsdpc260), annual European Community greenhouse gas inventory and annual European Community LRTAP convention emission inventory reports (http://www.eea.europa.eu)

Table 11.2: Urban population exposure to air pollution

	Urban population exposure to air pollution by PM10 particulate matter (micrograms per m³) (¹)					Urban population exposure to air pollution by ozone (micrograms per m³) (²)				
	1999	2001	2003	2005	2007	1999	2001	2003	2005	2007
EU-27	27.7	27.0	31.2	29.3	28.1	4 003	3 929	6 031	4 041	3 909
Belgium	34.5	33.9	36.5	28.8	25.1	3 804	3 380	5 136	2 722	2 371
Bulgaria	:	:	59.5	55.6	59.0	117	192	1 838	2 186	2 555
Czech Republic	28.0	35.7	47.0	39.6	32.0	4 760	3 464	7 041	5 532	4 870
Denmark	:	:	24.6	22.8	21.0	:	:	2 816	1 415	2 376
Germany	25.0	24.3	29.0	24.2	22.5	3 545	3 336	5 872	3 285	3 142
Estonia	:	18.2	19.4	20.7	18.6	:	4 255	2 524	1 321	2 308
Ireland	15.8	20.4	13.9	13.8	12.6	:	:	:	:	:
Greece	:	40.9	39.1	41.1	32.3	7 154	12 247	13 827	9 601	9 006
Spain	33.9	30.9	31.4	33.3	32.9	5 028	3 951	5 862	4 891	4 108
France	:	21.9	23.7	20.4	27.3	3 964	4 095	6 842	4 276	3 434
Italy	:	32.2	42.3	45.1	36.6	8 706	8 149	9 852	6 752	7 356
Cyprus	:	:	:	:	:	:	:	:	:	:
Latvia	:	:	:	:	:	3 801	:	863	308	:
Lithuania	:	:	:	22.9	20.2	:	:	:	5 048	1 995
Luxembourg	:	:	:	:	:	:	:	:	:	:
Hungary	:	:	40.1	37.7	29.7	:	:	:	5 091	7 622
Malta	:	:	:	:	29.3	:	:	:	:	8 156
Netherlands	33.1	29.0	32.9	28.5	29.6	2 300	1 888	2 880	1 490	1 157
Austria	:	32.0	32.2	28.9	23.8	5 344	5 299	8 318	5 711	6 043
Poland	45.6	38.5	45.3	38.9	34.0	3 308	3 812	5 232	4 037	3 610
Portugal	37.6	35.7	34.1	34.0	30.4	1 361	3 660	4 112	4 116	3 969
Romania	:	:	:	46.2	43.1	:	:	:	4 500	3 784
Slovenia	:	:	43.8	36.4	32.4	4 636	5 919	11 461	6 017	6 514
Slovakia	36.5	26.7	31.4	33.2	26.3	:	2 873	7 938	7 423	5 735
Finland	15.7	16.4	16.3	15.3	16.8	2 427	1 339	1 800	1 687	1 136
Sweden	14.1	17.9	19.6	19.6	17.5	2 196	1 362	3 276	2 920	1 728
United Kingdom	24.2	24.2	25.9	23.6	23.9	1 439	1 062	2 197	1 250	938
Iceland	:	:	21.3	19.6	11.5	:	:	2 645	66	:
Norway	:	:	19.6	24.0	20.7	:	:	:	:	380

(¹) Population weighted annual mean concentration of particulate matter.
(²) Population weighted yearly sum of maximum daily 8-hour mean ozone concentrations above a threshold of 70 microgram of ozone per m³.

Source: Eurostat (tsien110 and tsien100), European Environment Agency, European Topic Center on Air and Climate Change

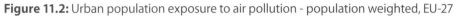

Figure 11.2: Urban population exposure to air pollution - population weighted, EU-27

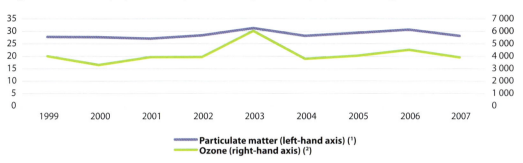

Particulate matter (left-hand axis) (¹)
Ozone (right-hand axis) (²)

(¹) Population weighted annual mean concentration of particulate matter (micrograms per m³).
(²) Population weighted yearly sum of maximum daily 8-hour mean ozone concentrations above a threshold of 70 microgram of ozone per m³ (micrograms per m³).

Source: Eurostat (tsien110 and tsien100), European Environment Agency, European Topic Center on Air and Climate Change

Figure 11.3: Weighted emissions of acidifying substances, by source sector, EU-27, 2006 (¹) (%, based on tonnes of acid equivalents)

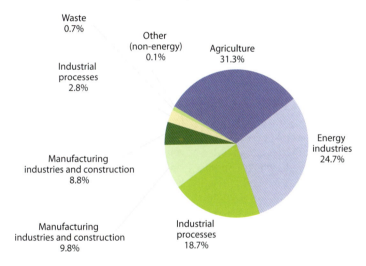

Waste
0.7%

Other
(non-energy)
0.1%

Agriculture
31.3%

Industrial
processes
2.8%

Energy
industries
24.7%

Manufacturing
industries and construction
8.8%

Manufacturing
industries and construction
9.8%

Industrial
processes
18.7%

(¹) Total emissions were 727 420 tonnes of acid equivalent; Figures do not sum to 100 % due to rounding.

Source: Eurostat (tsdpc260), European Environment Agency, Topic Centre on Air and Climate

11.2 Air emissions

Introduction

The term 'climate' covers meteorological phenomena over a lengthy period of time, for example, trends in temperature, storm activity or rainfall. Climate change results from natural phenomena and has occurred periodically throughout history – sometimes with catastrophic effects, such as the extinction of various species during the different ice ages. Over the past two decades a growing body of scientific evidence has been established that suggests that the most recent changes in the earth's climate have been substantially influenced by human activity, so-called anthropogenic effects.

Solar energy (heat from the sun), arrives in the earth's atmosphere as short wavelength radiation. Some of this is reflected by the earth's surface (especially from snow and ice covered areas) and atmosphere; however, the vast majority is absorbed, warming the planet. As the earth's surface gains heat, it starts to emit long wavelength, infra-red radiation back into the atmosphere. Despite their relative scarcity (less than 0.1 % of the total atmosphere, which consists mostly of nitrogen and oxygen), greenhouse gases are vital to life on earth because of their ability to act like a blanket, trapping some of this infra-red radiation and preventing it from escaping back into space; without this process the temperature on the earth's surface would be a lot colder. This layer of greenhouse gases has become thicker as a result of human activity and this process would appear to be disturbing the natural balance between incoming and outgoing radiative energy.

Substantial amounts of human-induced greenhouse gas emissions have come from the increased use of fossil fuels burned to power new machines, generate electricity and related to transport. The amount of emissions has accelerated in the last 200 years, reflecting increases in the world's population, economic development, and increased production and consumption in a globalised economy.

The Kyoto Protocol is an international agreement that committed industrialised nations to reduce or at least limit the growth of their greenhouse gas emissions. The protocol was adopted in 1997, setting legally-binding targets with the goal to reduce greenhouse gas emissions in developed countries by 2008-2012. However, it was not until 18 November 2004 when the Russian Federation ratified the protocol that the prescribed conditions were met and the Kyoto Protocol entered into force on 16 February 2005.

Kyoto established different commitments for each country according to their economic development. Globally, developed countries were required to reduce their collective emissions from 1990 base year levels by at least 5 % during the first commitment period (average emission levels for the period 2008-2012). Political negotiation and compromise resulted in different national targets: hence, while cuts of 8 % (relative to 1990 levels) were agreed for the EU-15, Switzerland and many central and eastern European countries, a number of other countries only agreed to stabilise their emission levels (New Zealand and Russia), while some countries were allowed to increase emissions (Australia and Iceland by 8 % and 10 % respectively).

The European Community agreed to an 8 % reduction in its greenhouse gas emissions for the EU-15 by 2008-2012. The reductions for each of the EU-15 Member States were agreed under the so-called 'burden sharing agreement', which allowed some countries to increase emissions, provided these were offset by reductions in others. Among the EU-15 Member States these range from decreases of 28 % for Luxembourg and 21 % for Denmark and Germany, to increases of 25 % and 27 % for Greece and for Portugal. Of the 12 Member States that have joined the EU since 2004, Cyprus and Malta are not party to the Kyoto Protocol, while the remaining ten countries have their own individual reduction targets, generally set at 8 %, although for Hungary and Poland the target is 6 %, and there are also base years other than 1990.

In an attempt to find alternative ways to reduce emissions, three market-based mechanisms were introduced to help countries meet their Kyoto commitments: joint implementation (JI); the clean development mechanism (CDM); and; international emissions trading (IET). These initiatives seek to aid those countries for which it may be easier and/or more cost-effective to enhance carbon sinks or cut emissions abroad – rather than on their national territory, based upon the premise that the overall effect of such actions (for the atmosphere) is the same regardless of where (geographically) the action is taken. Emissions trading schemes enable developed countries to acquire assigned amount units (AAUs) from other developed countries that are more able to reduce their emissions. This form of trading allows countries that have achieved emis-

sion reductions beyond those required by the Kyoto Protocol to sell their excess reductions to other countries that are finding it more difficult or expensive to meet their commitments.

One cornerstone of the EU's climate change strategy is an emissions trading system (ETS). The scheme covers about 12 000 factories and plants that together are responsible for about half of the EU's greenhouse gas emissions. Under the system, governments set limits on the amount of carbon dioxide and other greenhouse gases to be emitted by energy-intensive industries (such as utilities and steel producers) or other industries with high levels of greenhouse gas emissions arising from their production systems such as the cement industry. If these enterprises need to emit more greenhouse gases than their permits allow, they have to buy spare permits from the marketplace.

A revised Directive to improve and extend the greenhouse gas emission allowance trading scheme of the Community was adopted on 6 April 2009 ([6]). This is designed to achieve greater emissions reductions in energy-intensive sectors from the start of a third ETS period as of 1 January 2013. To stimulate the adoption of clean technologies, the new ETS provides that emissions permits will no longer be given to industry for free, but instead they will be auctioned. Each Member State will determine the use of its revenues from auctioning pollution permits (although at least half of the proceeds should be used to fight climate change in the EU and abroad and to alleviate the social consequences of moving towards a low-carbon economy).

([6]) Directive 2009/29/EC of the European Parliament and of the Council of 23 April 2009; for more information: http://eur-lex.europa.eu/LexUriServ/LexUriServ.do?uri=OJ:L:2009:140:0063:0087:EN:PDF.

Definitions and data availability

Data on **greenhouse gas emissions** are officially reported under the United Nations Framework Convention on Climate Change – UNFCCC ([7]). The Kyoto Protocol covers legally binding commitments in relation to the reduction of the following six types of greenhouse gases: carbon dioxide (CO_2); methane (CH_4); nitrous oxide (N_2O); sulphur hexafluoride (SF_6); hydrofluorocarbons (HFCs), and perfluorocarbons (PFCs). Note that while chlorofluorocarbons (CFCs) and hydrochlorofluorocarbons (HCFCs) are greenhouse gases, they are not included in the Kyoto Protocol (as they were previously covered by the Montreal Protocol on substances that deplete the ozone layer).

Each greenhouse gas has a different capacity to cause global warming, depending on its radiative properties, molecular weight and the length of time it remains in the atmosphere. The **global warming potential (GWP)** of each gas is defined in relation to a given weight of carbon dioxide for a set time period (for the purpose of the Kyoto Protocol a period of 100 years). GWPs are used to convert emissions of greenhouse gases to a relative measure (known as carbon dioxide equivalents: CO_2 equivalents), the following weighting factors are currently used: carbon dioxide = 1, methane = 21, nitrous oxide = 310, and sulphur hexafluoride = 23 900; hydrofluorocarbons and perfluorocarbons comprise a large number of different gases that have different GWPs.

The European Environment Agency (EEA) compiles an annual European Community greenhouse gas inventory report for submission to the UN. Within the inventory reporting requirements of Kyoto, estimates of greenhouse gas emissions are produced for a number of IPCC defined sectors which are delineated primarily according to process-technologies. The five main IPCC sectors include: energy (fuel combustion); industrial processes; solvent and other product use; agriculture; and waste. Note that the use of fuel in ships or aircraft engaged in international transport is excluded from the reporting mechanism. Information pertaining to land use changes and forestry are also reported but the view taken in this publication focuses only on the (gross) emissions rather than the emissions and the removals or sinks (net emissions).

Main findings

Greenhouse gas emissions in the EU-27 stood at 5 045 million tonnes of CO_2 equivalents in 2007. This figure marked an overall reduction of 9.3 % when compared with 1990, or some 519 million tonnes of CO_2 equivalents. There was generally a downward trend to emissions during the period 1990 to 1997 (aside from a relative peak in 1996, when a cold winter led to an increase in heating requirements). Since 1998, the evolution of greenhouse gas emissions within the EU-27 has remained relatively unchanged.

Carbon dioxide accounted for 83.0 % of EU-27 greenhouse gas emissions in 2007, followed by methane (8.2 %), nitrous oxide (7.3 %) and fluorinated gases (1.5 %). Fluorinated gases were the only group to record an overall increase in their amount of emissions between 1990 and 2007 (up 31.1 %); this may be entirely attributed to hydrofluorocarbons (HFCs),

([7]) For more information: http://unfccc.int.

which have, in recent years, been increasingly used as substitutes for ozone-depleting compounds such as chlorofluorocarbons (CFCs) in refrigeration, air conditioning, or the manufacture of insulating foams.

Across the Member States, greenhouse gas emissions were highest in Germany (19.0 % of the EU-27 total or 956.1 million tonnes of CO_2 equivalents in 2007), while the United Kingdom (12.6 %), Italy (11.0 %) and France (10.5 %) were the only other countries to record double-digit shares. EU-15 Member States accounted for 80.3 % of total greenhouse gas emissions within the EU-27 in 2007, some 4.2 percentage points above their corresponding share of 1990. The 'burden-sharing agreement' between EU-15 Member States foresees that four countries (Ireland, Spain, Greece and Portugal) may increase their emission levels through to the first commitment period (2008-2012). Some of the biggest overall increases in greenhouse gas emissions between 1990 and 2007 were recorded on the Iberian Peninsula, with gains of 53.5 % and 38.1 % in Spain and Portugal; Cyprus and Malta also recorded significant increases in their emission levels (although they are not parties to the Kyoto Protocol).

By far the most important source of greenhouse gas emissions across the EU-27 was energy use (in particular, oil and gas-fired power stations). This category was consistently the principal source of emissions throughout the period 1990 to 2007; the latest data available shows energy with a 59.8 % share of total emissions (or more than 3 000 million tonnes of CO_2 equivalents).

The transport sector (a subsector of the IPCC energy sector) was the next largest contributor (19.5 % of the EU-27's greenhouse gas emissions in 2007), and was also the IPCC sector where emissions were increasing at their fastest pace – within the confines of Kyoto reporting (road freight and passenger cars).

Agriculture accounted for 9.2 % of all greenhouse gas emissions in the EU-27 in 2007; contrary to other areas, where carbon dioxide was the principal greenhouse gas emitted, agricultural emissions are largely composed of nitrous oxide and methane. Emissions from industrial processes, solvents and product use accounted for a slightly lower share (8.8 %), while emissions from waste (which includes disposal, landfill sites and water treatment) accounted for the remaining 2.8 % of the EU-27's greenhouse gas emissions in 2007.

Figure 11.4: Greenhouse gas emissions, EU-27 (^{1})
(1990=100)

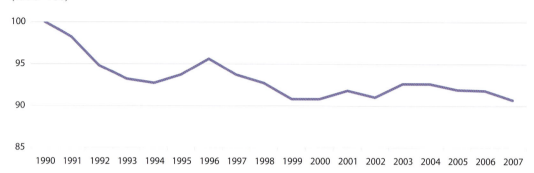

(^{1}) Weighted emissions of greenhouse gases represented 5 045 million tonnes in 2007.

Source: Eurostat (env_air_ind and ten00072), European Environment Agency, European Topic Center on Air and Climate Change

Figure 11.5: Total greenhouse gas emissions
(Kyoto base year=100)

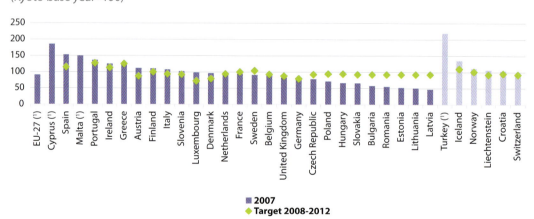

■ **2007**
◆ **Target 2008-2012**

(^{1}) No target under the Kyoto Protocol (1990=100).

Source: Eurostat (tsien010), European Environment Agency, European Topic Center on Air and Climate Change

Table 11.3: Greenhouse gas emissions

	Total greenhouse gas emissions (Kyoto base year=100) (¹)				Weighted emissions of greenhouse gases (million tonnes of CO_2 equivalent)			
	1997	2002	2007	Target 2008-2012	1997	2002	2007	Share in EU-27 (%)
EU-27	93.7	91.0	90.7	:	5 214.1	5 065.7	5 045.4	-
Euro area	:	:	:	:	3.365.1	3 414.5	3 364.1	66.7
Belgium	99.6	98.1	90.1	92.5	145.1	142.9	131.3	2.6
Bulgaria	63.2	50.2	57.2	92.0	83.8	66.5	75.8	1.5
Czech Republic	78.8	74.7	77.6	92.0	153.0	145.1	150.8	3.0
Denmark	115.1	99.0	96.1	79.0	79.8	68.6	66.6	1.3
Germany	86.6	81.7	77.6	79.0	1 067.6	1 006.4	956.1	19.0
Estonia	50.0	42.4	51.7	92.0	21.3	18.1	22.0	0.4
Ireland	113.0	123.7	124.5	113.0	62.8	68.8	69.2	1.4
Greece	110.4	119.4	123.2	125.0	118.1	127.8	131.9	2.6
Spain	114.8	139.1	152.6	115.0	332.7	403.1	442.3	8.8
France	100.1	97.4	94.2	100.0	564.6	549.3	531.1	10.5
Italy	102.3	107.5	106.9	93.5	528.7	555.8	552.8	11.0
Cyprus	136.4	170.6	185.3	:	7.5	9.3	10.1	0.2
Latvia	46.5	41.5	46.6	92.0	12.0	10.7	12.1	0.2
Lithuania	45.7	41.7	50.1	92.0	22.6	20.6	24.7	0.5
Luxembourg	74.7	86.1	98.1	72.0	9.8	11.3	12.9	0.3
Hungary	69.3	67.6	65.8	94.0	79.9	78.0	75.9	1.5
Malta	127.2	134.9	149.0	:	2.6	2.8	3.0	0.1
Netherlands	106.0	101.1	97.4	94.0	225.9	215.5	207.5	4.1
Austria	105.2	110.1	111.3	87.0	83.1	87.0	88.0	1.7
Poland	79.7	65.9	70.8	94.0	449.1	371.5	398.9	7.9
Portugal	118.8	147.6	136.1	127.0	71.4	88.8	81.8	1.6
Romania	59.9	52.7	54.7	92.0	166.7	146.7	152.3	3.0
Slovenia	96.4	98.5	101.8	92.0	19.6	20.1	20.7	0.4
Slovakia	69.3	68.0	65.2	92.0	49.9	49.0	47.0	0.9
Finland	106.6	108.2	110.3	100.0	75.7	76.8	78.4	1.6
Sweden	100.6	96.4	90.7	104.0	72.6	69.6	65.4	1.3
United Kingdom	91.2	84.5	82.0	87.5	708.1	655.8	636.7	12.6
Croatia	79.2	89.7	103.2	95.0	24.8	28.1	32.4	-
Turkey	150.3	159.1	219.1	:	255.5	270.6	372.6	-
Iceland	101.4	110.6	134.9	110.0	3.4	3.7	4.5	-
Liechtenstein	109.1	113.0	106.1	92.0	0.3	0.3	0.2	-
Norway	106.1	107.4	110.9	101.0	52.7	53.3	55.1	-
Switzerland	96.5	97.5	97.1	92.0	50.9	51.5	51.3	-

(¹) EU-27, Cyprus, Malta and Turkey, 1990=100 as there is no target (and therefore no base year) under the Kyoto Protocol.

Source: Eurostat (tsien010 and ten00072), European Environment Agency, European Topic Center on Air and Climate Change

Figure 11.6: Greenhouse gas emissions by source sector, EU-27
(%, based on data in million tonnes CO$_2$ equivalent)

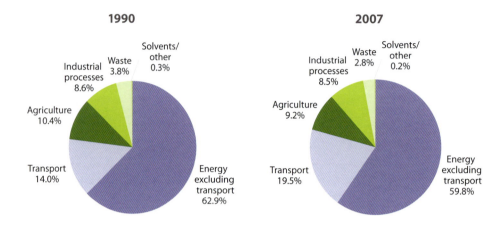

Source: Eurostat (env_air_emis), European Environment Agency

11.3 Waste

Introduction

Waste refers to materials for which the generator has no further use for their own purpose of production, transformation or consumption; the majority is landfilled, incinerated, composted or recycled. In some circumstances there may be statutory requirements on a producer to dispose of waste in a certain manner, for example, when waste materials are hazardous. The disposal of waste can have a serious environmental impact: for example, landfill takes up space and may cause air, water or soil pollution, while incineration can also result in emissions of dangerous air pollutants; both landfill and incineration result in the generation of greenhouse gas emissions.

In 2008, a revised Waste Framework Directive ([8]) was adopted by the European Parliament and the Council, with the dual aim of promoting the use of waste as a secondary resource, as well as simplifying existing legislation. The directive set new recycling targets: by 2020 each Member State should recycle 50 % of their household and similar waste and 70 % of their construction and demolition waste. The directive lays down a five-step hierarchy of waste management options (in descending order):

- waste prevention;
- re-use;
- recycling;
- recovery (including energy recovery); and
- safe disposal.

([8]) Directive 2008/98/EC of the European Parliament and of the Council of 19 November 2008; for more information: http://eur-lex.europa.eu/LexUriServ/LexUriServ.do?uri=OJ:L:2008:312:0003:0003:EN:PDF.

Waste prevention can be achieved through the use of cleaner technologies, eco-design, or more eco-efficient production and consumption patterns. Waste prevention and recycling can also reduce the use of resources by limiting raw materials' extraction and transformation. The EU's approach underlines that any waste that cannot be recycled or reused should, where possible, be safely incinerated, with landfill only used as a last resort.

The European Commission has defined several specific waste streams for priority attention, including: packaging waste, end-of-life vehicles, batteries, electrical and electronic waste. Member States are required to introduce legislation concerning the collection, reuse, recycling and disposal of these waste streams.

The EU's sixth environment action programme (EAP) identifies waste prevention and management as one of four priorities, underlining the relationship between the efficient use of resources and waste generation and management. The objective is to decouple the resource use and the generation of waste from economic growth, while ensuring that sustainable consumption does not exceed environmental capacity.

Economic growth and globalisation have led to an increase in the volume of waste that is shipped across borders (whether by road, rail or ship). The waste shipment Regulation ([9]) has introduced certain procedures and requirements to control the international movement of hazardous waste from Member States and by this ensure sound management of the waste. Shipments abroad for disposal are generally prohibited, as are exports of hazardous waste to developing countries (even if for

recovery). Shipments for recovery are usually permitted and these are governed by a series of annexes to the Regulation (which has been amended on three occasions to take account of scientific and technical developments).

Definitions and data availability

Waste statistics present data on the amounts and types of waste produced, as well as waste treatment methods. Regulation (EC) 2150/2002 on waste statistics ([10]) was adopted in 2002, creating a framework for harmonised statistics on waste; the Regulation requires Member States to provide data on the generation, recovery and disposal of waste every two years from 2004 onwards. The statistics collected within this framework are used to monitor the implementation of policy objectives across the EU, in particular compliance with the principles of recovery and safe disposal. The statistics are classified according to the economic activity (NACE Rev. 1.1) of the business responsible for handing over waste for treatment, such that waste flows from agriculture, mining, industry, construction, services and households may be distinguished.

Municipal waste consists of waste collected by or on behalf of municipal authorities. Such collection systems may well extend beyond waste from households to include waste collected from offices or small businesses. The treatment of municipal waste can be classified into three principal categories:

- **landfill:** which is defined as the depositing of waste into or onto land, including specially engineered landfill, and temporary storage of over one year on permanent sites;

([9]) Regulation (EC) No 1013/2006 of the European Parliament and of the Council of 14 June 2006; for more information: http://eur-lex.europa.eu/LexUriServ/site/en/oj/2006/l_190/l_19020060712en00010098.pdf.

([10]) Regulation (EC) No 2150/2002 of the European Parliament and of the Council of 25 November 2002; for more information: http://eur-lex.europa.eu/LexUriServ/site/en/consleg/2002/R/02002R2150-20050614-n.pdf.

- **incineration:** which refers to the thermal treatment of waste in specifically designed plant;
- **recovery:** which refers to any waste management operation that diverts a waste material from the waste stream and which results in a certain product with a potential economic or ecological benefit (for example, composting or recycling).

Main findings

On average, each individual in the EU-27 generated the equivalent of 524 kg of municipal waste in 2008, some 28 kg (or 5.3 %) more than a decade earlier; however, the amount of municipal waste generated per inhabitant has remained almost unchanged in the EU-27 since 2000.

Denmark recorded the highest level of municipal waste generated per inhabitant in 2008, at 802 kg per inhabitant; with waste volumes rising by more than one third (35 %) between 1998 and 2008. On a per capita basis, there were also relatively high levels of municipal waste generated in Ireland, Cyprus, Luxembourg, Malta and the Netherlands. Note these figures may reflect municipal waste collection policies, whereby local authorities seek to collect a growing volume of waste, based on the premise that waste represents additional resources and value (for example, the recycling of metals, glass, plastics or paper). The only Member States to report less than 400 kg of municipal waste per inhabitant in 2008 were Romania, Latvia, Poland, Slovakia and the Czech Republic; these relatively low figures may reflect lower levels of consumption per inhabitant or a limited

collection rate (for example, no municipal disposal facilities for used vehicles, hazardous goods or garden refuse).

During the period 1998 to 2008 the way in which municipal waste was treated changed significantly. In 1998 some 60 % of the municipal waste treated in the EU-27 was put into landfill, with a further 16 % being incinerated, the rest being treated in other ways, such as recycling (13 %) or composting (8 %). By 2008, the proportion of municipal waste that was put into landfill had declined to 40 %, while 20 % was incinerated. In contrast, the share of municipal waste treatment that was recycled (23 %) or composted (17 %) became increasingly important.

In Germany, the amount of municipal waste going into landfill shrank from 199 kg per inhabitant in 1998 to only 3 kg in 2008; there were also significant reductions in the Netherlands, Sweden, Austria and Belgium, where the volume of municipal waste sent to landfill was reduced to less than 25 kg per inhabitant. Those countries that reduced the use of landfill tended to have relatively high levels of waste incineration; note that newly installed waste incinerators are equipped with systems for energy recovery.

According to data collected through the waste statistics Regulation, some 2 953 million tonnes of waste were generated in the EU-27 by economic activities and households in 2006; this equated to an average of 6 tonnes per inhabitant. A high proportion of the total was generated by mining and quarrying industries (25 %) and by construction (including demolition) activities (also 25 %). Mining waste is spread particularly unevenly across the Member States as a function of indigenous supplies of raw materials and mining facilities. The share of mining and quarrying activities ranged from less than 5 % of the total volume of waste generated in 14 of the Member States to around one third of the total in Estonia, Greece and Finland, more than half of the total in Sweden and Romania, and as much as 93 % of the total in Bulgaria. The relative importance of construction and demolition activities in total waste also displayed a wide range, as nine Member States recorded shares below 10 %, while more than half of the waste generated in Germany, Ireland, Austria and the Netherlands was from construction and demolition activities, peaking at 71 % of the total in Luxembourg and 87 % in Malta. Services accounted for 5 % of the waste generated in the EU-27 in 2006, with nine

Member States recording double-digit shares. The relative importance of services as a source of waste was highest in Slovakia (22 % of the total waste generated) and Portugal (27 %).

More than 71 million tonnes of metallic waste were recovered across the Member States (excluding Luxembourg) in 2006, with a further 36 million tonnes of wood waste, 35 million tonnes of paper and cardboard, and 12 million tonnes of glass (2004). As may be expected, the highest levels of waste recovery were generally recorded among the largest Member States (Germany, Spain, France, Italy, Poland and the United Kingdom). Austria, Finland and Sweden together accounted for almost half (48 %) of the paper and cardboard recovery in the EU-27.

Figure 11.7: Municipal waste, EU-27 (¹)
(kg per inhabitant)

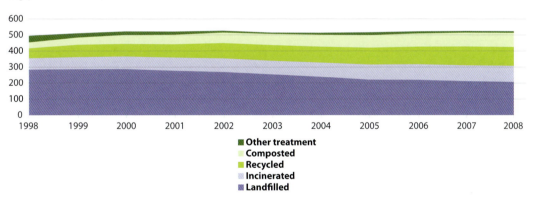

(¹) Data extracted on 2 February 2010.

Source: Eurostat (tsien120 and tsien130)

Table 11.4: Municipal waste (¹)
(kg per inhabitant)

	Municipal waste generated (²)			Municipal waste landfilled (³)			Municipal waste incinerated (⁴)		
	1998	2003	2008	1998	2003	2008	1998	2003	2008
EU-27	496	515	524	285	255	207	71	85	102
Euro area	538	555	558	256	221	177	91	107	127
Belgium	457	468	493	101	44	25	162	162	165
Bulgaria	495	499	467	382	407	440	0	0	0
Czech Republic	293	280	306	272	201	218	17	39	34
Denmark	593	672	802	67	34	35	312	363	433
Germany	647	601	581	199	115	3	112	137	193
Estonia	400	418	515	399	274	248	0	0	1
Ireland	557	736	733	478	480	440	0	0	19
Greece	378	428	453	344	393	347	0	0	0
Spain	566	655	575	317	364	327	38	42	53
France	508	508	543	230	193	193	167	172	172
Italy	472	524	561	365	314	276	34	55	69
Cyprus	664	724	770	601	653	672	0	0	0
Latvia	247	298	331	230	248	310	0	5	1
Lithuania	443	383	407	443	328	367	0	0	0
Luxembourg	629	684	701	146	129	131	288	266	248
Hungary	484	463	453	396	390	333	35	24	39
Malta	470	581	696	388	520	648	0	0	0
Netherlands	593	610	622	54	17	7	198	197	203
Austria	532	609	601	186	183	19	55	73	163
Poland	306	260	320	300	251	228	0	1	2
Portugal	423	447	477	310	293	307	0	96	91
Romania	277	350	382	224	277	287	0	0	0
Slovenia	584	418	459	512	348	341	0	3	7
Slovakia	259	297	332	181	233	254	34	30	29
Finland	466	466	522	294	278	265	28	49	90
Sweden	431	471	515	121	64	15	165	212	250
United Kingdom	543	593	565	456	440	308	37	45	55
Turkey	510	445	428	371	363	356	0	0	0
Iceland	452	485	555	338	364	380	70	45	54
Norway	647	403	490	417	86	88	85	131	184
Switzerland	613	670	741	66	8	0	279	343	371

(¹) Data extracted on 2 February 2010.
(²) Breaks in series: Estonia, 2001; Latvia, 2006; Lithuania, 1999; Hungary, 2000; Malta, 1999; Portugal, 2002; Slovenia, 2002; Slovakia, 2002; Turkey, 2004; Switzerland, 2004.
(³) Breaks in series: Estonia, 2001; Latvia, 2006; Lithuania, 1999; Hungary, 2000; Malta, 1999; Portugal, 2002; Turkey, 2004.
(⁴) Break in series: Italy, 2002.

Source: Eurostat (tsien120 and tsien130)

Table 11.5: Generation of waste, total arising and by selected economic activities
(1 000 tonnes)

	Total waste from economic activities and households		Mining and quarrying activities		Manufacturing industry		Construction and demolition activities		Other economic activities (services)	
	2004	2006	2004	2006	2004	2006	2004	2006	2004	2006
EU-27	2 913 252	2 953 087	862 157	740 745	380 021	364 206	:	:	146 439	154 094
Belgium	52 809	59 352	384	159	18 177	15 308	11 037	13 090	8 689	7 039
Bulgaria	252 058	242 489	222 231	225 338	5 611	4 316	2 999	1 023	9 181	1 473
Czech Republic	29 276	24 746	708	472	8 618	5 932	8 131	8 380	933	1 025
Denmark	12 589	14 703	2	2	1 553	1 643	4 274	5 802	1 290	1 486
Germany	364 022	363 786	55 880	47 222	30 163	31 705	191 563	196 536	16 343	15 107
Estonia	20 861	18 933	5 306	5 961	6 288	3 981	489	717	1 720	1 601
Ireland	24 513	30 005	4 046	4 793	5 356	4 067	11 287	16 599	1 184	1 327
Greece	34 953	51 325	1 902	14 888	4 554	5 285	3 324	6 829	1 518	1 518
Spain	160 668	160 947	21 780	26 015	28 377	22 427	46 320	47 323	14 194	15 376
France	429 153	445 865	166	1 040	21 434	22 973	:	:	24 158	24 158
Italy	139 806	155 025	761	1 005	39 472	39 997	49 151	52 316	3 860	5 534
Cyprus	2 242	1 771	119	60	557	412	488	307	313	313
Latvia	1 257	1 859	0	0	349	570	8	19	99	239
Lithuania	7 010	7 665	4	6	2 632	2 948	357	349	158	586
Luxembourg	8 322	9 586	46	56	725	604	6 985	6 775	179	243
Hungary	24 661	22 287	1 640	27	5 071	5 528	1 736	3 045	1 965	2 445
Malta	2 482	2 861	0	0	10	50	2 206	2 493	160	173
Netherlands	88 099	93 808	296	213	16 086	15 562	49 612	56 610	5 276	5 349
Austria	53 021	54 287	622	1 043	15 073	11 470	27 935	31 322	2 856	3 458
Poland	251 243	266 741	38 311	38 671	61 514	61 131	1 993	14 141	1 965	3 512
Portugal	29 272	38 714	4 761	3 563	10 123	14 699	2 626	3 607	4 202	10 352
Romania	371 503	331 863	326 553	199 138	11 156	9 184	54	34	3 096	3 841
Slovenia	5 771	6 036	129	377	1 960	2 385	908	995	426	429
Slovakia	10 668	14 502	211	332	3 878	5 527	1 404	916	761	3 236
Finland	69 708	72 205	23 819	21 501	18 613	17 976	20 843	23 146	1 276	1 668
Sweden	109 741	115 583	58 600	62 084	27 614	30 363	10 272	8 943	1 517	1 517
United Kingdom	357 544	346 144	93 883	86 779	35 056	28 161	99 234	109 546	39 120	41 088
Croatia	7 209	:	347	:	3 695	:	646	:	116	:
Turkey	58 820	46 092	:	:	16 325	:	:	:	62	:
Iceland	501	:	1	:	61	:	19	:	6	:
Norway	7 454	9 051	116	136	2 956	3 519	1 101	1 248	865	1 472

Source: Eurostat (env_wasgen)

Table 11.6: Waste treatment (non-hazardous), recovery, 2006
(1 000 tonnes)

	Metallic waste	Glass waste	Paper and cardboard waste	Rubber waste	Plastic waste	Wood waste	Textile waste
EU-27 (¹)	*63 453*	*11 948*	*34 932*	*1 451*	*6 429*	*36 181*	*1 717*
Belgium	2 711	282	630	8	130	440	10
Bulgaria	1 148	47	125	2	24	0	3
Czech Republic	1 307	50	201	13	89	120	18
Denmark	643	131	788	54	54	862	0
Germany	7 648	2 024	5 922	192	1 119	2 502	68
Estonia	4	7	6	6	10	398	0
Ireland	31	14	26	9	25	180	7
Greece	2 599	54	425	31	42	63	9
Spain	5 083	1 412	3 346	352	1 450	573	79
France	10 136	2 174	6 050	230	435	3 727	388
Italy	8 228	2 083	4 143	128	1 156	4 378	264
Cyprus	13	4	45	1	26	5	0
Latvia	9	1	18	1	8	0	0
Lithuania	15	26	141	11	36	34	1
Luxembourg	:	:	0	0	:	:	0
Hungary	760	21	344	10	49	174	1
Malta	0	1	3	1	0	1	0
Netherlands	1 928	495	2 731	71	252	705	92
Austria	1 160	249	1 425	30	164	2 282	34
Poland	8 004	136	212	785	446	419	1 294
Portugal	2 842	405	781	90	178	681	144
Romania	2 319	80	335	9	198	109	4
Slovenia	750	:	373	:	22	:	:
Slovakia	509	11	108	11	29	421	3
Finland	1 266	149	734	24	5	4 122	0
Sweden	1 866	:	1 846	35	:	10 916	0
United Kingdom	10 538	*1 198*	*4 174*	25	*426*	*2 747*	117
Croatia (²)	16	13	4	1	3	35	0
Turkey	9	7	23	2	13	0	1
Iceland (²)	0	*6*	*8*	*4*	2	23	1
Norway	880	91	670	39	36	348	13

(¹) Metallic waste, glass waste, rubber waste and textile waste, 2004.
(²) 2004.

Source: Eurostat (env_wastrt)

11.4 Water

Introduction

Water is essential for life, as well as an indispensable resource for the economy, while playing a fundamental role in the climate regulation cycle. The management and protection of water resources, of fresh and salt water ecosystems, and of the water we drink and bathe in are therefore major concerns all around the world. These issues often transcend national boundaries, and it is therefore often necessary for actions to be taken at EU or global level in order to ensure effective protection.

A study conducted for the European Commission ([11]) estimated that water use efficiency could be improved by nearly 40 % through technological improvements alone and that changes in human behaviour or production patterns could increase such savings further. In a scenario based on no changes in practices, it was estimated that water use by the public, industry and agriculture would increase by 16 % by 2030. Conversely, the use of water saving technologies and irrigation management in the industrial and agricultural sectors could reduce excesses by as much as 43 %, while water efficiency measures could decrease water wastage by up to a third.

In a Communication on water scarcity and droughts ([12]) adopted in July 2007, the European Commission identified an initial set of policy options to be taken at

European, national and regional levels to address water scarcity within the EU. This set of proposed policies aims to move the EU towards a water-efficient and water-saving economy.

Aside from the availability of water, another major concern is water quality: the pollution of rivers, lakes and groundwater remains of worldwide concern. Water quality in Europe may be affected by human activities such as industrial production, household discharges, or arable farming (a report on the protection of waters against pollution by nitrates from agricultural sources was issued in March 2007 ([13]). Another aspect of water quality relates to coastal bathing waters. The European Commission and the European Environment Agency present an annual bathing water report – the latest of these covers 2008 ([14]) and shows that 96.3 % of Europe's coastal bathing waters and 92 % of inland bathing waters met the minimum water quality standards. New legislation on bathing water was adopted in 2006 ([15]) and will provide for a more proactive approach to informing the public on water quality; it was transposed into national law in 2008 but Member States have until December 2014 to implement it.

Increasingly variable weather patterns and catastrophic floods (such as the those along the Danube and Elbe in 2002) prompted a review of flood risk management, which culminated in a European

([11]) For more information: http://ec.europa.eu/environment/water/quantity/pdf/water_saving_1.pdf.

([12]) COM(2007) 414 final; for more information: http://eur-lex.europa.eu/LexUriServ/site/en/com/2007/com2007_0414en01.pdf.

([13]) For more information: http://eur-lex.europa.eu/LexUriServ/LexUriServ.do?uri=COM:2007:0120:FIN:EN:PDF.

([14]) For more information: http://ec.europa.eu/environment/water/water-bathing/report2009/report.pdf.

([15]) Directive 2006/7/EC concerning the management of bathing water quality and repealing Directive 76/160/EEC; for more information: http://eur-lex.europa.eu/LexUriServ/LexUriServ.do?uri=OJ:L:2006:064:0037:0051:EN:PDF.

Commission Directive (^{16}) in November 2007 that aims to reduce and manage the risks that floods pose to human health, the environment, cultural heritage and economic activity.

The majority of the EU's population is connected to public water supplies, with the proportion rising close to 100 % in most Member States. Looking at the 'other end of the pipe', namely the treatment of wastewater, a number of countries reported that less than half of their population was connected to urban wastewater treatment; the European Commission releases regular reports on the implementation of the urban wastewater treatment Directive (^{17}).

Definitions and data availability

Water statistics are collected through the inland waters section of a joint OECD/Eurostat questionnaire which is continuously adapted to the EU policy framework. It currently reports on the following:

- **freshwater resources** in groundwater and surface waters – these can be replenished by precipitation and by external inflows (water flowing in from other territories);
- **water abstraction** – a major pressure on resources, although a large part of the water abstracted for domestic, industrial (including energy production), or agricultural use is returned to the environment and its water bodies, but often as wastewater with impaired quality;
- **water use**, analysed by supply category and by industrial activities;
- treatment capacities of **wastewater treatment plants and the share of the**

population connected to them – this gives an overview of the development status of the infrastructure, in terms of quantity and quality, that is available for the protection of the environment from pollution by wastewater;
- **sewage sludge production and disposal** – an inevitable product of wastewater treatment processes; its impact on the environment depends on the methods chosen for its processing and disposal;
- **generation and discharge of wastewater** – pollutants present in wastewater have different source profiles, and similarly the efficiency of treatment of any pollutant varies according to the method applied.

Statistics on water resources are usually calculated on the basis of long-term annual averages for at least 20 years, to take account of the fluctuations in rainfall and evaporation/transpiration from one year to the next.

Precipitation is defined as the total volume of atmospheric wet precipitation (mainly rain, snow and hail) and is usually measured by meteorological or hydrological institutes. **Evapotranspiration** is the volume of water that is transported into the atmosphere by evaporation from the ground, wetlands and natural water bodies or by transpiration of plants. **Internal flow** is defined as the total volume of river run-off and groundwater generated, in natural conditions, exclusively by precipitation into a territory; it is equal to precipitation less evapotranspiration and can be calculated or measured. **External inflow** is the volume of inflow derived from rivers and groundwater that originate in a neighbouring territory. Total

---

(^{16}) Directive 2007/60/EC of 26 November 2007: for more information:
http://eur-lex.europa.eu/LexUriServ/LexUriServ.do?uri=OJ:L:2007:288:0027:0034:EN:PDF.

(^{17}) For more information:
http://ec.europa.eu/environment/water/water-urbanwaste/implementation/pdf/implementation_report_summary.pdf.

freshwater resources refer to the volume of water resulting from internal flow and external inflow. **Outflow** is the volume of water that flows from rivers and groundwater into the sea and into neighbouring territories.

Water abstraction covers groundwater abstraction and surface water abstraction. **Surface water** is defined as water which flows over, or rests on the surface of a land mass; it may be a natural watercourse (such as rivers, streams, brooks and lakes), or an artificial watercourse (such as irrigation, industrial and navigation canals, drainage systems and artificial reservoirs). **Groundwater** is defined as water which is being held in, and can usually be recovered from, or via, an underground formation, including permanent and temporary deposits of water, both artificially charged and naturally, in the subsoil, of sufficient quality for at least seasonal use. Groundwater includes springs, both concentrated and diffused, which may also be subaqueous.

Wastewater is defined as water which is of no further immediate value to the purpose for which it was used or in the pursuit of which it was produced because of its quality, quantity or time of occurrence. However, wastewater from one user can be a potential supply to another user elsewhere. **Urban wastewater** is domestic wastewater or the mixture of domestic wastewater with industrial wastewater and/or run-off rain water. **Urban wastewater treatment** is all treatment of wastewater in urban wastewater treatment plants, which are usually operated by public authorities or by private enterprises working by order of public authorities. This includes also treatment plants in non-urban environments but fulfilling the conditions of the definition.

The **population connected to urban wastewater treatment** relates to persons who are connected to any kind of sewage treatment that is carried out in municipal treatment plants by public authorities or private enterprises on behalf of local authorities. There are three broad types of urban wastewater treatment that are distinguished in statistical information in this area: primary, secondary and tertiary wastewater treatment. **Primary treatment** of wastewater involves physical or chemical processes (such as sedimentation) in which the biological oxygen demand (BOD) and suspended solids are reduced by at least 20 % and 50 %, respectively. **Secondary treatment** generally involves biological treatment, with a secondary settlement procedure that should result in a BOD removal of at least 70 % and a chemical oxygen demand (COD) removal of at least 75 %. **Tertiary treatment** goes further and removes important percentages of nitrogen and/or phosphorous and/or any other pollutants affecting the quality of the water.

Main findings

The three main users of water are agriculture, industry and the domestic sector (households and services). The overall abstraction and use of water resources is generally considered to be sustainable in the long-term in most of Europe. Specific regions may face problems associated with water scarcity, especially in southern Europe, where it is likely that efficiency gains will need to be achieved especially in relation to agricultural water use in order to prevent seasonal water shortages.

Otherwise, regions associated with low rainfall, high population density, or intensive industrial activity may also face sustainability issues, which can be exacerbated by natural resource endowments, geographical characteristics and freshwater management systems. A number of Member States receive a significant proportion of their water resources as inflows from upstream rivers: this is particularly the case in the Danube basin and for the Netherlands, and to a lesser extent in Latvia, Germany and Portugal.

One measure of sustainability is the water exploitation index, calculated as water abstraction divided by long-term annual resources. The European Environment Agency (EEA) uses 20 % as a warning threshold for this indicator, while a ratio of more than 40 % indicates unsustainable water use. Using this measure and subject to data availability, a relatively high pressure exists on water resources in Spain, Bulgaria and Cyprus; although Cyprus was the only country to record a ratio of more than 40 %.

In absolute terms, total freshwater resources were broadly similar in Germany, France, Sweden, the United Kingdom and Italy, as each of these Member States reported a long-term average of annual freshwater resources of between 188 000 and 175 000 million m³. When expressed in relation to population size, Finland and Sweden recorded the highest freshwater annual resources per capita (more than 20 000 m³ per inhabitant). In contrast, relatively low levels (below 3 000 m³) were recorded in the six largest Member States (Germany, Spain, France, Italy, Poland and the United Kingdom), as well as Belgium, Bulgaria, Denmark, the Czech Re-

public and Romania, with the lowest level in Cyprus (420 m³ per inhabitant).

There are considerable differences in the amount of groundwater that is abstracted by the Member States, in part reflecting the resources available, but also abstraction practices for public water supply, industrial and agricultural purposes, as well as land drainage and land sealing. These differences are also apparent when looking at the breakdown of water abstraction between groundwater and freshwater resources. In Hungary surface water abstraction accounted for 32 times the volume of water abstracted from groundwater resources, while the difference was more than ten-fold in Bulgaria, Lithuania and Romania. At the other end of the range, larger volumes of water were abstracted from groundwater resources in Latvia, Slovakia, Cyprus and Malta.

Spain and France recorded the highest amounts of groundwater extracted in 2006 (subject to data availability), both with in excess of 6 000 million m³. Looking at the evolution of groundwater abstraction during the ten-year period to 2007, the volume of groundwater extracted generally fell, although Greece and Slovenia recorded abstraction levels that were between 15 % and 20 % higher, and Spain reported an increase of 41.7 %.

Spain and France also headed the ranking of Member States in relation to surface water abstraction, with more than 25 000 million m³ in 2006. Developments in surface water abstraction levels were even more contrasting than for groundwater, with the Netherlands reporting an increase of 68 % in the nine-year period to 2006, while the volume of surface

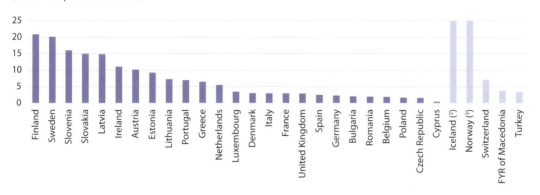

water abstracted in Latvia, Lithuania and Slovakia in 2007was almost half its 1997 level.

The proportion of the population connected to urban wastewater treatment covers those households that are connected to any kind of sewage treatment. This proportion was equal to or greater than 80 % in ten of the 24 Member States for which data are available (mixed ref-

erence years), with shares up to 99 % in the Netherlands where also some 95 % of the population was connected to a tertiary wastewater treatment facility. At the other end of the range, less than one in two households were connected to urban wastewater treatment in Bulgaria, Cyprus, Romania and Malta, where the lowest connection rate was recorded at 13 %; in the latter, however, new treatment plants are under construction.

Figure 11.8: Freshwater resources per capita – long-term average (^{1})
(1 000 m^3 per inhabitant)

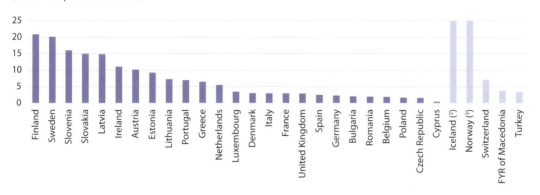

(^{1}) The minimum period taken into account for the calculation of long term annual averages is 20 years; population data are as of 1 January 2007; Hungary and Malta, not available.
(^{2}) Y-axis is cut, 552 500 m^3.
(^{3}) Y-axis is cut, 83 200 m^3.

Source: Eurostat (ten00001 and tps00001)

Table 11.7: Water resources – long-term annual average (¹)
(1 000 million m³)

	Precipitation	Evapotrans-piration	Internal flow	External inflow	Outflow	Freshwater resources
Belgium	28.9	16.6	12.3	7.6	15.3	19.9
Bulgaria	68.2	52.9	15.3	0.5	15.8	15.8
Czech Republic	54.7	39.4	15.2	0.7	16.0	16.0
Denmark	38.5	22.1	16.3	0.0	1.9	16.3
Germany	307.0	190.0	117.0	75.0	182.0	188.0
Estonia	29.0	:	:	:	12.3	12.3
Ireland	80.0	32.5	47.5	:	:	47.5
Greece	115.0	55.0	60.0	12.0	:	72.0
Spain	346.5	235.4	111.1	0.0	111.1	111.1
France	485.7	310.4	175.3	11.0	168.0	186.3
Italy	296.0	129.0	167.0	8.0	155.0	175.0
Cyprus	3.1	2.7	0.3	0.0	0.1	0.3
Latvia	42.7	25.8	16.9	16.8	32.9	33.7
Lithuania	44.0	28.5	15.5	9.0	25.9	24.5
Luxembourg	2.0	1.1	0.9	0.7	1.6	1.6
Hungary	:	:	:	:	:	:
Malta	:	:	:	:	:	:
Netherlands	29.8	21.3	8.5	81.2	86.3	89.7
Austria	98.0	43.0	55.0	29.0	84.0	84.0
Poland	193.1	138.3	54.8	8.3	63.1	63.1
Portugal	82.2	43.6	38.6	35.0	34.0	73.6
Romania	154.0	114.6	39.4	2.9	17.9	42.3
Slovenia	31.7	13.2	18.6	13.5	32.3	32.1
Slovakia	37.4	24.3	13.1	67.3	81.7	80.3
Finland	222.0	115.0	107.0	3.2	110.0	110.0
Sweden	313.9	141.2	172.7	11.8	194.6	183.4
United Kingdom	283.7	111.2	172.5	2.8	175.3	175.3
Croatia	63.1	40.1	23.0	:	:	:
FYR of Macedonia	19.1	:	1.4	6.3	:	7.6
Turkey	501.0	273.6	227.4	6.9	178.0	234.3
Iceland	200.0	30.0	170.0	:	170.0	170.0
Norway	470.7	112.0	377.3	12.2	389.4	389.4
Switzerland	60.1	20.0	40.2	13.1	53.5	53.3

(¹) The minimum period taken into account for the calculation of long term annual averages is 20 years.

Source: Eurostat (ten00001)

Table 11.8: Groundwater and surface water abstraction

	Groundwater abstraction (million m³)			Surface water abstraction (million m³)		
	1997	2002	2007	1997	2002	2007
Belgium	646	662	:	6 929	6 076	:
Bulgaria	798	493	473	6 735	6 096	5 708
Czech Republic	587	540	381	1 906	1 368	1 589
Denmark	917	650	:	16	18	:
Germany (¹)	6 710	6 204	:	33 880	31 802	:
Estonia	322	236	:	1 306	1 177	:
Ireland	:	:	213	:	:	517
Greece (²)	3 119	3 188	3 651	4 603	6 072	5 821
Spain (³)	4 250	5 310	6 022	30 353	32 210	27 738
France (³)	:	6 240	6 184	:	26 923	26 368
Italy	:	:	:	:	:	:
Cyprus (⁴)	143	145	145	34	62	64
Latvia	167	115	108	196	142	104
Lithuania	234	158	175	4 552	2 966	2 094
Luxembourg	:	:	:	:	:	:
Hungary (³)	851	730	541	:	20 303	17 432
Malta	20	16	14	0	0	0
Netherlands (⁵)	1 153	977	1 059	5 354	7 938	8 720
Austria	1 148	:	:	2 496	:	:
Poland	2 871	:	:	9 928	:	:
Portugal	:	:	:	:	:	:
Romania	1 260	860	508	8 000	6 379	5 426
Slovenia	159	208	191	:	691	745
Slovakia	498	410	358	812	684	330
Finland	:	*285*	:	:	:	:
Sweden	654	628	346	2 057	2 048	2 285
United Kingdom	:	:	:	:	:	:
Croatia	:	:	1 162	:	:	29 154
FYR of Macedonia	31	:	:	3 676	:	:
Turkey (⁶)	9 330	10 990	12 096	*26 222*	33 780	:
Iceland	154	160	:	6	5	:
Norway	:	:	:	:	:	:
Switzerland (³)	880	854	788	1 678	1 674	:

(¹) 1998 instead of 1997; 2001 instead of 2002.
(²) 1996 instead of 1997.
(³) 2006 instead of 2007.
(⁴) 1998 instead of 1997.
(⁵) 1996 instead of 1997; 2001 instead of 2002; 2006 instead of 2007.
(⁶) 2001 instead of 2002 for surface water abstraction.

Source: Eurostat (ten00004 and ten00005)

Table 11.9: Population connected to urban wastewater treatment
(% of total)

	1997	1998	1999	2000	2001	2002	2003	2004	2005	2006	2007
Belgium	35	38	39	41	46	48	52	53	55	56	60
Bulgaria	36	36	37	37	38	39	40	40	41	41	42
Czech Republic	59	62	62	64	65	70	71	71	73	74	75
Denmark	88	89	:	:	:	:	:	:	:	:	:
Germany	:	91	:	:	93	:	:	94	:	:	:
Estonia	72	69	69	69	69	70	70	72	74	74	74
Ireland	:	:	66	:	70	:	:	:	84	:	:
Greece	:	:	:	:	:	:	:	:	:	:	85
Spain	:	:	:	:	:	:	:	:	:	:	:
France	:	77	:	:	79	:	:	80	:	:	:
Italy	:	:	:	:	:	:	:	:	:	:	:
Cyprus	12	13	13	14	16	18	23	28	30	:	:
Latvia	:	:	:	:	:	65	70	66	66	65	65
Lithuania	:	:	:	:	:	57	59	:	69	69	69
Luxembourg	:	:	93	:	:	:	95	:	:	:	:
Hungary	24	26	29	46	50	57	59	62	54	57	:
Malta	13	13	13	13	13	13	13	13	13	13	13
Netherlands	98	98	98	98	98	99	99	99	99	99	:
Austria	:	81	:	85	86	86	89	89	:	92	:
Poland	47	49	52	54	55	57	58	59	60	61	62
Portugal	:	42	:	:	:	57	60	:	65	:	68
Romania	:	:	:	:	:	:	:	27	28	28	28
Slovenia	:	19	36	39	39	40	41	50	51	52	51
Slovakia	49	49	50	51	51	52	53	54	55	55	57
Finland	78	79	80	80	81	81	:	:	:	:	:
Sweden	:	93	:	86	:	85	86	86	86	86	:
United Kingdom	:	:	:	:	:	:	:	:	:	:	:
Turkey	14	17	23	26	27	28	30	36	39	42	:
Iceland	4	8	16	33	33	50	50	50	57	:	:
Norway	70	73	73	73	74	74	75	76	77	78	78
Switzerland	95	96	96	96	96	96	:	:	97	:	:

Source: Eurostat (ten00021)

Environment and energy **11**

Figure 11.9: Population connected to wastewater treatment, 2007 (¹)
(% of total)

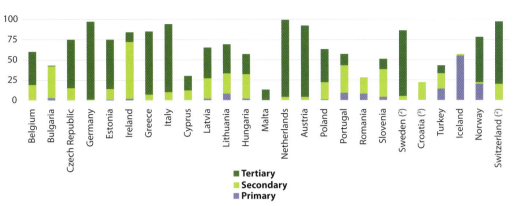

- **Tertiary**
- **Secondary**
- **Primary**

(¹) Hungary, the Netherlands, Austria, Sweden and Turkey, 2006; Germany, Ireland, Italy, Cyprus, Romania (only tertiary treatment), Iceland and Switzerland, 2005; Denmark, Spain, France, Luxembourg, Slovakia, Finland and the United Kingdom, not available.
(²) Primary, not available.
(³) Primary and tertiary, not available.

Source: Eurostat (ten00022, ten00023 and ten00024)

11.5 Environment and economy

Introduction

Resources are the backbone of every economy: in using and transforming them, capital stocks are built-up which add to the wealth of present and future generations. However, the extent of our current resource use may endanger economic growth for future generations and developing countries as they may face difficulties in accessing scarce resources. At the same time, the pace at which resources are being used may result in serious consequences for the environment. Such changes are only likely to accelerate as newly-industrialised countries and developing countries increase their economic activity.

In June 2006, the European Council adopted a comprehensive renewed Sustainable Development Strategy, the aim of which was to 'identify and develop actions to enable the EU to achieve continuous improvement of quality of life both for current and for future generations, through the creation of sustainable communities able to manage and use resources efficiently and to tap the ecological and social innovation potential of the economy, ensuring prosperity, environmental protection and social cohesion'. In response, a set of resource productivity indicators have been developed by Eurostat; these consider both the efficiency with which an economy uses energy and materials and an economy's ability to produce goods and services relative to environmental impacts.

In the absence of mechanisms and policies that require the polluter to pay, the costs resulting from pollution are met by society at large. However, policy development in relation to environmental and sustainable development initiatives has led to this financial burden being increasingly shifted to those enterprises or individuals who are causing/producing pollution; the 'polluter pays' principle.

Environmental accounts have been developed to analyse the environmental consequences of production and consumption patterns. From a production perspective, such accounts can be used to distinguish the environmental performance of different economic activities, an approach that can be extended through linking environment and economic output data, thereby providing measures of 'environmental performance', for example, emission intensities per unit of output.

A key component of the EU's environment and health action programme within the sixth environment action programme (sixth EAP) is the need for a complete overhaul of EU policy on chemicals management. A European Regulation ([18]) on the registration, evaluation, authorisation and restriction of chemicals (REACH) came into force in June 2007. The major objective of REACH is to ensure a high level of protection for human health and the environment, by increasing knowledge about the hazardous properties of chemicals.

The EU's eco-management and audit scheme (EMAS) is a management tool for enterprises and other organisations to evaluate, report and improve their environmental performance. Enterprises have been able to participate in the scheme since 1995 ([19]). It was originally restricted to enterprises within the industrial economy, however, since 2001 EMAS has been open to all economic sectors including public and private services. In addition, EMAS was strengthened by ISO 14001 an international standard for environmental management. These management systems aim to help organisations identify their procedures related to the environment and to minimise harmful effects on the environment caused by their activities, and continually improve their environmental performance ([20]). Organisations participating in EMAS are committed to evaluate and improve their own environmental performance, comply with relevant environmental legislation, prevent pollution, and provide relevant information to the public (via verified environmental audits). In July 2008 the European Commission proposed to revise EMAS to increase the participation of companies and reduce the administrative burden and costs, particularly for small and medium-sized enterprises. On 2 April 2009, the Council and the European Parliament reached agreement on the text for a revised EMAS Regulation ([21]); at time of writing, formal adoption of the Regulation and entry into force had yet to happen.

([18]) For more information: http://ec.europa.eu/environment/chemicals/reach/reach_intro.htm.

([19]) Council Regulation (EEC) No 1836/93 of 29 June 1993; for more information:
http://eur-lex.europa.eu/LexUriServ/LexUriServ.do?uri=CELEX:31993R1836:EN:HTML.

([20]) Commission Regulation (EC) No 196/2006 of 3 February 2006 amending Annex I to Regulation (EC) No 761/2001 of the European Parliament and of the Council to take account of the European Standard EN ISO 14001:2004, and repealing Decision 97/265/EC;
for more information: http://eur-lex.europa.eu/LexUriServ/site/en/oj/2006/l_032/l_03220060204en00040012.pdf.

([21]) For more information: http://ec.europa.eu/environment/emas/index_en.htm.

Definitions and data availability

Resource productivity measures the efficiency with which the economy uses energy and materials (the natural resource inputs needed to achieve a given economic output). Sometimes resource productivity is used as a proxy for environmental impacts, using the reasoning that if less goes into the economic system then less waste and pollution will be discharged into the environment. Using this approach it is thought that resource productivity also measures the economy's ability to produce goods and services relative to its environmental impacts. Resource productivity is defined as GDP divided by **domestic material consumption** (DMC), which in turn is related to the consumption activities of residents in the national economy (DMC = domestic extraction plus imports minus exports). It is important to note that the term consumption as used in DMC denotes apparent consumption and not final consumption.

Data on **environmental protection expenditure** are collected through a joint OECD/Eurostat questionnaire. Environmental protection expenditure covers all expenditure on activities directly aimed at the prevention, reduction and elimination of pollution or nuisances resulting from production or consumption. Note that activities which may be beneficial to the environment, but that primarily satisfy technical needs, or health and safety requirements, are excluded. These expenditures may be classified according to the economic sector (agriculture, industry, services, public sector, and households) carrying out the expenditure, according to a financial breakdown of the expenditure

(treatment and prevention investment, current expenditure, subsidies), or according to the environmental domain covered (air, waste, water, etc.) – of which there are nine areas distinguished in the classification of environmental protection activities (CEPA 2000) [22]. Investment expenditure includes outlays in a given year (purchases and own-account production) for machinery, equipment and land used for environmental protection purposes. Non-core expenditure consists of administrative costs such as labour costs associated with running environmental departments or government funded agencies.

Eurostat has developed a **production index of toxic chemicals**, broken down into five toxicity classes, presenting the trend in aggregated production volumes of chemicals which have been classified as toxic substances according to EU legislation. The toxicity classes, beginning with the most dangerous, are: carcinogenic, mutagenic and reprotoxic (CMR-chemicals); chronic toxic chemicals; very toxic chemicals; toxic chemicals; and harmful chemicals. These classes are derived from the risk phrases assigned to individual substances in annex 6 of the dangerous substance Directive, as last amended in 2001 [23]. Production volumes are extracted from PRODCOM (statistics on the production of manufactured goods) and are aggregated to the five classes according to their toxicity.

The **eco-management and audit scheme (EMAS)** is an EU voluntary instrument: organisations participating in EMAS are committed to evaluate and improve their own environmental performance, comply with relevant environmental legislation,

---

[22] For more information: http://ec.europa.eu/eurostat/ramon/nomenclatures/index.cfm?TargetUrl=ACT_OTH_DFLT_LAYOUT&StrNom=CEPA_2000&StrLanguageCode=EN.

[23] Commission Directive 2001/59/EC of 6 August 2001 adapting to technical progress for the 28th time Council Directive 67/548/EEC on the approximation of the laws, regulations and administrative provisions relating to the classification, packaging and labelling of dangerous substances; for more information: http://eur-lex.europa.eu/LexUriServ/LexUriServ.do?uri=CELEX:32001L0059:EN:NOT.

prevent pollution, and report on their environmental performance through the publication of an independently verified environmental statement. The scheme allows the use of ISO 14001 (international standard for environmental management system) as its environmental management system element. EMAS registered organisations are recognised by the EMAS logo, which guarantees the reliability of the information provided. To receive EMAS registration an organisation must comply with the following steps: conduct an environmental review; establish an effective environmental management system; carry out an environmental audit; and provide a statement of its environmental performance.

The EU's **eco-label scheme**, as laid down in a Regulation of the European Commission ([24]) is now part of a wider approach on integrated product policy (IPP). The Community eco-label is awarded to products and services with reduced environmental impacts. The existing scheme has been in operation since 1993. It is administered by the European eco-labelling board (EUEB), which includes representatives from industry environmental protection groups and consumer organisations.

Main findings

The efficient use of natural resources (many of which come from outside of the EU) contributes to economic growth, whereas disruption in supplies, inefficiencies and over-consumption are likely to put the sustainable future of economic systems under threat. Although the GDP of the EU-15 increased on average by 2.3 % per annum between 1995 and 2005, domestic material consumption grew at a much

slower pace, rising on average by 0.7 % per annum (with two main surges in 2000 and 2004); as a result, resource productivity in the EU-15 rose by 16.5 % overall between 1995 and 2005. This could be seen as a relative decoupling of the use of materials in relation to the economy, however, much of the economic growth during this time was due to a growth in services so any conclusions about the increasing efficiency of the EU-15 economies should only be made taking this into consideration.

An analysis of EU-27 environmental protection expenditure in 2004 within manufacturing industries shows that relatively similar amounts of expenditure were dedicated to tackling environmental concerns relating to wastewater (30.9 %), waste (27.2 %) and air pollution (25.9 %), while the remaining share (16.1 %) was used for none-core domains.

The chemicals industry is one of the largest European manufacturing sectors and it has a pivotal role in providing innovative materials and technological solutions which have a direct impact on Europe's industrial competitiveness. Manufactured chemicals can, however, have an environment impact on soil, water and air quality, and some chemicals such as hydrofluorocarbons (HFCs), perfluorocarbons (PFCs) and sulphur hexafluoride (SF_6) were included in the Kyoto Protocol because they contribute to global warming. Between 1997 and 2007 the total production of all chemicals in the EU-15 grew by 15.7 %. The output of all toxic chemicals increased at a much slower pace, rising 7.0 %, while the level of production for the most dangerous, carcinogenic, mutagenic and reprotoxic (CMR) chemicals expanded by 10.0 %; the out-

([24]) Regulation (EC) No 1980/2000 of the European Parliament and of the Council of 17 July 2000; for more information: http://eur-lex.europa.eu/LexUriServ/site/en/oj/2000/l_237/l_23720000921en00010012.pdf.

put of toxic and CMR chemicals peaked in 2004, since when both indices followed a downward trend.

Statistics on the production of toxic chemicals are available from 2004 onwards for the EU-25 (data for Bulgaria and Romania are not yet available). Toxic chemicals accounted for 58.2 % of the total output of the EU-25's chemicals industry in 2007. The volume of CMR chemicals produced in the EU-25 was around 36 million tonnes, equivalent to 10.2 % of total chemicals' production.

The eco-management and audit scheme (EMAS) is a management tool for companies and other organisations to evaluate, report and improve their environmental

performance. In the EU-27 there were almost 6 000 sites that had implemented EMAS by 2007 (an average of 11.9 sites per million inhabitants). The highest uptake of EMAS (relative to population size) was recorded in Austria, with 58.9 sites per million inhabitants, followed by Denmark (45.7) and Belgium (31.7); the only other countries to have ratios in double figures were Spain, Germany and Italy.

Denmark and Austria were also at the forefront of eco-label awards: with 5.3 and 3.0 awards per million inhabitants in 2007, compared with an EU-27 average of 1.0); the only other countries to have ratios above 2.0 awards per million inhabitants were Ireland, Italy and Malta.

Figure 11.10: Resource productivity, EU-15 (1995=100)

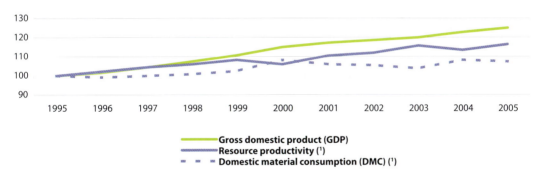

(¹) Estimates.

Source: Eurostat (nama_gdp_k, tsien140 and tsdpc230)

Figure 11.11: Environmental protection expenditure within manufacturing industries, EU-27, 2004 (¹)
(% of total)

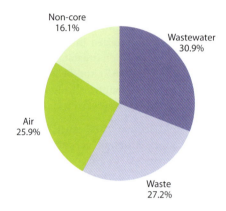

(¹) Figures do not sum to 100 % due to rounding.

Source: Eurostat (env_ac_exp1)

Figure 11.12: Production volume of toxic chemicals, EU-15 (¹)
(1997=100)

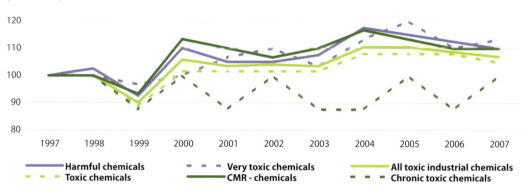

| Harmful chemicals | Very toxic chemicals | All toxic industrial chemicals |
| Toxic chemicals | CMR - chemicals | Chronic toxic chemicals |

(¹) In 2007, the volume of toxic chemicals produced in the EU-15 was: 317 million tonnes (EU-25: 354 million tonnes; an EU-25 time series is only available from 2004 to 2007). The share of substances classified as toxic was 183 million tonnes (EU-25: 206 million tonnes). Of the EU-25 production volume, starting with the most toxic substances, 36 million tonnes were classified as 'CMR-chemicals', 8 million tonnes as 'chronic toxic' chemicals, 39 million tonnes as 'very toxic', 74 million tonnes as 'toxic' and 49 million tonnes as 'harmful' chemicals in 2007.

Source: Eurostat (tsdph320)

Table 11.10: Environmental expenditure, EMAS and eco-label

	Environmental expenditure by the public sector, 2005 (% of GDP) (¹)	Environmental expenditure by total industry, 2005 (% of GDP) (²)	Sites having implemented an eco-management and audit scheme, 2007 (number)	Eco-label awards, 2007 (number)
EU-27	:	0.44	5 888	478
Belgium	0.62	0.53	336	6
Bulgaria	0.38	0.78	0	:
Czech Republic	:	0.87	30	7
Denmark	1.05	:	249	29
Germany	:	:	1 954	61
Estonia	0.24	0.35	2	0
Ireland	:	:	6	11
Greece	:	:	59	17
Spain	0.31	0.26	1 090	27
France	0.33	:	13	88
Italy	0.71	0.78	1 046	145
Cyprus	0.31	0.23	0	1
Latvia	0.06	0.19	13	3
Lithuania	:	0.42	0	0
Luxembourg	:	:	0	0
Hungary	0.64	0.64	16	1
Malta	:	:	1	1
Netherlands	:	:	15	8
Austria	0.47	0.36	488	25
Poland	0.43	0.74	7	5
Portugal	0.49	0.30	66	7
Romania	0.23	0.60	1	:
Slovenia	0.79	0.73	1	2
Slovakia	0.26	1.13	5	0
Finland	0.39	0.39	49	5
Sweden	0.27	0.39	72	17
United Kingdom	0.49	0.28	369	12
Croatia	0.08	0.73	27	:
Turkey	0.54	:	:	:
Iceland	:	:	:	0
Norway	:	:	27	6
Switzerland	:	0.29	:	:

(¹) Belgium, Spain, France, Cyprus, Portugal, Slovenia, Finland, Sweden and the United Kingdom, 2004.
(²) EU-27, Belgium, Spain, Italy, Portugal, Slovenia, Finland and the United Kingdom, 2004; Switzerland, 2003.

Source: Eurostat (ten00049, ten00052, tsdpc410 and tsdpc420)

11.6 Biodiversity

Introduction

Biodiversity, a contraction of biological diversity, reflects the number, variety and variability of living organisms, including mankind. We depend on natural resources and the variety of species found on the planet for tangible items that make life possible and drive economic development (food, energy, wood, raw materials, clean air and water). Many aspects of our natural environment are predominantly public goods (in other words, there are no markets or prices), as such the loss of biodiversity can often go undetected by economic systems. However, the natural environment also provides a range of intangibles, such as aesthetic pleasure derived from viewing landscapes and wildlife, or recreational opportunities. In order to protect this legacy for future generations, policies need to be developed in a range of areas to ensure that biodiversity is protected through the sustainable development of, among others, agricultural, regional, urban, energy and transport policy. Many of these issues were touched upon by a meeting of the G8 environment ministers held in Potsdam in March 2007, which launched an extensive study on the economic significance of the global loss of biological diversity ([25]).

Indeed, the global scale of the biodiversity issue has led to international action within this domain, the framework for which is the United Nations (UN) convention on biological diversity (CBD), which the EU ratified in 1993. At the United Nations world summit on sustainable development in Johannesburg in 2002, governments committed themselves to significantly reducing the rate of biodiversity loss by 2010. At a UN conference in Bonn in May 2008 decisions were taken on a number of concrete measures and a programme of funding to help achieve this goal.

In 1998 the EU adopted its own biodiversity strategy. Four action plans covering: the conservation of natural resources, agriculture, fisheries, and economic and development cooperation were subsequently agreed as part of this strategy in 2001. The European Commission released a Communication on stopping the decline of endangered species and habitats by 2010 ([26]); this underlined the importance of biodiversity protection as a prerequisite for sustainable development and set out an action plan. The biodiversity action plan addresses the challenge of integrating biodiversity concerns into other policy sectors. It also contains indicators to monitor progress and a timetable for evaluations, whereby the European Commission has undertaken to provide annual reporting.

EU policy on the conservation of natural habitats is part of the overall biodiversity strategy. It is essentially based on the implementation of two directives: the 'birds Directive' ([27]) for the conservation of wild birds and the 'habitats Directive' ([28]) which covers the conservation of natural habitats, wild fauna and flora; together these provide the legal basis for setting-

([25]) For more information: http://www.teebweb.org.

([26]) COM(2006) 216 final; for more information: http://eur-lex.europa.eu/LexUriServ/LexUriServ.do?uri=COM:2006:0216:FIN:EN:PDF.

([27]) Council Directive 79/409/EEC of 2 April 1979; for more information: http://eur-lex.europa.eu/LexUriServ/site/en/consleg/1979/L/01979L0409-20070101-en.pdf.

([28]) Council Directive 92/43/EEC of 21 May 1992; for more information: http://eur-lex.europa.eu/LexUriServ/LexUriServ.do?uri=CONSLEG:1992L0043:20070101:EN:PDF.

up an ecological network of sites under the title Natura 2000 – the largest network of protected areas in the world. The EU wants to expand Natura 2000, which currently counts around 25 000 different sites (and an area of almost 880 000 km²) where plant and animal species and their habitats must be protected.

Most of the work in this area has so far focused on the establishment of the Natura 2000 network which may be seen as the first pillar of action, relating to the conservation of natural habitats and habitats of various species. However, the legislation also foresees actions in relation to the establishment of a second pillar through the implementation of a strict protection regime for animal species (for example, the Arctic fox and Iberian lynx are both under serious threat of extinction).

Definitions and data availability

Annual data are available on **protected areas under the habitats Directive** and these are presented as a percentage of total country area. The indicator on protected areas is based on areas proposed by countries to be designated for the protection of natural and semi-natural habitats, wild fauna and flora according to the habitats Directive. **The index of sufficiency** measures the extent to which sites of Community importance proposed by the Member States adequately cover the species and habitats listed in the annexes I and II of the habitats Directive.

Birds are considered good proxies for biodiversity and the integrity of ecosystems as they tend to be at, or near, the top of the food chain, have large ranges and migrate, and thus reflect changes in ecosystems rather rapidly. By focusing attention on the population trends of rela-

tively large groups of abundant European species associated with different habitats, these indicators are designed to capture the overall, average changes in population levels of common birds and to reflect the health and functioning of ecosystems. For example, farmland and forest bird species have a high dependence on their habitats during the nesting season and for feeding during most of the year. The **population index of common birds** is an aggregated index (with base year 1990 or the first year the Member State entered the scheme) for population estimates of a selected group of common bird species. Indices are calculated for each species independently and are then combined by averaging with an equal weight used for each species. The EU index is based on trend data from 18 Member States, derived from annually operated national breeding bird surveys obtained through the pan-European common bird monitoring scheme (PECBMS) [29].

Main findings

About 13 % of the EU-25's territory was proposed as a protected area under the habitats Directive in 2007. Figures for the Member States show that protected areas account for a little above 30 % of the total area in Slovenia, while seven Member States reported shares below the threshold of 10 %. The protected sites generally provided an adequate level of cover for the species and habitats listed in the Directive, with an EU-25 average of 84 %; only Poland and Cyprus reported sufficiency ratios under 50 %.

Since 1990 there has generally been a downward trend in the evolution of common bird indices within the EU, in particular for common farmland species.

[29] For more information: http://www.ebcc.info/pecbm.html.

Part of the relatively steep decline (-25 % between 1990 and 2006) in numbers of common farmland birds may be attributed to changes in land use and agricultural practices. More recently, these indices have stabilised, with both the farmland and the forest bird index fluctuating around 80 % (of 1990 base year values), while the common bird index stands at around 90 % (of its 1990 level).

Figure 11.13: Protected areas for biodiversity: habitats Directive, 2007

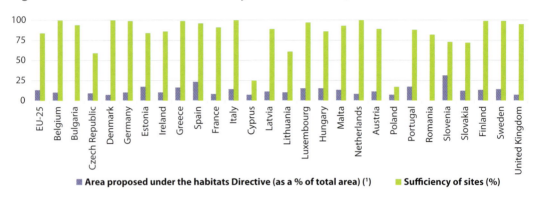

■ **Area proposed under the habitats Directive (as a % of total area) (¹)**   ■ **Sufficiency of sites (%)**

(¹) Bulgaria and Romania, not available.

Source: EEA/European Topic Centre on Biodiversity, Eurostat (env_bio1)

Figure 11.14: Common bird indices, EU (¹)
(aggregated index of population estimates of selected groups of breeding bird species, 1990=100)

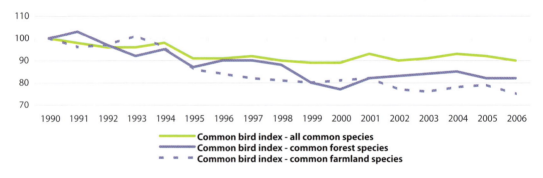

——— Common bird index - all common species
——— Common bird index - common forest species
‑ ‑ ‑ Common bird index - common farmland species

(¹) EU-12 up to 1994; EU-15 up to 2004; EU-25 up to 2006; 'all common species' covers information on 135 different bird species; 'common farmland species' covers 36 bird species; 'common forest species' covers 29 bird species.

Source: EBCC/RSPB/BirdLife/Statistics Netherlands, Eurostat (env_bio2)

11.7 Energy production and imports

Introduction

The EU's dependency on energy imports, particularly of oil and more recently of gas, forms the backdrop for policy concerns relating to the security of energy supplies. More than half of the EU-27's energy comes from countries outside the Union – and this proportion is rising. Much of this energy comes from Russia, whose disputes with transit countries have disrupted supplies in recent years – for example, between 6 and 20 January 2009, gas flows from Russia via Ukraine were interrupted.

The EU has set out plans for a new energy strategy based on a more secure, sustainable and low-carbon economy. In a Communication from November 2007, the European Commission put forward a strategic energy technology plan (SET-plan), titled 'towards a low carbon future' ([30]). This encouraged the development of carbon-free energy technologies, such as wind power, solar power (thermal, photovoltaic and concentrated), hydropower, tidal power, geothermal energy and second generation biomass. Aside from combating climate change through a reduction in greenhouse gas emissions, the use of renewable energy sources is likely to result in more secure energy supplies, greater diversity in energy supply, less air pollution, as well as the possibility for job creation in environmental and renewable energy sectors.

The European Commission adopted its second strategic energy review in November 2008. This addressed how the EU could reduce its dependency on imported energy, thereby improving its security of supply, as well as reducing its emissions of greenhouse gases. This agenda encourages energy solidarity among Member States, proposes an action plan to secure sustainable energy supplies, and adopts a package of energy efficiency proposals aimed at making energy savings in key areas, such as buildings and energy-using products.

Renewable energy has an important role to play in reducing carbon dioxide emissions. A sustainable energy policy is, in part, reliant upon increasing the share of renewable energy, which may at the same time help to improve the security of energy supply by reducing the Community's growing dependence on imported energy sources.

The integrated energy and climate change strategy adopted in December 2008 provided a further stimulus for increasing the use of renewables to 20 % of total energy production by 2020 (including a 10 % biofuels target for transport), while calling for energy consumption and greenhouse gas emissions to both be cut by 20 %. A Directive on the promotion of the use of energy from renewable sources ([31]) requires Member States to develop national action plans for the development of their renewable energy sources, as well as establishing sustainability criteria, for example, ensuring that the use of biofuels does not put food supply or forest protection at risk (either in the EU or in non-member countries).

The European Commission made a proposal at the end of 2008 to repeal Directive 2004/67/EC concerning measures to safeguard security of natural gas supply ([32]). In response to the Russian-Ukrainian

([30]) For more information: http://ec.europa.eu/energy/res/setplan/index_en.htm.

([31]) Directive 2009/28/EC of the European Parliament and of the Council of 23 April 2009; for more information: http://eur-lex.europa.eu/LexUriServ/LexUriServ.do?uri=OJ:L:2009:140:0016:0062:EN:PDF.

([32]) COM(2008) 769 final; for more information: http://eur-lex.europa.eu/LexUriServ/LexUriServ.do?uri=COM:2008:0769:FIN:EN:PDF.

gas crisis of January 2009, the European Council and the European Parliament called for an accelerated revision of the directive, arguing that the crisis demonstrated the need to define more clearly the roles of the gas industry, Member States and the Community institutions to deal with potential supply disruptions. As a result, the Council adopted a Directive in the second half of 2009 imposing an obligation on Member States to maintain minimum stocks of crude oil and/or petroleum products ([33]). These new measures for oil and gas markets are designed to ensure that all parties take effective action to prevent and mitigate the consequences of potential disruptions to supplies, while also creating mechanisms for Member States to work together to deal effectively with any major oil or gas disruptions which might arise; a coordination mechanism has been set-up so that Member States can react uniformly and immediately in emergency cases.

Definitions and data availability

In order to meet the increasing requirements of policymakers for energy monitoring, the legislation relating to energy statistics has in recent years undergone a period of renewal. The legal basis for energy statistics is a Regulation of 22 October 2008 on energy statistics ([34]). The data collection exercise covers all 27 Member States, Croatia, Turkey, Iceland, Norway and Switzerland; although not presented in this yearbook, monthly data are also available for certain indicators.

Energy commodities extracted or captured directly from natural resources are called primary energy sources, while energy commodities which are produced from primary sources in transformation plants are called derived products. **Primary energy production** covers the national production of primary energy sources and takes place when the natural sources are exploited, for example, in coal mines, crude oil fields, hydropower plants or in the fabrication of biofuels. Transformation of energy from one form to another, like electricity or heat generation from thermal power plants or coke production from coke ovens is therefore not considered as primary production.

Primary production of solid fuels (coal and lignite) consists of quantities of fuels extracted or produced, calculated after any operation for removal of inert matter. Primary production of crude oil covers all production within national boundaries, including offshore production. Natural gas is measured as the dry marketable production, after purification and extraction of NGLs (natural gas liquids) and sulphur; it does not include quantities re-injected, extraction losses, or quantities vented and flared. The heat produced in a reactor as a result of nuclear fission is regarded as primary production of nuclear heat. Renewable energy sources cover the production of energy from biomass, hydropower, geothermal energy, wind and solar energy:

- biomass is the heat content of the produced biofuels or biogas; heat produced after combustion during incineration of renewable wastes; this covers organic, non-fossil material of biological origin, which may be used for heat production or electricity generation, comprising wood and wood waste, biogas, municipal solid waste, and biofuels.

([33]) Council Directive 2009/119/EC of 14 September 2009; for more information:
http://eur-lex.europa.eu/LexUriServ/LexUriServ.do?uri=OJ:L:2009:265:0009:0023:EN:PDF.

([34]) Regulation (EC) No 1099/2008 of the European Parliament and of the Council; for more information:
http://eur-lex.europa.eu/LexUriServ/LexUriServ.do?uri=OJ:L:2008:304:0001:0062:EN:PDF.

- hydropower covers potential and kinetic energy of water converted into electricity in hydroelectric plants (the electricity generated in pumped storage plants is not included);
- geothermal energy comprises energy available as heat emitted from within the earth's crust, usually in the form of hot water or steam;
- wind energy covers the kinetic energy of wind converted into electricity in wind turbines;
- solar energy covers the solar radiation exploited for solar heat (hot water) and electricity production.

Imports represent all entries into the national territory, while exports cover all quantities exported from the national territory. **Net imports** of primary energy are calculated as imports minus exports; they exclude transit quantities (notably via gas and oil pipelines), except for electrical energy whose transit is recorded under external trade statistics.

The **energy dependency rate** is defined as net imports divided by gross consumption; gross consumption is equal to gross inland consumption plus the energy supplied to international marine bunkers. A negative dependency rate indicates a net exporter of energy. A dependency rate in excess of 100 % indicates that energy products have been stocked.

Main findings

Production of primary energy in the EU-27 totalled 849.6 million tonnes of oil equivalent (toe) in 2007. This continued the generally downward trend of EU-27 production, as supplies of raw materials become exhausted and/or producers considered the exploitation of limited

resources uneconomical. Production was dominated by the United Kingdom with a 20.4 % share of the EU-27 total, although this marked a considerable reduction when compared with a decade earlier (27.3 % of the EU-27 total in 1997). Indeed, the United Kingdom and Poland experienced the most significant reductions in their output of primary energy, with reductions of 88.8 million toe and 27.5 million toe respectively. France and Germany, in contrast, maintained their levels of production broadly in line with 1997; they were the only other Member States to report production of primary energy in excess of 100 million toe.

Primary energy production in the EU-27 in 2007 was spread across a range of energy sources, the most important of which was nuclear energy (28.4 % of the total); the significance of nuclear fuel was particularly high in Belgium, France, Lithuania, Slovakia and Sweden – where it accounted for more than half of the national production of primary energy. Around one fifth of the EU-27's total production of primary energy was accounted for by solid fuels (largely coal) and by natural gas, with shares of 22.0 % and 19.7 % respectively, while renewable energy sources (16.3 %) and crude oil (13.6 %) made up the remainder of the total.

The growth of primary production from renewable energy sources exceeded that of all the other energy types, with particularly strong growth since 2002. Indeed, there would appear to be something of a watershed since this date, as the production of renewables accelerated, rising by 38.4 % overall between 2002 and 2007. In contrast, the production levels of the other sources of primary energy all fell during

the period considered, with the largest reductions for crude oil (-28.7 %), natural gas (-18.1 %) and solid fuels (-11.1 %).

Among renewable energies, the most important source was biomass and waste, accounting for 96.2 million toe of primary production in the EU-27 in 2007. Hydropower was the only other significant contributor to the renewable energy mix (26.7 million toe). Although production still remains small, there has been a particularly rapid expansion in the production of wind energy, reaching 9.0 million toe in the EU-27 in 2007.

The downturn in the primary production of hard coal, lignite and crude oil has led to a situation where the EU-27 is increasingly reliant on primary energy imports in order to satisfy demand. The EU-27's imports of primary energy exceeded exports by some 988.4 million toe in 2007. The largest net importers of primary energy were generally the most populous Member States, with the exception of the United Kingdom and Poland (where some indigenous reserves of oil/natural gas and coal remain). Since 2004 the only net exporter among the Member States has been Denmark.

The origin of EU-27 energy imports has changed rapidly in recent years. In 2007, almost one third (30.3 %) of the EU-27's imports of crude oil were from Russia; this was 11.6 percentage points higher than seven years earlier. Russia also became the principal supplier of hard coal, its share of EU-27 imports rising from 7.9 % in 2000 to 22.6 % by 2007. In contrast, Russia's share of EU-27 imports of natural gas declined from 40.4 % to 30.7 % between 2000 and 2007; note, however, that during this period the volume of natural gas imports from Russia remained relatively unchanged.

The security of the EU-27's primary energy supplies may be threatened if a high proportion of imports are concentrated among relatively few partners. Almost two thirds (63.6 %) of the EU-27's imports of natural gas in 2007 came from Russia, Norway or Algeria. A similar analysis shows that 64.5 % of EU-27 imports of hard coal were from Russia, South Africa, Australia or Colombia, while 59.5 % of crude oil imports came from Russia, Norway, Libya or Saudi Arabia. Although their import volumes remain relatively small, there was some evidence of new partner countries emerging between 2000 and 2007. This was notably the case for crude oil imports from Libya and Kazakhstan, coal imports from Indonesia and Ukraine, or natural gas imports from Nigeria and Libya.

EU-27 dependency on energy imports increased from less than 40 % of gross consumption in the 1980s to 53.1 % by 2007, with the highest dependency rates recorded for crude oil (82.7 %) and for natural gas (60.3 %). The dependency on non-member countries for supplies of solid fuels and natural gas grew at a faster pace in the last decade than the dependency on oil (which was already at a high level). Since 2004, the EU-27's net imports of energy have been greater than its primary production; in other words, more than half of the EU-27's gross inland energy consumption was supplied by net imports. As it was a net exporter, Denmark was the only Member State in 2007 with a negative dependency rate. Among the other Member States, the lowest dependency rates were recorded by Poland, the Czech Republic and the United Kingdom; meanwhile, Cyprus, Malta and Luxembourg were almost entirely dependent on primary energy imports.

Table 11.11: Energy production
(million tonnes of oil equivalent)

	Total production of primary energy		Share of total production, 2007 (%)				
	1997	2007	Nuclear energy	Solid fuels	Natural gas	Crude oil	Renewable energy
EU-27	962.4	849.6	28.4	22.0	19.7	13.6	16.3
Euro area	453.0	453.6	41.6	16.3	17.3	3.2	21.5
Belgium	12.6	13.7	90.7	0.0	0.0	-	9.3
Bulgaria	9.8	9.8	38.5	48.7	2.4	0.3	10.1
Czech Republic	32.3	33.3	20.2	71.4	0.4	0.7	7.2
Denmark	20.2	27.0	-	-	30.6	57.5	11.8
Germany	138.5	135.3	26.8	40.4	9.5	2.5	20.8
Estonia	3.8	4.4	-	81.6	-	-	16.8
Ireland	2.8	1.4	-	42.0	26.2	-	31.7
Greece	9.9	12.2	-	85.4	0.2	0.7	13.8
Spain	30.7	30.2	47.1	18.1	0.3	0.5	34.1
France	127.9	134.0	84.6	0.0	0.7	0.8	13.9
Italy	30.3	25.9	0.0	0.4	30.7	23.0	46.0
Cyprus	0.0	0.1	-	-	:	-	100.0
Latvia	1.6	1.8	-	0.2	-	-	99.8
Lithuania	3.9	3.5	72.0	0.4	-	4.5	23.1
Luxembourg	0.0	0.1	-	-	-	-	100.0
Hungary	12.8	10.2	37.2	17.4	19.7	11.9	13.8
Malta	-	-	-	:	:	-	:
Netherlands	65.7	61.0	1.8	-	89.8	4.3	4.1
Austria	8.5	10.4	-	0.0	15.2	9.6	75.2
Poland	99.1	71.6	-	86.5	5.4	1.0	7.0
Portugal	3.8	4.6	-	0.0	-	-	100.0
Romania	31.6	27.6	7.2	24.8	33.4	17.5	17.1
Slovenia	3.0	3.4	42.7	36.0	0.1	0.0	21.1
Slovakia	4.6	5.6	70.3	9.8	1.9	0.4	17.5
Finland	14.8	15.7	38.4	6.9	-	-	54.6
Sweden	32.0	33.1	52.2	0.5	-	0.0	47.3
United Kingdom	262.3	173.6	9.4	5.6	37.4	45.1	2.5
Croatia	4.1	4.0	:	0.0	58.5	23.2	18.3
Turkey	28.0	27.3	:	54.2	2.7	7.9	35.2
Iceland	1.7	:	:	:	:	:	:
Norway	212.7	216.0	:	1.2	36.1	56.7	6.0
Switzerland	10.5	12.2	58.8	:	0.0	:	41.2

Source: Eurostat (ten00076, ten00080, ten00077, ten00079, ten00078 and ten00081)

Figure 11.15: Production of primary energy, EU-27, 2007
(% of total, based on tonnes of oil equivalent)

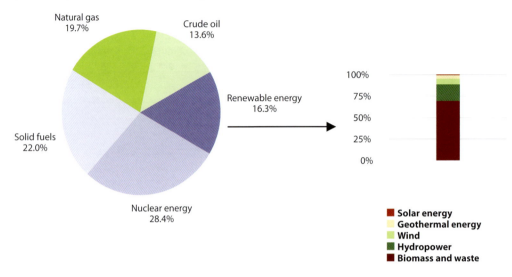

Source: Eurostat (ten00080, ten00077, ten00079, ten00078, ten00081 and ten00082)

Figure 11.16: Development of the production of primary energy (by fuel type), EU-27
(1997=100, based on tonnes of oil equivalent)

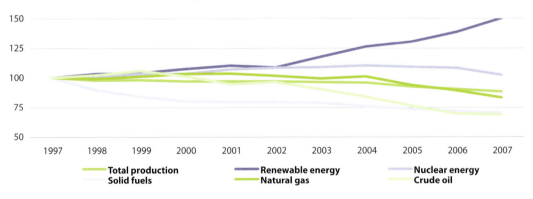

Source: Eurostat (ten00077, ten00081, ten00080, ten00077, ten00079 and ten00078)

Table 11.12: Primary production of renewable energy

	Primary production (1 000 toe)		Share of total, 2007 (%)				
	1997	2007	Solar energy	Biomass & waste	Geothermal energy	Hydropower energy	Wind energy
EU-27	92 390	138 831	0.9	69.3	4.2	19.2	6.5
Euro area	61 722	97 741	1.2	66.5	5.7	18.7	7.9
Belgium	633	1 273	0.4	93.4	0.2	2.6	3.3
Bulgaria	488	995	-	71.5	3.3	24.8	0.4
Czech Republic	673	2 404	0.2	91.9	-	7.5	0.5
Denmark	1 752	3 193	0.3	79.8	0.4	0.1	19.3
Germany	7 712	28 121	2.1	78.7	0.8	6.4	12.1
Estonia	587	745	-	98.7	-	0.3	1.1
Ireland	181	447	0.2	48.8	0.4	12.8	37.6
Greece	1 340	1 677	9.5	67.0	0.8	13.3	9.3
Spain	6 737	10 288	1.3	52.4	0.1	23.2	23.0
France	17 646	18 645	0.2	70.2	0.7	27.1	1.9
Italy	8 412	11 901	0.5	30.9	42.0	23.7	2.9
Cyprus	42	65	83.1	18.5	-	-	-
Latvia	1 530	1 794	-	86.7	-	13.1	0.3
Lithuania	542	813	-	94.2	0.2	4.4	1.1
Luxembourg	46	82	2.4	79.3	-	11.0	7.3
Hungary	513	1 404	0.2	91.7	6.1	1.3	0.6
Malta	:	:	:	:	:	:	:
Netherlands	1 547	2 496	0.9	86.9	-	0.4	11.9
Austria	5 985	7 839	1.4	56.5	0.4	39.5	2.2
Poland	3 873	5 018	0.0	94.9	0.2	4.0	0.9
Portugal	3 750	4 610	0.6	68.9	4.2	18.8	7.5
Romania	4 865	4 717	0.0	70.5	0.4	29.1	0.0
Slovenia	500	726	-	61.3	-	38.7	-
Slovakia	438	983	0.0	59.9	1.0	39.0	0.1
Finland	6 752	8 589	0.0	85.6	-	14.2	0.2
Sweden	13 774	15 639	0.1	62.8	-	36.4	0.8
United Kingdom	2 071	4 368	1.1	78.5	0.0	10.0	10.4
Croatia	854	737	0.1	49.7	0.4	49.4	0.4
Turkey	11 228	9 604	4.4	52.3	10.9	32.1	0.3
Iceland	1 682	:	-	:	:	:	:
Norway	10 670	12 876	0.0	10.0	-	89.4	0.6
Switzerland	3 947	5 040	0.6	36.0	3.2	60.1	0.0

Source: Eurostat (ten00081 and ten00082)

Table 11.13: Net imports of primary energy

	(1 000 tonnes of oil equivalent)					(tonnes of oil equivalent per inhabitant)				
	1999	2001	2003	2005	2007	1999	2001	2003	2005	2007
EU-27	790 677	858 357	905 367	986 618	988 354	1.64	1.77	1.86	2.01	2.00
Euro area	764 393	805 688	836 266	867 551	842 511	:	2.57	2.63	2.70	2.59
Belgium	49 161	51 272	53 244	53 775	51 452	4.81	5.00	5.14	5.15	4.86
Bulgaria	8 914	9 023	9 306	9 518	10 594	1.08	1.11	1.19	1.23	1.38
Czech Republic	9 880	10 721	11 397	12 887	11 592	0.96	1.04	1.12	1.26	1.13
Denmark	-3 434	-5 777	-6 850	-10 408	-5 486	-0.65	-1.08	-1.27	-1.92	-1.01
Germany	203 681	216 654	212 969	215 281	201 840	2.48	2.63	2.58	2.61	2.45
Estonia	1 887	1 785	1 580	1 671	1 877	1.37	1.31	1.17	1.24	1.40
Ireland	11 740	13 688	13 578	13 661	14 120	3.15	3.57	3.43	3.32	3.27
Greece	19 810	22 410	22 592	23 448	24 705	1.82	2.05	2.05	2.12	2.21
Spain	95 296	99 798	109 080	123 972	123 337	2.39	2.47	2.62	2.88	2.77
France	132 750	136 771	138 857	144 346	137 548	2.21	2.24	2.25	2.30	2.17
Italy	144 210	148 250	156 360	160 955	159 505	2.53	2.60	2.73	2.75	2.70
Cyprus	2 435	2 504	2 663	2 816	2 872	3.57	3.59	3.72	3.76	3.69
Latvia	2 194	2 534	2 796	2 995	3 039	0.91	1.07	1.20	1.30	1.33
Lithuania	4 354	3 923	4 105	5 119	5 778	1.23	1.13	1.19	1.49	1.71
Luxembourg	3 356	3 697	4 154	4 622	4 537	7.85	8.42	9.27	10.02	9.53
Hungary	13 942	13 895	16 346	17 514	16 589	1.36	1.36	1.61	1.73	1.65
Malta	984	1 626	1 818	1 600	1 786	2.60	4.15	4.58	3.97	4.38
Netherlands	26 929	32 644	36 691	38 390	38 784	1.71	2.04	2.27	2.35	2.37
Austria	19 175	19 979	23 098	24 661	23 347	2.40	2.49	2.85	3.01	2.81
Poland	9 558	9 408	11 933	16 600	25 064	0.25	0.25	0.31	0.43	0.66
Portugal	22 342	21 848	22 393	24 414	21 847	2.20	2.13	2.15	2.32	2.06
Romania	7 974	9 507	10 236	10 839	12 821	0.35	0.42	0.47	0.50	0.59
Slovenia	3 565	3 389	3 698	3 825	3 882	1.80	1.70	1.85	1.91	1.93
Slovakia	11 673	12 232	12 648	12 481	12 476	2.16	2.27	2.35	2.32	2.31
Finland	17 285	18 926	22 420	19 306	20 473	3.35	3.65	4.31	3.69	3.88
Sweden	18 234	19 293	22 835	20 179	18 976	2.06	2.17	2.55	2.24	2.08
United Kingdom	-47 220	-21 645	-14 583	32 152	44 999	-0.81	-0.37	-0.25	0.54	0.74
Croatia	4 361	4 174	4 996	5 252	5 336	0.96	0.94	1.12	1.18	1.20
Turkey	43 511	46 188	56 776	62 143	76 101	0.66	0.68	0.81	0.87	1.09
Iceland	972	947	937	1 063	:	3.53	3.34	3.25	3.62	:
Norway	-182 018	-203 323	-207 111	-200 643	-188 453	-40.95	-45.15	-45.50	-43.56	-40.26
Switzerland	14 082	15 262	14 739	16 244	14 120	1.98	2.12	2.02	2.19	1.88

Source: Eurostat (ten00083 and tps00001)

Table 11.14: Main origin of primary energy imports, EU-27
(% of extra EU-27 imports)

Hard coal								
	2000	2001	2002	2003	2004	2005	2006	2007
Russia	7.9	9.8	11.4	12.6	17.6	21.2	22.5	22.6
South Africa	21.3	23.2	26.8	27.1	23.6	22.7	21.5	18.6
Australia	15.1	13.9	14.6	14.8	13.4	11.9	11.0	11.7
Colombia	12.2	10.7	10.6	10.9	10.6	10.6	10.6	11.7
United States	10.8	9.5	7.0	6.0	6.7	6.9	7.0	8.4
Indonesia	4.8	4.8	5.7	6.2	6.1	6.5	8.5	7.1
Canada	3.4	3.3	2.7	1.8	1.9	2.9	2.5	2.9
Ukraine	1.1	1.4	1.7	1.1	1.9	1.8	1.3	1.5
Venezuela	1.8	1.4	1.7	2.3	1.0	0.9	0.8	1.0
Others	21.6	22.1	17.9	17.2	17.1	14.6	14.2	14.7
Crude oil								
	2000	2001	2002	2003	2004	2005	2006	2007
Russia	18.7	22.7	26.1	28.1	30.0	29.9	30.4	30.3
Norway	19.3	17.9	17.4	17.5	17.3	15.5	14.3	13.8
Libya	7.6	7.3	6.6	7.6	7.9	8.0	8.5	9.1
Saudi Arabia	10.8	9.5	9.0	10.1	10.2	9.7	8.2	6.4
Iran	5.9	5.2	4.4	5.7	5.7	5.6	5.8	5.6
Iraq	5.2	3.4	2.7	1.4	2.0	2.0	2.7	3.1
Kazakhstan	1.6	1.5	2.3	2.6	3.5	4.2	4.3	3.0
Nigeria	3.7	4.3	3.1	3.8	2.4	3.0	3.2	2.5
Algeria	3.6	3.2	3.0	3.1	3.4	3.6	2.7	2.2
Others	23.7	25.0	25.4	20.2	17.5	18.5	20.0	24.1
Natural gas								
	2000	2001	2002	2003	2004	2005	2006	2007
Russia	40.4	38.5	36.7	37.2	35.9	33.5	31.9	30.7
Norway	17.7	18.6	20.9	20.5	20.3	18.1	18.4	20.1
Algeria	19.6	17.0	17.2	16.4	14.8	15.3	13.8	12.8
Nigeria	1.5	1.9	1.8	2.6	3.0	3.0	3.6	3.9
Libya	0.3	0.3	0.2	0.2	0.3	1.4	2.1	2.5
Egypt	0.0	0.0	0.0	0.0	0.0	1.4	2.1	1.5
Qatar	0.1	0.2	0.7	0.6	1.2	1.3	1.5	1.8
Trinidad and Tobago	0.3	0.2	0.2	0.0	0.0	0.2	1.1	0.7
Croatia	0.0	0.0	0.0	0.0	0.0	0.0	0.3	0.2
Others	20.0	23.3	22.4	22.4	24.4	25.8	25.3	25.9

Source: Eurostat (nrg_122a, nrg_123a and nrg_124a)

11   Environment and energy

Table 11.15: Energy dependency rate, EU-27
(% of net imports in gross inland consumption and bunkers, based on tonnes of oil equivalent)

	1997	1998	1999	2000	2001	2002	2003	2004	2005	2006	2007
All products	45.0	46.1	45.1	46.8	47.5	47.6	49.0	50.3	52.6	53.8	53.1
Solid fuels	25.1	26.6	27.8	30.7	33.8	33.1	34.9	38.1	39.6	41.2	41.2
Crude oil	76.0	77.2	73.1	76.1	77.6	76.3	78.7	80.1	82.6	83.8	82.7
Natural gas	45.2	45.7	47.9	48.9	47.3	51.2	52.5	54.0	57.7	60.8	60.3

Source: Eurostat (nrg_100a, nrg_101a, nrg_102a and nrg_103a)

Figure 11.17: Energy dependency rate – all products, 2007
(% of net imports in gross inland consumption and bunkers, based on tonnes of oil equivalent)

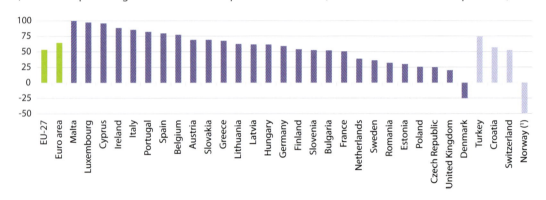

(¹) Y-axis is cut, -664.9.

Source: Eurostat (tsdcc310 and nrg_100a)

Europe in figures — Eurostat yearbook 2010 ■ **eurostat**

11.8 Consumption of energy

Introduction

As well as supply-side policies, there is a growing trend for policy initiatives to focus on improving energy efficiency in an attempt to reduce energy demand and decouple it from economic growth. This was given further impetus by the integrated energy and climate change strategy that committed the EU-27 to cut energy consumption by 20 % in relation to projected 2020 levels; by doing so, the EU hopes to cut greenhouse gas emissions by almost 800 million tonnes a year, while improving sustainability and security of supply.

To achieve these goals, the EU seeks to engage public opinion, decision-makers and market operators, while setting minimum energy efficiency standards and rules on labelling for products, services and infrastructure, in order to encourage significant reductions in consumption – for example, through the promotion of co-generation, improving the energy performance of buildings, or improving the information given to consumers with respect to the energy consumption of domestic appliances.

Daily life is becoming increasingly dependent on energy-consuming devices. Without compromising standards of living, there are a range of actions that could be employed to reduce energy consumption across many European households. Aside from making efficiency savings, these measures could also cut average fuel bills, for example, by: turning the thermostat down by one degree; using thermostatic radiator valves; not leaving tel-evisions, videos, music systems or DVD players on stand-by; defrosting fridges and freezers regularly; turning off lights when leaving rooms; using low-energy light bulbs; insulating hot-water tanks and heating pipes; or using loft insulation and cavity wall insulation.

The transport sector is the fastest growing consumer of energy and producer of greenhouse gases, even if advances in transport technology and fuel have resulted in marked decreases in emissions of certain pollutants. There are many factors that impact on energy use within the transport sector, for example, overall economic growth, the efficiency of individual transport modes, the take-up of alternative fuels, and lifestyle choices. The globalised nature of the economy has fuelled demand for international freight movements (principally by ship), while within the Single Market there has been a considerable expansion in the use of road freight transport (see Chapter 10 for more details concerning transport). This growth in the demand for energy from the transport sector is not confined to business, as it has been accompanied by an expansion in personal travel. The development of low-cost airlines, an increase in motorisation rates (the average number of motor vehicles per inhabitant), a trend for living in suburban areas, or the expansion of tourism (more frequent breaks, and more long-haul destinations) are among some of the factors that have contributed to an increase in the demand for energy as a result of personal travel.

In 2001, the European Commission adopted a policy to promote biofuels for transport, and a number of targets were set. The integrated energy and climate change strategy agreed at the end of 2008 foresees the share of renewables (such as biofuels) in total fuel consumption rising to at least 10 % by 2020.

Definitions and data availability

Gross inland energy consumption represents the quantity of energy necessary to satisfy inland consumption of the geographical entity under consideration. It may be defined as primary production plus imports, recovered products and stock changes, less exports and fuel supply to maritime bunkers (for seagoing ships of all flags). It describes the total energy needs of a country (or entity such as the EU), covering: consumption by the energy sector itself; distribution and transformation losses; final energy consumption by end users; and statistical differences.

Final energy consumption includes the consumption by all users except the energy branch itself (whether deliveries for transformation and/or own use), and includes, for example, energy consumption by agriculture, industry, services and households, as well as energy consumption for transport. It should be noted that the fuel quantities transformed in electrical power stations of industrial autoproducers and quantities of coke transformed into blast-furnace gas are not part of overall industrial consumption but of the transformation sector.

Energy intensity is measured as the ratio between gross inland consumption of energy and gross domestic product (GDP) for a given calendar year. It measures the energy consumption of an economy and its overall energy efficiency. The ratio is expressed as kgoe (kilogram of oil equivalent) per EUR 1 000, and to facilitate analysis over time the calculations are based on GDP in constant prices (currently using 1995 prices). If an economy becomes more efficient in its use of energy, and its GDP remains constant, then the ratio for this indicator should fall. The economic structure of an economy plays an important role in determining energy intensity, as post-industrial economies with large service sectors will, a priori, display relatively low intensity rates, while developing economies may have a considerable proportion of their economic activity within industrial sectors, thus leading to higher intensity.

Main findings

Gross inland energy consumption within the EU-27 in 2007 was 1 806 million tonnes of oil equivalent (toe), which marked a decline in consumption to a level not seen since 2003. The gross inland consumption of each Member State depends, to a large degree, on the structure of its energy system and the availability of natural resources for primary energy production; this is true not only for conventional fuels and nuclear power, but also for renewable energy sources. For example, although small in absolute levels, the use of solar power is relatively high in Mediterranean countries such as Cyprus, while the use of biomass is of increasing importance in some Member States with considerable forest areas, for example, Latvia, Finland and Sweden. In a similar vein, hydropower is particular-

ly important in mountainous countries with ample water supplies, such as Austria or Sweden.

Over the period 1997 to 2007 there was a gradual decline in the gross inland consumption of crude oil and petroleum products and solid fuels, while increasing amounts of natural gas and renewable energy sources were consumed. The combined share of crude oil, petroleum products and solid fuels fell from 58.8 % of total consumption to 54.1 %, reflecting changes in the EU-27's energy mix and a move away from the most polluting fossil fuels. Renewable energy sources accounted for 7.8 % of EU-27 gross inland consumption in 2007; however, their relative importance rose to almost one third of the total in Sweden and Latvia, and was close to one quarter of the total in Austria and Finland.

Final energy consumption in the EU-27, i.e., excluding energy used by power producers, was equivalent to just under two thirds (64.1 %) of gross inland consumption, at 1 158 million toe in 2007. An analysis of the final end-use of energy shows three dominant categories: as industry, road transport and households each accounted for around one quarter of the EU-27's final energy consumption in 2007; adding the figures for the different transport modes together, their total energy consumption amounted to 377.2 million toe in 2007, or approximately one third of the total.

There were, however, considerable differences in the evolution of energy consumption across transport modes in the EU-27, with the most rapid growth for aviation (42.3 % between 1997 and 2007) and a steady upward trend for road transport

(17.0 %), while the energy consumption of rail was relatively unchanged (-2.9 %). The largest increase, in absolute terms, was however recorded for road transport, where EU-27 energy consumption rose by 44.8 million toe between 1997 and 2007, compared with a 15.9 million toe increase for aviation. These changes in energy consumption reflect the popularity of each transport mode, but can also be influenced by technological changes, especially when these relate to fuel-efficiency gains.

In 2007, a minimum target was set for renewable energy sources (such as biofuels), requiring that they should account for at least 10 % of the petrol and diesel used within the road transport sector by 2020. Data for 2007 show that biofuels made the biggest contribution to fuel consumption in Germany (7.4 %) and Slovakia (4.9 %), while the EU-27 average was 2.5 %.

The lowest levels of energy intensity – a measure of an economy's energy efficiency – were recorded for Denmark and Ireland in 2007, while the most energy-intensive Member States were Bulgaria and Romania. It should be noted that the economic structure of an economy plays an important role in determining energy intensity, as post-industrial economies with large service sectors will, a priori, have considerably lower energy use than economies characterised by heavy, traditional industries, such as steel-making. Between 1997 and 2007, substantial energy savings were made in the Baltic economies of Estonia, Latvia and Lithuania, as the amount of energy required to produce a unit of economic output (as measured by GDP) was almost halved; the energy intensity of the Bulgarian and Romanian economies also fell at a rapid pace, by almost 40 %.

Table 11.16: Gross inland consumption of primary energy
(million tonnes of oil equivalent)

	1997	1998	1999	2000	2001	2002	2003	2004	2005	2006	2007	Share in EU-27, 2007 (%)
EU-27	1 704	1 723	1 711	1 724	1 763	1 758	1 803	1 824	1 826	1 826	1 806	100.0
Euro area	1 154	1 177	1 182	1 197	*1 227*	*1 228*	1 258	1 276	1 277	1 273	1 263	69.9
Belgium	59.0	60.1	61.1	61.5	60.3	58.4	61.6	61.5	61.1	60.4	57.4	3.2
Bulgaria	20.3	20.1	18.2	18.6	19.4	19.0	19.5	19.0	20.0	20.5	20.3	1.1
Czech Republic	42.8	41.2	38.5	40.5	41.5	42.0	45.6	45.9	45.3	46.4	46.2	2.6
Denmark	21.3	20.8	20.1	19.5	20.2	19.8	20.8	20.2	19.7	20.9	20.5	1.1
Germany	347.6	346.7	340.8	342.4	353.3	345.6	348.3	350.3	347.1	348.8	339.6	18.8
Estonia	5.7	5.4	5.0	5.0	5.1	5.0	5.5	5.7	5.6	5.4	6.0	0.3
Ireland	12.1	13.0	13.7	14.4	15.0	15.3	15.0	15.8	15.1	15.5	15.9	0.9
Greece	25.7	27.0	26.9	28.2	29.1	29.9	30.3	30.8	31.4	31.5	33.5	1.9
Spain	106.6	112.6	118.4	123.7	127.3	130.8	135.3	141.5	144.6	144.0	146.8	8.1
France	248.3	256.3	256.0	259.5	267.2	267.3	271.9	276.1	277.1	273.8	270.3	15.0
Italy	164.1	168.8	171.7	173.0	173.7	174.2	183.3	184.7	187.3	186.1	183.5	10.2
Cyprus	2.1	2.2	2.3	2.4	2.4	2.4	2.7	2.5	2.5	2.6	2.7	0.2
Latvia	4.4	4.3	4.0	3.7	4.1	4.0	4.3	4.4	4.5	4.6	4.8	0.3
Lithuania	8.9	9.3	7.9	7.1	8.1	8.6	9.0	9.1	8.6	8.4	9.2	0.5
Luxembourg	3.4	3.3	3.4	3.6	3.8	4.0	4.2	4.6	4.7	4.7	4.7	0.3
Hungary	25.8	25.6	25.5	25.0	25.5	25.9	27.1	26.6	28.0	27.8	27.0	1.5
Malta	0.9	0.8	0.9	0.8	0.9	0.8	0.9	0.9	0.9	0.9	0.9	0.1
Netherlands	76.3	76.2	75.7	77.0	*79.1*	*79.7*	81.9	83.8	82.5	80.5	84.5	4.7
Austria	28.8	29.2	29.3	29.1	30.8	31.5	33.2	33.5	34.3	34.8	33.8	1.9
Poland	102.5	96.2	93.8	90.8	90.8	89.4	91.8	92.2	93.6	98.1	98.0	5.4
Portugal	21.7	23.2	24.9	25.1	25.2	26.3	25.7	26.4	27.0	25.3	26.0	1.4
Romania	45.4	41.5	36.9	37.1	36.9	38.5	40.2	39.6	39.3	40.7	40.1	2.2
Slovenia	6.5	6.4	6.4	6.4	6.7	6.8	6.9	7.1	7.3	7.3	7.3	0.4
Slovakia	17.8	17.5	17.4	17.5	19.3	19.3	19.2	19.1	19.1	18.8	18.1	1.0
Finland	32.9	33.4	32.9	32.5	33.2	35.2	37.2	37.5	34.7	37.8	37.6	2.1
Sweden	50.3	50.8	50.4	47.9	51.4	51.1	50.5	52.6	51.7	50.3	50.6	2.8
United Kingdom	223.1	230.7	229.2	231.9	232.7	226.8	231.2	232.5	232.8	229.1	221.1	12.2
Croatia	7.8	8.0	8.0	7.8	8.0	8.3	8.8	8.9	8.9	9.0	9.4	-
Turkey	71.2	72.5	71.2	77.6	71.6	75.5	79.4	82.0	85.3	94.7	101.5	-
Iceland	2.5	2.7	3.1	3.2	3.4	3.4	3.4	3.5	3.6	*4.3*	:	-
Norway	24.5	25.6	26.8	26.1	27.0	24.3	27.3	28.3	32.3	25.0	27.7	-
Switzerland	25.8	26.1	26.1	25.9	27.4	26.5	26.6	26.9	26.9	28.1	26.9	-

Source: Eurostat (ten00086)

Figure 11.18: Gross inland consumption, EU-27
(% of total consumption)

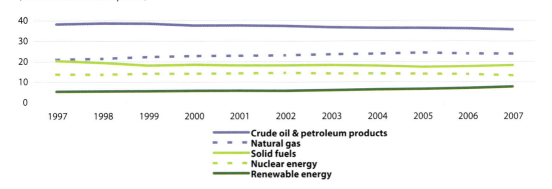

Source: Eurostat (nrg_102a, nrg_103a, nrg_101a, nrg_104a and nrg_1071a)

Figure 11.19: Share of renewables in gross inland energy consumption, 2007 (¹)
(%)

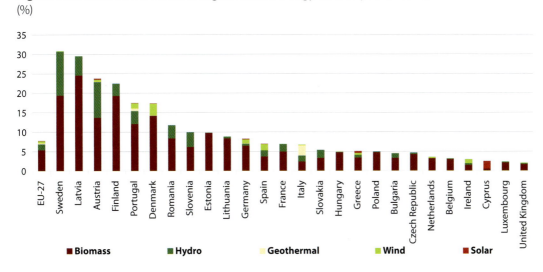

(¹) Malta, not available.

Source: Eurostat (tsdcc110)

Table 11.17: Final energy consumption
(million tonnes of oil equivalent)

	1997	1998	1999	2000	2001	2002	2003	2004	2005	2006	2007	Share in EU-27, 2007 (%)
EU-27	1 104	1 111	1 109	1 114	1 140	1 127	1 160	1 173	1 172	1 176	1 158	100.0
Euro area	752	767	770	778	801	793	817	825	823	825	810	70.0
Belgium	38.4	39.0	39.0	39.1	39.4	37.7	40.0	39.4	38.4	38.2	34.9	3.0
Bulgaria	9.3	9.9	8.8	8.6	8.6	8.7	9.4	9.2	9.6	10.0	9.8	0.8
Czech Republic	25.5	24.5	23.8	23.9	24.0	23.6	25.6	26.1	25.9	26.3	25.8	2.2
Denmark	15.0	15.0	15.0	14.6	15.0	14.7	15.1	15.3	15.4	15.6	15.7	1.4
Germany	225.3	223.5	218.7	218.1	223.9	219.2	222.3	220.7	217.3	221.6	210.3	18.2
Estonia	2.9	2.6	2.4	2.4	2.5	2.5	2.6	2.7	2.8	2.8	3.0	0.3
Ireland	8.6	9.3	9.9	10.7	11.1	11.2	11.5	11.8	12.5	13.1	13.2	1.1
Greece	17.3	18.2	18.2	18.6	19.2	19.5	20.5	20.3	20.8	21.5	22.0	1.9
Spain	68.2	71.9	74.5	79.6	83.5	85.6	90.7	94.5	97.5	96.2	98.7	8.5
France	147.6	152.7	152.5	152.5	158.3	153.8	157.7	159.7	159.2	157.7	154.0	13.3
Italy	115.7	118.9	123.5	123.5	126.2	124.7	130.3	131.2	132.6	130.7	132.1	11.4
Cyprus	1.5	1.5	1.6	1.6	1.7	1.7	1.8	1.8	1.8	1.8	1.9	0.2
Latvia	3.7	3.6	3.4	3.2	3.6	3.6	3.8	3.9	4.0	4.2	4.4	0.4
Lithuania	4.5	4.5	4.0	3.7	3.9	4.0	4.1	4.3	4.5	4.7	5.0	0.4
Luxembourg	3.2	3.2	3.4	3.6	3.7	3.7	4.0	4.4	4.4	4.4	4.4	0.4
Hungary	15.6	15.7	15.9	15.7	16.5	17.0	17.6	17.5	18.1	18.0	16.9	1.5
Malta	0.6	0.4	0.4	0.4	0.4	0.4	0.5	0.5	0.5	0.4	0.4	0.0
Netherlands	49.5	49.7	48.9	50.2	50.9	50.7	51.6	52.5	51.6	50.8	51.3	4.4
Austria	22.3	22.9	22.9	23.2	24.5	25.2	26.5	26.6	27.3	27.4	26.5	2.3
Poland	65.5	60.0	58.8	55.4	56.0	54.3	56.2	57.6	57.9	60.9	61.2	5.3
Portugal	15.3	16.2	16.7	17.7	18.1	18.4	18.4	20.2	18.7	18.5	18.8	1.6
Romania	28.7	26.2	22.4	22.5	23.0	23.1	24.2	25.5	24.7	24.8	24.0	2.1
Slovenia	4.5	4.3	4.4	4.4	4.6	4.6	4.7	4.8	4.9	4.9	4.9	0.4
Slovakia	10.7	10.5	10.3	10.3	10.9	11.1	10.7	10.8	10.6	10.7	10.5	0.9
Finland	23.5	24.3	24.7	24.2	24.1	25.1	25.6	26.1	25.2	26.8	26.6	2.3
Sweden	34.0	34.3	33.6	34.5	33.4	33.5	33.6	33.6	33.7	33.2	33.5	2.9
United Kingdom	147.5	148.5	151.5	152.2	153.3	149.0	150.8	151.9	152.3	150.4	147.9	12.8
Croatia	5.1	5.2	5.4	5.3	5.5	5.6	6.0	6.1	6.3	6.4	6.5	-
Turkey	50.3	49.9	49.2	55.5	50.2	54.7	58.7	60.4	63.2	69.0	72.8	-
Iceland	1.8	1.9	2.0	2.1	2.1	2.2	2.2	2.2	2.2	2.4	:	-
Norway	17.5	18.2	18.7	18.1	18.6	18.3	18.0	18.4	18.5	18.4	18.8	-
Switzerland	19.6	20.3	20.6	20.4	20.9	20.3	20.9	21.3	21.7	21.7	21.1	-

Source: Eurostat (ten00095)

Figure 11.20: Final energy consumption, EU-27, 2007 ([1])
(% of total, based on tonnes of oil equivalent)

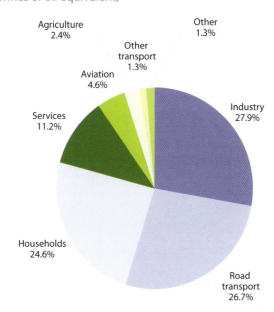

([1]) Provisional.

Source: Eurostat (tsdpc320 and tsdtr100)

Figure 11.21: Energy consumption by transport mode, EU-27 ([1])
(1997=100)

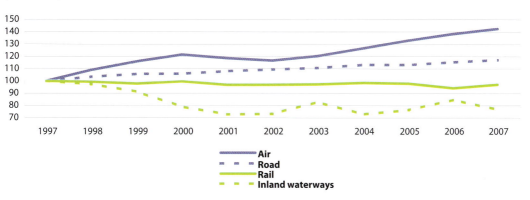

([1]) Provisional for all transport modes, 2002; provisional for road transport, 2006 and 2007.

Source: Eurostat (tsdtr100)

Figure 11.22: Share of biofuels in total fuel consumption of transport, 2007 (¹)
(%)

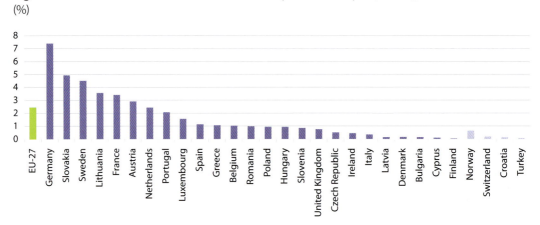

(¹) Estonia and Malta, not available.

Source: Eurostat (nrg_1073a and nrg_100a)

Figure 11.23: Energy intensity of the economy
(kg of oil equivalent per EUR 1 000 of GDP)

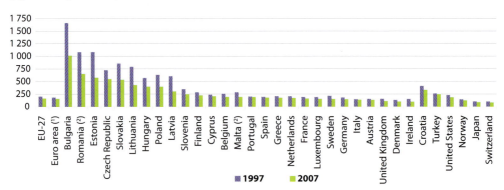

(¹) EA-15 instead of EA-16.
(²) Provisional, 1997.

Source: Eurostat (tsien020)

11.9 Electricity

Introduction

One of the reasons for the EU's increased dependency on imports of natural gas is a shift in the fuel mix towards this energy source for the purpose of electricity generation. Natural gas offers power generators the possibility to lower their greenhouse gas emissions (when contrasted with electricity generated from coal, lignite or oil). There has also been an increase in the use of renewable energy sources for electricity generation, particularly wind turbines (although their contribution remains relatively small). The use of nuclear power for electricity generation has also received renewed attention amid concerns about an increasing dependency on imported primary energy, rising oil and gas prices, and commitments to reduce greenhouse gas emissions; some Member States have recently started construction or have planned new nuclear reactors. These concerns are balanced against long-standing reservations concerning the safety of nuclear power plants and how to dispose of nuclear waste.

Since July 2004, small business consumers in the EU have been free to switch their gas or electricity supplier, and in July 2007 this right was extended to all consumers. Independent national regulatory authorities have been established across the Member Sates to ensure that suppliers and network companies operate correctly. However, a number of shortcomings were identified in the opening-up of markets, and it was therefore decided to embark upon a third legislative package of measures with the aim of ensuring that all users could take advantage of the benefits provided by a truly competitive energy market. A raft of legislation will come into effect as of March 2011, including:

- Regulation (EC) No 713/2009 of the European Parliament and of the Council of 13 July 2009 establishing an agency for the cooperation of energy regulators ([35]);
- Regulation (EC) No 714/2009 of the European Parliament and of the Council of 13 July 2009 on conditions for access to the network for cross-border exchanges in electricity and repealing Regulation (EC) No 1228/2003 ([36]);
- Directive 2009/72/EC of the European Parliament and of the Council of 13 July 2009 concerning common rules for the internal market in electricity and repealing Directive 2003/54/EC ([37]).

By opening-up European energy markets to competition, it is hoped that both households and industrial users will benefit from more choice, fairer prices, cleaner energy production, better services and improved security of supply. These issues are at the heart of the third legislative package, which proposes:

- to separate production and supply from transmission networks;
- to facilitate cross-border trade in energy;
- more effective national regulators;
- to promote cross-border collaboration and investment;
- greater market transparency on network operation and supply;
- increased solidarity among the EU Member States.

([35]) For more information: http://eur-lex.europa.eu/LexUriServ/LexUriServ.do?uri=OJ:L:2009:211:0001:0014:EN:PDF.

([36]) For more information: http://eur-lex.europa.eu/LexUriServ/LexUriServ.do?uri=OJ:L:2009:211:0015:0035:EN:PDF.

([37]) For more information: http://eur-lex.europa.eu/LexUriServ/LexUriServ.do?uri=OJ:L:2009:211:0055:0093:EN:PDF.

Definitions and data availability

Gross electricity generation at the plant level is defined as the electricity measured at the outlet of the main transformers. In other words, it includes the consumption of electricity in plant auxiliaries and in other transformers. **Gross national electricity consumption** comprises total gross national electricity generation from all fuels (including auto-production), plus electricity imports, minus exports. **Final consumption of electricity** covers the electricity delivered to the consumer's door (industry, transport, households and other sectors). It excludes deliveries for transformation and/or own use of energy producing activities, as well as network losses.

Electricity generated from renewable energy sources is the ratio of electricity produced from renewable energy sources compared with gross national electricity consumption. Electricity produced from renewable energy sources comprises that generated from hydropower plants (excluding pumping), wind, solar, geothermal installations, and biomass/wastes.

The indicator for the **market share of the largest generator in the electricity market** is based on net electricity production, and as such the electricity used by generators for their own consumption is not taken into account.

Main findings

Total gross electricity generation in the EU-27 was 3.4 million Gigawatt hours (GWh) in 2007, of which 29.5 % came from nuclear power plants. Natural gas-fired power stations accounted for around one fifth (20.1 %) of the total; while coal-fired, lignite-fired and oil-fired power stations accounted for 18.3 %, 10.3 % and 3.9 % respectively. Among renewable energy sources, the highest share of total electricity generation in 2007 was from hydropower, providing 10.2 %, followed by biomass-fired power stations and wind turbines, which generated 2.7 % and 2.4 % of the total respectively.

Germany and France were the principal electricity generators in the EU-27 in 2007, with shares of 19.0 % and 17.0 % respectively, while the United Kingdom was the only other Member State to report a share in double-digits (11.8 %). The relative weight of Spain in EU-27 electricity generation rose quickly between 1997 and 2007, gaining 2.3 percentage points to reach 9.0%.

Electricity generation in the EU-27 grew, on average, by 1.7 % per annum between 1997 and 2007. Some of the highest growth rates were recorded within the Czech Republic, Ireland, Greece, Malta and Portugal – all of which reported average increases of between 3 and 4 % per annum over the period under consideration. However, the most rapid growth in electricity generation was in Spain, Cyprus and, in particular, Luxembourg, where annual rates of change averaged 4.8 %, 6.0 % and 12.2 % respectively; the high rate for Luxembourg was largely due to a significant increase in generating output in 2002 as new gas-fired capacity was introduced. Lithuania and Denmark were the only Member States to generate less electricity in 2007 than in 1997.

Renewable energy sources can potentially play an important role in reducing greenhouse gas emissions. The European

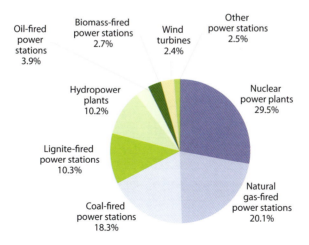

Parliament and Council set indicative targets in 2001 for the promotion of electricity from renewable energy sources: according to these, 21 % of the EU-27's gross electricity consumption should be sourced from renewables by 2010. The latest information available for 2007 shows that electricity generated from renewable energy sources contributed 15.6 % of the EU-27's gross electricity consumption. In Austria (59.8 %), Sweden (52.1 %) and Latvia (36.4 %) the share of renewable energy sources in gross electricity consumption was particularly high, largely as a result of hydropower and biomass, while in Denmark just over a quarter (26.9 %) of the electricity consumed came from renewables, largely from wind power and to a lesser extent biomass.

The growth in electricity generated from renewable energy sources during the period 1997 to 2007 reflects an expansion in two renewable sources; namely, wind turbines and biomass. Although hydro-

power remained the single largest source for renewable electricity generation in the EU-27 in 2007, the amount of electricity generated was almost the same as a decade earlier (-2.9 %). In contrast, the volume of electricity generated from biomass increased by 249 %, while that from wind turbines rose by 1 322 %.

One measure that is used to monitor the success of electricity market liberalisation is the market share of the largest generator. The small island nations of Cyprus and Malta were both characterised by a complete monopoly in 2007, with 100 % of their electricity being generated by the largest (sole) generator. Two other Member States – Estonia and Greece – reported shares for the largest generator of more than 90 %. In 11 of the 24 Member States for which data are available, the largest generator provided less than 50 % of the total electricity generated, with the share below 20 % in the United Kingdom and Poland.

Figure 11.24: Electricity generation by fuel used in power stations, EU-27, 2007 (% of total, based on GWh)

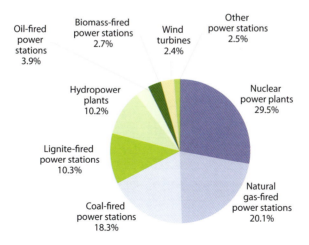

Source: Eurostat (nrg_105a)

Table 11.18: Gross electricity generation
(1 000 GWh)

	1997	1998	1999	2000	2001	2002	2003	2004	2005	2006	2007	Share in EU-27, 2007 (%)
EU-27	2 841	2 910	2 940	3 021	3 108	3 117	3 216	3 288	3 309	3 354	3 362	100.0
Euro area	1 930	1 976	2 018	2 091	2 142	2 159	2 234	2 297	2 307	2 350	2 354	70.0
Belgium	78.9	83.2	84.5	83.9	79.7	82.1	84.6	85.4	87.0	85.5	88.8	2.6
Bulgaria	42.8	41.7	38.2	40.9	44.0	42.7	42.6	41.6	44.4	45.8	43.3	1.3
Czech Republic	64.6	65.1	64.7	73.5	74.6	76.3	83.2	84.3	82.6	84.4	88.2	2.6
Denmark	44.3	41.1	38.9	36.0	37.7	39.3	46.2	40.4	36.2	45.6	39.2	1.2
Germany	551.6	556.7	555.5	571.6	586.3	571.6	599.5	616.8	620.3	636.6	637.1	19.0
Estonia	9.2	8.5	8.3	8.5	8.5	8.5	10.2	10.3	10.2	9.7	12.2	0.4
Ireland	20.0	21.2	22.0	24.0	25.0	25.2	25.2	25.6	25.4	27.5	28.2	0.8
Greece	43.5	46.3	49.9	53.8	53.7	54.6	58.5	59.3	60.0	60.8	63.5	1.9
Spain	190.3	195.2	209.0	225.2	238.0	246.1	262.9	280.0	294.0	299.5	303.3	9.0
France	504.5	511.0	524.0	540.7	549.8	559.2	566.9	574.3	576.2	574.6	569.8	17.0
Italy	251.4	259.8	265.6	276.6	279.0	284.4	293.9	303.3	303.7	314.1	313.9	9.3
Cyprus	2.7	3.0	3.1	3.4	3.6	3.8	4.1	4.2	4.4	4.7	4.9	0.1
Latvia	4.5	5.8	4.1	4.1	4.3	4.0	4.0	4.7	4.9	4.9	4.8	0.1
Lithuania	14.9	17.6	13.5	11.4	14.7	17.7	19.5	19.3	14.8	12.5	14.0	0.4
Luxembourg	1.3	1.3	1.0	1.2	1.2	3.7	3.6	4.1	4.1	4.3	4.0	0.1
Hungary	35.4	37.2	37.7	35.2	36.4	36.2	34.1	33.7	35.8	35.9	40.0	1.2
Malta	1.7	1.7	1.8	1.9	2.0	2.1	2.2	2.2	2.2	2.3	2.3	0.1
Netherlands	86.7	91.1	86.7	89.6	93.7	96.0	96.8	100.8	100.2	98.4	103.2	3.1
Austria	56.9	57.5	60.9	61.5	62.4	62.4	60.1	64.1	65.7	63.5	63.4	1.9
Poland	142.8	142.8	142.1	145.2	145.6	144.1	151.6	154.2	156.9	161.7	159.3	4.7
Portugal	34.2	39.0	43.3	43.8	46.5	46.1	46.9	45.1	46.6	49.0	47.3	1.4
Romania	57.1	53.5	50.7	51.9	53.9	54.9	56.6	56.5	59.4	62.7	61.7	1.8
Slovenia	13.2	13.7	13.3	13.6	14.5	14.6	13.8	15.3	15.1	15.1	15.0	0.4
Slovakia	24.5	25.5	27.7	30.7	32.0	32.4	31.2	30.6	31.5	31.4	28.1	0.8
Finland	69.2	70.2	69.4	70.0	74.5	74.9	84.2	85.8	70.6	82.3	81.2	2.4
Sweden	149.4	158.3	155.2	145.6	161.6	146.7	135.4	151.7	158.4	143.3	148.8	4.4
United Kingdom	345.4	362.0	368.4	377.1	384.8	387.2	398.2	393.9	398.4	397.9	396.1	11.8
Croatia	9.7	10.9	12.2	10.7	12.2	12.3	12.7	13.3	12.5	12.4	12.2	-
Turkey	103.3	111.0	116.4	124.9	122.7	129.4	140.6	150.7	162.0	176.3	191.6	-
Iceland	5.6	6.3	7.2	7.7	8.0	8.4	8.5	8.6	8.7	9.9	:	-
Norway	111.7	117.0	122.7	143.0	121.9	130.7	107.4	110.7	138.1	121.6	137.5	-
Switzerland	63.1	63.5	69.7	67.5	72.4	67.2	67.4	65.6	59.6	64.0	68.0	-

Source: Eurostat (ten00087)

Figure 11.25: Proportion of electricity generated from renewable energy sources (% of gross electricity consumption)

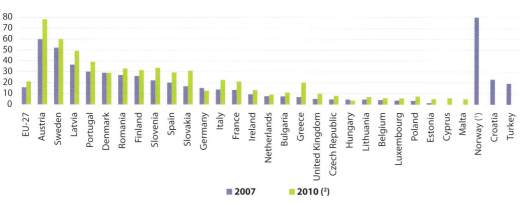

■ **2007**   ■ **2010** (²)

(¹) Y-axis is cut, 106.1.
(²) Indicative targets for 2010 are not available for Croatia, Turkey and Norway.

Source: Eurostat (tsien050)

Figure 11.26: Electricity generated from renewable energy sources, EU-27

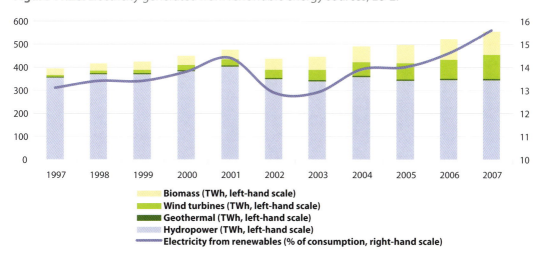

■ **Biomass (TWh, left-hand scale)**
■ **Wind turbines (TWh, left-hand scale)**
■ **Geothermal (TWh, left-hand scale)**
■ **Hydropower (TWh, left-hand scale)**
— **Electricity from renewables (% of consumption, right-hand scale)**

Source: Eurostat (nrg_105a and tsdcc330)

Figure 11.27: Market share of the largest generator in the electricity market, 2007 (¹)
(% of total generation)

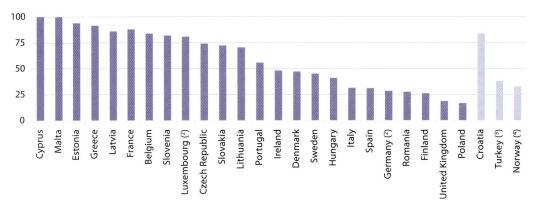

(¹) Bulgaria, the Netherlands and Austria, not available.
(²) 2004.
(³) 2005.
(⁴) 2006.

Source: Eurostat (tsier060)

Figure 11.28: Electricity consumption by households, 2007
(1997=100)

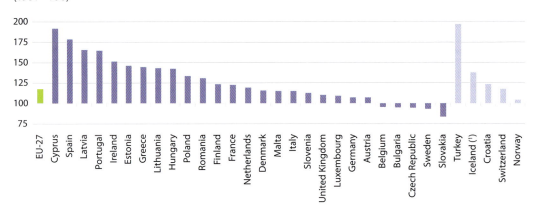

(¹) 2006.

Source: Eurostat (tsdpc310)

11.10 Energy prices

Introduction

Increasing energy demand, the global geopolitical situation, and severe weather conditions may all play a part in shaping energy prices. With rapid growth in demand for fossil fuels from the fast-growing developing economies of Brazil, Russia, India, and China (BRICs), imbalances arose between supply and demand, leading to crude oil prices rising significantly from 2004 to the middle of 2008. The price of crude oil later subsided somewhat, in part due to weaker demand as a result of the economic downturn, although there were signs of a rally in oil prices in the second half of 2009. Changes in oil prices have an impact on the price of energy substitutes, notably natural gas, and also feed into prices for other sectors that are heavy users of energy or use energy products as raw materials.

The price and reliability of energy supplies, electricity in particular, are key elements in a country's energy supply strategy. The price of electricity is important for a country's international competitiveness, as electricity usually represents a high proportion of total energy costs to businesses and households. In contrast to the price of fossil fuels, which are usually traded on global markets with relatively uniform prices, there is a particularly wide range of prices within the EU for electricity. The price of electricity is, to some degree, influenced by the price of primary fuels and more recently also by the cost of carbon dioxide emission certificates, and it is possible that resulting higher prices for electricity will provide

an incentive for greater energy efficiency and lower levels of carbon emissions.

These issues were touched upon in a Communication from the European Commission titled, 'facing the challenge of higher oil prices' ([38]), which called on the EU to become more efficient in its use of energy, and less dependent on fossil fuels – in particular by following the approach laid out in the climate change and renewable energy package.

The EU has acted to liberalise electricity and gas market since the second half of the 1990s. Directives adopted in 2003 established common rules for internal markets for electricity and natural gas. Deadlines were set for opening markets and allowing customers to choose their supplier: 1 July 2004 for all business customers and 1 July 2007 for all consumers (including households). Certain countries anticipated the liberalisation process, while others were much slower in adopting the necessary measures. Indeed, significant barriers to entry remain in many electricity and natural gas markets as seen through the number of markets that are still dominated by (near) monopoly suppliers. In July 2009, the European Parliament and Council adopted a third package of legislative proposals ([39]) aimed at ensuring a real and effective choice of suppliers, as well as benefits for customers.

Definitions and data availability

The transparency of gas and electricity prices should help promote fair competition, by encouraging consumers to choose between different energy sources (oil,

([38]) COM(2008) 384 final of 13 June 2008; for more information:
http://eur-lex.europa.eu/LexUriServ/LexUriServ.do?uri=COM:2008:0384:FIN:EN:PDF.

([39]) For more information: http://ec.europa.eu/energy/gas_electricity/third_legislative_package_en.htm.

coal, natural gas and renewable energy sources) and between different suppliers. For energy price transparency to be truly effective, prices and pricing systems must be published and broadcast as widely as possible.

The transparency of energy prices is guaranteed within the EU through the obligation of gas and electricity suppliers to send Eurostat information relating to prices for different categories of end-consumer (businesses and households), market shares, conditions of sale, and pricing systems. Electricity and gas tariffs or price schemes vary from one supplier to another. They may result from negotiated contracts, especially for large industrial consumers. For smaller consumers, they are generally set according to the amount of electricity or gas consumed along with a number of other characteristics; most tariffs also include some form of fixed charge. There is, therefore, no single price for electricity or gas. In order to compare prices over time and between countries, this publication shows information for two 'standard consumers' – one for domestic consumers and the other for industrial users. There are in total five different types of households for which electricity prices are collected following different annual consumption bands, while for natural gas prices statistics are collated for three different types of household. Across business/industrial users, electricity prices are collected for a total of seven different types of user, while for natural gas prices there are six different types of user distinguished.

Statistics on **electricity and natural gas prices** charged to industrial end-users are collected under the legal basis of

Commission Decision 2007/394/EC of 7 June 2007 amending Council Directive 90/377/EEC with regard to the methodology to be applied for the collection of gas and electricity prices. Directive 2008/92/EC of the European Parliament and of the Council of 22 October 2008 concerns procedures to improve the transparency of gas and electricity prices charged to industrial end-users. Note that gas and electricity prices for household end-users are collected on a voluntary basis.

The prices presented cover average prices over a period of six months (half-year/semester) from January to June and from July to December. The prices include the basic price of electricity/gas, transmission, system services, distribution and other services. Electricity prices for households are normally shown including taxes and value added tax (VAT) as this generally reflects the end price paid by consumers at home. All electricity price data are given in euro per kilowatt hour (kWh); a similar set of criteria are used for gas prices, except the unit changes to euro per gigajoule (GJ). For the purpose of comparison, industrial gas and electricity prices are also shown including taxes, although in practice enterprises can deduct the VAT paid.

Automotive fuel prices shown are at the pump prices of premium unleaded gasoline (petrol) 95 RON and automotive diesel oil. The prices are supplied to the Directorate-General for Energy and Transport of the European Commission by the Member States as being the most frequently encountered on the 15th of each month; as with gas and electricity prices these are averaged for a period of six months (half-year/semester); equally, the prices that are shown are inclusive of all taxes. Eurostat also publishes price information on heating oil and residual fuel oil.

Main findings

Due to a change in methodology, there is a break in series and hence a relatively short-time series available in relation to electricity and gas prices (from 2007 onwards). Nevertheless, even in this relatively short timeframe, electricity and gas prices have increased rapidly – in particular, gas prices. Between the second half of 2007 and the second half of 2008, both electricity and gas prices increased for households and industrial users in nearly all of the Member States. On average across the EU-27 the price of electricity for households rose by 9.6 %, while gas prices increased by 21.1 %. The price increases experienced by industrial users in the EU-27 over the same period were even higher – 13.8 % for electricity and 28.9 % for gas. There were a few notable exceptions to these trends, as the price of electricity for households fell in Poland (-6.2 %), Romania (-3.3 %), Luxembourg and Portugal (both -2.2 %), while gas prices fell in Denmark (-28.0 %), Portugal (-3.6 %) and Romania (-1.9 %).

In the second half of 2008, the price of electricity for households was nearly three and a half times higher in the most expensive Member State, Denmark (EUR 0.28 per kWh), than in the cheapest Member State, Bulgaria (EUR 0.08 per kWh). The range of prices for gas was similar in magnitude, as the highest prices for households were registered in Sweden (EUR 28.82 per GJ), at more than three times the lowest price recorded in Romania (EUR 9.33 per GJ). Household gas prices were also significantly higher in Denmark (EUR 26.57 per GJ) than in any of the other Member State (except Sweden), despite considerable price reductions. A large part of the energy price differences between the Member States may be attributed to taxes, as the range in prices between countries is narrower when taxes are excluded.

As with electricity and gas prices, petrol and diesel prices have also risen in recent years. The highest prices for unleaded petrol in the EU-27 during the first half of 2008 were found in the Netherlands, Belgium, Portugal and the United Kingdom, while the United Kingdom had, by some margin (EUR 0.20 per litre), the most expensive pump price for automotive diesel oil. While petrol and diesel prices rose considerably between the second half of 2004 and the first half of 2008, reflecting the evolution of crude oil markets, the range between the highest and lowest pump prices in the Member States narrowed (as variable taxes accounted for a lower share of the overall price). The lowest prices for petrol and diesel were recorded in the Baltic Member States, the islands of Cyprus and Malta, and in Slovenia, while diesel oil was also relatively cheap in Luxembourg and Spain.

Table 11.19: Half-yearly electricity and gas prices – including taxes
(EUR)

| | Electricity prices (per kWh) | | | | | | Gas prices (per GJ) | | | | | |
| | Households ([1]) | | | Industry ([2]) | | | Households ([3]) | | | Industry ([4]) | | |
	II-2007	I-2008	II-2008	II-2007	I-2008	II-2008	II-2007	I-2008	II-2008	II-2007	I-2008	II-2008
EU-27	0.15	0.16	0.17	0.11	0.12	0.12	14.44	15.12	17.48	9.94	11.07	12.82
Euro area ([5])	0.16	0.17	0.17	0.11	0.12	0.13	16.55	17.07	19.69	10.35	11.59	13.34
Belgium	0.17	0.20	0.21	0.11	0.13	:	13.89	16.26	20.24	9.46	11.06	12.67
Bulgaria	0.07	0.07	0.08	0.07	0.07	0.08	8.98	9.85	10.86	6.02	6.86	8.91
Czech Republic	0.11	0.13	0.13	0.11	0.13	0.13	10.06	12.20	14.69	8.11	10.56	13.03
Denmark	0.24	0.26	0.28	0.21	0.21	0.22	*36.89*	:	26.57	*9.18*	:	21.13
Germany	0.21	0.21	0.22	0.14	0.14	0.14	17.04	17.81	21.17	12.84	14.76	16.43
Estonia	0.08	0.08	0.09	0.06	0.07	0.07	7.30	9.30	10.30	5.94	8.23	10.34
Ireland	0.19	0.18	0.20	0.14	0.15	0.16	16.85	15.09	18.05	10.86	12.48	12.20
Greece	0.10	0.10	0.11	0.09	0.09	0.10	:	:	:	:	:	:
Spain	0.14	0.14	0.16	0.11	0.11	0.12	16.15	15.98	18.14	8.21	8.86	10.48
France	0.12	0.12	0.12	0.07	0.08	0.07	14.30	14.46	16.06	10.05	10.92	12.84
Italy	:	*0.21*	*0.22*	:	*0.16*	*0.17*	17.15	17.47	19.99	9.19	10.27	12.45
Cyprus	0.16	0.18	0.20	0.16	0.16	0.21	:	:	:	:	:	:
Latvia	0.07	0.08	0.10	0.07	0.08	0.09	8.65	8.70	13.88	9.10	9.33	12.99
Lithuania	0.09	0.09	0.09	0.09	0.10	0.10	6.52	9.15	10.63	7.98	10.37	14.33
Luxembourg	0.16	0.16	0.16	0.11	0.11	0.11	10.95	16.75	:	9.96	11.97	:
Hungary	0.13	0.15	0.16	0.14	0.14	0.15	10.62	11.24	12.93	10.29	11.62	14.06
Malta	0.10	0.10	0.15	0.13	0.13	0.17	:	:	:	:	:	:
Netherlands	0.17	0.17	0.18	0.12	0.12	0.12	19.14	19.37	21.03	10.83	11.44	12.66
Austria	0.17	0.18	0.18	0.11	0.13	0.13	16.95	16.88	17.72	:	:	:
Poland	0.14	0.13	0.13	0.11	0.11	0.11	11.15	11.56	14.30	8.80	10.20	11.39
Portugal	0.16	0.15	0.15	0.09	0.09	0.09	18.13	17.37	17.48	8.61	9.13	9.67
Romania	0.11	0.11	0.11	0.11	0.11	0.11	9.51	9.21	9.33	9.39	9.27	9.24
Slovenia	0.11	0.11	0.12	0.11	0.11	0.12	14.14	15.51	19.77	10.61	12.14	15.19
Slovakia	0.14	0.14	0.15	0.13	0.14	0.15	11.57	11.42	12.92	9.50	10.61	15.62
Finland	0.11	0.12	0.13	0.07	0.08	0.08	:	:	:	8.30	9.70	11.40
Sweden	0.16	0.17	0.17	0.07	0.07	0.08	25.56	26.53	28.82	20.94	17.95	18.37
United Kingdom	0.15	0.15	0.16	0.13	0.11	0.13	9.91	10.99	13.29	8.42	9.07	10.21
Croatia	0.10	0.10	0.12	0.09	0.09	0.11	7.60	7.59	7.70	7.77	7.72	7.82
Norway	0.15	0.16	0.17	0.09	0.10	0.11	:	:	:	:	:	:

([1]) Annual consumption: 2 500 kWh < consumption < 5 000 kWh.
([2]) Annual consumption: 500 MWh < consumption < 2 000 MWh.
([3]) Annual consumption: 20 GJ < consumption < 200 GJ.
([4]) Annual consumption: 10 000 GJ < consumption < 100 000 GJ.
([5]) EA-15 instead of EA-16.

Source: Eurostat (nrg_pc_204, nrg_pc_205, nrg_pc_202 and nrg_pc_203)

Figure 11.29: Half-yearly prices, premium unleaded gasoline (Euro-super 95) – including taxes (¹)
(EUR per litre)

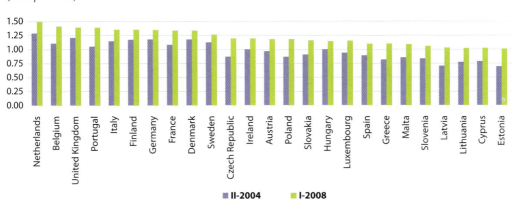

(¹) Bulgaria and Romania, not available.

Source: Eurostat (nrg_pc_201)

Figure 11.30: Half-yearly prices, automotive diesel oil - including taxes (¹)
(EUR per litre)

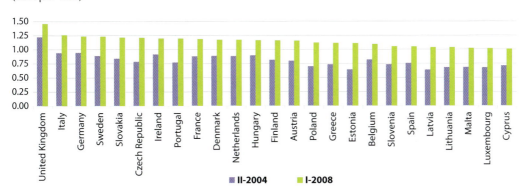

(¹) Bulgaria and Romania, not available.

Source: Eurostat (nrg_pc_201)

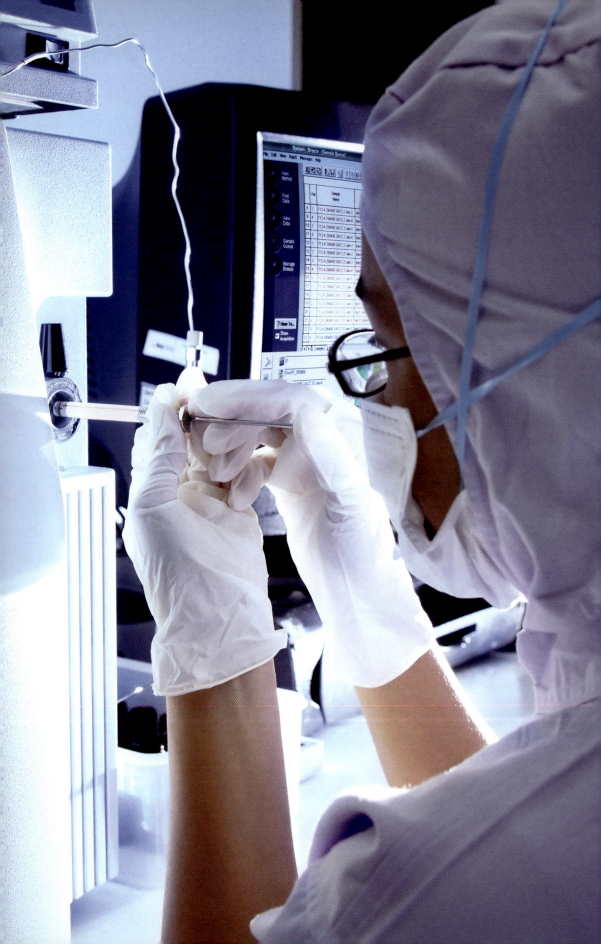

Science and technology

<p>12</p>

Research and development (R & D) is often considered as a driving force behind growth and job creation. However, its influence extends well beyond the economic sphere, as it can potentially, among others, resolve environmental concerns, ensure safer food, or lead to the development of new medicines to fight illness and disease.

The seventh framework programme for research and technological development (FP7) is the EU's main instrument for funding research in Europe ([1]); it runs from 2007-2013 and has a total budget of EUR 53 200 million. This money is generally intended to finance grants to research actors all over Europe, usually through co-financing research, technological development and demonstration projects. Grants are determined on the basis of calls for proposals and a peer review process.

The main aims of FP7 are to increase Europe's growth, competitiveness and employment. This is done through a number of initiatives and existing programmes including, the competitiveness and innovation framework programme ([2]), educational and training programmes, as well as regional development through structural and cohesion funds. FP7 is made up of four broad programmes – cooperation (collaborative research), ideas (European Research Council), people (human potential, Marie Curie actions) and capacities (research capacity). Through these four specific programmes, the aim is to create European 'poles of excellence' across a wide array of scientific themes, such as information technologies, energy and climate change, health, food and social sciences. FP7 also foresees specific programmes for EURATOM nuclear research and training

[1] For more information: http://cordis.europa.eu/fp7/home_en.html.

[2] For more information: http://cordis.europa.eu/innovation/en/policy/cip.htm.

activities, and direct research at the European Commission's own research institute (the Joint Research Centre (JRC)), where activities are focussed on: food, chemical products and health; environment and sustainability; and nuclear safety and security.

Science is becoming increasingly complex and costly. Today's researchers increasingly need to work together and they need access to advanced technical equipment. In 2000, the EU decided to create the European Research Area (ERA): a unified area all across Europe, which should:

- enable researchers to move and interact seamlessly, benefit from world-class infrastructures, and work with excellent networks of research institutions;
- share, teach, value and use knowledge effectively for social, business and policy purposes;
- optimise and open European, national and regional research programmes in order to support the best research throughout Europe and coordinate these programmes to address major challenges together;
- develop strong links with partners around the world so that Europe benefits from the worldwide progress of knowledge, contributes to global development and takes a leading role in international initiatives to solve global issues.

A debate was conducted during 2007 on what should be done to create a more unified and attractive research area to meet the needs of business, the scientific community and citizens. In May 2008 a set of ideas to develop the ERA were launched as part of what has become known as the 'Ljubljana process', including specific initiatives for five different areas: researchers' careers and mobility; research infrastructures; knowledge sharing; research programmes, and; international science and technology cooperation. In December 2008, the Competitiveness Council adopted a 2020 ERA vision ([3]), which foresees the introduction of a 'fifth freedom' across the ERA – namely, the free circulation of researchers, knowledge and technology.

12.1 Expenditure

Introduction

Research and development (R & D) comprises creative work undertaken to increase the stock of knowledge (of man, culture and society) and to devise new applications. The European Commission has placed renewed emphasis on the conversion of Europe's scientific expertise into marketable products and services. R & D lies at the heart of the EU's strategy to become the most competitive and dynamic knowledge-based economy by 2010; one of the original goals set by the Lisbon Strategy was for the EU to increase its R & D expenditure to at least 3 % of GDP by 2010.

One area that has received notable attention in recent years is the structural difference in R & D funding between Europe and its main competitors. Policy-makers in Europe have tried to increase R & D business expenditure so that it is

([3]) For more information: http://ec.europa.eu/research/era/2020_era_vision_en.html.

more in line with the ratios observed in Japan or the United States. The European Research Area (ERA) is designed to overcome some of these barriers that are thought to have hampered European research efforts, for example, by addressing geographical, institutional, disciplinary and sectoral boundaries.

In January 2006 the European Commission presented to the European Council its 2006 annual report on the revised Lisbon Strategy, in the form of a Communication – COM(2006) 30 – titled 'time to move up a gear – the new partnership for growth and jobs' ([4]). One of the four areas for priority actions was to invest more in knowledge and innovation, and to increase the proportion of national wealth devoted to research and development through to 2010. The Communication also referred to planned spending targets for R & D, stating that if these were met in the 18 countries that had set targets as part of their national plans then R & D expenditure was estimated to rise to 2.6 % of GDP by 2010. The Communication also stressed that while all Member States appreciate the importance of the spread and effective use of information and communication technologies and environmental technologies, the link between the identified challenges and the measures proposed to address them in national plans was not always clear.

In November 2009, the EU industrial R & D investment scoreboard was released ([5]). This presents information on the top 1 000 investors whose registered offices are in the EU and the top 1 000 companies registered elsewhere. The report shows that R & D investment by these EU companies grew by 8.1 % in 2008 despite the economic crisis that took hold in the second half of the year. This rate of growth was faster than that recorded for companies from either Japan or the United States, although higher R & D investment growth was registered by companies based in the emerging economies of China and India. Volkswagen had the highest level of R & D investment (EUR 5 930 million) among EU companies in 2008, while Nokia was also among the global top 10, which was led by Toyota Motors (Japan) and Microsoft (United States).

Definitions and data availability

Gross domestic expenditure on R & D (often referred to as GERD) is composed of four separate sectors of performance: business enterprises, government, higher education, and private non-profit organisations. Expenditure data consider the research spend on the national territory, regardless of the source of funds; data are usually expressed in relation to GDP, otherwise known as R & D intensity.

R & D expenditure is a basic measure that covers intramural expenditure, in other words, all expenditures for R & D that are performed within a statistical unit or sector of the economy. Expenditures made outside the statistical unit or sector but in support of intramural R & D (for example, purchase of supplies for R & D) are included; both current and capital expenditures are included.

Government budget appropriations or outlays for research and development (GBAORD) cover the amounts govern-

([4]) For more information: http://eur-lex.europa.eu/LexUriServ/site/en/com/2006/com2006_0030en01.pdf.

([5]) For more information: http://iri.jrc.ec.europa.eu/research/scoreboard_2009.htm.

ments allocate towards R & D activities and include all appropriations allocated to R & D in central (or federal) government budgets. Provincial (or state) government is only included if the contribution is significant, whereas local government funds are excluded. Comparisons of GBAORD across countries give an impression of the relative importance attached to state-funded R & D.

Main findings

Gross domestic expenditure on R & D (GERD) stood at EUR 228 681 million in the EU-27 in 2007, equivalent to 85 % of the total for the United States, but almost double the level of R & D expenditure in Japan (in 2006). In order to normalise these figures, GERD is generally expressed relative to GDP. This ratio increased marginally in the EU-27 during the five-year period up to 2002 from 1.78 % to 1.87 %. However, in 2003 it fell and this pattern was repeated again in 2004, while there was no change in the relative importance of R & D expenditure in 2005. The latest information available shows GERD increased and then stabilised, accounting for 1.85 % of the EU-27's GDP in both 2006 and 2007.

The EU-27's R & D expenditure relative to GDP tends to lag behind that of Japan (3.40 % in 2006) and the United States (2.67 % in 2007); this pattern has existed for a lengthy period. An analysis of the latest ten-year period for which data are available shows that the relative importance of GERD as a share of GDP rose by a modest 0.07 percentage points in the EU-27 between 1997 and 2007, while

a similar trend was witnessed in the United States (up 0.11 points). In contrast, there was a far higher increase in the relative importance of GERD in the Japanese economy, its share of GDP rising by 0.53 percentage points during the period 1997 to 2006; note however that Japanese economic growth was subdued during the period under consideration. The evolution of GERD (in current price euro terms) shows an overall increase of 64.9 % in the EU-27's R & D expenditure between 1997 and 2007, compared with growth of 43.5 % for the United States and 9.6 % for Japan (1997 to 2006).

Increasing investment in R & D is one of the key objectives of the Lisbon Strategy, in order to provide a stimulus to increase the EU's competitiveness. The Lisbon target of GERD representing 3 % of GDP remains the EU's objective for 2010, although most countries have specified their own targets in national reform programmes. Among the Member States, the highest R & D intensity was recorded in Sweden (3.60 % in 2007) and Finland (3.46 % in 2008), the only Member States to record ratios above the Lisbon target. Aside from Finland and Sweden (where a high proportion of research expenditure is focused on telecommunications), relatively high degrees of R & D intensity are found clustered in southern Germany (motor vehicles), through Switzerland into France (chemicals and pharmaceuticals) and on towards the Pyrenees (aerospace); regions containing capital cities also tend to be relatively R & D intensive. In contrast, there were ten Member States that reported R & D expenditure accounting for less than 1 % of their

GDP in 2007, with Bulgaria, Cyprus and Slovakia below 0.5 %; the regions with the lowest R & D intensity are generally found in southern and eastern Europe.

The differences in the relative weight of GERD among Triad members are often explained by referring to levels of expenditure within the business enterprise sector, as these are relatively low in the EU-27 (1.18 % of GDP) when compared with the United States (1.92 %) in 2007, and especially Japan (2.63 % in 2006). The relative importance of R & D

expenditure in the government and higher education sectors was broadly similar across all three members of the Triad.

When focusing on the breakdown of GERD by source of funds, slightly more than half (55.4 %) of the gross expenditure on R & D in the EU-27 came from business enterprises in 2006, while just over one third (33.5 %) was from government, and a further 8.6 % from abroad; business-funded R & D accounted for 77.1 % of total R & D expenditure in Japan and 66.4 % in the United States (2007).

Figure 12.1: Gross domestic expenditure on R&D (% share of GDP)

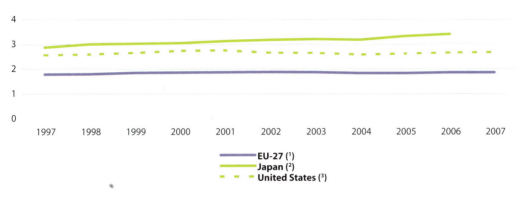

(¹) Estimates.
(²) Not available, 2007.
(³) Break in series, 1998; excludes most or all capital expenditure.

Source: Eurostat (tsc00001), OECD

Table 12.1: Gross domestic expenditure on R&D
(% share of GDP)

	1998	1999	2000	2001	2002	2003	2004	2005	2006	2007	2008
EU-27	1.79	1.84	1.85	1.86	1.87	1.86	1.82	1.82	1.85	1.85	:
Euro area	:	:	1.84	1.85	1.87	1.86	1.84	1.83	1.86	1.87	:
Belgium	1.86	1.94	1.97	2.08	1.94	1.88	1.87	1.84	1.88	1.87	:
Bulgaria (¹)	0.57	0.57	0.52	0.47	0.49	0.50	0.50	0.49	0.48	0.48	:
Czech Republic	1.15	1.14	1.21	1.20	1.20	1.25	1.25	1.41	1.55	1.54	:
Denmark	2.04	2.18	2.24	2.39	2.51	2.58	2.48	2.46	2.48	2.55	:
Germany	2.27	2.40	2.45	2.46	2.49	2.52	2.49	2.48	2.54	2.54	:
Estonia	0.57	0.69	0.61	0.71	0.72	0.77	0.86	0.94	1.15	1.14	1.29
Ireland	1.24	1.18	1.12	1.10	1.10	1.17	1.24	1.25	1.30	1.31	1.45
Greece	:	0.60	:	0.58	:	0.57	0.55	0.58	0.57	0.57	:
Spain	0.87	0.86	0.91	0.91	0.99	1.05	1.06	1.12	1.20	1.27	:
France (²,³)	2.14	2.16	2.15	2.20	2.23	2.17	2.15	2.10	2.10	2.08	:
Italy	1.05	1.02	1.05	1.09	1.13	1.11	1.10	1.09	1.13	:	:
Cyprus	0.22	0.23	0.24	0.25	0.30	0.35	0.37	0.40	0.43	0.45	:
Latvia	0.40	0.36	0.44	0.41	0.42	0.38	0.42	0.56	0.70	0.59	:
Lithuania	0.55	0.50	0.59	0.67	0.66	0.67	0.75	0.75	0.79	0.82	:
Luxembourg	:	:	1.65	:	:	1.65	1.63	1.56	1.66	1.62	:
Hungary (³)	0.68	0.69	0.78	0.92	1.00	0.93	0.88	0.94	1.00	0.97	:
Malta (³)	:	:	:	:	0.26	0.26	0.53	0.57	0.61	0.59	:
Netherlands (¹)	1.90	1.96	1.82	1.80	1.72	1.76	1.78	1.72	1.71	1.70	:
Austria	1.78	1.90	1.94	2.07	2.14	2.26	2.26	2.44	2.46	2.56	2.66
Poland	0.67	0.69	0.64	0.62	0.56	0.54	0.56	0.57	0.56	0.57	:
Portugal	0.65	0.71	0.76	0.80	0.76	0.74	0.77	0.81	1.00	1.18	:
Romania	0.49	0.40	0.37	0.39	0.38	0.39	0.39	0.41	0.45	0.53	:
Slovenia	1.34	1.37	1.39	1.50	1.47	1.27	1.40	1.44	1.56	1.45	:
Slovakia	0.78	0.66	0.65	0.63	0.57	0.57	0.51	0.51	0.49	0.46	:
Finland	2.87	3.16	3.35	3.30	3.36	3.43	3.45	3.48	3.45	3.47	3.46
Sweden (⁴)	:	3.61	:	4.17	:	3.85	3.62	3.60	3.74	3.60	:
United Kingdom	1.76	1.82	1.81	1.79	1.79	1.75	1.69	1.73	1.76	1.79	:
Croatia	:	:	:	:	0.96	0.97	1.05	0.87	0.76	0.81	:
Turkey	0.37	0.47	0.48	0.54	0.53	0.48	0.52	0.59	0.58	0.72	:
Iceland	2.00	2.30	2.67	2.95	2.95	2.82	:	2.77	2.99	2.75	2.90
Norway	:	1.64	:	1.59	1.66	1.71	1.59	1.52	1.52	1.64	:
Switzerland	:	:	2.53	:	:	:	2.90	:	:	:	:
Japan	3.00	3.02	3.04	3.12	3.17	3.20	3.17	3.32	3.40	:	:
United States	2.59	2.65	2.73	2.75	2.65	2.64	2.57	2.61	2.65	2.67	:

(¹) Break in series, 1999.
(²) Break in series, 2000.
(³) Break in series, 2004.
(⁴) Break in series, 2005.

Source: Eurostat (tsiir020), OECD

Table 12.2: Gross domestic expenditure on R&D by sector
(% share of GDP)

	Business enterprise sector		Government sector		Higher education sector	
	2002	2007	2002	2007	2002	2007
EU-27	*1.20*	*1.18*	*0.24*	*0.24*	*0.41*	*0.40*
Euro area	*1.18*	*1.19*	*0.27*	*0.27*	*0.40*	*0.39*
Belgium	1.37	*1.30*	0.14	*0.16*	0.41	0.41
Bulgaria	0.09	0.15	0.35	0.28	0.05	0.05
Czech Republic	0.73	0.98	0.28	0.29	0.19	0.26
Denmark	1.73	*1.66*	0.18	0.18	0.58	0.70
Germany	1.72	*1.77*	0.34	0.35	0.42	*0.41*
Estonia	0.22	0.54	0.12	0.10	0.34	0.48
Ireland	0.76	:	0.10	0.09	0.25	*0.35*
Greece	0.18	*0.15*	:	*0.12*	:	0.29
Spain	0.54	0.71	0.15	0.22	0.29	0.33
France ([1,2])	1.41	*1.31*	0.37	*0.34*	0.42	*0.40*
Italy ([3])	0.54	*0.55*	0.20	*0.21*	0.37	:
Cyprus	0.06	*0.10*	0.12	*0.12*	0.09	*0.19*
Latvia	0.17	0.19	0.08	0.14	0.17	0.26
Lithuania	0.11	0.23	0.22	0.17	0.33	0.41
Luxembourg	:	*1.36*	0.16	*0.22*	:	*0.05*
Hungary ([4])	0.35	0.49	0.33	0.23	0.25	0.23
Malta ([1])	0.07	*0.39*	0.04	*0.02*	0.16	*0.18*
Netherlands ([5])	0.98	*1.03*	0.24	*0.22*	0.50	0.45
Austria	1.43	*1.81*	0.12	*0.13*	0.58	*0.62*
Poland	0.11	0.17	0.25	0.20	0.19	0.19
Portugal	*0.25*	*0.61*	*0.14*	*0.11*	*0.29*	*0.35*
Romania	0.23	0.22	0.09	0.18	0.06	0.13
Slovenia	0.88	0.87	0.34	0.36	0.23	0.23
Slovakia	0.37	0.18	0.15	0.16	0.05	0.11
Finland	2.35	2.51	0.35	0.29	0.64	0.65
Sweden	:	2.66	:	0.17	:	0.77
United Kingdom	1.16	*1.15*	0.16	0.17	0.43	*0.44*
Croatia	0.41	0.33	0.21	0.21	0.34	0.27
Turkey	0.15	0.30	0.04	0.08	0.34	0.35
Iceland	*1.69*	1.50	*0.72*	0.49	*0.47*	0.69
Norway	0.95	0.88	0.26	0.25	0.44	0.51
Switzerland	:	:	0.03	:	0.64	:
Japan ([6])	2.36	2.63	0.30	0.28	0.44	0.43
United States	1.85	*1.92*	0.32	*0.29*	0.36	*0.35*

([1]) Break in series, business enterprise sector, 2004.
([2]) Break in series, higher education sector, 2004.
([3]) Break in series, higher education sector, 2005.
([4]) Break in series, government sector, 2004.
([5]) Break in series, government sector, 2003.
([6]) 2006 instead of 2007.

Source: Eurostat (tsc00001), OECD

Table 12.3: Gross domestic expenditure on R&D by source of funds
(% of total gross expenditure on R&D)

	Business enterprises		Government		Abroad	
	2002 (¹)	2007 (²)	2002 (¹)	2007 (²)	2002 (¹)	2007 (²)
EU-27	*54.6*	*55.4*	*34.3*	*33.5*	*8.9*	*8.6*
Euro area	*56.2*	*57.1*	*36.2*	*34.4*	*6.4*	*6.9*
Belgium	59.4	59.7	23.2	24.7	14.3	12.4
Bulgaria	24.8	30.6	69.8	61.9	5.0	6.5
Czech Republic	53.7	54.0	42.1	41.2	2.7	4.1
Denmark	61.4	59.5	28.2	27.6	7.8	10.1
Germany	*65.5*	68.1	*31.6*	27.8	*2.4*	3.8
Estonia	29.1	41.6	53.9	45.6	14.3	11.7
Ireland	63.4	*59.3*	27.5	30.1	7.1	8.9
Greece	33.0	31.1	46.6	46.8	18.4	19.0
Spain	48.9	47.1	39.1	42.5	6.8	5.9
France (³)	52.1	52.4	38.3	38.4	8.0	7.0
Italy	:	40.4	:	48.3	:	8.3
Cyprus	17.4	15.9	61.6	66.5	15.1	12.1
Latvia	21.7	36.4	42.7	55.2	35.6	7.5
Lithuania	27.9	24.5	65.1	47.9	7.1	19.6
Luxembourg	90.7	79.7	7.7	16.6	1.6	3.6
Hungary (⁴)	29.7	43.9	58.5	44.4	10.4	11.1
Malta	18.6	*45.4*	59.8	*3.3*	21.6	*28.4*
Netherlands	50.0	:	37.1	:	11.6	:
Austria	44.6	*47.7*	33.6	*35.6*	21.4	*16.3*
Poland	30.1	34.3	61.9	58.6	4.8	6.7
Portugal	*31.6*	36.3	*60.5*	55.2	*5.0*	4.7
Romania	41.6	26.9	48.4	67.1	7.0	4.5
Slovenia	60.0	58.3	35.6	35.6	3.7	5.8
Slovakia	53.6	35.6	44.1	53.9	2.1	10.2
Finland (⁵)	69.5	68.2	26.1	24.1	3.1	6.5
Sweden (⁶)	71.7	63.9	22.3	24.4	3.4	8.1
United Kingdom	43.5	*47.2*	28.9	*29.3*	21.5	*17.7*
Croatia	45.7	35.5	46.4	50.4	1.5	10.9
Turkey	41.3	48.4	50.6	47.1	1.3	0.5
Iceland	*46.2*	50.4	34.0	38.8	18.3	10.0
Norway	51.6	45.3	39.8	44.9	7.1	8.3
Japan	74.1	77.1	18.4	16.2	0.4	0.4
United States	65.2	66.4	29.1	*27.7*	:	:

(¹) Denmark, Greece, Sweden, Iceland and Norway, 2001; Luxembourg, 2000.
(²) EU-27, euro area, Bulgaria, Germany, Ireland, Spain, France, Italy and Japan, 2006; Belgium, Denmark, Greece, Luxembourg, Portugal and Sweden, 2005.
(³) Break in series, 2004.
(⁴) Break in series for government sector, 2004.
(⁵) Break in series for abroad, 2005.
(⁶) Break in series, 2005.

Source: Eurostat (tsiir030), OECD

12.2 Personnel

Introduction

One means of helping to achieve the goal of becoming the 'most competitive and dynamic knowledge-based economy in the world' is through an investment in human capital. Scientific and technological development has since been placed at the core of EU objectives, with an increasing interest in the role and measurement of skills within the labour force. The need for increasing human resources in this area may be tempered by a range of factors, including:

- young people's knowledge of careers in science;
- teaching in schools and universities preparing students for careers in science;
- a low level participation in scientific domains among women and minorities;
- the attractiveness of the EU for science students, scientists/engineers from the rest of the world;
- the professional status of researchers and science professionals;
- barriers to mobility within research and scientific professions.

As part of the European Commission's strategy to address the Lisbon goals, an independent group on increasing human resources for science and technology in Europe was appointed. Its objective was to identify actions or policy measures that would contribute towards increasing the number of research personnel (in particular) and science and technology professionals (in general). With the re-launch of the Lisbon Strategy in 2005,

policy focus switched to the concept of 'knowledge for growth', with renewed emphasis on improving the mobility of European researchers, encouraging networks between researchers from different Member States, and promoting R & D as an occupation for women. This latter point has been one particular area of concern for policymakers who consider that women's intellectual potential, and their contribution to society are not being fully capitalised upon. In particular, the participation of women is low in certain branches of the natural sciences, engineering and technology, which are considered key R & D areas. Furthermore, women are also under-represented in the business enterprise sector where the EU's R & D is most highly concentrated, as well as in senior academic grades and influential positions ([6]).

The European Research Area (ERA) aims at creating a unified area, in which researchers can move and interact seamlessly. As noted above, plans for the development of ERA by 2020 include the introduction of a 'fifth freedom' – the free circulation of researchers, knowledge and technology across Europe. In May 2008, the European Commission adopted a Communication to launch an initiative titled, 'better careers and more mobility: a European partnership for researchers' ([7]). Its goal was to improve mobility and to enhance the diffusion of knowledge throughout Europe, via: the creation of a partnership for mobility and career development; balancing demand and supply for researchers at a European level; helping create centres of excellence, and; improving

---

([6]) For more information: http://ec.europa.eu/research/science-society/index.cfm?fuseaction=public.topic&id=27.

([7]) For more information: http://eur-lex.europa.eu/LexUriServ/LexUriServ.do?uri=COM:2008:0317:FIN:EN:HTML.

the skills of researchers in Europe. It is hoped that ERA will inspire the most talented students to enter research careers, stimulate industry to invest more in European research, and contribute to the creation of sustainable growth and jobs. If such changes take place, then it may be hoped that improving career prospects for researchers will lead more young people to choose a research career, help keep researchers in Europe and attract more talented non-European researchers.

Definitions and data availability

Researchers are professionals engaged in the conception or creation of new knowledge, products, processes, methods and systems, and in the management of the projects concerned. The data on the number of researchers may be presented in the form of head counts or as full-time equivalents (FTEs).

Data on **R & D personnel** provide indicators for international comparisons of human resources devoted to R & D activity; they include all persons employed directly on R & D, as well as persons supplying direct services to R & D, such as managers, administrative staff and office staff. For statistical purposes, indicators on R & D personnel who are mainly or partly employed on R & D are compiled as head counts (HC) and as full-time equivalents (FTEs), or person-years.

Human resources in science and technology (HRST) are defined as stocks of persons having either successfully completed tertiary education, or persons who are employed in an occupation where such an education is normally required; those who fulfil both these criteria are classified

as the HRST core. HRST can be shown as absolute figures or relative total employment (among the age group 25-64). The data may be broken down by gender, age, region, sector of activity, occupation, educational attainment and fields of education (although it should be noted that not all combinations are possible).

Information pertaining to stocks of HRST (as shown here) provide details relating to the characteristics of the current labour force involved in science and technology. It is also possible to study flows of HRST, either from the perspective of job-to-job mobility, or flows of persons from education into the science and technology labour force. Information on HRST stocks and job-to-job mobility is derived from the labour force survey (LFS), while information on HRST flows from education are obtained from a UNESCO/OECD/Eurostat questionnaire on education. The latter can be used to provide a measure of the current and future supply of HRST from the education system, in terms of actual inflows (graduates from the reference period) and potential inflows (students participating in higher education during the reference period).

Education statistics are based on the international standard classification of education (ISCED); the basic unit of classification is the educational programme. Indicators based on the number of **PhD graduates** give an idea of the extent to which countries will have researchers at the highest level of education in the future. The data relate to numbers of new graduates in the reference year, not to the total number (stock) of graduates in the labour market that year. The number of PhD graduates is measured as graduates from ISCED level 6: a PhD is defined in terms of tertiary programmes which lead to the award of an advanced research degree, e.g. a doctorate in economics. These programmes should be devoted to advanced study and original research and are not based on course-work alone; a PhD usually requires 3-5 years. **Science and technology graduates** are defined as the number of new graduates from all public and private institutions completing science and technology-related graduate and post-graduate studies in the reference year; it is expressed relative to the total number of persons aged 20-29 years.

Main findings

The number of researchers in the EU-27 has increased considerably in recent years: there were 1.36 million full-time equivalents in 2007, which marked an increase of almost 250 thousand (or 22.5 %) when compared with 2000. A gender breakdown shows that men accounted for slightly less than three quarters (72 %) of the EU-27's research workforce in 2007; there was almost no change in the relative balance between male and female researchers during the period 2000-2007.

A breakdown of the number of researchers by institutional sector in 2007 shows that almost half (48.8 %) of all researchers in the EU-27 were concentrated in the business enterprise sector, while just over one third (36.1 %) were in the higher education sector and 13.8 % in the government sector. The relative importance of the different institutional sectors varied considerably across the Member States, with business enterprises accounting for 70 % of researchers in Luxembourg, and upwards of 60 % in Sweden, Austria, Denmark and

Germany; these shares were broadly in line with the latest data for Japan (68.1 % in 2006). Bulgaria was the only country to report a majority (55.1 %) of its researchers employed within the government sector, while more than half of all researchers working in the Baltic Member States, Slovakia, Poland, Greece and Cyprus were employed within the higher education sector.

One objective for European universities is to attract and maintain highly-qualified staff and students in order to support their research capabilities. Within the EU-27 there were 13.4 science and technology graduates per thousand persons aged 20 to 29 years in 2007, with particularly high ratios in France, Finland, Ireland, Lithuania and Portugal (all above 18). The number of science and technology graduates should be interpreted with care, insofar as some students could be foreigners who return home following their studies, whereas others may seek employment in a completely different domain as soon as they have graduated.

A similar (but more specific) measure of a country's potential research capability is provided by the number of PhD students; this may be broken down by their chosen subject. There were 525 800 PhD students in the EU-27 in 2007, compared with 396 200 in the United States and 75 500 in Japan. In relative terms, the broad subject group of science, mathematics, computing, engineering, manufacturing and construction-related studies accounted for more than one third (36.4 %) of the PhD students in the EU-27 in 2007, a proportion that was somewhat higher than in Japan (32.6 %) or the United States (30.2 %).

Across the whole of the EU-27, women accounted for 47.8 % of PhD students in 2007, a share that was not too dissimilar from that recorded in the United States, where women were in a slight majority (52.1 %); in contrast, men accounted for a much higher share of PhD students in Japan (almost 70 %). The gender split of PhD students across the Member States was typically quite balanced in 2007: with women accounting for more than half of all the PhD students in the Baltic Member States, Portugal, Italy, Finland, Spain and Poland, and at least 40 % of all PhD students in the remaining Member States for which data are available, with the exception of the Czech Republic (39.1 %) and Malta (34.7 %).

Human resources in science and technology (HRST) provide a broad measure of the stock of personnel employed in science and technology-related occupations. Some 64.5 million people were employed in the EU-27 within science and technology occupations in 2007; this amounted to 29.8 %

of total employment. Between 2004 and 2007 there was a modest increase in the relative importance of HRST within the EU-27 workforce, as their share rose by 0.9 percentage points. The HRST 'core' – made up of people with a university level degree who also work in a science and technology occupation – amounted to 35.2 million persons in 2007 (or 16.3 % of the total number of persons employed).

HRST accounted for almost 40 % of the workforce in Luxembourg and Sweden in 2007, while relatively high shares were also recorded in the Netherlands, Germany, Denmark and Finland. The most rapid growth in HRST between 2004 and 2007 (in relation to total employment) was reported for the Baltic Member States (in particular, Latvia), Malta, the Czech Republic and Italy, where the relative weight of HRST rose by at least 2 percentage points; Austria, Bulgaria, the Netherlands and Ireland were the only Member States where the share of HRST in the total employment fell.

Table 12.4: Researchers, by institutional sector, 2007 (^{1})

	Total - all sectors	Business enterprise sector		Government sector		Higher education sector	
	(1 000 FTE)	(1 000 FTE)	(% of total)	(1 000 FTE)	(% of total)	(1 000 FTE)	(% of total)
EU-27	1 355.7	661.9	48.8	186.7	13.8	489.3	36.1
Euro area	949.8	480.1	50.6	135.1	14.2	321.6	33.9
Belgium	35.9	18.4	51.3	2.5	7.1	14.8	41.1
Bulgaria	11.2	1.3	11.8	6.2	55.1	3.6	32.2
Czech Republic	27.9	12.5	44.8	6.6	23.8	8.7	31.1
Denmark	29.6	18.1	61.4	2.2	7.5	9.0	30.4
Germany	284.3	172.7	60.8	43.6	15.3	68.0	23.9
Estonia	3.7	1.0	26.0	0.5	14.8	2.1	56.5
Ireland (^{2})	12.2	7.0	57.5	0.5	4.1	4.7	38.4
Greece	20.8	6.1	29.3	2.2	10.6	12.4	59.5
Spain	122.6	42.1	34.3	21.4	17.5	58.8	48.0
France	211.1	114.1	54.0	25.6	12.1	67.9	32.2
Italy (^{3})	88.4	36.7	33.9	17.8	18.8	37.6	42.6
Cyprus	0.8	0.2	22.6	0.1	13.8	0.5	57.9
Latvia	4.2	0.5	11.0	0.7	17.6	3.0	71.4
Lithuania	8.5	1.3	15.4	1.7	19.7	5.5	64.9
Luxembourg	2.2	1.5	70.0	0.5	22.7	0.2	7.3
Hungary	17.4	7.0	40.2	4.6	26.3	5.8	33.5
Malta	0.5	0.3	50.9	0.0	3.3	0.2	45.8
Netherlands	44.1	26.1	59.2	6.9	15.5	11.2	25.3
Austria	31.4	19.8	63.3	1.4	4.6	9.9	31.7
Poland	61.4	9.8	16.0	12.8	20.9	38.6	62.8
Portugal	28.0	8.6	30.9	3.1	11.1	13.1	46.8
Romania	18.8	7.8	41.2	5.8	30.9	5.1	27.1
Slovenia	6.3	2.6	41.1	2.0	32.0	1.7	26.5
Slovakia	12.4	1.6	12.9	2.9	23.4	7.9	63.6
Finland	39.0	22.0	56.4	4.5	11.5	12.2	31.2
Sweden	47.8	30.9	64.8	1.9	4.1	14.8	31.1
United Kingdom (^{4})	175.5	91.5	52.2	8.5	4.8	71.5	40.7
Croatia	6.1	0.9	14.4	1.9	30.4	3.4	55.2
Turkey	49.7	15.3	30.8	4.8	9.7	29.5	59.5
Iceland	2.2	1.1	48.4	0.5	20.8	0.6	28.1
Norway	24.8	12.4	50.1	3.9	15.7	8.5	34.2
Switzerland (^{4})	:	:	:	0.4	:	12.7	:
Japan (^{2})	709.7	483.3	68.1	33.6	4.7	184.3	26.0
United States (^{5})	:	1 135.5	:	:	:	:	:

(^{1}) Shares do not sum to 100 % due to estimates, differences in reference years, the exclusion of private non-profit sector data from the table and the conversion of data to a count in terms of FTE.
(^{2}) 2006.
(^{3}) Total - all sectors and higher education sector, 2006.
(^{4}) Government sector and higher-education sector, 2006.
(^{5}) Business enterprise sector, 2006.

Source: Eurostat (tsc00004), OECD

Figure 12.2: Gender breakdown of researchers in all institutional sectors, 2007 (^{1})
(% of total researchers, based on FTEs)

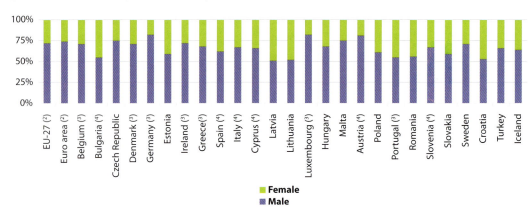

(^{1}) France, the Netherlands, Finland and the United Kingdom, not available.
(^{2}) Estimates.
(^{3}) 2005.
(^{4}) 2006.

Source: Eurostat (tsc00006)

Figure 12.3: Proportion of research and development personnel by sector, 2007
(% of active population)

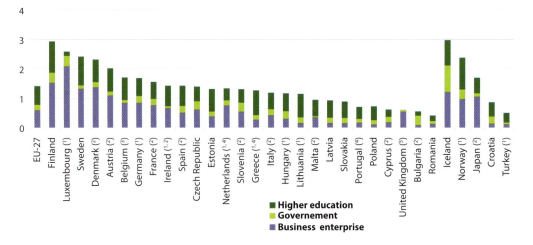

(^{1}) Private non-profit, not available.
(^{2}) 2006.
(^{3}) Business enterprises, 2006; government, higher education and private non-profit sectors, 2005.
(^{4}) 2005.
(^{5}) Higher education, not available.

Source: Eurostat (tsc00002)

Table 12.5: Science and technology graduates
(tertiary graduates in science and technology per 1 000 persons aged 20-29 years)

	Total		Male		Female	
	2002	**2007**	**2002**	**2007**	**2002**	**2007**
EU-27	*11.3*	13.4	*15.4*	17.9	*7.1*	8.7
Belgium	10.5	14.0	16.1	15.3	7.5	6.9
Bulgaria	11.7	8.4	13.9	14.2	4.8	5.1
Czech Republic	6.0	12.0	9.7	12.2	6.5	6.1
Denmark	11.7	16.4	:	9.1	:	7.8
Germany	8.1	11.4	6.8	9.2	2.8	3.5
Estonia	8.0	13.3	5.6	5.8	2.1	2.7
Ireland	20.5	18.7	15.7	20.8	7.5	11.9
Greece	:	8.5	7.3	14.0	4.4	9.8
Spain	11.9	11.2	4.5	8.5	1.7	5.5
France (¹)	20.1	20.5	13.8	10.0	9.5	6.8
Italy	7.4	8.2	10.1	15.1	5.3	8.6
Cyprus	3.8	4.2	27.2	23.8	13.3	11.0
Latvia	8.1	9.2	10.6	16.7	5.9	11.1
Lithuania	14.6	18.1	12.2	15.9	3.8	6.9
Luxembourg	:	:	15.7	20.4	5.2	7.6
Hungary	4.8	6.4	17.0	17.8	9.3	9.2
Malta	3.1	7.1	24.6	26.1	9.9	11.1
Netherlands	6.6	8.9	8.6	23.3	6.1	12.8
Austria	7.9	11.0	10.8	14.4	2.4	3.4
Poland	8.3	13.9	28.1	29.3	12.0	11.6
Portugal	7.4	18.1	9.6	16.0	6.4	10.4
Romania	5.8	11.9	18.3	24.0	10.9	12.0
Slovenia	9.5	9.8	12.4	16.6	3.4	5.3
Slovakia	7.8	11.9	:	:	:	:
Finland	17.4	18.8	8.3	16.6	3.5	7.2
Sweden	13.3	13.6	9.4	10.2	5.4	6.2
United Kingdom	20.3	17.5	26.4	25.5	14.6	11.8
Croatia	:	6.8	:	8.6	:	4.8
FYR of Macedonia	3.1	4.6	3.4	5.4	2.8	3.7
Turkey	5.0	6.7	6.7	9.1	3.1	4.3
Iceland	9.2	10.2	12.1	13.1	6.2	7.2
Liechtenstein	:	10.5	:	14.4	:	6.5
Norway	7.7	9.3	11.1	13.1	4.2	5.4
Switzerland	15.1	17.9	25.5	29.4	4.6	6.4
Japan	13.0	14.4	21.9	24.2	3.8	4.2
United States	10.0	10.1	13.3	13.5	6.6	6.4

(¹) 2001 instead of 2002.

Source: Eurostat (tsiir050)

Table 12.6: PhD students (ISCED level 6), 2007
(% of total PhD students)

	Total number of PhD students (1 000)	Male	Female	Social sciences, business & law	Teacher training & educ.; humani- ties & arts	Science, maths & computing; engineering, manuf. & construction	Agri- culture & vet- erinary	Health & welfare; services	Others (¹)
EU-27	525.8	52.2	47.8	21.8	21.0	36.4	2.9	14.5	2.0
Belgium	7.4	57.3	42.7	19.3	13.7	45.0	7.6	14.5	0.0
Bulgaria	4.8	50.4	49.6	19.5	22.3	41.8	2.9	13.5	0.0
Czech Republic	23.7	60.9	39.1	16.6	15.6	46.2	4.3	15.5	1.9
Denmark	4.8	53.6	46.4	12.6	14.9	34.7	8.7	29.1	0.0
Germany	:	:	:	:	:	:	:	:	:
Estonia	2.1	45.1	54.9	22.5	21.2	42.7	5.3	8.3	0.0
Ireland	5.6	53.0	47.0	17.0	23.2	47.3	1.7	8.9	1.8
Greece	21.7	57.5	42.5	14.3	24.7	34.3	4.4	22.4	0.0
Spain	72.7	48.2	51.8	22.8	21.7	21.3	2.1	19.9	12.3
France	71.6	53.5	46.5	29.3	25.6	41.7	0.1	3.3	0.0
Italy	40.1	47.8	52.2	19.7	14.9	42.5	6.1	16.4	0.5
Cyprus	0.4	52.4	47.6	16.0	32.2	51.9	0.0	0.0	0.0
Latvia	1.8	39.0	61.0	34.8	24.0	28.2	1.9	11.1	0.0
Lithuania	2.9	42.2	57.8	31.6	13.6	39.8	4.8	10.2	0.0
Luxembourg	:	:	:	:	:	:	:	:	:
Hungary	7.8	51.4	48.6	21.7	25.6	29.3	6.3	17.1	0.0
Malta	0.1	65.3	34.7	18.1	34.7	33.3	0.0	13.9	0.0
Netherlands	7.5	58.0	42.0	:	:	:	:	:	:
Austria	18.2	54.2	45.8	36.2	22.4	31.1	3.2	4.6	2.5
Poland	31.8	50.0	50.0	20.8	31.2	33.0	5.3	9.7	0.0
Portugal	18.7	44.2	55.8	29.6	20.8	31.4	1.6	16.6	0.0
Romania	27.7	54.4	45.6	17.2	15.4	43.0	7.0	17.4	0.0
Slovenia	1.3	52.2	47.8	13.3	17.1	49.2	3.0	17.4	0.0
Slovakia	11.1	55.1	44.9	20.9	18.1	37.1	3.2	20.8	:
Finland	21.9	47.9	52.1	22.6	24.2	39.8	2.1	11.4	0.0
Sweden	20.8	50.5	49.5	12.1	12.2	41.6	1.9	32.2	0.0
United Kingdom	99.4	54.8	45.2	21.1	21.6	40.3	1.3	15.3	0.3
Croatia	1.8	54.6	45.4	3.6	17.0	55.1	1.4	23.0	0.0
FYR of Macedonia	0.1	50.4	49.6	22.7	26.1	26.9	1.7	22.7	0.0
Turkey	33.8	59.0	41.0	23.9	22.6	34.0	7.8	11.7	0.0
Iceland	0.2	42.8	57.2	16.4	27.4	31.8	0.0	24.4	0.0
Liechtenstein	0.0	72.2	27.8	0.0	22.2	0.0	0.0	77.8	0.0
Norway	5.7	53.3	46.7	18.9	11.9	41.9	2.8	24.4	0.0
Switzerland	17.6	58.7	41.3	26.7	15.8	39.1	2.7	15.3	0.4
Japan	75.5	69.9	30.1	13.1	13.7	32.6	5.8	32.2	2.4
United States	396.2	47.9	52.1	26.9	24.4	30.2	0.8	17.7	0.0

(¹) Unknown or not specified.

Source: Eurostat (educ_enrl5)

Table 12.7: Human resources in science and technology (^{1})

	People working in a S&T occupation					People who have a third level education and work in a S&T occupation				
	(1 000)	(% of total employment)				(1 000)	(% of total employment)			
	2007 (^{2})	2004	2005	2006	2007	2007 (^{2})	2004	2005	2006	2007
EU-27	64 450	29.0	29.4	29.7	29.8	35 151	15.5	15.9	16.1	16.3
Belgium	1 441	31.5	32.7	33.0	33.0	967	20.9	21.2	21.6	22.2
Bulgaria	710	22.6	23.2	21.5	21.9	513	15.7	16.4	15.7	15.8
Czech Republic	1 638	30.9	32.6	32.6	33.3	540	10.2	10.8	11.1	11.0
Denmark (^{3})	995	35.6	36.7	37.0	36.2	592	22.9	23.7	24.1	21.5
Germany	13 782	35.7	36.2	36.6	36.4	6 610	17.2	17.5	17.2	17.4
Estonia	173	27.2	29.4	28.9	29.4	103	15.1	17.5	17.9	17.4
Ireland	486	23.6	23.1	23.2	23.4	338	15.7	15.4	16.1	16.2
Greece	1 038	21.9	22.0	22.8	23.1	778	16.4	16.4	17.0	17.3
Spain	4 928	24.1	24.9	24.0	24.2	3 592	17.6	18.0	17.8	17.7
France	7 935	30.9	31.2	31.6	31.8	4 525	17.3	17.8	18.3	18.1
Italy	7 403	29.9	29.7	31.1	32.0	2 797	10.9	11.2	11.5	12.1
Cyprus	102	25.6	25.7	26.1	27.0	75	18.0	17.7	18.4	19.8
Latvia	332	23.1	24.5	26.9	29.7	156	11.5	12.3	13.0	13.9
Lithuania	412	24.8	26.1	25.8	26.9	268	15.2	16.5	16.4	17.5
Luxembourg	80	39.5	38.7	39.0	39.5	52	22.7	25.1	23.2	25.9
Hungary	1 041	26.4	26.0	26.6	26.5	576	13.9	14.0	14.5	14.7
Malta	41	24.0	25.5	26.9	26.6	17	10.7	10.3	10.9	10.9
Netherlands	2 963	37.7	37.4	36.2	37.2	1 649	20.6	20.9	20.2	20.7
Austria	1 193	32.9	30.6	30.5	29.7	446	12.2	11.6	11.3	11.1
Poland	3 987	25.3	25.9	26.2	26.2	2 318	13.5	14.6	15.1	15.3
Portugal	893	16.7	17.0	17.7	17.6	527	9.5	9.6	10.3	10.4
Romania	1 739	17.3	17.8	18.6	18.6	973	8.6	9.3	10.1	10.4
Slovenia	299	29.6	30.8	31.7	30.9	168	14.7	16.0	17.1	17.4
Slovakia	690	28.5	29.6	29.7	29.3	272	10.4	11.5	11.9	11.5
Finland	854	33.4	33.6	34.1	34.5	562	22.2	22.0	22.4	22.7
Sweden	1 757	38.9	39.4	39.4	39.5	1 030	21.6	22.6	22.8	23.2
United Kingdom	7 539	25.8	26.0	27.0	26.9	4 710	16.0	16.2	16.7	16.8
Croatia	384	23.4	23.8	24.4	:	223	14.3	14.1	14.2	:
Turkey	2 646	:	:	12.5	12.5	1 470	:	:	6.7	7.0
Iceland	55	30.1	31.2	32.7	:	22	17.8	17.3	13.2	:
Norway	892	35.3	36.3	36.4	37.0	599	22.4	23.8	24.1	24.8
Switzerland	1 604	37.8	38.4	38.9	39.4	800	17.7	18.5	19.0	19.7

(^{1}) Break in series, 2006, with the exception of Belgium and Luxembourg.
(^{2}) Croatia and Iceland, 2006.
(^{3}) Break in series, 2007.

Source: Eurostat (hrst_st_nsec)

12.3 Innovation

Introduction

Innovation (ideas applied successfully in practice) provides the potential for society to tackle some of the world's major issues – for example, climate change, depleted energy resources, disease and illness.

Europe has a long-standing tradition of producing inventions. However, commentators often focus on an entrepreneurial gap in order to explain why some ideas for new products or services do not become a success in the marketplace, or why other ideas relating to new processes do not get implemented, thereby surrendering the opportunity to make efficiency gains on production lines or within industrial organisations. Hence, while Europe is very good at producing ideas, it is not as good at bringing them to market; as such, EU policy in this field increasingly aims to provide more focus to industry-driven, applied R & D.

Education is another area seen as key to developing an innovation-orientated society, through the acquisition of entrepreneurial, managerial, scientific, mathematical and foreign language skills, as well as digital literacy. Policymakers express concern at the numbers of science and technology graduates who directly apply their education once they move into the labour market, while a lack of job mobility between universities and industry may potentially hinder the transfer of ideas, thereby reducing the EU's innovation performance (see the previous subchapter for more details relating to labour-market issues).

Globalisation and the rising economic power of developing nations have resulted in some European enterprises needing to become more innovative just to maintain their competitive position. The European Commission is trying to make sure that innovation is thoroughly understood: indeed, 2009 was the European year of creativity and innovation. The EU seeks to contribute to greater competitiveness, sustainability and job creation, through the promotion of innovation (among others):

- providing financial support for innovators;
- providing innovation support services (notably for start-ups);
- encouraging venture capital;
- developing and testing new forms of business support;
- facilitating transnational cooperation;
- mobilising resources for the creation of a European innovation space.

Placing competitiveness at the heart of the European political agenda, the Lisbon Strategy aims to boost entrepreneurial initiative and create a productive environment where innovation capacity can grow and develop. With this in mind, on 29 October 2006, the European Parliament and the Council adopted a Decision 1639/2006/CE establishing a competitiveness and innovation framework programme (CIP) for the period 2007-2013 ([8]).

The European Council called for a plan on innovation in December 2008 and these reflections on future innovation policy

---

([8]) For more information: http://ec.europa.eu/cip/index_en.htm.

are likely to be part of a wider debate on the Lisbon Strategy post-2010 (EU 2020). This Council initiative provided the basis for a period of public consultation and business debate, for example, a first roundtable on future European innovation policy was held in June 2009; three months later the European Commission adopted a Communication 'reviewing Community innovation policy in a changing world' (⁹).

As part of these on-going reforms, the EU has set up a European Institute of Innovation and Technology (EIT); this is an independent Community body whose mission is to address Europe's innovation gap through the 'stimulation of world-leading innovation', such that Europe may capitalise fully on its innovation capacity and the capability of its actors (higher education staff, researchers, business leaders and entrepreneurs) through the creation of knowledge and innovation communities (KICs).

Definitions and data availability

Innovations are based on the results of new technological developments, new combinations of existing technology, or the utilisation of other knowledge acquired (by the enterprise). For the purpose of the Community innovation survey (CIS) an **innovation** is defined as a new or significantly improved product (good or service) introduced to the market, or the introduction within an enterprise of a new or significantly improved process. Such innovations may be developed by the innovating enterprise or by another enterprise. However, purely selling innovations wholly produced and developed by other enterprises is not included as an innovation activity, nor is introducing products with purely aesthetic changes. Innovations should therefore be new to the enterprise concerned: for product innovations they do not necessarily have to be new to the market, and for process innovations the enterprise does not necessarily have to be the first one to have introduced the process.

Enterprises with innovation activity include all types of innovator, namely product innovators, process innovators, as well as enterprises with only on-going and/or abandoned innovation activities. Enterprises may cooperate with other parties (for example suppliers, competitors, customers, educational/research establishments) when engaging in an innovative activity. The proportion of enterprises with innovation activity is also referred to as the propensity to innovate.

The CIS collects information pertaining to both product and process, organisational and marketing innovations. The legal basis for the collection of these statistics is Commission Regulation (EC) 1450/2004 of 13 August 2004 implementing Decision No 1608/2003/EC of the European Parliament and of the Council concerning the production and development of

(⁹) COM(2009) 442 final; for more information: http://eur-lex.europa.eu/LexUriServ/LexUriServ.do?uri=COM:2009:0442:FIN:EN:PDF.

Community statistics on innovation. Note that the European Commission accorded on 22 July 2005 a derogation to France concerning CIS 2006 data. As a result, CIS data for France for 2006 only cover the manufacturing sector (NACE Rev. 1.1 Section D) for enterprises with more than 50 employees.

Main findings

In 2006, some 38.9 % of EU-27 enterprises were considered as innovative. The highest propensity to innovate was recorded in Germany (62.6 %), while Belgium, Finland and Austria also reported that more than one in every two enterprises were innovative. At the other end of the range, the lowest propensity to innovate was registered by enterprises in Latvia (16.2 %), while Hungary, Bulgaria, Romania, Lithuania, Poland and Slovakia also reported that fewer than one in four enterprises innovated. Note that large enterprises tend to innovate more than SMEs and as such these figures may, at least to some degree, reflect the enterprise structure of each economy.

New or significantly improved products contributed a relatively small proportion of total turnover among innovative enterprises in 2006, some 10.0 % for the EU-27 in 2006, with 11 of the Member States reporting single digit shares. These products did however account for a much higher share of sales in the Czech Republic (16.0 %), Bulgaria (17.0 %), Greece (22.8 %) and Malta (where their relative importance rose to 33.4 % of turnover).

Almost half (47.5 %) of the large enterprises in the EU-27 (with 250 or more employees) brought product innovations to market in 2006, compared with 36.8 % of medium-sized enterprises (50 to 249 employees) and 29.7 % of small enterprises (10 to 49 employees). A similar size class breakdown for process innovations that are developed within the enterprise also showed that large innovative enterprises were also more likely to introduce processes innovations.

Figure 12.4: Proportion of innovative enterprises, 2006 (^{1})
(% of all enterprises)

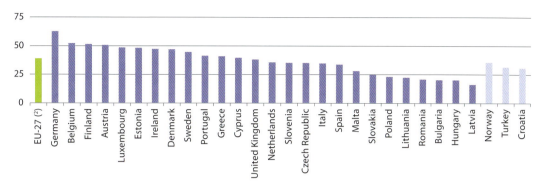

(^{1}) France, not available (derogation accorded on 22 July 2005).
(^{2}) Excluding France.

Source: Eurostat (inn_cis5_prod)

Figure 12.5: Turnover from new or significantly improved products new to the market, 2006 (^{1})
(% of total turnover of innovative enterprises)

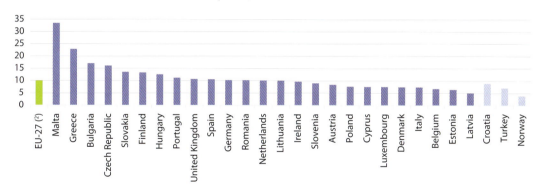

(^{1}) France (derogation accorded on 22 July 2005) and Sweden, not available.
(^{2}) Excluding France and Sweden.

Source: Eurostat (inn_cis5_prod)

Table 12.8: Proportion of innovative enterprises which introduced products new to the market or own-developed process innovations, 2006
(% of enterprises within size class or total)

	Process innovations: developed by the enterprise or group				Product innovations: new to market			
	Total	With 10 to 49 employees	With 50 to 249 employees	With > 250 employees	Total	With 10 to 49 employees	With 50 to 249 employees	With > 250 employees
EU-27 (¹)	:	:	:	:	32.6	29.7	36.8	47.5
Belgium	20.9	18.6	27.0	40.6	41.4	38.6	44.1	65.3
Bulgaria	7.7	6.3	10.1	21.8	41.3	38.6	46.2	45.7
Czech Republic	13.6	10.9	20.3	28.0	38.9	32.5	48.3	51.3
Denmark	16.4	13.7	24.6	33.3	33.8	30.9	37.9	50.6
Germany	19.3	15.8	23.3	43.8	30.4	25.9	35.3	47.7
Estonia	19.9	17.2	26.9	50.0	32.8	32.9	32.1	37.0
Ireland	20.0	17.6	26.3	44.1	40.8	38.0	47.0	51.6
Greece	19.8	17.4	31.1	35.3	49.5	48.1	50.2	70.7
Spain	16.1	13.9	25.2	39.0	18.3	14.8	26.0	39.5
France	:	:	:	:	:	:	:	:
Italy	:	:	:	:	29.5	26.8	37.2	50.1
Cyprus	12.5	11.5	17.9	10.7	34.5	30.9	42.3	52.2
Latvia	:	:	:	:	44.7	49.7	33.8	41.9
Lithuania	7.8	6.1	15.9	21.7	36.0	36.8	32.4	38.5
Luxembourg	22.0	18.3	28.9	44.9	58.9	59.3	52.6	75.4
Hungary	5.7	4.5	8.1	18.8	30.9	30.1	29.6	38.2
Malta	13.1	9.2	23.8	51.9	31.3	29.4	29.2	47.6
Netherlands	8.2	6.9	11.0	23.2	48.1	46.1	50.8	59.5
Austria	18.8	15.7	26.9	39.8	45.4	42.1	48.8	65.0
Poland	10.8	7.4	17.4	29.5	32.7	33.1	30.6	37.5
Portugal	19.1	17.1	26.9	36.8	29.8	26.5	37.1	48.5
Romania	14.3	12.0	18.1	28.4	24.7	22.1	26.6	33.9
Slovenia	13.8	11.4	18.0	30.8	51.1	52.5	44.9	59.4
Slovakia	7.9	5.0	13.1	21.6	37.6	34.7	39.8	43.8
Finland	19.7	17.8	23.3	35.0	44.6	44.3	40.7	58.1
Sweden	16.3	14.9	:	:	51.3	49.3	55.8	58.4
United Kingdom	:	:	:	:	31.6	31.0	31.7	39.8
Croatia	11.0	9.3	14.7	20.9	31.7	28.5	33.1	47.5
Turkey	20.2	19.1	23.4	30.4	59.6	62.3	50.5	52.9
Norway	10.4	9.1	14.3	21.1	39.9	40.6	37.0	42.0

(¹) Excluding France (derogation accorded on 22 July 2005).

Source: Eurostat (inn_cis5_prod))

12.4 Patents

Introduction

Intellectual property law establishes protection over intangibles – for example, when a manufactured product is sold, the product itself becomes the property of the purchaser, however, intellectual property rights allow intangible elements to remain in the ownership of the creator; these intangibles include (among others) the idea itself, or the name or sign/logo used to distinguish the product from others.

Patents and trademarks are common ways to protect industrial property. Patents are a limited term exclusive right granted to an inventor, maintained through the payment of fees. While patents are generally used to protect R & D results, they are also a source of technical information, which can potentially prevent re-inventing and re-developing ideas. A count of patents shows a country's capacity to exploit knowledge and translate it into potential economic gains; in this context, patent statistics are widely used to assess the inventive and innovative performance. Most studies show that innovative enterprises tend to make more use of intellectual property protection than companies that do not innovate. Enterprise size and the economic sector in which an enterprise operates are also likely to play an important role in determining whether an enterprise chooses to protect its intellectual property.

The use of patents is relatively restricted within the EU: this may be due to a range of influences: their relative cost; the overlap between national and European procedures; or the need for translation into foreign languages. Furthermore, the increasing number and complexity of patent applications worldwide has resulted in a backlog of pending applications, while the constant expansion of the human knowledge base makes it increasingly difficult for patent offices to keep abreast of technological developments.

The European Council held in Lisbon in March 2000 called for the creation of a Community patent system to address shortcomings in the legal protection of inventions, while providing an incentive for investments in R & D. In July of the same year the European Commission made a first proposal for the creation of a Community patent: this was discussed at various levels and despite a number of proposals and amendments for a Council Regulation during 2003 and 2004 no legal basis was forthcoming. In April 2007 the European Commission released a Communication titled, 'enhancing the patent system in Europe' ([10]); this claimed that European patent systems were more expensive, uncertain and unattractive compared with patent systems in non-member countries.

In July 2008 the European Commission ([11]) adopted a Communication titled, 'an industrial property rights strategy for Europe'. This foresees the development of legislation, arguing that the harmonisation of patent law could make it easier for European companies to patent their inventions both within and outside the EU.

On 4 December 2009, the European Council unanimously adopted conclusions on an enhanced patent system in the EU. The

([10]) COM(2007) 165 final; for more information: http://eur-lex.europa.eu/LexUriServ/site/en/com/2007/com2007_0165en01.pdf.

([11]) COM(2008) 465 final; for more information: http://eur-lex.europa.eu/LexUriServ/LexUriServ.do?uri=COM:2008:0465:FIN:EN:PDF.

package agreed covers two main areas: firstly, agreement on the approach to be adopted in order to move towards an EU patent regulation; secondly, an agreement on establishing a new patent court in the EU. It is hoped that these measures will together make it less costly for businesses to protect innovative technology and make litigation more accessible and predictable. However, the creation of the EU patent depends on a solution being found for translation arrangements which will be the subject of separate legislation.

Definitions and data availability

From 2007 onwards, Eurostat's production of European Patent Office (EPO) data has been based almost exclusively on the EPO's worldwide statistical patent database (PATSTAT) ([12]).The EPO grants European patents for the contracting states to the European Patent Convention (EPC), of which there are currently 32 – the Member States, Iceland, Liechtenstein, Switzerland, Monaco and Turkey.

European patent applications refer to applications filed directly under the European Patent Convention or to applications filed under the Patent Cooperation Treaty (PCT) and designated to the EPO (Euro-PCT). Patent applications are counted according to the year in which they are filed and are assigned to a country according to the inventor's place of residence, using fractional counting if there are multiple inventors.

In contrast, the United States Patent and Trademark Office (USPTO) data refer to patents granted; data are recorded by year of publication as opposed to the year of filing. This methodological difference im-

plies that any comparison between EPO and USPTO patents data should be interpreted with caution.

High-technology patents are counted following criteria established by the trilateral statistical report (drafted by the EPO, USPTO and the Japan Patent Office (JPO)), where the following technical fields are defined as high-technology groups in accordance with the international patent classification (IPC): computer and automated business equipment; micro-organism and genetic engineering; aviation; communication technology; semiconductors; and lasers.

Main findings

Having grown at a relatively fast pace during the 1990's the number of EU-27 patent applications filed with the EPO remained relatively stable (within the range of 50 253 to 54 216) during the period 2000 to 2006. Among the Member States, Germany had by far the highest number of patent applications to the EPO, some 22 675 in 2006 (43.0 % of the EU-27 total). In relative terms, Germany was also the Member State with the highest number of patent applications per million inhabitants (275.1), followed by Sweden (243.2), Luxembourg (228.3) and Finland (226.3).

EU-27 high-technology patent applications to the EPO represented an increasing share of total patent applications up until 2001 when they accounted for 22.8 % of all applications. Their relative importance declined somewhat after this, as did their absolute number. From a high of 11 543 high-tech patent applications in 2001, there was a relatively slow reduction through to 2004, followed by a collapse

([12]) For more information: http://www.epo.org/about-us/epo.html.

in the number of high-tech applications, falling to 3 754 in 2006. This pattern was observed across the majority of the Member States and particularly for the larger countries or those countries with traditionally the highest propensity to make patent applications. Luxembourg and Germany registered the highest number of high-technology patent applications per million inhabitants in 2006, the figures for both countries being around 20, while Belgium, France, Finland and Austria were the only other Member States to record double-digit ratios. The considerable reduction in high-technology patent applications filed with the EPO may reflect the length of patent procedures. Given the increasing speed of technological change and the rapid pace at which imitators are able to bring new technologies to market, it is perhaps not surprising that many enterprises increasingly choose to invest in continued innovation rather than spend time and resources to protect goods or services that may soon become copied or obsolete.

Figure 12.6: Patent applications to the European Patent Office (EPO), EU-27 (number of applications)

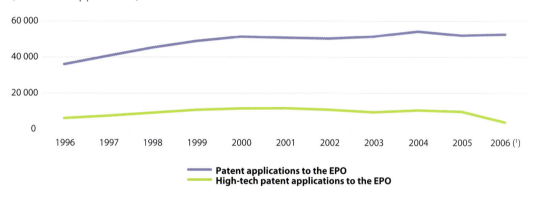

(¹) Estimate.

Source: Eurostat (tsc00009 and pat_ep_ntec), European Patent Office

Table 12.9: Patent applications to the European Patent Office (EPO) and patents granted by the USPTO

	Patent applications to the EPO			High-technology patent applications to the EPO			Patents granted by the US Patent & Trademark Office (USPTO)		
	(number of applications)		(per million inhab.)	(number of applications)		(per million inhab.)	(number of patents granted)		(per million inhab.)
	2001	2006	2006	2001	2006 (¹)	2006 (¹)	1998	2003 (²)	2003 (²)
EU-27	50 734	52 612	106.7	11 543	3 754	7.6	30 530	15 988	32.9
Euro area	41 924	44 277	139.3	9 076	3 344	10.5	23 750	13 161	42.2
Belgium	1 192	1 365	129.9	260	175	16.6	780	394	38.1
Bulgaria	16	20	2.6	3	2	0.3	7	3	0.4
Czech Republic	72	97	9.4	6	9	0.9	38	42	4.1
Denmark	896	1 011	186.3	227	27	5.0	564	219	40.8
Germany	21 757	22 675	275.1	3 889	1 617	19.6	12 747	7 258	87.9
Estonia	10	6	4.7	4	5	3.5	4	1	0.7
Ireland	243	251	59.7	80	17	4.1	164	117	29.6
Greece	71	116	10.4	13	9	0.8	33	25	2.3
Spain	861	1 333	30.5	151	69	1.6	351	249	6.0
France	7 234	7 891	125.3	1 848	876	13.9	4 602	2 085	33.7
Italy	3 960	4 736	80.6	396	240	4.1	1 893	1 226	21.4
Cyprus	16	17	22.1	4	0	0.2	0	2	3.1
Latvia	5	22	9.7	0	2	0.9	4	3	1.5
Lithuania	3	11	3.3	1	2	0.6	1	12	3.5
Luxembourg	73	107	228.3	8	10	21.0	40	29	64.7
Hungary	99	96	9.5	25	5	0.5	36	38	3.7
Malta	5	13	32.1	:	1	3.0	0	0	5.3
Netherlands	3 859	2 900	177.5	1 565	142	8.7	1 516	927	57.3
Austria	1 194	1 451	175.6	184	99	12.0	595	403	49.7
Poland	58	122	3.2	9	12	0.3	20	30	0.8
Portugal	41	129	12.2	8	18	1.7	13	13	1.3
Romania	10	29	1.4	4	0	0.0	6	9	0.4
Slovenia	48	102	51.1	7	2	0.8	28	19	9.5
Slovakia	12	30	5.5	5	3	0.6	7	6	1.1
Finland	1 371	1 190	226.3	663	70	13.3	987	425	81.6
Sweden	2 086	2 200	243.2	514	75	8.3	1 764	546	61.1
United Kingdom	5 543	4 691	77.7	1 667	274	4.5	4 329	1 925	32.4
Croatia	21	27	6.1	2	4	1.0	16	25	5.5
Turkey	45	154	2.1	0	12	0.2	18	18	0.3
Iceland	21	25	84.4	7	2	6.7	22	18	61.1
Liechtenstein	28	24	689.6	3	1	14.3	22	13	379.2
Norway	354	457	98.5	73	12	2.5	295	127	28.0
Switzerland	2 768	3 024	405.5	462	177	23.8	1 528	809	110.6
Japan	19 723	19 990	:	6 283	2 969	:	36 079	29 598	231.8
United States	29 899	31 403	:	10 407	1 347	:	100 276	86 574	297.4

(¹) Estonia, Cyprus and Latvia, 2005.
(²) Malta, 2002.

Source: Eurostat (tsc00009, tsiir060, pat_ep_ntec, tsc00010, pat_us_ntot and tsiir070), European Patent Office, USPTO

Figure 12.7: Co-patenting at the EPO according to inventors' country of residence, EU-27, 2005 (¹)
(% of total)

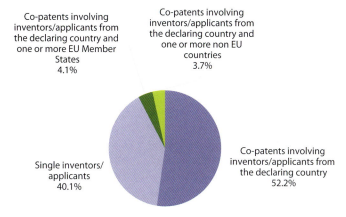

Co-patents involving inventors/applicants from the declaring country and one or more EU Member States
4.1%

Co-patents involving inventors/applicants from the declaring country and one or more non EU countries
3.7%

Single inventors/ applicants
40.1%

Co-patents involving inventors/applicants from the declaring country
52.2%

(¹) Figures do not sum to 100 % due to rounding.

Source: Eurostat (pat_ep_cpi)

Figure 12.8: Patent citations, EU-27
(number)

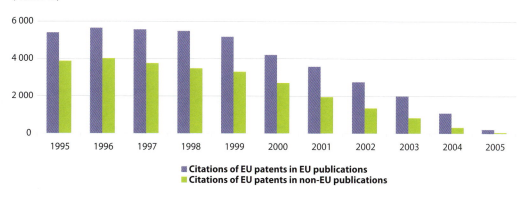

■ Citations of EU patents in EU publications
■ Citations of EU patents in non-EU publications

Source: Eurostat (pat_ep_cti)

Europe's regions

European regional policy is designed to further economic and social cohesion, by reducing the gap in development between regions and among Member States of the EU. Regional policy helps finance concrete projects for regions and towns, stimulating growth and competitiveness; as such, it is in line with the priorities set by the EU for growth and employment (the revised Lisbon Strategy). During the current programming period which covers 2007 to 2013, economic and social cohesion policy across the regions will benefit from EUR 347 410 million. The three main objectives are:

- **convergence**, under which the poorest Member States and regions (GDP per inhabitant less than 75 % of the Community average) are eligible, accounting for around 82 % of the funds for 2007 to 2013;
- regional **competitiveness and employment**, accounting for around 16 % of the funds; all regions which are not covered by the convergence objective or transitional assistance are eligible for funding;
- European **territorial cooperation**, accounting for around 2.5 % of the funds available.

Regional statistics are employed for a range of purposes, including the allocation of structural funds. NUTS, the common classification of territorial units for statistics, is used as an objective base to demarcate regional boundaries and determine geographic eligibility for funds, including:

- the **European Regional Development Fund** (ERDF) which operates in all Member States and co-finances physical investments and, to a limited extent, training; the fund can intervene in the three objectives of regional policy;

- the **European Social Fund** (ESF) which aims to make the EU's workforce and companies better equipped to face global challenges through the promotion of better skills and job prospects;
- the **Cohesion Fund** which co-finances mainly transport and environmental projects.

The ERDF supports regions covered by all three objectives. In relation to convergence, it focuses intervention on modernising and diversifying economic structures, as well as safeguarding or creating sustainable jobs. As regards regional competitiveness and employment, its priorities relate to innovation and the knowledge-based economy, environment and risk prevention, and access to transport and telecommunications services of general economic interest. Finally, in terms of its contribution to European territorial cooperation, the ERDF aims to develop economic and social cross-border activities, the establishment and development of transnational cooperation, and to increase the efficiency of regional policy through interregional promotion and cooperation, as well as the networking and exchange of experiences between regional and local authorities.

The ESF aims to improve employment and job opportunities through interventions that are made within the framework of convergence and regional competitiveness and employment objectives. The ESF supports actions in four key areas: increasing the adaptability of workers and enterprises (lifelong learning, designing and spreading innovative working organisations); enhancing access to employment and participation in labour markets;

reinforcing social inclusion by combating discrimination and facilitating access to labour markets among disadvantaged people; and promoting partnership for reform in the fields of employment and inclusion.

The Cohesion Fund supports actions within the framework of the convergence objective; it finances activities including trans-European transport network and environmental projects, as well as energy or transport projects, as long as these demonstrate environmental benefits (such as energy efficiency, the use of renewable energy, developing rail transport systems or improving public transport); this fund concerns Bulgaria, the Czech Republic, Estonia, Greece, Cyprus, Latvia, Lithuania, Hungary, Malta, Poland, Portugal, Romania, Slovenia and Slovakia; while Spain is eligible to a phase-out fund.

One particular focus of economic and social cohesion policy has been urban development. Europe's cities are centres of economic activity, attracting innovation and employment. Upwards of 70 % of the EU's population live in urban areas, yet a considerable proportion face problems such as crime, poverty, unemployment, housing, traffic or environmental pressures. The URBAN I Community initiative ran from 1994 to 1999 covering 118 urban areas, with projects focused on the rehabilitation of infrastructure, job creation, combating social exclusion and environmental improvements. URBAN II ran from 2000 to 2006 supporting development and regeneration strategies in 70 urban areas. As of 2007, the EU has reinforced the urban dimension of regional policy and fully integrated this into cohesion policy, with particular attention to promoting social cohesion and environmental sustainability. As such, the guiding principles of the URBAN Community Initiative have been incorporated into operational programmes; this change means that all cities are potential beneficiaries of funding, through support for different sectoral and thematic policies in the context of the revised Lisbon Strategy, the Sustainable Development Strategy and other EU priorities (for example, urban regeneration, urban transport, the rehabilitation of industrial sites and contaminated land areas, or housing developments).

Definitions and data availability

Regional data cover a broad range of statistical areas, for example: regional economic accounts; demography and migration; employment and unemployment; education and health; agriculture, industry, distributive trades and other services; tourism and transport; research and development. The concepts and definitions used for regional statistics are as close as possible to those used for the production of statistics at a national and European level.

The NUTS (nomenclature of territorial units for statistics) is the nomenclature subdividing the territory of the EU into regions at three different levels (NUTS 1, 2 and 3, respectively, from larger to smaller); above that there is the 'national' level of the Member States. The NUTS aims to provide a single and coherent territorial breakdown for the compilation of EU regional statistics. The current NUTS version of 2006 subdivides the territory of the EU and its 27 Member States into 97 NUTS 1 regions, 271 NUTS 2 regions

and 1 303 NUTS 3 regions. The NUTS is based on Regulation (EC) 1059/2003 on the establishment of a common classification of territorial units for statistics. An amending Regulation, extending the NUTS to the ten Member States that joined the EU in 2004, was adopted in 2005 and an amendment that extends the NUTS to cover Bulgaria and Romania, was adopted in 2008. This chapter presents regional information available at NUTS level 2 for a selection of key socioeconomic indicators, definitions of which are provided below.

GDP per inhabitant: the economic development of a region is, as a rule, expressed in terms of its gross domestic product (GDP). However, in order to take account of the different absolute sizes of regions, any comparison of economic development should take account of population. GDP per inhabitant should preferably be expressed in terms of a common currency that eliminates differences in price levels between countries. For this purpose, GDP is converted using conversion factors, known as purchasing power parities (PPPs), to an artificial common currency, called a purchasing power standard (PPS). Note that GDP per inhabitant is based on a measure of wealth (the GDP produced in the region) that relates to the 'place-of-work', which is subsequently divided by a 'place-of-residence' figure (inhabitants living in the region). This inconsistency can be particularly relevant wherever there are considerable commuter flows – i.e. more or fewer people working in a region than living in it (for example, Inner London, Wien, Hamburg, Praha or Luxembourg). As such, a more balanced picture of a region's economic situation may be obtained by analysing GDP per inhabitant figures alongside indicators that measure the regional distribution of income.

Disposable income per inhabitant: aside from interregional flows of labour (commuter flows), there are a number of additional factors that can result in the regional distribution of income deviating from the regional distribution of GDP. These include, for example, interregional flows of income from rent, interest or dividends received by the residents of a certain region, but paid by residents of other regions. In contrast to GDP per inhabitant, the disposable income of private households presents the balance remaining after these transactions have been carried out, based on the income received (wages, operating surplus, rent, interest, dividends and social benefits) from which are deducted taxes, social security contributions and other current transfers. The data are derived from household accounts and are (as with the GDP figures) presented in terms of an artificial common currency, a purchasing power consumption standard (PPCS) per inhabitant in order to eliminate differences in price levels between countries.

Population density: the ratio of average population, defined as the number of inhabitants, relative to the size of the territory in square kilometres (km²); the land area concept (excluding inland waters like lakes or rivers) is used wherever available.

Population change: the difference in population between two reference periods (at the beginning of each year) expressed in terms of an average annual growth rate.

Population change measures the sum of natural increase (births minus deaths) and net migration (immigration minus emigration).

Old-age dependency ratio: the ratio between the total number of elderly persons of an age when they are generally economically inactive (aged 65 and over) and the number of persons of working age (15 to 64).

The primary source of regional labour market information is the labour force survey (LFS); this is a quarterly household sample survey. The target population is made up of all members of private households aged 15 or over. The data presented refer to annual averages of the quarterly surveys.

Employment rate: employed persons are all persons aged 15 and over (16 and over in Spain and the United Kingdom, 15 to 74 in Denmark, Estonia, Latvia, Hungary, Sweden and Finland) who, during the reference week, worked at least one hour for pay or profit, or were temporarily absent from such work; family workers are included. The employment rate expresses persons employed as a proportion of the total target population.

Old-age employment rate: as above for the employment rate, but based on a target population of those persons aged 55 to 64 years old.

Unemployment rate: unemployed persons comprise those aged 15 to 74 (16 to 74 in Spain and the United Kingdom) who were (all three conditions need to be satisfied simultaneously): without work during the reference week (of the LFS); available for work; and actively seeking work. The latter involves taking specific steps in the four-week period ending with the reference week (of the LFS) to either: contact a public employment office to find work; contact a private temporary work or recruitment agency; apply directly to employers to find work; or finding a job to start within a period of at most three months. The unemployment rate expresses the number of unemployed persons as a proportion of the active population (which comprises all employed and unemployed persons).

One means of quantifying economic and social cohesion is through an analysis of the **dispersion of regional indicators** – in other words, how evenly an indicator is spread across EU regions, or among the different regions of the same Member State. Such measures of dispersion are presented here for GDP per inhabitant, employment rates and unemployment rates. In order to interpret the results, note that, for example, the dispersion of regional employment rates will be zero if the employment rate of each region is identical, and will rise the larger the differences in employment rates between regions. Given these indicators have been produced at NUTS level 2, they are not applicable for Estonia, Ireland, Cyprus, Latvia, Lithuania, Luxembourg, Malta or Slovenia, as these Member States comprise only one or two regions at this level of detail. The measure of dispersion is generally expressed in terms of the coefficient of variation, which presents the ratio of the weighted standard deviation of the regional measures compared with the overall national rate.

For more information on regional data collection and the NUTS classifica-

tion, please refer to: http://ec.europa.eu/ eurostat/ramon/nuts/introduction_ regions_en.html.

The main goal of the **urban audit** data collection is to provide information to assess the quality of life in European towns and cities. The urban audit provides statistical data for 321 cities across the Member States, as well as for five cities in Croatia, six in Norway, four in Switzerland and 26 in Turkey. These cities were selected in cooperation with the national statistical offices, and are geographically dispersed to ensure a representative sample, meaning that they are not necessarily always the largest cities.

Eurostat collects and publishes information on over 330 indicators relating to the quality of urban life and living standards, including information on: demography, housing, health, crime, the labour market, economic activity, income disparity, local administration, civic involvement, educational qualifications, cultural infrastructure and tourism. All definitions follow as closely as possible definitions employed for national and regional figures; in the event that a different definition is used, data providers are asked to estimate the data in line with the standardised definitions.

Data are collected at a number of different levels, namely: core cities, larger urban zones and sub-city districts (for a smaller subset of indicators). The urban audit defines a city as a legal entity (administrative concept), and delineates the 'core city' according to political and administrative boundaries; note that this concept is not always strictly comparable between countries due to the different structures of local government that may exist across countries. As economic activity, health services or air pollution, among others, cross the administrative boundaries of cities, the 'larger urban zone' is defined for analytical purposes as the core city and its commuter belt. Each core city is, in turn, divided into a number of 'sub-city districts', enabling information to be collected on possible disparities within cities.

For more information on the urban audit data collection, please refer to: http://epp.eurostat.ec.europa.eu/portal/page/portal/region_cities/city_urban.

Main findings

The maps presented on the following pages illustrate the diversity of the EU's 271 NUTS level 2 regions and show that large variations may exist for many economic and social characteristics, not only across the Member States, but also within countries; where available, information has also been included for candidate countries and for EFTA countries.

Economic trends across regions

GDP per inhabitant in the EU-27 averaged PPS 23 600 for 2006, while among the regions it ranged from a high of PPS 79 400 per inhabitant in Inner London to PPS 5 800 per inhabitant for Nord-Est (Romania); the factor between the two ends of the distribution was therefore 13.7:1. The next highest levels of GDP per inhabitant were recorded for Luxembourg (PPS 63 100) and Bruxelles/Brussels (PPS 55 100), while Hamburg (PPS 47 200) was the only other region to register a level that was at least twice

as high as the EU-27 average. Among the 20 regions with the highest levels of GDP per inhabitant, Praha (the Czech Republic) and Bratislavský kraj (Slovakia) were the only regions from the Member States that joined the EU since 2004, ranked in 12th and 19th place respectively. The nine 'poorest' regions (using this measure) were all in Bulgaria and Romania, with a number of Polish, Romanian and Hungarian regions making up the remainder of the bottom 20 in the ranking.

An analysis across those countries where there are several NUTS level 2 regions shows that Berlin, Rome, Amsterdam and Helsinki were the only capital city regions in 2006 not to record the highest levels of national GDP per inhabitant; Hamburg, the Provincia Autonoma Bolzano/Bozen and Lombardia (which contains Milan), Groningen (north east Holland), and Åland (south west Finland) reported higher levels of GDP per inhabitant than regions containing the capital city.

More generally, GDP per inhabitant tended to be relatively high in northern Belgium, southern Germany, northern Italy, the south of the United Kingdom, Ireland, Luxembourg, the Netherlands, Austria and Scandinavia, as well as the capital city regions of Prague, Madrid and Paris. GDP per inhabitant was relatively low in many of western regions of the Iberian Peninsula, southern Italy, Greece (aside from Athens) and eastern Germany, as well as in most of the Member States that joined the EU since 2004.

There were substantial regional differences within Member States as regards the distribution of GDP per inhabitant. The ratio between the highest and lowest values stood at a factor of 4.3:1 in the United Kingdom between Inner London and West Wales and the Valleys, while in France the ratio was 3.5:1 between the Île de France (which includes Paris) and Guyane (one of the French overseas departments). At the other end of the scale, the most 'equitable' distributions of GDP per inhabitant were recorded in Denmark, Ireland, Spain, the Netherlands, Portugal, Slovenia and Sweden, where the ratio between the highest and lowest regional values never rose above 2:1.

Data for GDP per inhabitant should be interpreted with care as this ratio is influenced by the number of commuters working in one region but living in another. Indeed, the relatively high levels of GDP per inhabitant within Inner London, Luxembourg and Bruxelles/Brussels (the three regions with the highest GDP per inhabitant) can, at least in part, be explained by a large daily influx of commuters from neighbouring regions or, in the case of Luxembourg, neighbouring countries. This effect can vary considerably and may reflect not only the propensity to commute or the distances that people are prepared to commute, but also the way NUTS level 2 regions are delineated and, in particular, how far the suburbs and surrounding areas of cities are included within the same NUTS region. Conversely, the counter-effect of commuters working in a neighbouring region tends to result in the GDP per inhabitant of 'commuter belts' or 'dormitory' regions being lower – examples include Lüneburg near Hamburg, Flevoland near Amsterdam, and several regions in Belgium (as Belgian commuters travel not only to Bruxelles/Brussels but also to Luxembourg).

When comparing the regional distribution of disposable income per inhabitant with that of GDP per inhabitant there are considerable differences, as income measures are not affected by commuter flows. A comparison between GDP per inhabitant for Inner London and for Surrey, East and West Sussex (a popular commuter belt to the south of London) shows that GDP per inhabitant was 2.69 times as high in Inner London. However, in terms of disposable income the difference between the two regions was much closer, as the disposable income figures reflect where each of these commuters lives (principally in areas around the capital). As such, disposable income in Inner London was PPS 25 403 in 2006, only 1.17 times as high as the figure for Surrey, East and West Sussex.

Inner London recorded the highest level of disposable income across all EU-27 NUTS level 2 regions in 2006. Of the nine regions in the EU-27 where disposable income per inhabitant was above the threshold of PPS 20 000 in 2006, five (including Inner London) were in the south east of the United Kingdom, three in Germany and one in France. Comparing the highest and lowest levels of disposable income per inhabitant across all EU-27 regions, incomes were higher in Inner London by a factor of 7.0:1 when compared with Nord-Est (Romania); this ratio was approximately half as pronounced as that recorded in terms of GDP per inhabitant for the same two regions (13.7:1).

Regional disparities (based on a comparison of the highest to the lowest levels of disposable income) within the same country were considerable in Greece and Romania; where disposable income per inhabitant in the two capital city regions was more than double that recorded in the region with the lowest levels of disposable income – Ionia Nisia (a group of islands off the west coast of Greece, including Corfu) or Nord-Est (Romania). Regional disparities were also generally high across Italy, Hungary, Slovakia and the United Kingdom, whereas the lowest disparities (using this measure) were recorded in Austria and Slovenia, followed by Ireland, the Netherlands, Finland and Sweden.

Demographic trends across regions and cities

Population density is measured in terms of the average number of inhabitants per square kilometre (km^2) of land area; this ratio stood at 122 inhabitants in 2007 for the EU-27. Information broken down by NUTS level 2 regions is generally available for 2007 and this shows that capital city regions are among the most densely populated regions in Europe, for example, Inner London and Outer London (United Kingdom), Bruxelles/Brussels (Belgium), Wien (Austria), Berlin (Germany), Praha (the Czech Republic), Istanbul (Turkey), Bucureşti-Ilfov (Romania) and Attiki (Greece). Each of these capital city regions had a population density above 1 000 inhabitants per km^2, as did the following non-capital city regions: West Midlands, Merseyside, Greater Manchester and West Yorkshire (United Kingdom), Hamburg and Bremen (Germany), the autonomous regions of Ceuta and Melilla (Spain), Malta (the whole island is defined as one NUTS level 2 region), and Zuid-Holland (Netherlands).

The least densely populated regions in 2007 were Guyane (France), Iceland (the whole country is defined as one NUTS level 2 region), and Övre Norrland (Sweden), all three with an average of three inhabitants per km^2. The next least densely populated regions, registering less than 20 inhabitants per km^2, were all in Sweden, Finland, the United Kingdom and Norway, while several regions across Spain (Aragón, Castilla-la Mancha, Castilla y León and Extremadura) and one in southern Portugal (Alentejo) were the only other EU-27 regions to record a population density of less than 30 inhabitants per km^2.

Around three quarters of the EU-27's population lives in cities or towns with more than 5 000 inhabitants. Information from the urban audit data collection shows that 26 of the more than 350 cities surveyed in 2007 had a population in excess of one million inhabitants (21 in the EU-27 and five in Turkey).

Istanbul was the largest of the urban audit cities, with a population of 9 million inhabitants (about the same number as the total population of Sweden), followed by London and Paris (7.4 million and 6.2 million respectively), Berlin, Ankara and Madrid (all in the range of 3 to 3.5 million inhabitants). Most of the agglomerations with more than 1.5 million inhabitants were capital cities, although Hamburg in Germany, Barcelona in Spain, and Istanbul and Izmir in Turkey were exceptions to this rule.

While Guyane (France) reported the lowest population density among EU-27 regions, it also reported the highest population growth (3.7 % per annum during the period 2002 to 2006). Of the 12 regions that reported population growth in excess of 2 % per annum during the period considered (generally 2003 to 2007), eight were in Spain, principally in the islands, easterly coastal regions, and around Madrid (the Comunidad de Madrid and Castilla-la Mancha which is south east of Madrid); the three other regions included both Irish regions (there are only two NUTS level 2 regions in Ireland) and another island region, namely, Corse (France).

Just over a quarter (25.8 %) of the 287 regions for which data are available reported a decline in their populations during the period 2003 to 2007. Of these, three regions recorded reductions in excess of 1 % per annum; two in eastern Germany (Chemnitz and Sachsen-Anhalt) and one in north west Bulgaria (Severozapaden).

Population ageing is likely to have a significant impact on a range of social and economic issues in the coming years, including education, the labour market, healthcare, social security and pension provisions. Relatively low fertility levels, combined with extended longevity have led to the demographic ageing of the EU-27 population, with older generations accounting for an increasing proportion of the total population, in contrast to the diminishing share of those of a working age.

Rural, agricultural areas of Greece, France, Italy and Portugal, as well as eastern regions of Germany (such as Chemnitz, Dresden or Sachsen-Anhalt) tended to record the highest old-age dependency ratios (the number of elderly persons aged 65 and over relative to the number of persons of working age (15 to 64)). The relatively high proportion of elderly persons is often a reflection of younger age groups finding it

necessary to leave the region in their quest to find work. The highest old-age dependency ratio was recorded in Liguria (Italy) at 43.2 % in 2008, while five other Italian regions Umbria, Toscana, Friuli-Venezia Giulia, Emilia-Romagna and Piemonte each reported rates of at least 35 %.

At the other end of the range, all 25 Turkish regions reported very low old-age dependency ratios – the lowest (5.9 %) was recorded for Van (eastern Turkey). There were also relatively low old-age dependency ratios recorded in Southern and Eastern Ireland, the French overseas departments of Guyane and Réunion, Flevoland (the Netherlands), the Polish regions of Lubuskie and Warmińsko-Mazurskie, Východné Slovensko (Slovakia), Inner London (United Kingdom) and the former Yugoslav Republic of Macedonia. These ratios may be associated with a range of influences, such as: relatively high fertility rates (boosting the share of the young in the total population); relatively low life expectancy (resulting in fewer persons aged 65 and over), or inward migratory patterns (whereby mainly younger persons move to a region in search of work, thereby lowering the relative share of older generations).

Labour market trends across regions

The Lisbon Strategy set an objective of attaining an overall employment rate of 70 % by 2010; the EU-27 rate stood at 65.9 % in 2008. A regional breakdown of this headline figure shows that 94 of the 271 NUTS level 2 regions (for which data are available) reported employment rates in excess of the Lisbon target. The range between the highest and the lowest regional employment rates in 2008 was considerable, as the high of 82.5 % in Åland (Finland) was almost double the figure recorded for Campania (Italy), 42.5 %.

A cluster of regions in southern Germany and Austria recorded relatively high employment rates, as did a number of northern European regions in Denmark, the Netherlands, Finland, Sweden and the United Kingdom. In contrast, generally low regional employment rates were often registered in many parts of southern Spain and southern Italy, as well as in eastern Europe. More specifically, there were 12 regions in the EU-27 that reported employment rates below the threshold of 50 % in 2008; five in southern Italy, the four French overseas departments, two in eastern Hungary, and the autonomous region of Melilla (Spain).

The Lisbon Strategy also set an objective for attaining a 50 % old-age (those aged 55 to 64 years) employment rate by 2010; the overall EU-27 rate stood at 45.6 % in 2008 (55.0 % for men and 36.9 % for women). The differences between regions and between men and women may often result from socio-economic and cultural forces – for example, the propensity of older generations to help look after children in their extended family, or differences in attitudes towards older persons continuing to work. Scandinavian countries, the Baltic Member States, the Netherlands and the United Kingdom recorded some of the highest employment rates among older workers. At the other end of the range, Belgium, France, Italy, Luxembourg, Hungary, Malta, Poland and Slovenia recorded some of the lowest rates.

The old-age employment rate ranged from a high of 75.9 % in Åland (Finland) to a low of 21.9 % in Dél-Dunántúl (Hungary)

in 2008. Some 113 of the 271 regions for which data are available within the EU-27 recorded an old-age employment rate that was in excess of the Lisbon target of 50 %. Of these, there were 31 with an old-age employment rate of more than 60 %, four of which – Åland (Finland), Småland med öarna, Stockholm and Västsverige (all Sweden) – recorded rates in excess of 70 %.

In the EU-27, some 38 of the 271 NUTS level 2 regions for which data are available for 2008 recorded double-digit unemployment rates; these were mainly located in eastern regions of Germany, the south of Spain, the French overseas departments, the south of Italy, as well as several regions in Belgium, Hungary and Slovakia. In contrast, the lowest levels of unemployment were recorded across the Netherlands and Austria, in the north of Belgium, in and around Praha (the Czech Republic), in the north of Italy and in the south of the United Kingdom. Eight of the 20 regions that recorded the lowest unemployment rates (3.0 % or less) in 2008 were Dutch, while there were three regions each from Austria and the United Kingdom, two from the Czech Republic, and one each from Belgium, Bulgaria, Italy and Finland.

Regional disparities within and between countries

The majority of funds for economic and social cohesion policy are attributed to those regions where GDP per inhabitant lies below the threshold of 75 % of the Community average. Twelve of the Member States (Belgium, Denmark, Germany, Ireland, Cyprus, Luxembourg, Malta, the Netherlands, Austria, Finland, Sweden and the United Kingdom) reported that none of their regions qualified for such funds, on the basis of the latest GDP per inhabitant figures for 2006.

The success of any regional policies designed to further economic and social cohesion can be analysed through studying regional disparities over time – for example, by measuring the convergence of regional GDP per inhabitant, regional employment rates or regional unemployment rates.

The dispersion of GDP per inhabitant across NUTS level 2 regions can be calculated in terms of a coefficient. When considering all EU-27 regions, this coefficient fell in successive years from 31.8 % in 2001 to 28.9 % by 2006. However, a number of Member States reported that disparities in regional GDP per inhabitant increased; this was notably the case between 2001 and 2006 in Bulgaria, Greece, Hungary, Romania and Slovakia.

The dispersion of employment rates (measured using the coefficient of variation) across NUTS level 2 regions stood at 11.1 % for the EU-27 in 2007. This marked a decrease of 1.8 percentage points when compared with the same ratio for 2003, having posted no change in the previous four-year period (1999 to 2003). Over the four-year period 2003 to 2007, there was a reduction in the regional dispersion of employment rates across the Czech Republic, Germany, Spain, Poland and Sweden (by more than 1 percentage point), while there was an increase of more than 1 percentage point across Hungarian and Romanian regions.

The largest disparities in employment rates in 2007 were observed among Italian and Hungarian regions. In the former, employment rates reached a high of 70.5 % for the northern Provincia Autonoma of Bolzano/Bozen, while the lowest rate was recorded for the southern region of Campania (42.5 %). Employment rates across the Netherlands and Sweden were, in contrast, characterised by a high degree of uniformity; maximum and minimum rates were 79.8 % for Utrecht and 73.0 % for Groningen among Dutch regions, and 77.4 % for Småland med öarna and 72.1 % for Övre Norrland among Swedish regions.

An alternative measure for measuring the performance of different regions within the same Member State is to compare regional employment rates with the national average. 'Underperformance' may be identified by comparing regional values against a particular threshold (for example, 90% of the national figure). Using this measure, at NUTS level 2, there were 26 underperforming regions out of a total of 265 for which data are available for 2008. Of these, France and Italy each accounted for six regions, Spain for five, Hungary for three, Belgium and the United Kingdom for two, and Germany and Finland for one region.

The dispersion of regional unemployment rates across NUTS level 2 regions in the EU-27 was 44.1% in 2007. As such, there was some degree of convergence when compared with 2003, as this ratio had previously stood at 58.7 %. Female unemployment rates converged at a more rapid pace than male unemployment rates during the period under consideration, although there was generally a higher degree of dispersion among female unemployment rates. During the period 2003 to 2007, regional unemployment rates in Italy and Portugal converged; in contrast, the dispersion of unemployment rates between the regions of Bulgaria, Belgium, Romania and Slovakia widened considerably.

The highest dispersion of unemployment rates in 2007 was observed across the regions of Belgium and Italy (despite the Italian figure being reduced considerably when compared with 2003). In Belgium, the unemployment rate peaked in Bruxelles/Brussels at 15.9 % in 2008, which was almost six times as high as the rate for the Prov. West-Vlaanderen (2.7 %). In a similar vein, the difference between the highest and lowest regional unemployment rates in Italy was also close to a factor of 6:1 between Sicilia (13.8 %) and the Provincia Autonoma of Bolzano/Bozen (2.4 %).

As for the employment rate, a similar measure exists for analysing 'underperformance' on the basis of unemployment figures, whereby those regions with unemployment rates that are more than 150 % of the national average are deemed to be underperforming. Using this criteria for NUTS level 2 in 2008, there were 33 out of a total of 264 regions for which data are available that were identified as underperforming, including: seven regions in Germany, six in Italy, four in Spain and in France, two in Belgium, Bulgaria, the Czech Republic, Hungary and the United Kingdom, and one in Greece and Austria.

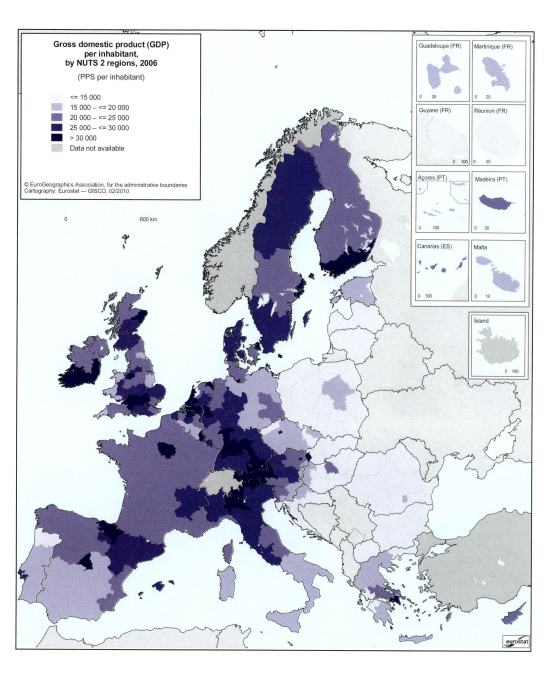

Gross domestic product (GDP)
per inhabitant,
by NUTS 2 regions, 2006

(PPS per inhabitant)

- <= 15 000
- 15 000 – <= 20 000
- 20 000 – <= 25 000
- 25 000 – <= 30 000
- > 30 000
- Data not available

© EuroGeographics Association, for the administrative boundaries
Cartography: Eurostat — GISCO, 02/2010

0   600 km

Guadeloupe (FR)   Martinique (FR)

0   25   0   20

Guyane (FR)   Réunion (FR)

0   100   0   20

Açores (PT)   Madeira (PT)

0   100   0   20

Canarias (ES)   Malta

0   100   0   10

Ísland

0   100

Source: Eurostat (tgs00005)

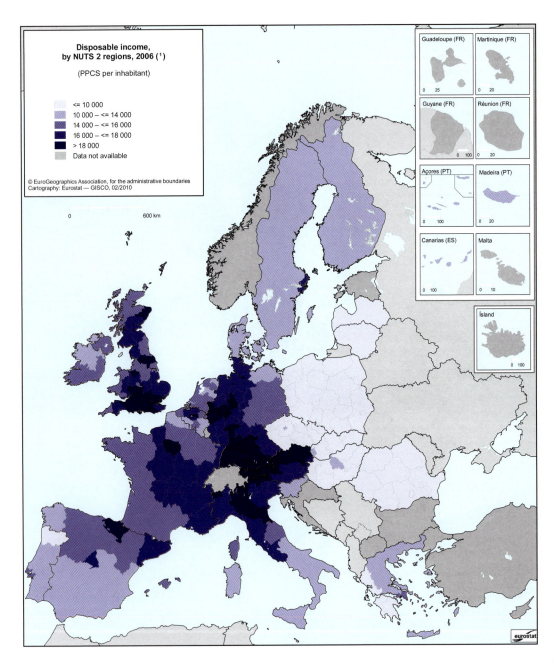

**Disposable income,
by NUTS 2 regions, 2006 (¹)**

(PPCS per inhabitant)

- <= 10 000
- 10 000 – <= 14 000
- 14 000 – <= 16 000
- 16 000 – <= 18 000
- > 18 000
- Data not available

© EuroGeographics Association, for the administrative boundaries
Cartography: Eurostat — GISCO, 02/2010

0   600 km

Guadeloupe (FR)   Martinique (FR)
0   25   0   20

Guyane (FR)   Réunion (FR)
0   100   0   20

Açores (PT)   Madeira (PT)
0   100   0   20

Canarias (ES)   Malta
0   100   0   10

Ísland
0   100

eurostat

(¹) Denmark, national level.

Source: Eurostat (tgs00026)

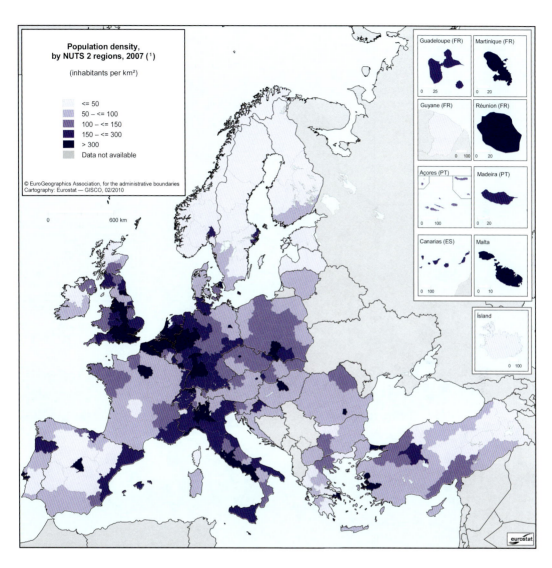

**Population density,
by NUTS 2 regions, 2007 (¹)**

(inhabitants per km²)

- <= 50
- 50 – <= 100
- 100 – <= 150
- 150 – <= 300
- > 300
- Data not available

© EuroGeographics Association, for the administrative boundaries
Cartography: Eurostat — GISCO, 02/2010

0   600 km

Guadeloupe (FR)   Martinique (FR)

0   25   0   20

Guyane (FR)   Réunion (FR)

0   100   0   20

Açores (PT)   Madeira (PT)

0   100   0   20

Canarias (ES)   Malta

0   100   0   10

Ísland

0   100

(¹) Spain, France, Cyprus, Luxembourg, Malta, Austria, Poland, Liechtenstein and Norway, 2006.

Source: Eurostat (tgs00024)

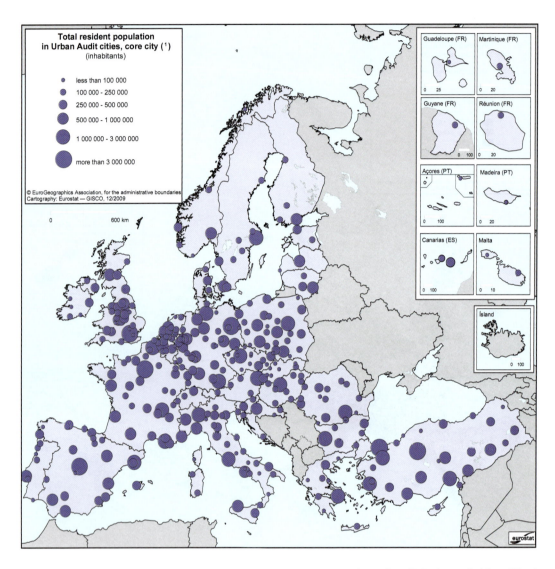

Total resident population in Urban Audit cities, core city (¹)
(inhabitants)

- less than 100 000
- 100 000 - 250 000
- 250 000 - 500 000
- 500 000 - 1 000 000
- 1 000 000 - 3 000 000
- more than 3 000 000

© EuroGeographics Association, for the administrative boundaries
Cartography: Eurostat — GISCO, 12/2009

0   600 km

Guadeloupe (FR)   Martinique (FR)
0   25   0   20

Guyane (FR)   Réunion (FR)
0   100   0   20

Açores (PT)   Madeira (PT)
0   100   0   20

Canarias (ES)   Malta
0   100   0   10

Ísland
0   100

(¹) The data is based on the most recent reference year. For København, Athina, Paris, Lisboa and Stockholm the so called "kernel" level data has been used.

Source: Eurostat (tgs00013)

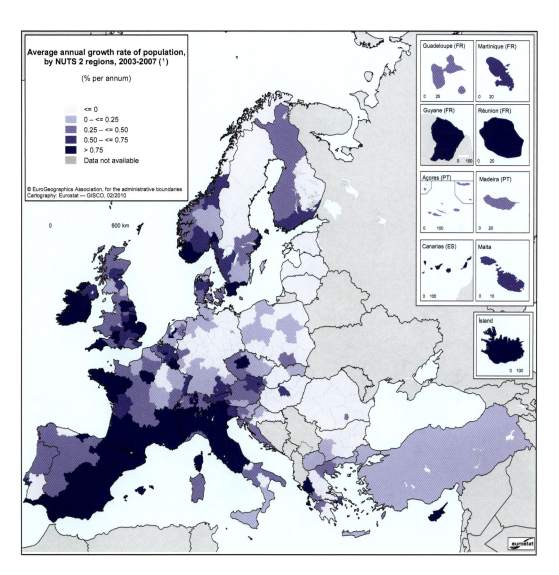

Average annual growth rate of population, by NUTS 2 regions, 2003-2007 (¹)

(% per annum)

- <= 0
- 0 – <= 0.25
- 0.25 – <= 0.50
- 0.50 – <= 0.75
- > 0.75
- Data not available

© EuroGeographics Association, for the administrative boundaries
Cartography: Eurostat — GISCO, 02/2010

0   600 km

Guadeloupe (FR)   Martinique (FR)
0   25   0   20

Guyane (FR)   Réunion (FR)
0   100   0   20

Açores (PT)   Madeira (PT)
0   100   0   20

Canarias (ES)   Malta
0   100   0   10

Ísland
0   100

eurostat

(¹) Denmark, 2006-2007; France, the United Kingdom, Liechtenstein and Norway, 2002-2006; Turkey, national level.

Source: Eurostat (tgs00001)

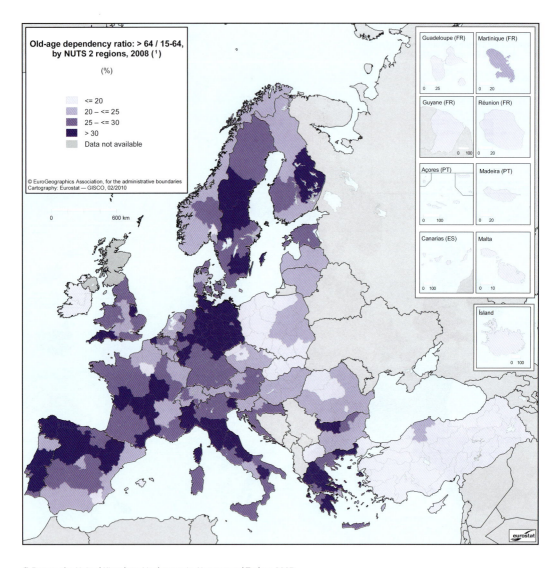

Old-age dependency ratio: > 64 / 15-64,
by NUTS 2 regions, 2008 (¹)

(%)

<= 20
20 – <= 25
25 – <= 30
> 30
Data not available

© EuroGeographics Association, for the administrative boundaries
Cartography: Eurostat — GISCO, 02/2010

0   600 km

Guadeloupe (FR)   Martinique (FR)

Guyane (FR)   Réunion (FR)

Açores (PT)   Madeira (PT)

Canarias (ES)   Malta

Ísland

(¹) France, the United Kingdom, Liechtenstein, Norway and Turkey, 2007.

Source: Eurostat (reg_d2jan)

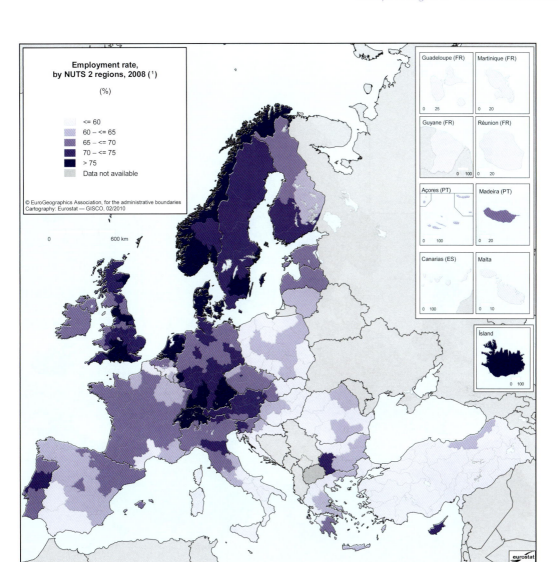

**Employment rate,
by NUTS 2 regions, 2008 (^{1})**

(%)

	<= 60
	60 – <= 65
	65 – <= 70
	70 – <= 75
	> 75
	Data not available

© EuroGeographics Association, for the administrative boundaries
Cartography: Eurostat — GISCO, 02/2010

0   600 km

Guadeloupe (FR)   Martinique (FR)

0   25   0   20

Guyane (FR)   Réunion (FR)

0   100   0   20

Açores (PT)   Madeira (PT)

0   100   0   20

Canarias (ES)   Malta

0   100   0   10

Ísland

0   100

eurostat

(^{1}) Croatia, Iceland and Switzerland, 2007.

Source: Eurostat (tgs00007)

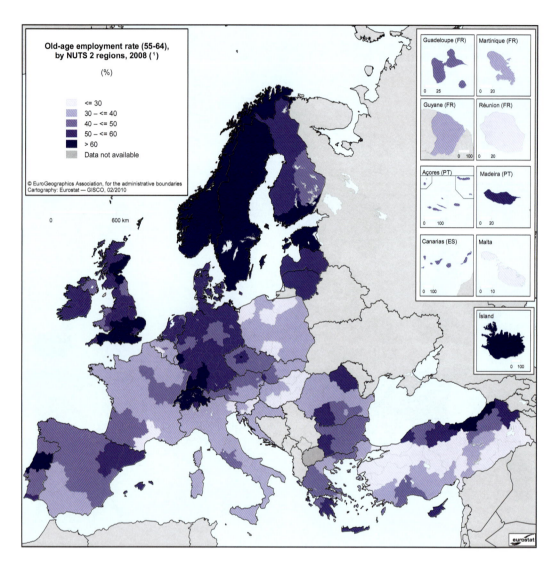

Old-age employment rate (55-64), by NUTS 2 regions, 2008 (¹)

(%)

- <= 30
- 30 – <= 40
- 40 – <= 50
- 50 – <= 60
- > 60
- Data not available

© EuroGeographics Association, for the administrative boundaries
Cartography: Eurostat — GISCO, 02/2010

0   600 km

Guadeloupe (FR)   0 25

Martinique (FR)   0 20

Guyane (FR)   0 100

Réunion (FR)   0 20

Açores (PT)   0 100

Madeira (PT)   0 20

Canarias (ES)   0 100

Malta   0 10

Ísland   0 100

(¹) Croatia, Iceland and Switzerland, 2007.

Source: Eurostat (tgs00054)

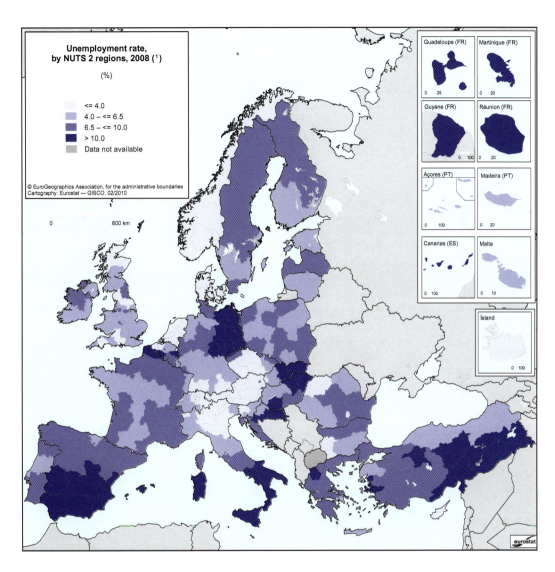

**Unemployment rate,
by NUTS 2 regions, 2008 (¹)**

(%)

	<= 4.0
	4.0 – <= 6.5
	6.5 – <= 10.0
	> 10.0
	Data not available

© EuroGeographics Association, for the administrative boundaries
Cartography: Eurostat — GISCO, 02/2010

0   600 km

Guadeloupe (FR)   Martinique (FR)
0   25   0   20

Guyane (FR)   Réunion (FR)
0   100   0   20

Açores (PT)   Madeira (PT)
0   100   0   20

Canarias (ES)   Malta
0   100   0   10

Ísland
0   100

(¹) Croatia, Iceland and Switzerland, 2007.

Source: Eurostat (tgs00010)

Table 13.1: Dispersion of regional gross domestic product (GDP) per inhabitant (^{1})
(%)

	1996	1997	1998	1999	2000	2001	2002	2003	2004	2005	2006
EU-27	:	:	:	:	:	31.8	30.9	30.3	30.0	29.5	28.9
Belgium	25.3	25.2	24.3	25.2	25.3	25.4	25.4	25.0	25.2	25.6	25.5
Bulgaria	18.0	18.6	17.7	21.3	17.4	20.3	23.7	23.7	26.0	26.4	31.0
Czech Republic	16.6	18.2	20.9	22.1	22.7	24.3	24.8	24.9	24.2	25.1	25.4
Denmark	:	:	:	:	:	:	:	:	14.4	16.3	15.7
Germany	17.0	17.0	17.2	17.5	17.6	17.9	17.9	17.8	17.6	17.3	17.3
Estonia	-	-	-	-	-	-	-	-	-	-	-
Ireland	-	-	-	-	-	-	-	-	-	-	-
Greece	:	:	:	:	20.6	21.8	24.2	24.5	26.2	25.6	26.8
Spain	19.1	19.7	20.1	20.5	20.5	20.3	19.8	19.1	18.8	18.4	18.4
France	19.9	18.9	19.6	20.7	20.9	20.5	20.6	20.9	19.9	20.3	20.4
Italy	24.8	24.4	24.5	24.1	:	24.3	24.2	24.3	24.2	23.8	23.4
Cyprus	-	-	-	-	-	-	-	-	-	-	-
Latvia	-	-	-	-	-	-	-	-	-	-	-
Lithuania	-	-	-	-	-	-	-	-	-	-	-
Luxembourg	-	-	-	-	-	-	-	-	-	-	-
Hungary	27.4	28.7	29.2	32.1	32.6	33.0	35.4	34.2	33.4	35.7	37.6
Malta	-	-	-	-	-	-	-	-	-	-	-
Netherlands	10.3	10.5	10.7	10.8	10.9	10.9	11.2	11.0	11.3	11.9	11.7
Austria	19.3	18.5	18.5	18.5	18.1	18.4	18.7	18.0	16.8	16.9	16.1
Poland	15.4	15.8	16.1	17.7	17.6	18.2	18.1	18.3	18.7	19.4	19.5
Portugal	19.8	20.8	23.0	21.3	22.8	22.1	23.0	22.8	23.0	23.3	22.6
Romania	:	:	:	:	23.8	24.7	23.3	23.7	23.0	27.0	27.5
Slovenia	-	-	-	-	-	-	-	-	-	-	-
Slovakia	26.0	26.5	26.1	26.0	26.5	27.3	28.3	27.8	28.3	31.7	30.1
Finland	15.1	15.5	17.2	17.8	17.6	17.5	16.8	15.4	15.7	15.4	15.5
Sweden	12.6	14.4	15.4	16.2	15.7	14.8	15.3	14.8	15.6	16.4	15.3
United Kingdom	17.6	18.8	19.6	20.1	21.1	21.3	22.0	21.9	22.1	22.4	22.4
Croatia	:	:	:	:	:	17.8	18.0	18.3	17.6	19.2	19.1

(^{1}) Dispersion of regional GDP at NUTS 2 level; for a detailed definition of the indicator please refer to the explanatory text on the Eurostat website.

Source: Eurostat (reg_e0digdp)

Table 13.2: Dispersion of regional employment rates (¹)
(coefficient of variation)

	Total			Male			Female		
	1999	**2003**	**2007**	**1999**	**2003**	**2007**	**1999**	**2003**	**2007**
EU-27	12.9	12.9	11.1	9.1	10.7	8.8	20.4	18.5	15.8
Belgium	8.0	7.7	8.6	6.6	6.9	6.9	10.5	9.1	10.7
Bulgaria	:	6.6	7.1	:	6.0	6.0	:	8.1	9.0
Czech Republic	5.6	5.8	4.6	4.3	4.9	3.5	7.8	7.4	6.4
Denmark	:	:	:	:	:	:	:	:	:
Germany	5.4	5.9	4.8	5.3	6.9	5.6	6.9	5.7	4.8
Estonia	-	-	-	-	-	-	-	-	-
Ireland	-	-	-	-	-	-	-	-	-
Greece	5.2	3.2	3.5	3.4	2.1	2.6	8.9	6.5	7.0
Spain	10.8	9.0	7.5	7.8	6.1	4.9	17.6	14.5	11.8
France	7.1	7.2	6.6	5.0	6.1	5.8	10.0	9.0	7.8
Italy	17.4	17.0	16.3	9.9	9.1	9.6	30.2	29.7	26.4
Cyprus	-	-	-	-	-	-	-	-	-
Latvia	-	-	-	-	-	-	-	-	-
Lithuania	-	-	-	-	-	-	-	-	-
Luxembourg	-	-	-	-	-	-	-	-	-
Hungary	9.1	8.5	9.7	8.8	8.1	9.3	10.0	9.2	10.3
Malta	-	-	-	-	-	-	-	-	-
Netherlands	2.3	2.3	2.2	2.5	2.0	2.0	3.4	3.2	2.7
Austria	2.3	3.0	3.8	2.2	3.6	4.1	4.2	3.8	3.4
Poland	4.8	7.2	4.5	4.1	6.4	3.4	6.5	8.7	6.7
Portugal	3.6	3.9	3.3	3.0	3.2	3.7	7.3	6.3	5.5
Romania	4.2	3.5	4.6	3.3	2.6	4.3	5.8	6.1	7.8
Slovenia	-	-	-	-	-	-	-	-	-
Slovakia	8.1	7.6	8.3	6.9	6.7	6.5	10.1	9.0	10.9
Finland	6.7	6.1	5.6	6.5	5.7	5.6	7.4	6.7	5.9
Sweden	4.8	4.3	2.4	5.2	4.1	1.9	5.6	4.8	2.9
United Kingdom	7.5	6.1	5.4	7.8	5.8	5.0	7.3	6.7	6.3
Croatia	:	:	7.5	:	:	4.8	:	:	11.4
Norway	2.4	1.6	2.5	1.9	1.8	2.2	3.0	2.3	3.1

(¹) Dispersion of regional employment rates for the age group 15-64 at NUTS 2 level.

Source: Eurostat (tsisc050)

Table 13.3: Dispersion of regional unemployment rates (¹)
(coefficient of variation)

	Total			Male			Female		
	1999	2003	2007	1999	2003	2007	1999	2003	2007
EU-27	54.6	58.7	44.1	51.6	59.6	47.3	66.0	64.4	46.6
Belgium	51.7	43.5	59.2	56.9	48.0	64.6	49.6	39.2	56.0
Bulgaria	:	22.0	39.1	:	17.0	39.6	:	28.8	41.0
Czech Republic	33.1	41.9	41.9	34.6	44.6	43.2	33.0	40.5	42.0
Denmark	:	:	:	:	:	:	:	:	:
Germany	42.0	45.8	43.5	40.7	44.7	46.2	46.2	49.2	41.7
Estonia	-	-	-	-	-	-	-	-	-
Ireland	-	-	-	-	-	-	-	-	-
Greece	13.4	15.9	15.2	15.8	16.1	15.0	15.5	18.3	19.0
Spain	35.9	32.3	30.6	41.7	33.7	29.1	33.6	33.9	34.3
France	24.1	37.1	35.2	28.0	42.9	38.4	23.9	34.6	33.0
Italy	68.9	78.0	56.7	77.3	83.2	62.7	66.8	79.1	56.2
Cyprus	-	-	-	-	-	-	-	-	-
Latvia	-	-	-	-	-	-	-	-	-
Lithuania	-	-	-	-	-	-	-	-	-
Luxembourg	-	-	-	-	-	-	-	-	-
Hungary	34.8	32.6	39.4	36.2	35.0	44.3	32.7	30.3	34.2
Malta	-	-	-	-	-	-	-	-	-
Netherlands	30.7	10.7	16.9	43.3	10.8	17.6	33.5	13.3	18.9
Austria	28.5	42.3	45.0	42.9	52.0	59.2	14.4	32.3	32.6
Poland	22.5	15.8	14.2	24.1	15.9	15.9	23.4	17.2	15.1
Portugal	31.0	29.6	20.3	37.9	33.7	30.4	32.6	27.9	20.5
Romania	13.0	13.9	27.7	13.4	13.7	24.8	14.2	15.6	32.2
Slovenia	-	-	-	-	-	-	-	-	-
Slovakia	27.4	26.7	38.0	30.1	28.5	39.1	24.7	24.8	38.4
Finland	23.8	22.0	25.8	25.2	20.4	24.6	25.6	24.9	28.3
Sweden	29.6	15.8	10.1	31.8	17.6	11.8	33.1	16.0	10.2
United Kingdom	33.9	30.5	24.8	39.3	34.2	28.7	29.1	27.5	24.3
Croatia	:	:	35.2	:	:	21.0	:	:	49.6
Norway	20.5	6.7	14.4	22.0	11.7	20.3	32.2	9.0	10.8

(¹) Dispersion of regional unemployment rates for the age group 15-74 at NUTS 2 level.

Source: Eurostat (reg_lmdur)

Annexes

NUTS (classification of territorial units for statistics)

European Union: NUTS 2 regions

Belgium

BE10	Région de Bruxelles-Capitale/ Brussels Hoofdstedelijk Gewest
BE21	Prov. Antwerpen
BE22	Prov. Limburg (B)
BE23	Prov. Oost-Vlaanderen
BE24	Prov. Vlaams-Brabant
BE25	Prov. West-Vlaanderen
BE31	Prov. Brabant Wallon
BE32	Prov. Hainaut
BE33	Prov. Liège
BE34	Prov. Luxembourg (B)
BE35	Prov. Namur

Bulgaria

BG31	Severozapaden
BG32	Severen tsentralen
BG33	Severoiztochen
BG34	Yugoiztochen
BG41	Yugozapaden
BG42	Yuzhen tsentralen

Czech Republic

CZ01	Praha
CZ02	Strední Cechy
CZ03	Jihozápad
CZ04	Severozápad
CZ05	Severovýchod
CZ06	Jihovýchod
CZ07	Strední Morava
CZ08	Moravskoslezsko

Denmark

DK01	Hovedstaden
DK02	Sjælland
DK03	Syddanmark
DK04	Midtjylland
DK05	Nordjylland

Germany

DE11	Stuttgart
DE12	Karlsruhe
DE13	Freiburg
DE14	Tübingen
DE21	Oberbayern
DE22	Niederbayern
DE23	Oberpfalz
DE24	Oberfranken
DE25	Mittelfranken
DE26	Unterfranken
DE27	Schwaben
DE30	Berlin
DE41	Brandenburg – Nordost
DE42	Brandenburg – Südwest
DE50	Bremen
DE60	Hamburg
DE71	Darmstadt
DE72	Gießen
DE73	Kassel
DE80	Mecklenburg-Vorpommern
DE91	Braunschweig
DE92	Hannover
DE93	Lüneburg
DE94	Weser-Ems
DEA1	Düsseldorf
DEA2	Köln
DEA3	Münster
DEA4	Detmold
DEA5	Arnsberg
DEB1	Koblenz
DEB2	Trier
DEB3	Rheinhessen-Pfalz
DEC0	Saarland
DED1	Chemnitz

DED2	Dresden		ES61	Andalucía
DED3	Leipzig		ES62	Región de Murcia
DEE0	Sachsen-Anhalt		ES63	Ciudad Autónoma de Ceuta
DEF0	Schleswig-Holstein		ES64	Ciudad Autónoma de Melilla
DEG0	Thüringen		ES70	Canarias

Estonia

EE00   Eesti

Ireland

IE01   Border, Midland and Western
IE02   Southern and Eastern

Greece

GR11   Anatoliki Makedonia, Thraki
GR12   Kentriki Makedonia
GR13   Dytiki Makedonia
GR14   Thessalia
GR21   Ipeiros
GR22   Ionia Nisia
GR23   Dytiki Ellada
GR24   Sterea Ellada
GR25   Peloponnisos
GR30   Attiki
GR41   Voreio Aigaio
GR42   Notio Aigaio
GR43   Kriti

Spain

ES11   Galicia
ES12   Principado de Asturias
ES13   Cantabria
ES21   País Vasco
ES22   Comunidad Foral de Navarra
ES23   La Rioja
ES24   Aragón
ES30   Comunidad de Madrid
ES41   Castilla y León
ES42   Castilla-La Mancha
ES43   Extremadura
ES51   Cataluña
ES52   Comunidad Valenciana
ES53   Illes Balears

France

FR10   Île-de-France
FR21   Champagne-Ardenne
FR22   Picardie
FR23   Haute-Normandie
FR24   Centre
FR25   Basse-Normandie
FR26   Bourgogne
FR30   Nord – Pas-de-Calais
FR41   Lorraine
FR42   Alsace
FR43   Franche-Comté
FR51   Pays de la Loire
FR52   Bretagne
FR53   Poitou-Charentes
FR61   Aquitaine
FR62   Midi-Pyrénées
FR63   Limousin
FR71   Rhône-Alpes
FR72   Auvergne
FR81   Languedoc-Roussillon
FR82   Provence-Alpes-Côte d'Azur
FR83   Corse
FR91   Guadeloupe
FR92   Martinique
FR93   Guyane
FR94   Réunion

Italy

ITC1   Piemonte
ITC2   Valle d'Aosta/Vallée d'Aoste
ITC3   Liguria
ITC4   Lombardia
ITD1   Provincia Autonoma Bolzano/
        Bozen
ITD2   Provincia Autonoma Trento
ITD3   Veneto

ITD4	Friuli-Venezia Giulia
ITD5	Emilia-Romagna
ITE1	Toscana
ITE2	Umbria
ITE3	Marche
ITE4	Lazio
ITF1	Abruzzo
ITF2	Molise
ITF3	Campania
ITF4	Puglia
ITF5	Basilicata
ITF6	Calabria
ITG1	Sicilia
ITG2	Sardegna

Cyprus

CY00	Kypros/Kibris

Latvia

LV00	Latvija

Lithuania

LT00	Lietuva

Luxembourg

LU00	Luxembourg (Grand-Duché)

Hungary

HU10	Közép-Magyarország
HU21	Közép-Dunántúl
HU22	Nyugat-Dunántúl
HU23	Dél-Dunántúl
HU31	Észak-Magyarország
HU32	Észak-Alföld
HU33	Dél-Alföld

Malta

MT00	Malta

Netherlands

NL11	Groningen
NL12	Friesland (NL)

NL13	Drenthe
NL21	Overijssel
NL22	Gelderland
NL23	Flevoland
NL31	Utrecht
NL32	Noord-Holland
NL33	Zuid-Holland
NL34	Zeeland
NL41	Noord-Brabant
NL42	Limburg (NL)

Austria

AT11	Burgenland (A)
AT12	Niederösterreich
AT13	Wien
AT21	Kärnten
AT22	Steiermark
AT31	Oberösterreich
AT32	Salzburg
AT33	Tirol
AT34	Vorarlberg

Poland

PL11	Łódzkie
PL12	Mazowieckie
PL21	Małopolskie
PL22	Śląskie
PL31	Lubelskie
PL32	Podkarpackie
PL33	Świętokrzyskie
PL34	Podlaskie
PL41	Wielkopolskie
PL42	Zachodniopomorskie
PL43	Lubuskie
PL51	Dolnośląskie
PL52	Opolskie
PL61	Kujawsko-Pomorskie
PL62	Warmińsko-Mazurskie
PL63	Pomorskie

Portugal

PT11	Norte
PT15	Algarve

PT16   Centro (P)
PT17   Lisboa
PT18   Alentejo
PT20   Região Autónoma dos Açores
PT30   Região Autónoma da Madeira

Romania

RO11   Nord-Vest
RO12   Centru
RO21   Nord-Est
RO22   Sud-Est
RO31   Sud – Muntenia
RO32   Bucureşti – Ilfov
RO41   Sud-Vest Oltenia
RO42   Vest

Slovenia

SI01   Vzhodna Slovenija
SI02   Zahodna Slovenija

Slovakia

SK01   Bratislavský kraj
SK02   Západné Slovensko
SK03   Stredné Slovensko
SK04   Východné Slovensko

Finland

FI13   Itä-Suomi
FI18   Etelä-Suomi
FI19   Länsi-Suomi
FI1A   Pohjois-Suomi
FI20   Åland

Sweden

SE11   Stockholm
SE12   Östra Mellansverige
SE21   Småland med öarna
SE22   Sydsverige
SE23   Västsverige
SE31   Norra Mellansverige
SE32   Mellersta Norrland
SE33   Övre Norrland

United Kingdom

UKC1   Tees Valley and Durham
UKC2   Northumberland and Tyne and Wear
UKD1   Cumbria
UKD2   Cheshire
UKD3   Greater Manchester
UKD4   Lancashire
UKD5   Merseyside
UKE1   East Yorkshire and Northern Lincolnshire
UKE2   North Yorkshire
UKE3   South Yorkshire
UKE4   West Yorkshire
UKF1   Derbyshire and Nottinghamshire
UKF2   Leicestershire, Rutland and Northamptonshire
UKF3   Lincolnshire
UKG1   Herefordshire, Worcestershire and Warwickshire
UKG2   Shropshire and Staffordshire
UKG3   West Midlands
UKH1   East Anglia
UKH2   Bedfordshire and Hertfordshire
UKH3   Essex
UKI1   Inner London
UKI2   Outer London
UKJ1   Berkshire, Buckinghamshire and Oxfordshire
UKJ2   Surrey, East and West Sussex
UKJ3   Hampshire and Isle of Wight
UKJ4   Kent
UKK1   Gloucestershire, Wiltshire and Bristol/Bath area
UKK2   Dorset and Somerset
UKK3   Cornwall and Isles of Scilly
UKK4   Devon
UKL1   West Wales and the Valleys
UKL2   East Wales
UKM2   Eastern Scotland
UKM3   South Western Scotland

UKM5	North Eastern Scotland
UKM6	Highlands and Islands
UKN0	Northern Ireland

Candidate countries: statistical regions at level 2

Croatia

HR01	Sjeverozapadna Hrvatska
HR02	Središnja i Istocna (Panonska) Hrvatska
HR03	Jadranska Hrvatska

The former Yugoslav Republic of Macedonia

MK00	Poranešna jugoslovenska Republika Makedonija

Turkey

TR10	Istanbul
TR21	Tekirdağ
TR22	Balikesir
TR31	Izmir
TR32	Aydin
TR33	Manisa
TR41	Bursa
TR42	Kocaeli
TR51	Ankara
TR52	Konya
TR61	Antalya
TR62	Adana
TR63	Hatay
TR71	Kirikkale
TR72	Kayseri
TR81	Zonguldak
TR82	Kastamonu
TR83	Samsun
TR90	Trabzon
TRA1	Erzurum
TRA2	Ağri
TRB1	Malatya
TRB2	Van
TRC1	Gaziantep
TRC2	Şanliurfa
TRC3	Mardin

EFTA countries: statistical regions at level 2

Iceland

IS00	Ísland

Liechtenstein

LI00	Liechtenstein

Norway

NO01	Oslo og Akershus
NO02	Hedmark og Oppland
NO03	Sør-Østlandet
NO04	Agder og Rogaland
NO05	Vestlandet
NO06	Trøndelag
NO07	Nord-Norge

Switzerland

CH01	Région lémanique
CH02	Espace Mittelland
CH03	Nordwestschweiz
CH04	Zürich
CH05	Ostschweiz
CH06	Zentralschweiz
CH07	Ticino

A full listing of the classification is accessible on the Eurostat website (http://ec.europa.eu/eurostat/ramon/nuts/codelist_en.cfm?list=nuts).

NACE Rev. 1.1 (classification of economic activities in the European Community)

A   Agriculture, hunting and forestry
B   Fishing
C   Mining and quarrying
D   Manufacturing
E   Electricity, gas and water supply
F   Construction
G   Wholesale and retail trade; repair of motor vehicles, motorcycles and personal and household goods
H   Hotels and restaurants
I   Transport, storage and communication
J   Financial intermediation
K   Real estate, renting and business activities
L   Public administration and defence; compulsory social security
M   Education
N   Health and social work
O   Other community, social and personal service activities
P   Activities of households
Q   Extra-territorial organisations and bodies

A full listing of the NACE Rev. 1.1 classification is accessible on the Eurostat website (http://ec.europa.eu/eurostat/ramon/nomenclatures/index.cfm?TargetUrl=ACT_OTH_BUILD_TREE&StrNom=NACE_1_1&StrLanguageCode=EN).

NACE Rev. 2 (classification of economic activities in the European Community)

A   Agriculture, forestry and fishing
B   Mining and quarrying
C   Manufacturing
D   Electricity, gas, steam and air conditioning supply
E   Water supply; sewerage, waste management and remediation activities
F   Construction
G   Wholesale and retail trade; repair of motor vehicles and motorcycles
H   Transportation and storage
I   Accommodation and food service activities
J   Information and communication
K   Financial and insurance activities
L   Real estate activities
M   Professional, scientific and technical activities
N   Administrative and support service activities
O   Public administration and defence; compulsory social security
P   Education
Q   Human health and social work activities
R   Arts, entertainment and recreation
S   Other service activities
T   Activities of households as employers; undifferentiated goods- and services-producing activities of households for own use
U   Activities of extraterritorial organisations and bodies

A full listing of the NACE Rev. 2 classification is accessible on the Eurostat website (http://ec.europa.eu/eurostat/ramon/nomenclatures/index.cfm?TargetUrl=LST_NOM_DTL&StrNom=NACE_REV2&StrLanguageCode=EN).

SITC Rev. 4 (standard international trade classification)

0   Food and live animals
1   Beverages and tobacco
2   Crude materials, inedible, except fuels
3   Mineral fuels, lubricants and related materials
4   Animal and vegetable oils, fats and waxes
5   Chemicals and related products, n.e.s.
6   Manufactured goods classified chiefly by material
7   Machinery and transport equipment
8   Miscellaneous manufactured articles
9   Commodities and transactions not classified elsewhere in the SITC

A full listing of the classification is accessible on the UN website (http://unstats.un.org/unsd/trade/sitcrev4.htm).

ISCED (international standard classification of education)

The classification comprises 25 fields of education (at two-digit level) which can be further refined into three-digit level. For the purpose of this publication only, the following nine broad groups (at one-digit level) and five detailed groups are distinguished:

0   General programmes
1   Education
2   Humanities and arts
3   Social sciences, business and law
4   Science
      42   Life sciences
      44   Physical sciences
      46   Mathematics and statistics
      48   Computing
5   Engineering, manufacturing and construction
      52   Engineering and engineering trades
6   Agriculture
7   Health and welfare
8   Services

Empirically, ISCED assumes that several criteria exist which can help allocate education programmes to levels of education. The following ISCED levels can be distinguished:

0   Pre-primary education
1   Primary education
2   Lower secondary education
3   Upper secondary education
4   Post-secondary non-tertiary education
5   Tertiary education (first stage)
6   Tertiary education (second stage)

A full listing of the classification and more details are accessible on the UNESCO website: http://www.uis.unesco.org/ev.php?ID=3813_201&ID2=DO_TOPIC.

Statistical symbols, abbreviations and acronyms

Statistical symbols

Statistical data are often accompanied by additional information in the form of statistical symbols (also called 'flags') to indicate missing information or some other meta-data. In this yearbook, the use of statistical symbols has been restricted to a minimum. The following symbols are included where necessary:

Italic Value is either a forecast, provisional or an estimate and is therefore likely to change

: Not available, confidential or unreliable value

– Not applicable or zero by default

0 Less than half the final digit shown and greater than real zero

Breaks in series are indicated in the footnotes provided with each table and graph.

In the case of the EU Member States, even when data are not available, these countries have been included in tables and graphs systematically (with appropriate footnotes for graphs indicating that data are not available, while in tables use has been made of the colon (:) to indicate that data are not available). For non-member countries outside the EU, when data are not available for a particular indicator the country has been removed from the table or graph in question.

Geographical aggregates

EU   European Union

EU-27   European Union of 27 Member States including Belgium, Bulgaria, the Czech Republic, Denmark, Germany, Estonia, Ireland, Greece, Spain, France, Italy, Cyprus, Latvia, Lithuania, Luxembourg, Hungary, Malta, the Netherlands, Austria, Poland, Portugal, Romania, Slovenia, Slovakia, Finland, Sweden and the United Kingdom. Note that unless otherwise stated, the EU aggregate in this publication refers to 27 countries, as if all 27 of these had been part of the EU in periods prior to 1 January 2007

EU-25   EU-27 other than Bulgaria and Romania (from 1 May 2004 to 31 December 2006)

EU-15   Belgium, Denmark, Germany, Ireland, Greece, Spain, France, Italy, Luxembourg, the Netherlands, Austria, Portugal, Finland, Sweden and the United Kingdom (from 1 January 1995 to 30 April 2004)

EU-12   EU-15 other than Austria, Finland and Sweden (from 1 January 1986 to 31 December 1994)

Euro area Note that unless otherwise stated, the euro area (EA) aggregate in this publication refers to 16 countries, as if all 16 of these had been part of the EA in periods prior to 1 January 2009

EA-16	Belgium, Germany, Ireland, Greece, Spain, France, Italy, Cyprus, Luxembourg, Malta, the Netherlands, Austria, Portugal, Slovenia, Slovakia and Finland
EA-15	EA-16 other than Slovakia
EA-13	EA-15 other than Cyprus and Malta
EA-12	EA-13 other than Slovenia

Other abbreviations and acronyms

AAU	assigned amount unit
ACP	African, Caribbean and Pacific states
AES	adult education survey
BMI	body mass index
BOD	biochemical oxygen demand
BoP	balance of payments
CAP	common agricultural policy
CBD	convention on biological diversity
CC	classification of types of construction
CDM	clean development mechanism
CFP	common fisheries policy
CIF	cost, insurance and freight
CIP	competitiveness and innovation framework programme
CIS	Community innovation survey
CLRTAP	convention on long-range transboundary air pollution
CMFB	committee on monetary, financial and balance of payments statistics

CMO	common market organisation
CMR	carcinogenic, mutagenic and reprotoxic (chemicals)
COD	chemical oxygen demand
COFOG	classification of the functions of government
COICOP	classification of individual consumption by purpose
CPA	classification of products by activity
CVT	continuing vocational training
CVTS	European survey of continuing vocational training in enterprises
DAC	development assistance committee
DMC	domestic material consumption
DSL	digital subscriber line
EAA	economic accounts for agriculture
EAP	environmental action programme
EBA	everything but arms
ECB	European Central Bank
ECHO	European Commission's Humanitarian Aid Office
ECHP	European Community household panel
EDP	excessive deficit procedure
EEA	1. European economic area 2. European Environment Agency
EEC	European Economic Community
EERP	European economic recovery plan
EES	European Employment Strategy
EFF	European Fisheries Fund

Annexes

EFTA	European free trade association	EUROFARM	a project for standardisation of methods for obtaining agricultural statistics; provides an overview of farm structure, agricultural holdings, wine growing and orchard fruit trees.
EIB	European Investment Bank		
EICP	European index of consumer prices		
EIT	European Institute of Innovation and Technology		
EITO	European Information Technology Observatory	EUROSTAT	statistical office of the European Union
EMAS	eco-management and audit scheme	FAO	Food and Agriculture Organisation (UN)
EMU	economic and monetary union	FOB	free on board
		FDI	foreign direct investment
EPER	European pollutant emission register	FP7	seventh framework programme
EPO	European Patent Office	FSS	farm structure survey
EPC	European patent convention	GBAORD	government budget appropriation or outlays on R & D
ERA	European research area		
ERDF	European Regional Development Fund	GDP	gross domestic product
		GERD	gross domestic expenditure on R & D
ERM	exchange rate mechanism		
ESA	system of national and regional accounts (ESA 95)	GFS	government finance statistics
ESAW	European statistics on accidents at work	GMES	global monitoring for environment and security
ESI	economic sentiment indicator	GNI	gross national income
		GSP	generalised system of preferences
ESF	European Social Fund		
ESS	European statistical system	GWP	global warming potential
ESSPROS	European system of integrated social protection statistics	HBS	household budget survey
		HDI	human development index
		HICP	harmonised index of consumer prices
ETS	1. external trade statistics 2. emissions trading system	HIS	health interview surveys
EU	European Union	HLY	healthy life years
EUEB	European eco-labelling board	HRST	human resources in science and technology
EU-SILC	European Union statistics on income and living conditions	ICD	international statistical classification of diseases and related health problems

ICHA	international classification for health accounts	NAFTA	North American free trade agreement (CA, MX, US)
ICT	information and communication technology	n.e.c.	not elsewhere classified
		n.e.s.	not elsewhere specified
IET	international emissions trading	NGL	natural gas liquid
ILO	International Labour Organisation	NGO	non-governmental organisation
		NMVOC	non-methane volatile organic compounds
IMF	International Monetary Fund	NPISH	non-profit institutions serving households
IPC	international patent classification	NUTS	hierarchical classification/nomenclature of territorial units for statistics (Eurostat) (NUTS 1, 2 and 3)
IPP	integrated product policy		
ISCED	international standard classification of education		
ISDN	integrated services digital network	ODA	official development assistance
IT	information technology		
IWG	inter-secretariat working group	OECD	Organisation for Economic Co-operation and Development
ITTO	international tropical timber organisation	OPEC	Organisation of Petroleum Exporting Countries
JI	joint implementation		
JFSQ	joint forest sector questionnaire	PCT	patent co-operation treaty
		PDA	personal digital assistant
JRC	Joint Research Centre	PECBMS	pan-European common bird monitoring scheme
JVR	job vacancy rate		
KIC	knowledge and innovation communities	PEEI	principal European economic indicator
LDCs	least developed countries	PES	public employment service
LFS	labour force survey	R & D	research and development
LLP	lifelong learning programme	REACH	(European Regulation on the) registration, evaluation, authorisation and restriction of chemicals
LMP	labour market policy		
MGDD	manual on government debt and deficit	RON	research octane number
MTO	medium-term budgetary objective	S & T	science and technology
		SBS	structural business statistics
MUICP	monetary union index of consumer prices	SDI	sustainable development indicator
NACE	statistical classification of economic activities within the European Community	SDS	Sustainable Development Strategy

SEIS	shared environmental information system	UIS	UNESCO institute for statistics
SEPA	single euro payments area	UNSC	United Nations statistical
SET	strategic energy technology		commission
SGP	stability and growth pact	UOE	United Nations/OECD/
SHA	system of health accounts		Eurostat
SII	summary innovation index	USPTO	United States patent and
SITC	standard international trade classification		trademark office
SME	small and medium-sized enterprise	UV-B	biologically harmful ultraviolet radiation
SMS	short message service	VAT	value added tax
SNA	system of national accounts (UN)	VET	vocational education and training
SPV	special purpose vehicle	WHO	World Health Organisation
STS	short-term (business) statistics	WTO	1. World Trade Organisation
TAC	total allowable catch		2. World Tourism
TEEB	the economics of ecosystems and biodiversity		Organisation

Units of measurement

UCITS	undertakings for collective investment in transferable securities	%	percent(age)
		AW	average worker
		AWU	annual work unit
UN	United Nations	BMI	body mass index
UNCAT	United Nations convention against torture and other forms of cruel or inhuman treatment	CHF	Swiss franc
		cm^3	cubic centimetre
		ESU	Economic size unit
		EUR	euro
		FTE	full-time equivalent
UNDP	United Nations development programme	GJ	gigajoule
		GRT	gross registered tonnage
UNECE	United Nations economic commission for Europe	GT	gross tonnage
		GWh	gigawatt-hour
UNEP	United Nations environment programme	Ha	hectare (1 ha = 10 000 square metres)
UNESCO	United Nations educational, scientific and cultural organisation	HC	head count
		JPY	Japanese yen
		kbit/s	kilobit per second
UNFCCC	United Nations framework convention on climate change	kg	kilogram
		kgoe	kilogram of oil equivalent
		km	kilometre
UNHCR	United Nations High Commissioner for refugees	km^2	square kilometre
		kW	kilowatt

kWh	kilowatt hour		PPP	purchasing power parity
l	litre		PPS	purchasing power standard
LSU	livestock unit		SDR	standard death rate
m	metre		t	tonne
mm	millimetre		t-km	tonne-kilometre
m³	cubic metre		toe	tonne of oil equivalent
MWh	megawatt-hour		TWh	terawatt hour
p/st	piece/unit		UAA	utilised agricultural area
p-km	passenger-kilometre		USD	United States dollar
PPCS	purchasing power consumption standard			

Subject index

A selection of Eurostat publications

Eurostat offers various types of publications on a wide range of statistical topics. Below there is a list of references for further reading, relating to some of Eurostat's most recent publications.

All publications are available in PDF format and can be downloaded free of charge from Eurostat's website at http://ec.europa.eu/eurostat. Moreover, the latest publications include a new feature – as access to on-line tables and databases is just one click away from the published table or graph, by means of hyperlinks that are inserted as part of each source.

Paper copies of publications can be ordered via the EU Bookshop at http://bookshop.europa.eu. Both websites allow searches to be made using the catalogue number (e.g.: KS-CD-09-001-EN-C) and offer guidance on how paper copies can be ordered.

News-oriented publications

Three collections are dedicated to the rapid release of key data: news releases, 'Statistics in focus' and 'Data in focus'. They are web-based publications that are freely available on the Eurostat website.

Statistical books

This collection contains publications which provide in-depth analysis, tables, graphs or maps for one or more statistical domains.

Eurostat regional yearbook 2009

Eurostat regional yearbook 2009 offers a wealth of information on life in the European regions in the 27 Member States of the European Union and in the candidate countries and EFTA countries. The texts are written by specialists in the different statistical domains and are accompanied by statistical maps, figures and tables on each subject. A broad set of regional data are presented on the following themes: population, European cities, the labour market, gross domestic product, household accounts, structural business statistics, the information society, science, technology and innovation, education, tourism and agriculture.

Available languages: DE, EN, FR
KS-HA-09-001-EN-C
Paper version: EUR 30

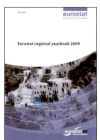

European economic statistics

This flagship publication on European economic statistics gives a wide-ranging overview of economic developments over recent years in the European Union, its Member States and selected partner countries. The publication covers key economic indicators available at Eurostat, including national accounts, government finances, balance of payments, foreign trade, prices, monetary and financial accounts, and the labour market. In addition, editorial and methodological sections provide commentary on topical issues and on the data presented. The statistical annex includes data covering the above mentioned areas.

Available language: EN
KS-31-09-001-EN-C
Paper version: EUR 20

Sustainable development in the European Union

The EU sustainable development strategy, launched by the European Council in Gothenburg in 2001 and renewed in June 2006, aims for the continuous improvement of quality of life for current and future generations. The Eurostat monitoring report, to be published every two years, underpins the European Commission's progress report on the implementation of the strategy. It provides an objective, statistical picture of progress, based on an EU set of sustainable development indicators. The data presented cover the period from 1990 to 2008 (or the latest year available).

Available language: EN
KS-78-09-865-EN-C
Paper version: EUR 30

European business

This publication gives a comprehensive picture of the structure, development and characteristics of European business and its different activities: from energy and the extractive industries to communications, information services and media. It presents the latest available statistics from a wide selection of statistical sources describing for each activity: production and employment; country specialisation and regional distribution; productivity and profitability; the importance of small and medium sized enterprises (SMEs); workforce characteristics; external trade, etc.

Available language: EN
KS-BW-09-001-EN-C
Paper version: EUR 25

Pocketbooks and brochures

This series of publications (pocketbooks and brochures) are available free of charge. They present essential statistical information from one or more domains and are generally around 100 pages in length. The flagship pocketbook 'Key figures on Europe' is also translated into German and French.

Key figures on Europe	Fishery statistics Data 1995-2008	External and intra-European Union trade	Principal European Economic indicators	Combating poverty and social exclusion	Using official statistics to calculate greenhouse gas emissions

     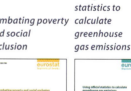 

KS-EI-10-001-EN-C   KS-DW-09-001-EN-C   KS-CV-08-001-EN-C   KS-81-08-398-EN-C   KS-EP-09-001-EN-C   KS-31-09-272-EN-C

Methodologies and working papers

Statistical manuals, classifications or nomenclatures are published under the collection 'Methodologies and working papers'. Intended for specialists, these publications are also only released through the Internet, they are freely available on the Eurostat website.

Please consult the Eurostat website for a full list of publications, at:

http://epp.eurostat.ec.europa.eu/portal/page/portal/publications/collections

European Commission

Europe in figures - Eurostat yearbook 2010

Luxembourg: Publications Office of the European Union

2010 — 657 pp. — 17.6 x 25 cm

Theme: General and regional statistics
Collection: Statistical books

ISBN 978-92-79-14884-2
ISSN 1681-4789
doi: 10.2785/40830
Cat. No. KS-CD-10-220-EN-C

Price (excluding VAT) in Luxembourg: EUR 30